SECURED TRANSACTIONS LAW REFORM

Secured transactions law has been subjected to a close scrutiny over the last two decades. One of the main reasons for this is the importance of availability of credit and the consequent need to reform collateral laws in order to improve access to finance. The ability to give security effectively influences not only the cost of credit but also, in some cases, whether credit will be available at all. This requires rules that are transparent and readily accessible to non-lawyers as well as rules that recognise the needs of small and medium-sized enterprises.

This book critically engages with the challenges posed by inefficient secured credit laws. It offers a comparative analysis of the reasons and the needs for a secured transactions law reform, as well as discussion of the steps taken in many common law, civil law and mixed law jurisdictions.

The book, written under the auspices of the Secured Transactions Law Reform Project, informs the debate about reform and advances novel arguments written by world renowned experts that will build upon the existing literature, and as such will be of interest to academics, legal practitioners and the judiciary involved in secured transactions law around the world.

Secured Transactions Law Reform

Principles, Policies and Practice

Edited by
Louise Gullifer and Orkun Akseli

• HART •
OXFORD • LONDON • NEW YORK • NEW DELHI • SYDNEY

HART PUBLISHING
Bloomsbury Publishing Plc
Kemp House, Chawley Park, Cumnor Hill, Oxford, OX2 9PH, UK

HART PUBLISHING, the Hart/Stag logo, BLOOMSBURY and the Diana logo are trademarks of Bloomsbury Publishing Plc
First published in Great Britain 2016

First published in hardback, 2016
Paperback edition, 2019

A catalogue record for this book is available from the British Library.

Library of Congress Cataloging-in-Publication Data

Names: Gullifer, Louise, editor. | Akseli, N. Orkun (Nazmi Orkun), editor.

Title: Secured transactions law reform principles, policies and practice / edited by Louise Gullifer and Orkun Akseli.

Description: Oxford ; Portland, Oregon : Hart Publishing, 2016. | Includes bibliographical references and index.

Identifiers: LCCN 2016024691 (print) | LCCN 2016025229 (ebook) | ISBN 9781849467438 (hardback : alk. paper) | ISBN 9781509903122 (Epub)

Subjects: LCSH: Security (Law) | Law reform. | Credit.

Classification: LCC K1100 .S415 2016 (print) | LCC K1100 (ebook) | DDC 346.07/4—dc23

LC record available at https://lccn.loc.gov/2016024691

ISBN: HB: 978-1-84946-743-8
PB: 978-1-50992-751-7
ePDF: 978-1-50990-311-5
ePub: 978-1-50990-312-2

Typeset by Compuscript Ltd, Shannon

To find out more about our authors and books visit www.hartpublishing.co.uk. Here you will find extracts, author information, details of forthcoming events and the option to sign up for our newsletters.

Secured Transactions Law Reform

Principles, Policies and Practice

Edited by
Louise Gullifer and Orkun Akseli

• HART •
OXFORD • LONDON • NEW YORK • NEW DELHI • SYDNEY

HART PUBLISHING
Bloomsbury Publishing Plc
Kemp House, Chawley Park, Cumnor Hill, Oxford, OX2 9PH, UK

HART PUBLISHING, the Hart/Stag logo, BLOOMSBURY and the Diana logo are trademarks of Bloomsbury Publishing Plc
First published in Great Britain 2016

First published in hardback, 2016
Paperback edition, 2019

A catalogue record for this book is available from the British Library.

Library of Congress Cataloging-in-Publication Data

Names: Gullifer, Louise, editor. | Akseli, N. Orkun (Nazmi Orkun), editor.

Title: Secured transactions law reform principles, policies and practice / edited by Louise Gullifer and Orkun Akseli.

Description: Oxford ; Portland, Oregon : Hart Publishing, 2016. | Includes bibliographical references and index.

Identifiers: LCCN 2016024691 (print) | LCCN 2016025229 (ebook) | ISBN 9781849467438 (hardback : alk. paper) | ISBN 9781509903122 (Epub)

Subjects: LCSH: Security (Law) | Law reform. | Credit.

Classification: LCC K1100 .S415 2016 (print) | LCC K1100 (ebook) | DDC 346.07/4—dc23

LC record available at https://lccn.loc.gov/2016024691

ISBN: HB: 978-1-84946-743-8
PB: 978-1-50992-751-7
ePDF: 978-1-50990-311-5
ePub: 978-1-50990-312-2

Typeset by Compuscript Ltd, Shannon

To find out more about our authors and books visit www.hartpublishing.co.uk. Here you will find extracts, author information, details of forthcoming events and the option to sign up for our newsletters.

FOREWORD

'Never a borrower nor a lender be, for loan oft loses both itself and friend, and borrowing dulls the edge of husbandry.'

The advice given by Polonius still hold good today, so far as loans between friends or workmates are concerned, but the position is quite different in the context of trade and industry. Here the availability and provision of loans and other forms of credit are essential elements, without which there is little prospect of these spheres of activity developing and flourishing.

In turn, those providing loans or other forms of credit usually (and not unreasonably) require some form of protection against the risk that the borrower will be unable to repay. Hence the development of numerous types of security, in the form of mortgages, charges, liens, retention of title clauses, hire purchase and the like.

English commercial law has a high reputation throughout the world. It is obviously in the interests of the United Kingdom that every effort should be made to ensure that this continues to be the case. But the reason for this reputation, namely its development over a very long time, also carries with it a danger of atrophy, of laws and practices becoming out of date and inefficient as the world of trade and industry changes in the light of technological and other developments.

I had personal experience of this some twenty years ago. London has for a long time been regarded as the leading world centre for international commercial arbitration. However, the English law of arbitration, again developed over a very long time, was not easily discoverable and some of it was beginning to look very out of date. Much of the law flowed from numerous court decisions, while the arbitration statutes were designed to deal with specific problems. Nowhere could be found a simple clear exposition of English arbitration law, and though the textbooks manfully attempted to steer a course through its many sources, it was often necessary to employ expensive specialized lawyers to find the way through.

It was becoming apparent that unless the law was restated and reformed, London risked falling behind, with other jurisdictions competing hard to attract international commercial arbitration to their shores. There was general agreement that something had to be done and I was privileged to take over the chairmanship of a committee charged with seeking to improve this part of the law, in particular bringing it into line with international arbitration principles, such as those contained in the Model Law produced by UNCITRAL, the United Nations Commission on International Trade Law. The end result was the English Arbitration Act 1996, in which we attempted to set out in simple, clear terms the law relating to arbitration. Whether we succeeded is hardly for me to say, but I understand that twenty years on, the Act seems to be working well.

There is a curious parallel between the situation as regards English arbitration law before 1996 and the law relating to secured transactions today. In both cases much of the law came from numerous court decisions, while statutes, such as the Bills of Sale Acts of 1878 and 1882, were the subject of criticism from the outset and hardly apt for the efficient conduct of trade and industry. Many other countries had modernized their laws while organisations such as UNCITRAL had proposed legislatives guides and a draft Model Law. As with arbitration law, there have been repeated calls for reform, stretching over decades.

I cannot improve upon the way in which Professor Gullifer, in one of the chapters of this book, sets out what is needed.

> It would be hard to disagree that the modern secured transactions law should (i) be as simple as possible but not simpler; (ii) be as transparent and certain as possible; (iii) promote contractual freedom and flexibility of transactions; (iv) promote efficiency of transactions and their enforcement; (v) balance the interests of those affected by the transactions; (vi) not unduly discriminate between market participants; (vii) to make full use of technology as far as possible.

This book contains a wealth of information on the subject of secured transactions, covering many jurisdictions and written by people with unparalleled knowledge and expertise. To my mind it is essential reading for anyone interested in the subject, particularly on the question of how best our law can be reformed. I for one am convinced that reform is needed and long overdue, while acknowledging that there are differing views on how best reform can be achieved. Again, there are parallels with our twenty-year-old endeavours to restate and reform the English law of arbitration. In that context there were differences over how best to proceed among the members of the committee and others. However, we were all so firmly convinced of the need to move forward that to achieve our aim we were able to work with a spirit of compromise, with the result that within a short time frame we were able to present a Bill for the consideration of Parliament. I have every hope that with so many convinced of the need for reform of the law of secured transactions such a spirit will enable progress to be made without undue delay.

I am honoured to be the present Chairman of the Steering Committee of the Secured Transactions Law Reform Project. I would like to take this opportunity to pay tribute to Professor Sir Roy Goode QC, who for many years has campaigned for the reform of the law, founded the Project and until recently was its Director. His knowledge, experience and enthusiasm has fired and continues to fire those anxious to see the law reformed. However, the Project is indeed lucky to have as his replacement Professor Louise Gullifer, who as Director is most ably carrying on the work to the standards set by Sir Roy.

Mark Saville
December 2015

CONTENTS

LIST OF CONTRIBUTORS

Orkun Akseli Senior Lecturer in Commercial Law, Durham University

Teresa Rodriguez de las Heras Ballell Associate Professor of Commercial Law, University Carlos III of Madrid and member of the UNIDROIT Study Group on a Fourth Protocol of the Cape Town Convention on matters specific to mining, agricultural and construction equipment (MAC Protocol Study Group)

Spyridon V Bazinas Senior Legal Officer and the Secretary of Working Group VI (Security Interests), International Trade Law Division (UNCITRAL Secretariat) Office of Legal Affairs, United Nations and University of Vienna Law School, Vienna, Austria

Hugh Beale, QC Professor of Law, University of Warwick and Visiting Professor, University of Amsterdam and University of Oxford

Moritz Brinkmann Professor of Civil Law, German and European Civil Procedure and Insolvency Law, University of Bonn

David Brown Associate Professor, Adelaide Law School, University of Adelaide

Frederique Dahan Chief Counsel, European Bank for Reconstruction and Development (EBRD)

Eric Dirix Professor of Law, University of Leuven

Marek Dubovec Senior Research Attorney, National Law Center for Inter-American Free Trade

Anthony Duggan Professor and Hon Frank H Iacobucci Chair, Faculty of Law, University of Toronto

Mike Gedye Professor of Commercial Law, University of Auckland

Roy Goode, QC Emeritus Professor of Law and Fellow of St John's College, University of Oxford

Louise Gullifer Professor of Commercial Law, University of Oxford, Fellow and Tutor in Law, Harris Manchester College, Oxford, the Executive Director of the Secured Transactions Law Reform Project and a Member of the British delegation to the UNCITRAL Working Group VI (Security Interests)

Cyprian Kambili Legal Adviser on Business Law Reforms for the Private Sector Department, Ministry of Industry and Trade of the Malawi Government and Part-time Lecturer, Faculty of Law, University of Malawi

Noel McGrath Lecturer in Law, University College Dublin

Hamish Patrick Partner, Shepherd and Wedderburn LLP

Magda Raczynska Lecturer in Law, University College London and the Deputy Executive Director of the Secured Transactions Law Reform Project

John Rainer Partner, Mourant Ozannes, Jersey

Jorge Feliu Rey Senior Lecturer in Commercial Law, University Carlos III of Madrid

Jean Francois Riffard Professor of Law, Universite D'Auvergne—Clermont I and a member of the French delegation to the UNCITRAL Working Group VI (Security Interests)

Andrius Smaliukas Partner, Valiunas Ellex and Associate Professor of Law, University of Vilnius

Andrew JM Steven Senior Lecturer in Law, University of Edinburgh and Scottish Law Commissioner

Anna Veneziano Deputy Secretary General, Unidroit and Professor of Law, University of Teramo, Professor of European Property Law, University of Amsterdam

Catherine Walsh Professor, Faculty of Law, McGill University and a member of the Canadian delegation to the UNCITRAL Working Group VI on Secured Transactions

Peter Winship Professor of Law, Southern Methodist University

TABLE OF CASES

United Kingdom

Australia

Australia

Belgium

Canada

Court of Justice of the European Union

France

Germany

Ireland

Jersey

Lithuania

Malawi

New Zealand

Scotland (pre union with England)

Spain

United States of America

United States of America

TABLE OF LEGISLATION

United Kingdom

Statutory Instruments

Other Measures

Australia

Regulations

Canada

Germany

Ireland

Italy

Jersey

Lithuania

Malawi

Slovak Republic

Spain

TABLE OF INTERNATIONAL INSTRUMENTS

1

Introduction

LOUISE GULLIFER

The importance of secured transactions law to the economic development of a country is well established. Numerous studies show a correlation between an efficient law for the creation, protection and enforcement of security interests, and increased access to credit, as well as a reduction in the cost of credit.[1] The World Bank, in its 'Doing Business' rankings of economies, includes an assessment of secured transactions laws in the data used in the ranking category of 'Getting Credit'.[2] It is perhaps not surprising that economies which have modern, integrated secured transactions regimes rank highly in that category, including many which have recently reformed their secured transactions law.

It is not difficult to work out why having an efficient secured transactions law increases access to credit. A creditor is more likely to want to lend to a business or an individual if it can be sure of being repaid, and being able to take an effective security interest in an asset, which can be protected against other claimants to that asset and enforced easily and quickly, is bound to reassure a creditor that it is likely to be repaid, even if the borrower becomes insolvent. A system for taking security, at least over some kinds of asset, has existed in most countries for many years. Over that period, the law is likely to have been developed in a piecemeal way, either through case law or legislative intervention, or a mixture of both. The resulting law, which is often complex, fragmented and inconsistent, is heavily path dependent. To understand it properly, one needs to be a historian, not just of the law, but of the economic imperatives which have shaped a particular country.

Given the benefits which come from an efficient secured transactions law, it is not surprising that many countries either have recently reformed their law, or are considering it. In addition to the basic reason discussed above, there are often other factors driving reform. One is the shift in the type of collateral available,

[1] Recent examples, some of which are referred to in Ch 21, are: R Haselmann, K Pistor and V Vig, 'How Law Affects Lending' (2010) 23(2) *Review of Financial Studies* 549; G Affaki, 'Increasing Access to Credit: Reforming Secured Transactions Laws' (2010) International Trade Centre; C Calomiris, M Larrain, J Liberti and J Sturgess, 'How Collateral Laws Shape Lending and Sectoral Activity', Working Paper, Draft, 2014.

[2] See www.doingbusiness.org/methodology/getting-credit.

first from immovable property (land) to movable property, and, more recently, from tangible property (goods and equipment) to intangible property (receivables, intellectual property and securities). Another is the ever-increasing ability of information technology to receive, hold and process information, so that many things which were not possible when a register had to be paper based (such as links between registers) are now part of the toolkit available to the reformer. A third is the growth of international business and the global markets. It is not only necessary, now, to take account of the law of secured transactions of a country's immediate neighbours: notice must be taken of international and transnational law reform and harmonisation initiatives. It is not conducive to global business to have a secured transactions law which is difficult to understand, or which is very different from the prevailing norms.

This volume provides an account of reform of the law of secured transactions in a number of important jurisdictions.[3] It is, in a sense, a snapshot of what is happening at the time of writing. The jurisdictions discussed include representatives of many different stages in the cycle of reform. Some jurisdictions, such as the United States and Canada, have had a reformed law for many years, and the concerns, therefore, are about points of detail which are uncertain or which themselves require reform. Others, such as New Zealand, Australia and France, introduced wide-ranging reforms more recently, and now are in a position to evaluate the impact of those reforms.[4] Others, such as Jersey, Belgium, Lithuania and Malawi, have had very recent wholesale reform, some of which is still ongoing, and there is still some time to go before a full evaluation is possible. More limited reform has recently taken place in Ireland, and in England and Wales: the chapters on these jurisdictions criticise these reforms and consider whether they have gone far enough. Further, there has been some piecemeal reform in Spain and Italy, and a more wholesale overhaul is being considered. Finally, there is Germany, which has never had legislative reform, and, indeed, does not even have a registration system. Even here, it seems that changes in the availability and structure of funding, and increasing globalisation, may soon have the effect of raising reform further up the legislative agenda.

The volume grew out of a conference hosted by the Secured Transactions Law Reform Project,[5] under whose auspices the volume is produced. The aim of this project is to look at the need for and shape of future reform of English law, involving all who are interested in this area of law: bankers, practising lawyers, judges and academics. The point of the conference, therefore, was to use the experience of other jurisdictions to inform the reform debate in relation to English law. There

[3] There has been reform in many other jurisdictions which are not included in the book. Short descriptions of reform in a large number of jurisdictions are included on the Secured Transactions Law Reform Project website at http://securedtransactionslawreformproject.org/reform-in-other-jurisdictions.

[4] Indeed, there has been a statutory review of the Australian reforms which reported in March 2015, and which is referred to extensively in Ch 7.

[5] See http://securedtransactionslawreformproject.org/.

is a huge amount that can be learnt from the experience of other jurisdictions, as to both the benefits and pitfalls of reform, and the process of reform. The jurisdictions represented at the conference were chosen for their closeness, both legally and geographically, to England and Wales. For this volume, the scope has been widened to include significant European civil law countries, such as France, Germany, Italy and Spain as well as European countries in which there has been recent reform, such as Belgium and Lithuania. Malawi was also included, as representing a country where recent reform has been informed by the UNCITRAL Legislative Guide on Secured Transactions.[6] As mentioned earlier, transnational law reform and harmonisation initiatives can be an important factor driving reform, and can also assist in the execution of such reform. Some of the international initiatives over the last 25 years are explored in the volume: there are chapters on the work of the European Bank for Reconstruction and Development, on the influence of the UN Convention on receivables financing and on the UNCITRAL Legislative Guide on Secured Transactions and the resulting Model Law, which is still at the drafting stage. Other harmonisation initiatives, such as the Cape Town Convention on International Interests in Mobile Equipment and the EU Financial Collateral Directive, are discussed in some detail in the individual chapters, both as drivers for reform and as an example of how national reform has to take account of international developments as well as interrelating areas of national law, such as insolvency and corporate law.

One obvious model for any common law jurisdiction considering reform to consider is that of the Uniform Commercial Code Article 9/Personal Property Security Act notice filing system, and the volume includes chapters from a number of jurisdictions where versions of that model have been enacted. In order to prevent each chapter explaining that model in detail, there is a chapter giving a generalised account of such a system. As a result, each other chapter can concentrate on the particular concerns of that jurisdiction in relation to the model. In relation to US, Canadian and English law, specific current issues are discussed, which are picked up again in the discussion of other jurisdictions.

The aim of this volume is to provide a resource both for those interested in the reform of English law, including the Secured Transactions Law Reform Project, and those involved in law reform throughout the world.

[6] There are a number of other jurisdictions where reform has recently been based on the UNCITRAL legislative guide, such as Ghana, Liberia and Jamaica, as well as many others where reforms have been based on similar models, such as the Organisation of American States' Inter-American Model Law on Secured Transactions (Mexico, Colombia, Costa Rica, El Salvador and Honduras). The UNCITRAL guide also influenced the reforms in Belgium, see Ch 18 M.

Part I

Modernisation of the Law of Secured Transactions in Common and Mixed Law Jurisdictions

2

An Outline of a Typical PPSA Scheme

HUGH BEALE

A. Introduction

The aim of this chapter is to provide the reader who is not familiar with any of the Personal Property Security Acts (PPSAs) or with Article 9 of the Uniform Commercial Code ('Article 9') with a short summary of the features that are typical of most of the PPSA schemes.[1] The chapters following this will consider the schemes in specific jurisdictions, and will therefore build on this basis analysis.[2]

The Canadian PPSAs follow fairly closely the original version of Article 9. However, the earlier schemes—notably the Ontario Personal Property Security Act of 1967—contain a number of significant differences from the later 'Western' model adopted in, for example, Saskatchewan.[3] The more important of these differences will be noted in this chapter, as will a few of the major amendments made in the revised version of Article 9 now in force in all the United States. The differences between the Canadian PPSAs and the PPSAs adopted in New Zealand and, particularly, Australia are much more substantial and are the subject of other chapters in the volume.

[1] A fuller account of the typical PPSA scheme will be found in H Beale, M Bridge, L Gullifer and E Lomnicka, *The Law of Security and Title-based Finance*, 2nd edn (Oxford, Oxford University Press, 2012), paras 23.81–23.142.

[2] Since so much of the material in this chapter is discussed in detail in relation to particular jurisdictions in subsequent chapters, cross-references in this chapter have been kept to a minimum.

[3] In this chapter, most of the examples given in the footnotes refer to the Saskatchewan PPSA 1993 ('SPPSA') or to the New Zealand PPSA 1999 ('NZPPSA'). In the footnotes Revised Article 9 is referred to as 'UCC'.

B. General Coverage

The typical PPSA covers most aspects of the law of secured transactions, dealing in particular with the following:

1. Aspects of the creation of a security interest. This is in the negative form that a security agreement will be enforceable as between the parties even though the debtor has not signed a security agreement or given possession of the collateral to the secured party.[4]
2. What is necessary for the security interest to become enforceable against a third party (such as another creditor claiming a security interest in the collateral): the debtor must either have given the secured creditor possession of the collateral or have signed a security agreement that describes the collateral in one of a number of ways,[5] and the security interest must have 'attached' to the relevant collateral. Attachment requires that the debtor has rights in the collateral and that the secured creditor has given value.[6]
3. Perfection of the security interest, so that it will be effective against, for example, execution creditors and in the debtor's insolvency. The principal methods of perfection are by registration or by taking possession of tangible collateral. Revised Article 9 provides that in the case of certain types of intangible collateral—broadly, what in England and Wales would be referred to as financial collateral—perfection may be by taking control of it.[7]
4. Priority of security interests, as against other security interests in the same collateral and as against buyers and lessees of the property.
5. The rights and duties of the parties before default.
6. Remedies on default.
7. Provisions for private international law issues.

C. Scope of Application

(i) Debtors

The scheme typically applies to security interests created by any debtor whether a company, a sole trader or partnership or a consumer (though many of the requirements are different for security interests created by consumers).

[4] SPPSA s 9(1).
[5] SPPSA s 10.
[6] SPPSA s 12(1).
[7] See Section E(ii).

(ii) Types of Security

(a) Traditional Forms of Security

Obviously the scheme will cover traditional security devices such as pledges, mortgages, charges and contractual liens. It does not normally distinguish between fixed and floating charges. In any security interest agreement the debtor may be given the right to dispose of some or all of the collateral that is subject to the agreement without obtaining the secured party's consent to the particular disposition. Even in the absence of such authorisation, the debtor has the power to dispose of cash, inventory and other items that it normally sells in the course of business unless the purchaser knows that the debtor has no right to dispose of the item.[8]

(b) 'Quasi-security'

Perhaps one of the most distinctive features of the typical PPSA scheme is that it applies not only to traditional security devices, but also to transactions that are considered to be the functional equivalent of traditional security, often called quasi-security devices. So a security interest is defined as 'an interest in personal property that secures payment or performance of an obligation'.[9] This includes, in particular, retention of title devices such as conditional sales (including retention of title over inventory that has been supplied), hire purchase agreements and finance leases.[10]

(c) A 'Unitary Notion' of Security Interest

It can be said that the Uniform Commercial Code and PPSAs have replaced the many different kinds of security and quasi-security with a 'unitary notion' of a security interest.[11] In so far as they apply to traditional forms of security and to 'quasi-security', this is true. For example, the schemes no longer distinguish between a charge taken by a financier over a machine to secure the advance of the purchase price and a finance lease or hire purchase agreement over the same machine between the finance house and the debtor. In each case the finance house is treated as a secured party. Both have to be perfected by filing a financing statement and, as we will see below, both are treated in the same way for purposes of priority and the same rights and remedies on default apply. Indeed, it is no longer necessary for the parties to characterise their agreement; it would be perfectly possible for the debtor

[8] SPPSA s 30(2), which provides the same for lessees also; UCC §§9-320–9-321 read with §1-201(9). See further below, Section I.

[9] SPPSA s 2(1)(qq). *cf* UCC §1-201(b)(35).

[10] SPPSA s 3(1).

[11] eg J White and R Summers, *Uniform Commercial Code*, 5th edn (St Paul, MN, West Publishing Co, 2000) 710; JS Ziegel, 'Canadian Perspectives on "How Far is Article 9 Exportable"?' (1996) 27 *Canadian Business Law Journal* 226, 232; RCC Cuming, 'The Internationalisation of Secured Financing Law' in R Cranston (ed), *Making Commercial Law: Essays in Honour of Roy Goode* (Oxford, Clarendon Press, 1997) Ch 22, 504–08.

simply to grant 'a security interest' over the machine and for the secured party to file accordingly. However, as the next two sections show, the schemes also usually include types of arrangement that do not have a security purpose and that in very important respects are not treated in the same way as security interests.

(d) Leases, Commercial Consignments, etc Without a Security Purpose

The schemes also cover what are termed deemed security interests. These are subject to only certain aspects of the scheme. Deemed security interests include outright sales of receivables (which, it may be argued, are functionally equivalent to security, at least when sold on a recourse basis) and some transactions which do not have a security purpose at all, such as operating leases and commercial consignments. Operating leases and commercial consignments are not covered by all schemes. They are outside the scope of Article 9 but in practice many operating leases in the US are registered just in case the lessor is wrong in treating the lease as an operating lease rather than a finance lease.[12] In the Western Canadian PPSAs and New Zealand they decided it would be simpler to require all operating leases lasting more than one year and commercial consignments to be registered. If they are not then the lessor or consignor may not be able to enforce its rights against other creditors, or may lose priority to other secured parties; but the lessor's or consignor's rights on default are not subject to the normal rules applicable to security and quasi-security interests.[13] Thus if the lessor or consignor repossesses the collateral and it is worth more than the sum secured, the lessor or consignor may keep the excess. In other words, the operating lease or commercial consignment is not wholly 'rechararacterised' as a security interest.

(e) Sales of Receivables

Outright sales of receivables are also covered by the priority and perfection rules but equally they are not wholly recharacterised as security,[14] even if the sale of the receivable is on a recourse basis. The buyer of the receivable—typically a receivables financier—will be able to collect the receivable in the normal way and keep the entire proceeds. There are a number of exceptions to the requirements to register outright sales, in particular when the receivable is transferred as part of the sale of the debtor's business, when the transfer is solely for the purpose of collection of the debt by the transferee[15] and, in Article 9, when a single assignment is made to satisfy an existing obligation.[16] The reason for these exceptions is that none of the cases is connected to receivables financing.

[12] J Ziegel and D Denomme, *The Ontario Personal Property Security Act Commentary and Analysis*, 2nd edn (Toronto, Butterworths, 2000) para 2.2.3.

[13] SPPSA s 3(2).

[14] SPPSA s 3(2).

[15] SPPSA s 4(g) and (h).

[16] UCC §9-109.

D. Notice Filing

(i) Filing Before or After Transaction

Article 9 and the PPSA schemes are often referred to as 'notice filing' schemes. This is because the secured party or its agent may 'file' (ie register)[17] at any time, including before it has taken a security interest, and a single filing may cover a succession of security interests provided that the parties remain the same and the collateral falls within the description used in the registration.[18] This is convenient when there are likely to be multiple transactions between the same parties. It means that a notice on the register is merely an indication that there may be a security interest over the debtor's property in favour of the named party.

(ii) Sanctions for Not Filing

Filing is voluntary but clearly advisable for any non-possessory security. If the security interest has not been perfected by filing or another permitted method when the debtor becomes insolvent, the security interest will not be effective in the debtor's insolvency.[19] Moreover, a security interest that has not been registered will lose priority to any subsequent security interest that is perfected first; and an unperfected security interest is also ineffective against execution creditors[20] and against any buyer or lessee of the collateral who takes without knowledge of the unregistered security interest.[21]

(iii) The Financing Statement

Notice filing merely requires the secured party or its agent to place a few particulars on the register, in the form of a financing statement. In the more recent schemes at least,[22] filing is done exclusively online and searching is similarly online. The

[17] Article 9 refers to 'filing', the SPPSA to 'registering'.

[18] SPPSA s 43(4) and (5). *cf* UCC §9-502(d).

[19] SPPSA s 30(2); UCC §9-317(a)(2) (priority of lien creditors, who include trustees in bankruptcy, see §9-102(a)(52). Note, however, that the NZPPSA does not render the security interest invalid if it is not perfected. The argument is that the invalidity rule in effect protects unsecured creditors but since they do not in practice rely on the register, they do not deserve protection. See M Gedye, R Cuming and R Wood, *Personal Property Securities in New Zealand* (Wellington, NZ: Thomson Brookers, 2002) 8 and Ch 7 F(i).

[20] SPPSA s 30(1); UCC §9-317(a).

[21] SPPSA s 30(3); UCC §9-317(b). 'Knowledge' here means actual knowledge, see below, text at n 43. Note the rule protecting purchasers of negotiable instruments in s 30(4).

[22] eg under the NZPPSA. It is common for the details of registration to be contained in separate regulations, eg Saskatchewan Personal Property Security Regulations, ch P-62 Reg 1, as amended.

financing statement will normally require the borrower's ('the debtor's') name and address, the creditor's ('secured party's') name and address and brief details of the property that is subject to the security interest.[23] Subsequent amendments may be added by a 'financing change statement' that will be linked to the original financing statement by a number given to the financing statement.[24] Any further information required by a searcher will have to be obtained from the debtor or the secured party, and there are provisions of varying elaborateness requiring secured parties to provide information of various kinds.[25] If the financing statement is inaccurate, for example it omits an item of collateral, the security interest will not be perfected in relation to that item; if the mistake prevents a searcher from finding the financing statement,[26] the security interest will not be perfected at all.

(iv) Filing and the Debtor

The debtor is generally not required to consent to filing. If a registration has been made without the debtor's consent and it does not cover an existing security interest or is incorrect, the debtor can require that it be removed or corrected.[27]

E. Methods of Perfection

(i) Filing or Taking Possession

The normal method of perfecting a non-possessory security interest is by filing a financing statement. An alternative when the property is tangible is for the secured party to take possession of the collateral, or for a third person who has possession to hold it to the order of the secured party.[28] If the method of perfection changes—for example, if the creditor first takes possession of the collateral but

[23] eg NZPPSA s 142. *cf* UCC §9-502(a).

[24] *cf* UCC §9-519.

[25] *cf* SPPSA s 18 and UCC §9-210.

[26] The test is whether the error in the financing statement is seriously misleading, which is usually interpreted to mean that the registration will be ineffective only if a reasonable search carried out in accordance with the permitted search criteria would not reveal the existence of the financing statement—for example, because the wrong person is named in the financing statement as the debtor: see UCC §9-515(c); *Coates v General Motors Acceptance Corporation of Canada Ltd* (case no 21546, 3/12/99, Sup Ct of BC); and see also *Gold Key Pontiac Buick (1984) Ltd v 464750 BC Ltd (Trustee of)* [2000] BCCA 435.

[27] SPPSA s 50. UCC §9-518 employs a different system; it allows the debtor to file a 'correction statement' which is added to the record. A copy of the financing statement or of a 'verification statement' sent by the registry to the secured party must be sent by the secured party to the debtor, unless the debtor has waived its right, on pain of a civil penalty: SPPSA s 65(1) (damages of not less than a prescribed amount).

[28] SPPSA s 27; UCC §9-313(b).

then gives back possession but registers its interest—the security interest will be regarded as having been perfected continuously from the date when the secured party first perfected it; and there also cases in which a security interest will be treated as perfected 'temporarily' for a period of time, for example if the secured party takes possession of goods but then releases them back to the debtor for a limited purpose such as resale under a trust receipt.

(ii) Control

As mentioned earlier, with non-possessory securities over financial collateral, under many schemes the secured party has the choice of perfecting by registration or of taking 'control' of the collateral.[29] The secured party will have control of the financial collateral if it is transferred into the name of the secured party; or if it remains held for the debtor by a third party such as an intermediary who maintains the account in which the investment property is held for the debtor, or a bank, if the secured party can direct the intermediary or bank to transfer or dispose of the collateral at its request without further reference to the debtor.[30]

Many schemes also provide for 'automatic perfection' of some security interests, for example when a finance house takes a purchase money security interest of goods it has supplied to a consumer,[31] or over proceeds of collateral.[32] This is no more than saying that once the security interest has attached to the collateral it is unnecessary for the secured party to take any further step in order to perfect the security interest.

F. Priority

(i) General Rules

The general priority rule for competing non-possessory security interests is that priority depends on the order of filing, not the order in which the security interests were created.[33] It will be noticed that this has the effect of changing the 'tacking' rule: even further advances made by the secured party who filed first will have priority over the second filer.

[29] For further discussion see, in particular, Ch 5 and Ch 6 C.

[30] This amounts to 'positive control', as compared to the 'negative control', preventing the debtor dealing with the collateral, which appears to be required by the Financial Collateral Arrangements (No 2) Regulations 2003, see *Gray v G-T-P Group Ltd, Re F2G Realisations Ltd (in liquidation)* [2010] EWHC 1772 (Ch).

[31] UCC §9-309, Security Interest Perfected Upon Attachment.

[32] Australian PPSA s 33(1)(c).

[33] SPPSA s 35; UCC §9-322.

In a contest between a possessory and a non-possessory security interest, priority depends on whether the filing took place before or after the perfection by possession.[34] With financial collateral, a secured party that has control of the collateral is given priority over one whose security interest was perfected only by registration.[35] This is because a secured party whose main interest is in the financial collateral will be expected to obtain control; a security interest over financial collateral that is perfected only by registration is likely to be just part of a global charge on all the debtor's assets.

(ii) Purchase Money Security Interests

An important exception to the 'first to file' rule occurs when an acquisition financier takes a security interest over just the asset that it has supplied (for example under a finance lease) or which has been acquired with the funds it supplied. Such a 'purchase money security interest' (PMSI) is given priority over previously registered security interests, as otherwise the other secured parties would benefit from an increase in the collateral available to them at the expense of the acquisition financier. However, 'PMSI priority' is dependent on the acquisition financier itself filing—with a security interest over equipment, it must do so within a short time after the equipment has been delivered to the debtor;[36] with inventory, it must not only have filed, but also have notified any other party who has already filed a security interest that would cover the inventory before delivering the inventory to the buyer.[37] 'Cross-collateralisation' is permitted: in other words, the secured party will have the same PMSI priority over other collateral that it supplied or paid for even if that collateral has been paid for.[38] The effect is similar to that of an 'all-monies' retention of title clause.

G. Proceeds[39]

The priority that is accorded to a security interest over original collateral normally applies to any 'proceeds' of the collateral[40]—for example, fruits obtained from the collateral, new products made from it (in the cases of commingling, accessions or

[34] SPPSA s 35; UCC §9-322.
[35] UCC §9-328.
[36] SPPSA s 34(2); UCC §9-324(a).
[37] SPPSA s 34(3); UCC §9-324(b).
[38] UCC §9-103(b)(2).
[39] See, in particular, Ch 5, Ch 6 D and Ch 13.
[40] SPPSA s 35(3); s 34 generally accords the proceeds of a purchase-money security interest the same priority as it had over the original collateral. Note that with proceeds other than cash in a bank account, if the kind of asset now involved does not fall within a previously-filed financing statement,

new goods: there are elaborate rules as to the secured party's proportionate share of new goods) and the proceeds of sale. Thus a supplier who uses a retention of title clause will have PMSI priority over not just the goods that are still in the buyer's possession in their original state, but also over new goods (in proportion to its contribution) and the proceeds of sales of the goods it supplied.[41] This may lead to a competition with a receivables financier who buys the receivables or takes a security interest over them 'as original collateral'. In this case, most schemes treat the PMSI supplier as a less important source of finance than the receivables financier and the PMSI priority is lost[42]—in other words, priority will depend again on which party was the first to file. This will normally be the receivables financier.

H. Priority Against Buyers and Lessees

(i) General

The schemes also set out rules on conflicts between secured parties and parties who buy or take a lease over the collateral. A buyer or lessee will take free of any unperfected security interest unless they had actual knowledge of it at the time.[43] A buyer or lessee will take subject to a perfected security interest unless the collateral is goods and either the goods were sold or leased in the ordinary course of the debtor's business[44] or the goods were of low value and were bought for private purposes.[45]

(ii) Motor Vehicles

PPSAs make special provision for motor vehicles and similar items that have a unique identifying number such as a chassis number. In this case the identifying number may be entered on the financing statement. If the number is included, a buyer or lessor will take subject to the security interest unless the security interest

a new financing statement must be filed or the security interest must be perfected by another method, within 15 days: SPPSA s 28(3).

[41] SPPSA ss 38, 39; UCC §9-335, 336. There are also provisions dealing with priority over fixtures and crops: SPPSA ss 36, 37; UCC §9-334.

[42] SPPSA s 34(6). The NZPPSA was amended to add such a provision (s 15 New Zealand Personal Property Securities Amendment Act 2004).

[43] SPPSA s 20(3); UCC §9-317(b).

[44] Unless the buyer also knows that the sale constitutes a breach of the security agreement pursuant to which the security interest was created: SPPSA s 30(2), which provides the same for lessees also; UCC §§9-320–9-321 read with §1-201(9).

[45] SPPSA s 30(3) (unless the consumer knows of the security interest). In this case the consumer buyer takes free not just of a security interest created by the seller, but of any security interest, such as one created by a previous owner.

was created by the party from whom they bought or leased the goods and the sale or lease was in the ordinary course of the debtor's business (when the rule stated above applies). If the number is not included, the buyer or lessee will take free of the security interest whoever was the secured party, eg a finance company that leased the vehicle to a previous owner.[46] This in effect makes sure that suppliers or other financiers of vehicles will register their interest against the vehicle as well as the debtor, and makes it much easier for a buyer to find out whether a vehicle is subject to an undischarged security arrangement.

Obviously it is not only serial-numbered equipment that may be bought and sold. In this case the buyer will not have such an easy way to discover whether the seller or some previous owner may have created a still-undischarged security interest over the goods. However, if the seller can provide complete information about the previous ownership, the buyer should be able to check by searching against each owner in turn—not so easy as with vehicles, but better than nothing.

(iii) Payments to Creditors

A debtor whose funds are subject to a security interest (for example, under a security interest over all the debtor's present and future assets) also has the power to make effective payments, free of the security interest, to creditors. A creditor who receives payment of a debt by the debtor making a payment by, for example, cheque or money transfer has priority over a security interest in the funds paid, the intangible that was the source of the payment and any instrument used to effect the payment, whether or not the creditor has knowledge of the security interest at the time of the payment.[47] It has rightly been pointed out that this is equivalent to the right that a debtor had under an uncrystallised floating charge.[48]

I. No Separate Concept of Floating Charge

The provisions that give the debtor an effective power of disposal of both its inventory[49] and its funds mean that Article 9 and the PPSAs enable a debtor to continue to trade in the ordinary course of business in much the same way as

[46] SPPSA s 30(6) and (7). Similarly, a party who takes a security interest over the vehicle will have priority: SPPSA s 35(4). This and s 30(6) and (7) are limited to cases where the vehicle is held as equipment. Buyers of inventory will normally take free in any event but secured parties will take subject to a security interest over vehicles held as inventory, even if the relevant financing statement did not list the serial numbers of the vehicles.

[47] SPPSA s 31(2) and (3); UCC §9-332.

[48] R Cuming and R Wood, *Saskatchewan and Manitoba Personal Property Security Acts Handbook* (Toronto, Carswell, 1994) §31[2]. See also Ch 7 C(ii).

[49] SPPSA s 30(2) does not protect a buyer who knows that the sale is in breach of the security agreement but this will be a rare case.

under a floating charge that has not crystallised. Further, the security agreement may give the debtor the right to dispose of any item of collateral free of the charge without obtaining the creditor's further consent. The security interest will still be valid and, subject to the rules of the scheme, effective if, at the crucial time, the item of collateral has not been disposed of.[50] The result is rather similar to saying that a charge over stock-in-trade and funds can only be a floating charge, while a security over any other collateral may be fixed or floating, but without drawing that distinction or requiring the creation of two separate charges.

J. Rights and Obligations Before Default

The schemes contain some provisions dealing with the rights and obligations of the parties to the security agreement before there is any question of default: for example, requiring a secured party which has possession of the collateral to take reasonable care of it;[51] allowing a secured party who receives income from the collateral either to remit it to the debtor or to apply it to reduce the amount of the secured obligation;[52] and on when the collateral may be used or on-pledged.[53]

K. Remedies

Article 9 and the PPSAs also set out a full set of 'remedies' for the enforcement of security interests, for the payment of any deficit and the distribution of any surplus after the collateral has been realised. These rules apply, it will be recalled, not only to traditional forms of security such as chattel mortgages and charges, but also to the 'quasi-security' devices such as finance leases. The schemes of remedies do not apply, however, or apply only in part, to 'deemed security interests' such as operating leases for over one year or commercial consignments that do not have a security purpose (even if these are within the scheme of registration and priority) or to outright sales of receivables.[54] The receivables financier who buys the receivables outright is left to collect the receivables in the normal way, save that if the sale was on a recourse basis, Article 9 requires the receivables financier to collect them in a commercially reasonable manner.[55]

[50] §9-205.

[51] SPPSA s 17; UCC §9-207.

[52] Compare SPPSA s 17(3) and UCC §9-207(c).

[53] See SPPSA s 17(4); UCC §9-208 (a)–(b). Article 9 allows a secured party who has possession of collateral or 'control' of it, for example over investment property, to create a security interest in it: UCC §9-207(c).

[54] SPPSA s 55(2).

[55] §9-607(c).

The scheme of remedies typically provides for at least the following:

— where the collateral is a receivable or other payment obligation, collection by the secured party, which may apply the money etc to the satisfaction of the secured obligation, after deducting reasonable expenses;[56]
— taking possession of the collateral in the event of the debtor's default;[57]
— disposal of the collateral in a commercially reasonable manner, and only after notice[58] unless the collateral is being sold in a ready market;[59]
— the buyer of the collateral to take free of the security interest, of any lower-ranked security interests and of any interest of the debtor;[60]
— that the secured party must account for and distribute any surplus;[61]
— the secured party keeping the collateral in full or satisfaction of the debt, but only if the debtor (or any other party who would be entitled to be notified of a sale) does not object;[62] and
— the debtor (or any other party who would be entitled to be notified of a sale) to be able to redeem the collateral at any time before it has been sold.[63]

The bulk of the rules are 'default rules' that will apply unless the parties had agreed otherwise. Some of the rules are mandatory; the number of mandatory rules varies from scheme to scheme. Rules that may affect third parties are usually mandatory[64] but the SPPSA, with limited exceptions,[65] prevents the parties from excluding or restricting the rules that are intended to protect the debtor.[66] The UCC lists specific provisions that cannot be altered against the interests of the

[56] SPPSA s 57. *cf* UCC §9-607.

[57] SPPSA s 58(2). *cf* UCC §9-609(a)(1).

[58] SPPSA s 59, which sets out detailed rules that must be followed.

[59] Thus there is no need for notice if the collateral 'is of a type that is to be disposed of by sale on an organized market that handles large volumes of transactions between many different sellers and many different buyers': s 59(16)(d); *cf* UCC §9-611(d).

[60] SPPSA s 59(14). UCC §9-617 is to similar effect. The NZPPSA has been criticised for omitting a similar provision: Gedye, Cuming and Wood (n 19) para 115.2.

[61] SPPSA s 60; UCC §9-615. It should be recalled that these rules do not apply to outright sales of accounts or other 'deemed security interests': see SPPSA s 55, UCC §9-615(e) and above, Section C(ii)(d) and (e).

[62] SPPSA s 61.

[63] SPPSA s 62.

[64] The original NZPPSA permitted debtors to waive their rights but provides that waiver will not affect third parties. This has now been amended: the Act now provides that the parties can only contract out of certain listed provisions. (The new s 107 was added as from 1 May 2002 by s 9 Personal Property Securities Amendment Act 2001.)

[65] eg, under the SPPSA, the debtor may waive the secured party's obligations to take steps to preserve the debtor's rights against third persons under an instrument or an investment security taken as collateral or to keep the collateral identifiable (s 17(1)–(2)). See also s 59(3)(d) (secured party may dispose of property by lease) and s 59(4) (secured party may dispose of collateral on deferred payment terms). A number of provisions allow for a post-default agreement, eg, s 60(2) (order of payment of surplus may be altered 'by the agreement of all interested parties') and s 62(1) (rights of redemption).

[66] Thus the SPPSA s 56(3) provides that, with listed exceptions, the rights, remedies and obligations provided by the Act, to the extent that the provisions give rights to the debtor or impose obligations on the secured party, cannot 'be waived or varied by agreement or otherwise'.

debtor. These include the duty to act in a commercially reasonable manner as to collection of outright sales of accounts, etc on a recourse basis; the rules on disposal of collateral and on giving notice, the distribution of surplus, and the right to redeem. Some schemes impose a general requirement that the secured party must exercise the remedies in good faith or in a commercially reasonable manner, but the parties are free to define what should be the proper manner if they wish to do so.

L. Private International Law Provisions

The schemes deal with many issues of private international law relating to security interests. Here Revised Article 9 has introduced a different system to that typically used in the PPSAs. The PPSAs provide, for example, that the validity, the perfection and the effect of perfection or non-perfection of security interests in goods in general and of possessory security interests in documentary intangibles is governed by the law of the jurisdiction where the collateral is situated when the security interest attaches.[67] If the collateral is then imported into another jurisdiction, it will be necessary to file there before the end of a short period of 'temporary perfection'.[68] With other intangibles or 'mobile' goods (goods that are commonly used in more than one jurisdiction, such as leased contractor's plant), the validity, the perfection and the effect of perfection or non-perfection of security interests is governed by the law of the place where the debtor has its principal place of business or, if the debtor has no place of business, principal residence.[69] As to enforcement rights, procedural issues are (except in relation to intangibles)[70] governed by the law of the place where the collateral is located at the time, and substantive issues by the proper law of the security agreement.[71] Under Article 9, issues of perfection, and the effect of perfection or non-perfection and of priority, of non-possessory security interests over most types of collateral are governed by the local law of the debtor's location.[72] This obviates any need to file in a second jurisdiction if the collateral is moved. There are special provisions for security interests over, for example, bank accounts[73] and investment property.[74]

[67] SPPSA s 5(1).
[68] SPPSA s 5(3).
[69] SPPSA s 7.
[70] These are governed by the law of the forum: SPPSA s 8(1)(b).
[71] SPPSA s 8.
[72] §9-301(1).
[73] §9-304 ('local law of the bank's jurisdiction', which may be a matter of agreement between the bank and the debtor).
[74] §9-305 (for example, with indirectly held investments this may be the law agreed between the intermediary and the entitlement holder, or in the absence of such agreement the law of the place where the account is to be maintained: §9-305(3) referring to §8-110(e)).

3

An Historical Overview of UCC Article 9

PETER WINSHIP

If Article 9 of the Uniform Commercial Code (UCC) were a computer code the present text of the article would be identified as version 3.1.[1] First adopted by its co-sponsors—the National Conference of Commissioners on Uniform State Laws (NCCUSL)[2] and the American Law Institute (ALI)[3]—in 1951 (version 1.0) and modified significantly in 1972 (version 2.0), the official text was thoroughly overhauled in 1998 and promulgated in 1999 (version 3.0). Since 1999 there have been several patches, most importantly in 2010 (version 3.1). As of July 2015, all States[4] have enacted the official text as modified in 2010, albeit with a number of relatively minor non-uniform amendments introduced by individual States.

This chapter adds flesh to this skeletal sketch of the evolution of UCC Article 9. The chapter first surveys the landscape of pre-Code secured transactions law as perceived by the drafters of Article 9 (A). It then describes the drafting of the first official text of Article 9 between 1947 and 1951 (B). The chapter goes on to identify developments between this first official text and the appointment in 1990 of a study committee to consider revision of Article 9 (C) and to report on the

[1] The latest official edition of Art 9 was published in September 2014. *Uniform Commercial Code: Official Text and Comments* (2014–2015 edn) (Thomson Reuters, 2014).

[2] The National Conference of Commissioners on Uniform State Laws (now known unofficially as the Uniform Law Commission) is a body of commissioners appointed by States to draft and promote uniform State legislation. The Commission maintains a website (www.uniformlawcommission.com/) which includes a description of the organisation, the texts of uniform laws, and information about current projects. For a history of the Commission, see RA Stein, *Forming a More Perfect Union: A History of the Uniform Law Commission* (Charlottesville, VA, Lexis/Nexis, 2013) (available in digital form on the Commission's website). Chapter 5 of the Stein book traces the evolution of the UCC.

[3] The American Law Institute is a non-governmental body whose members are prominent lawyers, judges and academics. The Institute, founded in 1923, is known principally for its Restatements of the Law. The Institute maintains a website (www.ali.org) which includes a description of its creation, the organisation and current projects. Unlike NCCUSL, the ALI is tax exempt and therefore prohibited from advocating adoption of legislation.

[4] Article 9 is also the law in the District of Columbia and non-State territories, such as Puerto Rico and the Virgin Islands. Where applicable (eg, when determining the rights and remedies of federal lending agencies), federal common law adopts the text of Art 9 in the absence of special federal concerns. See eg *United States v Kimbell Foods, Inc.*, 440 US 715 (1979).

drafting of the 1999 official text and subsequent modifications (D). The chapter concludes with a summary of major themes running through the history traced in the preceding parts (E). Readers interested in finding original materials on which the chapter is based will find sources in the appendix to this chapter.

A. Pre-Article 9 Security Law

Writing in 1947, Karl Llewellyn, the Chief Reporter of the Uniform Commercial Code project, listed the complex array of security devices then recognised in the United States:

> [T]he chattel mortgage, the conditional sale, the pledge of documents of title with its now rather well developed 'field warehouse' variant; there is the trust receipt; there are the two rather different types of assignment of contract rights: that of accounts receivable in bloc and that of a single executory production contract; there is the bailment variation of the sale on installments, familiar especially in railroad equipment financing as 'the Pennsylvania plan'; there is the true factor's (ie, selling agent's) possessory lien, and the banker-'factor's' statutory lien on the New York model.[5]

Grant Gilmore, an Associate Reporter for the original Article 9 and later historian of pre-Code law and Article 9, described these devices collectively as resembling 'the obscure wood in which Dante once discovered the gates of hell'.[6]

Complexity, if not obscurity, was enhanced by the fact that the law governing these devices was non-uniform State law—State law because it was assumed that the federal Constitution did not extend federal power to the law of property. This State law was judge-made law, statutory law or both, depending on the security device. Judges were often hostile to the claims of creditors alleging security. In those States that enacted legislation, the legislation addressed specific security devices, often requiring registration in separate public registries, and did not cover all possible issues even for a single device.

There were attempts to provide uniformity both by uniform laws and by non-binding restatements of the common law of security. NCCUSL had approved uniform statutes for several security devices—conditional sales (1918), chattel mortgages (1926) and trust receipts (1933)—but few of the 48 States and territories had enacted these statutes.[7] Attempts at restating security law were no more successful. In 1941 the ALI published a Restatement of Security, the last component

[5] KN Llewellyn, 'Problems of Codifying Security Law' (1948) 13 *Law & Contemporary Problems* 687, 687.

[6] G Gilmore, *Secured Transactions* (Boston, Little Brown & Co, 1964) I, 27. The first eight chapters of Gilmore's two-volume treatise describe the pre-Code devices. Elsewhere in the treatise, Gilmore contrasted the complexity of US security law with the simpler legal solutions found in English law. The reasons for the divergent development, however, he left to 'the patient labors of the historians': I, 25–26.

[7] Twelve states enacted the Uniform Conditional Sales Act, only one enacted the Uniform Chattel Mortgage Act and 34 ultimately enacted the Uniform Trust Receipts Act (1933). The Uniform Chattel

of its Restatement of the Law project. The Restatement, however, covered only the law of pledges, liens and suretyship. As the Introduction to the volume states, the Institute's object in preparing the Restatement was 'to present an orderly statement of those basic or especially important subjects of the general common law which have not been reformulated and codified in uniform statutes or which for various reasons are probably not now susceptible of useful restatement'.[8] In other words, the Restatement expressly excluded from its coverage chattel mortgages, conditional sales, trust receipts and security interests in land.[9]

The US Supreme Court played only a peripheral role in providing some order because of limits on its jurisdiction over disputes governed by State law. Several of its decisions did, however, have an impact on practice. The most notorious of these was Justice Brandeis' opinion in *Benedict v Ratner*[10] holding that the interest of a creditor to whom receivables had been assigned was a fraudulent transfer under New York law and therefore voidable by a bankruptcy trustee. The transfer was fraudulent because the creditor had not exercised sufficient control over the debtor's collection and subsequent use of the proceeds. Rather than discouraging receivables financing, however, the decision encouraged financers to develop control techniques that would avoid the fraudulent transfer trap.

When reviewing this pre-Article 9 history Grant Gilmore concluded that judicial distrust of security interests had encouraged the development of many of these different security devices. Noting that a legal device is 'a gimmick for getting around some prohibition imposed by the substantive law', Gilmore argued that the security devices were needed as face-saving ways to overcome judicial hostility to enforcing security rights of secured creditors.[11] As a consequence, despite judicial hostility, by 1940 creditors could obtain by means of one or another device a security interest in most of a debtor's present and future personal property.[12] 'In a sense', Gilmore wrote,

> the unified structure of personal property security law had already been built: all that remained was to knock down the scaffolding which had been a temporary necessity during construction. Article 9 is not so much a new start or a fresh approach as it is a reflection of work long since accomplished.[13]

The scaffolding, however, had led to a cadre of lawyers with specialised knowledge of the formalities required to create a valid interest, especially in inventory and receivables financing. The drafters of UCC Article 9 not only had to reveal the underlying structure, but also overcome the resistance of a specialist Bar.

Mortgage was withdrawn by NCCUSL just as the UCC project began, while the other two Acts were withdrawn in 1952.

[8] WD Lewis, 'Introduction' in American Law Institute, *Restatement of the Law of Security* (1941) vii.
[9] Note, 'Restatement of Security' in *Restatement of the Law of Security* 1–2.
[10] *Benedict v Ratner*, 268 US 353 (1925).
[11] G Gilmore, 'Security Law, Formalism, and Article 9' (1968) 47 *Nebraska Law Review* 659, 660.
[12] Gilmore (n 6) I, 288–90.
[13] ibid 290.

B. The First Official Text

(i) The Proposed Uniform Commercial Code

The idea of drafting a Uniform Commercial Code can be traced to 1940. At the end of his presidential address to the 1940 annual meeting of NCUSSL, William A Schnader[14] proposed the drafting of such a Uniform Commercial Code. Although uniform commercial laws—negotiable instruments (1896), sales (1906), warehouse receipts (1906), bills of lading (1909), stock transfer (1909), conditional sales (1918) and trust receipts (1933)—were the most successful of the NCCUSL's products, he argued that 'There does not seem to be the slightest excuse for the failure to have all of these acts universally adopted'.[15] Perhaps, he suggested, if the prior uniform commercial laws were packaged together, States might buy the package in a single Act without having to enact each law separately. Such a combined text would eliminate inconsistencies between prior uniform Acts, delete obsolete provisions and bring the laws up to date.[16] Among the reasons Schnader may have had for recommending a commercial code, however, there was no suggestion that banks, finance companies, sellers on credit, their legal advisers or lawyers generally demanded wholesale reform of the law governing security devices.

Schnader enlisted Karl Llewellyn as Chief Reporter.[17] Llewellyn, then a law professor at Columbia Law School, had been a uniform law commissioner since 1926 and by 1940 was chair of the Commercial Law section of the NCCUSL. Known in academic circles for his Realist jurisprudence and for his publications analysing the law of sales, Llewellyn had accumulated experience drafting legislative texts and knowledge of security devices. He cut his teeth on a Uniform Chattel Mortgage Act, which was withdrawn after only one State had enacted it, but he went on to draft a Uniform Trust Receipts Act, which by 1940 was proving popular despite its complexity.

Llewellyn promptly began drafting a substantial revision of the 1906 Uniform Sales Act. Schnader in the meantime led a successful campaign to persuade the ALI to participate in the preparation of the revised sales law as a possible title in the proposed Code project. In 1944 NCCUSL and the ALI approved a proposed

[14] Schnader ('General Schnader' because he had been Attorney-General of Pennsylvania) was at the time an officer of both NCCUSL and the ALI. This proved to be extremely helpful when he sought co-sponsorship from the ALI. He remained active in the promotion of the UCC until his death in 1968. See WA Schnader, 'A Short History of the Preparation and Enactment of the Uniform Commercial Code' (1967) 22 *University of Miami Law Review* 1.

[15] Handbook of the NCCUSL and Proceedings of the Fiftieth Annual Conference (Philadelphia, 1940) 35, 42.

[16] ibid 58.

[17] On Llewellyn, see W Twining, *Karl Llewellyn and the Realist Movement* (1st edn 1973; Cambridge University Press, 2nd edn 2014). Chapters 11–12 set out an excellent history of the drafting of the first official text of the UCC.

final draft of the Revised Uniform Sales Act and the ALI, having finished its Restatement project, debated whether to continue with the Commercial Code project or to dissolve. The ALI decided to continue.

(ii) The Initial Working Plan

On 1 December 1944 the NCCUSL and the ALI concluded a formal cooperation agreement with a tentative table of contents, a five-year timetable and a statement about how the work was to be organised.[18] An editorial board of five—two representatives from each body and the ALI Director as chair—was appointed to oversee the project. Llewellyn was appointed Chief Reporter and Soia Mentschikoff[19] the Associate Chief Reporter. Llewellyn was given a free hand to pick associate reporters for each topic. In the case of the 'chattel security' chapter he selected two young professors, Allison Dunham[20] and Grant Gilmore.[21] They brought research skills, knowledge of case law and fresh eyes to the subject but neither had practical experience with secured financing. A small group of 'advisers' were appointed to advise the reporters as to the substance and the form of the draft.

Drafts were to go through four stages, the first three of which were set out in the ALI-NCCUSL agreement. Review by the small group of advisers was the first stage. The Council of the ALI and the relevant Section of NCCUSL would then examine the text. If they approved, the draft would be submitted to the entire membership of the two sponsors for adoption. There was, in addition, an implicit fourth stage: approval by the House of Delegates of the American Bar Association (ABA).[22] By tradition,[23] the president of NCCUSL reported annually on the work

[18] For the text of the agreement between the ALI and NCCUSL, see ALI, '[Annual] Report of William Draper Lewis, Director' (1946). For a fuller history leading up to the agreement, see 'Report of the Committee on Cooperation with the American Law Institute in the Preparation of a Commercial Code' *Handbook of the NCCUSL and Proceedings of the Fifty-fourth Annual Conference* (Chicago, 1944) 143–71.

[19] Soia Mentschikoff had been Llewellyn's research assistant at Columbia Law School and she later became his wife. For her reflections on drafting the UCC, see 'Reflections of a Drafter: Soia Mentschikoff' (1982) 43 *Ohio State Law Review* 537.

[20] 'Reflections of a Drafter: Allison Dunham' (1982) 43 *Ohio State Law Review* 569. Dunham later became the Executive Director of NCCUSL and was drafter of the unsuccessful Uniform Land Transactions Act, which attempted to extend Art 9 principles to real property transactions.

[21] Descriptions of Gilmore's reflections on his experience as a drafter are scattered throughout his many publications. See eg Gilmore (n 6) I, 290–94; G Gilmore, '[Tribute to] Homer Kripke' (1981) 56 *New York University Law Review* 8; G Gilmore, 'The Good Faith Purchase Idea and The Uniform Commercial Code: Confessions of a Repentant Draftsman' (1981) 15 *Georgia Law Review* 605.

[22] The American Bar Association is a national voluntary membership organisation for lawyers. As of 2015 it had approximately 400,000 members. The ABA maintains a website (www.americanbar.org) with information about its history and goals. From its creation in 1878, the ABA has had as one of its goals the promotion of uniform law. NCCUSL was a spin-off of the ABA. For many years the ABA provided funds to NCCUSL and meetings of NCCUSL were held in conjunction with the annual meeting of the ABA.

[23] K Patchel, 'Interest Group Politics, Federalism, and the Uniform Laws Process: Some Lessons from the Uniform Commercial Code' (1993) 78 *Minnesota Law Review* 83, 88–91.

of NCCUSL and uniform acts were submitted to the ABA House of Delegates for endorsement.

It was understood that Llewellyn and his associates turn to security devices only after completing work on the other parts of the Code. This sequence was deliberate. As Llewellyn wrote in a 1943 memorandum reviewing possible topics to be included in a commercial code:

> [N]o field of the commercial code will elicit as much battle or political objection as the chattel security field. This portion of the code, though materially simpler to do in adequate fashion, thus requires to be postponed until after the preceding chapters have been taken care of. It may then be hoped that the prestige derived from the earlier work will carry weight in regard to the more controversial.[24]

A later memorandum identified as certain to cause political difficulty a single-type of purchase-money and book account financing, while auto title-certificate and certain chattel mortgages would probably cause political difficulty.[25] His experience as drafter of the uniform chattel mortgage and trust receipts acts no doubt informed this assessment.

(iii) Drafting the Secured Transactions Chapter

Unlike Schnader, who spoke as if it would be a simple task to collate the existing texts of the uniform commercial acts, Llewellyn returned again and again to the issue of what should go into a commercial code. With respect to a chapter on 'chattel security' he wrote at the end of 1943:

> The Code plan, as thus far developed, looks to the production of a complete battery of security devices covering every needed aspect of finance; but in general the plan looks to providing only a single device to fill any particular type of need. For example, purchase-money security in sales of goods seems unwisely left open to such three alternative forms as conditional sale, bailment-lease, and purchase-money chattel mortgage. One basic form, left properly flexible, is enough; this also provides a much clearer and simpler body of law.[26]

Under this plan each segment of the world of finance would be examined to determine what security device would be most appropriate.

Llewellyn's plan served as the starting point when work began on the 'chattel security' chapter at the end of 1947. Tentative Draft 1 consisted of a Part III

[24] K Llewellyn, 'Commercial Code, Sketch of Prospective Subject Matter (Prepared for W.E. Stanley October 12th, 1943)' *Llewellyn Papers* J.II.1.b at 5.

[25] K Llewellyn, 'Needed to complete what can fairly be called A COMMERCIAL CODE, with parentheses indicating *possible* additional material' (7 March 1944) *Llewellyn Papers* J.VI.1.c at 1–2.

[26] K Llewellyn, 'Uniform Commercial Code Project: Scope and General Plan (11-22-43)' *Llewellyn Papers* J.V.1.e at 4. A subheading to this document says 'Statement prepared for those who ask for more detailed information'.

devoted to inventory financing.[27] The text was promptly challenged. On reading this draft, Homer Kripke, who was then assistant to the general counsel of CIT Financial Corporation, thought the draft misguided. As he wrote later,

> The draftsmen in the beginning were overly impressed with the economic fact that inventory flows naturally into receivables and that both inventory and receivables constitute the basic working capital of the merchant. By a series of definitions they, therefore, tried to assimilate receivables into inventory for legal purposes. The resulting drafts failed to take into account the fact that many of the problems of receivables relate to the *assignment* thereof, and that these assignment problems involve three parties: the merchant, the buyer of the goods, and the assignee of the buyer's obligation. Inventory financing, on the other hand, involves only a two-party relationship between the merchant and his creditor. Moreover, there is little homogeneity between the problems of the goods on the shelf, the 30-day unsecured receivable, and the long-term secured installment receivable. The drafts constructed on this basis were wholly unworkable and the draftsmen were commendably quick so to concede.[28]

Kripke sought an interview with Llewellyn. They met. Llewellyn listened, conceded error and promptly took on Kripke to advise on commercial finance practices.[29]

The inventory financing provisions were revised but work continued to focus on a functional approach. By May 1949 the text included eight 'parts': short title and general provisions; pledge; inventory and accounts receivable financing; equipment financing; agricultural financing; consumer's goods financing; bulk sales/ bulk transfers; and vehicle liens.[30] When, however, the text was presented that May to a joint meeting of the ALI and NCCUSL, the members voted to remit this text to the reporters for further work.[31]

At the May 1949 meeting Dunham suggested the reporters might abandon the 'functional' approach.

> During the drafting it is becoming clearer to us that we have more and more sections in common that run across all of the transactions than we thought we originally would have, and over the summer we propose, if we can do so, to consider the possibility of instead of having six separate types of security interest based on function, to see whether we cannot put it together and have one set of rules that govern all security transactions with only limited numbers of sections defining special rules for a mortgage on stock in trade, for example, or a special rule for a consumer borrowing money to buy furniture.[32]

[27] Article 7, group 3, *Tentative Draft 1* (24 February 1948) (Confidential). The numbering of the Article was subsequently changed to Art 9 before the co-sponsors finally approved the Code.

[28] H Kripke, 'The Modernization of Commercial Security under the Uniform Commercial Code' (1951) 16 *Law & Contemporary Problems* 183, 184–85.

[29] 'Reflections of a Drafter: Homer Kripke' (1982) 43 *Ohio State Law Review* 577, 578.

[30] American Law Institute and National Conference of Commissioners on Uniform State Laws, *Uniform Commercial Code: May 1949 draft.*

[31] A transcript of the meeting may be found in the three volumes of the Proceedings of the twenty-sixth annual meeting of the American Law Institute in joint session with the National Conference of Commissioners on Uniform State Laws (1949).

[32] Proceedings of the twenty-sixth annual meeting I, 93.

Over the summer of 1949 Dunham and Gilmore proceeded to reorganise the text so that the draft approved by the next joint meeting of the sponsors closely resembles the organisation of the latest official text.[33]

Organisation of Article 9 may have been resolved satisfactorily, but agreement on substance continued to elude the reporters. The secured transactions provisions faced two principal objections: they were too 'leftist' and they needed technical revision.[34] Critics cited the regulatory provisions in the part on financing consumer goods as the principal example of the reporters' attempt to introduce social engineering. These provisions were designed to protect consumer debtors from abuse. Creditors would be required, for example, to disclose terms in a way that consumer debtors could make comparisons between creditors. Controversy over these provisions was, reports Gilmore, 'one of the most violent in the history of the Code's drafting'.[35] The objection that such controversial provisions would delay adoption of the Code, if not kill the project altogether, ultimately won the day and these provisions were withdrawn.[36]

As for technical deficiencies, Llewellyn and the reporters met the criticism by listening to practitioners and by being willing to modify the text. A 1951 ABA Section of Corporation, Banking and Mercantile Law report noted 'some tendency of the reporters (drawn exclusively from law school faculties) to adhere to the side of theory as distinguished from the hard realities of actual practice' but added that this tendency was offset by the willingness of the reporters 'to seek and listen to outside trade, industry and legal specialists in various fields (many of whom were furnished by this Section) and to adopt many of the suggestions offered by these specialists'.[37] A year earlier, however, the ABA Committee on the Proposed Commercial Code, while approving the attempt of the secured transaction chapter to rationalise the patchwork of existing security devices, concluded that the text 'needs a great deal of technical revision as well as further consideration of some of the underlying concepts'.[38]

Continuous technical revision and rethinking delayed presentation of a final text. Schnader was dismayed, complaining in 1950 to the Director of the ALI that

[33] Years later Dunham wrote that Gilmore and he were teaching summer school in Chicago. 'Neither of our families were present and we agreed that over the weekend we would come up with a draft. This was the 4th of July holiday weekend and it was the hottest weekend in the Chicago area in 1948 or' 49—I've forgotten the year—that was then imaginable. And we assembled in the Northwestern Law School all closed up for the holiday and went up on the third floor, took all of our clothes off, except our underwear, and produced a hot weather draft that survived thereafter.' Dunham (n 20) 569.

[34] AR Kamp, 'Downtown Code: A History of the Uniform Commercial Code: 1949–1954' (2001) 49 *Buffalo Law Review* 359, 435–48 (reporting criticism of secured transactions provisions).

[35] Gilmore (n 6) I, 293.

[36] Kripke (n 29) 582–83.

[37] 'Report of the Council to the House of Delegates on the Proposed Uniform Commercial Code' (1951–1952) 7 *Business Lawyer* 2, 5.

[38] 'Report of the Committee on the Proposed Commercial Code' (1949–1950) 5 *Business Lawyer* 142, 149.

Dunham and Gilmore were amateurs with no facility for the work. 'It seems to me to be just inexcusable for so many different drafts to have gone out on that article. It seems that nothing that is done is given enough thought to give it a semblance of finality.'[39] Schnader's frustration was no doubt related to the fact that the ALI and NCCUSL had planned to adopt the final text of the Code in 1950 and that money raised to support work on the Code was running out. When asked in 1950 by the Council of the ABA Section of Corporation, Banking and Mercantile Law to delay adoption for two years to allow further study, the co-sponsors pleaded the lack of funds but agreed to postpone adoption for one year. They also agreed to enlarge the size of the Editorial Board from five to 15 members and charged it with gathering input. The Enlarged Editorial Board itself convened a public meeting in New York City in January 1951 to listen to comments on the draft Code. In the light of these comments the Board approved changes to the text and the co-sponsors approved the amended text without 'Official Comments' in May 1951. NCCUSL and the ALI reaffirmed their approval in September. Less than a week later the ABA House of Delegates voted to approve the UCC, including Article 9. 'Official Comments' which accompany the text of each Code section were not ready so that it was not until 1952 that the first official text and comments edition was published.[40]

(iv) Contributions of the Original Text of Article 9

When the ABA House of Delegates voted to approve the Code in September 1951 it had before it a favourable report from the Council of the Section of Corporation, Banking and Mercantile Law. The report stated that Article 9 integrated prior statutes, filled gaps in the law, stated new principles and codified common law and commercial practices. This, the report concluded, was 'badly needed'.[41] This judgment is echoed in the Official Comment to §9-101.

Several contributions stand out. The integration of the multiple security devices into a unitary 'security interest' with common rules on creation, validity, perfection, priority and enforcement was a major achievement. Prior security devices, such as chattel mortgages and conditional sales, ceased to be treated separately. Terminology drawn from these devices could continue to be used but terms were to be characterised using Code concepts and terms (§9-102 (1)(a) and (2)). Separate filing offices for the different devices were no longer necessary. Filing a short notice (a 'financing statement') of a security interest was the principal means of

[39] Letter of 25 August 1950 from Schnader to Goodrich quoted in Kamp (n 34) 344 n 144.

[40] *Uniform Commercial Code: Official Draft* (Text and Comments edn) (ALI & NCCUSL, 1952).

[41] 'Report of the Council to the House of Delegates on the Proposed Uniform Commercial Code' (1951–1952) 7 *Business Lawyer* 2, 5.

giving public notice of a security interest in most types of collateral. Individual States retained flexibility when organising filing offices and filling in details on their operation.

The text also validates the 'floating lien'.[42] It does so by a variety of separate provisions that together permit a secured creditor to take a perfected[43] security interest in all a debtor's present and future assets to secure the debtor's present obligations to the creditor as well as future advances made by the creditor. Thus, a security agreement may provide that a security interest attaches to personal property when the property is acquired and that the obligation secured includes the creditor's future advances. Article 9 itself provides that the security interest automatically attaches to proceeds received on disposition of collateral. The Article also authorises a debtor to use or dispose of collateral, such as accounts and inventory, without having to account to its secured creditor, thus rejecting the rule in *Benedict v Ratner*. Notice filing allows a single filed financing statement to be effective as to subsequent transactions. Rules on the priorities of competing claimants to collateral are clarified by making the first to file or perfect priority; buyers of collateral in the ordinary course of business take free of security interests.

An Official Comment[44] explained that by recognising a floating lien Article 9 was merely recognising 'an existing state of things'. By 1950 it was possible in most States for a borrower to give a lien on all its present and future assets by the use of various security devices.[45] Although noting that there 'have no doubt been sufficient economic reasons' to reject hostility to the floating lien, the comment expressed regret. Earlier judicial prejudice against floating liens protected borrowers and provided unsecured creditors a cushion of assets free from secured claims—protection, the comment says, that has much to recommend itself. Article 9 'decisively' rejected the premise underlying this prejudice 'not on the ground that it was wrong in policy but on the ground that it has not been effective'.

[42] Although both the UCC lien and the English charge 'float', the two devices are conceptually distinct. The UCC floating lien attaches to collateral existing at the time the security interest is created and to after-acquired property when the debtor has rights in that property. The drafters were aware of the difference between the devices. PF Coogan, 'Article 9 of the Uniform Commercial Code: Priorities among Secured Creditors and the "Floating Lien"' (1959) 72 *Harvard Law Review* 838, 839 n 2.

[43] A security interest is 'perfected' when public notice of the interest is given, usually by filing a short notice in a public file. In most cases a perfected interest will prevail over subsequent unsecured creditors, the trustee in bankruptcy, and later security interests. A subsequent buyer of the collateral, on the other hand, takes free of a perfected interest unless the buyer is a 'buyer in the ordinary course of business or the secured party authorizes the sale.

[44] Official Comment 2 to §9-204 (UCC 1952).

[45] See Coogan (n 42) 850 (illustrating how a borrower could do so under pre-Code Massachusetts law).

C. The Interim Period (1952–1990)

(i) Further Study and Amendment of the 'Final' Text[46]

The decade following approval of the 1952 official text saw the 'political arm' of the UCC sponsors[47] promote the Code in key State legislatures and the reactivation of an Enlarged Editorial Board to review objections to various provisions of the Code. Critiques of the text came from all sides as it came under intense scrutiny by State legislative bodies, State Bar associations, lawyers and academics. The ABA continued to suggest modifications and to monitor the progress of the Code in State legislatures.[48]

Schnader, as chair of NCCUSL's Commercial Code committee, led the campaign for enactment. He submitted the Code to the Pennsylvania legislature, which in 1953 became the first State to enact the UCC. Other States, however, balked. To Schnader's disappointment, Governor Dewey of New York decided to refer the Code to the New York Law Revision Commission for review. The New York Commission began a three-year review. It solicited comments, held public hearings, and commissioned studies on each Code Article. The Commission's final report in February 1956 concluded that the UCC was 'not satisfactory without comprehensive re-examination and revision in the light of all critical comment obtainable'.[49] Article 9, however, was recognised as 'a significant reform of the law of personal property security'. The Commission believed that the Article's approach 'is sound in theory and satisfactorily developed in most of its elements'.[50]

While the New York Commission conducted its review, the Enlarged Editorial Board itself began responding to objections by proposing modifications of its own. The Board appointed sub-committees for each Article of the Code to analyse these objections. Changes and modifications recommended by the Editorial Board were approved by the ALI and NCCUSL in 1953 and a Supplement to the UCC was published in 1955. When the New York Commission's report appeared in early 1956 the Enlarged Editorial Board responded promptly, approving many but not

[46] For the history of this early period, see R Braucher, 'The Legislative History of the Uniform Commercial Code' (1958) 58 *Columbia Law Review* 798.

[47] Because the ALI could not engage in political activity, NCCUSL's Commercial Code committee organised the approach to State legislatures.

[48] Walter Malcolm, who had been chair since 1946 of the Committee on Commercial Code in the Section of Corporation, Banking and Mercantile Law, was appointed to the Enlarged Editorial Board in 1954. WD Malcolm, 'The Uniform Commercial Code: Current Status and Future Prospects' (1955) 10 *Business Lawyer* 3.

[49] 'Report relating to the Uniform Commercial Code' *1956 Report of the New York Law Revision Commission* 68.

[50] ibid 60.

all that report's criticisms. There followed the publication in quick succession of almost annual UCC official texts, culminating in the 1962 edition.[51]

Much of this activity was in response to increasing interest in the UCC in State legislatures. For despite the negative response in New York, other States began to adopt the Code. Massachusetts acted in 1957, followed by a growing trickle of States, until in 1962 the UCC was the law in 18 States. These States, however, adopted the Code with numerous non-uniform amendments, many of them to Article 9.

(ii) Non-uniform Amendments and the Permanent Editorial Board

Concerned about proliferating non-uniform amendments, NCCUSL and the ALI decided to make the Editorial Board permanent. They succeeded in their solicitation of funds to endow a Permanent Editorial Board (PEB) for the UCC. A formal agreement was drawn up in 1961 between the co-sponsors.[52] The PEB was 'to assist in attaining and maintaining uniformity ... and to this end to approve a minimum number of amendments to the Code'. The Board was to propose amendments when Code sections proved unworkable, court decisions raised doubts about their correct interpretation, or new commercial practices made sections obsolete or required new provisions.[53] The ALI Director was to serve as chair and each co-sponsor was to select five members, with a majority of selected members to come from States that had enacted the Code.

In several subsequent reports, the PEB proceeded to analyse each unofficial amendment to the Code, adopting some as uniform sections and rejecting others with explanations for doing so.[54] At its meeting in November 1966 the PEB noted that States had enacted 337 non-uniform, non-official amendments to Article 9, with 47 of its 54 sections amended.[55] By 1966 virtually all the States had enacted the UCC. Without the fear of inhibiting States from adopting the Code, the PEB concluded that it would be appropriate to restudy Article 9 'in depth'.

(iii) Substantial Review of Article 9 (1966–1972)

To carry out its 'in-depth' restudy of Article 9 the PEB appointed an Article 9 Review Committee in late 1966. Herbert Wechsler, then chairman of the Board,

[51] For 1952–1962 texts see *Uniform Commercial Code Drafts* vols XV–XXIII (ES Kelly compiler) (Littleton, CO, Fred B Rothman & Co, 1984).

[52] Agreement dated 5 August 1961 between the ALI and NCCUSL, Handbook of the NCCUSL and Proceedings of the Annual Conference Meeting in Its Seventieth Year (Saint Louis, MO, 1961) 168.

[53] ibid 169 ('Seventh' clause).

[54] PEB, *Report No 1* (1962); *Report No 2* (1964).

[55] PEB, *Report No 3* (1966).

chaired the study committee. The 10 other committee members were a mixture of judges, practising lawyers and academics; all had extensive experience with Article 9 in one capacity or another. There were also familiar faces. Homer Kripke was named Associate Reporter and effectively became the principal drafter when the Reporter, Robert Braucher, was appointed to the bench in Massachusetts. Grant Gilmore and Peter Coogan served as the two consultants.[56] For those who participated in drafting the original official text, this chance to revisit Article 9 was welcome. When they had published law review articles pointing out defects in the text Schnader had chastised them, saying that they should wait until all States had adopted the UCC.[57]

Between 1967 and 1970 the review committee studied an array of troublesome topics: fixtures; crops and farm products; timber; oil, gas and minerals; intangibles, proceeds and priorities; conflict of laws; motor vehicles and related problems of perfection; matters of scope; filing; and default.[58] When evaluating whether modifications to the existing texts were necessary, the committee followed the cautious policies of the PEB itself. As the 'general comment' in the committee's final report explained:

> The Reporters have reported to the Committee many instances in which the drafting could be improved for clarity or to answer questions that can be posed that are not now clearly answered. Yet the outstanding result of Article 9 in practice has been that it has been gratifyingly successful; that no errors with serious consequences have been disclosed; and that the demands for change have been in relatively narrow areas. The Committee has therefore felt that it is not its responsibility, consistent with the terms of creation of the Permanent Editorial Board, to seek perfection where the Code appears to be working satisfactorily without significant problems in practice, for to do so would run the risk of opening up still further problems.[59]

Although it reviewed confidential drafts behind closed doors, the review committee published several draft reports[60] and participated in several public panel discussions[61] before submitting its final report to the PEB. The Board in turn made recommendations to the ALI and NCCUSL, which approved the text published as the 1972 official text of the UCC. Of the amendments adopted, the most

[56] 'Foreword' Uniform Commercial Code: 1972 Official Text with Comments and Appendix showing 1972 Changes (ALI & NCCUSL, 1972) xxxi–xxxiii.

[57] Kripke (n 29) 581–82.

[58] The review committee's final report summarises its recommendations with respect to these topics. PEB Review Committee for Article 9 of the Uniform Commercial Code, *Final Report* (25 April 1971) 197–248.

[59] 'General Comment on the Approach of the Review Committee for Article 9' in PEB Review Committee, *Final Report* (25 April 1971) 195.

[60] The committee's confidential documents and reports may be found in digital form on the HeinOnline American Law Institute Library/Uniform Commercial Code database.

[61] See eg 'A Look at the Work of the Article 9 Review Committee: A Panel Discussion' (1970) 26 *Business Lawyer* 307.

significant were the revised treatment of fixtures and the clarification of priority with respect to future advances and proceeds.[62]

From the beginning, Article 9 covered security interests not only in personal property, but also in goods attached to real property (described, as of 1956, as 'fixtures'). Financiers of real estate transactions typically claim a mortgage interest not only in the real property, but also in fixtures. Financiers of goods that become fixtures, on the other hand, want to enforce a security interest in these fixtures by removing them from the real property when a debtor defaults. Balancing these interests—and the interests of other claimants—proved difficult. The drafters' very attempt to define what a 'fixture' is failed and the drafters ultimately incorporated the definition found in the real property law of the State in which that property is located. Real property law not being uniform among the different States, Article 9's incorporation of State definitions of fixtures necessarily is not uniform.

The 1972 amendments[63] recognise the right of an Article 9 secured creditor to remove fixtures on compensating other creditors for any damage caused by the removal. At the same time mortgagees and other encumbrancers of the real estate were presumed to have priority in the absence of an Article 9 rule to the contrary. The amendments clarified priority among the different interests. An Article 9 creditor that filed a 'fixture filing'—notice of an Article 9 security interest in fixtures filed in the real estate records—was given priority over mortgagees and encumbrancers in specified circumstances. Other competing claimants, such as a creditor with a judicial lien and a bankruptcy trustee, were subordinate to an Article 9 secured creditor that had either made a fixture filing or had filed notice (a 'financing statement') in the personal property office designated by Article 9. To meet objections from mortgagees financing construction, the drafters crafted special rules giving them priority over all fixtures affixed during construction. The resulting text of the amended Article 9 provision was necessarily complex and, if the transcript of a panel discussion is to be trusted, even the drafters were not fully satisfied with the final proposed amendments.[64]

Experience with priority issues related to future advances and proceeds revealed gaps and ambiguities in the pre-1972 official text.[65] For example, there was no answer to the question whether a creditor with a security interest in a debtor's receivables would have priority over a later creditor that took a security interest in the debtor's inventory (ie, collateral earlier in the business cycle). The 1972 amendments provided an answer: if the receivables financer duly filed a financing statement the financer would have priority over any subsequent creditor financing

[62] See generally PF Coogan, 'The New Article 9' (1973) 86 *Harvard Law Review* 477.
[63] Amendments were incorporated in UCC §9-313 (1972 edn); see §9-335 (2014–2015 edn).
[64] Panel discussion (n 61) 312–20; see Coogan (n 62) 483–505.
[65] See Coogan (n 62) 505–18.

inventory. When addressing this and other ambiguities, the drafters drew upon business needs and practices.[66]

(iv) Settling In (1972–1988)

The decade and a half that followed publication of the 1972 text was a period of settling in. No longer were the Article 9 provisions a novelty. Asset-based financing became commonplace for both financial institutions and borrowers. The 1972 amendments had addressed the most pressing issues that had led to non-uniform amendments, dubious judicial decisions, and uncertainties in practice. Although this period saw the beginnings of more sophisticated forms of financing, such as securitisation, the text of Article 9 remained relatively stable between 1972 and 1988. Four developments, however, were significant.

(a) *Security Interests in Investment Securities*[67]

Although often studied in isolation, Article 9 is a part of a commercial code. This means not only that the general provisions of Article 1 apply to secured transactions but also that changes to other parts of the UCC may require amendments to Article 9. This was the case in 1977 when the ALI and NCCUSL amended Article 8 (Investment Securities). As the Article 9 Review Committee was meeting at the end of the 1960s, the share markets suffered from a 'paperwork crunch' because the physical transfer of share certificates could not keep up with the sale and purchase of shares. An ABA Committee on Stock Certificates and a PEB committee considering the implications of electronic data processing had separately studied the problem and recommended recognition of 'uncertificated securities'. After reviewing the reports of these committees, the PEB approved a draft text spelling out the legal rights and obligations of parties to dealings in such securities. The 1977 text amended Article 8, but recognising that investment securities were often pledged the PEB also amended Article 9 to cross-reference relevant Article 8 provisions.[68]

Market practice, however, took a different turn. Instead of becoming uncertificated, the vast majority of publicly traded certificated securities were immobilised by depositing certificates with 'warehouses'. Owners of these securities held securities entitlements against securities intermediaries, such as clearing houses and brokers, which record these holdings in the owners' investment accounts on the intermediaries' books. To take into account this indirect holding system, the ALI

[66] This question has been one which requires a policy decision in every jurisdiction introducing similar reforms, see Ch 2 G, Canada [fn 43] and Australia Ch 7 F(ii).

[67] For further discussion of the Art 9 and PPSA provisions see Ch 4 E(ii).

[68] For a brief history of the 1977 amendments, see 'Foreword' to *Uniform Commercial Code Official Text and Comments* (1978 edn).

and NCCUSL adopted a revised Article 8 in 1994 with consequential amendments to Article 9.[69] The subsequent revision of Article 9 itself completed the absorption into Article 9 of the rules governing security interests in investment property with appropriate cross-references to Article 8. The 1977 revision of Article 8 became, in other words, an example of premature codification.

(b) Bankruptcy Code

Just as one must read Article 9 in the context of the full text of the UCC so one must consider Article 9 in the context of other laws that impinge on secured transactions.[70] By far the most important of these laws is the federal Bankruptcy Code. Under the federal Constitution the US Congress has the power to enact bankruptcy legislation and if it does so the bankruptcy law is the 'supreme law of the land', thus overriding contrary State law.[71] At the time Article 9 was first drafted, the relevant bankruptcy law was the Bankruptcy Act of 1898. Given its age and despite numerous amendments, the Act included concepts and terminology that differed from Article 9. These differences raised concerns that Article 9 security interests might be voidable in a bankruptcy proceeding. Recodification of bankruptcy law in the 1978 Bankruptcy Code resolved some but not all of these concerns.[72]

Prior to 1978 doubts had been raised about whether a 'floating lien' could withstand challenge.[73] A creditor's security interest attaches—ie, there is a transfer of a property interest—when, inter alia, the debtor acquires rights in collateral. Because inventory and receivables turn over in the ordinary course of business, the debtor transfers a property interest to the creditor as the debtor acquires new inventory items or receivables arise. Under the 1898 Act, transfers during a 'suspect' period (the four months immediately before commencement of bankruptcy proceedings) were void as preferential transfers. Were such transfers to a creditor with a floating lien over inventory or receivables therefore void? Although

[69] *Uniform Commercial Code: Official Text with Comments* (1994 edn). For a brief history of the evolution of Art 8, see 'Prefatory Note' to Art 8 in *Uniform Commercial Code: Official Text and Comments* (2014–2015 edn) (n 1) 672–75. Notwithstanding the focus of these amendments on the public market for investment property, a secured party may still perfect a security interest in an investment security by taking possession of a certificate. UCC §§9-313(a), 8-301.

[70] *United States Code*, Title 11. The relative priority of federal tax liens has also been of concern. *United States Code*, Title 26, §6321. Until the lien is duly recorded in an office designated by the relevant state, the lien is subordinate to an Art 9 perfected security interest. Ibid §6323(f). In 1978 NCCUSL adopted a Uniform Federal Lien Registration Act with registration provisions similar to those in real estate records and in UCC Art 9. Thirty-eight states have enacted the Uniform Act.

[71] *Constitution of the United States of America*, Art I, s 8, cl 4 (bankruptcy) and Art VI, cl 2 (federal legislation supreme law).

[72] Pub L No 95-598, 92 Stat 2549 (6 November 1978). The Bankruptcy Code was modified significantly in 2005. Pub L No 109-8, 119 Stat 23 (20 April 2005).

[73] See generally PF Coogan, 'Article 9—An Agenda for the Next Decade' (1978) 87 *Yale Law Journal* 1012, 1019–125.

the floating lien survived several judicial challenges,[74] it was thought desirable to amend the Bankruptcy Act. The National Bankruptcy Conference[75] appointed Grant Gilmore as chair of a committee charged with rewriting the preferential transfer section. The committee recommended comparing the secured creditor's position at the start of the suspect period with its position at the commencement of bankruptcy proceedings: the creditor's interest would be void only to the extent its position had improved. This recommendation was subsequently incorporated into the 1978 Bankruptcy Code.[76]

Other changes made by the 1978 Bankruptcy Code affected security interests—a stay of actions by a secured party to create or enforce a security interest became automatic on the commencement of a case under the Bankruptcy Code; the right to use collateral in a reorganisation proceeding was enhanced—but in general bankruptcy law recognised property rights created under State law and protected the value of these rights. Just as important as these substantive changes, however, was the increased publication of bankruptcy court opinions, a development encouraged by rules regularising the status and power of these courts. The number of opinions construing (and misconstruing) Article 9 increased significantly and ultimately led to calls for revision of Article 9.

(c) Academic Analysis of Secured Credit and Insolvency

Stimulated by the new Bankruptcy Code and by academic interest in the economic analysis of law in the late 1970s, a growing body of law review articles in this period examined the justification for secured transactions and priorities among creditors.[77] Most of the authors of these articles had little practical experience. Homer Kripke, who did have considerable experience, questioned the value of this theoretical literature.[78] The literature did, however, support calls at the end of the 1980s for a thorough review of Article 9.

[74] *DuBay v Williams*, 491 F.2d 1277 (9th Cir 1969); *Grain Merchants v United Bank & Savings Co* (7th Cir 1969).

[75] The National Bankruptcy Conference is a body of 60 leading US bankruptcy judges, practitioners and scholars. Membership is by invitation only. Since the 1930s the NBC has assisted Congress with the drafting of bankruptcy legislation and the development of relevant bankruptcy policies.

[76] 11 United States Code §547(c)(5).

[77] A small sampling of this literature includes TH Jackson and AT Kronman, 'Secured Financing and Priorities Among Creditors' (1979) 88 *Yale Law Journal* 1143; A Schwartz, 'Security Interests and Bankruptcy Priorities: A Review of Current Theories' (1981) 10 *Journal of Legal Studies* 1; JJ White, 'Efficiency Justifications for Personal Property Security' (1984) 37 *Vanderbilt Law Review* 473; and RE Scott, 'A Relational Theory of Secured Financing (1986) 86 *Columbia Law Review* 901. These authors and others continued to refine analysis of secured transactions in the 1990s.

[78] H Kripke, 'Law and Economics: Measuring the Economic Effect of Commercial Law in a Vacuum of Fact' (1985) 133 *University of Pennsylvania Law Review* 929. Professors Jackson and Schwartz responded: TH Jackson and A Schwartz, 'Vacuum of Fact or Vacuous Theory: A Reply to Professor Kripke' (1985) 133 *University of Pennsylvania Law Review* 987.

(d) Revamping the Permanent Editorial Board

In 1986 NCCUSL and the ALI replaced their earlier agreement creating the PEB with a more detailed agreement.[79] Recognising the continuing contribution of the ABA, the agreement expanded membership of the Board to include a non-voting representative of the ABA as an adviser and the possibility of inviting other interested groups to appoint non-voting representatives (para B.2).

The function of the PEB continued to be

> to discourage amendments or additions to the Uniform Commercial Code not authorized pursuant to this agreement, to assist in attaining and maintaining uniformity in State statutes governing commercial transactions, and to monitor the law of commercial transactions for needed modernization or other improvement (para B.5).

To carry out its function, the Board was given considerable leeway. A non-exhaustive list of steps it could take include (para B.5a–5e):

> a. making recommendations to the Institute and Conference for amendments, revisions or additions to the Uniform Commercial Code after studies conducted by the PEB upon its own motion or as suggestions by the American Bar Association or other groups indicate action is needed to correct unworkable provisions, to resolve divided interpretation of the law, to accommodate new or developing commercial practices, or to advance acceptance of a uniform commercial law, and thereafter commenting upon any drafting product;
>
> b. preparing and publishing supplemental Comments or Annotations to the Uniform Commercial Code and other articulations as appropriate to reflect the correct interpretation of the Code and issuing the same in a manner and at times best calculated to advance the uniformity and orderly development of commercial law; provided, however, that Annotations or Comments which suggest a substantial departure from an accepted interpretation of the Code shall first also be approved by the Executive Committees of the Conference and the Institute and if those bodies direct shall be circulated for suggestions by interested groups prior to their becoming final;[80]
>
> c. monitoring significant case law and statutory developments and the course of commercial practices either itself or in cooperation with the American Bar Association or other groups to detect significant divisions of authority, problem areas of commercial law and practice, and non-uniform amendments, and devising recommendations or other methods to deal with these matters including the publication of reports commenting on one or more developments;
>
> d. monitoring developments in federal law preempting or otherwise affecting the State commercial law and devising recommendations or other methods to deal with the issues raised; and

[79] ALI, *64th Annual Meeting Reports* (1987) 119. The 1986 agreement was revised in 1998. ALI, *79th Annual Meeting Reports* (1988) 189.

[80] In March 1987 the PEB adopted a resolution to implement this paragraph. PEB Resolution on Purposes, Standards and Procedures for the Adoption of PEB Commentaries, *Uniform Commercial Code: Official Text and Comments* (2014–2015 edn) (n 1) 1115–16.

e. coordinating the proper relationship between statutory commercial law and case law developments impacting upon it in the area of products liability and elsewhere and taking appropriate actions to reconcile the issues.[81]

The revamped Board promptly began to consider revising the UCC as a whole. Work began on other parts of the Code[82] but ample reasons were cited for also considering revision of Article 9.

> During the two decades since the [1967–1971] Review Committee's final report, the secured credit markets have seen continued growth and unprecedented innovation. In addition, many hundreds of judicial decisions applying Article 9 have been reported and a large volume of commentary on Article 9, both scholarly and practice-oriented, has emerged. Moreover, the enactment by Congress of the Bankruptcy Reform Act of 1978, which includes a new codification of bankruptcy law, has had a profound effect on secured transactions.[83]

The Board began revision on several fronts. It prepared 'Commentaries' analysing the interpretation of specific legal issues, many of which arose under Article 9. Five of the first seven Commentaries, for example, addressed Article 9 issues.[84] Typical is the issue analysed by Commentary No. 7:

> Secured party A and secured party B each has a perfected security interest in the same account, chattel paper, or general intangible, with A having priority over B. If the account debtor makes payment to secured party B, directly or through the debtor, may A recover the payment from B?

[81] The agreement was amended in 1998 to provide, inter alia, for the appointment of a research director whose duties include:

> (1) monitoring outside developments in technology, business practices, federal and state legislation that in any way may impact on or relate to the Code, international developments, and other matters considered relevant by the research director;
> (2) summarizing the same for the PEB at each meeting, along with (as required) recommendations to address the matters presented;
> (3) meeting with appropriate American Bar Association Committees, and other groups involved in matters concerning the Code at the direction of the PEB;
> (4) preparing drafts of and seeing through to completion PEB Commentaries, annual reports of the PEB, and such other matters as directed by the PEB;
> (5) receiving and, as directed by the chair of the PEB, acting on communications or requests to the PEB; and
> (6) reporting to the PEB or a designated subcommittee of the PEB at such times and in such manner as specified by the PEB as to the above matters.

ALI, 79th Annual Meeting Reports (1988) 189, 192.

[82] 'Foreword' Uniform Commercial Code: Official Text—1999 (ALI and NCCUSL, 1999) xiii.

[83] 'Report of the Article 9 Study Committee of the Permanent Editorial Board for the Uniform Commercial Code' (Dec 1992) I, 2.

[84] PEB Commentaries 1–7 (March 10, 1990), *Uniform Commercial Code: Official Text and Comments* (2014–2015 edn) 1114. Many of the Commentaries have been absorbed into subsequent revisions of the UCC Articles or amended to reflect these revised Articles. The texts of these Commentaries are reproduced in Appendix A of the 2014–2015 edition.

The Commentary discusses the issue and then sets out a conclusion, which it implements by amending the Official Comments published with the UCC black-letter text.[85]

By late 1989, however, the Board concluded that a more thorough revision might be desirable and it appointed a study group to examine the matter.

D. The 1999 Official Text

(i) The Study Group (1990–1992)

The Permanent Editorial Board appointed a study group in early 1990 to consider whether Article 9 should be amended.[86] William Burke, a prominent lawyer and ALI-appointed member of the PEB, chaired the 16-member group. To provide continuity with previous revision of Article 9, Homer Kripke was one of four advisers to the group. Professors Steve Harris and Charles Mooney, Jr, served as reporters.

The study group's primary task was to identify 'drafting imprecision, misinterpretations by the courts, gaps in scope and coverage, and the interaction of Article 9 with other articles of the UCC, with non-UCC State laws, and with an increasing number of federal laws and regulations'.[87] The review, however, was to be thorough, including both examination of Article 9 section by section and analysis of broad policy issues.

As a signal of how thorough the study was to be, the reporters circulated a 53-page list of preliminary issues at the beginning of the group's work in early 1990.[88] When listing questions that raised more basic questions of policy, the reporters suggested that explicitly asking and answering these questions would be useful because to do so would identify the group members' perspectives on policies and the role of the group. Even if the group spent little time discussing the questions in the abstract, they wrote, the questions might provide a useful backdrop for analysis of specific issues. The broad issues identified included such questions as whether the group should seriously consider the literature questioning the economic and social benefits of security interests, whether the group should seek consensus on the purpose of the 'public notice' rules, and how the group should address consumer transactions.[89]

[85] PEB Commentary 7, *Uniform Commercial Code: Official Text and Comments* (2014–2015 edn) 1139–41. The 1999 revision supersedes the commentary by answering the scenario directly with specific priority rules. UCC §§9-330, 9-331 and 9-332.

[86] PEB Study Group UCC Article 9, *Report* (1 December 1992) I, 3.

[87] ibid I, 2.

[88] SL Harris and CW Mooney, Jr, 'Preliminary List of Issues for Discussion and Study Concerning UCC Article 9' (18 April 1990).

[89] ibid 47–53.

Over a three-year period the study group met seven times to discuss working papers analysing a wide variety of issues.[90] The group commissioned some of the working papers; task forces established by groups of several ABA Sections also contributed studies on particular topics.[91] A total of 83 separate documents appear in the files of the study group and several additional reports appear in the volume of appendices submitted with the group's final report.[92]

Robert Scott, an academic member of the study group, later provided insight into the dynamics of the study group's deliberations. In a 1994 law review article Scott analyses the ALI and NCCUSL as 'private legislatures'.[93] These institutions, he argues, value expertise but not all expertise is equally valued. They value academic insights into the structure and social effects of secured transactions, but they value more highly knowledge of case law and they value most highly experience with how secured transactions work in the real world.

> Because operational expertise is the relevant criterion, it is unsurprising that eight members of the Study Group (including the chair) were commercial lawyers and house counsel whose practice specialty was the representation of secured creditors. These lawyers are the most knowledgeable concerning the questions the Study Group is asked to resolve, and they properly emerge as the most influential members of the group (other than the academic reporters). Their influence is further elevated because key members of this group also occupy prominent roles on the UCC Permanent Editorial Board.[94]

The dominance of these 'real-work' lawyers minimises the contributions of other members in the group's deliberations.

> Efforts by the [four] academic members to place on the agenda a discussion of the broader implications of the proposed changes in Article 9, including their cumulative effects on other societal interests, were uniformly unsuccessful. The several practicing lawyers who were seen as representatives of other interests were similarly marginalized by the focus on the technical task of 'fixing' Article 9. Ultimately, these members participated only sporadically in the discussions that led to the final report.[95]

Despite this dynamic, Scott points out that the result is not necessarily evidence that the recommendations have a special interest bias or that the

[90] An interim report published in the ABA Section of Business Law's widely circulated journal solicited comments from readers. WM Burke, SL Harris and CW Mooney, Jr, 'Interim Report on the Activities of the Article 9 Study Committee' (1991) 46 *Business Lawyer* 1883.

[91] PEB Study Group, *Report* (n 86) 4, fn 12 (listing special advisers and advisory groups).

[92] All of the documents before the study committee are preserved in the HeinOnline ALI Library/Uniform Commercial Code database. See Appendix to this chapter.

[93] RE Scott, 'The Politics of Article 9' (1994) 80 *Virginia Law Review* 1783. See also A Schwartz and RE Scott, 'The Political Economy of Private Legislatures' (1995) 143 *University of Pennsylvania Law Review* 595. See A Schwartz, 'The Still Questionable Role of Private Legislatures' (2002) 62 *Louisiana Law Review* 1147. One of the reporters later took issue with the Scott-Schwartz analysis. CW Mooney, Jr, 'Modeling the Uniform Law "Process": A Comment on Scott's Rise and Fall of Article 2' (2002) 62 *Louisiana Law Review* 1081.

[94] ibid 1808–09.

[95] ibid 1809.

recommendations will ultimately become law. In any event, no matter what the dynamics of its deliberations the group's final report records no dissents.

The study group submitted this final report in December 1992.[96] The report made 33 specific recommendations. These fall into three main categories: expanding the scope of Article 9, modifying and simplifying filing provisions, and introducing more detailed rules on enforcement with special attention to the obligations of account debtors on intangibles. The report does not have separate analysis of the broad questions asked initially but it is clear from the report that the group resolved any doubts about the utility of secured transactions in their favour. The report pays considerable attention to the appropriate use of filing in public records, but there is less concern about consumer debtors. Stressing that the group found the concepts in existing Article 9 to be fundamentally sound, the group nevertheless concluded that the benefits from proposed modifications outweighed the costs of re-education, unintended consequences, and temporary non-uniformity. To no one's surprise, the study group recommended the appointment of a drafting committee.

(ii) The Drafting Committee (1993–1998)

The co-sponsors accepted the recommendation and in 1993 the PEB appointed a drafting committee. William Burke was named chair of the drafting committee but the other members of the 12-person committee had not served on the study group. As with the 1967–1972 committee, membership included practitioners, judges and several academics. Steve Harris and Charles Mooney were asked to serve as reporters.

Work began promptly. Between November 1993 and March 1998 the drafting committee met 14 times. The annual meetings of NCCUSL reviewed drafts in 1995, 1996 and 1997. The Council of the ALI reviewed drafts in those same years, while the reporters made informational reports to the general ALI membership at the annual meetings in this same period. ALI members with a particular interest in the project constituted a Members Consultative Group and the reporters, the chair and some members of the drafting committee met with the group three times between 1994 and 1996. At the same time ABA committees, especially the Uniform Commercial Code committee of the Section of Business Law, prepared reports and monitored the progress of the drafting committee. In comparison with the 1968–1972 revision, the process was more transparent and open.

(a) Reconciling Consumer Interests

Notwithstanding this transparency and openness, the drafting committee's procedures were criticised for inadequate representation of consumer interests—

[96] PEB Study Group, *Report* (n 86) 2 vols.

a criticism already raised in connection with revision of other Code articles.[97] The Code sponsors responded by taking steps to support participation of representatives of consumer groups. In the case of the Article 9, the drafting committee appointed in 1995 a special subcommittee to consider 'whether and to what extent [the] Article 9 draft should contain consumer-protection provisions'.[98] As the drafters of the original Article 9 would have warned the committee, attempts to provide such protections proved to be controversial. Consumer representatives and consumer-finance creditors reached an impasse. As reported to the ALI membership in 1998, a compromise was brokered at the last minute by the chair of the drafting committee and presented to the committee as the only way to avoid 'widespread opposition, with pitched battles in the various legislatures during the enactment process'—delaying or inhibiting enactment.[99] Most of the compromises involved enforcement procedures. In several instances, the compromises left the resolution to judicial decisions without guidance.[100] The drafting committee approved the compromise but the drafters, who had not participated in the compromise negotiations, were not pleased.[101] Nor, more generally, was a principal representative of consumer interests.[102]

(b) Academic Debates

The openness and transparency of the UCC revision process encouraged the outpouring of academic analysis in the law reviews. The 1990s were halcyon days for commercial law academics. Distinguished reviews published articles and symposia issues exploring such topics as the justification (economic or otherwise) for secured transactions, the implications of the ALI and NCCUSL acting as private legislatures, whether unsecured creditors need protection from secured creditors, the value (or lack of value) of public filing systems, and whether the absence of empirical support for particular arguments was relevant. The Article 9 reporters—Professors Harris and Mooney—did not hesitate to contribute their analysis of these issues.[103]

[97] See eg comments on the revision of Arts 3 and 4 (Negotiable Instruments; Bank Deposits and Collections) in L Rubin, 'Thinking Like a Lawyer, Acting Like a Lobbyist: Some Notes on the Process of Revising UCC Articles 3 and 4' (1993) 26 *Loyola Los Angeles Law Review* 743; also Patchel (n 23).

[98] UCC Article 9: Proposed Final Draft (15 April 1998) xliv.

[99] ibid.

[100] See eg UCC §9-626(b); see also §9-103(h).

[101] CW Mooney, Jr, 'The Consumer Compromise in Revised UCC Article 9: The Shame of it All' (2007) 68 *Ohio State Law Journal* 215.

[102] G Hillebrand, 'What's Wrong with the Uniform Law Process?' (2001) 52 *Hastings Law Journal* 631.

[103] See eg SL Harris and CW Mooney, Jr, 'A Property-based Theory of Security Interests: Taking Debtors' Choices Seriously' (1994) 80 *Virginia Law Review* 2021; SL Harris and CW Mooney, Jr, 'Choosing the Law Governing Perfection: The Data and Politics of Article 9 Filing' (1995) 79 *Minnesota Law Review* 663; SL Harris and CW Mooney, Jr, 'Negotiability, Electronic Commercial Practices, and a New Structure for the UCC Article 9 Filing System: Tapping the Private Market for Information Technology' (1995) 31 *Idaho Law Review* 835; SL Harris and CW Mooney, Jr, 'Measuring the Social Costs and

The sometimes heated interchanges among academics, however, had little impact on the revised text of Article 9. Whether or not justified by empirical data, security interests continue to be recognised; the drafting process has not changed significantly; unsecured creditors may (or may not) be worse off by making it easier to perfect security interests in a common debtor's property; public filing remains the centrepiece of the system for determining priority; and empirical studies remain scarce. One example illustrates the point. Two Harvard scholars published an article in the *Yale Law Journal* questioning the priority of secured claims in bankruptcy.[104] Professor Elizabeth Warren followed up with a draft amendment to section 9-301 to allow an unsecured creditor to levy on 20 per cent of the value of collateral covered by a secured party with a perfected security interest.[105] Although her amendment interested some fellow academics, it had no support on the drafting committee and the proposal disappeared without trace.[106] Members of the committee showed little interest in the claims of unsecured creditors; they had their eyes focused primarily on responding to the recommendations of the earlier study group.

(c) The Final Text

From 1993 to 1998 the Article 9 drafting committee reviewed scrupulously the study group's recommendation and the draft texts prepared by the two reporters. The committee accepted most recommendations. As a result, the principal features of the final text submitted to the ALI and NCCUSL in 1998 are similar to those identified in the study group's report.[107] The scope of Article 9 is expanded to cover, inter alia, security interests in deposit accounts as original collateral, the sale of promissory notes and payment intangibles, and assignment of commercial tort claims. Agricultural liens are dealt with the first time. The filing provisions are extensively revised to encourage uniformity, reduce the cost of filing and address numerous details not previously covered. Details on enforcement of security interests fill broad and open-ended provisions, with particular attention to enforcing security interests in intangible property and to protecting consumer debtors.

Benefits and Identifying the Victims of Subordinating Security Interests in Bankruptcy' (1997) 82 *Cornell Law Review* 1349.

104 LA Bebchuk and JM Fried, 'The Uneasy Case for the Priority of Secured Claims in Bankruptcy' (1996) 105 *Yale Law Journal* 857; LA Bebchuk and JM Fried, 'The Uneasy Case for the Priority of Secured Claims in Bankruptcy: Further Thoughts and Replies to Critics' (1997) 82 *Cornell Law Review* 1279.

105 E Warren, 'Article 9 Set-Aside for Unsecured Creditors' (1997) 51 *Consumer Finance Law Quarterly Report* 323; E Warren, 'Making Policy with Imperfect Information: The Article 9 Full Priority Debates' (1997) 82 *Cornell Law Review* 1373.

106 Note that a version of this idea is now enacted in English law, see section 176A Insolvency Act, which provides that a percentage of floating charge assets ('the prescribed part') is set aside for unsecured creditors.

107 A useful summary of the revisions is found in Official Comment 4 to UCC §9-101. An overview of the text as revised is set out in the Official Comments to UCC §9-102.

Numerous definitions are added and the text reorganised. To help readers navigate what has become an extremely complex text bracketed captions are inserted at the beginning of subsections.[108]

The ALI and NCCUSL approved the official text in 1998 and the official text with comments in 1999.[109] The text was tweaked with the publication of errata, technical amendments and modifications in 1999 and 2000. To allow the text to come into force at the same time in all States, section 9-701 provided that it would take effect on 1 July 2001.

(iii) The 2010 Amendments

By the end of 2001 Revised Article 9 had come into force in all States. Some States, however, had enacted non-uniform amendments, many of which modified the public filing provisions. Filing officers and the International Association of Commercial Administrators (IACA)[110] proposed numerous changes to forms and procedures. Non-uniform treatment of the names of debtors, especially individuals, was particularly troublesome because financing statements are indexed under the names of debtors. Practice had also identified several other problems with the revised Article and several problematic court opinions were handed down.[111]

In January 2008 NCCUSL's executive committee approved the creation of a study committee to determine whether there were issues sufficiently significant that amendments were necessary. On the recommendation of the study committee, the Code sponsors appointed a Joint Review Committee chaired by Ed Smith, a member of the PEB and a prominent member of the ABA Business Law Section. Steve Harris agreed to be the Reporter. There was to be no change to policies adopted during the 1998 revision in the absence of significant problems in practice. The review committee was to recommend amendments to the statutory text only if these problems were substantial; otherwise other techniques, such as clarifying or amending the Official Comments, should be considered.

The ALI and NCCUSL adopted the final text in 2010, drafts of proposed amendments circulated in 2009.[112] The principal changes to the 1998 text relate

[108] LF Del Duca et al, 'Simplification in Drafting—The UCC Article 9 Experience' (1999) 74 *Chicago-Kent Law Review* 1309.

[109] Uniform Commercial Code: Official Text—1999 Appendix XVI.

[110] IACA is an association of administrators of official business organisation and secured transaction record systems. Originally established in the United States in 1978, IACA expanded its membership internationally in the 1990s. Although primarily an association of individual professionals, IACA amended its bylaws in 2013 to permit jurisdictions outside the United States and Canada to become members. See www.iaca.org.

[111] For the history of the 2010 amendments see EE Smith, 'An Updated Summary of the 2010 Amendments to Article 9 of the Uniform Commercial Code' (2013) 45 *Uniform Commercial Code Law Journal* 131.

[112] Uniform Commercial Code: Official Text and Comments (2014–2015 edn) Appendix AA.

to filing, although both text and comments were changed to address several other issues and the PEB issued a Commentary to clarify the issues in a troublesome 2007 case.[113] On the most problematic issue—the 'correct' name of an individual debtor—agreement could not be reached on a uniform solution so the official text sets out three alternative solutions, leaving it to each State to choose an alternative.[114]

E. Themes

The present Article 9 is complex. Much of its complexity can be attributed to changing financial practices, to expansion of the Article's coverage, and to the increasing demand for predictable answers. Financial practices have become more sophisticated. More intense competition among financial institutions has led to the search for new forms of potential collateral. A debtor's intangible property has become a far more significant part of its assets. At the same time, legal advisers have responded with demands for answers that provide certainty without the need to rely on litigation. Yet, notwithstanding this complexity, the basic concepts of the 1952 text—eg the distinction between attachment and perfection, the importance of filing financing statements—remain the foundation on which the complexity is built.

Article 9's success in responding to changes in the financial practice can be traced to the Permanent Editorial Board. The PEB has monitored developments and responded in a timely and measured way with a variety of measures ranging from proposed changes to the Article 9 text and separate commentaries. Its work has increasingly been aided by task forces and committees of the American Bar Association. It has found it more difficult, however, to obtain input from representatives of consumers continues.

Appendix

Sources

The historian of UCC Article 9 can draw upon a wealth of source material. Digital databases and paper-depositaries include official drafts, confidential drafts, explanatory introductions and comments to these texts, transcripts of meetings,

[113] 'PEB Commentary No 18: The *Highland Capital* case' (July 2014), *Uniform Commercial Code: Official Text and Comments* (2014–2015 edn) 1221.

[114] UCC §9-503. For discussion of the policy choices in this regard, see New Zealand Ch 6 F(ii).

committee reports, publications of drafters and other participants, reports and communications from other interested persons, and even anecdotal reminiscences of those intimately involved.

(i) Drafts of UCC Article 9 Texts and Reports

Paper copies kept in the Uniform Law Commission Archives at the University of Texas Law School (in process of being digitised) and in the American Law Institute Archives at the University of Pennsylvania Law School. A finding aid for the Uniform Commercial Code Records at the University of Pennsylvania may be found in ALI.04.004 (prepared by Jordon Steele) (last updated on 28 April 2011).

Uniform Commercial Code Drafts: Issued by the American Law Institute and the National Commissioners on Uniform State Laws through the 1962 Official Text with Comments (ES Kelly ed) (Littleton, CO, Fred B Rothman & Co, 1984) 23 vols (also available on HeinOnline: American Law Institute database)

Uniform Commercial Code Confidential Drafts: Issued by the American Law Institute and the National Conference of Commissioners on Uniform State Laws through the 1977 Revisions of Article 8 (ES Kelly and A Puckett compilers, 1955) (Littleton, CO, Fred B Rothman & Co, 1984) 10 vols (also available on HeinOnline: American Law Institute database)

HeinOnline: American Law Institute Library/Uniform Commercial Code

HeinOnline: National Conference of Commissioners on Uniform State Laws/ Archive Publications/Commercial Code database

Uniform Law Commission (NCCUSL) website: www.uniformlaws.org

(ii) Transcripts of Debates

Transcripts available in the archives mentioned above

HeinOnline: American Law Institute Proceedings of Annual Meetings

WS Hein & Co: Proceedings of ALI Annual Meetings (microfiches)

WS Hein & Co: Proceedings of the NCCUSL Annual Conference (microfiches)

(iii) Collected Papers

The papers of KN Llewellyn and the UCC papers of S Mentschikoff have been deposited at the University of Chicago in the Special Collections Department of the University Library. The Llewellyn UCC papers (Category J) were published on microfilm by WS Hein & Co.

Karl Llewellyn Papers: A Guide to the Collection (RM Ellinwood and WL Twining compilers, 1970) updated by *Karl N. Llewellyn Papers: A Supplemental Guide to the Collection* (SH Lewis compiler, 1994)

(iv) Reminiscences of the Drafters

(a) Original Official Text

'Symposium: Origins and Evolution: Drafters Reflect Upon the Uniform Commercial Code' (1982) 43 *Ohio State Law Journal* 535–642 (Mentschikoff, Coogan, Leary, Dunham, Kripke, Henson) (the publications of most of these authors often include comments on the drafting of the original official text and later amendments)

G Gilmore, '[Tribute to] Homer Kripke' (1981) 56 *New York University Law Review* 8

G Gilmore, 'The Good Faith Purchase Idea and The Uniform Commercial Code: Confessions of a Repentant Draftsman' (1981) 15 *Georgia Law Review* 605

(b) 1972 Amendments

H Kripke, 'A Draftsman's Wishes that He Could Do Things Over Again—UCC Article 9' (1989) 26 *San Diego Law Review* 1

(c) 1998 Amendments

SL Harris and CW Mooney, Jr, 'How Successful Was the Revision of UCC Article 9? Reflections of the Drafters' (1999) 74 *Chicago-Kent Law Review* 1357

CW Mooney, Jr, 'The Consumer Compromise in Revised UCC Article 9: The Shame of it All' (2007) 68 *Ohio State Law Journal* 215.

4

Transplanting Article 9: The Canadian PPSA Experience

CATHERINE WALSH

A. Introduction

Article 9 of the Uniform Commercial Code (UCC)[1] in the United States is famously based on a functional concept of security. In place of the traditional organisation of the effects of secured transactions according to their nominal form, a 'security interest' is defined as any interest in personal property that functions in substance to secure the performance of an obligation.[2] The great advantage of this organising structure was to enable the drafters 'to make necessary distinctions between the unlike elements of different security transactions and at the same time to formulate a single set of rules to cover the very large area of likeness common to all such transactions'.[3]

Often promoted as a model for secured transactions reform,[4] this chapter focuses on the first 'export' of the Article 9 model beyond United States borders. The Personal Property Security Acts (PPSAs) in effect in Canada's nine common law provinces and three federal territories are all modelled conceptually and structurally on Article 9.[5] While Article 9 and the early versions of the PPSAs also

[1] Unless otherwise indicated, references are to the official text of UCC Art 9 adopted in 1999, in effect from 1 July 2001, as revised in 2010, in effect from 1 July 2013.

[2] UCC §1-201(35).

[3] Grant Gilmore, 'The Secured Transactions Article of the Commercial Code' (1951) 16 *Law and Contemporary Problems* 27, 27.

[4] For an early account of the international influence of Art 9, see RCC Cuming, 'Internationalizing Secured Financing Law' in R. Cranston (ed), *Making Commercial Law: Essays in Honour of Roy Goode* (Oxford: Clarendon, 1997) 499–524.

[5] In order of implementation, see: ONTARIO, 1976 (SO 1967, c 73, in force 1 April 1976, replaced by SO 1989, c 16, in force 10 October 1989, RSO 1990, c P.10); MANITOBA, 1978 (SM 1973, c 5, in force 1 September 1978, replaced by SM 1993, c 14, in force 5 September 2000, CCSM c P35); SASKATCHEWAN, 1981 (SS 1979–80, c P-6.1, in force 1 May 1981, replaced by SS 1993, c P-6.2, in force 1 April 1995); YUKON TERRITORY, 1982 (OYT 1980, c 20, 2d Sess, in force 1 June 1982, RSY 2002,

influenced the civil law regime for movable security in Québec's 1994 Civil Code,[6] this chapter examines the Canadian transplant experience primarily through the lens of the PPSAs.

Section B reviews the origin and evolution of PPSA reform. As a result of the rather more spontaneous and bottom-up nature of the reform process compared to the United States, uniformity among the various PPSAs remains something of an elusive goal. Some insights into the reasons are offered.

If the PPSAs are not carbon copies of each other, still less are they carbon copies of Article 9. Space constraints preclude covering all points of difference. Section C focuses on what many consider to be the heart of the Article 9 model: the establishment of a comprehensive public registration regime for disclosing the potential existence of non-possessory security interests in a debtor's personal property. It will be seen that the PPSAs tend to favour the publicity function of registration vis-à-vis third parties whereas Article 9 puts greater emphasis on its 'claim staking' or priority ordering advantages for secured creditors.[7] Relatedly, the PPSAs have also tended to be more solicitous of the need to protect persons named as debtors in public registrations against the potential prejudice posed by 'false positives'.

Section D compares the broader transactional scope of the PPSA registration regime relative to that of Article 9. The analysis in this section reinforces the theme in Section C regarding the stronger emphasis placed by the PPSAs on the public notice function of registration.

Section E turns to the treatment of security interests in financial collateral. It will be seen that Canadian jurisdictions (including Québec) have followed Article 9's lead in exempting secured creditors who obtain 'control' of collateral in the form of investment securities from the public notice and temporal priority rules applicable to other categories of collateral. While this approach has roots in the traditional value assigned to negotiability in investment markets, the Article 9 control-based approach favours settlement finality in collateral transactions to a historically unprecedented degree. Article 9 extends similar treatment to security

c 169); ALBERTA, 1990 (SA 1988, c. P-4.05, in force 1 October 1990, RSA 2000, c P-7); BRITISH COLUMBIA, 1990 (SBC 1989, c 36, in force 1 October 1990, RSBC 1996, c 359); NEW BRUNSWICK, 1995 (SNB 1993, c P-7.1, in force 18 April 1995); NOVA SCOTIA, 1997 (SNS 1995–96, c 13, in force 3 November 1997); PRINCE EDWARD ISLAND, 1998 (SPEI 1997, c 33, in force 27 April 1998, RSPEI 1988, c P-3.1); NEWFOUNDLAND AND LABRADOR, 1999 (SNL 1998, c P-7.1, in force 13 December 1999); NORTHWEST TERRITORIES, 2001 (SNWT 1994, c 8, in force 7 May 2001); NUNAVUT, 2001 (in force 7 May 2001, SNWT (Nu) 1994, c 8). Generally, see Ronald CC Cuming, Catherine Walsh and Roderick J Wood, *Personal Property Security Law*, 2nd edn (Toronto: Irwin Law, 2012).

[6] Civil Code of Québec, CQLR c C-1991, Book Six—Prior Claims and Hypothecs. For a summary overview, see Cuming, Walsh and Wood (n 5) 99–113. See also Michael Bridge, Roderick Macdonald, Ralph Simmonds and Catherine Walsh, 'Formalism, Functionalism, and Understanding the Law of Secured Transactions' (1998–1999) 44 *McGill Law Journal* 567; Roderick Macdonald, 'The Counter-Reformation of Secured Transactions Law in Quebec' (1991) 19 *Canadian Business Law Journal* 239.

[7] On the public notice and claim staking functions of registration, see F Stephen Knippenberg, 'Debtor Name Changes and Collateral Transfers under 9-402(7): Drafting from the Outside-In' (1987) 52 *Missouri Law Review* 57, 61–63, and fn 22.

interests in deposit accounts with financial institutions and here too Canadian jurisdictions are in the process of enacting reforms aimed at emulating the Article 9 approach.

Section F offers concluding observations on what the Canadian PPSA experience teaches about the reasons for local adaptations of legal transplants as well as the potential for the transplant to revert to the original model in response to external market pressures for cross-border uniformity.

B. The Origin and Evolution of PPSA Reform in Canada

(i) Substantive Impetus for Reform

In the United States the pre-Article 9 jurisprudence imposed restrictions on financing against the security of a debtor's inventory and accounts receivable. A line of cases culminating in the Supreme Court's decision in *Benedict v Ratner*[8] required the creditor to police the debtor's dealings with the collateral and its proceeds on penalty of having its security interest declared fraudulent and void.[9] One important impetus underlying Article 9 reform in the United States was the desire to liberalise non-possessory secured financing on the security of circulating pools of assets.[10]

The pre-PPSA law in common law Canada did not suffer from any equivalent constraint.[11] The Canadian common law courts had early on embraced the English floating charge over inventory and receivables and the equitable mortgage and fixed charge over after-acquired assets.[12] The federal Parliament had

[8] *Benedict v Ratner*, 268 US 353 (1925).

[9] For a detailed examination of the impact of *Benedict v Ratner* on pre-Art 9 law and practice, see Grant Gilmore, *Security Interests in Personal Property* (Boston, MA: Little, Brown and Company, 1965) vol I at 250–86. For further discussion of the history of Art 9, see Ch 3.

[10] ibid 358–61. Gilmore famously came to regret that Art 9 had not preserved the substantive policy underlying the restrictions imposed by *Benedict* on all-assets secured financing: see Grant Gilmore, 'The Good Faith Purchase Idea and the Uniform Commercial Code: Confessions of a Repentant Draftsman' (1981) 15 *Georgia Law Review* 605, 627.

[11] Section 92(18) of Canada's Constitution Act 1867 places legislative authority over 'property and civil rights' in the 10 provinces. Constitutionally, the three northern territories are creations of the federal government, but the Parliament of Canada has devolved legislative powers to the territorial legislative assemblies generally equivalent to those granted to the provinces. Thus, there is no 'Canadian' law of secured transactions. Rather, there are 13 distinct provincial and territorial laws. The federal Parliament has ancillary authority over secured transactions in specific areas, including maritime law and banking, for which there exist specific regimes although these are not dealt with in this chapter. Bankruptcy and insolvency law is also a federal responsibility and necessarily intersects with the provincial and territorial secured transactions regimes.

[12] Cuming has frequently noted this difference in the motivations underlying Art 9 and PPSA reform: see, for example, Ronald CC Cuming, 'Article 9 North of 49: The Canadian PPS Acts and the Quebec Civil Code' (1996) 29 *Loyola of Los Angeles Law Review* 971, 972–73. But perhaps this difference

also enacted a special statutory regime empowering the federally chartered banks to take security over the inventory of commercial debtors.[13] On the other hand, like pre-Article 9 law in the United States,[14] the pre-PPSA legal framework for secured transactions was highly fragmented.[15] The law had evolved in an ad hoc fashion to recognise a complex mix of security devices. In addition to the forms of security derived from English law (the pledge, chattel mortgage, equitable assignment by way of security, and equitable charge in both its fixed and floating variants), other security devices in common use included the conditional sale and analogous lease agreements in which the creditor's reservation of ownership functioned to secure payment of the acquisition price. Each of these devices was subject to a discrete conceptual and legal framework as well as discrete and often highly technical public registration requirements.

(ii) First Steps: The 1976 Ontario PPSA

In the United States, secured transactions reform originated in 1940 as part of a larger national project aimed at unifying the entire body of commercial law in the various States under the co-sponsorship of the National Conference of Commissioners on Uniform State Law (NCCUSL) and the American Law Institute (ALI). The first official version of the UCC was published in 1951, with Article 9 on secured transactions considered by many to be its most innovative and valuable component.[16]

Reform in common law Canada was a more bottom-up process, originating at the provincial level with the formation in 1960 of a sub-committee of the Ontario Commercial Law Section of the Canadian Bar Association to make recommendations for the amendment of Ontario's various personal property

should not be overly emphasised. As Ziegel observes, citing Gilmore (n 9) 290, the difference was probably more one of degree than kind: Jacob Ziegel, 'The New Personal Property Security Regimes—Have We Gone Too Far' (1989–90) 28 *Alberta Law Review* 739, 749. On the commonalities and differences between the PPSA and pre-PPSA treatment of the types of assets covered by a floating charge, see Catherine Walsh, 'The Floating Charge is Dead; Long Live the Floating Charge—A Canadian Perspective on the Reform of Personal Property Securities Law' in Agasha Mugasha (ed), *Perspectives on Commercial Law* 129 (St Leonards, NSW: Prospect, 1999).

[13] On the Bank Act security regime, see Cuming, Walsh and Wood (n 5) 693–709.

[14] For a comprehensive examination of the pre-Art 9 law of secured transactions in the United States, see Gilmore (n 9) vol I, Part 1. And see Robert E. Scott, 'The Politics of Art 9' (1994) 80 *Virginia Law Review* 1783: 'The preexisting regime of pigeonholed classifications, each with its own filing system and/or special sets of rules, created unnecessary costs as well as traps for the unwary, and left—under virtually any rationale—odd holes in coverage and scope.'

[15] On the fragmented state of the pre-PPSA law, see Cuming, Walsh and Wood (n 5) 2–5. For detailed accounts, see Jacob S Ziegel, 'Canadian Chattel Security Law: Past Experience and Current Developments' in J.G. Sauveplannc (ed) *Security over Corporeal Movables* (Leiden: AW Sitjhoff, 1974) 73, 73–98; RCC Cuming, 'Harmonization of Canadian Personal Property Security Law' in *Harmonization of Business Law in Canada* (Toronto: University of Toronto Press, 1986).

[16] See Ch 3 B.

security registration statutes. After an initial attempt at piecemeal tinkering, the Committee concluded that a wholesale rationalisation and modernisation of the entire field was needed. The drafters quickly settled on Article 9 as the most workable—perhaps more accurately the only available—conceptual and structural blueprint.[17]

The Committee's draft Personal Property Security Act, as amended by the Ontario Law Reform Commission, was eventually enacted in 1967. Almost another decade elapsed before it was proclaimed in force in 1976. The principal reason for the delay was not a lack of faith in the basic Article 9 framework but rather in the registry infrastructure. Article 9 reform had been initiated before computers began to transform business operations and consumer life. The early State filing systems were predicated on a paper record and paper forms and often localised at the county level within each State.[18] By the time PPSA reform was initiated in Ontario, the technology to support a centralised computer-based registry record was available and the Ontario reformers were committed to that model from the outset. But the development of the necessary hardware and software proved to be a lengthier and costlier process than anticipated.[19]

(iii) Second and Third Generation PPSAs

Ontario's reform initiative early on attracted the interest of other Canadian common law jurisdictions. Not only did the new legislation promise to resolve shared problems, legal harmonisation was seen as important to facilitate cross-border financing transactions. The fact that PPSA reform was first pioneered by Ontario, Canada's most populous province and its financial centre, no doubt also played an important role in motivating other provinces to emulate its lead.

Nonetheless, the actual implementation of PPSA reform across common law Canada proved to be a slow process and some 25 years was to elapse between the coming into force of the original Ontario PPSA and the eventual adoption of PPSAs by all the common law provinces and territories.[20] In part the slow pace of take-up may have been due to a sense that immediate reform was not urgent given the general adequacy of the Canadian common law framework, despite its fragmented and complex nature, to accommodate financing against most important categories of consumer and enterprise assets.[21] In greater part, however, it was

[17] Ziegel (n 15) 99. On the two leitmotifs of rationalisation and modernisation associated with Art 9 and PPSA reform, see generally Ziegel (n 15).

[18] On the deficiencies of the early Art 9 filing systems, see Lynn M. LoPucki, 'Computerization of the Article 9 Filing System: Thoughts on Building the Electronic Highway (1992) 55 Law and Contemp. Probs. 5; Scott (n 14) 1829–30. See also Todd J. Janzen, 'Nationalize the Revised Article 9 Filing System: A Comparison of the Old Article 9 and Canadian Personal Property Filing Systems' (2001) 11 *Indiana International & Comparative Law Review* 389.

[19] Ziegel (n 12) 100.

[20] Above n 5.

[21] See above, text at nn 11–13.

likely due to the absence of a centralised organisational venue with the mandate and resources to lead and coordinate reform.

This was not for want of trying in the initial years. As early as 1963, the Commercial Law Section of the Canadian Bar Association (CBA) had established a special committee to develop model PPSA legislation. After a lengthy consultation period, the CBA endorsed a Model Uniform PPSA in 1970.[22] Some features of that model were incorporated as amendments to the original 1967 Ontario PPSA when it came into force in 1976. A year later, in 1971, the Uniform Law Conference of Canada (ULCC) adopted a Uniform PPSA based on the 1967 Ontario Act, with some features taken from the CBA Model.[23] But neither organisation attracted the political mandate and resources to retain an ongoing coordinating and updating role, no doubt in part due to their failure to coordinate efforts in the first instance. This left the reform initiative and the updating burden at the individual jurisdictional level.

Thus, while the 'second generation' PPSAs enacted by Manitoba, Saskatchewan and the Yukon Territory (in 1978, 1981 and 1982 respectively) incorporated features of the CBA Model, they also took account of the intervening 1972 revisions to Article 9 as well as technological advances in relation to the public registry infrastructure.

In the wake of the failure of broader harmonisation initiatives, the four western provinces and then two northern territories joined forces in 1989 to form the Western Canada Personal Property Committee composed of government representatives and academic experts from the member jurisdictions. Three of the six member jurisdictions had already enacted a PPSA (Manitoba, Saskatchewan and the Yukon Territory) but considered that these already needed updating. The other three jurisdictions (British Columbia, Alberta and the then Northwest Territories) had contemplated PPSA reform for some time but wanted to be sure that the legislation reflected current developments. While the Committee's initial goal was to foster harmonisation in western Canada, its work quickly attracted the interest of reformers from New Brunswick and subsequently the other three Atlantic Canadian provinces. A new constitution was ultimately proclaimed at the 1991 meeting of the Committee, reconstituting it as the Canadian Conference on Personal Property Security Law (CCPPSL) with a mandate 'to encourage and facilitate the harmonization and compatibility of provincial, territorial and federal personal property security law'.[24]

The CCPPSL's goals were largely successful. Between 1990 and 2001, 'third-generation' PPSAs adapted from the legislation developed by the Conference were enacted (or revised and re-enacted in the case of Saskatchewan and Manitoba)

[22] Ziegel (n 15) 100–01.

[23] ibid.

[24] The driving force behind the establishment of the Western Canada Personal Property Security Act Committee—and later the CCPPSL—was Prof Ronald Cuming of the College of Law at the University of Saskatchewan.

by all of the common law provinces and territories except Ontario.[25] Although derived from the 'second-generation' 1981 Saskatchewan PPSA, these third-generation Acts incorporated significant revisions to accommodate technological advances in the electronic registry infrastructure and intervening substantive developments in the jurisprudence and scholarship.[26]

(iv) Multiple PPSAs vs 'the PPSA'

Although largely uniform, even the CCPPSL-inspired third-generation PPSAs differ from each other on a number of points of substance and scope. The degree of divergence is relatively minor, however, compared to the differences between them and the Ontario PPSA.[27] When the original Ontario Act was substantially updated and re-enacted in 1989, the drafters incorporated only some of the features of the second-generation PPSAs. A second round of significant amendments to the Ontario Act in 2007 has brought it into closer harmony with the CCPPSL Acts.[28] These amendments implemented the recommendations of the Ontario Bar Association's Personal Property Security Law Committee, which has since made additional proposals directed at achieving even closer harmony. On the other hand, the Ontario Committee has also rejected conformity with the other PPSAs on a number of points in favour of an Ontario-specific approach.[29]

(v) Comparison with UCC Article 9: Harmonisation versus Uniformity

In its ongoing tolerance of interjurisdictional variation, the Canadian PPSA experience contrasts with the Article 9 story. As early as 1961, the UCC's co-sponsors established a Permanent Editorial Board (PEB) to ensure ongoing re-examination and updating of the Code and to discourage individual States from modifying the official texts. The efforts of the PEB have been successful at least in relation to Article 9 where the level of State variation is relatively minor.[30]

[25] The Yukon PPSA is also an exception but because the Yukon PPSA parallels the 1981 version of the Saskatchewan PPSA, which—as noted in the text—informed the work of the CCPPSL, the extent of variation is minor.

[26] There is no published version of the CCPPSL Model. The 'third-generation' Saskatchewan PPSA, above n 5, is usually taken as the prototype. See Law Reform Commission of Saskatchewan, *Proposals for a New Personal Property Security Act* (Saskatoon: 1992). See also: Cuming (n 12); Jacob Ziegel, 'The New Provincial Chattel Security Regimes' (1991) 70 *Canadian Bar Review* 681.

[27] For a summary overview of the more prominent differences among the non-Ontario PPSAs, and between the Ontario and non-Ontario PPSAs, see Cuming, Walsh and Wood (n 5) 64–70.

[28] See RCC Cuming, C Walsh and RJ Wood, 'Secured Transactions Law in Canada—Significant Achievements, Unfinished Business and Ongoing Challenges' (2011) 50 *Canadian Business Law Journal* 156. See also Cuming, Walsh and Wood (n 5) 65–67.

[29] Cuming, Walsh and Wood (n 5) 67–69.

[30] On State variations in Art 9, see Permanent Editorial Board for the Uniform Commercial Code, *Report on Effect of Non-Uniform Scope Provisions In Revised Article 9 of The Uniform Commercial Code,*

Efforts over the years to establish a stable centralised coordination mechanism for PPSA reform have not succeeded. While, as noted above, the CCPPSL exerted a strong harmonising influence on the non-Ontario PPSAs, its coordination role became secondary once the initial PPSA implementation phase was completed.[31] The Conference still meets annually with governmental members in attendance from all 13 Canadian jurisdictions including Ontario and Québec joined by associate members from academe. However, the government representatives today come from the staff of the PPSA Personal Property Registries. Unlike the representatives who attended during the earlier PPSA implementation stage, they are not directly involved in legislative reforms in their home jurisdictions except to the extent of recommending changes to the registry infrastructure. In very recent years, the CCPPSL has again begun to place substantive reform issues on its agenda for possible discussion and harmonisation. The possibility of these being implemented in the near term remains questionable in view of the limited political commitment of the members' home jurisdictions as evidenced in the very modest resources made available for members.

The ULCC—the Canadian equivalent to the NCCUSL in the United States—might seem to offer a more promising venue in the abstract. Like the NCCUSL, the ULCC is a national organisation with governmental representatives from all provinces and territories who meet annually to work on pan-Canadian harmonisation initiatives.[32] But, as noted earlier, the Conference's initial foray into the field—the adoption in 1971 of a Uniform PPSA[33]—never attracted significant support, with even the second generation PPSAs preferring the 1970 CBA Model. In the intervening years, the ULCC has solicited several reports aimed at updating and harmonising reform among the various PPSA jurisdictions but these have not received broad take-up.[34] An attempt in 2007 to reinvigorate the ULCC's coordination role likewise has not borne fruit.[35]

available at www.ali.org/media/filer_public/95/9c/959cdaeb-d4df-431a-8742-e7f4444b6886/peb1104.pdf; Penelope L Christophorou, Kenneth C Kettering, Lynn A Soukup, and Steven O Weise, 'Under the Surface of Revised Article 9: Selected Variations in State Enactments from the Official Text of Revised Article 9' (2002) 34 *Uniform Commercial Code Law Journal* 331, and 'Analysis of State Variations' (2002) 34 *Uniform Commercial Code Law Journal* 358.

[31] See Cuming, Walsh and Wood (n 28) 177.

[32] Detailed information on the ULCC's history, mandate, and current and past projects is available on its website: www.ulcc.ca. For an analysis of the origin and evolution of the ULCC, see Jacob Ziegel, 'Harmonization of Private Laws in Federal Systems of Government: Canada, the USA and Australia' in Cranston (ed) (n 4) 140–52.

[33] Above, text at n 22.

[34] See: Ronald CC Cuming and Catherine Walsh, 'Possible Implications of Revised UCC Article 9 for Canada Personal Security Acts' (1999); 'Possible Changes to the Personal Property Security Act' (2000); 'Study Committee Report on Reform of Secured Transactions Law (2001); Report of the Study Committee on Reform of Canadian Secured Transactions Law (2002). These reports are available at the ULCC website: www.ulcc.ca.

[35] See Ronald CC Cuming, 'Report on the ULCC Project for Changes to Personal Property Security Acts', presented to the 2007 ULCC Annual Meeting, available at www.ulcc.ca.

Compared to the ULCC, the NCCUSL in the United States is better financed and its State representatives reflect greater specialist expertise and a closer connection to the political constituencies needed to implement recommendations.[36] Even with these advantages, the NCCUSL has not generally achieved demonstrably greater success than the ULCC in terms of State take-up of its model law products with the important exception of the UCC.[37] The particularity of the UCC success story may in part be attributed to the co-sponsorship of the ALI, which brings additional deep expertise and resources to the table. The American Bar Association also provides some financial support as well as actively promoting adoption of Article 9 revisions and other UCC products in which it has a particular interest.[38] Perhaps more importantly, banks and other secured creditor industry groups are well represented in the Article 9 revision process ensuring their support at the State implementation level.[39]

Of course, the involvement of creditor industry groups, while bringing practical insight to the revision process also means that the NCCUSL and the ALI in many respects operate as private legislatures.[40] A similar cession of sovereignty may simply not be feasible in Canada's very different political culture. And even if one were to accept the proposition that secured transactions reforms involve purely technical considerations devoid of distributional and other policy choices, a UCC-style national uniformity project is not a feasible goal in Canada's bijuridical and bilingual private law context.[41] Spontaneous harmonisation from a perspective of enlightened self-interest is the more realistic option.[42]

Some level of disharmony may also be less disruptive of efficiency in Canada compared to the United States. With only 10 provinces and three territories, compared to the 50 States plus the District of Columbia that make up the US federation, one-tenth of the US population, and a smaller footprint in international financial markets, it is likely easier for Canadian practitioners and businesses to manage interjurisdictional variations in private law generally and secured transactions law in particular than it is for their US counterparts.[43]

[36] See Ziegel (n 32) 146–50, 153–54.

[37] ibid 154.

[38] ibid 159.

[39] ibid 155.

[40] See: Alan Schwartz and Robert E Scott, 'The Political Economy of Private Legislatures' (1995) 143 *University of Pennsylvania Law Review* 595; Alan Schwartz, 'The Still Questionable Role of Private Legislatures' (2002) 62 *Louisiana Law Review*.

[41] While Louisianan in the US is also a civil law jurisdiction, it is only one State among 50, whereas Québec is Canada's second most populous province and has the second largest GDP by expenditure.

[42] Benjamin Geva, 'Uniformity in Commercial Law: Is the UCC Exportable?'(1996) 29 *Loyola of Los Angeles Law Review* 1035–46: 'Unlike the United States, Canada is a federal country predominantly characterized by biculturalism and bilingualism, including dual provincial legal systems. Uniformity, UCC style, is not a realistic option … Rather than unification, greater harmonization efforts have been underway for some time'.

[43] For example, there are significant differences among the PPSAs in the rules governing priority in collateral in the form of accounts receivable as between the holder of a 'purchase money security interest' in inventory who is claiming the accounts as proceeds of the inventory and the holder of

In view of the above, it is noteworthy that all the Canadian jurisdictions, including the civil law province of Québec, have achieved perfect uniformity in recent years in reforming the legal framework governing the holding, transfer and grant of security in investment securities. A similar phenomenon is pending with respect to security in deposit accounts with financial institutions. The Canadian reforms in turn are uniform with earlier reforms effected to the UCC in the United States, implying that pressures emanating from markets outside Canada may be more likely to produce uniformity. This question is explored further in Section E of the chapter.

C. The Article 9 and PPSA Registration Regimes

(i) Introduction

Under both the PPSAs and Article 9, a security interest 'attaches' when a security agreement has been concluded between the parties, the debtor acquires rights in the relevant collateral, and the secured creditor has extended value.[44] In order for a security interest to be effective against third parties, however, the secured creditor generally must take an additional perfecting step. In both regimes, public registration is the usual perfection modality.[45] Physical possession (of tangible collateral) and control (of financial collateral) are alternatives about which more is said in Section E of the chapter. There are also exceptional instances of automatic perfection simply upon attachment, some of which are covered in Sections D and E. For the purposes of this part of the chapter, however, it is assumed that registration is generally required. Certainly, it is the only universally available perfecting step.

Under both regimes, failure to register or otherwise perfect does not render a security interest ineffective against the world.[46] Rather, it is a precondition to its effectiveness as against four principal types of competing claimants.[47]

a prior registered security interest in the accounts as original collateral. In practice, these difference have generated remarkably little controversy or litigation, suggesting that they are being dealt with effectively through inter-creditor agreements or other informal arrangements. See Cuming, Walsh and Wood (n 5) 70.

44 §9-203. For the PPSAs, see ibid 240–88.

45 §9-310(a). For the PPSAs, see ibid 301.

46 §9-201. For the PPSAs, see ibid 297. Compare Art 2663 of the Civil Code of Québec (n 6), which makes publication a precondition to the effectiveness of hypothecs against third parties generally. The Art 9 and PPSA drafters seem to have assumed that only third parties who part with 'value' should take free of a security interest in the absence of public notice. Yet restitution law teaches us that a donee who acquires an asset in the belief that it is unencumbered can also suffer prejudicial reliance by virtue of a change of position.

47 Note, however, that the PPSAs and Art 9, as a general rule, only apply to consensual security interests. See below n 224.

The first category comprises secured creditors with a competing perfected security interest in the same collateral. As a general rule, failure to register means a secured creditor will be subordinate to a prior-registered secured creditor, even one with actual knowledge.[48]

The second category comprises buyers and lessees of the collateral. Failure to register means that they will take free of the security interest although in this case only in the absence of actual knowledge.[49]

The third category comprises unsecured creditors of the debtor who have taken the steps necessary to acquire what Article 9 refers to as 'lien creditor' status before the security interest is registered.[50] Generally, this requires the unsecured creditor to obtain a judgment and then take an additional step to 'perfect' that judgment. Depending on the jurisdiction, the additional step may involve registration of a notice of the judgment or the completion of judgment enforcement proceedings.[51]

Finally, an unregistered security interest is ineffective against the debtor's trustee in bankruptcy.[52]

Most analysts accept the value of making public registration a precondition to the effectiveness or priority of a security interest against competing secured creditors and subsequent buyers and lessees. However, allowing the debtor's lien creditors and the trustee in bankruptcy to defeat an unperfected security interest is sometimes contested. It is argued that unsecured creditors do not rely on the public registry in making lending decisions since nothing prevents the debtor from granting a security interest after the credit has been advanced.[53] However, there is no empirical evidence to support this assumption. At least some unsecured creditors may adjust the terms of their lending to take account of the existence of

[48] §9-317(a), §9-322(a). For the PPSAs, see Cuming, Walsh and Wood (n 5) 301–02.

[49] §9-317(b)–(d). For the PPSAs, see ibid 376–82.

[50] §§9-317(a)(2)(A), 9-102(52) ('lien creditor'). For the PPSAs, see ibid 297, 494–504.

[51] Although registration of a notice of the judgment is sufficient in most PPSA jurisdictions, most US States require the judgment creditor to have completed execution of its judgment before the security interest is registered in order to prevail. See below text at nn 224–26.

[52] §9-301 provides that 'A security interest is subordinate to the rights of a person that becomes a lien creditor before the security is perfected'. The term 'lien creditor' is defined in §9-301(3) to include a trustee in bankruptcy. For the PPSAs, see Cuming, Walsh and Wood (n 5) 297, 542–51.

[53] See Steven L Harris and Charles W Mooney, Jr, 'A Property-Based Theory of Security Interests: Taking Debtors' Choices Seriously' (1994) 80 *Virginia Law Review* 2021, 2059 ('judicial lien creditors are "nonreliance" parties who have bargained for the right to enforce a judgment against whatever property the debtor may have on hand at the time'). Generally, see Douglas Baird 'Notice Filing and the Problem of Ostensible Ownership' (1983) 12 *Journal of Legal Studies* 53; James White, 'Revising Article 9 to Reduce Wasteful Litigation' (1992–93) 26 *Loyola of Los Angeles Law Review* 823. The drafters of the New Zealand Personal Property Securities Act rejected subordination of unperfected security interests to the debtor's unsecured creditors and insolvency representatives on this basis. See DF Dugdale, 'The Proposed PPSA' [1998] *New Zealand Law Journal* 383; New Zealand Law Commission Report No. 8, *A Personal Property Securities Act for New Zealand* (1989) 115. For detailed discussions of the counter-arguments summarised in the text above, see Jacob Ziegel, 'Canadian Perspectives on the New Zealand Chattel Securities Act' (2001) 7 *New Zealand Business Law Quarterly* 118; David Brown, 'New Zealand Personal Property Securities Act 1999' in John De Lacy (ed), *The Reform of UK Personal Property Security Law* (Oxford: Routledge-Cavendish, 2010) 328, 338–41. See also New Zealand Ch 6 F(i).

security interests either directly[54] or indirectly by relying on credit rating agencies who incorporate information on public registries in their credit assessments.[55] Public notice is also important to unsecured creditors at the stage of default in order to enable them to make an informed decision as to whether it is worthwhile to invest the time and effort in taking the steps necessary to acquire lien creditor status.[56] Finally, requiring a timely act of public registration addresses the concern—dating back to *Twyne's Case*[57]—with fraudulent and collusive arrangements entered into on the eve of insolvency.[58]

The rule entitling the debtor's trustee in bankruptcy to avoid an unperfected security interest has sometimes been separately criticised as an excessive penalty since it operates without regard to whether there were in fact any lien creditors or even judgment creditors in existence prior to bankruptcy. The policy justification, however, rests on the status of the trustee as the representative of the debtor's unsecured creditors. The intervention of bankruptcy prevents them from initiating or completing the steps necessary under non-bankruptcy law to obtain lien creditor status. The rule thus enables them to preserve, through the trustee as their representative, the same priority that they might have enjoyed had bankruptcy not intervened.[59] There are also efficiency benefits for the trustee in being able to rely on a public record to make a prima facie determination of the extent to which the debtor's assets are encumbered.[60]

[54] See Paul Shupack, 'Preferred Capital Structures and the Question of Filing' (1995) 79 *Minnesota Law Review* 787, 803–07. See also AL Diamond, *A Review of Security Interests in Property* (London: HMSO, 1989) [21.2]: 'There is the provision of information for persons proposing to deal with the company so that they can assess its credit worthiness; … The information may similarly be of use to financial analysts and to persons considering whether to invest in the company'. And see Gerald McCormack, *Registration of Company Charges*, 1st edn (London: Sweet & Maxwell, 1994) 25; Lynn M LoPucki, 'The Unsecured Creditor's Bargain' (1994) 80 *Virginia Law Review* 1887, 1924, 1935–36, 1943–44.

[55] See Charles W Mooney, 'The Mystery and Myth of "Ostensible Ownership" and Article 9 Filing: A Critique of Proposals To Extend Filing Requirements to Leases' (1988) 39 *Alabama Law Review* 683, 762, fn 301; David M Phillips, 'Secured Credit and Bankruptcy: A Call for the Federalization of Personal Property Security Law' (1987) *Law and Contemporary Problems* 53, 79; Law Commission for England and Wales Company Security Interests (Law Com R No. 296, 2005) at [3.77]; Diamond (n 54).

[56] Of course, this requires that an unsecured creditor be able to obtain adequate information to make an informed decision. On this point, see Section C(ii)(c) below.

[57] *Twyne's Case* 3 Coke Rep 80b, 76 Eng Rep 809 (KB 1601).

[58] See generally: Ziegel (n 53). And see Diamond (n 54): 'Registration … does away with the risk of fraud by inventing a security only when a receiver is appointed or the company goes into liquidation'.

[59] See: *Re Giffen* [1998] SCR 91 at [38]–[42]; Anthony J Duggan, 'The Status of Unperfected Security Interests in Insolvency Proceedings' (December 2007) University of Toronto, Legal Studies Research Paper No 08-01. Available at SSRN: http://ssrn.com/abstract=1076683. Of course, the intervention of bankruptcy prevents one also from knowing whether the unperfected secured creditor ultimately might have prevailed by perfecting before any unsecured creditors obtained lien creditor status. For a comprehensive analysis of why a bright-line rule relegating the unperfected secured creditor to unsecured status on bankruptcy nonetheless represents the preferable and least costly rule, see Thomas Jackson *The Logic and Limits of Bankruptcy Law* (Cambridge, MA: Harvard University Press, 1986) 70–79, responding to John McCoid, 'Bankruptcy, the Avoiding Powers, and Unperfected Security Interests' (1985) 59 *American Bankruptcy Law Journal* 175.

[60] See, for example, Diamond (n 54), observing that 'Registration can also ease the task of a receiver or liquidator in knowing whether to acknowledge the validity of an alleged mortgage or charge'.

(ii) Notice Filing and 'False Positives'

(a) Introduction

In contrast to the pre-reform 'transaction-filing' registration statutes, the PPSAs and Article 9 adopt a so-called 'notice filing' approach. Rather than having to file the underlying security documentation, a simple notice called a 'financing statement' is all that has be registered. Only minimal information needs to be set out in the financing statement: principally, the names and addresses of the secured creditor and the debtor and a description of the collateral.

Notice filing undoubtedly minimises the risk and complexity of the registration process for secured creditors while also enabling them to lock in priority against subsequent secured creditors without having to await the execution of the formal security documentation. On the other hand, it also means that registration does not provide even prima facie evidence that the security interest to which it refers actually exists. Registration signifies only that a security interest *may* exist or is contemplated.[61]

Notice filing thus increases the possibility that a search of the registry may disclose 'false positives'—that is, a search result indicating the potential existence of a security interest even though some or all of the assets described in the financing statement are not covered by any extant or contemplated security agreement between the parties.[62] The analysis that follows addresses the potential problems that 'false positives' present for the debtor and third-party searchers respectively and the manner in which Article 9 and the PPSAs have dealt with those problems.

(b) Debtor Protection Against 'False Positives'

Search results that disclose 'false positives' impair the putative debtor's practical ability to deal with assets covered by the registered financing statement. A potential buyer or new secured creditor generally will be unwilling to purchase or take security in the relevant assets because of the priority risk.

Both Article 9 and the PPSAs provide a procedure whereby a debtor may require its secured creditor to verify the scope of the collateral currently subject to a security interest in its favour.[63] A debtor could use this procedure to reassure potential buyers and secured creditors that the assets in which they are interested are not presently encumbered.[64] This is an insufficient palliative. Potential buyers and secured creditors generally will be unwilling to wait for the response. Even if they were, only an outright buyer would be safe in proceeding (since any

[61] §9-502, cmt 2. For the PPSAs, see Cuming, Walsh and Wood (n 5) 324–25.

[62] It was of course also possible in theory under the prior registration statutes for 'false positives' to be registered. But the risk is lower in a transaction filing system in view of the effort and expertise required to replicate a credible signed security agreement for the purposes of making a public filing.

[63] §9-210. For the PPSAs, see Cuming, Walsh and Wood (n 5) 326–27, 302–07.

[64] §9-210, cmt.3. For the PPSAs, see Cuming, Walsh and Wood (n 5) 327.

security interest that the secured creditor might later acquire could not attach to assets previously disposed of by the debtor.) However, a prospective secured creditor cannot assume it will have a first priority simply because the first registered secured creditor confirms that it does not currently have a security interest in the relevant assets. Under Article 9 and the PPSAs, priority among security interests perfected by registration generally dates from the time of registration, regardless of the order in which the security agreements are concluded.[65] It follows that if the debtor were to later grant a security interest in favour of the first registered secured creditor, that security interest would have priority over any intervening perfected security interests.[66]

In an attempt to provide *ex ante* protection to debtors against the risk of 'false positives', the early versions of Article 9 required the debtor's signature to appear on the financing statement.[67] This was not an effective precaution in the absence of any mechanism for verifying the authenticity of the signature. In recognition of this and in order to facilitate electronic registration, the requirement was eliminated in the 2001 revision to Article 9.[68] In its place, Article 9 now provides that the registration of an initial financing statement (or an amendment that adds collateral) is effective only if it is 'authorized' by the debtor.[69] Two modalities of authorisation are recognised. First, the conclusion of a security agreement between the parties automatically constitutes authority for a secured creditor to file a financing statement covering the assets described in the agreement without the need to include an express authorisation clause.[70] Alternatively, if the parties have not yet concluded a security agreement, the debtor's authorisation may be obtained in a separate off-record instrument.[71]

Closer analysis suggests that the authorisation requirement does little to relieve the problems posed for debtors by false positives. Indeed, it may well exacerbate those problems.[72]

To illustrate, suppose that a debtor (D) authorises a secured creditor (SC1) to register an 'all-assets' financing statement even though any actual or contemplated transaction between the parties is more limited in scope. While this may seem an unlikely scenario, commentators worry that the first secured creditor on the scene (SC1) will routinely require the debtor to authorise the registration of an all-assets financing statement in order to pre-empt any challenges to the adequacy of the description of the collateral in its financing statement or to ensure that it retains

[65] §9-322(a)(1), cmt. 4. For the PPSAs, see ibid 327.

[66] ibid.

[67] See former §9-402(1).

[68] §9-502 cmt 3. And see Harry C Sigman, 'Twenty Questions about Filing under Revised Article 9: The Rules of the Game under New Part 5' (1999) 74 *Chicago-Kent Law Review* 861, 871–72.

[69] See §9-509(a)(1) and §9-510(a).

[70] §9-509(b). And see Sigman (n 68) 873.

[71] §9-509(a)(1).

[72] See generally Lissa L Broome, 'Supergeneric Collateral Descriptions in Financing Statements and Notice Filing' (2011) 46 *Gonzaga Law Review* 435.

first priority should D subsequently wish to enter into a new security agreement covering additional assets.[73] Of course, SC1's financing statement, even if authorised, is effective to perfect its security interest only to the extent of the assets in which it actually holds a security interest.[74] Nonetheless, the risk of subordination under the first-to-register rule of priority means that a new secured creditor (SC2) will be unwilling to lend against any of D's assets as long as SC1's financing statement remains on the record.[75]

More worryingly, D's ability to obtain new financing from SC2 is equally impaired even if it did not authorise SC1 to register a financing statement or only authorised the registration of a financing statement covering a narrower range of collateral. Article 9 does not require a secured creditor to obtain the debtor's authorisation prior to filing. The post-registration conclusion of a security agreement automatically constitutes 'ratification' of an initially unauthorised registration.[76] Moreover, the time of registration, not the time the registration was subsequently authorised, is the relevant time for the purposes of applying the first-to-register priority rule.[77] Thus, even if SC1's registration is unauthorised at the time D grants a security interest to SC2, SC1 would still have priority if D were to subsequently enter into a security agreement with SC1 covering the assets subject to SC2's intervening security interest. In other words, SC2 faces the same potential risk of retroactive subordination to SC1 in the unauthorised registration scenario as in the authorised registration scenario.[78]

Apart from the limited deterrent value of a claim for actual and nominal statutory damages against the secured creditor of record,[79] Article 9 offers putative debtors in the position of D little effective relief against unauthorised registrations.

If D's complaint is that the collateral description in SC1's registered financing statement exceeds the scope of D's authorisation, D can file an 'information statement' setting out this 'belief'.[80] But the registration of an information statement

[73] As Broome observes, a standard form of security agreement prepared by the American Bar Association includes an authorisation clause of this kind in addition to the clause for describing the actual collateral covered by the agreement. See Broome ibid 439. See also Ray Warner, 'Attachment, Filing and Foreclosure under Revised Article 9' (2001) 916 *Commercial Law Bulletin* 10, 13: 'Since there is no prohibition against including an over-broad collateral indication in the financing statement (as long as it is authorized by the debtor), and since an "all assets" financing statement will provide maximum protection, lenders likely will file "all assets" financing statements even when the transaction is more limited in scope'.

[74] §9-509 cmt 2 and §9-510(a) cmt 2, ex 1.

[75] Broome (n 72) 439–41.

[76] See §9-509, cmt 3. And see Sigman (n 68) 873.

[77] §9-322 cmt 4. And see Sigman (n 68) 873. See also Broome (n 72) 438, 440, 443, 454.

[78] See Broome (n 72) 441–43.

[79] A person who is the victim of an unauthorised registration may recover damages for any actual loss caused thereby as well as nominal statutory damages of $500; see §9-625(b)(e). Article 9 recognises that actual damages may include 'Loss resulting from the debtor's inability to obtain, or increased costs of, alternative financing'. See §9-625(b). Proving a specific amount in this respect has proved difficult in practice. See Broome (n 72) 445–47. In addition, an action for damages is only of value if the person who effected the registration can be identified and has the means to satisfy any judgment.

[80] §9-518.

has no legal effect. It merely puts searchers on alert that there is a dispute as to the scope of the collateral for which the secured creditor was authorised to register a financing statement.[81]

A putative debtor is not much better off even if it has no intention of ever entering into a security agreement with the secured creditor of record and has not otherwise authorised the registration of a financing statement. Article 9 entitles a debtor to send a demand to a secured creditor of record to file a termination statement if the registration of an initial financing statement is not authorised (or if any obligations previously secured by collateral described in a registered financing statement have been satisfied).[82] If the secured creditor fails to comply within 20 days, the debtor itself is authorised to file the termination statement.[83]

In practice, this procedure provides little effective relief for the debtor. Although the registration of the termination statement is legally effective,[84] there is nothing on the public record to prove that the conditions justifying the debtor's filing were satisfied. Third-party searchers are expected to conduct off-record inquiries.[85] Moreover, Article 9 requires registered financing statements to remain on the publicly searchable record until at least one year after their normal expiration.[86] It follows that a debtor will continue to be impeded in its practical ability to deal with assets described in the unauthorised financing statement for what may be a considerable number of years after filing the termination statement.[87] While the secured creditor of record is liable for compensatory and nominal statutory damages for its failure to file a termination,[88] this is a costly and time-consuming remedy. Moreover, even if the secured creditor had filed the termination as requested, the debtor would still face the burden of having to provide off-record proof of this to potential buyers and secured creditors before they would feel safe in dealing with any of the assets covered by the ostensibly terminated financing statement.

The PPSAs take a very different approach. The Acts expressly provide that a financing statement may be registered in advance of the conclusion of a security agreement and may relate to successive security agreements covering the same collateral.[89] The secured creditor is required to send a copy of the information in

[81] §9-518 cmt 2.

[82] §9-513(c).

[83] §9-509(d)(2).

[84] §9-513(d), §9-509 cmt 6.

[85] See §9-518, cmt 2: 'Just as searchers [SP2s] bear the burden of determining whether the filing of an initial financing statement was authorized, searchers [SP2s] bear the burden of determining whether the filing of every subsequent record was authorized'. The quoted wording was added in conjunction with the 2010 amendments to Art 9.

[86] §9-519(g), §9-513, cmt 5.

[87] UCC §9-515 provides that a financing statement is effective for a period of five years unless the filing is renewed by registering a continuation statement for another five-year term. Thus, a search report will show financing statements and related termination statements and other amendments for at least six years after the filing of the initial financing statement.

[88] §9-625(b), §9-625(e)(4).

[89] See Cuming, Walsh and Wood (n 5) 327–30.

a registered financing statement to the debtor on pain of liability for actual and deemed damages for failure to do so.[90] But there is no requirement to obtain the debtor's off-record authorisation, either before or after registration. This is not because the PPSA drafters were unconcerned about the potential for debtor prejudice posed by 'false positives'. Rather it is because they recognised that a debtor authorisation requirement was an ineffective palliative and focused instead on providing more robust *ex post* protection.

Specifically, the PPSAs empower the debtor to issue a demand to the secured creditor to amend or discharge a registered financing statement to reflect the true state of any off-record transactions between them.[91] The right to demand an amendment is triggered if the collateral description in a registered financing statement includes an item or kind of collateral that is not currently covered by a security agreement between the parties. The right to demand a discharge is triggered if no security agreement exists between the parties or if the debtor's obligations under any security agreement to which the registration may have related have been performed. If the secured creditor does not comply within the specified time period, the debtor has the right to recover any actual damages suffered as well as deemed statutory damages. Most importantly, the debtor is empowered to compel the registration of the discharge or amendment, as the case may be, on proof of the secured creditor's unjustified non-compliance. While the Ontario PPSA requires the debtor to apply for a court order directed to the registrar to discharge or amend the registration, the non-Ontario PPSAs empower the person making the demand to directly bring about the discharge or amendment, as the case may be, on proof of the secured creditor's non-compliance, unless the secured creditor obtains a court order preserving the registration.[92]

As discussed in greater detail later in the chapter, an amendment or discharge registered under the PPSAs is legally effective upon registration.[93] Indeed, in the case of a discharge, the financing statement is expunged from the publicly searchable records. It follows that this procedure provides debtors with effective relief against the 'false positives' problem compared to Article 9.

The official comments to Article 9 acknowledge the problems created for debtors by 'bogus filings' and 'misuse of the public record' but take the position that the text cannot provide 'a satisfactory or complete solution'.[94] It is suggested that states should provide a summary judicial procedure to enable the record to be corrected in preference to authorising the State filing office itself to take *ex post* or *ex ante* corrective action.[95] A 2014 report of the National Association of

[90] See ibid 335–36. Although the effectiveness of the registration is not affected by non-compliance, this measure may be viewed as the functional equivalent to the Art 9 provisions that expose the secured creditor to liability for actual and statutory damages suffered as a result of an unauthorised registration.

[91] ibid 337–40. Cf the Australian approach discussed in Ch 7 E(iv).

[92] ibid.

[93] See Section C(ii)(c) below.

[94] §9-518 cmt 3.

[95] ibid.

Secretaries of State (NASS) documents the wide diversity of State strategies that have been implemented. Contrary to the recommendation in the official comments, the report concludes that, compared to the cost and delay associated with judicial remedies, a procedure that gives State filing offices the power to remove unauthorised filings from the record after due notice is likely to be the most effective strategy.[96]

(c) Third-party Protection Against 'False Positives': Access to Off-record Information

Despite the potential for search results to yield 'false positives', the Article 9 and PPSA notice filing systems sufficiently respond to the information needs of third parties in the position of potential secured creditors and buyers dealing with the debtor. They can protect themselves simply by refusing to proceed with the transaction unless the registration is discharged or amended, or unless the secured creditor of record agrees to subordinate or release any actual or potential priority to which it may be entitled.[97]

The debtor's unsecured creditors and their representatives are in a very different position. They need access to off-record information about the extent to which the collateral described in a registered financing statement is in fact subject to a current security interest and the amount of the indebtedness secured by that collateral. Without that information, they are unable to assess the impact of the grant of security on their own lending or to determine, in the event of default, whether it is worthwhile for them to obtain a judgment and initiate enforcement proceedings against the relevant assets. The potential for registered financing statements to reflect false positives (either absolutely or because of overly broad collateral descriptions) also increases the risk of collusive arrangements with the secured creditor of record on the eve of insolvency.[98]

The official comments to Article 9 recognise that the creditors of a debtor may have legitimate needs for more detailed information.[99] The drafters nonetheless decided to give only the debtor a statutory right to demand off-record information from the secured creditor.[100] For this reason, the adoption of notice filing was a matter of considerable debate among the early PPSA reformers. Although notice filing had been accepted for security in inventory granted to the federally chartered banks under the federal bank Act, the adoption of a comprehensive

[96] See National Association of Secretaries of State, *State Strategies to Subvert Fraudulent Uniform Commercial Code (UCC) Filings* (2014), available at www.nass.org/reports/surveys-a-reports.

[97] Cuming, Walsh and Wood (n 5) 325–26.

[98] On the rationales for requiring public registration vis-à-vis the debtor's unsecured creditors and trustee in bankruptcy, see the text at nn 53–60 above.

[99] §9-210 cmt 3. And see Lynn M LoPucki, Arvin I Abraham and Bernd P Delahaye, 'Optimizing English and American Security Interests' (2013) 88 *Notre Dame Law Review* 1785, 1801.

[100] §9-210.

notice-filing approach generated concerns that the legislation could be used to defeat or hinder the claims of the debtors' creditors and other interested parties. It was eventually decided to depart from Article 9 on this point.[101] The PPSAs give the debtors' creditors and their authorised representatives, as well as any person with an existing interest in the collateral described in a financing statement, a statutory right to obtain from the secured creditor a copy of the security agreement (or the ability to inspect it at a physical location) and to obtain other information about the current indebtedness and the current scope of the collateral.[102]

The official comments to Article 9 do not provide much insight as to why it was decided to limit the right to off-record information to the debtor. Perhaps the drafters assumed that the information needs of unsecured creditors would be met by having the debtor make the demand to the secured creditor on their behalf. But this is unrealistic. Once the credit has been extended, unsecured creditors and their representatives no longer have any leverage over the debtor to compel cooperation.[103]

Or perhaps the Article 9 drafters were concerned about protecting secured creditors from potential liability if it turned out that the person making the demand was not in fact a creditor of the debtor. The Ontario and Yukon PPSAs respond to this concern by empowering a court to exempt a secured creditor from having to comply when the person making the demand cannot prove that it is in a category of persons entitled to make the demand. The other Acts take a different approach. On the one hand, they entitle the secured creditor to respond to a demand for information made by a person who purports to be someone entitled to it unless it actually knows that this is not the case. At the same time, they give the courts the discretion to exempt the secured creditor from compliance in the case of a demand made by anybody other than the debtor (to the extent, for example, that broader confidentiality concerns might warrant restrictions on the information disclosed).[104]

As commentators have observed, the Article 9 public filing system apparently 'operates on the principle that existing liens are the business of no one but the debtor, and those to whom the debtor wishes to disclose them'.[105] In contrast, the PPSA drafters, in line with pre-PPSA registration policy, conceived the purposes of public registration as continuing to necessitate that sufficient information about security interests be provided to unsecured creditors and third parties with an existing interest in the collateral described in a registration to enable them to protect their rights.

[101] Ziegel (n 15) 106.

[102] In the event of non-compliance, the secured creditor is liable for actual and statutory damages. In addition, the PPSAs (other than the Ontario Act) empower the courts to issue an order compelling compliance and then to order the registration to be amended or discharged in the event of non-compliance. See Cuming, Walsh and Wood (n 5) 326–27, 302–07.

[103] LoPucki, Abraham and Delahaye (n 99).

[104] Cuming, Walsh and Wood (n 5) 304–05.

[105] LoPucki, Abraham and Delahaye (n 99) 1802.

(iii) 'False Negatives'

The PPSA and Article 9 registration regimes also create the potential for search results to disclose 'false negatives'—that is, a search result that either fails to disclose the existence of a perfected security interest in the relevant asset or suggests that any perfected security interest that a secured creditor may have had no longer exists. As the analysis that follows shows, the risk of false negatives is greater under Article 9 than the PPSAs.

(a) Erroneous and Unauthorised Cancellations or Discharges

Under Article 9, the registration of an amendment terminating the effectiveness of a registered financing statement must be 'authorized' to be legally effective.[106] As noted earlier, the debtor is 'authorized' to register a termination statement in limited circumstances.[107] Otherwise, the secured creditor's authorisation is needed.[108] As also noted earlier, Article 9 requires all filings, including purported terminations, to remain on the publicly searchable record for at least one year following the date the financing statement (or any renewal of it) would otherwise have lapsed.[109] There is nothing on the publicly searchable record to prove whether the person who registered the termination was authorised to do so. Third-party searchers are expected to verify this through off-record inquiries. If it turns out that the termination was filed without authority, the security interest remains perfected.[110]

This aspect of the Article 9 approach reduces the value and reliability of the filing system for third parties. Searchers may not have the legal sophistication to understand that a registered termination cannot be taken at face value. Even if they do, the need to conduct off-record inquiries to determine whether the termination was authorised adds cost and risk.

There is also considerable legal uncertainty surrounding what constitutes authorisation. A termination registered by the secured party of record, even if registered mistakenly, is considered to be authorised and therefore legally effective.[111] The situation is less clear where the error is committed by a person whom the secured creditor authorised to register the termination on its behalf. What constitutes authorisation is left to law outside Article 9, including principal and agency law.[112] The jurisprudence confirms that a secured creditor is bound under principles of actual authority if it reviewed an erroneous termination

[106] §9-510(a).
[107] §9-509(d)(2). And see above text at nn 82–83.
[108] §9-509(d)(1).
[109] §9-519(g), §9-513, cmt. 5. And see note 87 above.
[110] See nn 84–85 above.
[111] *In re Motors Liquidation Company, et al* 2015 WL 252318 (2d Cir Jan 21, 2014).
[112] See §9-502, cmt 3 cross-referencing UCC §1-103(b).

statement prepared by its agent in advance of filing and nonetheless authorised the filing.[113] What is less clear is whether the erroneous registration of a termination would also be considered authorised where a secured creditor delegates the task of filing to an agent—for example, its law firm—without bothering to review their work in advance of filing.[114] Also unclear is the extent to which a court may resort to the general law of mistake and unjust enrichment to preserve the perfected and priority status of a secured creditor who mistakenly authorises the filing of a termination as against competing claimants who did not in fact rely to their detriment on the registered termination.[115]

The PPSAs take a very different approach. The registration of a discharge, even if unauthorised, is legally effective to terminate the perfected status of the security interest to which it relates[116] and results in the removal of the related financing statement from the publicly searchable record.[117] In other words, the PPSAs place the legal risk of *both* erroneous and unauthorised cancellations on the secured creditor, not third parties. However, the various PPSA systems provide secured creditors with three important palliatives against this risk.

First, a number of the PPSA registry systems assign unique security codes or the equivalent to secured creditors or their representatives on the registration of an initial financing statement. Entry of that code is needed to register any subsequent amendments or discharges.[118] This minimises the risk of unauthorised or fraudulent discharges or amendments by the debtor and third parties.

Second, where a registration discharges or amends a registration, most PPSA registries notify the secured creditor of record.[119]

Third, the non-Ontario PPSAs entitle a secured creditor to reinstate the registration of a financing statement following an erroneous or unauthorised discharge or lapse. Reinstatement preserves the perfected and priority status of the

[113] Motors Liquidation Company (n 111).

[114] ibid. The Delaware Supreme Court confined its holding to circumstances in which the 'secured party of record has itself reviewed and approved the termination statement for filing'. For an analysis that favours attributing the errors of the agent to the secured creditor even in the absence of prior approval, see Bruce Markell, 'Oops: Official Comm. of Unsecured Creditors of Motors Liquidation Co. v. JPMorgan Chase Bank, N.A. (In re Motors Liquidation Co.)' (February 2015) Bankruptcy Law Letter, Thompson Reuters.

[115] ibid. See also Bruce Markell, 'Et Tu Ralph?: More on Motors Liquidation, and a Bonus on Attorney's Fees in Appeals of Involuntary Bankruptcies' (May 2015) Bankruptcy Law Letter, Thompson Reuters.

[116] For judicial confirmation, see *KBA Canada, Inc v Supreme Graphics Ltd*, 2014 BCCA 117.

[117] See, for example, Personal Property Security Act, 1993, SS 1993, c P-6.2, s 46(2).

[118] See, for example, the use of unique registration identification number (RINs) by the Saskatchewan Personal Property Registry: Personal Property Security Regulations, RRS c P-6.2 Reg 1, ss 2(1)(s), 5(4)(viii), 23.3(1)(c). Once a RIN has been assigned to a financing statement, renewals, amendments or discharges cannot be registered without providing the RIN. The aim is to ensure that the debtor or third parties cannot affect information in the registry record unless the registrant allows them to obtain the RIN. RINs are not assigned automatically but only at the request of registrants. Thus secured creditors must understand the importance of requesting a RIN at the time of initial registration and preserving its confidentiality.

[119] ibid, s 20.

security interest from the date of the original registration except as against competing claimants who acquire rights in the collateral during the period when the registry record indicated that the registration had been discharged or had lapsed. The Ontario PPSA contains a broadly similar saving provision but permits a registration to be revived at any time whereas the other PPSAs limit the opportunity for reinstatement to a 30-day period following registration of the discharge so as to limit the potential for circular priority competitions.[120]

The PPSA approach avoids drawing what may be difficult distinctions between unauthorised and erroneous registrations. It promotes legal certainty and the public notice function of the registry by enabling third parties to rely on a search result without having to conduct off-record inquiries. It enables secured creditors to regain their perfected and priority status following an erroneous and unauthorised discharge or lapse to the extent no intervening interests could have been prejudiced.

That having been said, PPSA jurisdictions have not always succeeded in protecting 'innocent' secured creditors from the priority risk posed by according full legal effect to unauthorised discharges. For example, in a recent British Columbia case, a secured creditor who had assigned its security interest to a new secured creditor mistakenly discharged the related financing statement.[121] It was able to do this because British Columbia had not instituted a secure code system for filing amendments and discharges.[122] Although the registry had sent a notice of the discharge to the new secured creditor of record, it was alleged that the notice had never been received. And while the error was eventually discovered, this was after the expiry of the 30-day window for reinstating a registration imposed by the non-Ontario PPSAs. In the result, the secured creditor was subordinated to two competing secured creditors over which it had had priority prior to the registration of the discharge. This represented a windfall in view of the absence of any detrimental reliance by them on the registered discharge. However, the court took the view that the policy goal of the PPSA drafters to ensure certainty and predictability in priority ordering precluded the exercise of equitable jurisdiction to reverse this result and also constituted a 'juristic reason' for denying a claim on the basis of unjust enrichment.[123]

The scenario that resulted in the mistaken registration in this case is being addressed by the implementation of secure access code procedures in PPSA jurisdictions where these have not already been instituted.[124] It is no doubt impossible

[120] See Cuming, Walsh and Wood (n 5) 361–62, 474–79.

[121] *KBA Canada* (n 116).

[122] ibid. As the court noted, the Personal Property Security Regulation, BC Reg 227/2002 does not require that the person seeking a discharge be the secured creditor or have any connection to the related security interest. Further, s 48 of the Regulation states that 'A registration may be effected in the registry without proof that … the registering party has authority to submit the registration'.

[123] *KBA Canada* (n 116) paras 20–42.

[124] Compare the Saskatchewan RIN code system (n 118) with the open access system in British Columbia (n 122).

to entirely eliminate the risk of unauthorised discharges in any system let alone the risk of error on the part of the secured creditor itself. Yet the imposition of secure code requirements for registering amendments and discharges would go a long distance in reducing those risks. If also implemented in the Article 9 filing systems, the practical consequences of the current divergence from the PPSAs on who should bear the risk of unauthorised registrations would also be greatly minimised.

(b) Effective Time of Registration: Who Bears the Risk of Registry Office Error or Delay?

Under Article 9, the registration of a financing statement is effective when it is accepted by the filing office for registration.[125] It follows that a security interest can be effective against third parties without being publicly searchable. Searchers also bear the risk of 'misindexing' errors on the part of registry staff even those that result in a financing statement being permanently unsearchable.[126]

In contrast, the PPSA computerised registries are programmed to assign the effective time of registration only as of the time that the information in a financing statement is entered into the record so as to be publicly searchable.[127] While this approach ensures the reliability of search results for third parties, it requires secured creditors to verify the time and accuracy of their registrations before acting in reliance on the perfected status of their security interests. The monitoring burden is negligible owing to the prevalence of direct electronic registration. Indeed, electronic registration is obligatory in most PPSA jurisdictions, and in those that still allow paper financing statements to be submitted, the incidence of use is minimal.[128] Electronic registration eliminates any significant delay between the submission of registration information to the registry and its public searchability. It also eliminates the risk of registry staff entry and indexing errors since the registration data is transmitted to the registry record directly by registrants.[129]

As noted earlier,[130] the PPSA drafters contemplated computerised registry records from the outset and electronic registration and searching facilities were implemented at an early stage in the reform process. In contrast, the early Article 9 filing systems were not just paper based but also plagued by administrative delay and error.[131] The drafters were presumably reluctant to require secured creditors who had submitted a properly completed financing statement to bear the risks

[125] §9-516(a). Note also §9-520(b) on the effectiveness of financing statements rejected for filing by the filing office if it turns out the rejection was unjustified.

[126] §9-518. And see Sigman (n 68) 885–86. See also Regions Bank v Official Comm of Unsecured Creditors (In re Camtech Precision Mfg, Inc), 471 BR 293 (SD Fla 2012).

[127] Cuming, Walsh and Wood (n 5) 334–35.

[128] ibid 333.

[129] ibid 363.

[130] Above n 19.

[131] Above n 18.

posed by deficiencies in the filing system.[132] Today, an increasing number of States offer direct electronic registration and it is even obligatory in some. The 2001 revision to Article 9 sought to facilitate the shift to electronic registration and one would have thought that making the legal effectiveness of the registration of a financing statement contingent on public searchability would have created a powerful incentive for States to accelerate the shift. Of course, once electronic registration becomes the norm in the United States, the practical impact of the difference between the PPSA and Article 9 rules will become less consequential.[133] On the other hand, the pragmatic considerations underlying the Article 9 rule will also become less defensible.

(c) Post-registration Change of Debtor Name or Transfer of Collateral to a New Debtor

The debtor's name is the principal search criterion under both the PPSA and Article 9 registration systems.[134] If a registrant makes a mistake in entering the debtor's name such that the financing statement would be irretrievable by a searcher using the correct name, the registration will be ineffective to perfect the security interest.[135] On this basic starting point, the PPSAs and Article 9 are in agreement.

But even if the debtor's name is correctly entered, the debtor's post-filing conduct may make the financing statement irretrievable by subsequent searchers. Suppose the debtor later changes its name (for example, as a result of a corporate amalgamation). Or suppose the debtor transfers the collateral in circumstances where the transferee takes subject to the security interest. A search according to the new name of the debtor or the name of the transferee will not disclose the security interest.

Article 9 and the PPSAs part company in their responses to these scenarios.

Under Article 9, a financing statement continues to be effective to perfect a security interest notwithstanding a post-filing transfer of the collateral.[136] Third parties who acquire rights in the collateral from the transferee are bound by the security interest notwithstanding the lack of notice. The same is generally true where the debtor changes its name.[137] This is subject to one important exception. If the security interest covers after-acquired collateral, the filed financing statement is effective to perfect the security interest only in collateral acquired by the debtor before or within the first four months after the change of name. For collateral acquired after the expiry of the four-month period, the security interest ceases

132 Knippenberg (n 7) 67–69.

133 §9-523(b) requires the filing office to acknowledge filings presented other than by means of a written record (ie electronically), but under subsection (a), an acknowledgment of the filing of a written record is required only if it is requested by the filer.

134 §9-519(c). For the PPSAs, see Cuming, Walsh and Wood (n 5) 330.

135 §9-506(c). And see Knippenberg (n 7) 67–68. For the PPSAs, ibid 364–66.

136 §9-507(a).

137 §9-507(c)(1).

to be perfected unless the secured creditor amends the record to disclose the new name of the debtor.[138]

Commentators have attributed the Article 9 approach to the drafters' assumptions about on-the-ground financing practices.[139] With the exception of purchase money financing where a second-in-time secured creditor has priority in any event,[140] it was assumed that there are few or no potential second-in-time creditors willing to lend against the security of a debtor's static assets.[141] Why burden secured creditors with the obligation to monitor for post-filling name changes and transfers if the absence of public notice is unlikely to mislead a significant number of real as opposed to hypothetical subsequent financers?[142] The likelihood of second-in-time secured financing was assumed to be greater where the security agreement covered after-acquired collateral such as inventory or accounts.[143] Moreover, the super-priority accorded to a subsequent purchase money financer of inventory is dependent on it giving notice to the holder of a prior-registered security interest in after-acquired collateral and thus depends on it being able to discover the existence of the prior creditor through a registry search.[144] The increased risk that a real as opposed to hypothetical second-in-time financer might be prejudiced by the absence of notice made it appropriate to impose an obligation to monitor for name changes in the case of after-acquired collateral. The four-month rule in effect divides the monitoring obligation, with the second secured creditor carrying the burden for the first four months after the name change, and the first secured creditor for collateral acquired thereafter.

This kind of cost-benefit analysis no doubt explains the Article 9 drafters' reluctance to impose an absolute obligation on secured creditors to monitor the debtor's post-filing conduct. On the other hand, once the secured creditor acquires actual knowledge of a change of the debtor's name or a transfer of collateral, it is in a position to correct the record at little cost or effort. Yet Article 9 does not require the secured creditor to refile even where it knows of or consents to a transfer of the collateral by the debtor.[145] Nor need it do so after acquiring knowledge of a change of name of the debtor. Its security interest remains perfected with respect to existing collateral and any collateral acquired before the expiry of the four-month grace period, even if it finds out about the name change at an earlier point.[146]

The PPSAs take a very different approach. The secured creditor is under no obligation to monitor for post-registration name changes or transfers regardless of whether the security interest covers fixed or after-acquired-assets. But the position

[138] §9-507(c)(2).
[139] Knippenberg (n 7) especially at fnn 107 and 108.
[140] §9-324(a). And see ibid at fn 130.
[141] ibid 102–04, and fn 107.
[142] ibid 88–89, 113–14, fnn 107 and 126.
[143] ibid 96–97.
[144] §9-324(b)–(c). And see Knippenberg (n 7) at fn 145.
[145] §9-507(a).
[146] §9-507(c)(1). And see Knippenberg (n 7) 99–103.

changes once the secured creditor acquires actual knowledge of a change of name or transfer.[147] The perfected status and priority of its security interest as against third parties whose rights arose *before* it acquired knowledge is unaffected.[148] But to preserve priority against interests acquired from the debtor after the secured creditor finds out about the change of name or from the debtor's transferee after it finds out about the transfer, the secured creditor must update the record before the expiry of a 30-day grace period.[149] If the correction is made before the expiry of this period, priority is preserved as against third parties whose rights arose after the secured creditor acquired the requisite knowledge but before the record was amended.[150] The secured creditor can still update the record after the grace period expires but it then loses protection against third-party rights arising in the grace period and therefore until the record is updated.[151]

In declining to require refiling in cases of actual knowledge, commentators have speculated that the Article 9 drafters wished to avoid the uncertainty associated with priority rules whose application depends on ad hoc factual inquiries concerning whether and when a person acquires 'knowledge' for fear that this might morph into a positive monitoring obligation.[152] But the drafters were not adverse to qualifying priority on the basis of actual knowledge in other contexts.[153] Nor were they averse to imposing an absolute refiling obligation for collateral acquired more than four months after a change in the debtor's name on the basis that the lack of public notice would be more likely to pose actual prejudice to subsequent secured creditors. So the better explanation may simply be Article 9's predisposition to favour the function of the filing system as a mechanism for ordering priorities among secured creditors as opposed to its broader public notice objectives vis-à-vis other categories of third-party searchers who might potentially be prejudiced, notably potential buyers and the lien creditors of the debtor or transferee.

Differences in the pre-reform law may also play a role in explaining the divergence in approaches. It has been suggested that the Article 9 rule requiring refiling

[147] See Cuming, Walsh and Wood (n 5) 356–59.

[148] ibid. But see the qualification in the case of the non-Ontario Acts in n 150 below.

[149] Note that the grace period is reduced to 15 days in the case of a transfer of the collateral to which the secured creditor gave its consent in advance. See Cuming, Walsh and Wood (n 147).

[150] The non-Ontario PPSAs recognise one exception: a buyer or lessee for value without knowledge takes free of the security interest if the sale or lease occurs during the grace period but before the secured creditor amends the registration: ibid 357.

[151] The Ontario approach is somewhat different. Failure to amend or otherwise perfect before the expiry of the grace period causes the security interest to become wholly unperfected even as against competing security interests that arose before the secured creditor acquired knowledge of the change of name or transfer. Priority can be regained if the secured creditor amends the registration or otherwise perfects even if this occurs outside the grace period. It follows that the difference in approach is consequential only in cases where no amendment is ever registered. In that event, the secured creditor is subordinated to the prior security interests whereas its priority would be preserved under the other Acts.

[152] Knippenberg (n 7) 101–03, 112.

[153] For example, an unperfected security interest remains effective against a buyer who acquires the collateral with actual knowledge of the security interest. See above n 49.

for collateral acquired more than four months after the debtor's change of name may in part also reflect the lingering influence of the pre-Code judicial hostility to recognising 'floating liens' over circulating assets such as inventory and receivables in the absence of active policing by the secured creditor.[154] As noted earlier, this was not a concern in the pre-reform Canadian context. In light of this, the general PPSA rule requiring the record to be updated only once actual knowledge is acquired would seem to offer sufficient protection to subsequent secured creditors. After all, a secured creditor who is relying on after-acquired collateral is more likely to be involved in monitoring the debtor and the collateral and is therefore more likely to learn about a post-filing change of name or collateral transfer before or soon after it occurs.[155]

(d) Applicable Law

The discussion to this point has suggested that the PPSAs on the whole are more solicitous of the public notice function of registration relative to Article 9. A variant of this policy difference is reflected in the choice-of-law rules of the two regimes.

Under the PPSAs, the perfected status of a non-possessory security interest in ordinary non-mobile goods and other tangible assets is governed, as a general rule, by the traditional *lex situs* rule.[156] It follows that third-party searchers can generally rely on a clean search of the registry in the jurisdiction where the relevant assets are located. This is true even in the case of a security interest in goods that attached when they were located outside the borders of the particular PPSA jurisdiction. If the goods are later brought into the jurisdiction, the security interest must be registered or otherwise perfected locally within a maximum grace period of 60 days to preserve its perfected status.[157]

While the initial versions of Article 9 adopted a similar approach (though with a longer four-month grace period), this was changed in the 2001 revision.[158] With some exceptions, the law applicable to the perfection of a non-possessory security interest in goods is now the law of the jurisdiction where the debtor is located.[159] Since that law also generally governs the perfection of security interests in mobile goods and intangible collateral, the new rule enables a security interest covering all

[154] Knippenberg (n 7) 93–97.

[155] Margit Livingston, 'Bewitched, Bothered and Bewildered: The Courts and Revised Article 9 of the Uniform Commercial Code Ten Years Later' (2010–2011) 9 *DePaul Business and Commercial Law Journal* 169, 186.

[156] See Cuming, Walsh and Wood (n 5) 193.

[157] ibid 194–96. Note that the non-Ontario PPSAs protect buyers and lessees who acquire rights in the goods during the grace period if the transaction occurs before the security interest is perfected locally. Ibid 196–97.

[158] See Ronald CC Cuming and Catherine Walsh, 'Revised Article 9 of the Uniform Commercial Code: Implications for the Canadian Personal Property Security Acts' (2001) 16 *Banking & Finance Law Review* 339, 357–62.

[159] §9-301(1).

assets of the grantor to be perfected by a single registration in the debtor's home jurisdiction.

Article 9's single registration venue rule is intended to reduce transaction costs for 'dominant classes of secured creditors such as general financers' who take security in all assets or significant categories of assets of a debtor.[160] Whether it actually achieves this goal is open to question owing to uncertainties in the practical effectiveness of the rule, especially in the international context.[161] But assuming it does, the gains for primary lenders come at the expense of increased transaction costs and decreased transparency for third-party searchers.[162] Potential buyers, purchase money financers of specific assets, and the debtor's unsecured creditors and their representatives reasonably expect a search of the local registry to disclose security interests in locally situated goods. The new approach puts them under the burden of having to verify whether the debtor is located in the same jurisdiction as the goods, and if not to incur the additional expense of having to search (and file in the case of subsequent secured creditors) in another State. Moreover, not all third parties will have the legal acumen to appreciate that the filing venue for locally situated goods may be located in a different State.

D. Transactional Scope of the Article 9 and PPSA Registries

(i) Security Interests in Motor Vehicles and Like Assets

The filing of a financing statement under Article 9 is ineffective to perfect a security interest in goods subject to a State statute that provides for the security interest to be perfected by a notation on the certificate of title issued by that State for the relevant goods.[163] A notation on the title certificate is instead the exclusive mechanism for perfection and public notice. The Article 9 filing regime applies only if the goods are held as inventory for sale or lease by a debtor in the business of selling such goods.[164]

Title certificate statutes began to be enacted by the various US States in the 1920s when the automobile first entered into widespread use. It is therefore

[160] Scott (n 14) 1826–29. See also Cuming and Walsh (n 158).

[161] ibid. See also Cuming, Walsh and Wood (n 5) 201–03.

[162] And see Scott (n 14) 1826-27.

[163] §9-311(a)(2). §9-102(10) defines 'certificate of title' to mean 'a certificate of title with respect to which a statute provides for the security interest in question to be indicated on the certificate as a condition or result of the security interest's obtaining priority over the rights of a lien creditor with respect to the collateral'.

[164] §9-311(d). This rule allows the inventory financier to perfect its security interest by filing a single financing statement without having to note its security interest on the title of each automobile.

understandable that the Article 9 drafters chose to defer to these systems. However, the interplay between these statutes and Article 9 has generated uncertainty and complexity owing to their non-uniform nature.[165] While all apply to road vehicles, some extend to other high-value goods such as mobile homes, boats and farm equipment.[166] This creates choice-of-law complexities when the goods move from an Article 9 filing State to a title certificate State. The choice-of-law problems are compounded because, owing to the absence of interstate coordination, the same goods may be subject to certificates of title issued by more than one State at the same time.[167] Additional 'confusion and uncertainty' is introduced by conflicts between the Article 9 rule for determining when perfection occurs and the equivalent rule in a number of the State statutes.[168] Even if these inconsistencies were resolved,[169] some residual uncertainty is likely inherent in any attempt to meld an external asset-based mode of public notice with Article 9's debtor-based filing regime.

Title certificate systems were not a feature of pre-reform Canadian law. Security devices covering motor vehicles and like assets were subject to the same registration regimes that applied to other types of collateral. So the PPSA drafters never contemplated a separate perfection venue. However, they incorporated the advantages of a title certificate system into the design of the PPSA registry. Because a title certificate follows the vehicle through successive owners, it does or should provide notice of a security interest granted by any owner in the chain of title. To duplicate this feature, the PPSA registry systems enable financing statements relating to security interests in motor vehicles to be registered and searched by reference to the vehicle identification number. The non-Ontario Acts extend this facility to other high-value goods for which there is a significant re-sale market and for which unique 'serial number' type identifiers are available (notably, trailers, mobile homes, aircraft, boats and outboard motors for boats).[170]

Entry of the VIN or serial number on a financing statement is necessary to perfect a security interest only if the asset is held by the debtor as consumer goods. If held as equipment, it is required only for the purposes of preserving priority against a subsequent buyer (and a subsequent secured creditor in the case of the

165 For a comprehensive summary of the certificate of title laws of each State, and how they relate (or fail to relate) to other laws including Art 9, see Alvin C Harrell, *Compendium of State Certificate of Title Laws* (Chicago: ABA, 2009).

166 These differences are recognised in the wording of §9-311(a)(2), which invites enacting States to 'list any statute covering automobiles, trailers, mobile homes, boats, farm tractors, or the like, which provides for a security interest to be indicated on a certificate of title as a condition or result of perfection'.

167 See §9-303, cmt 6.

168 See §9-311, cmt 5.

169 In 2005, the NCCUSL adopted a new Uniform Certificate of Title Act (UCOTA) aimed in part at achieving greater consistency with Art 9 but this has not yet received significant uptake. See Harrell (n 165) for a comparison between each of the existing State statutes and the new model.

170 See Cuming, Walsh and Wood (n 5) 331, 366, 395–97, 432–34.

non-Ontario PPSAs). For inventory collateral, it is unnecessary since here there is no risk of misleading third-party searchers.[171]

The PPSA approach avoids the choice-of-law and other complexities inherent in Article 9's deference to the State title certificate systems for perfection. It offers secured creditors and third parties the efficiency of a single registration and search venue. It is also more responsive to the information needs of the debtor's unsecured creditors and their representatives who may not have practical access to the VIN or other serial number of a debtor's goods by enabling them to at least search against the name of the debtor.

(ii) Purchase Money Security Interests in Consumer Goods

Unless covered by a State title certificate statute, Article 9 treats a purchase money security interest in consumer goods as automatically perfected upon attachment.[172] The filing of a financing statement is required only to preserve the effectiveness of the security interest against a consumer buyer.[173] As against other third parties, the security interest is effective despite the absence of public notice. The heavy burden of inquiry this imposes on potential buyers and secured creditors has been criticised as detrimental to consumers in view of its chilling effect on transactions that might otherwise have gone forward or gone forward at lower cost.[174]

The pre-PPSA conditional sales and chattel mortgage statutes did not include any equivalent exemption and no consideration was given by the PPSA drafters to introducing one. The official comments to Article 9 do not offer much insight into the rationale for the exemption beyond noting that the pre-reform conditional sales statutes did not apply to consumer goods.[175]

Commentators have suggested that requiring filing would put an unsustainable burden on filing offices.[176] While this has not been a problem in the PPSA context, it was noted above that the early Article 9 filing systems were far less efficient and reliable.[177] On the other hand, the vast majority of consumer goods registrations in the PPSA systems relate to security in motor vehicles and like goods. Since

[171] ibid.

[172] §9-309(1). A 'purchase money security interest' is defined in §9-103(a) to mean a security interest taken in collateral to secure loan or sale credit advanced for the purpose of enabling the debtor to acquire the collateral and in fact used for that purpose. 'Consumer goods' are defined in §9-102(a) to mean 'goods that are used or bought for use primarily for personal, family, or household purposes'.

[173] §9-320(b).

[174] See Douglas G Baird and Thomas H Jackson, 'Possession and Ownership: An Examination of the Scope of Art 9' (1983) 35 *Stanford Law Review* 175, 192–93; Gerald T McLaughlin, '"Seek But You May Not Find": Non-UCC Recorded, Unrecorded and Hidden Security Interests under Article 9 of the Uniform Commercial Code' (1985) 53 *Fordham Law Review* 953, 960–62.

[175] See §9-302 cmt 4 (1972); §9-309, cmt 3.

[176] See: William H Lawrence, William H Henning and R Wilson Freyermuth, *Understanding Secured Transactions* (LexisNexis, 12 October 2012) §7.01B; McLaughlin (n 174).

[177] Above n 18.

Article 9 requires purchase money security interests in these types of consumer goods to be perfected by a notation on the title certificate,[178] it is doubtful that requiring filing for the residual categories of consumer goods would have put that much additional strain on the early Article 9 filing systems.

It has also been suggested that because consumer goods often have a low and rapidly depreciating value, they are unlikely to be the subject of subsequent dealings so the burden that filing would impose on purchase money financers would exceed its possible public notice benefits.[179] This explanation is over-generalised since consumer goods can also include valuable objects. In any event, if this were really the concern, it could have been addressed by a rule along the lines of the non-uniform version of Article 9 enacted by the State of Maine, which limits the exemption to purchase money security interests in goods that have a purchase price of $10,000 or less.[180]

(iii) Sales of Accounts

With the exception of the rules on enforcement, the PPSAs apply to both the outright sale and the grant of security in accounts on the theory that both types of transactions raise the same public notice and priority ordering concerns.[181] While Article 9 takes the same approach, it carves out two significant exemptions from the requirement for public filing.

(a) The Article 9 'Non-Significant Part' Filing Exemption

Under Article 9, an assignment that does not 'transfer a significant part of the assignor's outstanding accounts' is automatically perfected on attachment.[182] The rationale for this exemption is a 'mystery'.[183] The wording implies that the aim was to 'to ensure that the bulk of any assignor's intangible property remained subject to claims of general creditors and later account transferees unless claimed by an assignee who had provided full public notice'.[184] But the official comments offer a different rationale—the purpose is said to be to exempt 'casual or isolated assignments' that 'no one would think of filing'.[185] The disconnection between the text

[178] See text at nn 163–69.

[179] See Baird and Jackson (n 174). See also Lawrence, Henning and Freyermuth (n 176).

[180] 11 ME Rev Stat §9-1309(1) (2012 through 125th Legis).

[181] Cuming, Walsh and Wood (n 5) 155, 157. The enforcement rules do not apply to outright sales of accounts for the obvious reason that the assignor does not retain any 'equity of redemption' in the assigned receivables.

[182] §9-309(2).

[183] Dan T Coenen, 'Priorities in Accounts: The Crazy Quilt of Current Law and a Proposal for Reform' (1992) 45(5) *Vanderbilt Law Review* 1061, 1083.

[184] ibid 1084.

[185] §9-309(2) cmt 4: 'The purpose of paragraph (2) is to save from ex post facto invalidation casual or isolated assignments—assignments which no one would think of filing. Any person who regularly takes assignments of any debtor's accounts or payment intangibles should file'.

and the official comments has led to a confusing proliferation of contradictory qualitative and quantitative tests in the case law for determining the scope of the exemption.[186]

Differences in the pre-reform law may explain the divergence between the PPSAs and Article 9 on this point. The pre-PPSA assignment of book debts statutes required the registration of general assignments of books debts whether outright or by way of security on pain of subordination to subsequent assignees and the assignor's general creditors and their representatives.[187] The aim of requiring registration was to deter fraudulent or collusive general assignments and to provide public notice to subsequent assignees.[188] However, the lack of clarity concerning the interaction of registration with the common law rule of priority in *Dearle v Hall*,[189] combined with the exclusion of specific assignments from the scope of the Acts, led to uncertainty in determining priority between successive assignees of the same debts.[190] The PPSAs resolved these problems by bringing all assignments of accounts, whether outright or by way of security, and whether general or specific, within the PPSA registration regime and the first-to-register rule of priority.[191]

Prior to Article 9, many of the US States had also enacted assignment statutes applicable to both sale and security assignments. While these statutes were all directed at protecting non-notification receivables financing transactions from the threat of avoidance under federal bankruptcy law, they differed widely as to the means.[192] Some made validation dependent on public recording but differed on whether this should be an exclusive mode of perfection or an alternative to notification of the account debtor. Others simply validated non-notification assignments without requiring any additional step. A few states had bookmarking statutes validating assignments if noted on the books of the assignor.

[186] See Coenen (n 183) And see Richard F Duncan, William H Lyons and Catherine Lee Wilson, *The Law and Practice of Secured Transactions: Working with Article 9* (New York, NY: Law Journal Press, 2016) §3.03(2). 1084–100.

[187] See, eg, the Assignment of Book Debts Act, RSS 1930, c 241. These statutes were all repealed with the coming into force of the PPSAs. Prior to their enactment, a general assignment of book debts was effective without the need for public notice although the assignor's or secured creditor's priority might be defeated by the first to give notice to the account debtor rule in *Dearle v Hall* (1823) 3 Russ 1. Their enactment was spurred by a provision in the 1919 federal Bankruptcy Act that declared a debtor's general assignment of book debts void against a trustee in bankruptcy unless registered under provincial law: Bankruptcy Act, SC 1919, c 36, s 30. The 1919 provision has been carried forward in successive iterations of federal bankruptcy legislation even though its original purpose has long been achieved.

[188] *Shubenacadie Band v Francis*, 1995 CanLII 4259 (NS CA). And see Catherine Walsh, 'Registration, Constructive Notice, and the Rule in *Dearle v. Hall*—Judicial Reform in Nova Scotia: *Martin v. Shubenacadie*' (1997) 12 *Banking & Finance Law Review* 129.

[189] Above n 187.

[190] Above n 188.

[191] Above n 181.

[192] For comprehensive reviews of the differences among the pre-Art 9 assignment statutes, see: Maximilian Koessler, 'Assignment of Accounts Receivable: Confusion of the Present Law, the Impact of the Bankruptcy Act, and the Need for Uniform Legislation' (1945) 33 *California Law Review* 40; Comment, 'Multistate Accounts Receivable Financing: Conflicts in Context' (1958) 67 *Yale Law Journal* 402. The latter article also addresses the choice of law complexities posed by the divergence in State laws.

The divergent responses of the different states reflected a deep division in the non-notification receivables financing markets. The commercial banks, late arrivals to non-notification financing, favoured public recording to eliminate the risk of double assignments.[193] The longer-established finance companies and factoring firms were hostile to public recording apparently because of concerns that their customers would be unwilling to publicise assignments and because they feared competitors would use the public records to discover and solicit their customers.[194] Against the backdrop of these deep divisions, the Article 9 drafters may have thought the 'non-significant part' carve-out offered an acceptable political compromise. In Canada, the banks had long been established players in the non-notification receivables financing market and their preference for public registration and the legal certainty provided by a first-to-register rule meant that there was no opposition to bringing all assignments within the scope of the PPSA regime.

(b) Scope of Extension to Sales of 'Accounts'

The definition of accounts in the PPSAs is broadly cast, encompassing all monetary obligations except for reified intangibles and investment securities. In contrast, the initial versions of Article 9 limited the concept to trade debts arising from the sale or lease of goods or services. As a result, the priority of an outright assignee of other types of payment obligations as against third parties was left to be addressed by other State law.[195]

In extending Article 9 to the outright sale of only a limited category of accounts, the early Article 9 drafters may have been influenced by a different view of the underlying justification. Rather than referring to the common public notice and priority ordering concerns presented by both sale and security assignments, they relied more on a kind of functionalist reasoning. Gilmore, by way of illustration, viewed factors as 'lenders in sheep's clothing', making it only 'just' that they be regulated as such.[196] A variant of this reasoning was reflected in the official comments to the 1972 iteration of Article 9, which referred to the 'blurred' distinction in commercial financing transactions between a security transfer and a sale as the reason for covering both categories of transactions.[197]

Critics contested that explanation, observing that the publicity problems inherent in the transfer of intangible assets whether by way of sale or security offered

[193] Koessler (n 192) 57–58.

[194] ibid 55, 60, 87, 99.

[195] For a detailed comparison of the Art 9 and the PPSA concepts of accounts, see Cuming and Walsh (n 158) 368–72.

[196] Gilmore (n 9) 334; see also at 128–29: 'factoring is a financing arrangement. … In substance the factor is a supplier of working capital, not a joint venturer in a business enterprise. In that sense one may properly describe him as a financier, a "banker", a lender of money against security'.

[197] See former §9-102 cmt 2: 'Commercial financing on the basis of accounts and chattel paper is often so conducted that the distinction between a security transfer and a sale is blurred, and a sale of such property is therefore covered by Section (1)(b) whether intended as security or not'.

a better explanation for the inclusion of both.[198] In the result, the 2001 revision brought the sale of most important types of monetary obligations within the scope of Article 9 and the rationale pointing to the blurred line between sale and security assignments was toned down in the official comments.[199]

While bringing Article 9 closer to the PPSA approach, the 2001 revision introduced a new difference. The applicable perfection rules under current Article 9 differ depending on whether the monetary obligation is an 'account' under the newly expanded definition of that term[200] or 'a payment intangible'.[201] Unlike sales of accounts, sales of payment intangibles are perfected automatically on attachment.[202]

The payment intangibles exemption was a concession to banks and other financial institutions that wished to be able to sell participations in commercial loans while relieving buyers of the burden of having to search for and file financing statements.[203] Commentators have criticised the exemption in view of the public notice problems it creates for potential assignees and other third parties.[204] Moreover, because of the drafting technique used to define a 'payment intangible'—by negative deduction from the highly detailed and complex definition of 'account'[205]—the precise scope of the exemption is difficult to predict with certainty.[206] There is also uncertainty as to whether the first-to-file priority rule applies to protect a buyer who files a financing statement covering future payment

[198] See Douglas G Baird, 'Security Interests Reconsidered' (1994) 80 *Virginia Law Review* 2249, 2267–69 (observing that sales of accounts produce the same publicity problems as security assignments and advocating notice through public filing for both). See also: Coenen (n 183) 1074 and fn 75, 1158–59, 1171–72; Bridge, Macdonald, Simmonds and Walsh (n 6) 580–86.

[199] See §9-109, cmt 4: 'This approach [extending Art 9 to sales of accounts] generally has been successful in avoiding difficult problems of distinguishing between transactions in which a receivable secures an obligation and those in which the receivable has been sold outright. In many commercial financing transactions the distinction is blurred'. The difficulties in the United States context in distinguishing between sale and security assignments seems to be due to an insufficient appreciation of the continued relevance of property analysis even in a functionalist framework: see Bridge, Macdonald, Simmonds and Walsh (n 6). And see Steven L Harris and Charles W Mooney, 'When is a Dog's Tail Not a Leg?: A Property-Based Methodology for Distinguishing Sales of Receivables from Security Interests that Secure an Obligation (2014) 82 *University of Cincinnati Law Review* 1029.

[200] See note 205 below.

[201] ibid.

[202] §9-309(3), (4).

[203] Cuming and Walsh (n 158) 369–70.

[204] ibid 370. See also Steven L Schwarcz, 'Automatic Perfection of Sales of Payment Intangibles: A Trap for the Unwary' (2007) 68 *Ohio State Law Journal* 273 276–77: 'automatic perfection makes it difficult, if not impossible, to know one's priority in purchased or pledged payment intangibles … The inability to know ownership priority in turn undermines the market for selling intangible rights and increases costs where sales do occur'.

[205] §9-102(a)(61) defines a 'payment intangible' to mean 'a general intangible under which the account debtor's principal obligation is a monetary obligation'. Thus, the scope of the concept can only be determined by examining what monetary obligations are excluded from the very long list of transactions listed in the definition of 'account' in §9-102(a)(2).

[206] See Cuming and Walsh (n 158) 370–71; Schwarcz (n 204) 274–76.

intangibles or whether priority between successive buyers is ordered by the time of attachment and automatic perfection.[207] Commentators seem to think that the first-filing buyer should be protected in order to induce buyers to file and search, the very burden that the exemption was intended to relieve them of.[208]

Thus far the UCC's co-sponsors have declined to address the uncertainty, either by an amendment to the Article 9 text or in the official comments.[209] It may be that the continuing uncertainty is seen as indirectly resolving the problem; that is to say, by creating an incentive for buyers to make prophylactic filings, uncertainty results in the de facto extension of the Article 9 filing requirement to most sales of payment intangibles.[210] Similar thinking may explain why the uncertainties with respect to the scope of the Article 9 'non-significant part' exemption discussed above also have not been explicitly addressed.

(iv) Commercial Consignments and Long-term Leases

A transaction may sometimes be cast in the form of a lease or consignment even though the real function of reserving ownership is to secure performance of the lessee's or consignee's obligation to pay the acquisition price of the leased or consigned goods. Disguised secured transactions of this kind fall within the scope of both the PPSAs and Article 9 pursuant to the functional concept of security interest.[211]

However, even true consignments and true long-term leases involve the separation of possession and property rights. As such, they raise the same public notice concerns as non-possessory security interests. For this reason, the PPSAs extend their scope of application to long-term leases (leases for a term of more than one year)[212] and (except for the Ontario Act) commercial consignments of inventory

[207] Steven L Harris and Charles W Mooney, Jr, 'Using First Principles of UCC Article 9 to Solve Statutory Puzzles in Receivables Financing (2011) 46 *Gonzaga Law Review* 297, 309–18.

[208] ibid 313: 'Applying FTFOP [the first-to-register or -perfect rule] provides an inducement for buyers of payment intangibles to search and file'. But note that filing will not protect a prospective buyer from the priority risk posed by the automatic perfection exemption—it will still be subordinated to a buyer who purchased the relevant payment intangible prior to the filing and whose interests were therefore automatically perfected as of the date of the sale. See Schwarcz (n 204) 276–77.

[209] Stephen L Harris and Charles W Mooney, 'UCC Article 9, Filing-Based Authority, and Fundamental Property Principles: A Reply to Professor Plank' Faculty Scholarship Paper 1014, 12–13. Available at http://scholarship.law.upenn.edu/faculty_scholarship/1014.

[210] Above n 208.

[211] See Cuming, Walsh and Wood (n 5) 125–37.

[212] ibid 155, 159–61. The PPSA drafters were committed to the inclusion of true leases within the PPSAs from the outset: see Jacob S Ziegel, 'Should Canada Adopt an Article 2A Type Law on Personal Property Leasing' (1989–90) 16 *Canadian Business Law Journal* 369, 386–89. See also Ronald CC Cuming, 'Article 2A for Canada—A Comment on Professor Ziegel's Paper' (1989–1990) 16 *Canadian Business Law Journal*. 439, 447–52. Ontario was the sole outlier until 2007 when its PPSA was revised to bring it into line with the other Acts on this point: see below n 221.

to a dealer for sale on behalf of the consignor.[213] These types of transactions are deemed to be security interests, more precisely, purchase money security interests (PMSIs). The deemed PMSI characterisation ensures that the consignor or lessor is able to preserve its ownership as against the consignee's or lessee's creditors by complying with the requirements applicable to true PMSIs for obtaining priority over a prior secured creditor who has filed a financing statement covering after-acquired assets of the same genre as the leased or consigned goods.[214]

Article 9 also treats true commercial consignments as deemed PMSIs with the result that the consignor must file a financing statement and comply with the relevant priority rules in order to preserve its ownership against competing claimants.[215] On the other hand, the Article 9 drafters have resisted calls to extend Article 9 to true long-term leases.[216] Leases are covered only to the extent that they operate in substance as true purchase money financing transactions. While the official commentary offers little insight on the reason for this decision, it has been argued that the informational benefits of requiring long-term leases to be published are outweighed by the potential costs to lessors (not just the cost of complying with the filing requirement but also the potential loss of ownership to the lessee's creditors and insolvency trustee for failure to file).[217]

Certainly, there is room for reasonable persons to reasonably disagree on whether the cost/benefit analysis of requiring filing should yield the same outcome as between non-possessory security interests and true leases. However, broader differences between the overall PPSA and Article 9 frameworks may also explain the divergence between them on this point. First, it will be recalled that security interests in motor vehicles and like goods are subject to the PPSA registration regime whereas Article 9 requires perfection under the State certificate laws if the goods are held by the debtor as consumer goods or equipment. Consequently, if Article 9 were extended to true leases of these types of assets, consideration would need to be given to whether public notice should also be accomplished via a notation on the title certificates,[218] exacerbating the already difficult coordination

[213] Cuming, Walsh and Wood (n 5) 155, 158–59. Note that the definition of 'commercial consignment' excludes consignments by or between consumers, as well as consignments to auctioneers and other consignees who are generally known by their creditors to be selling the goods of others. These arrangements are excluded because the separation of possession and property poses little or no risk of deception or prejudice to third parties dealing with the consignor. Ibid 159.

[214] ibid 445.

[215] §9-109(a)(4). The initial versions of the UCC brought commercial consignments within the scope of the Art 9 filing requirements and the purchase money security interest rules via a cross-reference to Art 9 in Art 2. The 2001 revision incorporated commercial consignments directly within the scope of Art 9 as deemed security interests. See §9-109(a)(4), cmt 6.

[216] See, for example, Baird and Jackson (n 174).

[217] See Mooney (n 55). See also Charles W Mooney, 'Filing Requirements for Personal Property Leases: A Comment and Response to Professor Ziegel' (1989–99) 16 *Canadian Business Law Journal* 419. Compare Baird and Jackson (n 174); Ziegel (n 212) 389–97, Cuming (n 212). Compare also the position in Australia, see Ch 7 C(vi).

[218] Mooney (n 55) 703, fn 82.

challenges between Article 9 and the State title certificate statutes.[219] Coordination challenges also exist within the structure of the UCC itself as between Article 9 and Article 2A on leasing; the experts, advisers and industry constituencies for the two articles are more than likely to have different perspectives on the filing issue. Finally, it will also be recalled that while PMSIs in consumer goods are automatically perfected without filing under Article 9, no such exemption exists under the PPSA filing regime.[220]

Ontario initially followed Article 9's lead in excluding true leases from its scope. It was not until 2007 that the Ontario PPSA was amended to bring it into line with the other PPSAs on this point.[221] That decision was motivated in part by harmonisation objectives but other considerations also played a role. One was the desire to increase certainty and limit litigation by minimising the need to determine whether a particular leasing arrangement is a true lease or a lease operating as security.[222] While the distinction is still relevant at the level of enforcement—since the PPSA enforcement rules do not apply to the deemed security interests—there is no longer any need to draw a distinction in the more litigation-intensive perfection and priority contexts.[223] Because of the re-characterisation risk, most Ontario long-term lessors had engaged in precautionary registrations in any event. So the Ontario reformers did not think that the reform would have that profound an impact on leasing industry costs and practices. Bringing true leases within the scope of the PPSA also offered other benefits to lessors, including the extension to true leases of the PPSA's modernised choice-of-law regime.

The Ontario experience with the true lease issue is interesting because it shows that the PPSA bottom-up reform process, in allowing for an interim period of experimentation by different jurisdictions with different solutions, may ultimately produce 'spontaneous' uniformity. In contrast, the UCC's centralised reform process requires uniform consensus for implementation of any change, thereby discouraging jurisdiction-specific experimentation and innovation.

(v) Judgment 'Liens'

Both Article 9 and the PPSAs apply only to security interests created by agreement. Priority competitions with security interests arising by operation of law are

[219] See Section D(i) above.

[220] See Section 4(b) above.

[221] See Cuming, Walsh and Wood (n 5) 65–66.

[222] On the difficulties of determining whether a lease is a true lease or a security lease, see Cuming, Walsh and Wood (n 5) 125–33. Characterisation is less of a challenge in the consignment context—problems are encountered only where the parties' actual conduct does not reflect the terms of the consignment agreement: ibid 133–37.

[223] This is not to say that the characterisation issue is inconsequential in the enforcement context. For example, if the lease is characterised as a true lease, the lessee may be liable for a damages claim that exceeds the value of the leased object if the lease includes an enforceable penalty clause: see *Equirex Vehicle Leasing 2007 Inc. v Verhage*, 2013 BCSC 1142. Conversely, if the lease is characterised

generally left to be dealt with by other law.[224] However, most PPSA jurisdictions have integrated their judgment enforcement law with the PPSA registry system and the PPSA perfection and priority rules.[225] Under the former law, the issuance of a writ of execution or enforcement order on behalf of a judgment creditor did not operate as an effective encumbrance because subsequent third parties who acquired an interest in the debtor's personal property typically took free of the judgment creditor's claim. Moreover, the judgment creditor was afforded priority under the PPSA over the holder of a prior unperfected security interest only if the judgment enforcement creditor actually caused the property to be seized under legal process before the security interest was registered or otherwise perfected. This has been altered in all PPSA jurisdictions (other than Ontario and British Columbia) to permit a writ or notice of judgment to be registered in the PPSA personal property registry. When registered, the right of the judgment creditor has substantially the same priority status as a perfected PPSA security interest against third-party competing claimants including obtaining the benefit of the first-to-register rule of priority as against subsequently registered security interests. From the perspective of the judgment creditor, this produces a more efficient form of 'passive' enforcement since the judgment debtor is compelled as a practical matter to satisfy the registered judgment in order to be able to sell or grant security in its assets.

Article 9 generally leaves the issue of priority between unperfected security interests and the debtor's judgment creditors to State law. While a few States have implemented regimes similar to that described above, the majority still require the judgment creditor to have completed the judgment execution process before being able to trump an unperfected security interest.[226]

as a security lease, the lessee may be entitled to the benefit of a statutory 'seize or sue' limitation on the lessor's default rights under a lease of consumer goods: *Mercedes Benz Financial v Wager*, 2010 BCSC 1090. See also *DaimlerChrysler Services Canada Inc v Cameron*, 2007 BCCA 144.

[224] For the PPSAs, see Cuming, Walsh and Wood (n 5) 494–515. The same is true for Art 9 with the exception of State agricultural liens, which were incorporated into the Art 9 perfection and priority structure in the 2001 revision: see §9-102(a)(5), §9-109(a)(2), §9-310(a), §9-322(a), §9-322(g). The complex interaction between Art 9's perfection and priority rules and the diverse State statutes giving rise to agricultural liens is beyond the scope of this chapter. The Art 9 drafters were urged to bring all non-possessory statutory liens within the Art 9 framework in order to provide greater legal certainty, particularly in the context of priority competitions involving consensual Art 9 security interests, but retreated in the face of the impracticality of assessing the implications given the diverse array of statutory liens provided by State statutes. See Stephen L. Harris and Charles W. Mooney, 'How Successful Was the Revision of UCC Article 9: Reflections of the Reporters' (1999) 74 Chi.-Kent L. Rev. 1357, 1387. In Canada, the perfection, priority and enforcement issues associated with non-possessory statutory liens in favour of private creditors have been dealt with in a number of jurisdictions by the enactment of comprehensive statutes adapted directly from the PPSAs. See, for example, the Commercial Liens Act, SS 2002, c C-15.1. And see: RCC Cuming, 'The Spreading Influences of PPSA Concepts: the Uniform Liens Act' (1999) 15 *Banking & Finance Law Review* 1; British Columbia Law Institute, *Report on the Uniform Liens Act* (BCLI Report No 23, January 2003), available at www.bcli.org/sites/default/files/Uniform_Liens_Act.pdf.

[225] See Cuming, Walsh and Wood (n 5) 494–503. And see RCC. Cuming, 'When an Unsecured Creditor is a Secured Creditor' (2003) 66 *Saskatchewan Law Review* 255.

[226] William J Woodward, 'New Judgment Liens on Personal Property: Does "Efficient" Mean "Better"?' (1990) 27 *Harvard Journal on Legislation* 1.

E. Alternative Modes of Perfection: Possession and Control

(i) Possession

The pre-PPSA and pre-Article 9 statutes generally required public registration only in relation to non-possessory secured transactions. Possessory pledges of tangible collateral were exempt on the theory that dispossession put third parties on notice that the relevant assets were potentially encumbered.[227] Article 9 and the PPSAs have carried forward the historical policy. Under both regimes, a security interest in goods or other tangible collateral may be perfected by either possession or filing,[228] with priority between competing security interests then determined, as a general rule, by the temporal order of these events.[229]

However, possession may sometimes constitute a superior mode of perfection. This is the case where the collateral is a cheque or other negotiable instrument. A 'purchaser for value'—whether taking by sale or security—who acquires possession has priority over a prior secured creditor who perfected by registration.[230] Only actual knowledge that the transaction violates the rights of the secured creditor can defeat this priority.[231] The policy reason lies in the negotiable character of the collateral. Negotiability necessitates that subsequent acquirers be able to rely fully on a person's possession as indicative of ownership without having to conduct further inquiries. Requiring them to search and file would be inconsistent with that goal.[232]

[227] Of course, the qualified character of the secured creditor's possession is not evident to the public. In this sense, admitting possession as an alternative to registration merely transfers the publicity problem from the debtor's creditors and transferees to those of the secured creditor. On the other hand, at least for pawnbrokers and other professional secured creditors, public knowledge of the nature of their general business offers a kind of implicit public notice that they are not holding assets for their own benefit. Douglas Baird and Thomas Jackson. 'Information, Uncertainty, and the Transfer of Property' (1984) 13 *Journal of Legal Studies* 299, 307. Possession also detracts somewhat from the priority-ordering function of the registry system, requiring potential secured creditors to also verify the debtor's possession. But this is usually part of a secured creditor's risk assessment process in any event. The public notice problems are also lessened by the typically short-term character of possessory secured financing of goods.

[228] §9-313. For the PPSAs, see Cuming, Walsh and Wood (n 5) 307–09.

[229] §9-322(a). For the PPSAs, see ibid 419–22.

[230] §9-330(d). For the PPSAs, see ibid 418, 404–08.

[231] ibid. Note that both regimes also grant a special priority status to a secured creditor or buyer who takes possession of 'chattel paper'. 'Chattel paper' is a statutory construct with no common law antecedent. It refers to secured transactions and leases entered into by dealers engaged in selling and leasing motor vehicles and other large-ticket consumer goods with their customers. The effect of this special priority is to give these contracts quasi-negotiable status so as to facilitate the financing of the dealers on the security of their rights to payment and associated property rights under these contracts. The utility of a dedicated chattel paper regime outside US and Canadian markets (or even within them) is doubtful: see Anthony Duggan, 'Chattel Paper' (2013) 43 *Australian Business Law Review* 171.

[232] See Baird and Jackson (n 174) 192.

Even broader protection is extended to possession where the collateral is money. Under both regimes, a transferee of money or funds from a bank account takes free of any security interest including one that may have been perfected by a prior filing.[233] The policy reason is the need to ensure that the grant of a security interest does not interfere with the free flow of money in the economy, including the ability of a debtor to pay its other creditors.[234]

(ii) Control of Investment Securities

Investment securities have long been vested with the quality of negotiability in order to facilitate liquidity in secondary investment markets.[235] Negotiability was traditionally achieved in a similar fashion to cheques and other negotiable bills. The intangible rights of an investor against the issuer were reified in a paper certificate so as to enable them to be sold or pledged free of adverse claims by delivery of the certificate to an acquirer without notice of any defects in the transferor's title. This technique became unworkable with the huge expansion in the volume and speed of trading on regulated exchanges in the latter part of the twentieth century. The US capital market responded by immobilising security certificates in central depositories and establishing an intermediated system for dealings in the securities.[236]

In the intermediated system, as least as it operates in the United States (and Canada), the acquisition and disposition of securities takes place solely through electronic credits and debits to securities accounts. The top tier intermediary—usually a central depository's nominee—establishes accounts to which it credits securities acquired from it by its bank and broker customers. These lower-tier intermediaries in turn establish accounts for their own clients, and so on down the chain of intermediaries until one reaches the securities account of the ultimate holder with its broker or bank. The intermediated system severs any direct link between the holder of the security and the issuer. The identity of the ultimate investor is recorded only on the books of its intermediary. The securities held by the investor's intermediary with its own intermediary are held in fungible bulk in its name and not in the name of the intermediary's customers and so on through the chain.

233 §9-332. For the PPSAs, see Cuming, Walsh and Wood (n 5) 404–05, 407–08. See also *Flexi-coil Ltd v Kindersley District Credit Union Ltd* 1993 CanLII 6650 (SK CA); but see *Bank of China v Fan* 2015 BCSC 590.

234 For the PPSAs, see ibid. For Art 9, see §9-332, cmt 2.

235 Eva Micheler, 'The Legal Nature of Securities: Inspirations from Comparative Law' in Louise Gullifer and Jennifer Payne (eds), *Intermediated Securities: Legal Problems and Practical Issues* (Oxford: Hart Publishing, 2010) 131–48; Philipp Paech, 'Market Needs as Paradigm: Breaking up the Thinking on EU Securities Law' (14 September 2012). LSE Legal Studies Working Paper No 11/2012, http://ssrn.com/abstract=2150156.

236 David C Donald, 'The Rise and Effect of the Indirect Holding Systems: How Corporate America Ceded its Shareholders to Intermediaries' (26 September 2007). Available at SSRN: http://ssrn.com/abstract=1017206.

Articles 8 and 9 of the UCC were significantly revised in 1978 and then in 1994 to address the legal challenges posed by the emergence of intermediated securities.[237] The principal task of the drafters was to provide for the negotiability of securities represented by entries in securities accounts. The solution centred on conceptualising the claims of account holders to securities held in a securities account with an intermediary as a distinct category of investment property called a 'security entitlement'. A person acquires a security entitlement simply by having a security or other 'financial asset'[238] credited (or accepted for credit) by her intermediary to her securities account.[239] The entitlement holder does not acquire a specific property right in the security. Rather she acquires a 'security entitlement' defined as 'the rights and property interest of an entitlement holder with respect to a financial asset specified' in part 5 of Article 8.[240] Under part 5, the property interest of entitlement holders is a 'pro rata property interest' in the fungible pool of all units of a particular security held by the intermediary for customers who have security entitlements with respect to that security.[241] To describe this as a 'property interest' is somewhat illusory since it is generally enforceable only by personal action against the intermediary to perform its obligations to entitlement holders under part 5.[242] In the event of the intermediary's insolvency, it is not enforceable against a 'purchaser' to whom the intermediary wrongfully transferred securities held for customers if the purchaser gave value and obtained control unless it is proved affirmatively that the purchaser acted in collusion with the intermediary to violate the intermediary's obligation to maintain sufficient quantities of securities to satisfy the claims of entitlement holders.[243]

The principal beneficiaries of the rule protecting non-colluding 'control' purchasers are secured creditors and their close cousins, repo purchasers.[244] Outright purchasers receive de facto protection from adverse claims asserted by former

[237] For comprehensive critical analyses of the revised framework, see: Francis J Facciolo, 'Father Knows Best: Revised Article 8 and the Individual Investor' (1999), 27 *Florida State University Law Review* 615; Russell A Hakes. 'UCC Article 8: Will the Indirect Holding of Securities Survive the Light of Day' (2002) 35 *Loyola Los Angeles Law Review* 661.

[238] §8-102(a)(9).

[239] §8-501.

[240] §8-102(a)(17). And see cmt 17: '"Security entitlement" means the rights and property interest of a person who holds securities or other financial assets through a securities intermediary. A security entitlement is both a package of personal rights against the securities intermediary and an interest in the property held by the securities intermediary. A security entitlement is not, however, a specific property interest in any financial asset held by the securities intermediary or by the clearing corporation through which the securities intermediary holds the financial asset. See Section 8-104(c) and 8-503. The formal definition of security entitlement set out in subsection (a)(17) of this Section is a cross-reference to the rules of Part 5. In a sense, then, the entirety of Part 5 is the definition of security entitlement. The Part 5 rules specify the rights and property interest that comprise a security entitlement.'

[241] §8-503 (a), (b).

[242] §8-503(c).

[243] §8-503(d), (e). Even in the rare case where these requirements are met, entitlement holders may enforce their collective proportionate property interests against the purchaser only if the trustee or other liquidator elects not to pursue recovery on their behalf. Ibid.

[244] Hakes (n 237) 721–22.

entitlement holders by virtue of the practical impossibility of tracing particular securities debited from a securities account through the netting processes of intermediaries and central clearing corporations in the settlement of trades. Tracing is possible, however, against purchasers who acquire control of securities directly from the intermediary.[245] A purchaser obtains 'control' of a security entitlement (and therefore an interest in a financial asset) if it 'becomes the entitlement holder'—that is, has the relevant security credited to its own securities account or that of its representative—or concludes a control agreement with the intermediary under which the intermediary agrees that it will comply with the purchaser's orders with respect to the financial assets credited to the securities account without the need to obtain further consent of the entitlement holder.[246]

The use of a no-collusion standard—as opposed to a no-notice or -knowledge test—to ensure near-absolute finality in collateral transactions in favour of control purchasers reflects the goal of the UCC drafters to facilitate the extension of financing to and among financial intermediaries.[247] The same tendency is reflected in the priority rules applicable specifically to secured creditors. While financial assets held by a securities intermediary for its entitlement holders are not subject to the claims of the intermediary's creditors,[248] this is subject to a significant exception. If the intermediary does not have sufficient interests in securities it holds to satisfy both its obligations to entitlement holders and a creditor to whom it has granted security interest in those securities, the secured creditor has priority if it obtains control.[249] Control also constitutes a mode of perfection and gives superior priority to the control secured creditor over competing secured creditors who perfect by filing.[250] Neither priority rule requires that the secured creditor take without notice or knowledge. Indeed priority is not even explicitly conditioned on a no-collusion requirement although the official comments suggest that positive evidence of collusion would defeat priority.[251]

[245] ibid.

[246] §8-106(d).

[247] Hakes (n 237) 784–85.

[248] §8-503(a), §8-511(a). In the event of the intermediary's insolvency, there is an evident overlap between this priority rule and the control purchaser rule in §8-503(d), (e), above text at n 243, reflecting the determination of the Art 8 drafters to ensure finality in collateral transactions involving intermediated securities.

[249] §8-511(b). Holders of security entitlements with clearing corporations—typically securities intermediaries—are also subordinated to the clearing corporation's secured creditors even if they do not have control: §8-511(c).

[250] §9-328(1), §9-322(f)(1). If more than one secured creditor has control (for example, because both concluded control agreements with the intermediary, they rank according to the time control was obtained: §9-328(2)(A). A securities intermediary with a security interest in its entitlement holder's security entitlement has control automatically and its security interest has priority over any other security interest including one held by an external secured creditor who obtained control by entering into a control agreement with the intermediary: §8-106(e), §9-328(3). The official comments state that margin loans are the type of transaction contemplated by the rule: §8-106(e), cmt 6.

[251] §8-511 cmt 1 states that the no-collusion requirement in the control purchaser rule in §8-503(e) applies to the §8-511(b) rule giving priority to the secured creditor of an intermediary over entitlement holders even though it is not explicitly incorporated in that rule. See Hakes (n 237) 782–83. §9-328,

The hyper-emphasis of the UCC drafters on settlement finality in collateral transactions in the intermediated system is controversial, particularly insofar as it leaves the protection of entitlement holders against wrongful conduct by their intermediaries in pledging 'their' securities almost entirely to other law, in particular regulatory rules requiring intermediaries to segregate customer securities and restricting their use as collateral for the intermediary's own financing, and investor insurance in the event that these regulatory controls fail.[252] Nonetheless, beginning in 2006, the Canadian provinces and territories enacted securities transfer Acts that substantively duplicate the Article 8 framework along with amendments to the PPSAs (and the Civil Code in the case of Québec) that mimic the corresponding Article 9 rules.[253] It is a moot question whether a made-in-Canada solution might have arrived at a different policy balance. In view of the close integration of the Canadian and US securities markets,[254] the drafters concluded that uniformity was essential. If the Canadian reformers had instead opted for a different regime, legal certainty would have been undermined. Owing to the very structure of the intermediated securities market, it is necessary to apply the law of the jurisdiction that governs the relevant intermediary–account holder relationship even though this means that what is de facto the same financial asset is subject at each tier of the chain to a distinct applicable law.[255] Under this choice-of-law approach, the content and characterisation of each account holder's rights is determined by the law applicable to the account relationship. It follows that if securities credited to a Canadian investor's accounts are located at the top tier of the intermediary chain in an account with a US central depository, US law would apply at that level. Any discrepancy between that law and the Canadian law applicable at the ultimate investor/intermediary level would have resulted in a potential mismatch between

cmt 8 states that 'the question whether a control secured party induced or encouraged its financing arrangement with actual knowledge that the debtor would be violating the rights of another secured party may, in some circumstances, appropriately be treated as a factor in determining whether the control party's action is the kind of egregious conduct for which resort to other law [to defeat the control secured creditor's priority under §9-328] is appropriate'. See further Hakes (n 237) 765–67.

[252] Hakes (n 237) 734–41, 784–85. As Paech has observed, while all legal systems must mediate between the conflicting policies of enhancing negotiability and protecting account holders from intermediary insolvency risk, the UCC security entitlement model 'is probably the paradigm of a legal framework ensuring negotiability'. See Paech (n 235).

[253] See Cuming, Walsh and Wood (n 5) 24–47. Canadian regulators have recently proposed stricter segregation requirements and rehypothecation and reuse restrictions on intermediaries and clearing corporations: see Canadian Securities Administrators (CSA), Proposed National Instrument 94-102, Derivatives: Customer Clearing and Protection of Customer Positions and Collateral (21 January 2016) www.osc.gov.on.ca/en/SecuritiesLaw_csa_20160121_94-102_derivatives-customer-collateral.htm.

[254] For example, approximately 40% of investors in Canadian companies are US residents. See William J Speirs, 'The Case to Make DRS Aa Canadian Listing Requirement, Securities Transfer Association of Canada' (21 March 2014) www.stac.ca/Public/PublicShowFile.aspx?fileID=236.

[255] For a persuasive analysis showing that private international law cannot resolve the legal uncertainty inherent in the holding and crediting and debiting of securities through accounts maintained by tiers of intermediaries across multiple jurisdictions with incompatible domestic legal frameworks, see Paech (n 235).

the rights of the ultimate investor and the rights of the US upper-tier account holder.[256]

(iii) Deposit Accounts with Financial Institutions[257]

Consistent with the general concept of a deposit account as a debt owed by the bank to its customer, the PPSAs traditionally have subjected security interests in funds deposited to an account with a bank or other financial institution to the same general rules that apply to security interests in other 'accounts'. The security interest must be 'perfected' by public registration and priority among secured creditors is ordered temporally according to the order of registration. The same rules have generally applied to a security interest granted by the customer to the depository bank itself, subject only to the bank's right, in its capacity as the debtor on the account, to set off any obligations owing to it by its customer that arise before it receives notice of a security right that otherwise would have priority.[258]

The initial versions of Article 9 did not include deposit accounts within its scope, leaving them to be dealt with under other State law. While the 2001 revision changed that, deposit accounts were treated as a distinct category of collateral subject to a distinct 'control'-based perfection and priority regime analogous to that applied to security interests in security entitlements.[259]

Writing in 2000, some Canadian commentators concluded that there was no justification for importing the Article 9 regime for deposit accounts into Canadian law.[260] In recent years, the tide of opinion has turned. The province of Québec already has implemented a control regime for hypothecs in deposits broadly in line with the Article 9 approach.[261] The principal aim of the new regime is

[256] Substantive uniformity provides legal certainty only within the Canadian and US cross-border markets. As long as other legal systems have a different substantive legal framework for intermediated securities, the potential for irreconcilable conflicts of law remains: Paech (n 235). The ambitious goal of the Geneva Securities Convention (UNIDROIT Convention on Substantive Rules for Intermediated Securities, adopted in 2009, not yet in force) is to establish a basic 'functionalist' common framework for the intermediated securities holding system. The framework is broadly in line with the US and Canadian regimes absent some of the most contentious features; for example, Art 20(2) awards priority to a control secured creditor who finances intermediaries over account holders unless it 'actually knows or ought to know that the interest granted violates the rights of one or more account holders' as opposed to requiring the account holders to show affirmative collusion. Nonetheless, its implementation therefore remains controversial. However, the only means of eliminating intermediary risk would be to establish a global structural framework that would allow securities to once again be held by investors directly in the books of the issuer: see further: Donald (n 236) and Paech (n 235).

[257] For further discussion see Ch 5 C.

[258] Cuming, Walsh and Wood (n 5) 664. The bank's set-off right, whether arising by operation of law or contractually, may be exercised regardless of whether or not it concurrently holds a security interest in the deposit account.

[259] §9-104, §9-312, §9-314 §9-327, §9-340.

[260] Cuming and Walsh (n 158) 364–68.

[261] Civil Code of Québec, CQLR c C-1991, Arts 2713.1–2713.9. See further: Sterling Dietze, 'Quebec is First Province to Propose Cash Collateral Regime', Stikeman Elliott (9 December 2014),

to facilitate the use of 'cash collateral' particularly in the securities lending and derivatives markets.[262] Citing the same policy priority, Ontario has designated the enactment of a new regime for deposit accounts in its PPSA as a priority.[263] Consequently, commensurate changes to the PPSA substantive and choice-of-law rules for deposit accounts are anticipated in the very near future.

F. Conclusion

The Canadian PPSAs reflect a stronger commitment than Article 9 to the reliability and integrity of their public registration systems and to the role of these systems in publicising security rights to third parties and in regulating priorities in a manner that enhances certainty and reduces litigation for all parties potentially affected by security interests, including unsecured creditors. This is evident in the PPSA rules addressing the operational aspects of registration explored in Section C and in the broader transactional scope of the PPSA registration regime reviewed in Section D. The reasons for this divergence can be attributed partly to timing and technology. The early embrace of computerised registry records and e-registration and e-searching enabled PPSA jurisdictions to establish more robust and reliable registration systems, reducing the need for legal rules aimed at protecting the first-registered secured creditor from the legal risk posed by imperfections in the registry system itself and motivating the drafters to extend the system to a broader range of transactions, including secured transactions involving PMSIs in consumer goods and long-term true leases.

There are additional path-dependent explanations for the differences in the transactional scope of the two regimes. The pre-PPSA registration statutes required public recording of both sale and security assignments of monetary obligations whereas this was a much more contested issue under pre-Article 9 law in the United States. This may partly explain the Article 9 exemptions from the filing of true sales of monetary obligations addressed in Section D. As also observed in Section D, the pre-reform establishment of State title certificate systems for

www.canadianstructuredfinancelaw.com/2014/12/Arts/derivatives/quebec-is-first-province-to-propose-cash-collateral-regime/print.html; Michel Deschamps, Mathieu Dubord and Mary Jeanne Phelan, 'New Regime in Quebec for Security on Bank Deposits and Other Monetary Claims', McCarthy Tetrault (15 May 2015), www.mccarthy.ca/article_detail.aspx?id=7105.

[262] The justifications offered in the official Art 9 commentary for the bank control regime are not very convincing; it is clear that in the Canadian context the principal pressure for reform has come from the financial industry: Catherine Walsh, 'Justifications for UCC Article 9's Treatment of Deposit Accounts' (2015) 4 *Pennsylvania State Journal of Law and International Affairs* 350.

[263] See Ontario Ministry of Government and Consumer Services, Business Law Agenda: Priority Findings and Recommendations Report 9 (2015). And see Ontario Bar Association, 'Perfecting Security Interests in Cash Collateral (6 February 2012)', available at www.oba.org/CMSPages/GetFile.aspx?guid=c020380c-6c0a-496f-b4b1-b44d6ac07eb5. See Ch 5 C.

providing public notice of security interests in motor vehicles and similar high-value tangible assets impeded the use of the Article 9 filing system as the public notice venue for this type of collateral.

Pre-reform law in the United States was also more hostile to all assets secured financing than in common law Canada and the Article 9 drafters have perhaps understandably been more concerned with prioritising the function of registration to protect the priority of the first registered secured creditor over its public notice function vis-à-vis third parties. Institutional differences may also play a role. Given the centralised nature of the Article 9 drafting process, and the incorporation of the industry perspective, the Article 9 drafters are more likely to view the primary function of secured transactions law as facilitating secured lending. The bottom-up nature of the PPSA enactment process makes it more likely that drafters must also take into account the perspectives of other players affected by the grant of security and particularly unsecured creditors. This difference in perspective is illustrated by the PPSA rules enabling unsecured creditors to obtain access to the parties' off-record security agreement examined in Section C and in the integration of judgments within the PPSA registration and priority system reviewed in Section D.

While the bulk of this chapter was focused on the differences between the PPSA and Article 9 regimes, Section E examined the almost perfect uniformity between them that has been achieved or will soon be achieved for security interests in intangible financial collateral deployed in investment markets. The demand for cross-border uniformity in this context was attributed to the increasing global character of securities markets, the resulting inability to manage cross-border differences in national law through the conventional mechanism of conflict of laws rules, and the demand of the globally dominant US capital market for absolute transactional finality in financial collateral arrangements. The financial collateral story illustrates how external market pressures may limit the ability of States to adapt transplanted legal models to local policies, perspectives and contexts.

5

Current Issues in Secured Transactions Law in Canada: An Ontario Perspective

ANTHONY DUGGAN

A. Introduction

I have been a member of the Ontario Bar Association's Personal Property Security Law Committee ('PPSL Committee') for the past 15 years. The committee comprises about 20 members, most of them legal practitioners specialising in secured lending or banking and finance law. The committee also includes two in-house bank lawyers, a representative of the motor vehicle industry, a provincial government representative and two law professors. The committee's main function is to make recommendations for reform of the Ontario Personal Property Security Act,[1] having regard, in particular, to new commercial developments, statutory developments in the other provinces, the United States and elsewhere and developments in the case law. The committee has achieved moderate success in persuading the government to adopt its recommendations. The most recent substantial round of PPSA amendments was in 2006, and most of these reforms resulted from recommendations made by the committee.

However, the pace of personal property security (PPS) law reform in Ontario has slowed over the past decade, in part because for some of this time there was a minority government in power and the politics of staying in office affected government priorities.[2] The PPSL Committee has remained active during this period and

[1] Personal Property Security Act RSO 1990, cP10 (OPPSA).

[2] The current Liberal government, which was elected in June, 2014, has committed itself to reforming and updating the province's commercial laws. In February, 2015, the government established a panel of experts with the task of mapping out a reform agenda. The committee submitted its report in mid-June, 2015: *Business Law Agenda Priority Findings and Recommendations Report*, available at www.ontariocanada.com/registry/view.do. PPSA reform is high on the list of priorities identified in the report.

has continued to make submissions to the government. None of the committee's more recent submissions has been acted on as yet, but they are all still on the table and the committee continues to press for their implementation.

In this chapter I discuss three of the PPSL Committee's more recent projects, the first dealing with security interests in statutory and contractual licences, the second with security interests in cash collateral and the third with security interests in proceeds collateral. I have chosen these topics because they involve interesting and important policy questions and so they are more likely to engage an international audience than other, more technical, topics I might have chosen instead.[3]

B. Security Interests in Statutory and Contractual Licences

(i) Statutory Licences

A question that has been much litigated in Ontario is whether a statutory licence qualifies as personal property for the purposes of the statute. Example 1, below, illustrates the context in which the issue typically arises.

> **Example 1.** Debtor runs a commercial fishing business and he holds a fishing licence from the relevant government authority. SP makes a loan to Debtor and takes a security interest in all Debtor's present and after-acquired personal property. Debtor ends up in financial difficulty and SP appoints a receiver. The receiver is keen to sell Debtor's business on a going-concern basis because this will bring in a higher return than the piecemeal sale of Debtor's assets. But the business is worthless without the licence.

Whether the receiver can transfer the licence as part of the sale depends on whether SP's security interest extends to the licence. This question, in turn, depends on whether the licence is 'personal property' within the meaning of the security agreement and the statute. OPPSA section 1(1) defines 'personal property' to mean: 'chattel paper, documents of title, goods, instruments, intangibles, money and investment property'. Each of these expressions is in turn defined. A statutory licence does not fit the definition of chattel paper, documents of title, goods, instruments, money or investment property. But it may fall under the catch-all definition of 'intangible', which reads as follows: '"Intangible" means all personal

[3] The three chosen topics were the focus for a presentation I gave at the England and Wales Secured Transactions Law Reform Project conference, *Secured Transactions Reform in Other Jurisdictions* (London, 18 June, 2014 and Durham, 20 June, 2014). Professor Peter Winship provided a U.S. perspective on the same topics, while Professor Louise Gullifer and Dr Magda Raczynska spoke to the position in England.

property, including choses in action, that is not goods, chattel paper, documents of title, instruments, money or investment property'. The question, therefore, is whether a statutory licence qualifies as personal property. There is a line of Ontario cases suggesting that the answer is 'no', or at least 'arguably not'.[4] The cases identify three related concerns:

— The licensing statute will typically give the licensing authority discretion to suspend or cancel a licence or to refuse to renew it. How can a licence qualify as property if the licensing authority has a discretion to take it away?
— The licensing statute may prohibit transfers or it may give the licensing authority a discretion to refuse a transfer. How can a licence qualify as property if it is not freely transferable?
— As a matter of public policy, the licensing authority needs to have control over who holds a licence. That control might be undermined if the courts allowed security interests in the licence.

The issue came before the Supreme Court of Canada in *Saulnier v RBC*,[5] where the facts resembled Example 1, above. The court rejected the earlier case law and concluded that a fishing licence was 'personal property', at least for the purposes of the PPSA and the bankruptcy laws. The judgment was written by Binnie J.

As Binnie J explained, there are two main policy considerations underlying the treatment of statutory licences as personal property. The first is the importance of facilitating access to credit in cases like Example 1, above. The second is the need to maintain the integrity of the licensing scheme. He expressed the first consideration as follows:[6]

> A commercial fisher with a ramshackle boat and a licence to fish is much better off financially than a fisher with a great boat tied up at the wharf and no licence. Financial institutions looking for readily marketable loan collateral want to snap up licences issued under the federal *Regulations*, which in the case of the lobster fishery can have a dockside value that fluctuates up to a half million dollars or more. Fishers want to offer as much collateral as they can to obtain the loans needed to acquire the equipment to enable them to put to sea.

Binnie J expressed the second consideration as follows:[7]

> Canada's fisheries are a 'common property resource' belonging to all the people of Canada. Under the Fisheries Act, it is the Minister's duty to manage, conserve and develop the fishery on behalf of Canadians in the public interest ... Licensing is a tool in the arsenal of powers available to the Minister under the Fisheries Act to manage fisheries.

[4] The cases are discussed in Jacob S Ziegel and David L Denomme, *The Ontario Personal Property Security Act—Commentary and Analysis*, 2nd edn (Toronto, Butterworths, 2000) 40–41.

[5] *Saulnier v RBC* [2008] 3 SCR 166.

[6] [2008] 3 SCR 166 at para 13.

[7] [2008] 3 SCR 166 at para 14, quoting *Comeau's Seafoods Ltd v Canada (Minister of Fisheries and Oceans)* [1997] 1 SCR 12 at para 37, Supreme Court of Canada.

By implication, the cost of treating a fishing licence as personal property lies in the danger of fettering the Minister's discretion.

However, as Binnie J goes on to point out, there is no such danger. The reason is that the PPSA gives the secured party no greater rights than the debtor himself had (*nemo dat quod non habet*). The debtor holds the licence subject to the Minister's discretion as provided by the licensing statute and, likewise, the debtor's right to transfer the licence is subject to the Minister's discretion. Therefore, the secured party's rights to hold and transfer the licence are also at the Minister's discretion:

> It may well be that in the course of a [receivership] the fishing licence will expire, or has already expired. If so, the [receiver] will have the same right as the original holder of an expired licence to go to the Minister to seek its replacement, and has the same recourse (or the lack of it) if the request is rejected. The debtor can transfer no greater rights than he possesses. The [receiver] simply steps into the shoes of the debtor and takes the licence 'warts and all'.[8]

To summarise, Binnie J's 'warts and all' principle has two implications:

(1) a security interest in a statutory licence does not interfere with the licensing authority's discretion and so there is no threat to public policy; and
(2) when a secured party is negotiating for a security interest in a licence, it must take account of the risk that the licensing authority might exercise its discretion contrary to the secured party's interests, for example by blocking a proposed future sale of the licence, or by cancelling or refusing to renew the licence. On all these fronts, the secured party is as vulnerable as the debtor/licence-holder and it must make a commercial decision about whether to assume the risk.

Ultimately, however, Binnie J did not rest his decision on these broad policy grounds. Instead, he reasoned that a fishing licence is at least analogous to a *profit à prendre* and that, given the *profit à prendre* is a well-established property right, fishing licences should also be treated as property.[9] The difficulty with this line of reasoning is that not all statutory licences are like *profits à prendre*. For example, the analogy between a taxi licence and a *profit à prendre* would be harder to draw and the same point could be made about nursing home licences and milk or tobacco quotas.[10] On the other hand, these licences, like a fishing licence, may represent major commercial assets. In summary, it is unclear, in the wake of *Saulnier*, whether licences which do not exhibit *profit à prendre* characteristics

[8] [2008] 3 SCR 166 at para 50.

[9] For similar reasoning, but in a different context, see *Harper v Minister for Sea Fisheries* (1989) 168 CLR 314, High Court of Australia.

[10] These examples are all taken from the Ontario cases referred to above.

would qualify as personal property for PPSA purposes. The policy considerations Binnie J advances in the first part of his judgment suggest that they should, but the second part of his judgment suggests otherwise.

(ii) Contractual Licences

A contractual licence is a form of agreement under which licensor A gives licensee B permission to use A's property. Licensing is a common method for the sharing of intellectual property rights (patents, copyrights, trademarks and the like). In form, a contractual licence is a promise by A to B that B may use A's property for the duration of the agreement. The licence may contain a provision prohibiting B from assigning its rights or, alternatively, stipulating that B may not assign its rights without A's consent. Can B use the licence as collateral? As in the case of a statutory licence, the answer depends on whether a contractual licence is 'personal property' within the meaning of the PPSA.

Saulnier was concerned with statutory licences, but the case has implications for contractual licences as well. In *Saulnier*, Binnie J remarked that 'a simple licence [probably could not] itself be considered property at common law'. But he went on to say that 'if not property in the common law, a fishing licence is unquestionably a major commercial asset'.[11] The same is true of a contractual licence such as an intellectual property licence and, applying the first part of Binnie J's judgment, this should lead to the conclusion that the licence is personal property in the PPSA context. Therefore, the licence may be used as collateral, but subject to the 'warts and all' limitation. In other words, if the licence agreement provides that the licensee may not transfer its entitlement without the licensor's consent, the secured party would be subject to the same limitation and therefore, if it wanted to enforce its security interest by selling the licence, it would first have to seek the licensor's approval. On the other hand, if the licence agreement absolutely prohibited transfer of the licence, the secured party would obtain no rights in the licence at all unless, perhaps, it was able to negotiate with the licensor for a waiver of the prohibition.

However, as indicated above, *Saulnier* is ambiguous and, on a narrower reading of the case, a licence is not personal property unless it is analogous to a *profit à prendre* or, at least, is part of a bundle of rights which includes a recognised proprietary entitlement. A contractual licence typically will not satisfy this requirement and therefore it is not personal property, even if there is no anti-assignment provision in the licence agreement.

[11] [2008] 33 SCR 166 at para 23.

(iii) Statutory Reforms

Two provinces, Saskatchewan and British Columbia, have expressly addressed the licence issue. Section 2(w) of the Saskatchewan PPSA[12] defines 'intangible' to include a licence and section 2(z) defines 'licence' to mean:

> a right, whether or not exclusive:
>
> (i) to manufacture, produce, sell, transport, or otherwise deal with personal property; or
>
> (ii) to provide services;
>
> that is transferable by the grantee with or without restriction or the consent of the grantor.

The provision applies to both statutory and contractual licences. A statutory licence falls outside the definition unless it is transferable. It follows that, if the governing statute absolutely prohibits transfers, the licence is not personal property to which the PPSA applies.[13] On the other hand, the fact that transfer of the licence is at the licensing authority's discretion does not take the licence outside the PPSA definition. Likewise, a contractual licence falls outside the definition if the licence agreement prohibits assignment. On the other hand, if there are no restrictions on assignment, or if assignment is permitted subject to restrictions, the licence is personal property and it may be used as collateral. Enforcement of the security interest will typically involve sale of the licence to a willing buyer, along with the business to which the licence relates. In this connection, Saskatchewan PPSA section 57(3) provides that the secured party may seize the licence upon giving notice to the debtor and also to the grantor of the licence, while section 59(18) provides that the licence may be disposed of only in accordance with the terms and conditions under which the licence was granted.[14] These provisions reflect the 'warts and all' principle.

In 1998, in a submission which pre-dated *Saulnier*, the PPSL Committee, through the Canadian Bar Association—Ontario, recommended amendments to the OPPSA along the lines of the Saskatchewan model.[15] As Binnie J was later to do in *Saulnier*, the submission stressed that the proposal constituted no threat to the licence grantor's interests because the secured party takes its security interest 'warts and all':

> Whatever restrictions exist in the terms of the license or in the relevant legislation imposing regulatory requirements will continue to apply. The explicit inclusion of

[12] Personal Property Security Act 1993, RSS 1993, cP-6.2 ('Saskatchewan PPSA'). The comparable British Columbia provisions are in the Personal Property Security Act, RSBC 1996, c359, s 1, 'intangible', 'licence' ('BCPPSA').

[13] Compare Revised Article 9, Uniform Commercial Code—Secured Transactions s 9-401(a), which is to similar effect.

[14] The comparable British Columbia provisions are in BCPPSA ss 58(2)(e) and 59(18).

[15] Canadian Bar Association—Ontario, Submission to the Minister of Consumer and Commercial Relations Concerning the Personal Property Security Act (1 October 1998).

> licenses simply means that the OPPSA applies to a security interest in a license. It leaves it up to the secured party, as a matter of commercial judgment, to decide whether the license is suitable collateral having regard to the contractual or statutory restrictions in the license.[16]

The proposal was not adopted, apparently because some government stakeholders, including the Ministry of Agriculture, Food and Rural Affairs, took the view that ministries responsible for the issue of government licences and quotas should have exclusive responsibility for the transfer, assignment and creation of interests in them. This concern seemingly overlooks the 'warts and all' qualification. In any event, the same proposal was put to the government again in 2006 and, again, it was rejected. It appears that, at the political level, the 'warts and all' idea is a hard one to get across.

The committee submitted a new draft proposal in 2009 with the aim of removing the uncertainty left by the *Saulnier* decision. In common with the earlier proposals, the 2009 version allows for security interests in a licence unless the governing statute prohibits the transfer of licences. However, in contrast to the Saskatchewan approach, the effect of a prohibition on licence transfers would be simply to prevent the secured party from enforcing its security interest by selling the licence and not to prevent the creation of the security interest in the first place. The thinking is that the licence itself may be viable collateral even if it is non-transferable because, for example, it may allow the secured party's receiver to operate the business. On the other hand, the proposed reform envisages that the licence statute might prevent the creation of security interests altogether by expressly providing that security interests are prohibited. The 2009 proposal is still on the table. The chances of its being adopted are uncertain but the fate of the earlier proposals does not provide much ground for optimism. Given the political challenges of selling the case for statutory reform, *Saulnier's* failure to unambiguously resolve the matter assumes added significance.

C. Security Interests in Cash Collateral[17]

Cash deposits are commonly used as collateral. For example, a bank may open a line of credit in its customer's favour on the basis that the customer or a related party deposits an agreed sum of money with the bank and gives the bank a security interest in the deposit to secure repayment of amounts outstanding from time

[16] ibid 7.

[17] This section is taken from A Duggan, 'The Australian PPSA from a Comparative Perspective: Some Canadian Reflections' (2014) 39 *Monash University Law Review* 59, 64–70. See also A Duggan and D Brown, *Australian Personal Property Securities Law* 2nd edn (Sydney, LexisNexis Australia, 2016) paras 3.49–3.59 and A Duggan, "Set-off, Flawed Assets and Security Interests in Cash Deposits" (2016) 31 *JIBFL* 201.

to time under the line of credit.[18] But the use of cash collateral is also widespread outside the context of bank lending. For example, a utility company might require a customer to deposit a sum of money as security for the customer's obligations to pay its bills. Cash collateral may also be used to secure a party's obligations under a derivatives contract or a securities lending transaction.

Revised Article 9 of the United States Uniform Commercial Code does not allow for perfection by registration of a security interest in a deposit account.[19] However, a secured party may perfect a security interest in a deposit account by taking control of the account.[20] In the case of a security interest taken by a secured party other than the deposit-taking institution itself (the bank), the secured party may obtain control either by becoming the bank's customer in respect of the deposit (account) or, alternatively, by entering into a control agreement under which the bank agrees to comply with the secured party's instructions directing disposition of the funds without the debtor's further consent. In the case of a security interest in the account taken by the bank itself, the security interest is automatically perfected by control; in other words, the bank obtains control simply by virtue of being the deposit-taking institution.[21] Revised Article 9, section 9-327(1) provides that a security interest perfected by control has priority over a conflicting security interest held by a secured party that does not have control.[22] This rule applies even if the conflicting security interest is perfected by some other method and regardless of the order in which the conflicting security interests became perfected. Examples 2 and 3, below, illustrate the application of these rules.

Example 2. On Date 1, SP1 takes a security interest in all Debtor's present and after-acquired personal property and registers a financing statement. On Date 2, SP2 provides

[18] See, eg, *Caisse Populaire Desjardins De L'Est de Drummond v Canada* [2009] 2 SCR 94, Supreme Court of Canada. This type of transaction is commonly known as a 'charge-back' arrangement. On the validity of charge-backs, see *Re Bank of Credit and Commerce International SA (No 8)* [1998] AC 214, overruling *Re Charge Card Services Ltd* [1987] Ch 150. There is no Canadian authority directly on point but the *Drummond* case proceeds on the assumption that charge-backs are permissible.

[19] United States Uniform Commercial Code—Secured Transactions, s 9-312(b)(1). Section 9-312(b) does not apply where a secured party holds a security interest in the deposit account as proceeds and s 9-315(c) applies instead. Section 9-315(c) provides that a security interest in proceeds is a perfected security interest if the security interest in the original collateral was perfected. For example: SP holds a security interest in Debtor's inventory perfected by registration. Debtor sells inventory in the ordinary course of business and deposits the sale proceeds. SP's security interest extends to the deposit as proceeds of its original collateral and, applying s 9-315(c), the security interest, as it applies to the deposit, is perfected by registration.

[20] ibid s 9-314.

[21] ibid s 9-104.

[22] As a general rule, security interests perfected by control rank according to priority of time in obtaining control: s 9-327(2). However, subject to s 9-327(4), a security interest held by the bank with which the deposit account is maintained has priority over a conflicting security interest held by another secured party: s 9-327(3); and a security interest held by the bank with which the deposit account is maintained is subordinate to a security interest where the secured party has obtained control by becoming the bank's customer with respect to the account: s 9-327(4).

credit to Debtor on the security of a cash deposit and obtains control over the deposit on the same date. On Date 3, Debtor defaults against SP1 and SP2 and they both claim the deposit.

SP2 may be either the deposit-taking institution itself or a third party. This variable may affect the steps SP2 must take to obtain control on Date 2, but it does not affect the final outcome. Applying Revised Article 9, section 9-312(b)(1), SP1's registration does not perfect its security interest in the deposit account and, since SP2's security interest is perfected by control, SP2 has priority over SP1. SP1 could have avoided this result by itself taking control of the account on Date 1 and parties in SP1's position can be expected to take this step if the account 'is an integral part of their credit decision'.[23] The official explanation for the rule, in its application to banks, is that it 'enables banks to extend credit to their depositors without the need to examine either the public record or their own records to determine whether another party might have a security interest in the deposit account'.[24] In other words, the purpose is to facilitate bank lending. The purpose of the rule in its other applications is to facilitate transactions which depend on cash collateral, for example derivatives trading and securities lending. It does this by avoiding the need for parties to register and search in advance of the transaction and by enabling the party taking security to be sure of its priority position before committing itself to the transaction.

In Example 2, SP1 claimed the disputed account as part of its original collateral. But the result will be the same in cases where the claim is to the disputed account as proceeds, as in Example 3.

Example 3. On Date 1, SP supplies Debtor with inventory on conditional sale terms and registers a financing statement. Debtor maintains an operating account with Bank. On Date 2, Bank opens a line of credit in Debtor's favour and takes a security interest in the account to secure repayment. On Date 3, Debtor, having sold SP's inventory for cash, deposits the proceeds into the account. On Date 4, Debtor defaults against both SP and Bank. SP claims the Date 3 deposit as proceeds of the inventory while Bank claims the deposit as part of its original collateral.

Since SP is claiming the deposit as proceeds of its original collateral, Revised Article 9, section 315(c) displaces section 9-312(b)(1) with the result that SP's Date 1 registration perfects its security interest in the deposit account. However, Bank's security interest was automatically perfected by control and so, applying Revised Article 9, section 9-327(1), Bank has priority over SP, even though Bank was later on the scene. According to the Official Comment, SP could avoid this outcome by requiring Debtor to deposit all inventory sale proceeds into a segregated account. But this precaution will not protect SP if Debtor breaches the agreement and pays the proceeds into the disputed account instead.[25]

[23] Official Comment on Revised Article 9, s 9-327, para 3.
[24] Official Comment on Revised Article 9, s 9-327, para 4.
[25] Official Comment on Revised Article 9, s 9-327, para 4.

The Canadian PPSAs currently make no provision for perfection by control of a security interest in a deposit account. A security interest in a deposit account may be perfected by registration and the ordinary first-in-time priority rule applies. The result is that in cases like Example 2, above, SP2 cannot obtain priority over SP1 except by negotiating a subordination agreement. The same is true in cases like Example 3 and, given the special priority rules for purchase-money security interests, it would still be true even if Bank had taken and perfected its security interest ahead of SP. Until recently, it was thought that banks and other deposit-taking institutions could avoid these outcomes by relying on the law of set-off as an alternative to claiming a security interest.[26] Banks have the right at common law to combine accounts, which is equivalent to a right of set-off. But a bank will not always be content to rely on the right of combination and it may insist on an express right of set-off in its agreement with the customer. The agreement may also include a promise by the customer to maintain (not to withdraw) the deposit so long as any amount is still owing to the bank under the loan agreement. This is commonly referred to as a 'flawed asset arrangement'.

The bank's agreement with its customer may give the bank set-off rights in combination with a flawed asset arrangement and it may also, for good measure, give the bank a security interest in the relevant deposit account. This type of transaction is commonly referred to as a 'triple cocktail'. Historically, the law of set-off was distinct from the law of secured transactions and the conventional wisdom was that the triple cocktail allowed the bank to pick and choose its remedies depending on the circumstances. In particular, in a case like Example 3, a triple cocktail arrangement would allow Bank to avoid the application of the PPSA by relying on the first two ingredients of the arrangement rather than the third and Bank's right of set-off would defeat SP unless SP had previously notified Bank of its security interest.[27] A right of set-off or combination combined with a flawed asset arrangement is functionally indistinguishable from a security interest in a deposit account; in both cases, the bank enforces its claim by helping itself to payment out of the deposit account. It follows that the difference between the various ingredients of the triple cocktail is a purely formal one and in a legal regime which elevates substance over form the distinction collapses.

The Supreme Court of Canada upturned the apple cart in the *Drummond* case by recognising the substantial equivalence of a contractual right of set-off exercisable against a flawed asset and a security interest. The case involved a line of credit transaction between a credit union and its customer supported by a triple cocktail

[26] See, eg, OPPSA s 40(1.1), dealing with the competing claims of the assignee of an account (including a secured party holding a security interest in the account) and a party with set-off rights in the account. This provision effectively codifies the common law rules governing the exercise of set-off rights against the assignee of an account.

[27] See R Derham, *Derham on the Law of Set-Off*, 4th edn (Oxford, Oxford University Press, 2010) para 17.34 (legal and equitable set-off), 17.54–17.57 (contractual set-off—set-off agreement preceding assignment); 17.59 (contractual set-off—set-off agreement following assignment). In Example 3, the date before which SP must give notice is probably Date 2 (the date the line of credit is opened), but possibly Date 4 (the date Bank claims set-off).

arrangement. The relevant terms were that: (1) the customer would deposit an agreed sum with the credit union; (2) the customer would maintain the deposit for a five-year term; and (3) the credit union could set off against the deposit any amount outstanding under the line of credit from time to time. The case was litigated in Quebec and the issue arose in the context of the federal Income Tax Act.[28] Nevertheless, the decision has clear implications for the other provinces in the PPSA context because the PPSAs apply to 'every transaction without regard to its form ... that in substance creates a security interest'.[29] On this basis, in a case like Example 3, assuming Bank's Date 2 agreement with Debtor involved a triple cocktail arrangement, it would make no difference whether Bank relied on its right of set-off or its security interest: either way, the PPSA applies and Bank's claim is subordinate to SP's prior perfected security interest in the account.

Partly in response to the *Drummond* case, the PPSL Committee, through the Ontario Bar Association, made a submission to the provincial government in February 2012 recommending new PPSA cash collateral provisions based on the Revised Article 9 approach discussed above.[30] The government responded quickly with an announcement in its 2012 budget that it planned amending the PPSA 'to make it easier for business and financial institutions to provide or obtain a first-priority security interest in cash collateral'.[31] But the proposal subsequently encountered opposition on the ground that, in cases like Example 3 above, it would unfairly advantage banks and other deposit-taking institutions at the expense of inventory suppliers and accounts receivable financiers. In response to this concern, the government established an Expert Working Group (EWG) to provide further advice. An EWG sub-committee was set up with the task of developing a compromise proposal, in other words to identify a set of reforms that would facilitate the taking of security interests in cash collateral by deposit-taking institutions and others, while at the same time providing a measure of protection for inventory suppliers and accounts receivables financiers against loss of their proceeds claims. As a result of this process, there is now a compromise proposal on the table but, at the time of writing, details had still not been made public and the government had not announced its intentions. In the meantime, Quebec has stolen a march on

[28] RSC 1985, c1. Section 227(4.1) of the ITA creates a deemed trust in favour of the Crown over property of an employer that has deducted income tax at source. The deemed trust secures the employer's obligation to remit the deductions to the government. The deemed trust is expressed to have priority over any competing security interest. 'Security interest' is defined in s 224(1.3) to mean: 'any interest in property that secures payment or performance of an obligation and includes an interest created by or arising out of a debenture, mortgage, hypothec, lien, pledge, charge, deemed or actual trust, assignment or encumbrance of any kind whatever, however or whenever arising, created, deemed to arise or otherwise provided for'. This provision is similar to the PPSA substance-over-form definition of security interest; hence the relevance of the *Drummond* case in the PPSA context.

[29] See, eg, Ontario PPSA s 2.

[30] Ontario Bar Association, *Perfecting Security Interests in Cash Collateral* (submission to the Ontario Ministry of Consumer Services and Ministry of Finance, 6 February 2012).

[31] *2012 Ontario Budget, Chapter 1: Transforming Public Services*, www.fin.gov.on./ca/en/budget/ontariobudgets/2012/ch.1.html#c1_secA_highlights.

Ontario by enacting its own reforms, based substantially on the Revised Article 9 provisions.[32]

D. Security Interests in Proceeds[33]

(i) The Secured Party's Cumulative Entitlements

Pre-PPSA, if the debtor sold or otherwise dealt with the collateral, the secured party had the choice of either enforcing its security interest against the original collateral in the transferee's hands or enforcing its security interest against the sale proceeds in the debtor's hands. But it could not claim both the original collateral and the proceeds because the remedies are inconsistent. The secured party's claim to the proceeds rested on its implied adoption of the sale, whereas its claim to the original collateral presupposed rejection of the sale.[34]

The position is different under the PPSAs. OPPSA section 25(1) provides as follows:

> Where collateral gives rise to proceeds, the security interest therein,
>
> (a) continues as to the collateral, unless the secured party expressly or impliedly authorized the dealing with the collateral free of the security interest; and
>
> (b) extends to the proceeds.

The corresponding provision in the other provincial PPSAs goes on to say:

> But where the secured party enforces a security interest against both the original collateral and the proceeds, the amount secured by the security interest in the collateral and the proceeds is limited to the market value of the collateral at the date of the dealing.[35]

[32] The reforms have been enacted by way of amendments to the Civil Code of Quebec. The amendments were assented to on 21 April 2015 and took effect on 1 January, 2016. The reason for the ongoing delay in Ontario has to do with the Supreme Court of Canada's decision in *Sun Indalex Finance LCC v United Steelworkers*, 2013 SCC 6, which was handed down after the events described in the text. Ontario's pension laws give pensioners a proprietary claim on the winding up of a pension plan in respect of the employer's unpaid contributions to the plan. In *Indalex*, a majority of the court read these provisions expansively, giving pensioners larger rights on the winding up of a pension plan than they were previously assumed to have had. The judgment responds to a number of high-profile cases in Canada where pensioners lost their pensions because the employer company became insolvent with substantial pension fund deficits. OPPSA s 30(7) provides that the pensioners' claim has priority over a security interest in an account or inventory and its proceeds. 'Account', as currently defined in OPPSA s 1, includes a bank deposit. The proposed cash collateral reforms would exclude bank deposits from the definition with the result that the pensioners' claim would no longer have priority under s 30(7) over a security interest in cash collateral. In other words, the reforms would take away from pensioners the enhanced protection the Supreme Court had so recently given them. Unsurprisingly, the Ontario government is reluctant to take that step.

[33] See Ch 13.

[34] L Gullifer (ed), *Goode on Legal Problems of Credit and Security*, 5th edn (London, Sweet & Maxwell, 2013) para 1-66. For criticism of this view, see Ch 13.

[35] See, eg, Saskatchewan PPSA s 28(1). See Ch 7 F(iii).

It is clear from the wording of OPPSA section 25(1) and the corresponding provision in the other provinces that under the PPSA, the secured party's rights are cumulative. The change from pre-PPSA law was deliberate and the purpose was 'to protect the secured party from deteriorations in value that occur after the dealing. Some of the proceeds may have been spent or otherwise lost, and the original collateral may have fallen in value through depreciation'.[36]

As indicated above, the non-Ontario PPSAs provide that if the secured party enforces its security interest against both the original collateral and proceeds, it can recover no more than the market value of the collateral at the date of the dealing. The purpose of the limitation is to prevent the secured party from obtaining a windfall as a result of the dealing. Example 4, below, illustrates the point.

> **Example 4.** SP holds a security interest in Debtor's printing press, perfected by registration. The security interest secures a $5,000 loan to Debtor. On Date 1, Debtor sells the printing press to Buyer without SP's consent and outside the ordinary course of business. The market value of the printing press is $2,700, but the parties agree on a price of $1,000. On Date 2, Debtor deposits the $1,000 in her bank account. There are no other funds in the account. On Date 3, SP learns about the sale and takes steps to enforce its security interest.

Assuming, for example, that Saskatchewan law applies, SP can enforce its security interest against both the printing press in Buyer's hands and the $1,000 sale proceeds, but for no more than $2,700, which was the value of the printing press on Date 1.[37] If there were no restriction on SP's cumulative claims, its collateral value would be $3,700 (representing the $2,700 value of the printing press and the $1,000 bank deposit), whereas if Debtor had not sold the printing press in the first place, SP's collateral value would have been only $2,700 or perhaps less if the value of the printing press had depreciated since Date 1. There is no reason in principle why SP should profit as a result of Debtor's actions.

There is no express limitation in the Ontario PPSA on the secured party's cumulative entitlements under section 25(1), but in *Bank of Nova Scotia v IPS*

[36] RJ Wood, 'Accounts, Proceeds and Conversion: *Bank of Nova Scotia v IPS Invoice Payment System Corporations*' (2011) 26 *Banking and Finance Law Review* 359, 363; RCC Cuming, C Walsh and RJ Wood, *Personal Property Security Law*, 2nd edn (Toronto, Irwin Law, 2012) 560–61.

[37] SP's security interest continues in the printing press unless SP expressly or impliedly authorised Debtor's sale to Buyer: OPPSA s 25(1)(a). OPPSA s 28(1) provides that a buyer of goods from a seller who sells the goods in the ordinary course of business takes them free of any security interest given by the seller even though the security interest is perfected and the buyer knows of it, unless the buyer also knew that the sale constituted a breach of the security agreement. In Example 4, SP's security interest continues in the printing press because SP did not authorise the sale and Buyer cannot rely on s 28(1) because the sale was not in the ordinary course of Debtor's business. Example 4 bears a passing resemblance to the facts of *Fairfax Gerrard Holdings Ltd v Capital Bank plc* [2007] EWCA Civ 1226, an English case which also involved the sale of a printing press. The difference is that in *Fairfax*, the printing press was inventory and the sale was in the ordinary course of business. This means that if Ontario law had applied, the buyer would probably have won on the basis either that the secured party expressly or impliedly authorised the sale or alternatively that the sale was in the ordinary course of the debtor's business. See S Thomas, 'The Role of Authorization in Title Conflicts Involving Retention of Title Clauses: Some American Lessons' (2014) 43 *Common Law World Law Review* 29.

Invoice Payment System Corporations,[38] the court held that the limitation was implicit. The court's interpretation of section 25(1) was a creative one, but it can be justified having regard to the policy considerations outlined above. The PPSL Committee has recommended codifying this aspect of the *IPS* case by enacting a statutory version of the limitation along the lines of the approach the other provinces have taken.

(ii) Enforcing a Security Interest

Example 5, below, is a simplified version of the facts in the *IPS* case.

> **Example 5.** On Date 1, Bank opens a line of credit in Debtor's favour and takes a security interest in Debtor's present and after-acquired inventory and accounts to secure repayment. Bank registers a financing statement on the same day. Debtor draws $500,000 on the line of credit. On Date 2, Debtor enters into a factoring agreement assigning a block of accounts to Factor. The face value of the accounts is $275,000 and the agreed price is $200,000. Factor pays Debtor and Debtor pays the money into his line of credit account with Bank. Bank is unaware of the factoring agreement and is also unaware of where Debtor's $200,000 deposit came from. On Date 3, Factor collects on the accounts, recovering a total of $225,000; Factor pays this money into a bank account where it remains traceable. On Date 4, Bank finds out about the Date 2 and Date 3 events and takes steps to enforce its security interest, claiming the $225,000 Factor has collected.

As indicated above, all the Canadian PPSAs permit a secured party to enforce its security interest against both the original collateral and proceeds that have been generated by a dealing in the collateral. In provinces other than Ontario, there is a statutory limitation on the secured party's cumulative entitlements, while in Ontario, it has now been established that OPPSA section 25(1) is, by implication, subject to the same limitation. The limitation applies 'where the secured party *enforces* [its] security interest against both the original collateral and the proceeds'. In the *IPS* case, the factor's payment to the debtor was proceeds of the bank's original collateral (the accounts) and the court treated the bank as having enforced its security interest against these proceeds when the debtor used them to pay down its line of credit with the bank. In other words, the court read the statutory limitation as covering not only the case where the debtor is in default and the secured party recovers payment by enforcing its security interest, but also the case where the debtor is not in default and makes a voluntary payment to the secured party in reduction of the debt. Applying this reasoning to the facts of Example 5, Bank's claim against Factor is limited to $75,000. The court gave no reasons in support of this construction and it appears simply to have assumed that the limitation applied in both cases.

[38] *Bank of Nova Scotia v IPS Invoice Payment System Corporations* (2010) 318 DLR (4th) 751 (Ontario Superior Court of Justice).

However, the issue was directly addressed in *Toronto-Dominion Bank v Kerwin Capital Corp*.[39] In that case, the bank argued that the statutory limitation 'is not intended to cover "voluntary" payments' and it only applies 'when the proceeds are "captured" by the [secured party] and applied to the indebtedness of the parties through enforcement on default'.[40] The court rejected the argument on both statutory interpretation and policy grounds. It held that the statutory limitation 'does not make [the distinction contended for by the bank], and if it was pivotal for the operation of the section, then one would expect it to be set out in the PPSA'.[41] The court also held that the exclusion of voluntary payments from the statutory limitation would place 'an undue burden on third parties'.[42] 'A third party should not risk losing its interest simply because a payment is made by a debtor to its secured creditor when the secured creditor is not enforcing the debt'.[43]

The decision in *Kerwin* is open to question as a matter of statutory interpretation. The word 'enforcement' is typically used when the debtor is in default under the security agreement and the secured party asserts its rights over the collateral. There is nothing in the statute to indicate that the legislators intended a different meaning.[44] On the contrary, the legislative history of the provision clearly indicates that it was intended to operate only where the secured party is enforcing its security interest upon default.[45]

The court's policy argument in *Kerwin* is also open to criticism. Wood states the argument more fully as follows:[46]

> Suppose that the secured debt is $100 and the collateral is worth $50. The debtor then sells the collateral to a buyer for $50. Why should it matter if the secured party simply receives the $50 from the debtor by way of a voluntary payment rather than taking enforcement action against the $50 while it is still in the debtor's hands? To permit the secured party to enforce against the collateral permits it to move from a partly secured to a fully secured status. Should the secured party have its cake and eat it too?

But Wood goes on to state the counter-argument:[47]

> Suppose that a secured party takes a security interest in collateral to secure an operating line of credit. The debtor later sells the collateral to a buyer and the proceeds are used to reduce the operating line of credit. The secured party may be unaware that the collateral has been sold or that the proceeds have been used to reduce the indebtedness on the line

[39] *Toronto-Dominion Bank v Kerwin Capital Corp* 2013 SKQB 376 (Court of Queen's Bench for Saskatchewan).

[40] ibid at para 43.

[41] ibid at para 48.

[42] ibid at para 50.

[43] ibid at para 51. These comments were strictly obiter because the court found that the bank had authorised the dealing with the collateral free of the security interest and therefore its security interest did not continue in the original collateral: Saskatchewan PPSA s 28(1)(a).

[44] Wood (n 36) 365.

[45] ibid note 16, citing Saskatchewan Law Reform Commission, *Proposals for a New Personal Property Security Act* (1992) 111–12.

[46] ibid 364.

[47] ibid 364–65.

> of credit. The secured party may advance further funds in the belief that it will be able to look to the full value of the collateral. The secured party may argue that it did not know that the funds deposited into the bank account were proceeds, and that it would not have allowed the debtor to draw on the line of credit had it known that its ability to claim against the collateral was diminished.
>
> An incorrect assessment of risk can occur even when the security interest does not secure future advances. A secured party, in deciding whether to forbear or to enforce its security interest, will likely consider, among other things, the extent to which its obligation is secured by the value of the collateral. This risk assessment assumes that the secured creditor can readily determine that it has priority to the collateral to the full extent of its obligation.

In summary, there are strong arguments, on both statutory interpretation and policy grounds, in support of the conclusion that the statutory limitation on the secured party's cumulative enforcement rights only applies where the secured party takes enforcement action to recover proceeds. These arguments were overlooked in both the *IPS* case and *Kerwin*. The Ontario PPSL Committee has recommended statutory reforms to reverse the decisions.

(iii) The Meaning of 'Proceeds'

OPPSA section 1(1) defines 'proceeds' to mean:

> Identifiable or traceable personal property in any form derived directly or indirectly from any dealing with collateral or the proceeds therefrom [including]
>
> …
>
> (d) any payment made in total or partial discharge or redemption of an intangible, chattel paper, an instrument or investment property.

In the other provincial PPSAs, the definition is limited to property 'in which the debtor acquires an interest'.[48] Applying this limitation to the facts of Example 5, above, the $225,000 collected by Factor on Date 3 is not 'proceeds' and so Bank's security interest does not extend to these funds.[49]

In the *IPS* case, the court held that the money collected by the factor on the assigned accounts was 'proceeds' within the meaning of OPPSA section 1(1). On a literal reading, this conclusion is correct because the provision does not limit proceeds to property 'in which the debtor acquires an interest'. In other words, there is no 'debtor interest limitation' in Ontario as there is in the other provinces. On the other hand, the court recognised that 'sequential dealings with collateral could

[48] See eg Saskatchewan PPSA, s 2(1)(hh).

[49] However, Bank might have a personal claim against Factor for recovery of an amount up to the value of its collateral shortfall ($75,000): see Section D(iv).

generate more than one set of proceeds and create uncertainty with respect to the extent of a third party's liability'.[50] As explained in more detail below, the debtor interest limitation addresses this concern and the court in the *IPS* case could have read the Ontario definition as by implication being subject to the limitation. The court was prepared to take an expansive approach to the interpretation of OPPSA section 25(1)[51] and it is unclear why it failed to take a similar approach to the interpretation of the proceeds definition.[52]

Wood summarises the reasons for the debtor interest limitation as follows:[53]

> The first [reason] concerns the geometric multiplication of proceeds claims. The second concerns the relative strength of the proceeds claim. Both can be illustrated through use of an example. Suppose that SP is granted a security interest in D's auger. D sells it to B1 and it is later resold by B1 to B2, and then by B2 to B3. In addition to SP's claim to the auger in the hands of B3, SP will have a right to enforce against the proceeds in the hands of D, B1 and B2. This opens up the possibility to a further multiplication of proceeds claims. Every time the proceeds are dealt with, additional proceeds claims arise. Suppose that B1 and B2 acquire rights in trade-in implements in respect of their respective sales. The trades are later sold by B1 to B4 and by B2 to B5. SP can assert a claim to the trades in the hands of B4 and B5, and can also claim the proceeds received by B1 and B2 in connection with these re-sales. Because SP is not required to elect between enforcement against the collateral and enforcement against its proceeds and is permitted to claim against multiple generations of proceeds, this soon produces an astonishing number of proceeds claims in the absence of a debtor interest restriction.
>
> Under prior law, the problem of geometric multiplication of claims was ameliorated by the fact that the proceeds claim was subject to a significant limitation. It could not be asserted against a bona fide purchaser who acquired legal title for value and without knowledge. An innocent party who acquired the asset for value and without knowledge was therefore protected. The same does not hold true under the PPSA. Subject to a few exceptions, a claim to proceeds enjoys the same priority status as the claim to the original collateral. Consider the position of B4 and B5 who purchase the trades that are held by B1 and B2 as proceeds. Despite the fact that they may have bought the goods for value and without knowledge, they are subject to SP's proceeds security interest in the trades. This holds true even though the sales may have occurred in the ordinary course of business. The ordinary course buyer rule of the PPSA allows the buyer to take free of any security interest granted by the seller. The rule is inapplicable because the security interest was not granted by their seller, but by a former owner (D).
>
> Nor can B4 and B5 protect themselves by conducting a search of the registry. SP's claim to proceeds is perfected under the OPPSA so long as the registration in respect of the collateral remains effective. A search by B4 or B5 using the name of their sellers (B1 or B2) would not reveal the security interest, as it was D who granted it. The outcome

[50] (2010) 318 DLR (4th) 751 at para 32.
[51] See Section D(i).
[52] Wood (n 36) 365–66.
[53] ibid 366–67.

> will differ only if SP knew of the unauthorized sale and failed to amend its registration within 30 days. In this event, the security interest in both the collateral and the proceeds will become unperfected, and a buyer who thereafter takes without knowledge will prevail.

On the other hand, Ziegel and Denomme oppose the debtor interest limitation for the following reasons:[54]

> [The] difficulties are exaggerated and it is open to question whether the difficulties of searching in the case of non-cash proceeds are greater than in the case of original collateral. In any case, in many cases the transferee will have the protection of one of the provisions in ss. 28–29. Even if this were not so, to restrict the secured party to proceeds that were received by the debtor would err too much in the opposite direction. Consider, for example, the following hypothetical. D, a debtor under a security agreement with SP, sells the collateral, a used vehicle (V1), to M, a used car dealer. M resells the vehicle to T and receives in part payment another used vehicle (V2). If SP's rights were restricted to the original collateral (V1) and to proceeds received by D, SP would be entitled to follow V1 into T's hands but not to claim V2 from M. This would be true even though M was in a much better position to search D's title (and therefore to learn of SP's interest) than was T.

Ziegel and Denomme do not explain why they think the difficulties caused by an unrestricted definition of proceeds are exaggerated; on the contrary, the Wood passage quoted above suggests that there is legitimate cause for concern. Ziegel and Denomme argue that in many cases, the transferee will have the protection of the cut-off provisions in OPPSA sections 28–29; but Professor Wood effectively refutes this argument. Finally, Ziegel and Denomme argue that a debtor interest limitation is undesirable because it would prejudice parties like T in their example; but this argument overlooks the potential prejudice to parties like B4 and B5 in Wood's example if there is no debtor interest limitation.

There are additional arguments in support of the debtor interest limitation. First, the debtor interest limitation simplifies the law (by eliminating the potential for the geometric multiplication of proceeds claims) and therefore it reduces litigation costs. Secondly, the debtor interest limitation on the secured party's rights can be seen as a quid pro quo for the secured party's cumulative entitlements under OPPSA section 25(1). Under pre-PPSA law, the secured party was required to elect between the original collateral and the proceeds and, in this respect, it is substantially better off under the PPSA. By facilitating proceeds claims, the PPSA increases the potential prejudice to third parties. The debtor interest limitation ameliorates this consequence and it can reasonably be characterised as a small price for the secured party to pay for its improved position under the PPSA. The Ontario PPSL Committee has recommended that for these reasons, and also in the interests of inter-provincial harmonisation, Ontario should adopt the same restriction.

[54] Ziegel and Denomme (n 4) 198.

(iv) The Secured Party's Personal Claim

Example 6, below, is a further variation on the facts of the *IPS* case.

> **Example 6.** On Date 1, Bank opens a line of credit in Debtor's favour and takes a security interest in Debtor's present and after-acquired inventory and accounts to secure repayment. Bank registers a financing statement on the same day. Debtor draws \$500,000 on the line of credit. On Date 2, Debtor enters into a factoring agreement assigning a block of accounts to Factor. The face value of the accounts is \$275,000 and the agreed price is \$200,000. Factor pays Debtor and Debtor deposits the money in a separate account where it remains traceable. On Date 3, Factor collects on the accounts, recovering a total of \$225,000; Factor pays this money into a bank account where it remains traceable. On Date 4, Bank finds out about the Date 2 and Date 3 events and takes steps to enforce its security interest, claiming the \$200,000 Debtor received from Factor on Date 2 and the \$225,000 Factor collected from the account debtors on Date 3.

Outside Ontario, Bank's security interest does not extend to the \$225,000 in Factor's hands because these funds are not proceeds of Bank's original collateral. The position would be the same in Ontario if the reforms discussed in Section D(iii), above, were adopted. However, although Bank cannot assert a proprietary claim against Factor, it may have a personal claim for damages on the basis that, by collecting the accounts on Date 3, Factor wrongly interfered with Bank's collateral. Bank's cause of action may lie in conversion, although there is considerable doubt as to whether the doctrine of conversion applies to intangible property.[55] Alternatively, Bank may have a cause of action based on unjust enrichment, although again the law is unsettled.[56] Assuming Bank can sue Factor in addition to enforcing its security interest against Debtor, in principle it should recover no more in total than the market value of its collateral on Date 2 (\$275,000). In other words, if Bank claims the \$200,000 in Debtor's hands and subsequently sues Factor, its damages should be no more than \$75,000. Correspondingly, if Bank successfully sues Factor for the \$225,000, its claim against Debtor should be limited to \$50,000.

The PPSAs, as currently drafted, provide (or in Ontario's case, imply) that where a secured party enforces its security interest against both the original collateral and proceeds, the amount secured by the security interest in the collateral

[55] The conventional view is that the tort of conversion only protects possessory interests and so it does not apply to intangible property: *OBG v Allen* [2008] 1 AC 1 (HL). But there was a strong dissent in *Allen* and the decision has been criticised: see, eg, Sarah Green and John Randall, *The Tort of Conversion* (Oxford, Hart Publishing, 2009) 128–29; Wood (n 36) 369–70; Martin Davies, 'Conversion of Intangible Goods: Some Modern Approaches' (2014) 88 *Australian Law Journal* 235.

[56] The basis of the unjust enrichment is 'interceptive subtraction': Factor was enriched at Bank's expense in the sense that the account debtors conferred a benefit on Factor that was destined for Bank, and that would have accrued to Bank but for Factor's interception: see RCC Cuming, 'Secured Creditors' Non-Statutory Remedies: Unfinished Business' (2012) 91 *Canadian Bar Review* 243, 267, citing C Mitchell, P Mitchell and S Watterson, *Goff & Jones' Law of Unjust Enrichment*, 8th edn (London, Sweet & Maxwell, 2011) paras 6-52–6-662.

and the proceeds is limited to the market value of the collateral at the date of the dealing which gave rise to the proceeds. This provision only applies where the secured party enforces its security interest against both the original collateral in the transferee's hands and the proceeds in the debtor's hands; it does not cover the case where the secured party enforces its security interest against the debtor and brings a damages claim against the collateral transferee.[57]

E. Conclusion

The Secured Transactions Law Reform Project is an investigation into the desirability or otherwise of reforming the law of secured lending in England and Wales along the lines of the Article 9 and Canadian PPSA models. The issue is a contentious one and its resolution has been a long time coming. But even if the decision is ultimately against wholesale adoption of Article 9/PPSA reforms, many of the specific issues that arise under the Article 9/PPSA model should still be of interest to English readers (as well as to readers in Article 9/PPSA jurisdictions). Keeping an eye on current developments in the Article 9/PPSA jurisdictions may draw attention to issues that English courts have not yet had an opportunity to consider and it may facilitate a richer debate on issues that have previously come to light. These, of course, are the benefits of comparative scholarship and they are worth pursuing independently of the ongoing debate in England and Wales (and other parts of the world) over the Article 9/PPSA model's commitment to substance over form.[58]

The three topics discussed in this chapter—security interests in statutory and contractual licences, security interests in cash collateral and security interests in proceeds—all transcend the substance-over-form debate in the sense that all three issues are just as likely to surface in an English court applying English law as it currently stands, as they are in a Canadian court charged with applying the PPSA. All three issues have proved to be challenging in the Canadian context, as indicated by the failure so far to achieve definitive solutions. But the debates have been illuminating and with luck the Ontario PPSL Committee's efforts will bear fruit in the end. In the meantime, the committee's work should at least serve as a catalyst for further scholarship in Ontario, Canada and perhaps also internationally.

[57] The Ontario PPSL Committee considered these issues in some detail but in the end concluded that it would be difficult to craft an appropriate legislative response and that therefore the issues should be left to the courts.

[58] For example, see the discussion on some of the same points as those discussed in Ch 13 D.

6

The New Zealand Perspective

MIKE GEDYE

A. Introduction

On 1 May 2002 New Zealand became the first Commonwealth country outside North America to implement a secured transactions regime based on the principles first introduced some 50 years earlier by Article 9 of the Uniform Commercial Code of the United States of America. While conceptually following the broad principles of Article 9, in form the New Zealand Personal Property Securities Act 1999 (PPSA)[1] most closely resembles the legislative model adopted by most of the Canadian provinces, with the comparisons included in the New Zealand Act being mainly to the Saskatchewan legislation. The raison d'etre and history of the New Zealand legislation have been extensively canvassed elsewhere and it is not intended to replicate that here.[2] Nor is it the intention to describe the nature of an Article 9-derived secured transactions regime; that topic is covered elsewhere in this volume.[3] Rather, this chapter is intended to consider how the new regime has been received in New Zealand and to highlight those aspects of the New Zealand experience that may be of interest to jurisdictions considering similar reforms. In particular, the author will review those areas where New Zealand has departed from the Canadian models on which the New Zealand Act was based.

Before the PPSA, New Zealand's secured transactions law was broadly similar to English law. The partly fixed, partly floating charge (with the former used to the maximum but uncertain extent permitted by law) was the most common form of security taken over corporate assets. Retention of title arrangements were ubiquitous when goods were supplied on credit to either businesses or

[1] In New Zealand and Australia, the legislation is called the Personal Property Securities Act. In the Canadian provinces, the name is the Personal Property Security Act. In this chapter, 'PPSA' will refer to the New Zealand Act unless otherwise specified. 'PPS' means personal property security[ies] and generally refers to the legislation and regimes in all jurisdictions that have adopted a secured transactions law derived from Article 9 of the Uniform Commercial Code of the United States of America.

[2] See, for example, the New Zealand Law Commission Preliminary Paper No 6 (1988) 26–60.

[3] See Ch 2.

consumers. But apart from a limited statutory exception in relation to inventory,[4] unincorporated businesses and natural persons could not utilise the floating charge. When the floating charge was available, negative pledge and automatic crystallisation clauses, with their attendant uncertainties, were commonly employed in an effort to minimise the inherent weaknesses of that form of security. Registration with the Registrar of Companies was mandatory for many, but not all, company charges, whether fixed or floating. On the other hand, while in theory retention of title devices, whether given by individuals or companies, often required registration under the New Zealand Bills of Sale legislation,[5] in practice there were no serious consequences of failing to register.[6] From as early as the late 1950s, questions had been asked about why the law imposed different rules and registration requirements depending on the status of the debtor (ie, incorporated or unincorporated) and the form chosen for the transaction (eg, a mortgage or a title retention arrangement) when such distinctions did not seem to have any logical justification. This and other questions and criticisms about the then law led to broadly based calls for reform.

B. The Comprehensive New Zealand Reform and its Reception

Eventually, New Zealand took the view that comprehensive reform was better than incremental change. While it may have been possible to improve, say, just the registration or priority regime for corporate security interests, it was felt preferable to implement the elegant logic of a comprehensive secured transactions regime deliberately designed around the commercial function of transactions rather than their legal form. This view was pretty much universally held by law reform bodies,[7] legal academics and the legal profession. Extensive consultation did not elicit any significant opposition from relevant stakeholders such as banks and after some delay the Personal Property Securities Act was finally passed in 1999 with the new regime becoming operative in 2002.

It is now 14 years since the PPSA came into force and there is little doubt that the legislation has generally been well received in New Zealand and is regarded as a significant improvement on prior law. A survey conducted by the author

[4] Section 26(1)(d) Chattels Transfer Act 1924 (NZ) (repealed).

[5] The Chattels Transfer Act 1924 (NZ) (repealed).

[6] One reason for this was because the Chattels Transfer Act invalidated unregistered instruments rather than attacking the underlying ownership interest. If an instrument providing for a retention of title arrangement was invalidated, the owner could simply rely on its ownership interest, which was (because the owner's title always pre-dated, and was independent of, the retention of title arrangement) the fallback position once the instrument was set aside.

[7] See the New Zealand Law Commission Preliminary Paper No 6 (1988) and Report No 8 (1989).

indicated around a 95 per cent approval rating for the regime.[8] For the most part, the courts, practitioners and other stakeholders have readily embraced the concepts that underpin a comprehensive secured transactions regime based on Article 9 principles. Since the legislation makes it very simple for financiers to take security over all of a debtor's present and after-acquired personal property, including circulating assets such as inventory and accounts receivable, it is generally regarded as favourable for the banks and, as far as the author is aware, no bank has expressed dissatisfaction with the regime. Likewise, those financiers who rely on title retention arrangements, such as the leasing industry, can also adequately protect their position provided they comply with the basic and inexpensive formalities required by the Act.[9]

It may seem contradictory to suggest that both all-assets financiers and title retention financiers are better off under the PPSA but this observation can be explained by the enhanced predictability of outcome wrought by the Act. For example, under prior law there was often considerable doubt about whether an alleged retention of title arrangement was truly a term of a sale contract and hence which of a supplier or general financier would prevail. Under the PPSA, retention of title suppliers (including lessors) who comply with the required formalities win; if they do not comply they lose. Some initial opposition from lessors (and others wedded to the sanctity of title) to the prospect of losing their goods if they failed to follow the formalities required by the Act has since diminished and can now be viewed as a transitional issue that demonstrates the need both before and after the implementation of such a significant reform for the comprehensive education of all those that will be impacted by the reforms.[10]

Those recurring issues that have arisen in New Zealand are often a consequence (intended or otherwise) of New Zealand drafting innovations, whether of style or of substance, and are not indicative of shortcomings in Article 9-derived regimes generally.

[8] M Gedye, 'Practitioner Attitudes to the PPSA' [2012] *New Zealand Law Journal* 118.

[9] For title retention arrangements to be fully effective under the PPSA, they must be in writing and a registration is required. This obviously requires greater discipline and care on the part of those relying on title retention arrangements compared to prior law, under which even informal retention of title clauses agreed orally or implied by conduct could be effective.

[10] Two of the early PPSA cases involved lessors who failed to register their interest and consequently lost their goods to an all-assets secured party (*Graham v Portacom New Zealand Ltd* [2004] 2 NZLR 528 and *NZ Bloodstock Ltd v Waller* [2005] NZCA 254). This outcome would not have followed under prior law where the lessors could have simply relied on their title and the common law *nemo dat quod non habet* rule. The cases illustrate the Act working as intended but appear to be a radical result to those not familiar with secured transactions regimes based on Article 9. Similar teething issues have arisen in Australia. The *Review of the Personal Property Securities Act 2009 Interim Report*, 31 July 2014, a report prepared by Mr B Whittaker for the Australian Attorney-General, states that 'An insufficient appreciation of the Act has had particularly severe impacts on the equipment hiring industry' and goes on to note: 'The Australian Bankers' Association suggests that part of the difficulty stems from the fact that small businesses have not been able to accept that they are no longer sufficiently protected by being the owner of their assets' (p 16). Both comments highlight the vital role that educating affected stakeholders plays in transitioning to a new secured transactions regime rather than any shortcomings in the regime.

C. The Floating Charge

(i) The 'Abolition' of the Floating Charge

Since the seminal case of *Re Panama, New Zealand and Australian Royal Main Co*,[11] the floating charge has satisfied, at least until the advent of personal property securities legislation in Canada, New Zealand and most recently Australia, the need in Commonwealth jurisdictions for a security device that could cover circulating assets. It is the impact of personal property securities legislation on this form of security that is sometimes raised as a concern by banks and other all-assets financiers and their advisers in jurisdictions that have not yet adopted such legislation. Any such concern is misplaced. In New Zealand (and Canada and Australia), the PPSA does not abolish the floating charge. Rather, it abolishes the prior law's formalistic distinction between fixed and floating charges. Essentially, this is achieved by doing away with the 'floating' or pre-crystallised status of the floating charge and substituting statutory rules that determine when a charge, whether described as fixed or floating, 'attaches' (to use the statutory term) to collateral. The parties may continue to use floating charge terminology if they so choose (although there is no reason to do so) but for the avoidance of doubt the New Zealand Act makes it clear that doing so does not resurrect traditional floating charge jurisprudence, including the uncrystallised state of the floating charge.[12]

The statutory examples of security interests set out in section 17(3) of the Act also expressly include floating charges but, because there are potentially some downsides of continuing to employ this terminology, express references to floating charges have quickly disappeared from New Zealand's legal lexicon. What once might have been referred to as a 'debenture' or 'secured debenture' (which commonly were secured by fixed and floating charges) is now popularly referred to as a 'general security agreement'. Although the term 'general security agreement' is not defined in the legislation, it is widely taken to refer to a security agreement that covers substantially all of a debtor's present and after-acquired assets in contrast to a security agreement that covers only specific assets or classes of assets; the latter generally being referred to as a specific security agreement.

The term 'floating charge' may have fallen into disuse but the concept of a security device that covers all of a debtor's present and after-acquired assets, including circulating assets, remains as relevant under personal property securities legislation as it is under equitable floating charge law. In fact, so far as the secured party is concerned, the form of security over circulating assets that is recognised by personal property securities legislation is clearly superior to the

[11] Re Panama, New Zealand and Australian Royal Main Co (1870) LR 5 Ch App 318.

[12] Section 40(4) of the PPSA provides that 'a reference in a security agreement to a floating charge is not an agreement that the security interest created by the floating charge attaches at a later time than the time specified in [s 40(1)]'.

equitable floating charge, which being so easily defeated was always a relatively weak form of security. The general security interest recognised under the PPSA effectively has the status of a fixed legal interest,[13] even though it covers circulating assets, and is less amenable to defeasance than the floating charge. Uncertain concepts such as automatic crystallisation, the refloating of crystallised charges and the degree of control required to achieve fixed status over circulating assets are eliminated. The PPSA all-assets security interest can even allow the secured party to take assets not owned by the debtor.[14] Because personal property securities legislation modelled on Article 9 permits such a pro-bank form of security, opposition to it from the banking sector would be surprising.

The initial (though in the author's opinion misconceived and unjustified) concerns voiced in New Zealand by title retention financiers such as lessors and those that rely on Romalpa-type clauses was more understandable and is now replaying in Australia.[15] But while it can be argued that personal property securities legislation, and the security interest over all present and after-acquired assets that it authorises (which can perhaps be regarded as a turbo-charged version of the traditional floating charge), is too favourable to general secured creditors, as noted below, policy choices open to the legislature allow the balance to be shifted towards other stakeholders, where Parliament considers this to be warranted.

In short, the floating charge has not been abolished in New Zealand, it has simply been superseded by a superior form of security and if this is regarded as too generous to all-assets financiers such as banks, there are ways the legislation can address this concern and improve the relative position of other secured or unsecured creditors.

(ii) Statutory Provisions Replace Floating Charge Jurisprudence

Any form of security that encompasses circulating assets, whether the traditional floating charge or the PPSA's general security interest, must allow the debtor some licence to deal with the charged assets and to pass title clear of the security interest. For example, the holder of security over a debtor's inventory generally expects the debtor to sell the inventory and to use the proceeds for various purposes such

[13] See New Zealand Law Commission, Report No 8, *A Personal Property Securities Act for New Zealand*, Wellington, 1989, 80 where it was noted: 'the distinction between fixed and floating charges under current law ceases to be of significance under this statute. The "floating security" authorised by this statute amounts, in effect, to a fixed charge over an ever changing pool of assets which typically consists of inventory, accounts, chattel paper and equipment'. See also *Royal Bank v Sparrow Electric Corp* [1997] 1 SCR 411 (Supreme Court of Canada).

[14] For example, under the PPSA, a supplier who retains title to goods supplied on credit is in effect recharacterised as a secured party and such a supplier who fails to comply with the formalities required by the Act will lose the goods to a creditor secured under a general security agreement who has met the required formalities. This is obviously a significant exception to the common law *nemo dat* rule that would not be available to a creditor secured by a traditional floating charge.

[15] See n 10.

as replenishing the inventory and/or paying down the debt. Obviously, the buyer of such inventory should take free of the secured party's interest. There are different theories as to how this desired outcome is achieved under floating charge law, and accordingly there exists a degree of uncertainty over what transactions are permitted.[16] But under the PPSA, the position is quite clear: the secured party's interest remains attached to the collateral despite any dealing by the debtor, and will prevail over any competing claims, including those of buyers, unless the Act or some other law provides otherwise.[17]

Necessary and permitted dealings that allow assets to be transferred free of a security interest include paying debts and, crucially, sales in the ordinary course of business.[18] The scope of transactions permitted under a floating charge may not be well defined but under personal property securities legislation, the range of transactions that will defeat a prior security interest is determined by the legislature according to policy objectives. The essential section 53 of the New Zealand PPSA allows a person who buys goods in the ordinary course of the seller's business to take free of a security interest given by the seller.[19] Although sales in the ordinary course of business may seem similar in scope to the transactions permitted under a floating charge, it is a much more limited concept.[20] Because it is a statutory test, a degree of fine tuning is available to the legislature to satisfy local policy and requirements. In New Zealand (and in most of Canada) the concept is limited to the ordinary course of business '*of the seller*'. Thus it is necessary to inquire into the particular seller's way of doing business rather than looking to what is ordinary in the particular industry or even commerce generally. There is no such limitation in the Ontario Act where the test is accordingly the ordinary course of commercial practice generally. On the other hand, under the Australian Act, a buyer prevails only where the sale was in the ordinary course of business '*of the seller's … business*

[16] See, for example, P Blanchard and M Gedye, *The Law of Company Receiverships in New Zealand and Australia*, 2nd edn (Wellington, Butterworths, 1994) paras 1.13–1.17.

[17] That this is the appropriate starting point for resolving competing claims is made clear by s 35 of the PPSA.

[18] See s 94 (holder of money takes free of a security interest), s 95 (specifying when a creditor who receives payment of debt has priority over a security interest) and s 53 (a buyer or lessee of goods sold or leased in the ordinary course of business of the seller or lessor takes free of a security interest given by the seller or lessor).

[19] It is essential because in a system that does away with the uncrystallised state of the floating charge and that does not distinguish between legal and equitable interests, such a section is a necessary part of the statutory regime, which allows buyers to shop with confidence. In the absence of this provision, any shopper would be at risk of the shop's secured creditor taking back goods that the shopper had bought and paid for.

[20] For a detailed analysis of the meaning of ordinary course of business under the New Zealand and Australian PPSAs, see M Gedye, 'A Hoary Chestnut Resurrected: The Meaning of "Ordinary Course of Business" in Secured Transactions Law' (2013) 37 *Melbourne University Law Review* 1. Any reform of the magnitude of the PPSA will at least initially introduce an element of uncertainty around the precise meaning and application of novel provisions and so it proved in New Zealand over the scope of s 53 and the meaning of ordinary course of business in this context. However, guiding principles have now been laid down by the Court of Appeal in *StockCo Ltd v Gibson* [2012] NZCA 330.

of selling … personal property of that kind'.[21] Arguably, the Australian provision only protects buyers of inventory that was held by the seller for resale. One hopes that this was a deliberate policy choice because drafting innovations such as this can have a significant impact on the functioning of the regime and should only be adopted after careful consideration of the need for them. The difference between the New Zealand and Australian approach is easily illustrated. Take, for example, a debtor whose business was the leasing out of cranes but who occasionally sold a crane that was surplus to the debtor's requirements. Under section 53 of the New Zealand PPSA, a seller of such a crane would likely be found to be selling the crane in the ordinary course of its business and the buyer would therefore acquire the crane free of any security interests given by the seller.[22] But because the seller's business was leasing and not selling cranes, this would appear not to follow in Australia.[23]

Policy choices can also have an impact on the security interests of which a buyer can take free. In New Zealand, Canada and Australia, buyers in the ordinary course of business take free of only those security interests that were 'given by the seller'. This leaves buyers vulnerable to security interests given by the seller's predecessors in title, unless the seller has itself previously taken free of such interests. For example, say a private individual sells to a second-hand boat dealer a boat that the private individual uses for recreational fishing and over which he or she had previously given a security interest. This sale would not discharge the security interest under section 53 of the PPSA because such a sale would not be in the ordinary course of business of a private individual who is not in the business of selling boats. If the boat dealer then resells the boat to a customer in the ordinary course of the boat dealer's business, the customer would not take free of the prior security interest under section 53 (or under the equivalent Canadian and Australian provisions) because that security interest was not given by the boat dealer who sold to the customer.[24]

[21] Personal Property Securities Act 2009 (Cth) (Aus) s 46. The article mentioned in the previous footnote was discussed in *Warehouse Sales Pty Ltd (in liq) v LG Electronics Australia Pty Ltd* [2014] VSC 644 (see Ch 8 F(v) especially at n 186) in which the differences between the Canadian, New Zealand and Australian formulations were noted.

[22] See *Alberta Pacific Leasing Inc v Petro Equipment Sales Ltd* [1996] 1 WWR 552, a decision on the Alberta provision that is similarly worded to s 53 of the New Zealand Act.

[23] See the Australian *Replacement Explanatory Memorandum, Personal Property Securities Bill 2009 (Cth)* [2.92] (NB: confusingly, different official versions of the Explanatory Memorandum use different paragraph numbering systems.)

[24] Although the analysis given here was referred to in *StockCo Ltd v Gibson* [2012] NZCA 330 at [148]–[153] as the 'orthodox view', the Court of Appeal expressly declined to decide the point. Of course, the boat dealer's customer may be protected by one of the other buyer protection provisions, such as s 52 (buyer takes free of unperfected security interests) or s 54 (buyer of low-value consumer goods can take free of any outstanding security interests). In the hypothetical example, the buyer from the second-hand boat dealer would, under s 53, take free of any security interests given by the dealer itself, assuming as stated that the sale by the dealer was in the ordinary course of the dealer's business.

Some commentators and courts have suggested that this outcome is inappropriate,[25] but in the author's view it is a deliberate and valid policy choice to prefer an innocent secured party over an innocent buyer in this circumstance.[26] While buyers of inventory can reasonably expect to take free of security interests given by the seller (because the seller's secured party, as a financier of inventory, can be assumed to have either expressly or impliedly authorised the sale of the inventory or at least accepted that the sale would discharge its security) the same cannot be said of a buyer of a non-inventory item (because the seller's secured financier cannot be taken to have impliedly authorised the sale). Consumer protection policy is satisfied by another section of the Act that further protects consumer buyers of low-value goods by allowing them to take free of all security interests, whether given by the seller or by a prior owner.[27] But otherwise, it is quite proper for a prior secured party that has publically notified its claim by complying with the registration requirements of the legislation to prevail where there has been an unauthorised sale of which the secured party was unaware.[28] In the hypothetical example given above, the secured party did not voluntarily enter into a contract with the second-hand boat dealer. It was the customer that chose to contract with the boat dealer and arguably therefore it is the customer who should bear the risk of the dealer's insolvency or take other measures to protect itself. Nevertheless, if it were believed that this policy choice were too favourable to secured parties, it would be a simple matter to delete the words 'given by the seller' from the provision protecting buyers in the ordinary course of business. Ordinary-course buyers would then be protected from security interests given by any previous owner.

However, it must not be forgotten that the existing versions of Article 9-derived legislation have a long history and the decision to enact local variations should not be taken lightly. It is easy to overstate the differences in commercial practice between jurisdictions and the alleged need for a local approach. Further, where local variations are adopted, it is important that they are adequately justified, explained and recorded in an official record. This was not done in Australia and accordingly in many places in the Australian Act, such as the modified wording of

[25] For example, J White and R Summers, *Uniform Commercial Code*, 5th edn (West Group, St Paul, MN, 2002) 316 and *Royal Bank v Wheaton Pontiac Buick GMC Ltd* (1990) 1 PPSAC (2d) 131, 136.

[26] See B Whitaker, Review of the [Australian] PPSA 2009 Final Report (2015) (hereafter the Australian Review Final Report) 7.6.7.2, where this policy choice is affirmed after consultation. However, because of the arcane workings of the Australian defective registration provisions (ss 164–166) and temporary perfection provisions (ss 34 and 52), the policy provides little practical protection to secured parties in Australia: see Gedye (n 20) 38 and 39.

[27] Section 54 PPSA. The level of consumer protection offered by this section can be extended or restricted by modifying the parameters of the section (such as the maximum value of goods to which the section can apply).

[28] The legislation expressly takes account of the possibility that a debtor may unlawfully sell collateral to an innocent buyer and has already addressed the issue by imposing on the secured party an obligation to update its registration on becoming aware of an unauthorised disposition. See, for example, s 90 PPSA.

the ordinary-course-of-business test referred to above, it is unclear whether the departure from the New Zealand and Canadian precedents was purely stylistic or was intended to implement a local policy choice.

D. Restricting the Reach of a General Security Interest Through the Priority Regime

Registration by secured parties, and the time of registration, plays a central role in the New Zealand PPSA and the other Article 9-derived regimes. Where there are competing security interests, the general priority rule most commonly applicable gives priority to the secured party that registered first.[29] The easily verifiable time of registration accordingly settles most priority disputes, generally without regard to other considerations such as whether the first registered secured party had knowledge of any prior secured parties that had not registered.[30] Because a debtor's principal financier, such as its bank, will usually take care to ensure that it is the first to register, this priority rule could further entrench the favoured position of financiers secured over all present and after-acquired assets. But the prime position of the secured party that is first to register is then tempered by a special priority given to what are known as purchase money security interests (PMSIs).

A PMSI can arise where a secured party, whether a seller, lessor or third party financier, provides credit to allow a debtor to acquire specific assets. Provided the purchase money financier complies with the formalities required by the Act, the purchase money financier is given priority over financiers secured over all assets (except in the unusual case where the security interest of the all-assets financier also comes within the definition of a PMSI and satisfies the purchase money formalities). This is so even where the all-assets financier was the first to register. Aside from the extra level of formality required of the purchase money financier to gain priority under the PPSA, this result is very similar to the favourable treatment accorded to retention of title suppliers under the prior New Zealand (and current English) law.

To gain priority under the PPSAs of New Zealand, Canada and Australia, the purchase money financier must register promptly but under the Canadian legislation a purchase money financier of inventory is additionally required

[29] See, for example, PPSA s 66(b)(i). If one or more of competing security interests were possessory, priority under the general priority rule would go to the first to register or take possession.

[30] The Register is fully computerised; there are no paper-based registrations. Registration is instantaneous and real time and is undertaken by the registering party so there cannot be any registrations pending that require action by the Register's staff. With this system, there is no doubt as to when a registration was effected and it is not possible for two registrations to occur at the same time. Of course, this system puts the responsibility for getting a registration right onto the registering party but provided the registering party knows what he or she is doing, the system is essentially fool proof.

to serve notice on prior registered financiers.[31] This is another area where the Australasian legislation has adopted a different policy. The Canadian notice requirement is justified on the basis that it is appropriate to inform a prior general secured party of the risk that its prior security interest in inventory may be subordinated to the inventory financier's subsequent interest so that the general financier may make an informed decision on whether to continue giving credit secured over the inventory. But this is one of two areas where the Australasian legislation intentionally places more emphasis on the time of registration than any Canadian jurisdiction.[32] Unlike Canada, in Australia and New Zealand there is no requirement that in order to gain priority a purchase money supplier of inventory who registers in time must also give notice to a prior general secured party.[33] In the author's opinion, the Australasian approach can be supported on several grounds. For example, one can argue that the use of purchase money finance for the acquisition of inventory is so common that prior general financiers should simply assume that they will be subordinate to inventory suppliers/financiers and make their lending decisions on that basis. Also, one can argue that any benefits of giving notice to prior general secured parties are outweighed by the additional transaction costs and uncertainty created by a priority rule that turns not on the easily verifiable time of registration but on proving that a notice has been given.

In any event, the supposed benefits of the Canadian requirement that inventory purchase money financiers must serve notice of their claim on prior general secured parties can largely be achieved automatically through technology without imposing any additional legal requirements on inventory financiers. In January 2015, the Australian PPS Registry announced that secured parties who have registered against a business debtor can choose to be automatically notified by the Registry of subsequent registrations against that debtor by another secured party.[34] Coupled with the current Australian requirement that registrations in respect of PMSIs must self-identify as such, this technological innovation essentially

[31] See, for example, Saskatchewan PPSA s 34(3).

[32] The other area is in the priority given to buyers over unperfected security interests (which generally refers to a security interest in relation to which no registration has been undertaken). In Canada, a buyer defeats an unperfected security interest only if the buyer had no knowledge of the security interest. In Australia and New Zealand, a buyer defeats an unperfected security interest regardless of the buyer's knowledge.

[33] The Australian PPSA does currently require a registration to identify when a PMSI is claimed (see ss 62(2)(c), 62(3)(c) and 153(1) item 7 of the Australian PPSA and Schedule 2 Part 3 clause 3.1 of the Australian Personal Property Securities Regulations 2009). The Australasian approach that allows purchase money inventory financiers to claim priority without first notifying prior secured parties has been criticised elsewhere: see, for example, Roderick Wood 'Acquisition Financing of Inventory: Explaining the Diversity' (2013) 13 *Oxford University Commonwealth Law Journal* 49. The Australian Review Final Report recommends that the requirement to identify when a PMSI is claimed should be deleted, but does not recommend that it be replaced by an obligation to notify prior secured parties: see 7.7.8.11. See also Ch 8 F(ii).

[34] See http://ppsr.govspace.gov.au/attention-ppsr-practitioners-account-users-and-b2g-customers-do-you-need-to-monitor-another-organisations-ppsr-activity/.

allows prior general secured parties automatically to receive notice of subsequent inventory financiers to whom the earlier general financier will be subordinated, without the disadvantages of the Canadian manual notice regime.[35]

E. Scope of the Act

(i) Inclusion of the Title-based Interests

In common with other Article 9-derived secured transactions laws, the New Zealand PPSA brings within its scope certain ownership interests in personal property but excludes most interests in real property. These are two issues that must be addressed by any jurisdiction contemplating secured transactions law reform. The New Zealand experience with the inclusion of title-based interests within the PPSA is considered in this subsection. Some comments on the exclusion of real property are offered in the next subsection.

One of the defining features of Article 9-derived secured transactions law is the inclusion within the regimes of what are sometimes referred to as the 'quasi-security devices'; that is, those transactions that function economically and commercially as security devices but that the prior law did not consistently regulate as secured transactions. Most significantly, such transactions include those under which an owner retains title to goods, but parts with possession of them, where the function or substance of the transaction is to secure performance of an obligation owed by the party that takes possession: for example, a transaction under which a seller retains title to goods until the buyer has paid for the goods. This concept also extends to a lease of goods that in commercial and economic substance secures the performance of an obligation, even though under the terms of the lease the lessee may never acquire ownership.

Although determining when a lease fits the concept of securing performance of an obligation can at times be challenging, the legislation, official commentaries and case law provide the guidance that will help to resolve most cases. An obvious example of a lease that comes within this concept would be a lease for the entire economic life of an asset where the lessee is obliged to make rental payments that in aggregate exceed the cash price of the goods. Because the lessee has the use of the asset until it has fully depreciated, and pays more than its cash price, in

[35] This solution will not be as effective if the Australian Review Final Report's recommendation that the requirement to self-identify PMSIs be abolished is enacted. Earlier general financiers would still receive notice of a subsequent registration and from the collateral description they would know that it covered inventory but they would need to make their own assessment whether the subsequent security interest was a PMSI. As most specific security interests over inventory are probably PMSIs, earlier general financiers would likely just assume a subsequent security interest over inventory was a PMSI.

economic effect, the lease functions as a disguised secured credit disposition even though the lessee may never take title to the asset. In economic substance, such a lease is no different to a credit sale secured by a charge over the goods sold or a credit sale where title is retained until the purchase price is paid.

Any residual difficulties with classifying a lease as securing performance of an obligation have largely been obviated in Canada, New Zealand and Australia by the expediency of simply deeming all leases of more than one year to give rise to security interests. This is a purely pragmatic choice to simplify the classification issue at the expense of conceptual purity and is not followed in all PPS jurisdictions. The automatic inclusion within the regime of leases for more than one year, and the breadth of the definition of such leases, proved, at least initially, to be of concern to the hire industry in New Zealand and Australia.[36] In the author's opinion, such concerns are overstated. Provided lessors are aware of the need to register in these cases, their interests are protected by the legislation's giving them priority over all other possible claims.[37]

The definition of security interest, largely based as it is on economic and functional grounds,[38] effects what to common lawyers schooled in the tradition of *nemo dat quod non habet* is one of an Article 9-derived regime's most radical concepts: when the definition applies, it essentially recharacterises ownership as a mere security interest so that the owner is effectively recharacterised as a secured party and the debtor is effectively recharacterised as an owner.[39] Some jurisdictions have explicit examples of this process. For example, Articles 1-201(37) and 2-401 of the American Uniform Commercial Code expressly provide that a retention of title by a seller in goods delivered to a buyer is limited in effect to a security interest. While this recharacterisation (as security interests) of those title-based interests that come within the statutory definition of security interest (and the concomitant recharacterisation of the debtor's interest) is not expressly spelt out in other PPS jurisdictions, it is in the author's opinion implicit. In New Zealand and Canada,

[36] The initial concern in New Zealand, as highlighted by the business media in the article 'Oi, That's My Horse', 5 August 2005, *National Business Review* 14, can be seen as a transitional issue that settled down once lessors became aware of the need to register. In Australia, where the legislation has been in force only since 2012, it appears lessors and their advisers have yet to accept that leases for a term of more than one year should automatically come within the regime: see, for example, Oliver Shtein, 'How the Law Is Robbing Hire Companies and Must Be Changed', 3 February 2015, *Business Review Weekly*, brw.com.au. This concern has been addressed in the Australian Review Final Report at 4.3.5, where some reform is recommended, so that leases for an indefinite term that do not secure performance of an obligation will only come within the definition of security interest if they in fact run for more than one year (see 4.3.5.4.3).

[37] See, for example, s 73 PPSA.

[38] As noted above in respect of leases for a term of more than one year, to simplify the classification process, several categories of transaction are brought within the definition even where they do not in economic substance secure performance of an obligation. The other two categories are transfers of certain receivables and some consignment arrangements: see, for example, s 17(1)(b) PPSA.

[39] Some pre-Article 9 debate on this issue is noted in M Gedye, 'The Development of New Zealand's Secured Transactions Jurisprudence' (2011) 34 *University of New South Wales Law Journal* 696, 700 and 701.

both the courts and commentators have on the whole readily accepted this to be an essential feature of PPS logic,[40] but the question remains as to whether aspects of an Article 9-derived regime could be adopted without including the quasi-security devices. While this would certainly be possible, it would in the author's opinion be a mistake. To exclude transactions that function as security from a secured transactions regime would perpetuate the unjustified legal consequences that flow from fine legal distinctions that are not based on the purpose or commercial effect of a transaction.

Excluding retention of title arrangements from secured transactions laws is sometimes baldly justified on the grounds that title retention is not security,[41] but this argument is no different to the argument that was made and lost in the United States in the early twentieth century,[42] and fails to explain why transactions that have the same economic and commercial purpose should be regulated differently simply because the parties chose a different wording.[43] It also ignores English law's current ability to look through the form of a transaction and, in appropriate cases, recharacterise a transaction documented as a retention of title as a charge.[44] Contrary to assertions that retention of title is not security, many such arrangements do function as secured transactions and in New Zealand their regulation as security interests alongside the traditional security devices such as the charge is now well accepted.[45]

Another benefit of including title-based interests in any reform of secured transactions law is the ability to improve the position of such interests through statutory intervention and the enactment of rules designed to achieve commercially sensible outcomes. Prior to the PPSA, suppliers could often

[40] See, for example, *Graham v Portacom New Zealand Ltd* [2004] 2 NZLR 528 at [17]–[28] and the authorities and commentaries referred to therein. Not all commentators wholeheartedly accept this recharacterisation as essential to Article 9-derived regimes. See, for example, S McCracken, 'Construing the Personal Property Securities Act 2009 (Cth): Interpretation or Interpolation' Dec 2013–Feb 2014, *Commercial Law Quarterly* and L Meehan, *The PPS Guide* (Woof Creative, 2001) 21.001–21.046.

[41] See The City of London Law Society, *Discussion Paper: Secured Transactions Reform*, November 2012 at para 1.13: 'We do not see that there is any merit in bringing reservation of title or similar devices into the ambit of the law on secured transactions—largely because they are not secured transactions'.

[42] See n 39.

[43] The justification cannot be freedom of contract because the parties' choice affects third parties.

[44] See, for example, *Re Curtain Dream PLC* [1990] BCLC 925, 935 where the Court noted that 'it is the substance of the transaction that has to be looked at and not just the form'. However, the case involved a sale to the financier and a sale back to the debtor and it is clear that the circularity of this transaction was influential (at 939). The Court made it clear (at 938) that a single sale with a retention of title would not be reclassified as a security interest (unlike the case under the PPSA) and so does not go as far as the PPSA in giving emphasis to substance over form.

[45] Although, as noted above, this is yet to be fully accepted by businesses and their advisers in Australia: see above notes 10 and 36. There are a number of reasons for the different attitudes to this issue in New Zealand and Australia, including the novelty of the concept to Australians (whose Act only came into force in 2012) and the far more severe consequences that follow in Australia for failing to understand that a title-based interest can be recharacterised as a security interest. In Australia, a title-based interest that does not follow the requisite (but straightforward) formalities required by the legislation is lost upon the debtor's insolvency. Controversially, this is not the case in New Zealand (see Section F(i)).

protect their position through the informal practice of inserting a retention of title clause in an invoice. Under the PPSA, suppliers can still achieve the same protection but greater formality is required: essentially it is now necessary to obtain written assent from the debtor and to undertake a registration. One could argue that the additional formalities reduce uncertainty and in any event are a good discipline for suppliers but clearly they involve some cost that suppliers did not previously incur.[46] In a sense, retention of title suppliers are then compensated for this additional cost by being given a statutory right to any goods that the supplies are attached to, mixed with or converted into and to trace into the proceeds of any of the supplies that are dealt with.[47] These statutory rules obviate the need to draft complex contractual provisions designed to achieve a similar effect (such as clauses claiming title to goods into which supplied components are manufactured or purporting to create trusts over proceeds) and overcome the common law's uncertainty as to the status of such provisions and when they are effective.

Although in the author's opinion any departures from precedent legislation need to be fully explained and justified,[48] and it is a truism that uniform laws work best when they are uniform, it is neither easily achievable nor essential for the Article 9-derived regimes of different jurisdictions to be identical. States within the United States have adopted non-uniform versions of Article 9, the Canadian Acts vary in form and substance from Article 9 and the New Zealand Act, while in most respects closely aligned to the Act in force in Saskatchewan, nevertheless departs from the Canadian legislation in some significant respects. The Australian Act draws from both the Canadian and New Zealand legislation, and even from Article 9 directly, as well as including many home-grown drafting innovations. But despite such differences, all of the North American and Australasian Article 9-derived regimes accept the desirability of encompassing title-based interests and the logic for doing so. Indeed, as each jurisdiction has adopted its Article 9-derived regime, issues have generally arisen not from the inclusion of title-based interests but from the adoption of the non-uniform variations to the legislation. Failure to include the title-based security interests in any comprehensive reform of secured transactions law can be likened to renovating a bathroom without updating all of the fittings. Doubtless the new bathroom would be better than the old, but the partial renovation would be a lost opportunity and would not present as a modern and cohesive facility.

[46] Where ongoing supplies are involved, such as the supply of inventory, the debtor's written assent and registration is required only once, not for each separate transaction, so the costs are not great. Where a one-off supply is involved, such as a hire purchase transaction, it is likely that a written agreement would have been signed even absent the PPSA requirements and the only additional cost is the small registration fee.

[47] See, for example, ss 16 (definition of proceeds), 45, 78 and 82.

[48] Regrettably, this ideal was not adequately realised in either New Zealand or Australia. The magnitude of the unexplained drafting innovations in Australia will likely there lead to additional uncertainty, a cost that could have been avoided by either following the precedent legislation more closely or by properly explaining, in the Australian Explanatory Memorandum, the drafter's intention.

(ii) A Comprehensive Security Interest that Includes Real Property

The PPSA (and its foreign counterparts), as the name implies, essentially applies only to personal property.[49] It has been suggested that this is a weakness and that, instead of a regime such as the PPSA, which is comprehensive in the sense of applying to both incorporated and unincorporated debtors and encompassing both the traditional security interests and title-based interests, what is required is a security interest applicable only to incorporated businesses but that is comprehensive in the sense of applying to both real and personal property.[50] This proposal confuses what can be achieved under a statutory regime with what can be achieved under a security agreement. It is perfectly possible under New Zealand law to have a simple single security agreement that covers both real and personal property, and this is common in practice, so the alleged shortcoming in the New Zealand PPSA does not arise.[51]

However, in New Zealand at least, it would not be sensible, even if it were technically feasible, to regulate both real property security and personal property security under the one statutory regime. The New Zealand real property regime is a title-based Torrens regime that is indexed according to the identity of the land, essentially guaranteeing title to all types of registered interest. On the other hand, the personal property securities regime is indexed according to the debtor's name, does not guarantee title and only records security interests. Clearly, the real property title-based regime is superior in a number of respects. Perhaps in an ideal world a single secured transactions regime would apply to both real and personal property but then the nature of personal property would preclude the use of a title-based regime. The uniqueness, stability and value of real property make it feasible to utilise the superior title-based form of register for all interests in land. Because most items of personal property lack these characteristics, it is not practical to have a comprehensive register of title for interests in personal property.[52] At most, a register that recorded security interests in both the real and personal property of incorporated debtors could protect the secured party from

[49] Where particular property has characteristics of both personal and real property, such as mortgages of land, leases of land and fixtures, the PPSA can apply but the real property regime will generally prevail where there is any conflict: see, for example, *Marac Finance Ltd v Greer* [2012] NZCA 45.

[50] See R Calnan, 'What Makes A Good Law of Security' (Proceedings of the Personal Property Security Law: Local and Global Perspectives Conference, University of Adelaide, February 2013) 6.

[51] Where a security agreement is intended to encompass all of a debtor's real and personal present and after-acquired property it is probably prudent to include words to the effect that it functions as a security interest over personal property and as a charge over real property (to foreclose any possible argument that the term 'security interest' is by definition under the PPSA limited to personal property) but little more is required. Where it is desired to take a legal mortgage over the real property, it is also prudent to provide that the debtor will execute registrable mortgages if called upon to do so.

[52] It is of course possible to have a title register for certain types of personal property that can be uniquely identified and are of sufficient value to justify such a register, such as motor vehicles, aircraft, ships and various intellectual property rights.

insolvency invalidation (which, as noted in Section F(i) below, is not an issue in New Zealand) but could never give priority over interests registered under a title-based real property regime that conferred indefeasible title like the existing New Zealand land registration regime.

F. Registration

(i) No Mandatory Registration in New Zealand

The concept of 'perfection', which satisfies public notification goals, is crucial to the efficacy of security interests under Article 9-derived regimes. In simple terms, perfection determines priority status and protects against unauthorised dispositions of the collateral.

Perfection is generally achieved through registration in a public register.[53] A permitted alternative to registration is the taking of possession of the collateral by the secured party, but obviously this is not convenient for most secured transactions. Registration, then, is the principal device by which security interests are publically notified. But controversially, New Zealand does not insist upon public notification of security interests through either registration or possession. Registration is not mandatory in the sense of either its being an offence not to register or its being required for a security interest to be valid in the debtor's insolvency. In New Zealand, a security interest that is not perfected (which essentially means that the secured party has neither registered nor taken possession of the collateral) is vulnerable to other proprietary claims to the collateral (such as those of competing secured parties or buyers) but is fully effective against a liquidator or bankruptcy administrator.[54] This approach has not been adopted elsewhere; even in Australia, where the recent legislation followed other New Zealand innovations.

[53] The New Zealand Register uses the Article 9 system of 'notice registration', requiring registration of what is known as a financing statement. Individual security agreements are not registered; instead what is registered is a description, which in most cases can be general in nature, of collateral. This is a very efficient and cost-effective system that has several significant advantages over a regime that requires registration of security documents. In particular, registration can take place before a security agreement is entered into (which reduces risk for the secured party and facilitates settlement) and a single registration can cover multiple security agreements provided the collateral description is adequate (which again gives the secured party greater certainty while reducing the time and cost involved in both initial and ongoing registrations). The simplicity of notice registration comes at the cost of providing less information to a searcher who will not be able to discover the terms of a security agreement. However, notice registration fully satisfies the searcher's legitimate need to discover whether it is safe to deal with particular assets of the debtor and it is not clear that a searcher should be entitled to other information that may be commercially sensitive or confidential to others.

[54] The risk of subordination to other secured parties and buyers provides an incentive to register so even without mandatory registration prudent secured parties will do so.

Mandatory registration of non-possessory security interests has, among other things, traditionally been seen as helping to mitigate the 'scandal' of a creditor who held an undisclosed security from taking all of a debtor's assets and leaving unpaid the ordinary trade creditors who were unaware of the security.[55] But the rationale for mandatory registration was hotly debated in New Zealand. The committee that prepared the Law Commission's report on secured transactions law reform did not reach consensus on the issue.[56] Commentators in favour of mandatory registration, which included the author, argued that registration was a small price for secured creditors to pay for their priority over ordinary trade creditors. Mandatory registration, it was argued, would promote both the integrity of the register and an informed market, while facilitating insolvency administrations and reducing the risk of fraud.[57] Further, mandatory registration was the international norm as well as having always been required under companies and bills of sale legislation and there was no good reason to change the status quo. Those against mandatory registration suggested that the world had moved on from the doctrine of reputed ownership and that no legitimate interest was adversely impacted by non-registration. Buyers and other secured creditors were already adequately protected by the buyer protection and priority rules of the Act and unsecured creditors could not claim to be detrimentally affected by non-registration. Further, while registration was essentially mandatory under the prior company charges regime, it was for all practical purposes never required for the title retention devices that were thenceforth to be considered security interests; so whichever option was chosen the status quo would change for either the traditional security interests or the title-based security interests.[58]

Fourteen years on, it is possible to offer some comments on how the New Zealand experiment has panned out. In the author's experience, it seems that the vast majority of all-assets security interests are perfected by registration even though it is not mandatory. This is unsurprising: commonly such creditors are either related to the debtor and seeking to steal a march over other creditors or are sophisticated financial institutions and the risk of subordination to buyers and other secured creditors is a powerful incentive to register. Anecdotal evidence suggests that it is the title retention creditors who are more likely to fail to register and this is not the group that mandatory registration has traditionally been aimed at.

[55] The history of this 'scandal' is canvassed in *Agnew v Commissioner of Inland Revenue* [2001] UKPC 28; [2001] 2 AC 710; [2002] 1 NZLR 30 at [8]–[10]. The term 'scandal' was coined by Lord Macnaghten in *Salomon v Salomon & Co Ltd* [1897] AC 22, 53.

[56] New Zealand Law Commission (n 13) para 7.

[57] See, for example, M Gedye, R Cuming and R Wood, *Personal Property Securities in New Zealand* (Wellington, Thomson Brookers, 2002) Intro 5.

[58] See D Dugdale, 'The Proposed PPSA' [1998] *New Zealand Law Journal* 268; New Zealand Law Commission (n 13) 115. The argument goes that unsecured creditors cannot claim to have been harmed by the non-perfection of a security interest because they are in any event exposed to security interests that are perfected after the unsecured credit was provided and the prudent assumption that unsecured creditors must make is that they will be subordinated to such security interests.

The frequency with which it seems title retention creditors fail to register points to one unexpected consequence of New Zealand's refusal to make registration mandatory: the equitable doctrine of marshalling assumes greater significance than in other Article 9-derived regimes.[59] Under the PPSA, title retention creditors who register promptly are entitled to priority over all-assets secured creditors. But if a title retention creditor fails to register properly, it may be subordinated to an all-assets secured creditor. The all-assets secured creditor, by virtue of its resultant superior priority, may then enforce against the title retention creditor's collateral, potentially leaving the latter unsecured. However, where the debtor's total assets are sufficient to repay the all-assets secured creditor in full, with something left over, the subordinated title retention creditor may seek to be subrogated to the all-assets security interest under the equitable doctrine of marshalling, even if the title retention creditor's collateral has already been exhausted. While the doctrine of marshalling can apply in other PPS jurisdictions, it would not avail a title retention creditor who had failed to register because the bankruptcy administrator would then prevail. This constraint does not apply in New Zealand because registration is not required for validity in insolvency.[60]

Although, arguably, mandatory registration (or possession) can reduce fraudulent behaviour, the New Zealand cases so far do not disclose any widespread evidence of fraud. Doubtless there have been cases where security agreements have been backdated or fictitious agreements put forward but ironically in the only reported case where this was in issue, the secured creditor had in fact registered and the case turned on whether the security agreement had been executed prior to the appointment of a liquidator.[61]

Undoubtedly, the absence of mandatory registration complicates insolvency administrations. Liquidators are obliged to give effect to security interests that they may have difficulty independently verifying. They may find themselves unintentionally dealing with assets that will not benefit unsecured creditors because a secured creditor of whom the liquidator was unaware can come along and claim the proceeds. Potentially, liquidators may even be exposed to claims in conversion for improperly dealing with the collateral of an unknown secured creditor. Nor do liquidators now have the benefit of an easily verifiable date of registration to help them determine the date that a security interest was given when applying New Zealand's voidable 'charges' regime.[62] However, such difficulties can be

[59] For a comprehensive discussion of the principles of marshalling of securities, see P Ali, *Marshalling of Securities: Equity and the Priority-ranking of Secured Debt* (Oxford, Clarendon Press, 1999).

[60] A separate issue is whether the equitable doctrine of marshalling should ever apply in the face of the statutory principles and priorities of the PPSA. This issue is yet to be fully explored in New Zealand.

[61] *The Healy Holmberg Trading Partnership v Grant and Khov* [2012] NZCA 451. Registration may help to resolve allegations of fraud but is not the complete answer. This is because under a notice registration regime there is no necessary connection between the date of registration and the existence or date of a particular security agreement.

[62] Section 293 Companies Act 1993. This provision invalidates 'charges' securing past advances given within two years before liquidation and was never modernised to refer to the broader concept of

overstated. In a notice registration regime, registration is not evidence of the existence of a security agreement and the date of registration does not necessarily bear any relationship to the date any security agreement was entered into. Registration may take place before or after a security interest has been granted (and even in the absence of a security agreement) so that even where registration has taken place, the prudent practice that insolvency practitioners have widely adopted is to require production of the underlying security agreement. This practice mitigates some of the difficulties referred to and would still be essential if mandatory registration were required.

One benefit of the New Zealand non-mandatory registration approach that should not be underestimated is the huge reduction in litigation that would otherwise transpire and the consequent cost savings. Many Canadian cases have been brought by insolvency administrators challenging technically defective registrations. A surprisingly large proportion of the cases under the Australian PPSA have been brought by secured creditors seeking leave to register out of time so that their otherwise unperfected security interest may survive the debtor's liquidation. Such cases simply do not arise in New Zealand since security interests are effective in insolvency whether or not they are perfected by valid registrations.

It is worth noting that while in Australia registration is generally required for non-possessory security interests if the secured party is to prevail in insolvency, the Australian Act has adopted a novel technique to achieve this outcome. In North America, an unperfected security interest is simply made ineffective against the insolvency administrator.[63] In Australia, most unperfected security interests are 'vest[ed] in the grantor [ie the debtor] immediately before [the commencement of the formal insolvency procedure]'.[64] The Australian approach, which divests the secured creditor of its proprietary interest, achieves a broadly similar result to that of North America. Perhaps the novel Australian technique was adopted to dispose of any remnant arguments along the lines that a bankruptcy administrator only succeeds to the property of the debtor so that a secured party who retained title could fall back on its underlying ownership interest and would not be affected by the invalidation of merely its security interest.

The New Zealand approach to validity in insolvency probably explains why, as compared to Australia, there has been far less hostility from the leasing industry

a PPSA security interest. There are conflicting dicta in the cases as to whether the term 'charge' should now be taken to incorporate title retention arrangements: *cf Dunphy v Sleepyhead Manufacturing Co Ltd* [2007] 3 NZLR 602 (Court of Appeal) (post-PPSA, title retention arrangements are to be considered as 'charges') and the subsequent High Court decision of *Mercedes-Benz Financial Services New Zealand Ltd v Quadrant Wholesalers Ltd* [2014] NZHC 814, decided without reference to the Court of Appeal decision in *Sleepyhead* (title retention arrangements are not 'charges').

[63] For example, see Saskatchewan PPSA s 20(2).

[64] Australian PPSA s 267. Note that this does not apply to certain security interests created by the transfer of debts or by the consignment of goods (see s 268). In leaving some security interests unaffected by s 267, the Australian approach is something of a halfway house since such security interests do not require registration to survive the debtor's insolvency.

to the classification of lessors' interests as security interests.[65] In New Zealand, a lessor who fails to register will risk being subordinated to any buyers or perfected secured parties but otherwise can recover its property from an insolvency administrator. Currently, in Australia, in addition to the risk of subordination to buyers and perfected secured parties prior to insolvency, the lessor cannot recover its goods if the debtor is put into insolvency.[66]

On balance, it might be said that in New Zealand the jury is still out on whether registration should be mandatory. The doctrinal arguments both ways can still be made and this tension is now mirrored in practice. Certainly, the sky has not fallen in. However, the anecdotal and intuitive analysis set out above is not an adequate basis for rational law making. What is required is a formal review of the New Zealand approach where submissions are invited from interested parties and the issues properly considered in the light of the experience so far. One failing of the New Zealand regime, both in this context and more generally, is the lack of any formal process for reviewing the legislation and rectifying any flaws. The Ministry of Business Innovation and Employment, which is the responsible Ministry, does not appear to have tasked its staff with this responsibility and there is no review planned. This can be contrasted to the position in Australia, where the legislation itself mandated a formal review within three years of its implementation.[67]

(ii) The Operation of the New Zealand Register

The register plays a central role in the operation of any Article 9-derived secured transactions regime. As such, operational aspects of the register should not be regarded as an afterthought. The design of the register is almost as important as the design of the legislation and the two should be carefully integrated. Reference has already been made to the concept of notice registration under Article 9-derived regimes,[68] but it is worth highlighting the pertinent features of notice registration and its application in New Zealand. An essential function of the registration regime is to enable third parties to determine the existence of security interests in assets in which the third party may be intending to acquire an interest. Accordingly, under a notice registration regime (where security documents are not registered) the way in which the assets are described in the register and

[65] See nn 10 and 36 and the surrounding text.

[66] The Australian Review Final Report recommends that the Act be amended so that only leases that secure performance of an obligation will vest in an insolvency administrator if they are not perfected: see 8.7.4. If this proposal were enacted, it would mean that what can broadly be described as operating leases would no longer require registration for validity in insolvency. This would lessen the hostility of the leasing industry but would make the difficult classification issue of when a lease secures performance of an obligation far more significant. It would also make Australia more of a halfway house (see n 64).

[67] See Australian PPSA s 343.

[68] See n 53.

(because the register is indexed primarily under the debtor's name) the way in which the debtor's name is set out are fundamental considerations.

Because the New Zealand Register is wholly computerised, with no paper-based registrations and minimal involvement of the Registrar in the registration process, the design of the software used by the register plays a key role in its functioning. Rather than taking one of the Canadian registers as a blueprint, New Zealand designed its own register and imposed collateral description requirements different to those applicable in any of the Canadian provinces. While overall the functionality of the New Zealand Register is highly regarded, this has meant that, without the guidance of Canadian precedents, there is some doubt as to how detailed the collateral description needs to be when a security interest is taken over only some of a debtor's assets.[69] Although the Court of Appeal has given some guidance,[70] this uncertainty has encouraged some New Zealand practitioners to utilise unhelpful collateral descriptions (such as 'all the debtor's assets except those that are not goods or proceeds of goods supplied by the secured party') that make it difficult for a searcher to identify the precise collateral of interest. Clearer regulations governing the way collateral must be described would obviate the need for such artifices.

The way in which the searching function of a register operates is also fundamental. The policy choice here is between disclosing only those registrations that exactly match the index criteria that are searched (known as exact match searching) or allowing some latitude so that registrations that closely resemble the searched criteria are also disclosed (known as close match searching). As the primary indexing and searching criterion is the debtor's name, the debtor's name must be recorded in a registration sufficiently accurately to allow a searcher to locate the registration. Where the register utilises an exact match searching system, complete accuracy is required of the registering party when entering the debtor's name because any difference between the way the name is written in a registration and the way it is written in a search request will prevent the search from disclosing the registration.[71] Even apparently minor typographical errors can invalidate a registration.[72] This places a high onus on the registering party to get it exactly right.[73]

[69] Where the security covers all of the debtor's present and after-acquired personal property, a simple all-assets description suffices (except in the case of motor vehicles and other prescribed assets that are required to be described, inter alia, by serial number) and this makes it very simple for banks and the like to perfect comprehensive security interests.

[70] See *Service Foods Manawatu Ltd v Shephard and Dunphy* (2007) 10 NZCLC 264263 at [25]–[34].

[71] See *Polymers International Ltd v Toon* [2013] NZHC 1897 at [11]–[26].

[72] Although the system allows for rectification of such errors at any time, the validity of the registration will date from the time of rectification.

[73] Under the technically modern New Zealand register, all registrations are done remotely by the registering party (ie, the secured party or its agent). Apart from some basic automated checks (for data such as impossible dates) the Registrar has no involvement with the registration process and takes no responsibility for errors. It is the registering party who bears the responsibility for any mistakes, which would include recording the debtor's name incorrectly. However, there is an

On the other hand, under a close match searching system, a search will disclose such variations of the searched criteria as are provided for by the register's software, thus allowing the registering party some leeway. Where the register employs close match searching, minor errors may not invalidate a registration. But under this system, a search may disclose closely matching registrations that actually relate to debtors of no interest to the searcher. The close match system requires the searcher to distinguish between relevant and irrelevant registrations, reducing the accuracy expected of the registering party at the cost of placing a greater onus on the searching party. It will be more likely in a bigger jurisdiction, with a correspondingly larger number of registrations, that there will be a large number of false positive searches that the searching party must deal with. Perhaps partly for this reason, the bigger jurisdictions of Ontario and Australia have adopted exact match searching so that a searcher is not required to deal with a potentially large number of irrelevant search results while the smaller jurisdictions of the other Canadian provinces have all adopted close match searching to lighten the burden on the registering party.[74] New Zealand, being a relatively small jurisdiction, might have been expected to follow the lead of the smaller Canadian provinces by adopting close match searching and the New Zealand legislation appears to have been drafted with this in mind. Nevertheless, the New Zealand Register was programmed for exact match searching. While this may be a legitimate policy choice, obviously it would have been preferable for the legislation and the functionality of the register to match.

G. Drafting Deficiencies

Concerns are most commonly expressed in respect of the New Zealand PPSA where it has departed from the Canadian model, rather than where the North American precedents have been followed. It is the author's opinion that while a number of the New Zealand innovations are worthwhile (for example, giving buyers, absent bad faith, priority over unperfected secured creditors regardless of knowledge) they have not all proven to be clearly beneficial. Arguments can be made for and against some of the New Zealand innovations (for example, making unperfected security interests effective against an insolvency administrator) and there are yet others that have clearly been problematic.

important safeguard that makes the entry of the debtor's name almost foolproof when the debtor is an incorporated company: the company's incorporation number must also be recorded and the system does not allow an erroneous name and number combination.

[74] Also, there are potentially privacy issues with close match searching where registrations may be disclosed to a searcher that relate to persons other than the person that the searcher is legitimately interested in.

Without a proper official explanation of what was intended, sometimes the New Zealand variations have simply created uncertainty until they have come before the courts. For example, modifying the Canadian concept of a lease for a term of more than one year by something as seemingly inconsequential as referring also to bailments caused uncertainty until the matter was addressed by the Court of Appeal in *Rabobank New Zealand Ltd v McAnulty*.[75] Until such issues are resolved by the courts, practitioners responding to the uncertainty may create other difficulties. For example, the New Zealand regulations are not always clear on how collateral must be described in registrations. As noted above, to get around this, some practitioners are using an all-assets-based description in a registration when in fact the collateral is more limited. This can create difficulties for subsequent searchers who may not be able to determine accurately which of the debtor's assets are subject to the earlier security interest.

In other cases, New Zealand departures from the Canadian precedents have produced substantive difficulties for financiers. For example, the failure of the New Zealand Act to deal with fixtures leaves fixtures financiers vulnerable unless they are able to negotiate a suitable priority under the land registration regime. In yet other cases, New Zealand has failed to follow through with the reforms by neglecting to bring other legislation into line with PPS concepts. This is particularly noticeable where provisions in other legislation, such as the Companies Act 1993 and the Property Law Act 2007 (which imposes certain duties on secured parties seeking to enforce) still refer to mortgages or charges rather than to the PPS concept of a security interest. For example, despite some consideration by the courts, it is still unclear which security interests come within the definition of a mortgage under the Property Law Act and are thus subject to the obligations imposed under that legislation when a secured party enforces against the collateral.[76]

None of the above issues imply any fundamental shortcomings in Article 9-derived legislation. What they do point to is the need when basing legislation on a foreign precedent to explain and record departures from it in a comprehensive and transparent way that can be openly critiqued. One of the oddest New Zealand departures from the Canadian precedents was to provide in section 109 of the New Zealand PPSA that only a first priority secured party could enforce its security interest. Following disclosure requested by the author under the Official Information Act 1982, it transpired that this innovation was based on a mistaken belief that enforcement by one secured party discharged all other security interests in the realised collateral.[77] Eventually, the offending provision was amended but this flaw would likely have been remedied much sooner had the faulty reasoning behind it been published.

[75] *Rabobank New Zealand Ltd v McAnulty* [2011] NZCA 212.

[76] See n 62.

[77] Copies of the information disclosed are on file with the author.

The original section 109 was not the only flaw in the New Zealand enforcement regime. One of the benefits of PPS legislation is the ease with which a fully effective security interest can be created with simple wording. Provided the basic formalities required by the legislation are observed, even lay people can draft an effective security agreement, leaving any gaps to be filled in by the provisions of the Act. Transaction costs are reduced both where the parties act without taking legal advice and where legal advisers are engaged. For example, the legislation can provide standard enforcement remedies and regulate their application so there is less need to provide for these matters in a security agreement. Unfortunately, in New Zealand the enforcement of security interests is regulated across multiple statutes, including Part 9 of the PPSA, and many of the relevant provisions in the PPSA can be contracted out of. Originally, it was possible for a debtor to contract out of protections as fundamental as the right to receive an accounting for the proceeds of any collateral sold by the secured party (see section 107(2)(a)) and to recover any surplus (see section 107(2)(b) as originally enacted). Section 107(2)(b) has since been repealed and it is no longer possible to contract out of the debtor's right to recover a surplus but section 107(2)(a) remains so it is unclear how a debtor who was not entitled to receive an accounting would know there was any surplus to recover!

Even with the various amendments that have been made to the enforcement regime under the PPSA as originally enacted, the hotchpot of relevant statutes and the ability to contract out of key provisions leaves the New Zealand regime for the enforcement of security interests overly complex yet still incomplete. What is required is a full review of the rationale and required scope of a statutory enforcement regime. Such a review could encompass all of the disparate New Zealand legislation that currently regulates the enforcement process and should lead to a more comprehensive and integrated mandatory regime to govern the enforcement of all types of security interest. Subject to any perceived need to provide for additional consumer protection measures in consumer finance transactions, the inconsistencies between the various current enactments could be eliminated by legislating for enforcement rights and obligations that no reasonable debtor or creditor would object to and that could not be contracted out of. Eliminating the present disparities in the New Zealand enforcement regime that currently arise from the form of security agreement adopted would also align with the objective of Article 9-derived legislation of creating a unitary and functionally based security interest.

More broadly, New Zealand should undertake a thorough review (along the lines of that mandated under the Australian Act) of the drafting and policy innovations introduced in the New Zealand PPSA. This would facilitate the rectification of any conceptual or technical flaws that have arisen in New Zealand as a consequence of home-grown drafting and would help to inform international debate on the development of Article 9-derived legislation.

H. The Courts and the PPSA

Credit is essential to a modern economy and while secured transactions are pervasive they are often inherently costly and complex. One of the goals of the New Zealand PPSA was to reduce these transaction costs and to simplify this branch of the law. There will inevitably be transitional costs of any reform,[78] so to be successful on a cost-benefit measure the present value of the future savings must exceed the transitional costs. Unfortunately, it is not easy to make such an assessment precisely but the favourable reception given to the New Zealand reforms by practitioners and the finance industry and the lack of adverse commentary suggests that economic benefits have been achieved despite any indigenous drafting deficiencies. Further, given the ubiquitous nature of secured transactions, one would have expected much more litigation had there been serious problems in practice. The relative infrequency of litigation (approximately 70 substantive cases over 14 years) in comparison to the number of secured transactions entered into (more than 7 million Personal Property Securities Register registrations over the same period)[79] suggests that in the vast majority of transactions, the law is working satisfactorily and as intended. If this is so, and the law is clear in most instances, then, after an initial settling in period, those cases that do reach the courts can be expected to deal mainly with the few areas where there is some remaining doubt and room for different interpretations. Such circumstances, where the majority of transactions proceed smoothly and generally only the harder cases get to court, can occasionally give rise to wayward or even contradictory first instance decisions until an issue is settled by the appellate courts. This is consistent with the New Zealand experience.

Overall, the PPSA has been well received by the New Zealand courts. The novel concepts have generally been well understood and given appropriate recognition. Even prior to its enactment, senior members of the judiciary supported the proposed reforms. Justice O'Regan, who subsequently became the president of the New Zealand Court of Appeal and is now a judge of the Supreme Court, was, in his then capacity as a senior commercial law partner in a large law firm, the co-author of the New Zealand Law Commission's preliminary report

[78] Transitional costs include retraining stakeholders such as legal practitioners, credit providers and the judiciary, educating other stakeholders and drafting new documentation. Any losses incurred by those who initially neglected to become sufficiently familiar with the new law or to comply with it (such as lessors who lost ownership to their assets because they were unaware of the need to register or simply failed to do so) might be regarded as a transitional cost to the losing party but overall are a zero-sum game because there is an offsetting gain to another party.

[79] The number of registrations has been estimated by extrapolating the available data. Since registration is not mandatory and many secured creditors choose not to register (and also because a single registration can cover multiple transactions), the number of secured transactions entered into would be far greater than the number of registrations.

advocating for the reforms.[80] Justice Blanchard, later of the New Zealand Supreme Court and also in his then capacity as a senior commercial lawyer, was a member of the committee established by the Law Commission that endorsed the proposed reforms and prepared draft legislation.[81] Justice Hansen, the judge who sat on the first New Zealand PPSA decision (*Graham v Portacom New Zealand Ltd*),[82] was the president of the New Zealand Legal Research Foundation, a private law reform body that had published as long ago as 1970 what could claim to be the catalyst for the New Zealand reforms[83] and which hosted symposia and presented seminars on the new regime.

Portacom and other early cases involved disappointed owners testing the extent to which their traditional ownership rights were impacted by the PPSA.[84] As such, they dealt not with difficulties in the legislation but with bringing to the fore core doctrinal issues including the nature of a security interest and the extent to which a debtor could convey to a third-party buyer or subsequent secured party a greater interest than the debtor had itself contracted for. There are no great surprises in these cases; their value lies in the demonstrated willingness of the courts to acknowledge the conceptual changes brought about by the legislation and to apply the appropriate foreign jurisprudence. In *Portacom*, Justice Hansen, noting that the New Zealand Act was modelled on the North American counterparts and that the North American authorities had direct application in New Zealand,[85] applied Canadian judicial and academic analysis to the effect that the legislation had redefined traditional ideas of ownership and required a fresh approach based not on a common law *nemo dat quod non habet* analysis but on an application of the statutory rules.[86]

The decision in *Portacom* was reinforced by the subsequent High Court and Court of Appeal decisions in the *New Zealand Bloodstock* litigation where a lessor once more failed to comply with the simple statutory formalities required to protect its claim to the leased assets and was consequently defeated by a competing security interest.[87] As with *Portacom*, this outcome would not have followed under the *nemo dat* rule of the prior law.

One of the hallmarks of personal property securities litigation in Canada has been the willingness of the courts not only to apply foreign precedents but also to look to academic commentary to help to interpret the legislation. Doing so

[80] J Farrar and M O'Regan, *Reform of Personal Property Security Law* (Wellington, Law Commission, 1988).

[81] A Personal Property Security Act for New Zealand (Wellington, Law Commission, 1989).

[82] *Graham v Portacom New Zealand Ltd* [2004] 2 NZLR 528.

[83] S Riesenfeld, *The Quagmire of Chattels Security in New Zealand* (Auckland, Legal Research Foundation, 1970).

[84] For example, see also the first Court of Appeal decision on the legislation: *Waller v New Zealand Bloodstock Ltd* [2006] 3 NZLR 629.

[85] [2004] 2 NZLR 528 at [20].

[86] ibid at [22]–[28].

[87] *Waller v New Zealand Bloodstock Ltd* [2005] 2 NZLR 549 (High Court) and [2006] 3 NZLR 629 (Court of Appeal).

has greatly facilitated the development of the law. Although *Portacom* is an endorsement of this approach, in the Court of Appeal decision in *Bloodstock* it is possible to discern some reluctance to rely unequivocally on Canadian authorities and New Zealand commentaries. The majority at one point opined: 'Our decision turns on the legislation adopted by the Parliament of New Zealand'.[88] Nevertheless, any such reluctance has not been evident in more recent cases and the use of foreign cases and foreign and local commentaries has allowed the law in New Zealand to develop in a reasoned and consistent fashion.

Those few cases that have strayed from accepted PPS concepts are generally those that fail to consider the appropriate PPS learning, be it local or foreign precedents or commentary. The status of lessors under the PPSA was well settled by the *Portacom* and *Bloodstock* decisions but despite these authoritative decisions a more recent High Court decision reverted to a traditional analysis and failed to recognise properly that the PPSA has redefined a lessor's property rights. In the case of *Hughes and Hughes v Fea and Heenan*, without reference to any New Zealand or foreign authority or commentary, the Court, using reasoning that, with respect, is inapt for PPS legislation, held that the particular lessor's interest did not fall within the statutory definition of a security interest because it had existed prior to the execution of the lease.[89] If this reasoning took hold, it would undermine the Act's inclusion of all forms of title-based security interests (because the owner will invariably have held title prior to entering into the impugned transaction) and, in the author's respectful opinion, is clearly incorrect. While this case may be regarded as a wayward decision in the face of the earlier strongly reasoned decisions of the High Court and Court of Appeal, it is a timely reminder of the need always to bear in mind the conceptual changes introduced by Article 9-derived legislation and to ensure that all stakeholders are well educated about them.[90]

From the start, the courts at all levels have mostly had no trouble recognising and applying the conceptual changes wrought by the PPSA. Typically, the courts

[88] [2006] 3 NZLR 629 at [76]. More curiously, the majority placed a good deal of emphasis on the English Law Commission's 2002 Consultation Paper No 164 *Registration of Security Interests: Company Charges and Property other than Land*: see [2006] 3 NZLR 629 at [72].

[89] [2013] NZHC 2863 at [18]. At [16] the judge stated a lease was a security interest only if it 'gave' the lessor an interest in personal property. This wrongly conflates the statutory wording in s 17(1) of 'created *or provided for*' and ignores the express reference to leases in s 17(3).

[90] The New Zealand experience seems to be that those cases that expressly refer to these matters, and that cite appropriate precedent or commentary, tend to produce more reliable outcomes. In Australia, the concerns of the leasing industry identified in Mr Bruce Whittaker's *Review of the Personal Property Securities Act 2009 Interim Report*, 31 July 2014 appear largely to stem from a lack of awareness by industry of the implications of the reforms due to insufficient training. See also the Australian Review Final Report at 3.1. There is room to debate whether in Australia the training opportunities were inadequate or whether stakeholders simply failed to engage with the process but either case emphasises the need for comprehensive training and education both leading up to the implementation of the reforms and afterwards until they have bedded in. Unlike in Australia, in New Zealand, since the early decisions in *Portacom* and *New Zealand Bloodstock*, there is little evidence of ongoing angst within the leasing industry and even in *Portacom* and *Bloodstock* it seems likely that the lessors were aware of the new regime but were testing its boundaries, whereas in Australia there appears to be genuine ignorance in at least some sectors of the business community.

have also successfully dealt with any operational issues that have arisen and where this has not been the case the matter has generally been promptly rectified by the Court of Appeal. For example, in the author's respectful opinion there were initially some surprising rulings on the important question of what constituted a sale in the ordinary course of business of the debtor.[91] Although under the PPSA this is in large measure a question of fact, the guidance given by the Court of Appeal in the leading case of *StockCo Ltd v Gibson* has now largely settled the relevant legal principles.[92] As far as the author is aware, there has only been one issue that has given rise to a significant divergence of opinion in the High Court and that has not yet been considered by the Court of Appeal. This involves merely a procedural point, though an important one, concerning debtor challenges to allegedly inappropriate registrations.[93] It is also noteworthy that although one section of the PPSA has been considered by the Supreme Court,[94] no significant PPSA issue has yet been sufficiently contentious to warrant appeal to that Court.

I. Conclusion

It is the view of the author that the New Zealand Personal Property Securities Act is a great improvement on the prior New Zealand law (which in large measure mirrored the current English law). A survey of practitioners reinforces this assessment. Barely 3 per cent of practitioners surveyed preferred the prior regime. This is hardly surprising. The PPSA is based on the well-tested North American model that has its genesis in Article 9 of the American Uniform Commercial Code. It is conceptually coherent and designed to achieve sensible commercial outcomes. For the vast majority of transactions, its application is easy. Inevitably, there are some hard cases but these tend to be where the parties have chosen to employ novel and complex transactions or which otherwise concern unusual circumstances.

New Zealand could have chosen a less comprehensive reform. Although it may have been possible to implement a partial reform, New Zealand reformers were convinced by the logic of Article 9. It was believed that lesser reforms would not have yielded the same gains. Treating alike all transactions that functioned as security and not perpetuating illogical distinctions based on the form

[91] This is important because under s 53 of the PPSA, a sale by the debtor in the ordinary course of business effectively extinguishes a security interest in the asset sold. It is one of the key provisions of the Act that replaces the old floating charge jurisprudence but under the PPSA the ordinary course of business is a more limited concept than it was under floating charge law. The cases on this issue are analysed elsewhere by the author: see Gedye, 'Financing transactions structured as sales of goods' (2013) 25 *New Zealand University Law Review* 1076 and Gedye (n 20).

[92] [2012] NZCA 330.

[93] See, for example, *Working Capital Solutions Holdings Ltd v Pezaro* [2014] NZHC 1020.

[94] Section 95, dealing with the priority of a creditor who receives payment of a debt, was considered in *Stiassny v Commissioner of Inland Revenue* [2012] NZSC 106.

of the transaction or whether or not the debtor happened to be incorporated made good sense. Consistent with Article 9, the PPSA logically brings within its purview title retention arrangements that function as secured transactions but, at the same time, it preserves the priority status that title-based financiers enjoyed under the prior law (provided that they adhere to some basic formalities). The Act permits a comprehensive all-assets security that is clearly superior to the equitable floating charge and that is available to incorporated and unincorporated debtors. While all-assets security interests can easily be drafted to encompass both real and personal property, the legislation itself only applies to the latter. It is difficult to see how it could be otherwise under the Torrens title-based real property regime that operates in New Zealand.

Local policy choices (such as fine tuning when buyers defeat security interests and the greater emphasis given in Australasia to the time of registration as a priority point) can easily be accommodated by Article 9-derived regimes. But any departures from tried and true precedent legislation should be adequately justified and fully explained and documented, an ideal not entirely achieved in New Zealand. Australia similarly failed to justify or explain properly many of the drafting innovations in its PPSA but that country wisely stipulated for a comprehensive review of the new regime to be carried out within three years. In New Zealand, it is disappointing that no formal review is planned and there is apparently no agenda for remedying drafting defects.

Some New Zealand innovations have been well received but others remain controversial. In particular, there is ongoing debate over whether allowing unperfected security interests to be effective in insolvency is warranted. This again points to the desirability of a formal process, missing in New Zealand, for monitoring the successes and shortcomings of any reform of this magnitude.

It is not only the formal law that is important in this area. The proper functioning of the registration regime is also critical. The Article 9 concept of notice registration provides a number of benefits and the New Zealand iteration is highly regarded and generally works well. However, further enhancements could be made. Any future review of the New Zealand regime should include a consideration of how collateral should be described when registering and should revisit the choice of exact match searching functionality.

Enough time has now elapsed since the PPSA was implemented to assess how the courts have dealt with the regime. Although there is still the occasional wayward decision where the court fails to apply PPS concepts properly, overall the New Zealand experience has been very positive. The courts have generally had no difficulty in applying the conceptual and operational aspects of the new law and any divergent views that have arisen at first instance have generally been promptly settled by the Court of Appeal.

Throughout the reform process, the New Zealand initiatives were widely supported by law reform agencies, the profession and even members of the judiciary. When the PPSA first became operational, there were some concerns expressed by lessors who discovered that they could no longer merely rely on traditional ownership rights and that compliance with additional formalities was required to preserve their traditional status. Two of the early cases involved such lessors testing the boundaries of the new law. But since then, any such fears seem to have dissipated as title retention suppliers have become familiar with the regime's requirements. The mindset initially adopted in New Zealand by some lessors and the more vociferous and ongoing opposition apparent in Australia from some players in the equipment leasing industry highlight the vital role that education plays in transitioning to an Article 9-derived regime. It seems that in Australia businesses and other stakeholders are not yet sufficiently informed.

Although generally well done, the New Zealand reform process was not perfect in every respect. Inadequate consideration was given to the explanation and drafting of some of the New Zealand innovations and insufficient care was taken to ensure consistency with other legislation. But stakeholder engagement and support was high throughout and the vital educative function was more successful than appears to be the case in Australia. Every indication suggests that while improvements could certainly be made to the new regime, few would wish to return to the old law.

7

Australian Secured Transactions Law Reform

DAVID BROWN

A. Background and Context

The Personal Property Securities Act 2009 (Cth) (PPSA) came into operational effect on 30 January 2012.[1] It established a single national scheme and register. Australia is the only federal jurisdiction to have achieved this. Before this, the law was a patchwork of Commonwealth and State legislation, common law and equity. Much commercial legislation is at State and Territory level. On the other hand, intellectual property, bankruptcy and maritime law are federal matters.[2]

The prior law derived from a number of sources. The common law landscape was familiar to English readers. Pledges and liens existed as possessory forms of security, as well as chattel mortgages and charges. Mortgages and charges, both legal and equitable, existed; priority depended largely on the equitable doctrine of notice, and the rule in *Dearle v Hall*.[3] The floating charge existed, with a system of registration of company charges and priority almost identical to the English Companies Acts.[4] As in England and Wales, the concept of retention of title evolved and was subject to similar judicial limitations.[5]

The federal landscape was inevitably more complex than in the UK. Most States and Territories required registration of motor vehicle security, hire purchase

[1] Section 306, ss 310–318 Personal Property Securities Act 2009 (Cth) ('PPSA'); Personal Property Securities (Migration Time and Registration Commencement Time) Determination 2011(Cth).

[2] Patents Act 1990 (Commonwealth 'Cth'), Trade Marks Act 1995 (Cth), Designs Act 2003 (Cth), Plant Breeder's Rights Act 1994 (Cth), Admiralty Act 1988 (Cth), Shipping Registration Act 1981 (Cth), Bankruptcy Act 1966 (Cth), Corporations Act 2001 (Cth).

[3] *Dearle v Hall* 38 ER 475; (1828) 3 Russ 1 (ChD). The rule is now enshrined in Australian property legislation, eg s 15 Law of Property Act 1936 (South Australia 'SA').

[4] Corporations Act 2001 (Cth), Chapter 2K (now repealed). *Whitton v ACN 003 266 886 Pty Ltd* (1996) 42 NSWLR 123.

[5] *Associated Alloys Pty Ltd v ACN 001 452 106* (2000) 202 CLR 588.

agreements, bills of sale and chattels security.[6] However, between States, there were differences of definition, coverage and effect. In addition, for corporate debtors, the national law required registration of company floating charges, and fixed charges over certain collateral.[7] Registration of ships and intellectual property are Commonwealth matters. The Australian consumer law contains a code of obligations which also impacts on credit and security.[8] The latter legislation, as well as that governing corporations, and now the PPSA, are examples where States and Territories have 'referred' their law-making power to the Commonwealth, enabling the latter to enact national law.[9] This involves negotiation and inevitable compromise, as discussed below.

Thus, the rules varied, depending upon the type or location of debtor, the type or location of the collateral, and the form of the transaction—for example, whether a charge, pledge, lease or retention of title arrangement. With the introduction of the PPSA, at least 70 State, Territory and Commonwealth Acts or provisions were repealed, and 40 existing registers closed.[10] Most important in volume and economic significance were motor vehicle security registers, and the Register of Company Charges.

B. History and Legislation

Secured transactions law reform has been mooted in Australia since the 1970s.[11] In the early 1990s, various State Law Reform Commissions and the Australian Law Reform Commission (ALRC) tackled the subject, and an ALRC Interim Report was published; although they agreed on the need and direction for reform, there was no consensus with regard to the model.[12] In 1995 the Commonwealth

[6] eg Bills of Sale Act 1886 (SA); Goods Securities Act 1986 (SA), Stock Mortgages and Wool Liens Act 1924 (SA).

[7] Section 262 Corporations Act 2001 (Cth) (now repealed).

[8] National Consumer Credit Protection Act 2009 (Cth) sch 1.

[9] Corporations Act 2001 (Cth) National Consumer Credit Protection Act 2009 (Cth), Consumer and Competition Law Act 2010 (Cth), PPSA. For referral legislation, see eg Personal Property Securities (Commonwealth Powers) Act 2009 (New South Wales 'NSW').

[10] *Explanatory Memorandum, Personal Property Securities Act 2009*, Commonwealth of Australia, Outline, p 10. For the list of replaced registers, see www.ppsr.gov.au/AbouttheRegister/TransitionalRegisters.

[11] Committee of the Law Council of Australia, Report to the Attorney-General for the State of Victoria on Fair Consumer Credit Laws (1971) ('Molomby Committee'). See further E Sykes and S Walker, *The Law of Securities*, 5th edn (Sydney, Law Book Co, 1993) 548–600; A Duggan and D Brown, *Australian Personal Property Securities Law* (Sydney, LexisNexis, 2012) 16–19.

[12] Queensland Law Reform Commission and Law Reform Commission of Victoria, *Personal Property Securities Law: A Blueprint for Reform* (QLRC Discussion Paper No 39 and VLRC Discussion Paper No 28, August 1992). Australian Law Reform Commission and NSW Law Reform Commission, *Personal Property Securities*, ALRC Discussion Paper No 52, NSWLR Discussion Paper No 28 1992). ALRC, *Personal Property Securities*, Interim Report No 64, 1993.

Attorney-General issued a Discussion Paper, and a conference was organised by the late Professor David Allan.[13] No further action was taken for some years, but Professor Allan continued work, with a further conference out of which came a draft Bill in 2002.[14]

These discussions did not occur in a domestic vacuum. International bodies such as the United Nations Committee on International Trade Law and the European Bank for Reconstruction and Development produced important guidelines,[15] and the influence of individual North American jurists was clear.[16] Closer to home a major political driver was the Memorandum of Understanding on Commercial Law with New Zealand, first signed in 2000.[17] New Zealand enacted the PPSA in 1999, and it came into force in May 2002.[18] In 2005, Professor Allan's work engaged the attention of the Commonwealth Attorney-General.[19] This led to a round of consultation papers,[20] and was taken up by the incoming government. A draft Bill was circulated in 2008 and after extensive Parliamentary and inter-governmental discussion of various versions,[21] the PPSA received royal assent in December 2009.[22]

The operational commencement of the PPSA and Personal Property Securities Register (PPSR) was postponed a number of times, to allow the legislative and technological machinery of both government and major users to be prepared, particularly the PPSR.[23] On 30 January 2012 the PPSA took full effect, the PPSR opened for new entries, the existing registers were closed, and the subordinate legislation, consequential amendment legislation, and two sets of amendments to the Corporations Act, all came into force.[24] The government 'migrated' over

[13] Attorney-General's Department, Discussion Paper, Personal Property Securities: A National Approach, Canberra, January 1995; Report of the Bond University Personal Property Securities Law Workshop, 14–17 December 1995.

[14] 'Special Issue: Proceedings of a Workshop on Personal Property Security' (2002) 14(1) *Bond Law Review*.

[15] *Legislative Guide on Secured Transactions Law* (New York, United Nations, 2010) (see Ch 24) chapter X; European Bank for Reconstruction and Development Model Law, 1994 (revised 2004) (See Ch 22).

[16] Submissions to the Australian consultation process included influential ones from leading PPSA experts Professors Ron Cuming, Jacob Ziegel and Anthony Duggan.

[17] Memorandum of Understanding between Australia and New Zealand on Coordination of Business Law, Ministry of Economic Development (New Zealand), Australia Treasury (revised 2010).

[18] PPSA Commencement Order 2002, SR 2002/60. See Ch 7.

[19] See A Duggan and M Gedye, 'Personal Property Security Law Reform in Australia and New Zealand: The Impetus for Change' (2009) 27 *Penn State International Law Review* 655, 657–58.

[20] Standing Committee of Attorneys-General, *Options Paper: Review of the Law on Personal Property Securities*, April 2006, Canberra; *Registration and Search Issues*, Canberra, Commonwealth of Australia, 2006.

[21] Inter-Governmental Personal Property Securities Law Agreement (2 October 2008).

[22] Senate Committee Report, Exposure Draft of Personal Property Securities Bill 2008, March 2009.

[23] The administration of the PPSA and PPSR lies with the Australian Financial Security Authority, within the Attorney-General's Department, see www.afsa.gov.au. However, the PPSR website is www.ppsr.gov.au.

[24] Personal Property Securities (Corporations and other Amendments) Acts 2010, 2011 (Cth), Personal Property Securities (Consequential Amendments) Act 2009 (Cth), Personal Property Securities Regulations 2010 (Cth).

4 million entries from pre-existing registers, so these were already entered on the PPSR immediately before 30 January 2012.[25] This was a major logistical exercise, intended to reduce the burden on secured parties and encourage them to embrace the new system. However, there were significant teething problems, largely stemming from the inconsistency between the data fields and rules for the pre-existing registers compared to those under the PPSA and its Regulations.[26]

The last section of the PPSA prescribed a mandatory review of the operation of the Act to be completed within three years of its commencement.[27] This review was commenced in 2014 and consisted of an Interim Report (requested by the government to focus on the impact on small business), four consultation papers, and a Final Report submitted in March 2015.[28] Reference has been made throughout this chapter to various recommendations in the Final Report.

C. The Scope and Design of the PPSA

(i) Objectives of the Legislation

The discussion in Chapter 1 and that above has focused on the advantages, particularly in the Australian context, of introducing such a system. In the Explanatory Memorandum to the Bill, the government stated that one national register 'would result in more certain, consistent, simpler and cheaper arrangements for personal property securities for the benefit of all parties'.[29] In the recent statutory review of the PPSA, the Final Report noted the three overarching goals as (1) to increase consistency and certainty in secured finance; (2) reduce complexity and cost of secured finance, and (3) enhance the ability of businesses and consumers to use their assets as security, and improve their ability to access cost-effective finance.[30]

The Final Report goes on to suggest that some of the stated advantages have yet to reach their full potential for stakeholders and the wider economy.[31] Nevertheless, as it also acknowledges, the Commonwealth Attorney-General recently stated that the PPSA was a significant factor in Australia improving its ranking in the

[25] Sections 306, 332–334 PPSA; Personal Property Securities (Migration Time and Registration Commencement Time) Determination 2011 (Cth).

[26] R Hope, 'Migrated Security Interests: Lost in Transition' (2011) 34 *University of New South Wales Law Journal* 646.

[27] Section 343 PPSA.

[28] See www.ag.gov.au/consultations/pages/StatutoryreviewofthePersonalPropertySecuritiesAct2009.aspx.

[29] Explanatory Memorandum to the Personal Property Securities Bill, Commonwealth of Australia, p 10.

[30] Review of the Personal Property Securities Act 2009, Final Report, para 2.1.2.

[31] ibid, para 3.3.1.

World Bank's 2013 'Doing Business—Smarter Regulations for SMEs' report.[32] The PPSR is being well used. As at the last available quarter,[33] the Register contained 8.6 million registrations, 50 per cent related to motor vehicles, and 20 per cent to 'all present and after-acquired property'. 2.02 million searches, the highest number for any quarter to date, were conducted.

(ii) Design Issues

A policy decision was taken to provide a two-year 'transitional period', expiring on 31 January 2014; during this period, interests arising under pre-30 January 2012 security agreements would retain their pre-existing priority even if not registered on the PPSR.[34] This was particularly relevant to title-based interests brought within the new definition of security interest, such as retention of title, and some leasing and consignment arrangements. Prior to the PPSA, these did not generally have to be registered anywhere. However, there is sometimes argument on the facts as to whether an interest (for example under a retention of title clause contained in a purchase order) arose under a new agreement at the date of the order, or under a pre-30 January 2012 'master' agreement containing the terms of trade. This has been a source of ongoing dispute notwithstanding the end of the transitional period.[35]

It may be questioned whether a transitional period, or such a lengthy one, was needed, given that, as events transpired, there was more than a two-year gap between the PPSA's enactment and operational commencement. Other jurisdictions have not had such a generous approach.[36] On the other hand, despite the 'grace period', there is still concern that small businesses and others are still unaware of the PPSA, or its relevance to them.[37]

Another design issue relates to the relationship between the PPSA and other legislation. In relation to a number of Commonwealth registers, for example patents, registered designs and ships, which exist for other purposes than recording security interests, it was decided to retain parallel registration of those interests.[38] It will be possible, though optional, to register security interests on these registers as before, but priority and enforceability will require registration on the PPSR.

[32] ibid and see media release, George Brandis QC, Attorney-General, *Review of Personal Property Securities Act*, 4 April 2014, www.attorneygeneral.gov.au/Mediareleases.

[33] June 2015, see www.afsa.gov.au/about-us/ppsr/ppsr-statistics/ppsr-quarterly-statistics.

[34] Sections 307–308, 311, 320–324 PPSA.

[35] *Central Cleaning Supplies v Elkerton* [2014] VSCA 92, *Industrial Progress Corporation v Wilson* [2013] WASC 225; D Brown, 'PPSA and Transitional Provisions: When the ROT Starts' (2012) 12 *Insolvency Law Bulletin* 208–11.

[36] eg in New Zealand there was merely a six-month transitional period which was confined to permitting re-registration of pre-PPSA registered company charges, chattel or motor vehicle securities, s 193 PPSA (NZ).

[37] *Interim Report, Review of the PPSA*, Canberra, Commonwealth of Australia, 2014.

[38] eg patents (Patents Act 1990 (Cth)), ships (Shipping Registration Act 1981 (Cth)).

While they are separate unconnected registers, some degree of harmony exists in that the 'serial number' for the PPSA as specified in the PPS Regulations 2010 is the same number as that used in the other registers, for example the number issued by IP Australia for designs, patents and plant varieties.[39] Australia has recently ratified the Cape Town Convention on Security Interests in Mobile Equipment, and its Protocol on Aircraft Security.[40] Its international online register of security interests in aircraft takes precedence over the PPSA, and the appropriate definitions in the PPSA were originally drafted to align with the Protocol's terminology. Two further design issues concerning the PPSA's interaction with consumer credit legislation, and insolvency legislation, are discussed below.[41]

Lastly, there is an obvious difference between the Australian PPSA and its overseas comparators, namely the length of the legislation. For example, the Saskatchewan PPSA has 75 sections, whereas the Australian one has 343. Even allowing for provisions dealing with constitutional issues, it is still more than twice as long. No rational explanation exists for the extent of this departure from Canadian and New Zealand models in this respect. The Final Report on the statutory review does comment that, in building on overseas precedents, the 'architects of the Act may have tried too hard to be helpful. They tried to produce a "best of breed" by picking the best elements and then adding more detail in an effort to explain more clearly what exactly is required'.[42] The statutory review has noted the length of the PPSA as contributing to the complexity of the system, and among other improvements, has recommended that the constitutional provisions, and those establishing the Registrar's office and functions, be removed to separate legislation.[43]

(iii) Terminology

The PPSA uses the concept of 'grantor' for most purposes connected with giving a security interest, whereas most other PPSAs only use the term 'debtor'.[44] The grantor of a security interest may not always be the debtor, for example in relation to a guarantee. In addition, since the PPSA covers 'deemed' security

[39] Designs Act 2003 (Cth), Patents Act 1990 (Cth), Trade Marks Act 1995 (Cth), see Personal Property Securities (Consequential Amendments) Act 2009 (Cth) sch 2, and PPS Regulations 2010, reg 2.1.

[40] Australia ratified the Convention and Protocol on 26 May 2015, effective from 1 September 2015, having earlier passed legislation to enable this, and to amend the PPSA and other legislation. see International Interests in Mobile Equipment (Cape Town Convention) Act 2013, and International Interests in Mobile Equipment (Cape Town Convention) Consequential Amendments Act 2013 (Cth); UNIDROIT 'Cape Town' Convention on International Interests in Mobile Equipment, adopted 2011. Aircraft Protocol. See *Official Commentary on the Convention on International Interests in Mobile Equipment and the Protocol thereto on Matters specific to Aircraft Equipment* (UNIDROIT, revised edn 2008); R Goode, 'Security Interests in Mobile Equipment: Lawmaking Lessons from the Cape Town Convention' (2014) 35 *Adelaide Law Review* 59.

[41] Section H.

[42] Final Report, 30.

[43] Final Report, para 9.4.1.1.

[44] Section 10 PPSA, 'debtor', 'grantor'. *cf* s 2(1)(m) Personal Property Security Act 1993, SS 1993 CP-6.2 (Saskatchewan).

interests, such as leases where there is no financing element, it is not appropriate to refer to the lessee as the debtor, absent a creditor–debtor relationship. Hence, in chapter 4 (Remedies) a distinction is made, where relevant, between the 'debtor' and the 'grantor'.[45]

(iv) Scope of the PPSA

The PPSA only extends to personal property, not land. There are some borderline cases in relation to creation and transfer of interests in land, but the PPSA attempts to create a bright line by excluding dealing in the latter from the Act.[46]

As mentioned above, the achievement of agreement for a national PPSA came at a cost—there were a number of areas where the States wished certain collateral to remain outside of the regime. It was agreed that these could be reviewed in future, and this was one of the purposes behind the statutory review provided for in the Act. The review has now recommended that all of these three aspects be re-examined by State and Commonwealth governments with the general objective of bringing them within the scope of the Act.[47]

The first of these was fixtures. While at common law, title to a fixture follows the land,[48] under some PPSA regimes, security interests in chattels continue notwithstanding that they become affixed and would otherwise satisfy the common law test. This is the case in Canadian PPSAs, and requires interaction between the land registration system and PPS register so as to alert those dealing with the land.[49] However, in Australia, land title is a State matter,[50] and despite the clear advantages of making finance readily available on goods that become affixed, the States were not prepared to include fixtures in the PPSA regime, so goods that can be shown to be 'affixed' are excluded.[51]

Water rights are subject to State regulation, depending on the source and nature. In Australia, given scarcity, the agricultural and domestic demands upon water, and the interstate flow of major rivers, these rights are extremely controversial. At the time the PPSA was proposed, a government Commission had suggested a national register of water rights, so these, defined very broadly, are for now excluded from the PPSA.[52] The review recommends that those which are *not* covered by the national register of water rights should be subject to the PPSA.[53]

[45] For example, s 123 uses 'debtor' in relation to default; sub-s 121(4) requires the 'grantor' to be given notice to enforce liquid assets.

[46] Sub-section 8(1)(f)(i), (ii) PPSA.

[47] Final Report, para 4.5.10.2 (fixtures); 4.5.9 (water rights); 4.4.6 (statutory licences).

[48] *TEC Desert Pty Ltd v Commissioner of State Revenue* (2010) 273 ALR 134 (High Ct of Australia).

[49] Section 36 PPSA (Saskatchewan).

[50] See, eg, Law of Property Act 1936, Real Property Act 1886 (SA).

[51] Sub-section 8(1)(j), s 10 ('fixtures') PPSA. See *Cancer Care Institute of Australia Pty Ltd (Administrator appointed)* [2013] NSWSC 37 (linear accelerator installed in dedicated radiography suite, and subject to retention of title clause registered on PPSR, was held a chattel).

[52] Sub-sections 8(1)(i), 8(5) PPSA.

[53] Final Report, para 4.5.9.

Lastly, and of great economic significance, the PPSA excepts statutory licences and similar rights.[54] On the other hand, 'private' commercial licences, for sale, use, manufacture or distribution of goods or services, or intellectual property licences, are within it, provided that the licence is 'transferable', even if consent to transfer is required.[55] The question of whether licences are 'property' has always been a boundary issue between contract and property,[56] but the PPSA has adopted the approach of Saskatchewan and British Columbia in enacting that commercial licences, at least, are property for PPSA purposes.[57] The reluctance of Australian governments to permit statutory licences and rights to be collateral within the PPSA is regrettable, and probably stems from an unwarranted belief that to do so would be to cede regulatory control over the field of economic activity. The Supreme Court of Canada in *Saulnier v Royal Bank of Canada*[58] made it clear that the secured party could still take the licence 'warts and all', thereby preserving its economic value subject to the regulatory regime. Given the range of areas in Australia which are governed by statutory licensing, including mineral extraction, farming quota, fishing and taxi licences, the inability of small businesses to offer these as secured collateral is in need of review. The recent statutory review emphasised the importance of this to contribute to the PPSA achieving its full potential, and called on State and Commonwealth governments to revisit this issue.[59]

The method by which the above types of collateral are excluded from the PPSA is through section 8. Yet that section covers two types of case, and some other provisions appear to be there for the avoidance of doubt. First, it excludes certain types of collateral.[60] Secondly, it excludes certain types of security interest, such as pledging chattels with a pawnbroker.[61] Thirdly, it excludes proprietary arrangements which would probably not amount to PPSA security interests anyway, such as liens and rights arising by operation of law, 'Quistclose' trusts, and set-off.[62]

(v) The Scope of 'Security Interests'

The heart of the PPSA is the definition of 'security interest' in section 12(1):

> [A]n interest in personal property provided for by a transaction that, in substance, secures payment or performance of an obligation (without regard to the form of the transaction or the identity of the person who has title to the property).

[54] Sub-section 8(1)(k), s 10 PPSA.
[55] Section 10 ('licence').
[56] Ch 6 B.
[57] eg sub-s 2(1)(w), (z) PPSA 1993 (Saskatchewan).
[58] *Saulnier v Royal Bank of Canada* [2008] SCR 166, discussed at Ch 6 B.
[59] Final Report, para 4.4.6.
[60] Sub-section 8(1(j), (jb), (k) PPSA.
[61] Sub-section 8(1)(ja).
[62] Sub-section 8(1)(c), (d), (h).

The wording applies a functional test and makes clear that it is substance not form, and that it even extends to agreements where the creditor retains title.

While stated to be only examples, section 12(2) gives a list of familiar pre-PPSA forms of transaction that, assuming the in-substance test is also met, fall within section 12(1). These include the fixed charge, floating charge, pledge and chattel mortgage, but also include 'conditional sale agreement (including an agreement to sell subject to retention of title)', hire purchase agreement, consignment, lease of goods, assignment, transfer of title, and a flawed asset arrangement. While the inclusion of examples may have been intended to make users comfortable with the transition, it is doubtful if this is necessary or helpful. It may even perpetuate usage of those 'old' terms. Furthermore, some of the section 12(2) examples have caused confusion. For example, trust receipts may be commercially relevant in North America, but not in Australia. The difference between an 'assignment' and 'transfer' of title is unclear, and flawed asset agreements, whose categorisation as security interests was controversial even prior to the PPSA, have had the controversy enhanced by their inclusion, particularly given the exclusion in section 8 of 'set-off' arrangements.[63]

(vi) 'Deemed' Security Interests

There are three situations where, irrespective of whether or not a transaction secures payment or performance of an obligation, the PPSA 'deems' a security interest to arise.[64] The justification is that these are situations where it is difficult to tell in a particular case whether or not an in-substance security interest exists, and also where 'apparent ownership' of property in the possession of the debtor might mislead searchers, absent registration.[65] The first of these 'deemed' interests for PPSA purposes is consignments. Consignments are listed in section 12(2) as an example of an 'in-substance' security consignment within section 12(1). The term 'consignment' itself is not defined in the Act. Nevertheless, for the purpose of deeming certain consignments to be security interests under section 12(3) the Act defines a 'commercial consignment'. This will apply where goods are delivered for sale, lease or other disposal by a consignor and both parties are entering into such transactions in the ordinary course of their business, unless it is known to creditors that the consignee takes goods on consignment.[66]

[63] D Loxton, 'One Flaw Over the Cuckoo's Nest—Making Sense Of The "Flawed Asset Arrangement" Example, Security Interest Definition and Set-off Exclusion in the PPSA' (2011) 34(2) *University of New South Wales Law Review* 472.

[64] Sub-section 12(3) PPSA.

[65] See A Duggan and D Brown, *Australian Personal Property Securities Law* (Sydney, LexisNexis, 2012) 53–56.

[66] Sub-section 12(3)(b), s 10 ('commercial consignment') PPSA. The statutory review also recommended that the exemption for the 'regularly engaged' test should be where it is or should reasonably be known to anyone, not just creditors, that the consignee takes goods on consignment for sale, lease or disposal, para 4.3.4.2.3.

The effect of inclusion in section 12(3) is that most regular consignment arrangements will be security interests, irrespective of whether any credit element was given by the consignor. There was some discussion in the statutory review about whether it was really necessary to have this category of deemed security interests, as consignments are not the basis of vehicle financing in Australia, and the visual arts sector submitted that they should be exempted from it. Nevertheless, the review recommended that there should not be any such ad hoc exemption, as it would be generally known in the arts community that galleries generally often receive goods on that basis, and further it was confirmed that the category of 'commercial consignment' should remain as a deemed security interest. There has been at least one PPSA consignment case already, so it clearly is relevant in Australia, as most submitters testified.[67] Secondly, assignments of accounts or chattel paper are 'deemed' security interests, the transferee being the secured party.[68]

Lastly, the PPSA 'deems' leases or bailments of goods to be security interests if the lease is for a term of either more than one year, or capable of or actually lasting more than one year.[69] The Final Report of the statutory review stated that this category garnered the most submissions, and that there was 'surprise and dismay', in particular from lessors of operating leases, that they were subject to the Act.[70] It noted that lease financing is worth $4.9 billion a year for motor vehicles and plant and equipment, and just under half of that was operating leases. Using the review's criterion of 'significant disruption' if this entire category were *not* included, and endorsing the publicity and characterisation reasons which have led overseas PPSA regimes to include such leases, the review concluded that the commercial impact was so great that the PPSA should continue to apply to some of these leases, and noted that most respondents agreed with that view.[71] In relation to leases for indefinite terms, however, the review acknowledged that this was a genuine concern for the hiring industry, where small businesses argued that the burden of compliance was overwhelming. There was no logic in excluding fixed terms for less than one year but subjecting indefinite ones which *may* endure beyond one year. Rather than recommend that indefinite terms of less than one year be excluded, which would have been a 'cleaner' solution, it recommended a 'wait and see' rule, so that the lease would become subject to the PPSA once it did in fact last for more than one year.[72] It may be that the generous 24-month transitional period has only served to prolong the adjustment in the leasing sector,

[67] *Re Arcabi Pty Ltd* [2014] WASC 310.

[68] Sub-section 12(3)(a) PPSA. It is noted elsewhere that the statutory review has recommended removal of references in the Act to 'chattel paper'.

[69] Sub-section 12(3)(c), s 13.

[70] Para 4.3.5.1.1.

[71] Final Report, para 4.3.5.12.

[72] Para 4.3.5.4.3.

and the review's recommendations in relation to education, particularly for small businesses, combined with the above recommendation, should see a medium-term adjustment of business practice in the hiring sector.

In the case of serial-numbered goods prescribed by the PPS Regulations, a lease for 90 days or more (for example a motor vehicle) or which could last more than 90 days in the ways described above, wasl also a security interest within the PPSA until recently.[73] But this category has been removed, from 1 September 2015[74]—as the new government wished to identify regulatory 'red tape' and some sectors of the plant hire industry lobbied to remove this category of short-term arrangements. It had no equivalent in other PPSA jurisdictions. The statutory review has also endorsed the removal.[75] To come within any of the above categories as a 'PPS lease' the lessor or bailor must also have been regularly engaged in the business of leasing or bailing goods.[76]

One unusual extension from the situation in Canada is the reference to 'bailment'. The concept appears to derive from the New Zealand PPSA. In the New Zealand Court of Appeal case of *Rabobank v McNulty*[77] it was found that a horseracing syndicate that had left a stallion with a stud for agistment and training was not regularly engaged in that business and so there was no bailment. While that element is common to the Australian definition, the Court noted additional wording in the Australian PPSA, whereby the bailee must provide value for the bailment.[78] In *Rabobank*, the payment was made by the bailor, for agistment and other services. This has proved confusing in Australia; for example, it has been debated whether it brings storage, warehousing and agistment arrangements within the definition of 'security interest'. While it is suggested that this is not the case,[79] the recent statutory review has recommended removal of references to bailment, and it is thought that this would cure the uncertainty without any corresponding detriment.[80]

'Deemed' security interests are shielded from the effects of non-registration of security interests should the debtor become insolvent.[81] Further, chapter 4, Enforcement, does not apply to them, because it provides default remedies for the creditor–debtor relationship, and most of the chapter's provisions would therefore be inappropriate.[82]

[73] Sub-section 13(1)(e) PPSA.
[74] Personal Property Securities Amendment (Deregulatory Measures) Act 2015.
[75] Final Report, para 4.3.5.2.
[76] Sub-section 13(2) PPSA.
[77] *Rabobank v McNulty* [2011] NZCA 212.
[78] Sub-section 13(3) PPSA.
[79] See *re Arcabi Pty Ltd.* [2014] WASC 310
[80] See Ch 7G and Final Report para 4.3.5.3.
[81] Sub-section 268(1) PPSA.
[82] Section 109.

D. Attachment and Enforceability

The concept of attachment has been discussed in Chapter 2.[83] Mention will be made of particular Australian features. First, under section 19(2), a security interest usually attaches when the grantor has rights in the collateral or the power to transfer rights, and either value is given or the grantor does an act by which the security interest arises. As in other jurisdictions, the meaning of 'rights in the collateral' is not spelt out, so that the question of whether possessory rights will suffice is left to case law.[84] However, section 19(5) provides some assistance in that it states that 'a grantor has rights in goods that are leased or bailed to the grantor under a PPS Lease, consigned to the grantor or sold under a conditional sale agreement (including an agreement to sell subject to retention of title) when the grantor obtains possession of the goods'.

In relation to floating charges, the PPSA makes it clear that while parties can agree that a security interest attaches at a later time than that laid down for attachment in section 19(2), a reference to a floating charge is not, without more, an agreement that the security interest attached at a later time than that.[85] There are 'statute of fraud' evidential requirements for enforceability of the security interest against third parties, as discussed in Chapter 1. In Australia these extend to acts which reasonably appear to be done by the grantor with the intention of adopting or accepting the writing.[86] This is thought to cover such matters as a 'course of dealing' in retention of title, for example.

E. Perfection

(i) Perfection Generally

The concept of perfection has been discussed in Chapter 2.[87] There are three statutory methods.[88] The principal one in terms of practical relevance to most security interests, and to the centrality of the PPSR, is registration. Possession

[83] See Ch 2 B.

[84] See, eg, *iTrade Finance Inc v Bank of Montreal* [2011] 2 SCR 260; *Gray v Royal Bank of Canada* (1997) 143 DLE (4th) 179 (BCSC), *JS Brooksbank and Co (Australasia) Ltd v EXFTX Ltd* (in rec and liq) [2009] NZCA 122. See also B Whittaker, 'The Scope of "Rights in the Collateral" in Section 19(2) of the PPSA—Can Bare Possession Support Attachment of a Security Interest?' (2011) 34 University of New South Wales Law Journal 524.

[85] Sub-section 19(4) PPSA.

[86] Section 20(1)(b).

[87] Ch 2 B.

[88] Section 21 PPSA.

is still relevant for pledges and contractual liens: actual rather than constructive possession is required, and repossession does not qualify.[89] This is important because continuous perfection is required to be shown at the relevant date for priority purposes[90] and can be achieved through a combination of perfection methods.[91]

The third method of perfection is control. However, it does not apply to *any* collateral. It is only available for ADI accounts (banks and other authorised deposit takers),[92] various financial property such as shares, intermediated securities, cheques and some letters of credit, and satellites and space objects.[93] In relation to each of these categories of collateral, the PPSA sets out a special meaning for 'control',[94] though it approximates to the right to give instructions or direct the transfer of the collateral. It is notable that the New Zealand PPSA functions without control, and the concept has been adopted from Article 9 of the revised United States Uniform Commercial Code, which for the first time brought security interests in cash deposits as original collateral within its scope.[95] The importance of control as a method of perfection in Australia, particularly over bank accounts and financial property, can be seen when we examine priority below.[96]

Lastly, there are some cases of 'temporary perfection', where a grace period is given in which to perfect by one of the above three means, for example on transfer of the collateral.[97]

(ii) Perfection by Registration

The concept of notice filing has been explained in Chapter 2.[98] The PPSA achieves notice filing through a 'financing statement', which is an online form with prescribed data fields for the secured party or its agent to complete.[99] The Australian experience is that this has been a paradigm shift for those familiar with the old system, particularly registration of company charges and other registers where lodgement of a copy of the security instrument was required. There has been a failure by many, particularly insolvency practitioners, to understand the macroeconomic benefits of a notice filing system. Nevertheless, nearly all submissions

89 Sub-section 21(2)(b), and see sub-s 123(4).
90 Sub-section 55(6).
91 Section 56.
92 Section 10 ('The Dictionary').
93 Sub-section 21(2)(c); s 10 ('The Dictionary').
94 Sections 25–29.
95 Section 9-109(a)(1) Uniform Commercial Code (US).
96 Section F.
97 Sub-section 21(1)(a)PPSA. See eg s 22, sub-s 33(2), ss 34, 36.
98 Ch 2 D.
99 Sections 148, 150, 153 PPSA, PPS Regulations sch 1.

to the statutory review opposed a return to instrument filing and the reviewer, rightly in this author's opinion, felt it would be a retrograde step and would increase the burden on secured parties[100] filing.

The PPSA provides that the grantor and other interested searchers, including insolvency practitioners as 'authorised representatives' of the grantor,[101] can call for the secured party to provide a copy of the security instrument, and other details including the outstanding debt and inventory of claimed collateral, and the secured party has 10 business days to provide it.[102] It does not have to respond if there is a confidentiality agreement with the debtor.[103] Failing any response, or any adequate or accurate one, and subject to time extensions by the court, an interested party may apply to court, which has discretion to extinguish the security interest.[104] Despite this procedure, there have been complaints that many secured parties have not responded at all, or expedititously, to such requests, and that the system is thus insufficiently responsive to cope with a vast number of registrations against a debtor, especially in an insolvency situation where there are tight timelines. One counter to this criticism is that prior to the PPSA, it would have been even more time consuming and difficult to ascertain the extent of claims against property in the possession of the debtor. The generous transitional period may have continued the uncertainty for searchers. The statutory review, while reinforcing the point made above that the situation is certainly no worse and arguably better than it was prior to the PPSA, referred the issue to the insolvency policy section of government to consider whether there should be a shorter response period in insolvency cases, with greater finality, for example if no response was received from secured parties within 21 days to a request that they verify their security interest, it would be rendered ineffective.[105]

The procedure for obtaining information about the security agreement is buttressed by the 'amendment demand' procedure, whereby secured parties can be forced to amend the financing statement on the register to reflect the discharge of debt or other changes,[106] and this is supported by recourse to the Registrar if the secured party does not amend the registration within the requisite period. There is a parallel procedure by application to the court, and the current administrative process, with the parallel judicial process, is regarded as unduly complex. The statutory review has recommended that a simpler process along the lines of that in New Zealand be adopted.[107]

[100] Final Report, para 6.11.2.

[101] Section 275, sub-s 275(9) PPSA.

[102] Section 277.

[103] Sub-section 275(6).

[104] Section 280.

[105] Final Report, para 9.2.4.1.3.

[106] Sections 177–178 PPSA.

[107] Sections 179–182. See Final Report, para 6.10.5.8.3. See *Davidson v Registrar of Personal Property Securities* [2015] AATA 649, for an example of an appeal from the administrative process undertaken by the Registrar.

(iii) Registration

An important design issue for the PPSR is the nature of the search results which the chosen system returns.[108] Australia adopted an exact-match search system. The advantage of this is that, it being a national register, and thus a relatively large database, a search will return a more manageable number of results, which can then be followed up as necessary with secured parties or their agents. The chosen system has little tolerance for error, and is supported by a 'waterfall' of registration fields in the PPS Regulations 2010, which put the onus on the secured party to register against the correct grantor name or serial number.[109] A search which cannot be discovered using the relevant search criteria will likely lead to an ineffective registration, so that the security interest loses priority and/or cannot be enforced.[110] While it contains the broader concept of a 'seriously misleading defect' as in Canadian PPSAs, the PPSA provides that any defect in the name or (in consumer cases) serial number, renders the registration ineffective.[111] In all cases of seriously misleading defects, it is provided that it is irrelevant whether anyone is actually misled.[112]

While registration and search against grantor name is the norm, the exception, important in terms of volume of transactions, is serial-numbered collateral. By far the largest category of prescribed serial-numbered property is motor vehicles,[113] but it also includes aircraft, watercraft and various intellectual property rights.[114] Where the property is 'consumer property', registration against these forms of collateral *must* be by serial number. There is no option of registering against the name of the individual. In the case of commercial property, registration *may* be by serial number.[115] The justification given for the inability to register security over consumer property against the name of a grantor is privacy.[116] This does not seem to have been a concern in other PPSA jurisdictions, so may reflect government sensitivity in light of Australian privacy law. But that rationale cannot explain why one can register against the name of an individual for *non*-serial-numbered collateral.[117]

[108] See Duggan and Brown (n 65) 121–23. See also Ch 7 F(ii).

[109] Section 153 PPSA, PPS Regulations 2010, sch 1.

[110] Sections 164–165 PPSA.

[111] Section 165.

[112] Sub-section 164(2).

[113] The definition of 'motor vehicle' in s 10 was narrowed, as from 1 July 2014, by an amendment to PPS Regulations 2010, reg 1.7(2), resulting from complaints that the original definition captured low-powered, low-speed vehicles. Now the motor must be above 200W *and* capable of going above 10 kmh.

[114] Section 10 ('The Dictionary') PPSA and PPS Regulations, sch 1, reg 2.2.

[115] Section 53(1), Table—Item 4.

[116] Personal Property Securities Bill 2009, *Replacement Explanatory Memorandum* (Parliament of Commonwealth of Australia, 24 June 2009), paras 5.7, 5.37. See also s 173 PPSA (protection of privacy on searches against individual grantors).

[117] The anomaly was noted in the statutory review, but no change was ultimately recommended, see Final Report para 6.6.1.3.

The PPS Regulations prescribe a 'waterfall' of criteria to use for ascertaining the name of an individual grantor, corporations, partnerships and trusts.[118] These are supposed to be relatively intuitive and designed to minimise error. Thus, the Australian Company Number (ACN), which all corporations must have and display, is the 'grantor name', as opposed to the incorporated or trading name.[119] In the case of individuals, the usual criterion will be the name given on a driving licence.[120] The rationale is probably that most adults have one, and are obliged to carry it if driving, so would usually have it when entering into any financing transaction in person.[121] It is expected that the Regulations would be known to regular users of the PPSR, and assumed that the grantor data is accessible to them. Practical uncertainty has arisen in relation to trusts behind a corporate structure, for example as to whether to search against the ACN, or the Australian Business Number, used by trading entities for tax and other regulatory purposes,[122] but these problems stem from the nature of trusts. As a trust is not a separate legal entity, the statutory review has recommended that registration should be against the grantor name of the trustee, whether corporate or individual.[123]

The financing statement must specify the collateral under one of a number of prescribed classes.[124] These are fewer than the types of collateral defined under the PPSA. The main collateral categories are 'all present and after-acquired property', 'motor vehicles', 'financial property', 'intangible property', 'agriculture', 'other goods'.[125]

In addition, it is required to select consumer or commercial property.[126] The definition of 'consumer property' for this purpose is property held by an individual other than in furtherance to any degree of an enterprise for which an Australian Business Number is required.[127] (This differs from the approach in chapter 4 of the PPSA, which reflects that in the National Credit Code, and focuses on the use made of the collateral.)[128] In the case of commercial property, the financing statement must state whether or not it is held as inventory.[129] In relation to the data

[118] PPS Regulations, sch 1.

[119] ibid, reg 1.3.

[120] ibid, reg 1.2, Item 3. There are two items prior to this in the hierarchy: first, the name on any transitional register; and secondly, the grantor name as known to a secured party through the Anti-Money Laundering and Counter-Terrorism Financing Act 2006. The statutory review recommends the latter be removed, since searchers would not be able to discover the exact grantor details used internally by banks and other affected secured parties, see Final Report, para 6.7.1.1.

[121] Duggan and Brown (n 65) 125.

[122] Schedule 1, reg 1.5.

[123] Final Report, para 6.7.4.1.3.

[124] Sub-section 153(1), item 4 PPSA; PPS Regulations, regs 1.6 (Definitions), 2.3.

[125] Section 10 PPSA ('The Dictionary'), PPS Regulations, regs 1.6 (Definitions), 2.3.

[126] Sub-section 153(1), Item 4 PPSA.

[127] Section 10. Such a number is required by the Australian Taxation Office.

[128] Section 47, sub-s 109(5) PPSA. (Chapter 4 PPSA covers 'Remedies'.) See also PPSA (New Zealand) s 16(1).

[129] Sub-sections 148(a), 153(1) PPSA, item 8; PPS Regulations, sch 1, cl. 4.1, Item 1.

required to be entered on a financing statement by a secured party, the statutory review acknowledged that the current requirements were overly complex, particularly for non-legally trained users. A number of the fields which are required to be entered do not provide information to most searchers that is of any great consequence or material use, or only address one specific situation in the legislation. The review has made a number of recommendations which 'declutter' the financing statement by removing these fields (for example the requirement to specify whether the collateral is 'inventory', whether it is 'commercial' or 'consumer' property, whether or not it is a purchase-money security interest, whether or not 'control' is being asserted over the collateral, and the optional field to specify whether or not there is 'subordination').[130] Furthermore, the review found that the collateral classes could be reduced.[131]

One of the most criticised aspects of the design of the PPSR has been that other than 'all present and after-acquired property', the system only permits of a single class of collateral to be specified on one financing statement.[132] This sometimes necessitates multiple filings, and the cost quickly mounts up for commercial secured parties. The statutory review recommended that this impediment be reversed.[133]

Lastly, the PPSR is used by governments and enforcement agencies as a depositary for other information about the collateral than that about security interests. It is a convenient way of notifying searchers of restrictions placed upon particular collateral. These relate to proceeds of crime orders, impounding of vehicles, and other criminal or regulatory steps against personal property.[134]

(iv) Liability

One unique, and arguably draconian, feature is that civil liability is imposed on a secured party or its agent who registers or maintains a financing statement covering collateral where there is no belief on reasonable grounds that the collateral was, or is still, subject to a secured obligation.[135] Given that the PPSA has the 'amendment demand' system,[136] it is not immediately obvious why this civil liability is required. Its purpose may be to deter vexatious registrations, but the uncertainty in some areas as to whether or not something is a 'security interest', for example bailment or consignment, means that this potentially exposes unsophisticated or poorly advised parties to liability, and may deter them from

[130] Final Report, para 6.2.
[131] ibid, para 6.3.3.
[132] Section 153(1), item 4(d).
[133] Final Report, para 6.3.3.
[134] Section 154 PPSA, PPS Regulations, regs 5.3–5.4, sch 2.
[135] Section 151 PPSA.
[136] Section E(ii).

protecting their secured position. It has not proved necessary in other PPSA jurisdictions, and the answer to any risk of vexatious registrations may lie in strengthening or using the powers of the Registrar to keep the PPSR 'cleansed' of obsolete or vexatious registrations.[137]

F. Priority

(i) Default Priority Rules

One of the principal advantages of the PPSA is that it contains a simpler and clearer set of priority rules from the web of different rules stemming from statute, common law and equity.[138] Section 55 sets out priority rules, which are 'default' in two senses. First, they only apply where no other PPSA priority rule applies (for example, section 62 in relation to purchase-money security interests). Secondly, secured parties can 'contract out' of the statutory priorities through subordination.[139]

The section 55 rules generally apply a 'first in time' rule, meaning first to register, or otherwise perfect.[140] In that respect, they are no different to other Article 9-based systems. Nevertheless, there are two features worthy of specific comment. First, provision is made for priority between two unperfected security interests, namely that the order of attachment will prevail.[141] Secondly, the PPSA does not state the point in time at which priority disputes should be determined by the rules in section 55. In Canada it has been held that it is when the security interests 'come into conflict';[142] for example, the time when a receiver is appointed under a security interest. A later registration will not be able to achieve a better priority than it had at the date of receivership. This view has been approved recently in New Zealand,[143] and the statutory review has recommended that the Act be amended to make that view clear.[144]

Lastly, perfection by control will prevail over other perfected security interests irrespective of time of their perfection.[145] Where more than one security interest is perfected by control, the earlier so perfected prevails.[146] Security interests over

[137] Sections 184–185 PPSA.

[138] See text to n 2.

[139] Sub-section 18(1), s 61 PPSA.

[140] Note that first in time means first to perfect or register, not first to *create* the security interest, as is the general rule, with exceptions, in the UK system or common law generally.

[141] Sub-section 55(2) PPSA. Arguably that issue could have been left to the common law, but the result will not always be the same, given the technical definition of 'attachment' in the PPSA, see s 19.

[142] *Sperry v Canadian Imperial Bank of Commerce* (1985) 17 DLR (4th) 236 (ONCA).

[143] *Gibbston Downs Wines Ltd v Perpetual Trust Ltd* [2012] NZHC 1022.

[144] Final Report, para 7.7.1.3.

[145] Section 57 PPSA.

[146] Sub-section 57(2).

ADI accounts[147] are in an even stronger position, as in the United States, albeit that the Australian position is more extensive than in the United States.[148] The Australian PPSA confirms that a security interest may be taken by a secured party over its own obligation.[149] Moreover, where an ADI has perfected a security interest by control over an account held by that ADI, this is automatically perfected and has priority over any other interest in the ADI account.[150] This provision, combined with the ability to perfect solely by control, represents a major concession to the banking sector, largely at the expense of suppliers claiming perfected security interests in proceeds paid into the account. There is no official Australian explanation for this, but the US Commentary would suggest that it was regarded as necessary to the smooth operation of banking and financial markets transactions.[151] The statutory review endorses the automatic effect of the priority, and this was supported by most submitters. The review recommends that the government should consider further the appropriateness of automatic priority in all the categories of financial collateral that have such priority through control—however, in the case of an ADI's control over an ADI account, the reviewer's expressed view is that the automatic priority is justified, partly because it reflects the widely known set-off and combination rights which banks have always had, and therefore there is no need for publicity through registration.[152]

(ii) Purchase-money Security Interests

The concept of a purchase-money security interest (PMSI) in Article 9-based systems has been elucidated in Chapter 2. Satisfaction of the requirements for a PMSI provides a special priority rule in the Australian PPSA, reversing the 'first in time' default rule.[153]

The definition of a PMSI covers the traditional 'seller PMSI' such as a supplier of goods on retention of title, or other title-based security or deemed security over goods, namely leased or bailed goods amounting to a 'PPS Lease', and goods on commercial consignment.[154] Secondly, it extends to 'lender PMSIs' where funds

[147] An ADI is an authorised deposit-taking institution under the Banking Act 1959, and an ADI account is one held at such an institution which is payable on demand or some future agreed time, s 10 ('Dictionary').

[148] Sections 9-312(b)(1), 9-327(1) Uniform Commercial Code (US). See ch 5C.

[149] Sub-section 12(3A) PPSA. In English law, the House of Lords held in *Re BCCI (No 8)* [1998] AC 214 that a charge-back could validly be created, *cf* the earlier case of *Re Charge Card Services* [1987] Ch 150, and see G McCormack, *Secured Credit in English and American Law* (Cambridge, Cambridge University Press, 2004) 249–57 for the history and discussion of charge-backs.

[150] Sections 21(2)(c), 25, 75 PPSA.

[151] See Duggan and Brown (n 65) 104, 152–53. See ch 5C.

[152] Final Report, paras 5.3.7.3.3, 7.7.4.1.3.

[153] Section 62 PPSA.

[154] Sub-section 14(1)(a), (c), (d).

are advanced for acquisition of the secured collateral by a grantor.[155] In case of any conflict, a seller PMSI will take priority over a lender PMSI.[156] However, the PMSI definition in Australia is closely tied to the particular goods which were acquired, or their proceeds.[157] It does not extend to cross-collateralisation, ie does not give a PMSI over any non-purchase-money obligations or collateral. Thus the 'all-monies' clause approved in *Armour v Thyssen*,[158] would not be covered by a PMSI, and to the extent of the all-monies obligation, would simply be a 'normal' security interest. The statutory review has recommended that this be amended, noting that this is the case with Article 9 of the US Uniform Commercial Code.[159] The amendment deals with the difficulty of identifying inventory and thus evidencing whether it related to unpaid stock, and thus extends the PMSI to non-serial-numbered items of inventory, if not separately identifiable. Neither does a PMSI extend to personal, domestic or household collateral, other than serial-numbered collateral, and the statutory review points out that since in any event this exclusion did not cover serial-numbered property, it was of limited use and it was difficult to see a policy justification for it; there was speculation that it may have been based on the view that directors' guarantees would be undermined if they could grant a PMSI for other finance, but the reviewer took the view that this was not a strong enough reason for departing from the policy that a PMSI should be recognised where there was a facilitation of acquisition of new assets for the grantor.[160]

An unusual feature is that, in order to be effective as a PMSI, it must be perfected by registration as such.[161] In some jurisdictions, written notice of the PMSI registration must be given to perfected secured parties.[162] The latter approach may be more effective to alert them.[163] There are also timing requirements for PMSI registration in Australia. Where the collateral is inventory, registration must occur prior to the grantor taking possession, (if not goods, then prior to attachment).[164] In the case of non-inventory, there are 15 business days from possession or attachment.[165] This latter concession is designed to recognise the difficulty for secured parties of processing larger equipment finance transactions, but is probably not necessary given the PPSR is almost always open for registrations.

Lastly, as in New Zealand,[166] a policy decision was taken that in a priority dispute between a PMSI claimant (such as inventory financier) to an account

155 Sub-section 14(1)(b).
156 Section 63.
157 Sub-sections 14(1), (3), (4), (7).
158 *Armour v Thyssen* [1991] 2 AC 339 (HL, Scot).
159 Final Report, para 7.7.8.5.3.
160 Sub-section 14(2A) PPSA.
161 Sub-sections 62(2)(c), 153(1), item 7; PPS Regulations, sch 1, reg 3.1.
162 See, eg, s 34(3) Personal Property Security Act 1993, SS 1993, c.P-62 (Saskatchewan).
163 See further Ch 7D.
164 Sub-section 62(2) PPSA.
165 Sub-section 62(3).
166 Section 75A PPSA 1999 (NZ). On the policy in New Zealand, see D Brown, 'The New Zealand Personal Property Securities Act 1999' in J de Lacy (ed), *The Reform of UK Personal Property Security Law: Comparative Perspectives* (Abingdon, Routledge Cavendish, 2010) 328–65, 357–58.

as proceeds, and a non-PMSI claimant to the account as original collateral (for example a factor), the latter would prevail notwithstanding the usual 'superpriority' of the PMSI.[167] In order to obtain this priority, the non-PMSI claimant must give notice to the PMSI claimant 15 business days or more prior to registration or attachment, whichever is earlier. While this policy choice is controversial, it was necessary to at least protect accounts financiers from the effects of the PMSI 'superpriority' over inventory proceeds, though this could have been achieved by using the default priority rule.[168] The statutory review pointed out that this provision still only gives the receivables financier priority over earlier *PMSIs*, not over other earlier registered security interests, irrespective of whether or not they are held by the same inventory financier or some other secured party.[169] The Final Report therefore recommended that the receivables financiers should obtain 'superpriority' over *any* earlier registered security interests held by the *same inventory financier*, not just PMSIs.[170] This is because otherwise, the inventory financier who had a non-PMSI for other obligations owed, could frustrate the policy behind section 64 by registering it over 'accounts' to secure its claim to the proceeds of inventory, and thus defeat the policy behind section 64.

(iii) Proceeds

Although the PPSA applies to a broader spectrum of 'security interests' than previously, one of the advantages in the extended ability of secured parties to claim proceeds of original collateral. A key element is section 32, which facilitates the express or implied licence by the secured party to the grantor to deal with collateral, as in the case of the floating charge over inventory.[171] In such a case, the secured party's interest will be limited to the 'proceeds'. Where there is no authorisation for the dealing, the secured party will have a security interest in the original collateral and the proceeds up to the value of the collateral at the time it became proceeds.[172]

The definition of 'proceeds' requires a 'dealing' with the original collateral, but there is then automatic attachment of the security interest to any direct or indirectly derived proceeds which are 'identifiable and traceable'.[173] While this otherwise preserves common law and equitable rules regarding identification and tracing, the PPSA removes a major obstacle by obviating the need to show any fiduciary relationship.[174] Moreover, the definition of 'proceeds' extends to

[167] Section 64.
[168] See Duggan and Brown (n 65) 177.
[169] Final Report para 7.7.9.
[170] ibid para 7.7.9.3.3.
[171] Sub-section 32(1) PPSA.
[172] Sub-section 32(2).
[173] Sub-section 31(1).
[174] Sub-section 31(2).

insurance payments and compensation for damage to the collateral, irrespective of whether these could be said to derive from a 'dealing' with the original collateral in the sense of some form of exchange taking place.[175] Where proceeds are paid into an ADI account, an ADI will have perfected by control over that account, and this will defeat a registered secured party in respect of a claim to the collateral in the account as proceeds.[176] Note also the comments in the previous paragraph about the 'superpriority' over proceeds in the situation where receivables financiers give the prescribed notice to registered inventory financiers.

To avoid multiplication of proceeds claims and to recognise the information available to searchers, the grantor must have an interest in the proceeds or the power to transfer rights in them to the secured party.[177]

Perfection over proceeds is facilitated under the PPSA and PPS Regulations.[178] The latter, combined with a design feature of the financing statement, mean that proceeds claims are by default selected as 'all present and after-acquired property', which covers all possible proceeds.[179] If they are in the form of cash, insurance or compensation, or if of the same type as the original collateral (for example vehicle trade-ins), then they are automatically perfected irrespective of any reference to the proceeds on the PPSR.[180] Lastly, if none of the above apply, there is a 'temporary perfection' period whereby the secured party can register in respect of the proceeds within five business days from attachment of the security interest to the proceeds.[181]

(iv) Accessions and Commingling

Another advantage of the PPSA for suppliers is the relative ease, compared with the common law, of continuing a security interest into an accession or commingled goods.

In relation to accessions, generally at common law once a component was determined to be an accession it was regarded as part of the 'host'. There was judicial uncertainty at common law as to the test for defining an accession.[182] The PPSA makes two important changes. First, it provides a clear definition, namely 'goods that are installed in, or affixed to, other goods, unless both the accession and the other goods are required or permitted to be described by serial number'.[183]

[175] Sub-section 31(1)(b).
[176] Section 75.
[177] Sub-section 31(3). See R Cuming, C Walsh and R Wood, *Personal Property Security Law*, 2nd edn (Toronto, Irwin, 2012) 563–64.
[178] Section 33, sub-s 153(1), item 4(d) PPSA; PPS Regulations sch 1, reg 2.4.
[179] Sub-sections 33(2), (3).
[180] Sub-section 33(1)(c).
[181] Sub-sections 33(2), (3).
[182] *Industrial Acceptance Corporations v Firestone Tire & Rubber Co. of Canada Ltd* [1971] SCR 357.
[183] Section 10 PPSA.

An example of the latter would be aircraft engines and the aircraft itself. Secondly, once a component falls within the definition, the PPSA states that security interests in the component continue into the accession.[184] The common law rule was that a component which could be removed without causing damage did not become part of the whole. The PPSA reflects that by providing that security interests in accessions may be enforced by removal of the collateral, albeit on notice.[185] The PPSA provides rules for determining priority between security interests in the component and any property interests in the whole.[186] The ability to continue a security interest into an accession is not wholly dependent on perfection. Provided the security interest in the component attached before it became an accession, it will have priority over interests in the whole.[187] Perfection becomes important, however, to assure priority over subsequent perfected interests in the whole.[188]

In relation to commingling,[189] the PPSA again improves on the common law and makes it easier for suppliers to make a claim to a mass where their inputs can no longer be separately identified. While proportionate property interests could be claimed where homogeneous goods were combined, such as grain or oil,[190] the common law was less generous in treatment of inputs into processed or manufactured items.[191] This was particularly relevant to retention of title clauses where generally, the courts regarded 'aggregation clauses' purporting to retain title to an input as 'charges' over the newly made or processed item, and as often as not, these charges were not registered under the corporations legislation.[192] The PPSA theoretically improves the position of suppliers of inputs on credit. It currently covers manufactured, processed, assembled or commingled goods, where the identity of the input is lost in the mass, or else it is not economically practicable to restore the input to its original state.[193] This latter wording goes further than some PPSA jurisdictions, for example by extending to an expensive chemical reversal process, or where the costs of investigating and identifying ownership of many components is prohibitive.

The PPSA provides special priority rules for security interests in these situations. The main provision is that a security interest in the goods continues into the mass.[194] Perfection in the inputs is sufficient for perfection in the mass.[195] There

[184] Section 88.

[185] Sections 92–97, 123.

[186] Sections 90–91.

[187] Section 89, sub-s 91(a).

[188] Section 90, sub-s 91(b).

[189] Commingled goods 'includes goods mixed with the same kind of goods' (s 10, 'The Dictionary'). The PPSA, in ss 99–103, uses the term 'processed or commingled goods' as a general heading, but 'commingled' is also mentioned in s 100 distinctly from 'manufactured, processed or assembled' goods.

[190] *Re Gillie, ex parte Cornell* (1996) 150 CLR 110 (FCA).

[191] *Associated Alloys v ACN 001 45 106 Pty Ltd, (in liq)* [2000] HCA 25.

[192] *Re Peachdart* [1984] Ch 131.

[193] Section 99 PPSA.

[194] Sub-section 99(1).

[195] Section 100.

are two notable features of these rules. First, to prevent a windfall, they are limited to the value of the secured debt at the time the input was commingled; at least that is the case where there are competing security interests in the mass.[196] Secondly, where there are competing perfected security interests over the inputs, or competing unperfected interests, they share the mass proportionate to the size of their respective secured obligation, again limited to the value of inputs, and with the obligation limited by the value of the goods at the time of the input.[197] The rules do not provide for recognition of the value of non-collateral inputs such as the labour and materials of the grantor or others. While these rules in theory provide an improved position to input suppliers from that at common law, there are still practical and commercial issues of evidencing such claims, especially through to proceeds of sale of the mass. In addition, the current rules are complex, and the statutory review has recommended some degree of simplification.[198] It notes that the rules seem to have been designed with processed, rather than commingled, goods in mind. Therefore it proposes separation of the provisions governing processed goods from those for mixed or manufactured goods. In the latter case, the situation should be much as it was at common law, namely that interests in the mass should be proportionate to the contributions to the mass. If enforcement became necessary, the secured party would need to separate its share of homogeneous goods. In the case of processed goods, the rule regarding the 'cap' on recovery should be recast as limited to the amount recoverable by the secured party on the input, rather than, as currently, cast as a limit on 'priority'.[199] Lastly, the current rules do not deal with priority disputes between security interests over the input and those over the mass, and it recommends that the default priority rules apply in this situation, as if it was a priority conflict in relation to the same collateral.[200]

Lastly, in recognition of the economic importance of agricultural finance in Australia, there is special priority for crop security interests.[201] Many States and Territories had crop liens and similar interests prior to the PPSA, which replaces them with unified rules. Growing crops are 'goods' under the PPSA.[202] Security interests in crops will not have priority over existing registered mortgages or other interests over the land, since a land title search would have revealed the position.[203] Conversely, perfected security interests over the crops will not be affected by any later dealings with the land, since a PPSR search would have revealed the interest.[204]

[196] Section 101.
[197] Section 102.
[198] Final Report, para 7.10.1.3.
[199] ibid, para 7.10.3.1.3.
[200] ibid, para 7.10.3.2.3.
[201] Section 84 PPSA.
[202] Section 10 ('The Dictionary'), s 84A.
[203] Sub-section 84(1).
[204] Sub-section 84(2).

Priority between perfected interests over growing crops will be given to secured obligations which helped the crops to be produced, for example supply of fertiliser, provided the security agreement is made during growth or the crops are planted within six months.[205] A similar priority is given for perfected security interests over livestock enabling the livestock to be fed or developed, such as hormone suppliers.[206] This is a special priority, similar to a PMSI, though the priority is not over the input, but the crop or livestock to which it is applied. The statutory review has queried whether this priority, which may be making it harder to raise bank or receivables finance, is necessary. The majority of submitters wanted to remove it, but the review recommended that there should be further consultation with affected stakeholders.

(v) Third Parties and Transfers of Collateral

We have seen that if dealings with secured collateral are unauthorised, the secured party has a continued security interest in the collateral, as well as in any proceeds from it. However, in some circumstances, set out in Part 2.5 PPSA, third parties receiving this collateral by way of sale or lease may 'take free' of the security interest. A buyer or lessee for value will always take free of an *unperfected* security interest.[207] But further rules apply to *perfected* security interests.

A number of the taking-free rules apply to a 'buyer or lessee'. Neither 'buyer' nor 'sale' is defined in the PPSA, so the better view is that it must take its meaning from the Sale of Goods Acts. This view, taken in Canada and New Zealand,[208] has recently been confirmed in Australia.[209] In that case, customers under layby sales arrangements were not buyers under State law, so in contrast to outright sale transactions, they were not able to take free of the security interest. In relation to lessees, 'taking free' here must mean that the lessee takes the limited leasehold interest from the lessor who granted the security interest in question.[210] A buyer or lessee of serial-numbered collateral such as motor vehicles, unless as inventory, will take free of a registered security interest if a search by serial number would not have disclosed the security interest.[211] Thus, any omitted or incorrect serial number will be fatal against transferees, even though in the case of commercial property, registration against serial number is not mandatory.[212] A second rule, inaccurately known as the 'garage sale' rule, enables transferees of domestic

[205] Section 85.

[206] Section 86.

[207] Section 43.

[208] *Royal Bank of Canada v 216200 Alberta Ltd* (1987) 51 Sask R 47 (SKCA); *Orix New Zealand Ltd v Milne* [2007] NZHC 507.

[209] *Warehouse Sales Pty Ltd (in liq) v LG Electronics Australia Pty Ltd* [2014] VSC 644 at [47], [73] Sifris J.

[210] Cuming, Walsh and Wood (n 177) 377.

[211] Section 44 PPSA.

[212] Sub-section 153(1), Item 4.

low-value, non-serial-numbered goods to take free of security interests.[213] Thus it does not cover vehicles. It can apply to sellers who are dealers. The limit in Australia is $5,000 market value, though if the transferee has actual or constructive knowledge[214] that the transfer is a breach of the security agreement, or that the market value is greater, she will not be able to take free.[215] Where a non-dealer buys or leases a vehicle from a licensed dealer, the PPSA protects the buyer/lessee, as some State legislation did previously.[216] Provided the purchaser/lessee does not know of a breach of the security agreement, she should not have to search the register in such cases.

The most important 'taking-free' rule is the 'ordinary course of business' rule. The precise wording of the phrase in section 46 PPSA should be observed. It is that a 'buyer or lessee takes free of a security interest given by the sellor/lessor if the sale/lease was in the ordinary course of the seller or lessor's business of selling/leasing property of that kind'. The words 'of that kind' do not appear in overseas equivalent provisions,[217] and could be argued to suggest a narrower approach in some cases.[218] That view has received judicial support.[219] Nevertheless, early indications are that the Australian courts will draw upon New Zealand and Canadian precedent in this area.[220] The phrase 'ordinary course of business' has been used in a number of contexts, for example in floating charges and in former legislative provisions on unfair preferences. The New Zealand Court of Appeal[221] implied that the insolvency cases were relevant in the PPSA context, but an Australian court has correctly pointed out that the context and wording is different, in particular the need to focus on 'course of the sellor/lessor's business', not business generally.[222] Lastly, overseas cases reveal a policy tension between viewing this as a buyer protection policy, to obviate the need for searches in ordinary dealings, and as a policy to protect secured parties from unauthorised dealings.[223] It will be interesting to see how the Australian courts approach this tension, if called upon to do so.[224] Section 46 and its overseas equivalents have generated more case law than most areas of the PPSA.

213 Section 47.

214 Section 297 PPSA defines 'constructive knowledge', but not 'actual knowledge'. See Duggan and Brown (n 65) 211–12. There are also provisions dealing with knowledge of bodies corporate and other entities, and presumptions in case of family or associated entities, ss 298–299.

215 Sub-section 47(2)(b), (c).

216 Sub-section 45(3) PPSA, PPS Regulations 2010, regs 2.1, 2.2.

217 Section 53 PPSA(NZ).

218 See Ch 7 C(ii).

219 *Warehouse Sales Pty Ltd (in liq) v LG Electronics Australia Pty Ltd* [2014] VSC 644 at [83].

220 ibid at [82]–[98].

221 *StockCo Ltd v Gibson and Stiassny* [2012] NZCA 330 at [43]–[44].

222 *Warehouse Sales Pty Ltd (in liq) v LG Electronics Australia Pty Ltd* [2014] VSC 644 at [81].

223 *Agricultural Commodity Corp v Schaus Feedlots Inc* [2001] OJ No 2908 (Ontario), cf *StockCo Ltd v Gibson and Stiassny* [2012] NZCA 330 at [49].

224 See *Warehouse Sales Pty Ltd (in liq) v LG Electronics Australia Pty Ltd* [2014] VSC 644 at [30] where Sifris J acknowledges the balance in the buyer protection provisions.

The relationship with other laws is relevant here. Taking free from licensed vehicle dealers is an example of an attempt to preserve aspects of pre-PPSA law, and there is a further provision in relation to purchase of vehicles, to enable a purchaser to rely on a search undertaken within a 'day and a half' of the purchase, which derives from chattel securities legislation.[225] While many Acts have been repealed as a consequence of the PPSA, there are other State provisions concerning 'buyer in possession' and 'mercantile agent' protections in the sale of goods and similar legislation, which are still arguably relevant.[226] In some States, sale of goods legislation has been amended to state that nothing in it shall affect the PPSA.[227] However, the PPSA provides that other legislation may operate, provided it is not inconsistent with the PPSA, in which case the latter prevails.[228]

A number of further rules in the PPSA are either expressed as 'taking-free' rules or as priority rules, and are designed to parallel or reflect pre-PPSA law, and preserve the flow of commerce and financial transactions. The most important one relates to currency, so that a recipient of cash takes free provided they have no actual or constructive knowledge of a security interest over it (note that the knowledge is of the interest, not of breach of the security agreement, as in some of the other taking-free rules).[229] Similar rules apply to investment instruments such as shares, and negotiable instruments reflecting the 'holder in due course' provisions in the Cheques Act 1986.[230] Lastly, section 69 states that a creditor receiving certain payments of debts, other than by cash or pre-authorised debit or transfer, will have priority over a secured party. It applies provided the creditor recipient does not have actual or constructive knowledge of a breach of security agreement (again note that this is different from, say, the knowledge requirement for currency).

G. Remedies

Chapter 4 of the PPSA deals with enforcement against the grantor following default. The range of forms of security and quasi-security interest now within 'PPSA security interests' traditionally have their own remedies, either in the contract, or in relevant statute or common law. The form of transaction dictated, to some extent, the remedy that existed pre-PPSA. For example, foreclosure was a feature of the mortgage transaction. Some State legislation also regulated

[225] Sub-section 45(1) PPSA; sub-s 8(3)(b) Registration of Interests in Goods Act 1986 (NSW).

[226] See Duggan and Brown (n 65) 214–17.

[227] See *Warehouse Sales Pty Ltd (in liq) v LG Electronics Australia Pty Ltd* [2014] VSC 644 at [36], Sifris J pointing out that Victoria does not have such an amendment, but New South Wales and New Zealand do.

[228] Section 254 PPSA.

[229] Section 48.

[230] Section 70 (negotiable instruments); ss 49–51 (investment instruments and intermediated securities).

contractual termination of hire purchase contracts.[231] The PPSA provides a unified set of enforcement provisions.

While the existence of chapter 4 provides a useful set of remedies provisions modelled on the mortgage, it was not thought that this should be mandatory, at least for non-domestic collateral. Most of the provisions are therefore capable of exclusion or modification by the parties.[232] There are the following exceptions: chapter 4 contains a general duty to act in good faith and in a commercially reasonable manner in relation to exercise of remedies arising under chapter 4.[233] This obligation, which in this broad form had no previous parallel in secured transactions law, is in any event narrower than the equivalent in Canada and New Zealand, where it applies to the whole of the PPSA, not just to the remedies provisions.[234] Secondly, section 131 provides for a separate duty to obtain the best price reasonably obtainable in the circumstances at time of sale—this reflects the standard in the previous case law, and mirrors section 420A Corporations Act 2001 (Cth), which applies to receivers of corporate property. There is much useful case law which can be drawn upon in that context. Thirdly, section 140 provides a statutory order of distribution, albeit that it largely reflects what would happen absent the PPSA.

The PPSA provides that the enforcement provisions in chapter 4 do not apply to receivers of corporate property,[235] as there are already overlapping statutory duties in Part 5.2 Corporations Act 2001 (Cth). While New Zealand takes the same approach, this is in contrast to Canada, where a receiver is within the definition of 'secured party' for the purposes of the enforcement provisions.[236] The resulting situation in Australia is confusing, since receivers of the property of an individual must still comply with Part 4 PPSA, and 'controllers' (defined in the Corporations Act, Part 5) who are *not* receivers are also still bound by the relevant provisions of Part 4 PPSA.[237]

Another unique aspect of the PPSA is alignment with the National Credit Code (NCC).[238] Part 5 regulates enforcement of security over consumer collateral. The NCC applies only if the obligations secured are for 'personal, domestic or household purposes', irrespective of whether the secured collateral is used for those purposes.[239] While the PPSA applies to a security interest to which the NCC applies, clearly there is overlap between the two regimes. Both, for example, provide for notices of disposal of the collateral to be given to the grantor/debtor, and the obligation to obtain market value or the best reasonable price.[240] However, the provisions are not identical, for example regarding time periods. The PPSA and Regulations

231 eg Hire Purchase Act 1959 (Victoria).
232 Sections 115, 110 PPSA.
233 Section 111.
234 Section 65 PPSA 1993, SS 1993 c P 6.2 (Saskatchewan), s 25 PPSA 1999 (NZ).
235 Section 116.
236 Section 56 PPSA (Saskatchewan).
237 Section 116.
238 National Consumer Credit Protection Act 2009, sch 1.
239 National Credit Code, ss 4, 5 and 7.
240 See PPS Regulations 2010, reg 4.1, Items 1 and 2.

ameliorate this situation by providing that compliance with the relevant provision of the NCC will be deemed compliance with the parallel provision in Part 4 PPSA, and vice versa.[241] If there is still any inconsistency, the NCC prevails.[242] The statutory review recommends that the government should consider a much simpler approach that whenever the NCC applies, Chapter 4 of the PPSA does not.[243]

Chapter 4 provides for seizure 'by any method permitted by law', provided there has been default, though the latter is not statutorily defined.[244] Equivalent collection methods are defined for intangible property including accounts, and for seizing crops and livestock.[245] Chapter 4 also provides for the right to dispose of collateral on notice, and provides that third parties receive good title from the secured party disposing of the collateral.[246] A statutory power akin to foreclosure, a right to retain collateral, subject to no objections being received, is provided,[247] and the secured party has a reasonable period of time to store collateral and consider whether to dispose of or retain it.[248] Section 142 provides that at any time prior to disposal, the grantor or other secured party may redeem the collateral by payment of the secured obligation and expenses. This right may be excluded in commercial arrangements.[249] This is in contrast to some North American PPSA statutes, which assume this right is fundamental; however, there is strictly no right to redeem in relation to the PPSA statutory security interest, unlike with a common law mortgage.

Lastly, there is a statutory right of reinstatement, on a once-only basis, where the grantor must pay all arrears and expenses, cure other defaults, and may then recover its interest in the collateral, with reversal of any acceleration clause.[250] The security agreement stays on foot, unlike with redemption. This provision can also be excluded for commercial collateral.[251]

H. Insolvency Law

Insolvency legislation is contained in the Bankruptcy Act 1966 (Cth), and Corporations Act 2001 (Cth) Part 5. The PPSA was designed to be 'insolvency neutral'.[252] Nevertheless, jurisdictions have taken varying approaches to achieving

241 Sub-section 119(2) PPSA, PPS Regulations reg 4.1.
242 Section 258.
243 Final Report, para 8.1.11.3.
244 Section 123(1) PPSA.
245 Sections 120–121, sub-s 123(2).
246 Sections 128–133.
247 Sections 134–136.
248 Section 125.
249 Sub-section 115(1)(q).
250 Section 143.
251 Sub-section 115(1)(r).
252 Explanatory Memorandum to Personal Property (Corporations and other Amendments) Act 2010, Commonwealth of Australia, para 1.2.

this. In Canada the PPSA is provincial legislation, while insolvency is federal law.[253] In New Zealand, that problem does not exist, but nevertheless Parliament decided to take a relatively laissez-faire attitude to the relationship between the PPSA and insolvency legislation[254] Thus, no attempt was made to amend the terminology in the Companies Act other than in relation to priority debts.[255] In Australia, initially the Bill did not address this, but the government later decided to attempt to harmonise the terminology and some of the operative provisions in the insolvency legislation.[256]

(i) Effect of Failing to Perfect a Security Interest

The most important issue is the effect of failure to perfect a security interest before the grantor becomes formally insolvent. In Australia, as with Canada, the policy in the corporations legislation in relation to company charges, and in certain other statutes, was continued in the PPSA, namely that unregistered charges, motor vehicle or chattel securities would be void on insolvency, but that is now widened to encompass PPSA security interests, and also to include bankruptcy alongside liquidation, voluntary administration and deeds of company arrangement.[257] In the case of personal insolvency, inexplicably this does not extend to rehabilitation procedures, such as debt agreements and personal insolvency agreements.[258]

Two peculiar features of this issue in the Australian context are worthy of comment. First, as in Canada, and as was the case pre-PPSA with unregistered company charges and some motor vehicle and other chattel securities, unperfected security interests will effectively lose out to unsecured creditors on formal insolvency.[259] However, rather than stating that an unperfected security interest would be 'void' or 'not effective', section 267 PPSA states that the security interest 'vests in the grantor'.[260] The effect seems to be the same, and insofar as the rationale for the language can be gleaned, it may be a concern with rendering title-based claims such as leases 'void' or 'ineffective'.[261] Nevertheless, this has not been a concern in Canada.[262]

[253] R Wood, 'The Structure of Secured Priorities in Insolvency Law' (2011) 27 *Banking and Finance Law Review* 25.

[254] Companies Act 1993 (NZ) and Insolvency Act 2006 (NZ). See *Dunphy v Sleepyhead Manufacturing Co Ltd* [2007] 3 NZLR 602 (Court of Appeal).

[255] Section 312, Seventh Schedule, Companies Act 1993 (NZ). See *Strategic Finance Limited v Bridgman and Sanson* [2013] NZCA 357.

[256] Personal Property Securities (Corporations and other Amendments) Acts 2010 and 2011 (Cth); Personal Property (Consequential Amendments) Act 2009 (Cth).

[257] Section 267 PPSA.

[258] Under Parts IX and X Bankrutpcy Act 1966 (Cth).

[259] See s 20 PPSA 1993 (Saskatchewan).

[260] Sub-section 267(2). See also s 588FL Corporations Act 2001 (Cth).

[261] See Ch 7 F.

[262] *Re Giffen* (1998) 155 DR (4th) 332 (SCC). The New Zealand PPSA does not render unperfected security interests void or ineffective on insolvency.

Secondly, a layer of unnecessary complication, possibly from the motive of not wanting to interfere too much with existing corporations law, is that alongside section 267 PPSA, the Corporations Act attempts to preserve the idea of the former provision, which rendered unregistered corporate charges void if the instrument was not lodged within 45 days from execution.[263] The amended provision vests the security interest in the grantor if the interest is not registered on the PPS register either within 20 business days from the security agreement, or at least six months prior to the insolvency event.[264] As with the unamended Corporations Act and on the same grounds, there is some discretion for the court to extend the time limit,[265] although this discretion cannot extend beyond the insolvency event, because of section 267 PPSA. This parallel provision in the case of corporate grantors has led to much confusion and the statutory review recommends that it be removed from the Corporations Act.[266] Not all security interests will vest in the grantor in this way. Broadly, it was decided that this consequence would be too draconian for 'deemed' security interests such as non-finance leases and consignments, or non-security account transfers.[267] Nevertheless, if they do not perfect, these types of secured parties may lose priority to other security interests.[268]

(ii) Fixed and Floating Charges

The second aspect of alignment with insolvency law relates to terminology. Wherever the Corporations Act referred to 'charges', 'pledges' or 'liens', amendments have substituted 'PPSA security interests' or 'possessory security interests'.[269] Parliament also anticipated that parties will continue for some time to use the language of fixed and floating charges. Therefore it provided that wherever such terms appear in post-PPSA security agreements or in Commonwealth legislation,[270] they will be interpreted as their PPSA equivalents, for example 'floating charge' will be interpreted as security taken over a 'circulating asset'.[271] The Guide to the relevant Part states that 'these rules are expected to have less relevance over time, as the scheme provided for by this Act provides an alternative to reliance on those

[263] Chapter 2K Corporations Act 2001 (Cth), repealed.

[264] Section 588FL Corporations Act 2001 (Cth). See *In re Carpenter International Pty Ltd (administrators appointed)* [2016]VSC 118. The provision was also moved into the Part of the Act which deals with recovery of property for the benefit of creditors (Part 5.7B), which also includes voidable transactions.

[265] Section 588FM Corporations Act, see *Re Barclays Bank plc* [2012] NSWSC 1095, *In re Cardinia Nominees Pty Ltd* [2013] NSWSC 32, *In re Appleyard Capital Pty Ltd* [2014] NSWSC 782.

[266] Final Report, para 9.2.2.1.3.

[267] Section 268 PPSA, s 588FN Corporations Act 2001 (Cth).

[268] Section 55 PPSA.

[269] Sections 51, 51A, 51B, 51D Corporations Act 2001 (Cth).

[270] See s 318 PPSA.

[271] Section 339.

techniques';[272] however it was arguably unnecessary and may actually serve to prolong the use of old terminology in security agreements.

For these purposes, floating charges and fixed charges have been redefined as security interests over circulating and non-circulating assets respectively,[273] with reference to two criteria: first, a list of 'current assets', which broadly correspond to the categories of floating charge assets previously;[274] alternatively, whether or not the secured party has given the grantor express or implied authority to transfer the property in the ordinary course of the grantor's business, free of the security interest.[275]

The PPSA states that these provisions only apply to charges where title is in the grantor.[276] The Corporations Act mirrors this, as it defines a 'circulating security interest' as a PPSA security interest attaching to a circulating asset as defined by the PPSA, and where the grantor has title to the asset.[277] It seems, prima facie, contrary to the spirit of the PPSA for 'title' to be brought back into the equation, but the purpose is to clarify that references to charges do not apply to retention of title and similar title-based security interests, notwithstanding that these may encompass current (circulating) assets.[278]

The Corporations Act thus defines security interests by incorporation of the terminology of the PPSA, and the definitions in sections 339–341A PPSA. The reason for its redefining the concepts is so that the priorities on insolvency distribution may be preserved, particularly priority over (the previous) 'floating charge realisations'.[279] Just as prior to the PPSA, Australian law, as in the UK, distinguished fixed and floating charges based on legal and factual control over the collateral in question, the post-PPSA amendments have attempted to preserve that distinction, notwithstanding that the PPSA abolishes the distinction.[280] Thus, an asset will not be a 'circulating asset', despite the other features mentioned above, if a registered financing statement discloses that the secured party has 'control' of the asset, and it does have control, or if the secured party has perfected by possession.[281] However, confusingly, 'control' in this context, as a distinction between circulating and non-circulating assets, has a wider meaning from its meaning for perfection purposes.[282] In sections 341–341A, the PPSA attempts to reflect the pre-existing law as to when a chargor would have been found to have sufficient control to give it a fixed charge. For these purposes the Act provides separate definitions for control of inventory,

[272] Section 338.
[273] Section 340.
[274] Sub-section 340(5).
[275] Section 340.
[276] Section 339(1)(b).
[277] Section 51C Corporations Act 2001 (Cth).
[278] Section 340(5) PPSA.
[279] Sections 433, 556 Corporations Act.
[280] J Stumbles, 'Personal Property Security Law in Australia and Canada' (2011) 51 *Canadian Business Law Journal* 425, 443, arguing that this perpetuates the floating/fixed distinction.
[281] Sub-sections 340(2), (3) PPSA.
[282] Section 341 PPSA.

accounts, and ADI accounts respectively. These definitions are relevant to the Corporations Act's insolvency provisions referring to 'circulating security interests', mainly in relation to dealing with property, and to priorities on distribution.[283] One of the attractions of the PPSA was that its wider, statutory, 'security interest' removed the controversial and complex requirement for distinguishing fixed from floating charges (and the related concept of crystallisation),[284] while nevertheless preserving contractual freedom to achieve the same outcomes. Nevertheless, these provisions will enable continuation of arguments in insolvencies about whether or not an agreement, and the actual circumstances, achieves control. It is true that in Australia, the arguments may be fewer than elsewhere, as employees are the only creditors to whom circulated security interests are subordinated.[285] Nevertheless, Parliament's bold attempt to replicate the fixed/floating charge distinction using PPSA terminology, without changing consequences for insolvency priorities, has resulted in a complex set of provisions. An alternative to the attempt to provide a statutory encapsulation of the control test for the purposes of this distinction, is to refer to the categories of collateral that are ordinarily subject to 'circulating', or 'non-circulating' security interests respectively. This solution was that chosen in New Zealand, after some amendments to the legislation.[286] The Australian statutory review has now recommended that a similar approach be adopted. Thus, it suggests that a 'circulating asset' would be confined to the category of inventory (and its proceeds), other than inventory subject to a PMSI.[287] While this goes half way to replicating the New Zealand provision, in relation to 'accounts', it suggests further consultation as to whether government wishes to take a policy decision to include accounts within circulating assets. In New Zealand, 'accounts receivable' are subject to statutory insolvency priority creditors.[288] In Australia, the definition of 'accounts' is narrower, as it does not extend to 'any monetary obligation'.[289] The Final Report of the statutory review, where it discusses transfers of an account as deemed security interest, recommends that 'account' should be clarified to confine it to trade receivables (as there has been some confusion as to whether it extended to corporate loans). Neverthless, it also recommends that governments should consult further about whether the definition should extend more generally to 'monetary obligations', as in New Zealand.[290] This earlier discussion of transfers of an 'account' is not reflected in the later discussion about circulating assets for insolvency priority purposes. Obviously a broader meaning of 'account' will

[283] eg ss 433 (receivership), 442B, 443E (voluntary administration), 561, 588FJ (liquidation).

[284] See *Whitton v ACN 003 266 886 Pty Ltd* (1996) 42 NSWLR 123, cf re Spectrum Plus [2005] 2 AC 680.

[285] Section 562 Corporations Act 2001 (Cth).

[286] For the history, and interpretation, of the New Zealand provisions, see *Strategic Finance Ltd v Bridgman and Sanson* [2013] NZCA 357.

[287] Final Report, para 9.2.1.1.3.

[288] Companies Act 1993 (NZ), Seventh Schedule.

[289] Section 10 PPSA.

[290] Final Report, para 4.3.2.2.3.

impact on the extent of the subordination to priority creditors. Nevertheless, it is clear that insolvency policy prior to the PPSA was that a floating charge, including such a charge to the extent that it was over book debts, was subordinated to priority creditors, and therefore it is unclear why the statutory review does not directly recommend that 'accounts' be a circulating asset. The review also rightly points out that, whatever happens, these provisions of the PPSA should be moved to the Corporations Act,[291] since they are only relevant to insolvency priority, and the current references in them to 'control' are apt to confuse, given that 'control' is also a form of perfection in the PPSA.

(iii) Title-based Claims

The last aspect is an attempt to deal with the title-based claims, to the extent that these are now 'PPSA security interests'. In the Corporations Act there are many references to the 'property of the corporation', particularly as regards the powers and duties of liquidators and administrators to deal with that property, and on distribution.[292] Prior to the PPSA, a title-based claimant would have recourse to the collateral; it would not form part of the property of the corporation for the purposes of distribution, for example. Since the PPSA now regards the debtor as granting a security interest, doubt would arise as to whether it could be said that personal property belonged to a corporate grantor or to the party retaining title to it. The Australian approach is to define such interests as 'PPSA Retention of Title Property', which is defined as property used by or in possession of the corporation, where the corporation does not have title, and where a PPSA security interest is attached for which the corporation is the grantor.[293] Despite the phrase 'PPSA Retention of Title Property', the definition extends to leases, consignments or other title-based claims.

While the Corporations Act states that such property will *not* be 'property of the corporation', unless expressly or impliedly provided to the contrary,[294] for some specific purposes it *is* included—for example Part 5.3A, Voluntary Administration.[295] Since a secured party with a security interest in the whole or substantially the whole of the corporation's property may appoint an administrator, or 'veto' the appointment of one, and appoint a receiver instead,[296] it might be argued that the statutory inclusion of 'PPSA Retention of Title Property' in Part 5.3A may result in the secured party not having security over the whole or

[291] ibid, para 9.2.1.2.3.
[292] eg, ss 477, 478, 501, 561, 562 Corporations Act 2001 (Cth).
[293] Section 51F Corporations Act.
[294] Sub-section 51F(2) Corporations Act.
[295] Section 435B Corporations Act.
[296] Sections 436C, 441A Corporations Act.

substantially the whole of the property.[297] In addition, where the security interest over 'PPSA Retention of Title Property' is unperfected and falls within section 267 PPSA, it will vest in the grantor and becomes 'property of the corporation', for example on a liquidation.[298]

(iv) General Approach

The Australian approach is unique in its attempt to harmonise the PPSA and insolvency law. It has certainly been a criticism in Canada, where this has not been attempted by provincial and federal governments.[299] New Zealand's amendment of the insolvency provisions, while it did amend some of the terminology, was less ambitious, though this left some interpretation issues for the courts.[300] It can be seen from the statutory review that Australia's approach was overly complex and that the attempt to find the optimal solution to the marriage between insolvency and secured transactions terminology is a work in progress.

I. Conflict of Laws

The main provisions are in Part 7.2. These provide rules for ascertaining, in Australian proceedings, which jurisdiction's laws govern validity, perfection, and the effect of perfection and non-perfection.[301] Separate rules deal with security interests in goods, relocation of goods, and goods frequently moved between jurisdictions; intangible property, accounts, and financial property, and proceeds. In relation to goods generally, the location of the goods at time of attachment applies, other than that jurisdiction's conflict of law provisions.[302] In relation to intangibles, the location of the debtor at the time of attachment applies.[303]

However, there are two particular features of the Australian provisions which cloud application of these rules. First, the PPSA contains a 'territorial' provision in section 6. It states that the PPSA applies where the grantor is an Australian entity, where the goods or financial property are located in Australia, where accounts are payable in Australia, and to ADIs and Australian intangible property. Section 6

297 This argument led to an early amendment before the PPSA came into operational effect, but it only applies to transitional security interests, see s 1501A Corporations Act 2001 (Cth). Post-PPSA security agreements might be drafted so as to make the position clear.

298 eg ss 461, 513A Corporations Act.

299 Wood (n 253).

300 See Brown (n 166) 354–56, and *Strategic Finance Ltd v Bridgman and Sanson* [2013] NZCA 357.

301 Sub-section 234(1) PPSA.

302 Section 238.

303 Section 239.

seems to limit the operation of the rules in Part 7.2. Where the grantor is a foreign entity, or, for example, where goods are located outside Australia, the rules in Part 7.2 cannot be used to determine the choice of law in Australian proceedings. This leads to a lacuna, since section 6 does not say that the other jurisdiction's law will then apply. Common law would have to be relied upon. Thus the statutory review has recommended that the government consider whether section 6 is needed, and suggested it should either be deleted or at least amended so that it does not impede Part 7.2.[304]

Section 237 enables the parties to include a provision in the security agreement nominating Australian law as the governing law, but only if the grantor is an Australian entity.[305] This does not apply to accounts, intellectual property, or transfers of accounts or chattel paper;[306] effectively this confines it to non-mobile goods, since that is the only situation where selecting Australian law would result in a different outcome from the other Part 7.2 rules. For example, it might allow Australian law to apply notwithstanding the location of the goods was in New Zealand. The statutory review concluded that section 237 was contrary to the objective of certainty in the PPSA and in conflicts rules, and recommended that it be deleted.[307]

J. Conclusion

While it is still early in the life of the PPSA, the statutory review, completed in March 2015, has provided an opportunity to consider some of the features of the PPSA and PPSR, and whether they are necessary, or are of optimum design to achieve its purposes. While the submissions have covered many detailed aspects of the legislation and its practical operation, many of which have been referred to above, the two main themes in the Final Report, which its recommendations are designed to address, are lack of awareness of the legislation and its impact (particularly among small businesses) and secondly, a perception that the Act generally, and particularly the registration process and terminology, are unnecessarily long and complex.[308] Even before the review, an incoming government with an 'anti-red tape' agenda entertained submissions from some, particularly in the equipment hire sector, who wished to restrict the scope of the PPSA. Given that the scheduled review was imminent, this piecemeal approach to law reform in such a

304 Final Report, para 9.1.1.3.

305 Section 236 provides that a Commonwealth law may state that it, or any other Commonwealth law, governs the security interest, despite any other provisions in Part 7.2.

306 Sub-section 237(2).

307 Final Report, para 9.1.6.1.3.

308 Review of the Personal Property Securities Act 2009, Commonwealth of Australia, 2015.

complex area with interdependent provisions is unwelcome, though fortunately the reviewer recommended the proposed amendment should proceed.[309] Another early observation is that the Australian courts, in the first few decisions on the substantive aspects of the PPSA, have readily adopted the new concepts and terminology, and looked to New Zealand and Canadian case law authority to assist where necessary, including as to the objectives of the legislation.[310] The citation of overseas caw law to such an extent is a refreshing development in Australian commercial jurisprudence.

Notwithstanding initial teething problems and some issues raised in the review, the achievement of the PPSA, in bringing about a single national system and register in a federal jurisdiction, and the large number of registrations and searches to date, suggest that in the medium term the economic benefits to users and the wider economy will start to become apparent and will amply justify the initial investment by government, and costs and adjustments incurred by affected parties.

[309] Final Report recommendation 19. See also Personal Property Securities Amendment (n 74 above).

[310] *Re Maiden Civil Pty Ltd* [2013] NSWSC 852, *Warehouse Sales Pty Ltd (in liq) v LG Electronics Australia Pty Ltd* [2014] VSC 644.

8

Secured Transactions Law Reform in Malawi: the 2013 Personal Property Security Act

MAREK DUBOVEC AND CYPRIAN KAMBILI

This chapter examines some aspects of the secured transactions legal reform in Malawi which led to the adoption of the Personal Property Security Act Number 8 of 2013 (PPSA). The PPSA entered into force 23 November 2015 upon establishment of the registry. In addition to the PPSA, this chapter also examines some of the other related reforms that have been undertaken with the objective of increasing access to credit and that affect secured transactions indirectly, including the reforms related to corporate law, insolvency and warehouse receipts and the establishment of commercial courts.

A. Introduction—Why the Reform?

Most secured transactions reforms have been preceded by studies of the legal and economic framework of the given country and whether it provides an environment conducive to access to credit, in general, and secured lending, in particular. Prior to the reform in Malawi, several such studies had been conducted highlighting the inefficiency and outdated nature of the country's legal framework that pertained to access to credit. One such study prepared by the World Bank—the Malawi Investment Climate Assessment[1] (ICA) provided a picture of Malawi's private sector and an effective baseline assessment. According to the ICA:

> A good investment climate is one that provides a sound legal and regulatory framework for enterprises, promotes competition, strengthens governance and reduces bureaucratic inefficiencies, improves access to key financial and infrastructure services.[2]

[1] World Bank Group, Africa Private Sector Group, 'Malawi Investment Climate Assessment' (2006).
[2] ibid 11.

Among other conclusions, the ICA showed that Malawi's manufacturing sector is small, accounting for just 11 per cent of the gross domestic product, and inward orientated as only 14 per cent of manufacturing output is exported. Additionally, it was shown that Malawi's low-cost labour advantages are being eroded by poor productivity resulting from inadequate infrastructure, unreliable utilities and difficulties in accessing affordable finance. The ICA also showed that some of the main constraints to improving trade performance lie in the supply side of the economy. The ICA suggested that expansion of Malawi's domestic private sector into regional markets is essential for the country to diversify away from its vulnerable reliance on exports of tobacco, sugar and tea. With the private sector structure made up of a few large firms at the top, many small ones at the bottom and a missing middle, a key policy challenge suggested for Malawi was to encourage the large number of small enterprises, many of which operate in the informal sector, to expand by reducing the costs of formalisation and doing business, including by increasing access to finance.[3]

In response to these challenges facing the economy, the government—through the Ministry of Industry and Trade—was entrusted with leading the Private Sector Development Strategy and Reform Programme (PSD Programme). The main task of the PSD Programme is to draw upon and implement the recommendations from the World Bank's ICA and Doing Business Surveys. These assessments and surveys also serve as the analytical foundations and as the basis for monitoring the progress of these reforms. Malawi is ranked 164 out of 189 economies in the World Bank's 2015 Doing Business Survey.[4] To some extent, this low ranking may be attributed to the absence of a credit information registry, a strong collateral law and an electronic collateral registry.[5]

In response to these assessments, the government of Malawi, through the Ministries of Justice and Industry and Trade, prepared a study on the prioritisation of economic laws in urgent need of revision.[6] One of the major criteria in the review of the then existing Malawian laws was their actual impact on economic activity and their compliance with international standards and the current best practices.[7] The Ministry of Industry and Trade carried out a follow-up study specifically focusing on credit supply to small and medium-sized enterprises (SMEs) in December 2008.[8] The study concluded that 'transparent and well defined

[3] See generally M Dubovec and C Kambili, 'Using the UNCITRAL Legislative Guide as a Tool for Secured Transactions Reform in Sub-Saharan Africa' (2013) 30 *Arizona Journal of International and Comparative Law* 163.

[4] World Bank Group, 'Doing Business Survey Malawi', www.doingbusiness.org/rankings.

[5] World Bank Group (n 1).

[6] Government of Malawi, Ministry of Justice, 'Report on Prioritisation of Economic Laws for Reform' (Lilongwe, Malawi, 2008).

[7] ibid 9.

[8] Government of Malawi, Ministry of Industry and Trade, 'SME Credit in Malawi: Supply Side Study' (Lilongwe, Malawi, 2008).

property rights need to be established in order to improve access to finance and reduce banking diffidence'.[9]

In addition to analysis and assessments, these studies catalogued the laws that existed before the enactment of the PPSA.[10] Many gaps, inefficiencies and other deficiencies had been identified resulting in the unnecessarily high cost of credit and its limited supply to a narrowly identifiable set of borrowers. A conscious decision to modernise the legal framework was made in line with the best international standards. Following a study of model laws, guides and actual legislation that is in effect in other jurisdictions, it was proposed that the New Zealand PPSA 1999, which is based on the Saskatchewan PPSA 1993,[11] be adapted to the local legal and economic environment in Malawi. At that time, it was felt that the New Zealand PPSA presented a fairly recent model that could easily be adapted to Malawi unlike the Australian PPSA 2009, which was deemed rather complex.[12,13] It was envisaged that in the course of developing the Malawi PPSA, international guides, such as the United Nations Commission on International Trade Law Legislative Guide on Secured Transactions (UNCITRAL Guide), would inform the process where guidance was lacking or sought.[14]

B. Fundamental Aspects of the PPSA

The scheme of the Malawian PPSA follows its New Zealand model. It is organised in Parts that cover the fundamental elements of a secured transaction, opening with the scope and ending with transitional provisions. The following paragraphs examine some of the features governed by the 11 Parts into which the Malawian PPSA is divided. PPSA in this chapter refers to the Malawian PPSA unless specifically noted.

(i) Scope of the Act

The personal scope provisions set forth in section 3 allow any person, whether natural or legal, to create a security interest or act as a secured party. In terms of the transactional scope, in addition to security interests created by an agreement,

[9] ibid 24.

[10] Dubovec and Kambili (n 3).

[11] New Zealand Law Commission, *A Personal Property Securities Act for New Zealand: Report No. 8* (NZLC R 8, Wellington, New Zealand, 1989) and D Brown, 'The New Zealand Personal Property Securities Act 1999' in J de Lacy (ed), *The Reform of UK Personal Property Security Law, Comparative Perspectives* (Abingdon, Routledge-Cavendish, 2012). See Ch 7.

[12] See Ch 8 C(ii).

[13] Both authors were very closely involved in the drafting of the Malawi PPSA.

[14] See Ch 24.

as defined in section 2, the PPSA applies to non-consensual liens created by judgments and operation of the law, but only with regard to their perfection, registration and priority. The High Court of Malawi defined one such type of lien given to a service provider in *Small Holder Farmers Fertiliser Revolving Fund of Malawi v Export Trading Co Limited*[15] as 'a right at common law in one man to retain that, which is rightfully and continuously in his possession belonging to another until the present and accrued claims of the person in possession are satisfied'.

The PPSA is based on a functional approach that subjects all transactions with the purpose of securing an obligation to the same legal regime. It thus supersedes all pre-existing laws that govern hire purchase, conditional sale agreements, and charges as well as the common law that allows the debtor to transfer outright its intangible rights to secure an obligation. The definition of a security interest in section 2 may strike the reader as limiting somewhat the transactions to which the PPSA applies. Looking at the definition alone, the reader might come to a conclusion that outright transfers of receivables, consignments and long-term operating leases are excluded because in these transactions there might not be an obligation that the debtor purports to secure. However, the PPSA must be read as a whole, including the definitions of debtor and secured party, which clearly state that these non-security transactions are also within the scope of the law. For parties involved in secured transactions, it is critical that they understand the effect of this approach. Before the adoption of the PPSA debtors and creditors were used to structuring their transactions according to form and expected the courts to enforce these transactions according to their intentions as reflected in the terms of the agreement. For instance, in *Chanyumbu Transport & Chanyumbu Trading v Standard Bank Limited*[16] the High Court of Malawi held that according to the lease contract:

> The leased assets were only leased and not sold by the defendant bank to the plaintiff as is clearly evident by clause 6 of exhibit 'YM8' which in reference to the Leased Assets clearly stated that they were to remain the property of the lessor to wit the defendant bank and that nothing was to be construed as conferring on the lessee namely the plaintiff, any right or interest in the Leased Assets other than the lease.

Under the PPSA, leases of the kind involved in this case would be characterised as creating security interests if they fell under the definitions of either a financial lease or operating lease. Accordingly, the lessee would have sufficient rights in the leased asset to create a security interest competing with that of the lessor.

The PPSA is also somewhat ambiguous in its application to outright transfers of intangible rights in general as opposed to more limited outright transfers of

[15] *Small Holder Farmers Fertiliser Revolving Fund of Malawi v Export Trading Co Limited* [2005] No 1651 (High Court of Malawi, Principal Registry, unreported).

[16] *Chanyumbu Transport and Chanyumbu Trading v Standard Bank Limited* [2008] No 1128 (High Court of Malawi, Principal Registry, unreported).

accounts receivable. This deviation may cause some confusion but also practical difficulties for buyers of intangible rights such as intellectual property. Its model, the New Zealand PPSA, applies to outright transfers of only accounts receivable and chattel paper.[17] Section 84 of the Malawi PPSA states that the Part on Enforcement of Security Interests does not apply to outright transfers of only accounts receivable and chattel paper, which may lead to somewhat troublesome interpretation that outright transfers of other intangible rights are subject to the PPSA for all purposes.

In relation to assets that can be used as collateral, section 3(5)(c) of the PPSA excludes from its scope real property, wages, salary and other compensation owed to workers, annuities and life insurance policies, claims to damages arising from non-commercial torts, ships, licences and concessions. Following the New Zealand model, the PPSA also does not apply to fixtures.[18] The New Zealand PPSA excluded fixtures from its scope which, under the common law, become part of the immovable and the interest of the third party in the chattel is lost.[19] During the drafting of the Malawi PPSA, a concern was raised as to the potential effect on the applicable land laws which were, at that time and still today, mired in controversy. It was felt that interference of the PPSA with the rights of land owners, mortgagees and buyers, however remote, could raise some eyebrows and even lead to delays. Even though the drafting group understood and explained that the inclusion of fixtures would not alter the rights of those under the land law, a decision was made to proceed strategically focusing on the passage of the PPSA at the expense of dropping fixtures from its scope.

(ii) Creation of Security Interests

Section 4 sets forth the fundamental rule for the creation of a security interest that depends on the conclusion of a security agreement between the debtor and secured party. At this moment the security interest becomes effective as between the two parties. Section 17(2) imposes a special requirement on the creation of a security interest in crops that the debtor grows on land that is subject to a mortgage or that she leases from the owner. In both situations the PPSA requires the consent of the mortgagee or lessor as a condition of creation of the security interest. This additional condition was included for the same reason that fixtures were excluded from the scope of the PPSA.

Section 4 does not expressly require either party to sign the security agreement. Nonetheless, a signature of the debtor is a mandatory condition to the

[17] L Widdup, Personal Property Securities Act: A Conceptual Approach, 3rd edn (Lexis Nexis, 2013) 35.

[18] United Nations Commission on International Trade Law, *The UNCITRAL Legislative Guide on Secured Transactions* (Vienna, United Nations, 2010) (UNCITRAL Guide) refers to fixtures as attachments to immovable property.

[19] Widdup (n 17) 67. See also New Zealand Ch 7 G.

enforceability of the security interest. Pre-PPSA Malawian courts rendered security mechanisms unenforceable against the debtor based on the failure of the secured party to produce a writing signed by the debtor indicating her consent to the creation of a security mechanism. In *Chilongwe v Chilembwe Lodge*[20] the secured party refused to release some collateral belonging to the debtor claiming that the collateral also secured another facility that had not yet been fully satisfied by the debtor. The High Court of Malawi held that:

> The secured creditor was unable to produce a duly signed copy of the letter to prove that the debtor agreed to the changed terms of the overdraft facility ... The logical consequence of this is that the overdraft facility and the bank guarantee remain distinct. It is only the bank guarantee, which was secured with a collateral undertaking.

(iii) Perfection of Security Interests

Part III of the PPSA, in only two sections, governs the perfection of security interests. Section 9(1)(b) provides for three fundamental methods of perfection, namely: (1) registration, (2) possession and (3) control.[21] They are supplemented by two special methods which are automatic and temporary. For instance, under section 14 a security interest automatically continues in cash proceeds even though the registration does not refer to cash proceeds and the secured party has taken neither possession nor control of such proceeds.[22] Sections 15, 18 and 19 then recognise temporary perfection. Under section 18, the secured party may return an instrument or certificated security, the possession of which it previously took to perfect its security interest, back to the debtor. Such security interest will remain temporarily perfected for 10 working days, thus allowing the debtor, for instance, to present the security certificate to the issuer to collect a dividend.

Registration is the universal method of perfection available for security interests in any type of asset subject to the PPSA. The other four methods are limited to specific types of asset or transaction—possession may only be taken over tangible assets, control applies only to deposit and securities accounts, automatic perfection is available with respect to a particular kind of proceeds and temporary perfection may be used only for negotiable documents of title and certificated securities.

The PPSA covers registration in great detail in Part VII. It provides the framework for the establishment of a notice-filing registry and allows the secured party

[20] *Chilongwe v Chilembwe Lodge* [2006] No 17 (Industrial Relations Court, Blantyre, Malawi, unreported).

[21] Compare with Recommendations 32, 34 and 35 of the UNCITRAL Guide. Control is the least well-known perfection mechanism of the three. NO Akseli, *International Secured Transactions Law, Facilitation of Credit and International Conventions and Instruments* (Abingdon, Routledge, 2012) 162.

[22] On the instances in which the security interest may be automatically perfected under the Canadian Provincial PPSAs see generally RCC Cuming, C Walsh, and R Wood, *Personal Property Security Law* (Toronto, Irwin, 2005) 218–23.

to submit only summary information about an existing or potential transaction presented in a financing statement. All PPSA registries in Australia, Canada and New Zealand are based on the same concept.[23] Sections 109–115 allow a third party to obtain further information about the secured obligation and the collateral from the secured party. It is noteworthy that the UNCITRAL Guide does not include any recommendations entitling the debtor or a third party to request information even though such rules are an integral part of modern secured transactions laws.[24] The draft UNCITRAL Model Law does include a comparable provision. Consistently with the other PPSAs, the secured party has a duty to respond to requests for information received only from the debtor. The Malawian registry will be designed to allow secured parties to attach files to their financing statements, which can include summaries of security agreements or more detailed collateral descriptions.[25]

As a consequence of the notice-filing approach, the role of the registrar and the registry system is administrative. When processing financing statements, the registry merely ensures that all the required information has been provided by the secured party. Pursuant to section 52, the registry does not verify whether the debtor actually authorised the registration of the financing statement, whether the security interest has been validly created or even whether the information in the financing statement is factually and legally correct.[26]

Section 54 is one of the most critical in the entire structure of the PPSA because it tells the secured party how to identify the debtor in a financing statement and consequently informs the registry where to place the financing statement in its records. Finally, it also gives direction to the searcher for determining what information to enter into a search request. Section 54 distinguishes among three types of debtors: (1) individuals, (2) registered companies and (3) unregistered companies. For all three, it requires the secured party to identify them according to their unique identifiers as defined in the Registry Regulations, which were adopted and published in the *Malawi Gazette* of 17 April 2015. It is vitally important for a secured party to establish the correct identifier for the debtor and then to enter it accurately in the relevant field in a financing statement.

[23] For Australia see generally A Duggan and D Brown, *Australian Personal Property Securities Law* (Chatswood, NSW Lexis Nexis Butterworths, 2012) 118.

[24] For Canada, see Cuming, Walsh and Wood (n 22) 231–33 and for Australia, Duggan and Brown (n 23) 130.

[25] See *In re Management by Innovation Inc* (2005) 321 BR 744 where the financing statement included the following language: 'The property and/or the equipment and all other types of collateral as described in this attached entire agreement [the equipment lease] and in any schedule attached thereto. The attached security agreement and any schedule attached thereto are being submitted for filing as a financing statement'.

[26] Compare with Recommendation 7 of the *UNCITRAL Guide on the Implementation of a Security Rights Registry* (Vienna, United Nations, 2014). See also M Dubovec, 'UCC Article 9 Registration System for Latin America' (2011) 28(1) *Arizona Journal of International and Comparative Law* 133–35. See generally International Finance Corporation, *Secured Transactions Systems and Collateral Registries Toolkit* (IFC Toolkit) (Washington, DC, 2010) 68, which highlights that 'reasons for rejection must be objective so that no discretionary judgments are involved in the decision-making process'.

An error in the identifier of the debtor that is seriously misleading may be fatal for the effectiveness of a security interest. Section 65 applies the test of seriously misleading errors to two specific elements of registration information: (1) the identifier of a debtor and (2) the serial number of collateral.[27] Unlike Recommendation 34 of the UNCITRAL Registry Guide, the Malawian PPSA follows the Australian, Canadian and New Zealand models which provide for indexing and searching according to a serial number for a narrowly defined list of assets and regulate the resulting legal effects.[28] A financing statement shall be seriously misleading if it cannot be retrieved in a search against the correct identifier of the debtor. Since one of the system requirements for the Malawian registry is strict search logic that does not retrieve close matches, any errors, however trivial, will render the financing statement ineffective and the security interest vulnerable against competing claims. Sections 79 and 81 establish the right of all persons, whether natural, legal, domestic or foreign, to search the registry. Unlike its counterparts in Australia and New Zealand, the Malawian registry was not designed to require the searcher to indicate a reason for the search.[29]

(iv) Priority

The priority rules of the PPSA are divided into two chapters—one that sets forth the general rules governing conflicts between secured parties and another that provides special rules for conflicts between secured parties and other competing claimants, such as buyers of collateral and holders of liens. This division follows the UNCITRAL Guide and the other PPSAs. The priority rules are based on two fundamental notions. First, subject to a narrow list of exceptions, the secured party to first perfect its security interest or register a financing statement with respect to a security interest perfected subsequently has priority over another secured party that perfected or registered later.[30] Sections 26–31 of the PPSA regulate the priority for secured parties that have taken a purchase money security interest (PMSI). As long as they satisfy the requirements of these sections, the PMSI secured parties may obtain priority even over earlier perfected security interests. Second, knowledge of the secured party is immaterial in resolving general priority conflicts. However, knowledge does remain relevant in the context of special priority rules that may require, for instance, a buyer not to have knowledge that its action

[27] Recommendation 64 of UNCITRAL Guide (n 18) imposes a similar test with respect to the identifier and address of the secured creditor and a description of the encumbered assets. For the application of the seriously misleading test in Australia see Duggan and Brown (n 23) 135 and in Canada see Cuming, Walsh and Wood (n 22) 269.

[28] For Canada see Cuming, Walsh and Wood (n 22) 238.

[29] While in New Zealand this requirement affects all types of searches, in Australia it is limited to searches of the name of a debtor who is an individual. Duggan and Brown (n 23) 129. The IFC Toolkit (n 26) 70 refers to such requirements as misguided.

[30] Malawi PPSA s 60 allows the secured party to register a financing statement before conclusion of a security agreement subject to proper authorisation of the debtor.

would violate the rights of the secured party in order to take free of such a security interest.

Buyers of collateral may take either subject to or free from a security interest depending on the application of the relevant section of the PPSA. Debtors may sell assets in the ordinary course of business but may also do so when the collateral is not held as inventory or farm products. Section 38 invalidates any restrictions, such as in the form of a negative pledge clause, on the ability and power of the debtor to transfer its rights in the collateral. This override of contractual restrictions applies to any assets that are sold primarily outside the ordinary course of business, but any transfer of collateral subject to such a restriction does not prejudice the rights of the secured party, including the rights to (1) follow the collateral into the hands of the transferee, (2) claim proceeds received from the transferee, and (3) declare the debtor in default. Knowledge of a contractual limitation on the part of the transferee outside the ordinary course of business would not affect the availability of these rights to the secured party. At times, secured parties may also include contractual limitations that apply to inventory that is to be sold in the ordinary course of business, such as for higher-value items like boats, the sale of which may require specific authorisation of the secured party. In this case, the right of the secured party to follow the collateral into the hands of the transferee is cut off unless the buyer has knowledge that such a transfer violates the rights of the secured party. As a result, the override of contractual limitations only affects the power of the debtor to transfer rights in the collateral but not necessarily the priority of the transferee who may take subject to or free of the security interest depending on the state of its knowledge. Sections 42–44 of the PPSA also protect the purchasers of negotiable instruments, chattel paper, documents of title and security certificates as well as transferees of money and funds credited to a bank account.

In addition to the priority rules for conflicts between a secured party and competing claimants that acquired an interest in the collateral by an agreement, the PPSA also covers three particular priority conflicts of secured parties and holders of non-consensual claims and liens. First, section 20(2) preserves the rights of workers and similar claimants that remain unaffected by the PPSA. In *Standard Bank Limited & Raymond Davies v ML Luka and 1162 Others & Import and Export (Malawi) Ltd (in Liquidation)*[31] the Malawi Supreme Court of Appeals decided a dispute between a secured creditor of a business and the former employees of that business whose employment was terminated. The former employees claimed terminal benefits in the form of pension and severance allowances under section 35 of the Employment Act, but the priority of these claims as against a security interest was challenged by the secured party. The Court rejected the argument of the secured creditor that section 35 confers the priority of employees' claims only

[31] *Standard Bank Limited and Raymond Davies v ML Luka and 1162 Others and Import and Export (Malawi) Ltd (in Liquidation)* [2012] No 01 (Malawi Supreme Court of Appeal, MSCA Civil Appeal, unreported).

against unsecured creditors and interpreted that section to subordinate the claims of all kinds of creditors, including those with some security in the debtor's assets, to the claims of employees. However sections 94 and 297 of the Insolvency Act 2016 overturn this decision, making clear that the priority of payments to employees extends only in relation to unsecured creditors.

Second, section 41 of the PPSA provides for the priority of third parties that have furnished services or materials in respect to the collateral, limited to the value of those services and materials. Third, section 46 of the PPSA provides a priority rule for a conflict between a secured party and a judgment creditor. The judgment creditor will receive priority only if it has taken a step to execute its judgment before the security interest is perfected. This step may either be physical seizure of the collateral or serving a garnishee order on a third party that holds debtor's assets, such as a bank account.

(v) Remedies

Part VIII of the PPSA addresses default, enforcement of a security interest and remedies available to secured parties. According to section 84, this Part does not apply to outright transfers of an account receivable or chattel paper, long-term operating leases and commercial consignments: in relation to these transactions, the deemed secured party can proceed as the full owner of the asset. With some exceptions listed in section 86, Part VIII defers to the parties' agreement with respect to the application of default remedies. A peculiar feature of the PPSA is the necessity to register an enforcement form in the PPSA registry in order to alert third parties about the initiation of enforcement proceedings against some property of the debtor under section 87(3).[32] Such registration is required for both judicial and extrajudicial enforcement.

The enforcement of a security interest is conditioned on the occurrence of default which is defined in section 2(1) as 'any event that gives the secured party the right to enforce a security interest'.[33] The parties may thus agree on any events the occurrence of which would constitute default, including the failure to make an instalment payment or the changing of an address without prior notification to the secured party. Pre-PPSA Malawian courts have already decided disputes involving questions as to whether the debtor defaulted on its obligations and these precedents should remain equally guiding under the PPSA. In *Chanyumbu Transport & Chanyumbu Trading v Standard Bank Limited* the High Court of Malawi

[32] For a similar requirement see Dubovec (n 26), M Dubovec and B Osei-Tutu, 'Reforming Secured Transactions Laws in Africa: The First African Collateral Registry in Ghana' (2013) 45 *Uniform Commercial Code Law Journal* 77.

[33] The PPSAs in Canada and New Zealand include a similar definition but there is no comparable definition of default in the Australian PPSA. Duggan and Brown (n 23) 267. The Uniform Commercial Code Article 9 also does not define default.

concluded that the debtor indeed defaulted because of the following clause in a financing agreement, which defined cross-default:[34]

> If the Borrower should fail to make payment by due date of any amount due in terms of the Short Term Loan Facility or any other facilities that the Bank has accorded to the Borrower or shall become insolvent the full amount of the facility and any other facilities accorded to the Borrower by the Bank together with additional interest as defined in this Facility Letter shall immediately become due and payable. In addition the bank shall have the right to exercise all other remedies available to them in terms of the Laws of Malawi.

The Malawian courts have also held that employees of the debtor have no standing to petition the court for an injunction that would suspend enforcement of the secured party's rights.[35] Similarly the courts have also rejected an application for an injunction if it is based on the debtor's claim that the enforcement would merely disadvantage the debtor.[36]

The secured party may either proceed extrajudicially or take an enforcement action pursuant to a court order. The secured party may repossess the collateral or render it unusable extrajudicially, pursuant to section 87 as long as the debtor does not resist. The debtor's resistance is based on the concept of breach of the peace expressly incorporated in the US Uniform Commercial Code Article 9 (UCC 9) and the other PPSAs. However, under UCC 9 and the other PPSAs the secured party would not be allowed to proceed if the debtor did not resist but there are some other circumstances that could lead the court to the conclusion that the peace was breached, such as the reaction of third parties or the place from which the collateral was repossessed.[37]

It may happen that after the collateral has been repossessed, the debtor files for insolvency. Section 298 of the Insolvency Act empowers the secured party to realise its security interest or otherwise deal with the collateral. Thus this section does not limit the power of the secured party to take the collateral in possession of an insolvent debtor. However the secured party's powers are not unfettered and require an authorisation from the court under sections 27 and 110 of the Insolvency Act, for company reorganisation and winding up, respectively.

For intangible assets, such as accounts receivable, the secured party may simply collect debts by informing account debtors to channel payments directly to itself.

[34] *Chanyumbu Transport and Chanyumbu Trading v Standard Bank Limited* [2008] No 1128 (High Court of Malawi, Principal Registry, unreported).

[35] *Mwapasa and another v Stanbic Bank Ltd* [2003] Misc Civil Cause No 110 (High Court of Malawi, Principal Registry, unreported).

[36] *Harz Co Ltd v National Seed Cotton Milling Ltd* [2001] Civil Cause No 229 (High Court of Malawi, Principal Registry, unreported).

[37] See Cuming, Walsh and Wood (n 22) 529 and *Kerry A Clarin v Repossessors Inc* (1999) US App LEXIS 31549 7 in which a US Appellate Court for the 8th Circuit identified five elements that should guide the courts in assessing actions of the secured party against the requirement not to commit a breach of the peace: (1) where the repossession took place, (2) the debtor's express or constructive consent, (3) the reactions of third parties, (4) the type of premises entered, and (5) the creditor's use of deception.

Based on the New Zealand model, section 89(1) authorises only the secured party with priority over all other secured parties to collect and apply the collateral.[38] Recommendation 168 of the UNCITRAL Guide, the Canadian PPSAs and UCC §9-607 do not impose a similarly impractical limitation.[39]

The secured party may dispose of the collateral in a public or private sale or by any other method agreed to by the parties in a security agreement, pursuant to section 93. Alternatively, the secured party may dispose of the collateral by appropriating it to the secured obligation, effectively becoming its owner. This appropriation remedy is available only to the secured party with the highest priority. It may be utilised only when the entire outstanding secured obligation is to be extinguished, and may be exercised only if a person entitled to receive a notice of the disposition does not object to the secured party's proposal.[40] Both of these forms of enforcement require the secured party to send a notice to affected parties, including the debtor and other secured parties who perfected their security interests by registration against the same collateral.

There seems to be a gap in the PPSA in terms of the requirements on the content of the notice of sale. Recommendation 151(b) of the UNCITRAL Guide clearly states that a law should provide for the minimum contents a notice must reflect, and UCC §9-613 and §9-614 even detail the content requirements separately for disposition of consumer and commercial collateral thus providing safe harbour forms of such notice.[41] Though safe harbour forms have been included in the Regulations courts, they may still be called on to apply the requirement of commercial reasonableness with respect to the content of the notices. The PPSA also does not provide for legal consequences stemming from the secured party's failure to provide a notice of sale.

In a number of aspects, the PPSA protects the rights and interests of debtors. In addition to requiring the secured party to (1) proceed in a commercially reasonable manner, (2) refrain from repossessing the collateral over resistance of the debtor, and (3) send a notice of disposition, section 105 provides for the right of redemption and section 106 for the right of reinstating the security agreement. The Malawi common law already recognised and the courts enforced the right of redemption pre-PPSA. In *First Merchant Bank v Lorgat*[42] the High Court of Malawi held that:

> A chargor or mortgagor has, therefore, up to the date of the contract or at the fall of the hammer on an auction, to pay arrears and restrain the mortgagee or chargee from

[38] Widdup (n 17) 416.

[39] *cf* the New Zealand PPSA, which does impose this limitation (s 108).

[40] See Malawi PPSA ss 100 and 101. In this respect, s 100 deviates from Recommendation 156 of the UNCITRAL Guide (n 18), which makes this remedy available to any secured party, even the one holding a junior security interest. Compare also with UCC §9-620(a), which allows any secured party to accept collateral in satisfaction of obligation. *cf* the New Zealand PPSA which limits this to the senior secured creditor (s 108).

[41] Canadian PPSAs contain similar requirements. Cuming, Walsh and Wood (n 22) 542.

[42] *First Merchant Bank v Lorgat* [2002] Civil Cause No 3917 (High Court of Malawi, Principal Registry).

exercising the power of sale. If the chargor or mortgagor does not pay before a contract of sale to the mortgagee or chargee or into court, a court will not restrain by injunction the lawful exercise of the power of sale.

(vi) Miscellaneous Matters

Finally, Part IX deals with miscellaneous matters, such as the manner in which notices may be sent. Part X, entitled Applicable Laws, provides for the conflict of laws rules that determine when the PPSA applies, such as when tangible collateral is located in Malawi, and Part XI deals with transitory measures. Part IX empowers the Ministry to issue Regulations to implement the PPSA, in particular with respect to establishing the registry system. It also includes a savings and repeal clause in section 123, under which the Bills of Sale Act, the Hire Purchase Act, the Farmers' Stop Order Act and the Commercial Credits Act are repealed. Part X follows the other PPSAs as well as the UNCITRAL Guide, which provide for two connecting factors for its application: (1) location of the collateral for tangible property and (2) location of the debtor for intangible property.[43] Unfortunately, the Malawian PPSA has not incorporated the substance of Recommendations 219 and 220 of the UNCITRAL Guide, which clearly determine at which point in time the location of the collateral or the debtor should be established. The PPSA includes special rules for certain kinds of collateral, including mobile goods that regularly move between multiple jurisdictions, deposit and investment accounts, and proceeds.[44]

Even though Part XI is supposed to provide a comprehensive regulation of transitory issues, other sections of the PPSA also address matters that have a bearing on the transition to the PPSA. An example is contained in section 123 referred to in the preceding paragraph. Sections 131–133 address the transition of pre-existing security devices into the PPSA, preserving their effectiveness but only during the period of six months after the PPSA enters into force. If the secured party fails to take an action to perfect its pre-PPSA security interest within this transitional period, under section 135 its security interest will become ineffective against third parties.[45]

Since the PPSA came into operation, secured parties were required to perfect their prior security interests, including by registration of financing statements. The pre-existing interests were divided into two categories for purposes of the Act. Firstly those created under prior law such as fixed and floating charges, bills of sale, and commercial credits which required registration under prior law.[46] Secondly,

[43] See generally Akseli (n 21).

[44] Malawi PPSA ss 124(2), 126 and 127.

[45] Under the Australian PPSA, the Australian government took the responsibility for migrating the pre-PPSA registrations into the PPSA registry. Australian PPSA s 332 includes a definition of migrated security interest.

[46] Malawi PPSA s 132.

registration under the Act is now also required for those security interests that did not require registration under prior law, such as financial leases under the common law, retentions of title under the Sale of Goods Act and hire-purchase (conditional sales) under the Hire Purchase Act.[47] Secured parties have six months to register financing statements from the commencement date of the PPSA if they are to retain the original date of perfection and priority established under prior law.

C. PPSA Registry and Regulations

The Registry Regulations implement the relevant provisions of the PPSA that deal with the registration of financing statements included under Part VII. One of the challenging issues for the Regulations was to implement the requirement of section 54 to identify the debtor by a unique identification number. This section left the issue deliberately undefined to allow for a more detailed discussion as to how individual and entity debtors must be identified in financing statements. Regulations 15 and 16 provide the criteria according to which different types of individual debtors, including citizens and foreigners, as well as different types of entities, including registered and unregistered companies, must be identified and what their respective unique identification numbers are. Unique numbers were chosen as the indexing/search criteria because of the commonality of names and the fact that names could be presented differently in various identification documents.

The Regulations also include Schedules that contain the forms that are to be used in connection with accessing the registry, including the initial financing statement, amendment, search request, rejection of registration, etc. One of the Schedules separates the Malawian Regulations from similar instruments adopted under the other PPSAs in that it includes model forms that are contemplated by the PPSA, including a bailee acknowledgement, pre-registration authorisation letter, demand to discharge registration, notification to the account debtor to pay the secured party, notice of public disposition of collateral, and notification of proposal to retain collateral. These forms have been included not only as examples, but as a safe harbour, which, when used, protects the sender against the claims of an affected party that the acknowledgement, notification, letter, demand or notice did not substantially comply with the requirements of the PPSA.[48] Regulation 34 clearly specifies that the forms included in the Third Schedule are deemed to provide sufficient information. This approach was adopted to provide guidance to the users, reduce the cost for lenders to develop these forms, and to minimise the potential for disputes, although the affected party could always challenge the sufficiency of the form based on the information filled in by the sender, such as an incorrect identification of the secured party in a demand to discharge registration.

[47] Malawi PPSA s 133.

[48] Compare with UCC §§9-613 and 9-614.

D. Post-adoption Developments

(i) Control

This section examines a few questions that have already arisen in connection with the PPSA. Unlike its New Zealand model, the Malawian PPSA allows security interests in specific assets to be perfected by control.[49] Section 2(1) includes a definition of control that can be taken only over deposit and securities accounts. It recognises two forms of control depending on the nature of the secured party: (1) taken by a person that actually maintains the relevant deposit or securities account, or (2) taken by a third-party creditor that has executed a control agreement with the debtor (the holder of the relevant deposit or securities account) and the person, such as a bank or other financial institution that maintains the same account. However, control is not available with respect to other types of intangible rights for which a security interest may be perfected only by registration. The UNCITRAL Guide similarly limited the availability of control, as a perfection mechanism, to the right to payment of funds credited to a bank account.[50]

(ii) Electronic Documents

Increasingly, documents that embody certain rights, either to payment or delivery of goods, are being issued and transferred electronically. Electronic bills of lading, warehouse receipts and cheques have been around for over a decade.[51] When these electronic documents are utilised in secured transactions as collateral, a question arises as to how the security interest should be perfected. Most secured transactions laws provide for specific rules on the perfection and priority of security interests in these documents but only when they have been issued in paper.[52] In the absence of specific rules the general perfection and priority rules of the secured transactions law become applicable. Accordingly if one were to take a security interest in an electronic warehouse receipt (EWR) under the Malawian PPSA, it would be

[49] Malawi PPSA s 9(1)(iii).

[50] See Recommendation 49 of the Guide (n 18). Recommendation 4(c) excludes from the scope securities, as a result of which the Guide does not cover any aspects of taking security interests in securities, including securities accounts.

[51] On electronic bills of lading see generally M Dubovec, 'The Problems and Possibilities for Using Electronic Bills of Lading as Collateral' (2006) 23 *Arizona Journal of International and Comparative Law* 437.

[52] See the Guide (n 18) Recommendations 51–53 but compare with UCC §9-314, which provides for the perfection of a security interest by control in electronic documents, such as bills of lading and warehouse receipts and the Australian PPSA s 21(2)(c) which allows a security interest in an uncertificated negotiable instrument but not an electronic document of title to be perfected by control. See further Duggan and Brown (n 23) 104.

necessary to register a financing statement to perfect it.[53] Whether this is efficient depends on the manner in which EWRs are used in the particular jurisdiction.

Malawi has two commodity exchanges—AHL Commodity Exchange (AHCX)[54] and Agricultural Commodity Exchange for Africa (ACE)[55]—that actively trade EWRs. Many African commodity exchanges trade actual EWRs rather than or in addition to contracts for the delivery of commodities, such as futures, options and forwards traded at the Chicago Mercantile Exchange and the London Metal Exchange. In a typical transaction, a Malawian farmer deposits her crops to one of the Exchange-accredited or -owned warehouses, obtains a confirmation of delivery and then the Exchange's system creates an EWR that is uploaded to its trading platform. Interested parties may either buy the EWR or take a security interest in it. For the latter, the two Malawian Exchanges have a mechanism whereby they suspend the depositor's trading authority and empower the secured party to dispose of the EWR on the Exchange or off-Exchange by reclaiming and selling the goods in case of the depositor's default. The manner in which this operation is structured and the allocation of rights and powers bear similarities to the perfection by control with respect to bank accounts.[56] Requiring registration would not impose an undue burden on the secured party. However, the potential to mislead a third party is minimal in these transactions because the only way to buy or take a security interest in an EWR or goods covered thereunder is through the Exchange, which would have already clearly marked the EWR as being encumbered. Further arguments for allowing control over EWRs would be the quick turnaround in transactions, such as situations in which EWRs are sold after they have been encumbered and then encumbered again which is not the case in Malawi, yet. In addition, if the registry system operates inefficiently or charges high fees for registrations, perfection by control would reduce the cost for secured transactions of this kind. For these reasons, the Warehouse Receipts Bill, pending adoption by the Parliament, included special rules on perfection by control over EWRs that will supplement the PPSA.

(iii) Vehicles

Another area of interest is the interaction of the PPSA with the law that governs the registration of vehicles, including the title thereto and any encumbrances.[57] Vehicles are expected to be the most common type of collateral to be utilised under the PPSA. Currently a creditor is registered as the 'title holder' of the vehicle

[53] An electronic warehouse receipt would fall under the definition of 'intangible' included in s 2(1).

[54] See www.ahcxmalawi.com/.

[55] See www.aceafrica.org/default.aspx.

[56] See further M Dubovec, 'Fundamentals of Taking Security Interests in Bank Accounts' in F Dahan (ed), *EBRD Research Handbook on Secured Lending in Commercial Transactions* (Cheltenham, Edward Elgar, 2015).

[57] Road Traffic Act 1998 (C 69:01 Laws of Malawi).

while the debtor is registered as its 'owner'. Non-consensual lien holders such as the Malawi Revenue Authority may also be registered as title holders. This type of registration and the fact that the title holder retains possession of the certificate of ownership prevents the owner from selling the vehicle without the title holder's consent. On the one hand, these procedures perfect the security interest and prevent the debtor from selling the collateral, but on the other hand they limit the debtor's power to create multiple security interests over the same vehicle. The vehicle registration system is being upgraded to interface with the Revenue Authority as well as the police system to integrate the relevant information relating not only to the title and encumbrances, but also to any liens for owed taxes and claims of rightful owners who might have been defrauded by a thief. The Road Traffic Department is working to establish connections with banks to be able to collect registration fees remotely but also to allow them to register notices of their interests electronically. In addition, this connection should allow the banks to verify and validate the authenticity of driver licences of potential borrowers and identify them accordingly in a PPSA registration. With respect to the interaction with the PPSA registry, the two government authorities responsible for their establishment and maintenance contemplate an interconnection that would automatically alert the Road Traffic Department every time a registration in the PPSA registry is completed against a particular serial number of the vehicle. The practice whereby secured creditors get themselves registered as title holders and retain certificates of ownership is expected to continue to minimise the risk of the debtor selling the vehicles without the creditor's authorisation.

(iv) Stamp Duty

The Stamp Duty Act was enacted in 1969 to impose a stamp duty on certain instruments.[58] In practice, the registrar responsible for the registration of those particular instruments will not register them in the relevant registry if the stamp duty has not been paid. When duty is paid, an instrument will be physically stamped to confirm the fact of payment.[59] The instruments and the stamp duty payable are specified in the Schedule to the Act.[60] There are two types of stamp duty: (1) fixed stamp duty, which specifies an amount payable on the instrument, and (2) *ad valorem* stamp duty, which varies depending on the amount involved in the transaction. The Act applies to instruments that may be created under

[58] C 43:01 1969 (Laws of Malawi). Legislation to impose duties was first introduced in England in 1694, as a temporary measure. DG Hill, *Stamp, Death, Estate and Gift Duties: NSW, Commonwealth and ACT*, 1st edn (Sydney, Law Book Co, 1970).

[59] See also WDM Cannon, 'Fundamental Principles of Stamp Duty' (1996) 19 *University of New South Wales Law Journal* 3.

[60] The stamp duty originated as a tax on instruments rather than transactions. D Cominos, 'Queensland Stamp Duty Aspects of Financing Transactions' (1990) 6 *Queensland University of Technology Law Journal* 39.

other laws, including charges and mortgages. However, certain instruments that are covered by the PPSA now have been exempt from stamp duties. For instance, section 12 of the Farmers' Stop Order Act expressly exempted farmers' stop orders from stamp duty. During several workshops conducted by the authors in Malawi, a number of commercial banks suggested that secured transactions subject to the PPSA be similarly exempted.

The PPSA did not alter the Act, which raised a question as to whether a duty should be imposed on security agreements at all, and, if so, which duty should be applicable. Since the PPSA has replaced charges with security interests, one could argue that the security agreement falls under the category of loan agreements that attract a duty of the equivalent of US$1. However, several issues have already come up. First, since the PPSA allows registration to take place in the absence of a security agreement, unlike previously, a registration could be completed before stamp duty is even payable. Second, nowhere does the PPSA refer to stamp duty. Third, the trend is to exclude personal property from the application of stamp duty. In addition to farmers' stop orders, in 1986 when the Companies Act 1984 was brought into force, transactions involving shares in companies were exempted from stamp duty. An express exemption of security interests in personal property was one possible direction that the government contemplated, given its policy on financial inclusion and the costs that stamp duty might impose on borrowers. However, the Government eventually decided to impose stamp duty on financing statements through the Personal Property (Fees & Stamp Duty) Regulations 2015.[61] Stamp duties are payable in addition to registration fees which are about the equivalent of USD$5 for the registration of initial financing statements, amendments and discharges do not attract any fees, and searches could be conducted for approximately USD$2. The peculiar feature of the Malawian registry fee schedule is the right of microfinance institutions to pay an annual subscription fee of approximately USD$555 to gain unlimited access to the registry services.

E. PPSA-Related Modernisation

(i) Corporate Law

The above-mentioned assessments also highlighted the need to modernise the areas closely related to the PPSA. For secured transactions reforms, it is critical that the factors that enable the efficient application of the substantive law be examined and modernised, when necessary. For instance, the ICA highlighted the barriers that exist to the entry of firms to formal entrepreneurship due to the high costs

[61] Government Notice Number 42/2015, 27th November 2015.

of formalisation. The Malawian financial institutions prefer to lend to formally constituted businesses so it was important to enable the many informal SMEs to transition into the formal sector, in which opportunities for accessing credit are significantly greater. The response was the Business Registration Act 2012, which replaced the Business Names Registration Act 1916. Further reforms to the legislation governing incorporation of companies followed.

Malawi's Companies Act 1984 had been drafted along the lines of the English Companies Act 1948.[62] There was a general feeling that the Act was dated and required reform.[63] The Ministry of Industry and Trade prepared a paper entitled *Company Law Review: A Working Paper* which, inter alia, concluded:

> The rights of shareholders, and in particular minority shareholder actions is one area that has developed an immense technical thicket based on judge made law that could benefit from a well thought out and careful review. There is a need for accurate and timely corporate financial reporting to improve governance and access to credit. The World Bank's *Report on the Observance of Standards and Codes: Accounting and Audit in Malawi* and *Report on the Observance of Standards and Codes: Corporate Governance* clearly identified the gaps in the present legal framework.[64]

An additional reason for reforming the Companies Act was the need to conform its provisions on the registration of charges to the PPSA. The first draft of the Companies Bill was modelled after the Companies Act 2008 of Mauritius. The reason was that the Mauritius companies law was one of the most highly regarded laws on companies. In the process leading to the enactment of the Malawian Companies Act No 15 of 2013, the Registrar of Companies in Mauritius shared much of their country's reform experience with the local drafting group of Malawi. However, in the area of protecting minority shareholders and issues of corporate governance, Malawi opted to follow the English Companies Act 2006. The Companies Act 2013 states that for the avoidance of doubt the PPSA applies to debentures that are secured by personal property. Accordingly, since the PPSA entered into force, fixed and floating charges over personal property are no longer governed by the company law and subjected to registration in the Companies Registry.

(ii) Corporate Insolvency Law

The modernisation of Malawian company law also necessitated a review of its insolvency law as the 1984 Companies Act also governed some insolvency aspects

[62] M Nzunda, 'The Company Law of Malawi' (PhD thesis, University of Cambridge, 1987). The thesis contains an unpublished short report on the preparation of the Companies Act 1984 by Prof Len Sealy of the University of Cambridge.

[63] National Steering Committee, 'Malawi: Country Action Plan for the Implementation of Reforms to Strengthen Corporate Financial Reporting' (Lilongwe, Malawi, 2009).

[64] Malawi Government, Ministry of Industry and Trade, 'Company Law Review: A Working Paper' (Lilongwe, Malawi, 2009) 13.

with respect to registered companies.[65] A major influence for the review of the insolvency provisions was the recommendations of the *World Bank's Doing Business, Closing a Business in Malawi Report* which, inter alia, recommended the introduction of corporate rescue provisions.[66] The Report identified a deeply entrenched liquidation culture attributed to the existing insolvency framework and a lack of oversight of insolvency practitioners. The Report also noted that the framework in this area, both for personal and corporate insolvency, was outdated.

Having followed the Companies Act of Mauritius, it was inevitable that Malawi would substantially follow the Insolvency Act 2010 of Mauritius except in the areas of insolvency practitioner regulation and administration and corporate reorganisation, the reform of which was modelled on English law. The Malawi Insolvency Act received assent on 24th January 2016[67] as Act number 9 of 2016. The Act imposes a moratorium on all proceedings against the property of the company on the onset of a company re-organisation or winding up.[68] However a secured party retains the power to take possession of, realise and otherwise deal with property over which it has a security interest.[69] The right is not subject to the claims of preferential creditors or expenses of the proceedings other than those related to maintenance of the collateral. Finally the Insolvency Act incorporates the cross-border insolvency provisions of the UNCITRAL Model Law on Cross-Border Insolvency.[70] Following its enactment, its accompanying PPSA and Companies Act reforms, the Insolvency Act 2016 provides a complete scheme for a modern credit legal infrastructure in Malawi. The reason for delaying the enactment of the Insolvency Act was mainly its complicated technical nature and size, which required a more engaged discussion in the relevant Parliamentary Committees before it was formally presented for discussion in the Parliament.

(iii) Dispute Resolution

Another important reform undertaken in Malawi relates to judicial dispute resolution mechanisms. In response to the concerns about timely and cost-efficient commercial justice by the private sector, the Malawi government established the Commercial Division of the High Court to clear the backlog of commercial

[65] On the desirability and necessity to reform secured transactions laws in conjunction with insolvency laws see AH Raymond, 'How May International Standards Assist Law Reform in England?' in NO Akseli (ed), *Availability of Credit and Secured Transactions in a Time of Crisis* (Cambridge, Cambridge University Press, 2013).

[66] World Bank Group, 'World Bank's Doing Business, Closing a Business in Malawi Report' (Washington, DC, 2010).

[67] Malawi Gazette Supplement dated 5th February 2016

[68] Sections 26, 27 and 149.

[69] ibid s 298(6)(a) and (7).

[70] www.uncitral.org/uncitral/en/commission/working_groups/5Insolvency.html#1995-1999.

cases.[71] Efficient judicial mechanisms are critical, particularly for the enforcement of security interests. Secured parties will need to rely on such mechanisms when, for instance, the debtor resists repossession of the collateral, which leaves no option but to proceed pursuant to judicial process, as mandated by section 87(2) of the PPSA. One year after its establishment, a report reviewing the operations of the Commercial Court highlighted:[72]

> The lobby for the establishment of the Commercial Court was born out of frustration with long delays experienced in prosecuting commercial cases in what may now be called the 'General Division' of the High Court (eg mortgage, debt collection, arbitration cases). There was also a view that the creation of the Court would allow for specialisation of judges and lawyers in commercial litigation. Further, the Commercial Court was to function in such way that the Court was responsible for case management and control so that the pace of litigation is determined by the Court and not the parties and/or their lawyers.

Some concerns were raised in connection with the minimum monetary threshold in dispute for the Commercial Division to assume jurisdiction, which was set at the equivalent of US$2,000. The review report highlighted that this minimum threshold had been considered by some as being so high as to make the Commercial Court an epitome of the law being used as a tool of capitalists to oppress the masses. It had been argued that there is no justification for the government to provide resources for an expedited service that is available only to the rich when the masses also have commercial and business disputes that need efficient resolution.[73] However, contrary to this suggestion, in 2010 the threshold was doubled due to the depreciation of the currency and the view of the Commercial Court itself that a low threshold might open the floodgates for petty disputes that could overburden the judges and lead to delays in resolving commercially significant disputes. The rules of the Commercial Court have enabled disputes to be resolved in less than 100 days as compared to over a year prior to its establishment.[74]

(iv) International Conventions

This dramatic reform of the domestic commercial law landscape also aligned Malawi's framework with the relevant international conventions in the area of

[71] Courts Act 2007 (C 3:03 Laws of Malawi), High Court Commercial Division Rules Malawi Government Notice No 5 of 2007 as amended by Government Notice No 21 of 2008 issued by the Chief Justice under the Courts Act.

[72] High Court of Malawi, Final Report on Review of the High Court (Commercial Division) Rules 2007 and High Court (Commercial Division) (Mandatory Mediation) Rules, 2007 (Blantyre, Malawi, 2008) and Audit of Commercial Matters in the General Division of the High Court of Malawi (Blantyre, Malawi, 2008) unpublished, p 3.

[73] High Court of Malawi, Final Report on Review of the High Court (Commercial Division) Rules 2007, 6.

[74] ibid 3.

secured financing, enabling it to become a party to the instruments that facilitate financing on a cross-border basis. By way of background, section 3(5) of the PPSA includes a list of transactions to which it does not apply. Security interests in aircraft objects such as frames and engines have not been excluded, as has been done in many secured transactions laws. This seemingly unusual deviation is, however, compatible with the relevant recommendation of the UNCITRAL Guide that the law not apply to 'aircraft … in so far as such asset is covered by a national law or an international agreement'. Malawi does not have a special law that governs the registration of mortgages in aircraft objects. The Civil Aviation Act[75] nowhere provides how an interest in an aircraft may be created and perfected, so a creditor would need to register a charge in the Companies Registry to protect its interest in the aircraft against third parties. On 16 January 2014 Malawi acceded to the Convention on International Interests in Mobile Equipment (Convention).[76] Both the Convention and its Aircraft Protocol entered into force for Malawi on 1 May 2014. The impetus to ratify the Convention and the Aircraft Protocol came from Ethiopian Airlines (ET), which, as a strategic partner of the Malawi government, expressed an interest in acquiring Malawian Airlines, which was a successor of Air Malawi, voluntarily wound up in 2012. As a condition of its investment, ET requested that the government accede to the Convention and the Aircraft Protocol.[77]

In its accession package, Malawi made a number of declarations that are largely compatible with the PPSA. Under Article 39(1)(a) of the Convention, Malawi declared that a number of non-consensual claims (eg payments due to workers) will retain priority. Under Article 40, Malawi declared that specified non-consensual rights shall be registrable, most notably the rights of judgment creditors. Finally under Article 54(2), Malawi declared that any remedies available to the creditor may be exercised without court action and any leave of the court. Malawi also elected to be bound by a number of credit-friendly provisions of the Aircraft Protocol, including the application of the insolvency Alternative A of Article XI. All of these declarations have set a clear path for Malawi to create an environment that is protective of creditors' rights in aviation finance.

F. What is Going to Happen Next?

Modernisation of a secured transactions law requires much more than adoption of a new statute. In addition to the related reforms, many of which were examined above, the users of the new framework must be adequately informed and

[75] Civil Aviation Act 1971 (C 70:01, Laws of Malawi).

[76] The Convention on International Interests in Mobile Equipment, Cape Town, 16 November 2001.

[77] Before its first scheduled flight on 31 January 2014, ET delivered two planes to Malawian Airlines. See www.nyasatimes.com/2014/01/26/malawi-airlines-launches-first-flight/.

trained.[78] Such training is typically conducted on multiple fronts. Before the PPSA registry was launched, the designer of the system had rolled out a robust training programme to its potential users. The International Finance Corporation, as part of its reform projects, also provides training on the fundamentals of asset-based lending and such training will be delivered to Malawian lenders.[79]

An obvious need for additional awareness on the legal implications of the PPSA remains. Over the last four years of delivering workshops, both authors no longer hear questions about what is going to happen to the floating and fixed charges and why they have been replaced with the new functional concept of a security interest. The lenders' thinking is now shifting to the security title devices that allow them to retain ownership of an asset until the debtor fully satisfies the obligation. Most of these lenders have a difficult time grasping the transition from an environment in which there are no priority conflicts because they effectively hold title to a new environment in which title is immaterial and the three forms of perfection determine priority. They are surprised when the authors explain to them that no matter how they allocate ownership in their agreement with the debtor, the PPSA will disregard such allocation and bestow a security interest on them. They are also bewildered when they hear that the fact that they are named in the Registry of Vehicles as title holders of the vehicle for which they provided financing is immaterial. Granted that such designation should eliminate the risk of the debtor fraudulently selling the vehicle, it is still no shield against a competing security interest that was first registered in the PPSA registry or against an insolvency trustee, as these competing claimants are not concerned with an indication that the lender owns the vehicle according to the records of the Registry of Vehicles. The PPSA changes these ingrained perceptions about the legal framework.

The Malawian PPSA took effect on 23 November 2015 when the registry became available for online registrations. An IT company that has designed and implemented the collateral registries of Ghana, Liberia and Nigeria customised the software to fit the requirements set out in the PPSA and the Regulations. Malawi has joined the group of African economies that have already reformed their secured transactions laws and launched fully electronic registries. A handful of other countries (eg Kenya, Sierra Leone, Zambia, and Zimbabwe) will soon join this group.

Nonetheless, some implementation challenges remain. Further training and educational campaigns are key for the success of the PPSA. It will be interesting to see how quickly sophisticated commercial banks and microfinance institutions that extend low-value loans secured with inventory and household assets will embrace the new framework. In Ghana, the largest users of its Collateral Registry are microfinance institutions catering to women entrepreneurs. Microfinance

[78] For more comment on the need for education, see Ch 22 D.

[79] As noted by many commentators, 'the beneficial economic results cannot be achieved by legislation alone'. G McCormack, *Secured Credit and the Harmonisation of Law: The UNCITRAL Experience* (Cheltenham, Edward Elgar, 2011) 1, 67.

institutions are expected to be one of the largest users of the Malawian registry too. Some concerns about the adequacy of technological infrastructure and connectivity remain. One of the authors encountered similar concerns in Liberia before the launch of its Collateral Registry in June 2014. Thus far, Liberian lenders have not experienced difficulties accessing the registry, which is a positive sign for Malawi. Still, there are some outstanding tasks to complete, primarily the adoption of the Warehouse Receipts Bill. Hopefully, the Malawian policymakers will revisit the application and economic impact of the Stamp Duty Act on secured transactions and other commercial instruments. The success of the Malawi PPSA is expected to have ramifications beyond the domestic landscape as there are a number of African economies patiently waiting on the side-lines, monitoring the impact of these kinds of reforms on economic development and contemplating their own reform projects.

9

Reforming the Law of Secured Transactions in Jersey

ROY GOODE AND JOHN RAINER

Part 1: The Security Interests (Jersey) Law 2012

ROY GOODE

A. A Brief History

Law reform takes time. It was way back in July 1998 that I was asked by Richard Syvret, then Director General of the Jersey Financial Services Commission, to make proposals for the modernisation of Jersey law governing security interests in movable property in the light of a report prepared many years earlier by a working party set up by the Financial & Commercial Law Sub-Committee of the Jersey Law Society. A primary concern was to ensure that Jersey, a significant offshore financial centre, did not lose business to competing financial centres because of concerns of prospective foreign lenders and investors as to the effectiveness of security interests under the Security Interests (Jersey) Law 1983. Jersey lawyers had long been aware of the deficiencies in Jersey's security law and Jersey's economic adviser, David Morgan, introduced an ambitious project to modernise the law along the lines of Article 9 of the American Uniform Commercial Code (UCC), but though the Jersey Law Society had been persuaded of its merits it came to nothing and instead the 1983 Law was enacted.

I produced a discussion document identifying what seemed to me to be the main weaknesses of Jersey secured transactions law at that time, including the inability to take global security over present and future assets, the restricted forms of security available, the limited range of default remedies and the absence of any machinery for registration of security interests, which were therefore invisible to third parties. This was followed by a separate paper on the conflict of laws aspects.

The original conception of the working party was to cover all forms of asset, tangible and intangible, movable and immovable, but it was sensibly decided to exclude security interests in immovable property because of the distinctive features of interests in land and to limit the project to security interests in intangible movables in the first instance. There followed an extended period of consideration by the Jersey Financial Services Commission and others. In April 2003 I produced a detailed blueprint for the reform of the law, which was revised in July. Unfortunately there was then a hiatus of several years while the Commission's focus shifted to other matters and it was not until 2007 that the project was revived by James Mews, the Director of Jersey's Finance Industry Department. By then Jersey's law draftsman, Chris Anderson, had produced a comprehensive draft law based on the blueprint. This was a major step forward. Equally significant were the distinctive working methods adopted. In the first place the law draftsman proved unusually open to suggestions both on substance and on drafting and produced a series of drafts as the text developed. Secondly, there were numerous meetings with practising lawyers and industry experts as the project progressed. The banking lawyers in particular made a valuable contribution not only to the substance of the provisions, but also, through their comments and suggestions, to the language of the drafts.[1] Thirdly, faced with a choice between highly sophisticated, complex rules of the kind embodied in Article 9 and a simpler set of provisions which would be rough at the edges and leave more leeway for the court but would be much easier to understand, the banking lawyers—wisely, in my view—opted for the latter. So the path adopted was to paint with a broader brush and to focus on relative simplicity rather than seeking to provide solutions to every conceivable problem.

It is fair to say that in the early stages some sectors of the Jersey legal profession, as with lawyers in other jurisdictions, were rather sceptical of the need for the reforms but they very soon became convinced that the 1983 Law was inadequate and needed to be replaced by much more comprehensive legislation. Jersey had £246 billion of funds under management in 2007, and its finance industry contributed 60 per cent of the island's gross domestic product. The project drew heavily on the English Law Commission's 2004 excellent consultative report *Company Security Interests*, produced under the direction of Professor Hugh Beale,[2] and on legislation in other common law jurisdictions that had been influenced by Article 9 of the American UCC, in particular the Saskatchewan Personal Property Security Act 1993 and the New Zealand Personal Property Securities Act 1999; and close attention was paid to their registry systems by those engaged in the establishment of the Jersey register of security interests.

[1] See Part 2 B.

[2] Law Commission, *Company Security Interests: A Consultative Report*, Consultation Paper No 176 (2004).

The draft Law (known informally as SIJL 1 because it was the first of two parts, Part 1 being confined to intangible movables) was sent to Whitehall to receive the imprimatur of the Privy Council. It was unfortunately delayed for nearly a year through adoption of a consultation process within the UK government which failed to take account of Jersey's special status, but eventually the Law received the royal assent on 10 July 2012 and was registered by the Royal Court on 27 July 2012, entering fully into force on 2 January 2014. But that was not quite the end of SIJL 1. First, the trust lawyers belatedly entered the scene, successfully pressing for security by certain private trusts to be exempted from registration.[3] Second, certain defects were found in the legislation. Fortunately the Law itself provides for certain amendments to be made by regulation and others by Ministerial order, so these issues were fixed.[4] There will be a further opportunity to rectify errors or omissions not so far detected when SIJL 2, extending the Law to tangible movables, is introduced.

B. Purpose and Scope of the New Law

The overriding aim of the new Law is to facilitate the creation and perfection of security interests in intangible movables and their proceeds ('collateral') with the minimum of formality and to lay down priority rules that meet the reasonable expectations of the business community. In order for a security interest to be created so as to be enforceable under the Law six conditions must be fulfilled:

1. There must be a security agreement creating or providing for the security interest. The Law does not apply to non-consensual security interests.
2. The subject matter (the collateral) must be intangible movable property. The Law will not apply to goods or documents of title to goods until extended by SIJL 2, which is still in draft.
3. There must be a connection to Jersey as provided by Article 4 of the Law,[5] though the parties to a security agreement can agree on the application of the Law in their relations with each other even where Article 4 does not apply.[6]
4. The security interest must have attached to the collateral as provided by Articles 18–20.
5. The interest must not be one which is excluded by Article 8 of the Law.
6. The transaction must not be one which is excluded by Article 9.

[3] See Part 2 C below.

[4] The 2012 Law was amended by the Security Interests (Amendment of Law) (Jersey) Regulations 2013 (R & O 102/1013) and the Security Interests (Amendment of Law) (No 2) (Jersey) Regulations 2013 (R & O 128/2013), and the consolidated text as at 2 January 2014 has been published in a Revised Edition.

[5] As modified by Article 2 of the Security Interests (Application of Law) (Jersey) Order 2013.

[6] See Section H.

Assignments of receivables by way of security fall within the ordinary provisions governing security interests but are also subject to the special provisions of Articles 39 and 41.[7] But outright assignments are also brought within the provisions of the Law governing perfection and priorities in order to create transparency in receivables financing, though the enforcement provisions, which are geared to default, do not, of course, apply to them. Unless otherwise stated an assignment means an outright assignment,[8] so that in the priority rules, for example, an assignment by way of security is not referred to as an assignment, it simply falls within the umbrella of security interest.

The Law is in nine Parts:

Part 1 Interpretation
Part 2 Scope of Law
Part 3 Attachment and Perfection
Part 4 Priority in General
Part 5 Taking Free
Part 6 Assignments of receivables
Part 7 Enforcement of Security Interests
Part 8 Registration
Part 9 Miscellaneous

For reasons of space only an outline can be given here.

C. Some Key Definitions

Article 1 contains a long list of definitions. We begin with some basic definitions; others will be encountered as we go along.

(i) Security Agreement

A security agreement is defined as an agreement that creates or makes provision for a security interest and includes an agreement that varies, renews or extends a security agreement and any writing that evidences a security agreement.

(ii) Security Interest

Following UCC/PPSA legislation elsewhere Article 1A(1) defines 'security interest' as 'an interest in intangible movable property, being an interest that, under

[7] See Section M.
[8] See Article 1.

a security agreement, secures payment or secures performance of an obligation'. 'Security interest' is thus used in a broad sense to cover mortgages, pledges and contractual liens and 'any other encumbrance that is by way of security',[9] in particular a charge, or hypothec. These terms have disappeared, all of them being subsumed under a single rubric, the security interest. Contracting parties remain free to use the old terminology but this will have no significance. The purpose is to replace the existing security devices, each with its own creation, perfection and priority rules, with a generic security interest which, with some exceptions, applies a common set of rules.

The security interest concept, which embodies the traditional approach, will expand when the Law is extended to goods, since if the text put out for consultation some years ago is maintained the provisions applicable to security will also embrace the reservation of title by a seller under a conditional sale agreement or by a supplier under a hire purchase agreement, the interest of a lessor under a lease for a term of more than one year and the interest of a consignor under a commercial consignment, though as regards the last three categories the enforcement provisions would be inapplicable if the relevant agreement did not transfer substantially all the risks and rewards of ownership of the relevant goods to the hirer, lessee or consignee, so that in the absence of such a transfer the proposed new Law would be limited to attachment, perfection and priority.

Article 6 also provides that where a bank holds money on deposit or a securities intermediary holds securities for a customer maintaining a securities account the bank or intermediary, as the case may be, may take a security interest in its own obligation thus giving legislative effect to a dictum of Lord Hoffmann in *Re Bank of Credit and Commerce International SA (No 8)*,[10] and that a company incorporated with a share capital may take a security interest from any of its shareholders in its own shares.

(iii) Secured Party

The secured party is the person who holds the security interest, whether for the benefit of itself, of a third party or of both.

(iv) Grantor; Obligor

The grantor is the person granting the security interest and typically will be the person owing the secured debt. However, security may be taken not only for the grantor's own indebtedness, but also for that of a third party. In such a case

[9] Article 1A(3).
[10] *Re Bank of Credit and Commerce International SA (No 8)* [1996] Ch 214 at 226–28.

the third party is known as the obligor, to distinguish him from the grantor of the security. The distinction is particularly relevant to the enforcement provisions, which refer to the grantor when dealing with the collateral or proceeds but obligor when referring to a monetary liability for a deficiency.[11]

(v) Collateral

Intangible movable property that is subject to a security interest.

D. Security in After-acquired Property

The floating charge has never featured in Jersey law and does not do so now. Article 18(3) provides that the attachment of a security interest to collateral is not affected just because the grantor retains, in the absence of a contrary direction from the secured party, the right to deal with the collateral free from the security interest and without a duty to account for the proceeds or to replace the collateral, though a disposition within the scope of the debtor's authority to deal precludes the secured party from asserting a continuing security interest in the disposed-of collateral.[12] Nothing in the Law precludes the grant of a floating charge over assets in another jurisdiction which recognises floating charges, but if the assets are removed to Jersey they come within the ambit of the 2012 Law. Under Article 19(1) a security agreement may provide for a security interest in after-acquired property, and by Article 19(2) the security interest attaches automatically to a newly acquired asset without the need for any post-acquisition act of transfer or other appropriation.

English law has never been explicit as to the time *from which* a security interest in after-acquired property attaches, but it is implicit in the working of the priority rules that once the new asset has been acquired priority goes back to the time of the security agreement.[13] In those unusual cases under the Jersey law where priority is governed by the order of attachment it is expressly provided that a security interest in after-acquired property shall be taken to have attached at the time of making of the security agreement.[14]

[11] See Ch 8 C(iii): the Australian legislation makes the same distinction (unlike many other PPSAs), but uses 'debtor' instead of 'obligor'.

[12] Article 24(a).

[13] This principle was first articulated by the writer in *Legal Problems of Credit and Security* (London, Sweet & Maxwell, 1982) 6–8. See now Louise Gullifer (ed), *Goode on Legal Problems of Credit and Security*, 5th edn (London, Sweet & Maxwell, 2013) para 2-13.

[14] Article 29(3).

E. Intangible Movable Property

Intangibles are divided into documentary intangibles[15] and non-documentary (or 'pure' intangibles). The former are susceptible to possession and are thus capable of pledge as if they were goods. Not all documentary intangibles are currently within the scope of the Law but only negotiable instruments and negotiable investment securities. Documents of title to goods will feature in SIJL 2 as part of the general extension of the Law to security interests in goods. Broadly the same rules apply to negotiable instruments and negotiable investment securities, but the former remain governed by negotiable instruments law, so that nothing in the security interests Law affects the rights of a holder in due course.[16] A pure intangible is anything that is not a documentary intangible and includes cash that is not money[17] and licences and quotas having commercial value even if not transferable,[18] but not money or intangibles excluded under Article 9.[19] Among the other items of intangible property are securities accounts,[20] ordinary debts,[21] contract rights, including contractual rights to the delivery of goods but not an interest in the goods themselves. So while the Law covers security in the interest of an investor in an unallocated gold or other precious metals account, where there has been no appropriation of precious metals to the sale contract, merely a contractual obligation to deliver precious metals of a specified quantity, a security interest in precious metals that have been appropriated to the sale contract is an interest in goods falling outside the present Law, though prospectively within SIJL 2.

F. Receivables

Receivables are a particular form of debt, being defined as a monetary entitlement, whether or not earned by performance, arising from the supply of goods or services (other than insurance services) or the supply of energy, but the term

[15] The phrase 'documentary intangibles' was coined by the Crowther Committee in its report on consumer credit (Cmnd 4596, March 1971) vol 2, Appendix III, para 8.

[16] Article 37.

[17] That is, cheques or drafts and deposit accounts in banks or similar deposit-taking institutions (see definition of 'cash proceeds' in Art 1) but not currency, ie coins and notes.

[18] See Ch 6 B.

[19] Article 1.

[20] A securities account means an account maintained by an intermediary to which investment securities may be credited or debited and includes a reference to the investment securities so credited (Art 1). So the account holder may either grant a security interest over the account as a whole as it stands from time to time, including future investment securities credited to the account, or all or identified securities in the account at a given time.

[21] Of which a subset consists of receivables, for which there are distinct provisions. See Section M.

does not include a loan, a deposit account or a right to payment embodied in a negotiable instrument or investment security.[22] Receivables financing is typically undertaken by factors and invoice discounters, who buy receivables outright from suppliers of goods or services, and by banks and other financiers lending on the security of receivables. There are three reasons for treating receivables as a distinct category. The first is that the rules governing registration and priorities are extended to outright assignments to give transparency for types of transaction involving a continuous flow of dealings between assignor and assignee. Such considerations do not apply to the categories of transaction excluded from the definition. The second is that receivables are not susceptible to control in the same way as securities accounts and deposit accounts. Thirdly, it is necessary to impose restrictions on the effectiveness of prohibitions against the assignment of receivables in order to avoid a serious obstacle to this form of trade finance.[23]

G. Proceeds

A security interest in collateral that is dealt with or otherwise gives rise to proceeds continues both in the original collateral and in the proceeds, so far as these are of a kind falling within the Law.[24] So if investment securities given in security are wrongfully disposed of by the debtor and the proceeds paid into a deposit account in the name of the debtor the secured party can follow the securities into the hands of the transferee, subject to any overriding rights given to the transferee by the Law, and can also assert a security interest in the deposit account. Of course the secured party is not entitled to recover both the original collateral and the proceeds but will have to elect which to follow. If the proceeds had taken the form of tangible movables, such as a motor car, this would not constitute proceeds, being a form of asset outside the Law.

'Proceeds' covers identifiable or traceable intangible movables derived directly or indirectly from a dealing with the collateral (and thus extends to proceeds of proceeds), as well as insurance proceeds but, in contrast to the Article 9/PPSA legislation and the Law Commission's proposals in its consultative report, proceeds do not include interest, dividends or other income derived from the proceeds. The reason for the exclusion was twofold. In the first place income does not in fact constitute proceeds, the original asset still being in the hands of the debtor. Secondly, dividend and other income is typically left in the hands of the debtor. However, this may need review, since it is based on a formal concept of disposition as a transfer of title, whereas to be consistent with the functional approach embodied in the Law part dispositions, such as the grant of a lease, should be recognised

[22] Article 1.
[23] See Section M.
[24] Article 26.

as diminishing the value of the asset in the hands of the lessor and giving rise to proceeds such as the lease rentals. Meanwhile there is nothing to preclude the parties from entering into a security agreement providing for security over income as original collateral.

H. Connection to Jersey

Article 4 lays down a variety of connecting factors which link a secured transaction to Jersey in order to make the Law applicable. Article 4 was later extensively revised by regulations to increase the range of connecting factors.[25] Article 5 is a unique provision that parties may agree to apply the Law to the relations between themselves even without the Jersey connection that would otherwise be required. Obviously this cannot extend to registration or other means of perfection or to priority rules or the impact of insolvency.

I. Exclusions and Exemptions

Articles 8 and 9 exclude various categories of transaction from the scope of the law. Some of the exclusions relate to transactions that do not in law constitute security at all but are stated for the avoidance of doubt. Included among these are rights of set-off, netting or combination of accounts, assignments for the general benefit of creditors, sale and repurchase transactions ('repos') and stock lending. Others reflect the fact that the transaction in question is not fulfilling a security function, for example, assignments in discharge of a pre-existing indebtedness and assignments of receivables for collection, the assignor remaining the beneficial owner. Moreover, outright assignments are in general outside the scope of the Law altogether, but outright assignments of receivables, though not treated as security interests, are brought within the Law solely for the purpose of registration and priority, in order to alert third parties to their existence.

Further, an Order has been made pursuant to Articles 4A, 60(2)(b), 62(1) and 92 of the Law exempting security interests granted by prescribed unit trusts over trust property not situated in Jersey or where the security interest is created and perfected under the law of a jurisdiction other than Jersey.[26]

In addition to total exclusions from the Law various more limited exemptions have been prescribed by Order pursuant to Articles 4A and 92 of the Law. In particular, security interests granted by trustees of private trusts are perfected by mere attachment, without registration, except in the case of Jersey property unit trusts

[25] Security Interests (Amendment of Law) (Jersey) Regulations 2013.

[26] Security Interests (Application of Law—Exceptions) (Jersey) Order 2013, R & O 168/2013.

(JPUTs).[27] This exemption was made after the Jersey trust lawyers belatedly awoke to the potential impact of the registration system on the much-prized privacy of Jersey private trusts.[28] However, it seems unlikely that banks will lend to a trust on the basis of a security interest perfected by mere attachment, because it then risks subordination to a subsequent security interest perfected by control,[29] so the likelihood is that the lender will insist on perfecting by control.

J. Attachment and Perfection

The Law borrows these terms from Article 9 and the PPSAs.

(i) Attachment

'Attachment' denotes the act or event by which the security interest becomes enforceable against the grantor with respect to the collateral.[30] Usually three conditions have to be satisfied in order for a security interest to attach:

1. value must have been given, though an antecedent debt or liability suffices;
2. the grantor must have rights in the collateral, though these need not necessarily be ownership rights, a limited interest suffices;
3. the grantee of the security interest must have possession or control or there must be a written security agreement signed by the grantor containing a description of the collateral sufficient to enable it to be identified, for which purpose a description is sufficient if it identifies the collateral by item, by type, by a statement that the security agreement covers all present and future collateral or by a statement that the security agreement covers all present and future collateral except for specified items or types, and the collateral is not within those exceptions.[31]

Where these conditions are satisfied a security interest over after-acquired property takes effect upon acquisition as described earlier. Exceptionally attachment occurs

[27] Security Interests (Registration and Miscellaneous Provisions) Order 2013, R & O 130/2013.

[28] See Part 2 C.

[29] Article 30A(5). As to control, see Art 3 and Section J(iii).

[30] Articles 1, 17.

[31] Article 18(1), (2). Article 18(2) is taken directly from Art V(5) of the Luxembourg Protocol to the Convention on International Interests in Mobile Equipment on Matters specific to Railway Rolling Stock 2007 (the Cape Town Convention on International Interests in Mobile Equipment 2001). By Art 18(3) attachment is not affected just because the grantor retains, in the absence of a contrary direction from the secured party, the right to deal with the asset free from the security interest and without a duty to account for the proceeds or replace the collateral. Under English law such a right would result in characterisation of the security interest as a floating charge, so that attachment would be treated as deferred. Article 18(3) is designed to make it clear that attachment is not deferred merely because of the grantor's continued dealing power, though the parties can expressly agree to deferment (Art 18(1)). See Ch 7 C(ii).

automatically as regards investment securities held with an intermediary and given as security for advances by the intermediary of the purchase price of investments bought for the account holder.[32] The conditions can be satisfied in any order.

(ii) Perfection

Attachment is not normally sufficient to make the security interest effective against third parties. For that a further step, 'perfection', is required. The concept of perfection broadly encompasses a step that will enable a third party to discover the existence of the security interest. The principal methods of perfection are possession, control and registration. Possession is confined to negotiable instruments and negotiable investment securities. Control is effected by one of the methods described below. Registration is available for security interests in any type of collateral except for automatically perfected security interests in favour of a securities intermediary under Article 20[33] and is the only method of perfecting a security interest in collateral which does not consist of documentary intangibles, non-documentary investment securities or deposit accounts. So a security interest in debts or contract rights must be perfected by registration. It is not sufficient for the creditor to take a written assignment and give notice in writing to the account debtor. Perfection, though an essential ingredient of priority, does not guarantee it. The ranking of perfected security interests is governed by the priority rules. Perfection is also necessary in order to maintain the efficacy of the security interest in the debtor's insolvency.[34]

In addition to the three types of perfection described above—registration, possession and control—there are three other types provided by the Law, namely automatic perfection, continuous perfection and temporary perfection. A security interest is automatically perfected if it is in favour of a securities intermediary to finance the purchase of investment securities for a customer before the customer has paid for them. A security interest in proceeds of collateral is considered as continuously perfected where the security interest in the original collateral has been perfected by registration and the proceeds are described in the financing statement and are of a kind to which the Law applies or are of the same description as the original collateral or are cash or insurance or compensation proceeds.[35] There are certain cases where a security interest in proceeds that have not been continuously perfected is temporarily perfected for a period of 30 days without

[32] Article 20.

[33] Article 22(5).

[34] This is a requirement in every Art 9/PPSA jurisdiction except New Zealand, which is alone in preserving an unperfected security interest in the debtor's insolvency. This reflects a view that, where perfection is by registration, the ordinary criteria for avoiding an unregistered interest (want of value, preference, etc) are not applicable. But there are good policy reasons for avoiding an unperfected security interest in insolvency. See Roy Goode, *Principles of Corporate Insolvency Law*, 4th edn (London, Sweet & Maxwell, 2010) para 13-124. See also Ch 7 F(i).

[35] Article 25.

any further step. If the security interest is re-perfected within that period it will be considered continuously perfected as from the time of the original perfection but otherwise only from the time it is in fact re-perfected.[36]

(iii) Control

The concept of control is of central importance in the new Law. The usual method of perfection of a non-possessory security interest is by registration but this is unsuitable for dealings in investment securities, which are regularly turned over in high volume. Article 3 provides for the means of control over three classes of asset, certificated investment securities, securities accounts and deposit accounts. Other categories of intangible, such as receivables or other debts, are not susceptible to control. Control, where available, may be exercised either directly or through a trustee or other person who has control for or on behalf of the secured party.[37]

(a) Investment Securities

Under the Financial Collateral Directive (FCD)[38] no registration or other formality is permitted where the secured creditor takes possession or control of financial collateral. The Directive does not apply to Jersey, and the 2012 Law permits security interests in investment securities to be perfected by registration except in the case of a security interest in favour of a securities intermediary to secure a purchase money advance to the intermediary's customer where perfection is automatic.[39] However, there is little point in registering a security interest in investment securities already perfected by possession or control.

As stated above, perfection of investment securities by possession is limited to negotiable securities as a form of documentary intangible.[40] Other securities, even if certificated, have to be perfected by registration or by control. Under Article 3(5) a secured party has control of a certificated non-bearer security if he or she is registered with the issuer of the security as holder or is in possession of the certificate. But the great bulk of securities are now held through a securities account with an intermediary, where the root of title to securities is their credit to the customer's securities account. The two principal methods of control of a securities account maintained by an intermediary are transfer of the account into the name of the secured party with the written consent of the grantor and the intermediary and an agreement by all three that the intermediary will comply with instructions from

[36] Articles 26–28.

[37] Article 3(7).

[38] Directive 98/26/EC on settlement finality in payment and settlement securities systems of 6 May 2009, OJ L166 dated 11.6.98, p 45, as amended by Directive 2009/44/EC of 6 May 2009, OJ L146/37 dated 10.6.2009 ('FCD'). The Directive was implemented in the UK by the Financial Collateral Arrangements (No 2) Regulations 2003, SI 2003/3226, as amended by SI 2009/2462 ('FCARs').

[39] Articles 21(4), 20. The definition of 'investment security' in Art 1 broadly corresponds to the definition of 'financial instruments' in reg 3(1) of the FCARs.

[40] Articles 22(1), 1.

the secured party as to the disposition of the securities.[41] The grantor remains free to deal with the securities until such instructions are given. Of these two methods the former is the stronger in that the secured party has priority over the holder of an earlier interest perfected by control by the latter method.[42]

There is a third method of control available only to an intermediary. Where the intermediary is the secured party it has control without need for anything further,[43] for the obvious reason that the grantor cannot deal with the securities account without the intermediary's cooperation. Thus charge-backs benefit from automatic perfection without the need for registration. The definition of 'intermediary' in Article 1 includes a person maintaining accounts on its own account as well as for others, so that the grantee under a charge-back retains its status as an intermediary. But a bank acting purely as portfolio manager for another bank and maintaining a parallel account purely for record purposes is not an intermediary.

(b) Deposit Accounts

Control of a deposit account[44] may be effected in the same three ways as control of a securities account,[45] but Article 3(3)(c) adds a fourth method of control, namely by assignment in writing by the grantor to the secured party followed by written notice of assignment to the bank or other institution with which the deposit account is held.

K. The Registration System

Much attention was devoted to the development of an efficient registration system, which proved more complex than originally envisaged but is operative and functioning smoothly. Indeed, in July 2014 the Jersey Companies Registry was given an award by the International Association of Commercial Administrators for 'outstanding achievement in secured transaction registry innovation'. The Security Interests Register is run by the Companies Registry, an arm of the Jersey Financial Services Commission.[46] Following the approach adopted in other jurisdictions the registration system is based not on transaction filing but on notice filing and the registration is against the name of the debtor, not against an asset.[47]

[41] Article 3(4).

[42] See L(ii).

[43] Article 3(4)(c).

[44] Defined as 'a current, deposit, or other, account maintained with a bank, or another deposit-taking institution, and evidencing a depositor's right to the payment of money'. This broadly corresponds to the definition of 'cash' in reg 3(1) of the FCAR, a definition which does not include money in the sense of coins or notes.

[45] Article 3(3).

[46] The Jersey registry won a merit award from the International Association of Commercial Administrators award in 2014 for its innovation and effectiveness. See www.iaca.org/about-iaca/merit-awards/.

[47] In contrast to the registration system established by the Cape Town Convention (n 31), which is asset based. This, of course, requires that the asset be uniquely identifiable.

The secured party or intending secured party files a financing statement stating that he or she has taken or intends to take a security interest in a given item or class of collateral. The information on the register is kept to a minimum and for further details a searcher must approach the secured creditor. In short, the object is to give a searcher notice of the existence of a security interest or prospective security interest over an item or class of collateral.

The registration system is wholly electronic, so that there is no physical filing of documents. Indeed, the only electronic document that has to be filed is the financing statement; there is no obligation to file a copy of the security agreement. This helps to ensure that the terms of the agreement, some of which may be commercially sensitive, are not put in the public domain. The other great advantage of the notice-filing approach is that a financing statement can be filed before the security interest has been created, with priority back to the time of filing once the three conditions of attachment have been fulfilled, and a single filing can cover all future transactions relating to the same classes of collateral; it is not necessary to file in relation to each financing transaction. In the case of loans, that result could be achieved anyway by registering an all-moneys, all-assets security interest, but notice filing is particularly useful for transaction-based finance embodied in conditional sale and hire purchase agreements, to which SIJL 2 will apply.

Transfers, assignments, subordinations, amendments and discharges may be registered by filing a financing change statement. Registration of a financing statement or financing change statement lasts for 10 years or such other period as is specified in the statement.

L. Priority Rules

These are necessarily somewhat complex and only an outline can be given here. They divide into general rules and special rules for particular types of collateral.

(i) General Rules

Under the general rules a perfected security interest has priority over an unperfected security interest, while as between two perfected security interests priority goes to whoever took the first perfection step, that is, registration, possession or control. So where two security interests are perfected by registration priority goes to the first to register; and where one security interest is perfected by registration and another by possession or control, priority is determined according to whether registration preceded or followed possession or control. If both interests are unperfected they rank in order of attachment, but of course the priority of the first attached security interest is provisional only in that the subsequent interest may jump ahead by being the first to be perfected. The second of these priority rules deserves particular attention. A, who is negotiating terms on which it will provide secured finance to D, files a financing statement on 1 January stating it intends to finance on the security of motor vehicle stock. On 10 January B concludes a security agreement with D, gives value and files a financing statement perfecting its security interest. On 20 January A enters into a security agreement with D and gives value. Though B's security interest was perfected first, A has priority as the first to file. A's financing statement put B on notice that its priority was only provisional and was liable to be displaced. B should therefore have procured a subordination from A. Another example is where A takes control on 1 May without yet having concluded a security agreement, B registers a financing statement on 10 May and enters into a security agreement on 12 May, while A enters into its security agreement on 15 May. In this case, although B was the first to enter into a security agreement and thus to perfect its security interest A has priority because it took the first perfection step, control, before B filed its financing statement.

There are similar rules governing competing assignments of the same receivable and priority as between a security interest and an assignment of a receivable.

(ii) Special Rules: Certificated Securities, Securities Accounts and Deposit Accounts[48]

It is necessary to have special rules governing the priority of security interests in certificated securities, securities accounts and deposit accounts because all of these are subject to perfection by control, a form of perfection which is given an enhanced priority status compared with perfection by registration for much the same reasons as those motivating the FCD provisions disapplying registration requirements for security interests in financial collateral. Where the secured party has control of these categories of collateral he or she has priority over another secured party who does not have control.[49] Where both have control priority is determined by the order of control.[50]

In general, a security interest in favour of the bank or intermediary where a deposit or securities account is held has priority over security interests in favour of another secured party[51] but this does not apply where the deposit or securities account is transferred into the name of the other secured party.[52] The point here is that the new account constitutes an entirely separate root of title which in general is unaffected by encumbrances on or other defects in the original account. The same principle applies in cases outside Article 30(3) and (8), ie where the earlier security interest is held by a party other than the intermediary. So if creditor A has

[48] See also discussion in Ch 6 C.

[49] Article 30(5).

[50] Article 30(6).

[51] Article 30(8).

[52] Article 30(2), (4). This will need review in the consideration of SIJL 2 because the case is one which more properly falls within Article 38(3).

control of a deposit or securities account in the name of the debtor while creditor B takes a transfer of such an account into his own name by way of security, creditor B, even if later in time, is unaffected by creditor A's security interest,[53] because, as stated above, the asset in which he holds security is not the same asset as that which is the subject of creditor A's security interest. Moreover, the fact that at the time he took his interest B was aware of A's interest is irrelevant;[54] B loses priority only if he was aware not only of the existence of A's security interest, but also of the fact that the disposition to B was in breach of the security agreement creating that interest.[55] The rules on this point are silent in relation to security interests in deposit accounts.[56] Nothing affects the right of set-off of a bank or other deposit-taking institution or an intermediary.[57]

(iii) Further Advances

A security agreement may secure further advances and as to these the security interest has the same priority as it does in relation to the initial advance, whether or not the further advances are made under an obligation.[58]

(iv) Purchase Money Security Interest

A purchase money security interest is a security interest in collateral taken in favour of a seller to secure the price of the collateral or a security interest to the extent that it is taken to secure value given to enable the grantor to acquire rights in the collateral and used for that purpose. For example, a reservation of title in favour of the seller of intangible movables is a purchase money security interest, as is a security interest in investments taken to secure an advance made to the grantor for the purchase of the investments and so utilised. A purchase money security interest in intangible movable property and proceeds is given priority over a non-purchase money security interest.[59] There are two policy reasons for this priority. The first is that where a security interest has been granted to A covering

[53] Article 38(3).

[54] Article 14(2), 38(3).

[55] Art 38(4). This provision too may need to be reviewed. There are cases in Canada and New Zealand courts have taken the view that a subsequent secured creditor is not concerned with contractual relations between the debtor and first secured creditor and is not to be considered acting in bad faith merely because taking with knowledge even that the grant of the second security interest is in breach of the earlier security agreement. In order to constitute bad faith the later secured creditor must have taken some positive action constituting a waiver or supporting an estoppel or actively misleading or hindering the perfection of the prior interest. See, for example, *Canadian Imperial Bank of CommerceBank of Nova Scotia v Gaudreauy* (1984) 48 OR (2d) 478 at 518–519; *Canadian Imperial Bank of Commerce v AK Construction (1988) Ltd* (1995) 8 WWR 120. *Gibson and Stiassny v Stockco Ltd* [2011] NZCCLR 29.

[56] Article 30 does not contain any provision equivalent to Article 38(4).

[57] Articles 30A, 30B.

[58] Article 33(3).

[59] Article 34.

after-acquired property and later a new asset is acquired with funds advanced by B it would unjustly enrich A to give him priority over B when the asset would not have come into the debtor's estate without B's new money. The second is that without such a rule A would have a complete monopoly over the debtor's financing. The special status of a purchase money security interest is likely to be of more significance in relation to goods than to intangibles.

(v) Taking Free

A person acquiring collateral for value takes free from an unperfected security interest[60] even if having actual knowledge of it. This is not expressly stated in Article 35(1) but is to be implied from the fact that the only exception stated is where the unperfected security interest was created or provided for by a transaction to which the person was a party. The general principle that actual knowledge of an earlier security interest does not affect priority is stated in Article 14(2) and (3) and is applied to a person taking free in cases covered by Articles 36(2) and 38(1) and (3). The purpose of the rule is to give predictability and avoid factual disputes as to the existence of knowledge. So, as stated earlier, in a case outside Article 30, one who has given value[61] for an investment security held with an intermediary and has it transferred to a securities account in his name with the same or another intermediary takes free from a security interest in favour of another party in the original account.[62] Again, the underlying principle is that the transfer to the new account creates a new root of title. Other cases of taking free relate to a creditor who receives payment of a debt,[63] a person who takes possession of a certificate to an investment security[64] or a transfer into his own name of an investment security previously held in an account with an intermediary and subject to a security interest.[65] The taking-free rule does not apply to a person who takes with knowledge of the fact that the disposition to him was in breach of the terms of a security agreement.[66]

M. Assignments of Receivables

Part 6 has special provisions governing the assignment of receivables, for the reasons given earlier.[67]

[60] Article 35.
[61] ie as an outright purchaser, not as grantee of a security interest, whose rights would be governed by Art 30.
[62] Article 38(3).
[63] Article 36.
[64] Where the person's acquisition is itself by way of security this overlaps with the priority rule in Art 30(5).
[65] Article 38(1), (3).
[66] Article 38(2), (4).
[67] Section F.

(i) Anti-assignment Clauses[68]

Article 39 is aimed at a term of a contract prohibiting assignment. This is seen as inimical to the free flow of receivables in the stream of trade, for example under factoring and invoice discounting agreements. Though a debtor may have good commercial reasons for prohibiting assignment—for example, not wanting to deal with a different and potentially tougher creditor—the argument is not a wholly persuasive one. In the first place, it is not only in cases of assignment that the debtor may face a tougher approach. It could also happen because of a change in the policy of the creditor company or a more stringent credit controller. Secondly, anti-assignment clauses are not designed to protect the weaker party, since it is the debtor, not the creditor, who is in the stronger bargaining position, for otherwise it would not be able to impose such a term. If the debtor is not willing either to furnish security or to allow its supplier to offload risk by assignment this puts the supplier in a very difficult position. Finally, if Jersey law follows English law an assignee can anyway get over the prohibition by requiring the assignor to sue or, if the assignor is unwilling, by joining it as a debtor, with a view to obtaining an order for payment by the debtor to the assignor, who would then be accountable to its assignee.[69] So Article 39(1), while preserving the assignor's right to damages for breach of an anti-assignment clause, provides that the clause is not binding on the assignee and does not affect the validity of the assignment. Article 39(1) applies both to outright assignments and to assignments by way of security.

(ii) Debtor's Duty to Assignee

Where the assignment is not a security assignment Article 40 crystallises the account debtor's duty in traditional terms. The debtor does not have to pay the assignee unless he receives a written notice of assignment identifying the account assigned and requiring the account debtor to pay the assignee. Until the debtor acquires knowledge of the assignment it can safely pay the assignor. Article 40 does not apply to security assignments because an underlying concept of the Law is that the creditor's interest is limited to a security interest, so that full ownership of the assigned claim remains with the security assignor.

(iii) Qualification of Assignee's Rights

In line with the case law the assignee, whether under an outright or a security assignment, takes subject to defences of the debtor against the assignor and to

[68] See Ch 15.

[69] See *Barbados Trust Co Ltd v Bank of Zambia* [2007] 1 Lloyd's Rep 495 and Roy Goode, 'Contractual Prohibitions against Assignment' [2009] *Lloyds Maritime and Commercial Law Quarterly* 300, 313–15.

rights of set-off accruing before the account debtor acquired knowledge of the assignment or which are closely connected with the assigned claim.[70] This does not apply if the debtor has entered into an agreement containing a cut-off clause precluding the debtor from asserting defences.[71]

N. Enforcement

Part 7 is devoted to enforcement in respect of a security interest. In contrast to the 1983 Law, under which sale was the sole default remedy and could not be effected without leave of the court unless otherwise agreed, Part 7 provides a battery of remedies which do not require leave of the court. Thus the following remedies, which may be enforced cumulatively so far as not conflicting, are exercisable in relation both to the collateral and to its proceeds after an event of default and service on the grantor of a written notice specifying the event of default.[72]

(i) Appropriation

This is the taking of the collateral or proceeds in total or partial satisfaction of the debt. This is to be distinguished from the English law remedy of foreclosure, which the Law does not provide, in that the debt is not extinguished unless the net value is at least equal to the amount of the debt, and if there is a deficiency the debtor remains liable for it, while conversely the secured party is accountable for any surplus

(ii) Sale

Again, the debtor is liable for any deficiency following sale and, subject to the rights of other encumbrancers, is entitled to any surplus.

(iii) Ancillary Actions

These are:

— taking control or possession of the collateral or proceeds;

[70] Article 41(1).

[71] Article 41(2).

[72] Article 43(1)–(4). By an 'event of default' is meant the failure to pay or otherwise to perform the obligation secured under the security agreement when due or an event that, under the security agreement, gives the secured party the right to enforce the security.

— exercising any rights of the grantor in relation to the collateral or proceeds (eg the grantor's right to sue a third party for rentals payable under a lease from the grantor or for damages for loss or damage caused to the collateral by the third party); and
— instructing any person who has an obligation in relation to the collateral or proceeds to carry out the obligation for the benefit of the secured party.

(iv) Contractual Rights

The secured creditors can also take such other action as is permitted by the security agreement and is not in conflict with the Law.

(v) Protection of the Grantor and Others

The interests of the grantor, other persons having an interest in the collateral (eg junior encumbrancers) and the obligor are protected by various provisions requiring notice of intended action and the imposition of duties on the secured party, for example to take all commercially reasonable steps to obtain fair market value when selling collateral and otherwise to act in a commercially reasonable manner (Article 46(2)) and to distribute surplus in a specified order of priority.[73]

O. Effect of Grantor's Insolvency

Effectiveness in insolvency is the acid test of the strength of a security interest. In order for a security interest to survive the grantor's bankruptcy it must be perfected before the grantor becomes bankrupt, otherwise it will be void.[74] Similarly an outright assignment of a receivable is void if not perfected before the assignor's bankruptcy.[75] In addition, the security interest or assignment may be affected by the ordinary bankruptcy rules[76] governing transactions at an undervalue, preferences and extortionate credit transactions.[77] Subject to these provisions bankruptcy does not affect the secured party's power to appropriate or sell collateral or otherwise act in relation to collateral.[78] In effect the collateral does not form part of the bankrupt's estate to the extent of the security interest.

[73] Article 49.
[74] Article 59(1).
[75] Article 59(2).
[76] Bankruptcy (Désastre) (Jersey) Law 1990, Arts 17–17C.
[77] Article 57(2).
[78] Article 56.

P. On to SIJL 2

Work on SIJL 2, which will extend the Law to cover goods and documents of title to goods, is already underway. The text has already been available in draft for some years although a consultation paper was issued as a White Paper in November 2011 it did not attach any draft legislation. Work on SIJL 2 has also been held up because the Jersey government had other priorities but it is now about to resume. It will be necessary to put out for consultation the text already prepared but incorporating amendments to SIJL 1 already made or found to be necessary, so as to have a complete consolidation. With the enactment of SIJL 2 Jersey will have an advanced, modern personal property security law that will provide rights and facilities that even now, despite its sophistication, are not available under English law. It is hoped that the new Law will give additional impetus to the Secured Transactions Law Reform Project set up some years ago and now directed by Professor Louise Gullifer, with Lord Saville as Chairman of the Project's Steering Committee. The advantages of a similar enactment for England could be substantial.

Part 2: The Security Interests (Jersey) Law 2012: A Practitioner's Perspective

JOHN RAINER

A. Introduction

The Security Interests (Jersey) Law 2012 (SIJL 1) came into force on 2 January 2014. SIJL 1 is principally inspired by the Personal Property Security Act (PPSA) legislation of New Zealand and the Canadian Provinces. What follows is a brief practitioner's perspective on Jersey's transition to its new PPSA regime, along with reflections on what went well, what could have been done better and how the PPSA regime might be improved.

B. What Went Well?

Jersey's transition to a PPSA regime has gone more smoothly than could have been anticipated for the following main reasons.

First, practitioners were embedded in the law-drafting process. This was unprecedented in Jersey as, before, practising lawyers were not permitted to participate in law drafting. This meant that practitioners had the opportunity to mould SIJL 1 into a law suitable for Jersey. The importance of this should not be underestimated because although Jersey's law draftsman used the Personal Property Securities Act 1999 of New Zealand (NZPPSA) as his starting point,[79] the NZPPSA was unsuitable in a number of respects. The NZPPSA is primarily concerned with taking security over tangibles, whereas the primary concern in Jersey was taking security over intangibles; the NZPPSA is too debtor friendly whereas Jersey needed a creditor-friendly statute; and the NZPPSA contains some unsuitable provisions such as those regulating the priority of security interests in transferred collateral. It took at least a year to craft a law that practitioners were happy with.

Secondly, there was an uncharacteristic amount of cooperation between law firms. The big firms in Jersey came to a common understanding on numerous issues before SIJL 1 came into force, with input from Professor Goode on more technical questions as he had advised the government of Jersey on the SIJL 1

[79] See Ch 6.

project as a whole. This significantly reduced the time taken by firms negotiating each other's security agreements once SIJL 1 came into force.

Thirdly, a market standard security agreement was prepared by the author, with input from Professor Goode, which is publicly available on the Jersey Bankers Association website. This exercise had two aims: to provide Jersey banks and small Jersey law firms with a precedent that could be used with minimal adaptation; and to try and generate consistent market practice.

Finally, practitioners were also closely involved with the establishment of the online Jersey Security Interests Register (SIR). A great effort was made to make the SIR interface as simple and as intuitive as possible and it was tested comprehensively as, for reputational reasons, Jersey could not afford to have the SIR crash or fail. The author drafted the SIR guidance notes and they are contained in a single document. This was considered preferable to a maze of linked guidance that is encountered on other registers. In short, the SIR is as simple as it possibly can be. As stated above, the SIR was an International Association of Commercial Administrators 2014 Merit Award winner.

C. What Could Have Been Done Better?

There has only been one problematic issue that practitioners have had to grapple with since SIJL 1 came into force. When the transitional provisions of SIJL 1 were drafted, the aim was to fully grandfather security interests created under the old regime without the need for them to be registered under SIJL 1 in order to preserve their priority. The intention was that SIJL 1 would only end up applying to old security if new collateral was added to it after SIJL 1 came into force. It was intended that it would be possible to amend an old security interest in other respects without SIJL 1 applying. However, that aim was not entirely achieved because what has come to be called the 'tipping point' question was not addressed. When finance documents are amended, it is necessary to assess whether the amendments, particularly new lending, constitute a new agreement necessitating new security, even if the security agreements under which security was taken secured liabilities as amended from time to time. This involves an assessment of what was in the general purview of the parties at the time the security was originally taken, which is a question of degree. Consequently, an assessment of whether the tipping point has been met arises. Fortunately, this problem will fade away as transactions are refinanced.

Secondly, the Jersey trusts industry realised rather late that the security registration regime was originally going to require security interests granted by trustees to be registered and that the registration would require the identification of the name of the trust. This was viewed as trust registration by the back door, which could have made Jersey unattractive to private client business. Registration of security granted by trustees and nominees was exempted from registration under SIJL 1 unless the trustee is the trustee of a Jersey unit trust holding real estate (commonly referred to as a Jersey property unit trust or JPUT). This outcome was preferable to having a system of registration under which the fact that a grantor is acting as trustee is disclosed but the name of the trust is not since, without the name of the trust, it would not be practical to search against large trust companies that may have granted numerous security interests in respect of the many trusts that they administer.

Thirdly, another area where SIJL 1 requires further refinement is in terms of its scope. Jersey conflict of laws rules provide that security should be taken under the *lex situs* of an asset. Nevertheless, SIJL 1 provides that it is possible to take Jersey security over the assets of a trust governed by Jersey law (irrespective of the situs of those assets) and Jersey-situated trust assets (irrespective of the governing law of the trust). Similarly, it is possible to take Jersey security over the rights under a Jersey law-governed agreement (irrespective of whether the person owing the obligations is based in Jersey) and over the rights under a foreign law-governed agreement if the person owing such obligations is Jersey resident.

The thinking was that it should be possible to take security where there is a Jersey connection, despite the conflict of laws rules on the applicability of the *lex situs*. However, this created a different problem. This was that foreign law-governed security over contractual rights arising under a foreign law-governed agreement granted by a Jersey grantor would have fallen within the scope of SIJL 1 and would therefore have to have been perfected by registration in order not to be set aside in a Jersey bankruptcy of the grantor. A similar problem arose in relation to foreign security granted by the trustees of a JPUT. In the end all such foreign security was exempted from the ambit of SIJL 1 altogether (which was always intended). Accordingly, there remain unresolved underlying complexities of private international law for which SIJL 1 will need to be amended to provide express conflict rules.

D. Can the PPSA Regime Be Improved?

Although the PPSA system is both evolved and comprehensive, it is possible to identify at least some minor improvements that could usefully be made. A general recommendation that can be made is that wherever there is an abundance of case law in PPSA jurisdictions that fails to settle an issue, the matter should be resolved definitively by statute since the PPSA system is intended to be a codified regime. Two examples can be given of this.

The first is whether a purchase money security interest loses its PMSI status as to priority on a refinancing with a new secured party. In Australia this point has been addressed with a rule to the effect that purchase money status is not lost.

Secondly, while a more pragmatic approach to tracing proceeds is taken in PPSA case law, it would be helpful for PPSA statutes to specify that this approach should be adopted. For example, in *Republic of Brazil v Durant*,[80] the Jersey courts adopted a pragmatic test for tracing in equity that is consistent with the approach to tracing proceeds required in the PPSA context. The test adopted in Jersey is that the plaintiff has to establish a sufficient link between his original property and the property into which he is seeking to trace. The Jersey courts are not constrained either to adopt or reject any particular rules such as the lowest intermediate balance rule or backwards tracing or to adopt specific labels to describe the links they identify or that are missing in any particular case.[81]

A number of specific recommendations can also be made. First, the PPSA system introduced a unitary concept of security interest and a substance-over-form test to determine whether a security interest has been created. The result is that even personal rights can be classified as a security interest. This approach is exemplified by the Canadian Supreme Court decision in *Caisse Populaire Desjardins de L'Est de Drummond v Canada*,[82] which held that the combination of a right of set-off, a flawed asset provision and a negative pledge (together called here 'the Personal Rights') constituted a security interest.[83] It is submitted, however, that as none of these Personal Rights create a proprietary interest, they should not be treated as creating a security interest either individually or when used in combination. SIJL 1, in line with Canadian PPSA statutes, provides that rights of set-off do not constitute a security interest, but it is silent as regards flawed asset arrangements and negative pledges. The PPSA statutes of Australia and New Zealand, however, provide that flawed assets arrangements are security interests. It would be helpful for SIJL 1 to be amended to provide that Personal Rights do not create security interests either individually or when used in combination.

Personal Rights are relevant in the context of investment management where the assets under management are held by a custodian. Investment management agreements often contain a lien for fees which will have to be registered to be perfected. Like investment banks, investment managers do not want to disclose their customers on a public register. As such, the only alternative for them is to resort to Personal Rights instead of a lien, but this will only work if they do not constitute security interests. It is submitted that public policy arguments for registration do not apply in the context of investment management since assets under management will, in effect, be removed from circulation so no one should be misled into believing that they are unencumbered. Alternatively, liens taken by investment managers should be exempt from registration.

Secondly, one of the conditions for attachment of a security interest is that value is given in respect of the security. In *Agricultural Credit Corp of Saskatchewan v*

[80] *Republic of Brazil v Durant* [2013] JCA 71.

[81] For discussion of tracing under English law, see Ch 13.

[82] *Caisse Populaire Desjardins de L'Est de Drummond v Canada* [2009] 2 SCR 94 (Saskatchewan Court of Appeal).

[83] For discussion of this case see Ch 5 C.

Pettyjohn[84] it was held that a binding commitment to lend is sufficient to fulfil the requirement to give value. However, it is not clear whether value has been given if the conditions precedent to the drawdown of a loan have not been fulfilled. For the purposes of giving legal opinions, it would be helpful to have statutory clarification that it would.

Thirdly, it would be helpful to have statutory provisions regarding the effect of contractual restrictions on assignment and prohibitions on the grant of security on the attachment, perfection and enforceability of security interests. While it may be that a prohibition on assignment does not preclude the attachment of a security interest that does not take effect by way of assignment,[85] the author is not aware of any PPSA case law as to whether contractual prohibitions on the creation of security preclude attachment. It would be helpful to have clarity on these important points.

Finally, there should be a period of temporary perfection for a security interest in after-acquired investment securities pending the issue of certificates. It would then not be necessary to register in order to perfect a security interest in after-acquired investment securities provided certificates are delivered within the period of temporary perfection. Similarly, possession or control should be a method not only of perfecting a security interest in investment securities, but also of perfecting a security interest in the income, voting and other rights attaching to them. It should not be necessary to register in order to perfect a security interest in such other rights. This is more consistent with the spirit of the PPSA regime that possession or control is an alternative to registration as a method of perfection.

E. Conclusion

SIJL 1 represents a major development in the Jersey law of security interests. The ability to take debenture-style security, register security interests and exercise a comprehensive range of enforcement remedies under SIJL 1 has enhanced Jersey's attractiveness as a jurisdiction in which to undertake secured lending. While SIJL 1 is more complex than the law it replaced, it is, nevertheless, simpler and more creditor friendly than other PPSA statutes as it has been tailored to meet the needs of Jersey as a leading international financial centre. Practitioners and banks have adapted to SIJL1 without difficulty and are taking advantage of the flexibility that it affords.

[84] *Agricultural Credit Corp of Saskatchewan v Pettyjohn* (1991) 1 PPSAC (2d) 273.

[85] Goode (n 69) 309. Moreover, Art 39 of SIJL 1 renders restrictions on the assignment of receivables ineffective (whether the assignment is absolute or by way of security).

10

Reforming the Company Charge Register in Ireland

NOEL MCGRATH

A. Introduction

The law of credit and security in Ireland is largely similar to its English counterpart. As is the position in England, Irish law lacks a unitary security interest and instead retains the traditional distinctions between pledges, liens, mortgages and charges. Irish courts have eschewed the application of 'functional, economic analysis to contractual devices framed as being other than mortgages and charges'[1] and have, in consequence, recognised a range of quasi-security interests such as reservation of title clauses and the assignment of receivables. As a result, Irish lawyers struggle with many of the same difficulties which beset our English neighbours. These problems include difficulties in the characterisation of transactions,[2] problems of complexity and uncertainty in the application of the priority rules,[3] as well as the inherent problems of inaccessibility and vagueness associated with an uncodified common law system of rules.

Irish perfection law is likewise similar to its English counterpart. The two principal systems of registration, those covering bills of sale and security interests created by companies over their property, are the result of Westminster legislation carried forward into Irish law after independence in 1922.[4] The British system for the registration and priority of ship mortgages also continued in force in Ireland

[1] H Beale, M Bridge, L Gullifer and E Lomnicka, *The Law of Security and Title Based Financing*, 2nd edn (Oxford, Oxford University Press, 2012) [1.26].

[2] See, for example, the distinction between fixed and floating charges as set out in *Re Keenan Brothers Ltd* [1985] IR 401 (SC); as is the case in England and Wales the boundary between charges and retention of title arrangements continues to be problematic: see *Carroll Group Distributors v G&JF Bourke Ltd* [1990] ILRM 285 (HC).

[3] See *Re JD Brian Ltd* [2015] IESC 62.

[4] The Bills of Sale (Ireland) Acts 1879–1883 and the Companies (Consolidation) Act 1908 were continued in force by Article 73 of the Constitution of Saorstát Éireann and were subsequently carried forward in Ireland's current constitutional structure by Article 50 of the Constitution of Ireland.

until 1955.[5] Only in respect of security interests over real property has Irish law historically charted its own course.[6]

In the decades since independence, the law of credit and security has rarely been the subject of detailed examination by academics or by official law reform bodies. A specialised system of perfection and priority was introduced in the 1920s to tackle some of the problems experienced by the farming community in accessing credit using the bills of sale machinery. The Agricultural Credit Act 1927 created two special forms of statutory chattel mortgage which enabled licensed banks and other credit institutions to take fixed and floating security over agricultural stock and other farming assets. The legislation provided for local registration of the creation of such interests in Circuit Court offices and further provided that competing chattel mortgages would rank in priority in the order in which they were registered. Rather strangely to modern eyes, the legislation prevented members of the general public from searching the register, confining access to representatives of banks and to public officials such as the sheriff.[7] It would appear that the Oireachtas was concerned that Irish farmers would decline to borrow money on a secured basis if the fact of their having done so might become known to their neighbours.[8] The agricultural credit legislation, which has been re-enacted with minor amendments several times since 1927, remains on the statute books but is only rarely, if ever, used in modern practice.

Like their English counterparts, the Bills of Sale (Ireland) Acts 1879–1883 have attracted little or no parliamentary attention since the late nineteenth century. The Irish legislation differs slightly from English law in that the Bills of Sale Acts 1890 and 1891 were never applied to Ireland. With that exception, the law in both jurisdictions is materially identical and in Ireland, as in England, bills of sale have long been all but abandoned by commercial practice in favour of quasi-security techniques such as conditional sales and hire purchase agreements.[9]

The registration of company charges suffered an early set back in Ireland when, on 25 May 1921, the Customs House in Dublin, in which the records were stored, was destroyed by military action during the Irish War of Independence.[10]

[5] See Part I, Merchant Shipping Act 1894. The ship mortgages provisions have benn re-enacted without substantial amendment by Part II of the Mercantile Marine Act 1955 and now form part of the Merchant Shipping (Registration of Ships) Act 2014; however this legislation has not yet been commenced.

[6] Unregistered conveyancing in Ireland has historically involved the registration deeds under the Registration of Deeds (Ireland) Act 1707, an act of the pre-Union Irish parliament. Registered conveyancing, first introduced by the Local Registration of Title (Ireland) Act 1891, is likewise distinct from its English counterparts. For details see A Lyall, *Land Law in Ireland*, 3rd edn (Dublin, Roundhall, 2010) 160–69 and 930–65.

[7] See s 25(6) Agricultural Credit Act 1927, now re-enacted with minor amendments as s 26(6) Agricultural Credit Act 1977.

[8] Dáil Debs vol 19 cols 2165–2185 (5th May 1927).

[9] For details see B Maguire, 'The Bill of Sale: The Forgotten Relation?' (1997) 4 *Commercial Law Practitioner* 3.

[10] For contemporaneous press reports see Anonymous, 'The Ruined Custom House', *The Irish Times* (Dublin, 30 May 1921) 4.

The charge register was swiftly reconstituted by special legislation, which required the return to the registrar of certified copies of certificates of registration of company charges so as to facilitate the reconstitution of the charge register.[11] Thereafter the legislature did not return to the law of company charges until the enactment of the Companies Act 1963 which was in force in Ireland until June 2015.

The drafting of what was to become the Companies Act 1963 was preceded by a committee on company law under the chairmanship of Arthur Cox, a prominent Dublin solicitor of the time, which reported in February 1958.[12] In its report, the Cox Committee recommended a series of changes which, in effect, brought Irish law up to date with developments in England following the Companies Act 1948. This chiefly involved the expansion of the categories of registrable charge to include charges on calls made but not paid, charges on goodwill, charges on ships or shares in ships and charges over patents and trademarks. The Cox Committee considered whether charges or pledges over goods in bond and pledges over documents of title to goods should be included in the system but recommended against such a course of action lest registration requirements become unduly onerous. Legislation giving effect to the Committee's proposals was duly drafted and placed before the Houses of Oireachtas. While the Bill was at report stage in its passage through Dáil Éireann (Ireland's lower house), an amendment was made to section 100 to remove the requirement that the company supply the original charge document to the registrar when registering a charge over its property. In explaining the thinking behind the amendment, the then Minister for Industry and Commerce, Jack Lynch TD, stated that the government intended it to implement the recommendations of the Jenkins Committee in England and Wales, which had criticised the English registrar's function in checking the accuracy of the particulars submitted against the original charge document.[13]

The passage of the 1963 Act marked the last major change[14] to Ireland's perfection systems for secured transactions until Ireland's ratification and implementation of the Cape Town Convention on International Interests on Mobile Equipment in 2005.[15] In contrast to the English experience, neither the Irish civil service nor the Law Reform Commission has given serious public consideration to the possibility of a systematic reform of the law in this area. The latter made brief reference to Article 9 of the Uniform Commercial Code when examining

[11] See s 3(c) Companies (Re-Constitution of Records) Act 1924.

[12] See Report of the Company Law Reform Committee (Dublin, Stationary Office, Pr 4523, 1958) (hereafter 'the Cox Committee').

[13] Dáil Deb, Special Committee on the Companies Bill 1962, 21 February 1962. For the relevant passage in the Jenkins Report see Board of Trade, *Report of the Company Law Committee* (Cmnd 1749, 1962) paras 302–03.

[14] The company charge register was further extended to include interests in aircraft by section 122 Companies Act 1990. The same legislation conferred a power on the Minister for Enterprise, Jobs and Innovation to extend the categories of registrable charge by statutory instrument but this power has never been used.

[15] See International Interests in Mobile Equipment Act 2005.

the impact of retention of title clauses on the process of debt collection, but the Commission did not examine the case for comprehensive reform. Instead, it opted for a recommendation that retention of title arrangements become registrable in the same manner as a company charge.[16] That proposal has not been implemented. Similarly there has been little academic attention paid to secured credit, with almost no major monograph or textbook making more than a passing reference to the need for law reform in this area.[17]

In the absence of systematic reform, Irish law can be subjected to many of the same criticisms as its English counterpart.[18] Irish personal property security law is complex, unwieldy and frequently irrational. The presence of multiple systems of registration leads to problems of duplication and uncertainties in the determination of priorities. The individual registration systems each have their own difficulties with the result that they provide, at best, only a partial solution to the problems faced by third parties in a jurisdiction whose law recognises and gives effect to secured transactions.[19]

B. The Companies Act 2014

The remainder of this chapter will focus on the Companies Act 2014 ('the 2014 Act'), which was signed into law by the President of Ireland on 22 December 2014 was commenced on 1 June 2015.[20] The 2014 Act introduces a number of significant changes to the registration and priority of charges over company property in Ireland. The Act is largely the product of two reports published by the Company Law Reform Group (CLRG) published in 2001[21] and 2004.[22] The CLRG was established as a statutory body following an ad hoc review which had recommended that Ireland must 'combine modernisation and codification of its company law in a period of major company law reform'.[23] Its functions include monitoring and advising the Minister for Jobs, Enterprise and Innovation in relation to the implementation and amendment of the Companies Acts.[24] In carrying out its advisory

[16] Law Reform Commission, Report on Debt Collection (2): Retention of Title (LRC-28, 1989).

[17] For a recent exception to this trend see M Donnelly, *The Law of Credit and Security* 2nd edn (Dublin, Roundhall, 2015) 511-514–79. For journal contributions see M Donnelly, 'Reforming Personal Property Security Law: Is There a Case for a Single Securities Register?' (2000) 22 *Dublin University Law Journal* 50; N McGrath, 'Chopping down Dante's Wood: Article 9 of the Uniform Commercial Code and Personal Property Security Law in Ireland' (2006) 13 *Commercial Law Practitioner* 279.

[18] For a comprehensive overview of the English criticisms see Beale et al (n 1) ch 23.

[19] See Donnelly, *The Law of Credit and Security* (n 17) 512.

[20] See Companies Act 2014 (Commencement Order) 2015 SI 169 of 2005.

[21] Company Law Review Group, First Report (2000–2001) (Dublin, Stationary Office, 2001).

[22] Company Law Review Group, Second Report (2002–2003) (Dublin, Stationary Office, 2004). (hereafter 'the Second Report').

[23] Report of the Working Group on Company Law Compliance and Enforcement (Dublin, Stationary Office, PN 6697, 1998) [1.3].

[24] Section 68(1) Company Law Enforcement Act 2001.

function, the CLRG is required to 'seek to promote enterprise, facilitate commerce, simplify the operation of the Companies Acts, enhance corporate governance and encourage commercial probity'.[25]

Although the 2014 Act makes significant amendments to the company charge register, it should be clearly understood from the outset that a comprehensive reform of credit and security law was never an objective of the CLRG process. In its Second Report the CLRG noted the various proposals for comprehensive reform in England, including the Diamond Report[26] and the consultation paper published by the Law Commission of England and Wales,[27] but did not engage in a substantive discussion of the contents of these proposals. Instead, the CLRG confined its review to the registration and priority of mortgages and charges and proposed a series of amendments to the existing system of charge registration aimed at ensuring that the register provides 'timely information on a company … so that those dealing with a company can make themselves familiar with the company's financial soundness and credit position'.[28] The remainder of this section will consider the more significant elements of the changes introduced by the 2014 Act.

(i) Scope of the Register

The first major alteration to the company charge register concerns its scope. Section 408(1) of the 2014 Act establishes a general principle that all charges and mortgages, whether created orally or in writing are to be included within the registration system. The CLRG explained the rationale for this change by reference to simplicity and certainty, arguing that the existing list of registrable charges was an anachronism which had become cumbersome in practice.[29]

The expansion of the requirement register to include all charges raises issues for the implementation of the Financial Collateral Directive,[30] Article 3 of which requires, inter alia, the disapplication of perfection requirements from transactions within the scope of the Directive. Section 408(1) therefore excludes charges over certain categories of asset from the definition of a charge for the purposes of the registration requirement. These assets include:

(a) cash;
(b) money credited to an account of a financial institution, or other deposits;
(c) shares, bonds or debt instruments;

[25] Section 68(2) Company Law Enforcement Act 2001.

[26] AL Diamond, A Review of Security Interests in Personal Property (London, HMSO, 1989).

[27] Law Commission, Registration of Security Interests: Company Charges and Property other than Land (Consultation Paper No 164, 2002).

[28] The Second Report (n 22) [8.2.3].

[29] ibid [8.2.5]–[8.2.7].

[30] Directive 2002/47/EC of the European Parliament and the Council of 6 June 2002, on Financial Collateral Arrangements [2002] OJ L168/43.

(d) units in collective investment undertaking or money market instruments;
(e) claims and rights (such as dividends or interest) in respect of categories (b) to (d).

A number of points can be made about this list. First, the Financial Collateral Directive has already been implemented in Irish law by statutory instrument.[31] The Companies Act 2014 does not repeal that statutory instrument so it is not entirely clear why it was felt necessary to address the perfection of financial collateral for a second time in drafting Part 7 of the Act.

Second, the list of excluded charges in section 408(1) does not quite accord with the categories of financial collateral affected by the Directive. The list, as currently drafted, does not include credit claims, which were added to the definition of financial collateral as a matter of EU law in 2009.[32] This problem may be rectified in the future by adding credit claims to the list by statutory instrument.[33] More significantly, there appears to be an error in the drafting of the second item on the list, which refers to 'money credited to the account of a financial institution'. The phrase 'account of a financial institution' appears to refer to a charge over an account in which the account holder is itself a financial institution. Presumably what was intended here was to cover a charge over money held by a company in an account held with a financial institution but a literal reading of the language employed does not make this clear.

Third, insofar as section 408(1) excludes charges over financial collateral from the registration system, its effects go well beyond those of the Directive itself. A financial collateral arrangement only qualifies for the protection of the Directive and 2010 Regulations where the collateral is 'delivered, transferred, held, registered or otherwise designated so as to be in the possession or under the control of the collateral taker or of a person acting on the collateral taker's behalf'.[34] The meaning and scope of the possession and control concept has been the subject of considerable difficulty in England and Wales.[35] The Irish courts have not yet had an opportunity to consider the meaning of these terms in Ireland, and significant doubts remain about whether a floating charge gives rise to a sufficient degree of possession or control to come within the scope of the 2010 Regulations. As a result, floating charges over financial collateral are sometimes registered in the company charge register as a matter of caution.[36] This practice of defensive

[31] See European Communities (Financial Collateral Arrangements) Regulations 2010, SI 626 of 2010 ('the 2010 Regulations').

[32] See Directive 2009/44/EC of the European Parliament and the Council of 6 May 2009, amending Directive 98/26 on settlement finality in payment and securities settlement systems and Directive 2002/47 on financial collateral arrangements as regards linked systems and credit claims [2009] OJ L146/37.

[33] See s 408(2).

[34] See Art 2(2), Dir 2002/47/EC and reg 2(2) of the 2010 Regulations.

[35] See Re F2G Realisations Ltd; Gray v G-T-P Group Ltd [2010] EWHC 1772 (Ch) and Re Lehman Brothers International (Europe) [2012] EWHC 2997 (Ch).

[36] Donnelly, *The Law of Credit and Security* (n 17) 602.

registration should now cease, at least for those transactions which are squarely caught by section 408(1). This is because all excluded charges will be exempt from the obligation to register and the associated sanction of invalidity regardless of whether the chargee has possession or control of collateral. It is notable that having relieved the parties of the requirement to register the transactions as a company charge or, alternatively the requirement to take possession or control under the Directive, section 408 provides no alternative safeguards to enable third parties to discover the existence of the charge.

Finally, it is interesting that the exclusion of these categories of charge from the registration system results in a subtle shift in Irish public policy on the treatment of financial collateral. The Financial Collateral Directive provides an option for Member States to confine its effects to transactions between certain categories of company and/or public authority.[37] In the 2010 Regulations, the Irish authorities took up this option and provided that both parties to a financial collateral arrangement must be, in effect, either a public institution such as a central bank, or a regulated entity.[38] Section 408(1) partly alters this position by disapplying the perfection requirements for the listed categories of financial collateral for charges created by all companies. The CLRG seems to have expressly intended that this change would occur. In its report it argued that restricting the Financial Collateral Directive to certain classes of entity might hinder access to the capital markets 'to the detriment of the companies themselves and ultimately to the economy of the State'. There are difficulties with the substance of this argument—as has been pointed out in English writing on the subject, while there might be good reasons for disapplying perfection requirements to transactions between systemically important institutions, it is far from obvious that the same reasoning applies when the debtor company is an ordinary trading company with no connection to the capital markets.[39] Whatever view one takes of the substance, section 408(1) creates an unnecessary complexity in the law. If the Irish state takes the view that all financial arrangements, regardless of the nature of the parties, should attract the protection of the Directive, then the appropriate course of action is to extend the implementation of the Directive by amending the 2010 Regulations accordingly. Section 408(1), by contrast, creates a complex multi-tier system for financial collateral in Ireland. Transactions where both parties are either public authorities or regulated entities will attract the full protection of the Directive. Where one party is neither a public authority nor a regulated entity a charge will be exempted from the registration requirements of the Companies Act, provided that the collateral in question can be brought within the categories listed in section 408(1). Where one party is neither a public authority nor a regulated entity, and the collateral is a credit claim, the registration requirement under the 2014 Act will

[37] See Art 1(3), Dir 2002/47/EC.

[38] See reg 3(2) of the 2010 Regulations.

[39] See L Gullifer, 'What Should We Do about Financial Collateral' (2012) 65 *Current Legal Problems* 377, 402–03.

continue to apply to the transaction. However one looks at it, it is difficult to describe section 408(1) as having created a simple rule.

(ii) Registration Procedures

The 2014 Act makes major changes to the procedures for registering a charge in Ireland. Section 410 places a duty on the company to comply with the registration procedures, though the existing provisions which permit any person with an interest in the charge to attend to registration have been retained.[40] Although, the company is still duty bound to register charges created over its property, the criminal sanction for non-registration has been abolished.[41] Where a charge is not registered in accordance with the registration procedures, it will continue to be void against the liquidator and any creditor of the company, and any debt secured by an unregistered charge will continue to become immediately repayable.[42]

One of the major innovations of the 2014 Act is the introduction of a new procedure for registering a charge. Companies will still have the option of choosing to register charges in the traditional manner, ie by the delivery of the prescribed particulars to the Companies Registration Office (CRO) within 21 days of the date of creation of the charge.[43] Alternatively, the company may opt for a two-step procedure. The two-step procedure requires that the company file a notice of its intention to create a charge. The notice must contain all of the particulars of the charge. Once the charge has been created, the company must then send a second notice to the CRO confirming the creation of the charge. If the second notice is received within 21 days of the first notice, then the charge is deemed to have been registered at the date when the first notice was received. The advantage of the two-step procedure is that it enables a prospective lender to secure its priority position while a prospective transaction is under negotiation. This has consequences for the operation of the new priority rules introduced by section 412 of the Act, which will be considered in more detail below.

The 2014 Act also makes changes to the particulars of the charge which must be submitted to the CRO for registration. Section 414 requires the CRO to maintain a register of charges for each company containing:

(a) the date of creation of the charge;
(b) the date of submission of the particulars (including the date of the advance notice of creation where the two-step registration procedure is followed);
(c) short particulars of the property charged; and
(d) details of the person entitled to the charge.

[40] See s 410(2) and (3) of the 2014 Act.
[41] Section 411 of the 2014 Act has retained a criminal sanction for a failure to register charges existing on property subsequently acquired by the company.
[42] Section 409(5) and (6) of the 2014 Act.
[43] Section 409(2) of the 2014 Act.

In contrast to the English position,[44] Irish law does not require companies to send a copy of the charge document to the CRO when particulars of a charge are submitted. The CRO therefore has no means of checking that the particulars of the charge are an accurate reflection of the contents of the charge document. Instead, the new statutory form which must be used to effect registrations, Form C1,[45] continues the pre-2014 practice of providing a space for the signature of one or both of the parties to the charge in a section of the form entitled 'Verification'.[46] The use of this term might be taken to imply that the person or persons signing the form are attesting to the accuracy of its contents; however, the form itself contains no statement to this effect, nor is any sanction imposed upon a person who, whether acting negligently or otherwise, signs a form which contains a material inaccuracy.

The CLRG acknowledged that this position has resulted in problems in the past where inaccurate or incomplete information has been submitted to the CRO and entered onto the register.[47] The CLRG considered the imposition of a requirement for both parties to the charge to sign the Form C1 but was concerned that such a requirement might make electronic filing difficult to develop and that it might be practically difficult to secure both signatures within the 21-day time period. Instead the Group suggested that a form signed by the solicitor should be sufficient in all circumstances.[48] The new Form C1 adopts a requirement that the forms must be signed by an officer or the solicitor of the chargor company and by an authorised person acting on behalf of the chargee.[49]

The Companies Act 2014 conferred a power on the Minster for Jobs, Enterprise and Innovation to introduce a mandatory requirement that certain categories of CRO filings be made in electronic form.[50] Once the Minister has made an order under the section for a given category of documents, the CRO may then establish an electronic system for the filing of those documents.[51] This power has now been exercised in relation to the company charge register.[52] Company charges may now

[44] See s 859A(3) Companies Act 2006.

[45] See Part 27, Companies Act 2014 (Forms) Order 2015 (SI. 147 of 2015).

[46] See Form C1 as provided for in the Companies (Forms) Order 2001 SI 466 of 2001. Until the introduction of the new scheme, where only one party to the charge signed the form, there was an administrative requirement to submit a certified copy of the charge document. Anecdotal evidence suggests that in such cases the CRO made a cursory check to ensure that the date of the charge and the names of the parties had been correctly recorded. The other particulars (including the description of the property subject to the charge) were not verified by the CRO. It would appear that this practice will cease under the new scheme.

[47] The Second Report (n 22) [8.11.4].

[48] ibid.

[49] See Companies Registration Office, 'Draft Form C1 version 2.6', www.cro.ie/Portals/0/2014%20Act%20Draft%20Forms_NOT_IN_USE/C1%20v2.6%20draft.pdf.

[50] See s.897 Companies Act 2014.

[51] See s.897(2). In specifying the requirements of any such system, the CRO is obliged under s.12(1)(b) of the Electronic Commerce Act 2000 to ensure that its requirements are made public and are "objective, transparent, proportionate and non-discriminatory".

[52] See r.3 Companies Act 2014 (Section 897) Order 2015 (SI 203 of 2015).

only be registered using the section of the CRO website known as the Companies Online Registration Environment ('the CORE system'). The CORE system permits a person registering a charge to fill out an electronic version of the Form C1 and to sign it using a digital signing certificate.[53] The digital signing certificate is issued by the Revenue Online Service ('ROS'). The ROS system, which has been in operation since 2003, allows individuals, companies and other business entities to file tax returns and other documentation with the Revenue Commissioners through a web-based system.[54] Use of the system is free of charge, and since Irish companies and most individual Irish taxpayers are now required to file tax returns using it,[55] most Irish companies and the business community at large can be expected to be familiar its operation. Documents filed through ROS are electronically signed using a digital signature which associated with the individual identity of every Irish taxpayer. The ROS system also permits professional advisors to obtain digital signatures in respect of their clients where they are authorised to do so.[56]

The introduction of electronic filing is clearly a welcome development from an efficiency perspective. The use of the ROS system to facilitate digital signing has the advantage of utilising a pre-existing state technology and one in which there is a high degree of public trust.[57] The link between the CORE system and its ROS counterpart has the further advantage that there is a reliable record of the identities of those who have signed the Form C1,[58] a measure which should serve to prevent the some of the difficulties associated with false or vexatious registrations which have caused concern in other jurisdictions.[59]

(iii) The Certificate of Registration

The certificate of registration has long been a source of controversy in Irish company law. Under section 104 of the Companies Act 1963, the certificate provides conclusive evidence that the requirements of the Act as to registration have been complied with. This position has attracted academic criticism,[60]

53 The legal effect of such a digital signature is identical to a traditional signature on a paper form under s.13 of the Electronic Commerce Act 2000. For a detailed description of the new system www.cro.ie/Services/E-Filing/Digital-Signing-Certificate.

54 For details see: https://www.ros.ie/helpcentre/help.html#/?a=gettingStarted/about-ros. The legal basis for the system is to be found in Part 38 Chapter 6 of the Taxes Consolidation Act 1997 as inserted by s.202 Finance Act 1999.

55 See Tax Returns and Payments (Mandatory Electronic Filing and Payment of Tax) Regulations 2011 (SI 223 of 2011).

56 See www.ros.ie/PublisherServlet/info/faq_roscust#Question18.

57 See Revenue Commissioners, *Survey of SME Taxpayers 2013*, (Dublin, 2013), 30-31.

58 See www.cro.ie/Services/E-Filing/Mandatory-E-filing-of-Charges

59 See Law Commission (n 27), [4.44].

60 See Donnelly, *The Law of Credit and Security* (n 17) 536, P Ussher, *Company Law in Ireland* (Dublin, Round Hall, 1986) 469; L McCann and T Courtney (eds), *Companies Acts 1963–2012* (Dublin, Bloomsbury Professional, 2013) 229; N McGrath, 'The Certificate of Registration and the Company Charge Register' (2013) 36 *Dublin University Law Journal* 35.

and its compatibility with both the Constitution of Ireland and Article 6 of the European Convention on Human Rights has been questioned.[61] The 2014 Act retains the certificate of registration but significantly dilutes its effect.

Section 415(1) and (2) obliges the CRO to issue a certificate of registration and provides that the certificate shall be conclusive evidence that the requirements of Part 7 of the Act have been complied with. Subsection 3 provides as follows:

> To the extent that the particulars of a charge delivered to the Registrar in purported compliance with this Part omit the required particulars in respect of one or more properties to which the charge relates, the evidential effect of the certificate … shall not extend to the particular property or properties in respect of which that omission occurs.

The effect of this section appears to reverse the result in cases similar to the well-known English decision in *National Provincial and Union Bank of England v Charnley*,[62] in which the Court held that a mortgage by demise over a leasehold interest in a mill together with the plant used on the premises was enforceable notwithstanding the fact that the particulars of the charge made no mention of the plant. If a similar situation were to arise before an Irish court after the 2014 Act, it would certainly be open to the court to conclude that the property had not been sufficiently described in the particulars. As I have argued elsewhere,[63] section 415(3) opens up a new and potentially difficult question of interpretation for Irish courts. What standard of description is required when producing 'short particulars of the property charged'? The statute provides no guidance for answering this question, but there is some evidence that the Irish courts may take a more relaxed approach than has been the case in comparable systems for registering interests in real property.[64] In *Re Valley Ice Cream (Ireland) Ltd*[65] the court considered a document which purported to create a charge over a list of items that were described in the charge document as being set out in the fifth schedule. In the particulars the property charged was described as 'equipment in the form attached in the first schedule'. From what little that can be gleaned from the judgment, it would appear that the certificate of registration was not relied upon in argument. McCracken J held that the charge had been properly registered notwithstanding the mention of an incorrect schedule number in the particulars. It remains to be seen if subsequent courts will take a similarly relaxed attitude in light of the language of section 415(3).

[61] G Hogan and D Gwynn Morgan, *Administrative Law in Ireland*, 4th edn (Dublin, Roundhall, 2010) para 11-79 and N McGrath, 'The Company Charge Register and the Constitution' (2014) 52 *Irish Jurist* 20.

[62] *National Provincial and Union Bank of England v Charnley* [1924] 1 KB 431.

[63] See N McGrath, 'The Company Charge Register in Ireland: Some Reflections on the Reform Proposals in the Companies Consolidation and Reform Bill 2012' [2013] *Journal of Business Law* 303, 310–11.

[64] See in the context of the Registry of Deeds (Ireland) Act 177, *Stephenson v Joyce* (1856) 5 ICR 401 and *Re Monsell* (1856) 5 ICR 529; *cf Wyatt v Barwell* (1815) 19 Ves Jr 435.

[65] *Re Valley Ice Cream (Ireland) Ltd*, unreported, High Court, 22 July 1998, McCracken J.

(iv) The Registration of Negative Pledge and Crystallisation Clauses

In Ireland, as elsewhere, it is a near universal practice for floating charges to be accompanied by negative pledge clauses whereby the chargor agrees not to create security over charged assets that rank prior to, or *pari passu* with, the interest of the floating charge holder.[66] The CLRG reported that:

> It has become customary to insert additional details on a Form C1, the most common of which is that where a floating charge is created the company covenants in the deed, creating the floating charge, that it will not create any further charge ranking pari passu with or in priority to the floating charge.[67]

The reason for this practice can be found in the decision of the Irish Supreme Court in *Welch v Bowmaker (Ireland) Ltd.*[68] There the court held that a negative pledge clause affects the position of a subsequent chargee who has notice of it even where that subsequent chargee is not party to the contract containing the clause. The majority of the court made it crystal clear that actual rather than constructive notice is the standard of knowledge to be applied in such cases. Henchy J stated:

> Since [a negative pledge clause] is more or less common form in modern debentures, there would be much to be said for applying the doctrine of constructive notice to such a situation were it not that it is settled law that there is no duty on the bank in a situation such as this to seek out the precise terms of the debenture … Whatever attractions there may be in the proposition that priority should be deemed lost because a duty to inquire further was called for but ignored, and that such inquiry would have shown that the company was debarred from entering into a mortgage which would have priority over the debenture, the fact remains that it would be unfair to single out the bank for condemnatory treatment because of their failure to ascertain the full terms of the debenture when what they did was in accord with judicially approved practice and when such a precipitate change in the law would undermine the intended validity of many other such transactions. If the proposed extension of the doctrine of constructive notice is to be made, the necessary change in the law would need to be made prospectively and, therefore, more properly by statute.[69]

Parke J concurred and specifically expressed his agreement with Henchy J that any change to the law on this issue would require specific legislation after 'a careful consideration of a number of factors including current commercial practice and the provisions of certain statutes'.[70] Kenny J dissented on the basis that he considered the charge to have been a fixed one, which rendered it unnecessary for

[66] Donnelly, The Law of Credit and Security (n 17) 538.
[67] The Second Report (n 22) [8.5.1].
[68] *Welch v Bowmaker (Ireland) Ltd* [1980] IR 251 (SC).
[69] ibid at 256.
[70] ibid at 262.

him to express any opinion on the issue of constructive notice.[71] Following the *Welch* decision, there was an incentive to include details of a negative pledge in the particulars submitted to the CRO in order to affix parties searching the register with actual notice of the negative pledge clause.[72]

Section 412(6) deals with negative pledge clauses and associated matters. The relevant parts read as follows:

> (6) Subject to subsection (7) in relation to particulars of a charge received by the Registrar pursuant … the following provisions apply so far as those particulars consist of particulars of a negative pledge, any events that crystallise a floating charge or any restrictions on the use of any charged asset (and particulars of any such matter are referred to subsequently in this subsection as 'extraneous material'):
>
> (a) the Registrar shall not enter in the register … particulars of the extraneous material pursuant to that section;
>
> (b) the fact that the Registrar has received the particulars of the extraneous material shall have no legal effect;
>
> but nothing in the foregoing affects the validity of the receipt by the Registrar of the other particulars of the charge.

The effect of this section is to prevent parties from using the register to place third parties who search it on actual notice of the existence of negative pledge clauses or of automatic crystallisation clauses. The CLRG explained the reasoning behind this section in the following terms:

> It is recommended that this additional material should be discontinued and any such material on a form submitted be ignored by the Registrar (which he currently does ignore) when transcribing details onto the register of charges applicable to the charging company. The amending legislation, or statutory instrument enacting the form, should so provide. It would be quite exceptional for a floating charge not to contain a restriction on subsequent charges or even not to have an automatic crystallisation clause. Accordingly, it should be regarded by the public as a given that a floating charge will contain these clauses just as a fixed charge over book debts will contain a provision that the proceeds are to be paid to a designated account.[73]

Four points should be made with respect to the above passage. First, with the greatest of respect to the CLRG, I suggest that this passage is based on a view of the law that is wholly irreconcilable with the decision of the Supreme Court in *Welch*. The majority of the Court made it clear on that occasion that specific legislation would be required to alter its central holding that a party is not affected by constructive notice of a negative pledge clause simply because such clauses are commonly encountered in practice. No such legislation has been passed in the

[71] ibid at 258–59.

[72] See M Donnelly, 'Company Charges and the Company Charge Register: Implications of the Companies Bill 2012 for Secured Lending' (2014) 21 *Commercial Law Practitioner* 3, 7.

[73] The Second Report (n 22) [8.5.2].

interim period since *Welch* was decided and the Companies Act 2014 contains no provision which would have this effect.

Second, the reasoning of the CLRG cannot be defended on the basis of its assertion in the first paragraph that the CRO does not transcribe details of 'additional material' onto the register itself. No doubt the CLRG correctly recorded what the current practice was in 2004 when the Second Report was published; however in the years since, the company charge registration system has become partially electronic and its records are publicly available for consultation via the CRO's website. When a search is carried out through the website, the searcher, having paid the relevant fee, obtains a scanned copy of the Form C1 which was submitted to the CRO. There is no evidence that the scanned copies are redacted or altered in any way to conceal 'additional information' such as notice of negative pledge clauses. According to the CRO's most recent annual report,[74] 97 per cent of searches of the CRO's records are performed using the online system and therefore it seems likely that inserting notices of negative pledge clauses onto the Form C1 is, in practice, an effective means of communicating their existence to third parties who search the register.

Third, the CLRG's reasons for prohibiting the inclusion of additional information do not, in fact, provide any substantive account of why this practice should be prohibited. The effect of these changes will be to make it more difficult for floating charge holders to ensure that others dealing with the company are placed on actual notice of the existence of a negative pledge clause. As a practical matter, most subsequent creditors will insist on sight of the prior charge document or will seek to negotiate an inter-creditor agreement and are thus likely to have actual notice of the negative pledge clause by this means; however, the difficulty for the prior creditor is ensuring that this in fact occurs. As I have argued elsewhere,[75] if the law is to be changed to abolish or prohibit a practice which the commercial community has clearly found to be practically useful, then a positive justification for that change is called for. The CLRG's report does not provide such a justification and it is not apparent, as Donnelly has pointed out, why the effectiveness of the floating charge should be undermined in this manner.[76] In contrast to the practice adopted in formulating recent changes to the company charge register in the United Kingdom, the CLRG did not hold a public consultation on the proposals contained in the Second Report.[77] For this reason the views of the Irish commercial community on the issue are unknown, but it may be significant that British banking and commercial interests strongly favoured the position of including a requirement to

[74] Companies Registration Office, *Annual Report 2013* (Dublin, 2013) 4. See www.cro.ie/Portals/0/Publications/2013_CRO_Annual_Report_Final.pdf.

[75] McGrath (n 63) 310–15.

[76] Donnelly (n 72) 7.

[77] A brief public consultation on the entirety of the Companies Bill was held by the Select Committee of the Houses of the Oireachtas on Jobs, Enterprise and Innovation in advance of the committee stage debates in the Oireachtas in August 2013. The results of this consultation were not made public.

reveal negative pledge clauses in the reform of the UK charge register,[78] a proposal ultimately adopted in the UK regulations.[79]

Finally, there are two practical objections to the wording of section 412(6). Subsection (a) prohibits the CRO from entering extraneous information into the register. The prohibition is clearly intended to be mandatory and is addressed to the registrar. Thus it is at least arguable that the CRO, if it is to observe the letter of the law, has an obligation to check each set of particulars received and redact any extraneous information contained within them prior to entering the particulars on the register. If this view is correct, then section 412(6) is open to the criticism that it involves the CRO in inefficient bureaucracy. Subsection (b) is clearly intended to address a situation in which extraneous information has been entered into the register in error by ensuring that the presence of the information on the register has no effect. In some situations, the effect of this provision might be to protect a person who has knowingly acquired an interest in the collateral in the full knowledge that the company is in breach of a negative pledge clause agreed with its prior creditor. To take the case at its most charitable, such a person might be described as having engaged in sharp practice and it is difficult to understand why the law should protect such behaviour.

(v) Changes to the Priority Rules

The Companies Act 2014 makes significant changes to the priority of charges. The existing companies legislation, like its English counterpart, does not directly regulate the priority of charges—section 99 of the Companies Act 1963 declares void a charge which is not registered within 21 days of creation—but aside from this the priority of competing mortgages and charges is left to the common law. This results in the well-known problem of the 21-day 'blind spot' in the company charge register—A Ltd grants a charge to C1 on 1 January which is registered on 10 January. On 5 January A Ltd grants a charge to C2, which is registered on 7 January. In a priority conflict, C1 will succeed as the person whose charge was created first in time in spite of the fact that C2 could not have discovered the existence of the prior charge.

Recognition of the 21-day blind spot led the CLRG to conclude that the company charge register was 'open to abuse' although it also pointed out that the problem had not occurred in practice.[80] The CLRG proposed 'that priority be given to

[78] Department of Business, Innovation and Skills, Summary of Responses—Consultation on Registration of Charges created by Companies and Limited Liability Partnerships (2010) 15. See www.gov.uk/government/uploads/system/uploads/attachment_data/file/31494/10-1230-summary-responses-consultation-registration-of-charges.pdf.

[79] See s 859D Companies Act 2006 as inserted by reg 2 Companies Act 2006 (Amendment of Part 25) Regulations 2013 (SI 2013/600).

[80] The Second Report (n 22) [8.3.4].

the creditor who files first in time' as a means of remedying this potential abuse, arguing that when combined with the two-step procedure for registration it would remove any potential for abuse.[81] The CLRG's report also addresses a second well-known problem in jurisdictions which operate several distinct systems of registration of security interests—that of a conflict between priority rules attached to different systems. The Irish courts have encountered this problem in connection with charges over agricultural chattels created by companies which attract a dual registration requirement. In *Re Castlemahon Poultry Products Ltd*[82] the Court held, in apparent defiance of the wording of the agricultural chattel legislation,[83] that there was no requirement for registration of the charge in both systems. Although there is no direct authority on this point, it is commonly assumed that a different result is likely in relation to charges over land and that dual registration of charges over land is required.[84] The CLRG endorsed this latter assumption by recommending that the first-to-register rule for company charges should not affect the rules attaching to other systems of registration.[85]

When the legislation which has now become the Companies Act 2014 received its first reading in Dáil Éireann, the CLRG's proposals in relation to priority were contained in clause 413 of the Companies Bill 2012. This clause established that the priority of competing charges, unless governed by another act of the Oireachtas or an inter-creditor agreement,[86] was to be determined in accordance with the order in which the CRO received the particulars of the charge (where the one-step procedure was adopted), or the other in which the CRO received a notice of intention to create a charge (where the two-step procedure was adopted).

During the committee stage of the passage of the Bill through Seanad Éireann, the government amended the wording of clause 413 to create what was ultimately enacted as section 412 of the Act. The relevant parts of the section read as follows:

(1) For the purposes of this section—
 (a) 'relevant rule of law' means a rule of law that governs the priority of charges created by a company, and for the avoidance of doubt, any enactment governing the priority of such charges is not encompassed by that expression,
 (b) the reference in subsection (2) to any priority that one charge, by virtue of a person's not having notice of a matter, enjoys over another charge or charges shall be deemed to include a reference to any priority that an advance made on foot of a charge, by virtue of a person's not having notice of a matter, enjoys over a subsequent charge or charges.

[81] ibid [8.2.5] and [8.3.6].

[82] *Re Castlemahon Poultry Products Ltd*, unreported, High Court, 13 December 1985, Carroll J.

[83] See s 26(5) Agricultural Credit Act 1978.

[84] Statements to this effect are to be found in most of the major commentaries on Irish company law; see, for example, T Courtney, *Law of Companies*, 3rd edn (Dublin, Bloomsbury Professional, 2012) 1260–62.

[85] The Second Report (n 22) [8.3.7].

[86] See Companies Bill 2012 (as initiated) www.oireachtas.ie/documents/bills28/bills/2012/11612/b11612d.pdf.

(2) On and from the commencement of this section, any relevant rule of law shall stand modified in the manner specified in subsection (3), but not so as to displace any priority, whether before or after that commencement, that one charge, by virtue of a person's not having notice of a matter, enjoys over another charge or charges.

(3) That modification is that, for the part of the rule that operates by reference to the time of creation of the 2 or more charges concerned, there shall be substituted a part that operates by reference to—

(a) the dates of receipt by the Registrar of the prescribed particulars of the 2 or more charges concerned, or

(b) if the date of receipt by the Registrar of the prescribed particulars of the 2 or more charges is the same, the respective times, on the date concerned, of receipt by the Registrar of those particulars.

In explaining the need for this amendment the Minister of State at the Department of Jobs, Enterprise and Innovation, Seán Sherlock TD, explained that:

> The current rule of priority is that the first mortgage has priority over the subsequent mortgage, subject to an exception where the second mortgagee gives notice to the first of the creation of the second mortgage, in which case the second mortgage will have priority over amounts secured by the first mortgage advanced after the date of such notice. This is known as the tacking of further advances. As far as charges on land are concerned, the exemption is contained in section 111 of the Land and Conveyancing Law Reform Act 2009 and section 75 of the Registration of Title Act 1964. However, there is no equivalent legislation which governs assets other than land, rather the same result is arrived at under common law.
>
> As the Bill stands, section 412 provides that unless their priority is otherwise governed by another enactment, charges will rank in priority in accordance with their date of registration in the CRO and makes no provision for the tacking of further advances. Accordingly, … the position on the tacking of further advances will vary, according to whether the assets charged are land or assets other than land. The holder of a second charge over land will be able to get priority over further advances, whereas the holder of a second charge on other assets will not as there is no legislative provision for it. This would not be a desirable outcome.[87]

The government's desire to amend the Bill in order to avoid impacting the right to tack further advances is understandable. The common law of tacking in Ireland where the collateral is not land is uncertain owing to the near complete absence of Irish authority in point.[88] In all probability the position is the same as that represented by the rule in *Hopkinson v Rolt*,[89] whereby a first mortgagee loses the right to tack a later advance made after receiving notice of a second mortgage. Where registration systems have impacted the right to tack future advances in the

[87] Seanad Debates, 17 June 2014 (Committee Stage).

[88] See *Re O'Bryne's Estate ex p Hawkes* (1855) 15 LR Ir 373 and *Bank of Ireland v Purcell* [1989] 1 IR 327 (SC) in the context of real property.

[89] *Hopkinson v Rolt* (1861) 9 HL Cas 514.

context of real property, the general practice in Ireland has been to legislate for the position that the giving of express written notice of a second charge puts an end to the right to tack.[90] In the context of this uncertainty, it is understandable that Minister Sherlock sought to avoid further complications by amending the law of tacking in the context of companies legislation. The drafting adopted to achieve this object is open to criticism in that it undermines the clarity and possibly the effect of the move to use of registration as the priority point. This is because subsections 412(2) and (3), as amended, have the combined effect of continuing all common law rules of priority which depended on notice. What the government appears not to have considered is that notice does play a role in determining common law priority outside the context of tacking. When combined with the retention of the 21-day period for registration this opens potential problems.

The following scenario illustrates the point: A Ltd grants a fixed charge to C1. A Ltd then grants a legal mortgage over the same asset to C2. Provided that both interests are registered within 21 days of the date of their creation, section 412(2) appears to require a court to consider favouring C1 unless C2 is a bona fide purchaser for value without notice of the prior charge, just as would have been the case in the past. Admittedly, provided both charges are registered, it is likely that C2 will have constructive notice of the first charge on the basis that C2 would have been expected to search the register, so the problem is unlikely to pose many practical difficulties, but I suggest that it would have been preferable for the government to have provided a savings clause for tacking, rather than altering the basis of the priority rule when amending the legislation.

Section 412 represents a welcome development in Irish company charge law, which resolves some of the shortcomings in the present system. Its most significant effect is to abolish the 21-day blind spot in the register which, though it may never have caused significant practical problems, was a deeply unsatisfactory aspect of the system. It will also have the effect of reducing the likelihood of certain irregularities in the registration process as secured parties will have a greater incentive to ensure that charges taken by them are registered with the utmost dispatch. This should reduce the incidence of irregular conduct such as that encountered in *Lombard & Ulster Bank v Amurec Ltd*,[91] in which registration of a charge was procured some 16 months after completion of the transaction by means of inserting an artificial date of creation into the particulars delivered to the CRO and then relying on the conclusive effect of the certificate of registration to uphold the effectiveness of the charge.

Though generally welcome, section 412 does have its shortcomings. The retention of the 21-day time limit for registration is curious. In a system where priority is to be determined by order of registration there is a powerful incentive for

[90] See s 75 Registration of Title Act 1965, s 111 Land and Conveyancing Law Reform Act 2009.
[91] Lombard & Ulster Bank v Amurec Ltd [1976–1977] ILRM 222 (HC).

secured parties to ensure that registration is attended to in a timely manner. It is not clear, therefore, what role the 21-day time limit now plays in the law of charge registration. The existence of the limit is likely to increase costs for users of the registration system because an application to the High Court is still required for leave to present late particulars in the event that registration is mistakenly left uncompleted after 21 days.[92] In view of the new priority rules, and of the universal practice that leave to effect a late registration is always accompanied by a saver protecting any third-party rights acquired prior to the making of the actual registration,[93] it seems that such applications are merely wasteful of time and costs and serve no useful function. Furthermore, the retention of the 21-day time limit may have been the inspiration for the requirement that confirmation of the creation of the charge be delivered within 21 days of the notice of intention to create a charge where the two-stage registration procedure is adopted. The relatively short period of time allowed may make this procedure less attractive to practitioners.

C. Conclusion

There is an old joke told in Ireland in which a tourist, sometimes portrayed as an Englishman, asks an elderly gentleman for directions to Dublin. The man pauses for a moment, thinks carefully, and then replies 'Well, if I were you, I wouldn't start from here'. Those tasked with carrying out a piecemeal reform of Irish personal property law are faced with a similar dilemma. The reforms to the company charge register in Ireland, while broadly positive, are far from fully satisfactory; however, one must make allowances for the difficult position in which the CLRG found itself. The law of credit and security in Ireland, like its English counterpart, is a complex amalgam of common law rules and equitable principles with some legislation, largely of Victorian origin, bolted on to it. It is understandable that the CLRG chose not to attempt systematic reform of the entire system. Indeed, given that its statutory objectives are confined to the realm of company law, it could well be argued that to do so would have been ultra vires the Group.

Having made that acknowledgement, the Irish experience of reforming the company charge register illustrates both the potential benefits and the undoubted pitfalls of engaging in a limited review of the law of credit and security. After the commencement of the Companies Act 2014, the company charge register in Ireland is a more efficient and useful instrument. The Act has delivered a clearer, more rational and more certain system for secured creditors, their debtors and

[92] See section 417 Companies Act 2014, which re-enacts the existing law without material amendment.

[93] See *Re Farm Fresh Frozen Foods Ltd* [1980] ILRM 131, 136 (HC).

those tasked with providing legal advice to both sides of secured transactions. This much is to be welcomed; however, if one were to sit down and design a system of company charge registration beginning from a blank sheet of paper, it seems unlikely that the result would bear any resemblance to the contents of Part 7 of the Companies Act 2014. Reading the CLRG report, it is clear that radical change to the existing structure was never truly considered and that the Group struggled to escape the tendency to chart the future through a close analogy with the past. The watering down of the revisions to the priority rules should also serve as a warning to those considering a piecemeal approach to law reform in this area. The legal framework for secured credit is a complex jigsaw; changes in one area may have to be carefully shaped in order to fit together with others. This fact adds a further pressure on the would-be reformer to avoid proposals which strike at the overall structure of the system. In the short term, it seems unlikely that the Irish commercial and legal communities can be convinced to give their support to another major overhaul of commercial law so soon after accommodating their practices to the new Companies Act and thus progress on systematic reform is likely to be slow. That said, the forces of legal inertia are unlikely to be sufficient in the long run to prevent the ultimate adoption of an Article 9-type regime at some future date.

11

Reforming the Law of Secured Transactions in Scotland

ANDREW JM STEVEN AND HAMISH PATRICK

A. Introduction

The year 1897 saw the publication in Edinburgh of Gloag and Irvine's magisterial *Law of Rights in Security*.[1] The fact that this remains the leading work on the subject in Scotland in the early years of the twenty-first century of itself says much.[2] In that book, the authors write:

> The law on the subject of security-rights over corporeal moveables [chattels] is beset with difficulties; and is not perhaps in a very satisfactory state, as a result of its rules is often to deprive the owners of such property of the power to make use of it as a security for its debts. It is open to question whether the rigidity of the law of Scotland on this subject should not now be relaxed by the adoption of a system analogous to the English bill of sale.[3]

But Scotland never adopted such a system[4] and the law on rights in security in relation to both corporeal moveables and incorporeal moveables (intangible personal property) remains in an unsatisfactory state. With the exception of the introduction of the floating charge in 1961[5] there has been little reform.

[1] WM Gloag and JM Irvine, *Law of Rights in Security, Heritable and Moveable including Cautionary Obligations* (Edinburgh, W Green & Sons, 1897, reprinted 1987). See AJM Steven, 'One Hundred Years of Gloag and Irvine' 1997 *Juridical Review* 314.

[2] It has been stated in relation to Scottish private law literature that 'the largest hole … gapes in the area of security'. See R Zimmermann and J Dieckmann, 'The Literature of Scots Private Law' (1997) 8 *Stellenbosch Law Review* 3, 10. Scotland is in much need of an equivalent to H Beale, M Bridge, L Gullifer and E Lomnicka, *The Law of Security and Title-Based Financing*, 2nd edn (Oxford, Oxford University Press, 2012).

[3] Gloag and Irvine (n 1) 187–88.

[4] Perhaps wisely as the system has been heavily criticised and is now being reviewed by the Law Commission for England and Wales. See http://lawcommission.justice.gov.uk/areas/bills-of-sale.htm.

[5] See Section B(ii)(c).

This chapter will be structured as follows. After this introduction, Section B will provide an overview of the current law and in particular the division between 'true' and 'functional' securities. Section C will look at some of the difficulties caused in practice by the outdated and restrictive nature of the current law. Section D will consider reform and in particular the large moveable transactions project being carried out by the Scottish Law Commission. Section E is the conclusion.

B. The Current Law

(i) General

In private law terms, Scotland is a mixed legal system.[6] That is to say, its law is a mixture of both civil (Roman) law and English common law. But, unsurprisingly, the mix is an uneven one. Scottish property law, that is to say the law of assets and the basis of personal property security law, is thoroughly civilian.[7] As in other civilian property systems, a fundamental distinction is made between personal rights (rights against a person or a limited group of persons, such as contractual rights) and real rights (rights in things which are enforceable against the world). Ownership is the principal real right and a right in security is a subordinate real right. Thus John may own a watch but if he pawns it the pawnbroker acquires a subordinate real right of pledge in the property. In contrast with England, there is no dualism between law and equity. Thus George Joseph Bell, one of the so-called Scottish institutional writers,[8] noted that the idea of an equitable mortgage is 'inconsistent with the genius of the Scottish law'.[9]

Rights in security over property can be divided into those created by the voluntary act of the owner of the property and those which are involuntary. The latter category will not be discussed further here as the focus is on securities which can be voluntarily granted.[10] As we shall see, there are several ways in which

[6] See VV Palmer (ed), *Mixed Jurisdictions Worldwide: The Third Legal Family*, 2nd edn (Cambridge, Cambridge University Press, 2012). See also KGC Reid, 'The Idea of Mixed Legal Systems' (2003–04) 78 *Tulane Law Review* 5.

[7] See, eg, GL Gretton, 'Security over Moveables in Scotland' in J de Lacy (ed), *The Reform of UK Personal Property Security Law: Comparative Perspectives* (Abingdon, Routledge-Cavendish, 2010) 270.

[8] See K Luig, 'The Institutes of National Law in the 17th and 18th Centuries' 1972 *Juridical Review* 193 and JW Cairns, 'Institutional Writings in Scotland Reconsidered' (1983) 4 *Journal of Legal History* 76.

[9] GJ Bell, *Commentaries on the Law of Scotland and the Principles of Mercantile Jurisprudence* (7th edn by J McLaren) (1870, reprinted Edinburgh, The Law Society of Scotland/Edinburgh, 1990) II, 24.

[10] The main examples of involuntary securities in Scotland are the possessory lien, which is broadly similar to its English counterpart, and the landlord's hypothec, which can be compared to distress for rent. See further GL Gretton and AJM Steven, *Property, Trusts and Succession*, 2nd edn (Haywards Heath, Bloomsbury Professional, 2013) paras 20.57–20.66.

Scots law allows a debtor to grant security over its property, while retaining ownership. In other words there is a limited number of what can be termed *true* securities. As a result of this, security is often achieved by means of the creditor being given or retaining ownership in the asset, or by using trusts. Such securities can be termed *functional* securities.

(ii) True Securities

(a) Pledge

The principal security right over corporeal moveable property is pledge,[11] a security which is familiar in most legal systems. Like its Roman ancestor *pignus*[12] it requires the creditor to have possession of the asset. The reason for this is to publicise the security to third parties. The default position is that a court order is required for a pledge to be enforced, but it is long settled that the parties may agree on an extrajudicial power of sale.[13]

(b) Hypothec

The sister security to *pignus* in Roman law was *hypotheca*, where the debtor retained possession of the property.[14] This meant that the security was not publicised and would-be creditors risked lending against an item which was already encumbered, possibly a number of times. Scots common law, like other European systems generally, eschewed the hypothec because of this difficulty.[15] Thus in a 1695 case the court stated that:

> [A] hypothec of a great flock of sheep … *retenta possessione*, is unknown in law; and such pledges were very inconvenient, for there is no register to certiorate [tell] the lieges [people] of such impignorations when they continue in the impleger's [*sic*] hand.[16]

The only express hypothecs recognised at common law are the wonderfully named but now disused bonds of bottomry and respondentia, which are maritime securities.[17]

[11] See, generally, in relation to the Scots law, AJM Steven, *Pledge and Lien* (Edinburgh, Edinburgh Legal Education Trust, 2008) chs 2–8.

[12] On which, see, eg, JAC Thomas, *Textbook of Roman Law* (Amsterdam, North Holland, 1976) 329–34.

[13] *Murray of Philiphauch v Cuninghame* (1668) 1 Br Sup 575.

[14] See, eg, Ulp. D. 13, 7, 9, 2. *Hypotheca* developed out of *pignus*. See B Nicholas, *An Introduction to Roman Law* (Oxford, Clarendon Press, 1962) 152.

[15] See AJM Steven, 'Rights in Security' in K Reid and R Zimmermann (eds), *A History of Private Law in Scotland: Vol 1 Introduction and Property* (Oxford, Oxford University Press, 2000) 345–50.

[16] *Ker of Greenhead v Scot and Eliot* (1695) Mor 9122.

[17] Both securities are granted by the owner of a ship or its captain, the former security over the ship and the latter over its cargo. See WM Gloag and RC Henderson, *The Law of Scotland*, (13th edn, by Lord Eassie and HL MacQueen) (Edinburgh, W Green, 2012) para 36.27.

(c) Floating Charge

In a 1951 case, Lord President Cooper, arguably the most distinguished Scottish judge of the twentieth century,[18] said: 'It is clear in principle and amply supported by authority that a floating charge is utterly repugnant to the principles of Scots law'.[19] Yet only 10 years later in 1961 the security was introduced to Scotland by statute followed by the introduction of receivership in 1972.[20] The adoption of the floating charge had been recommended in a report by the Law Reform Committee for Scotland, which stated that the common law was too restrictive because pledge was in effect the only security available and it required delivery of the assets to the creditor.[21]

The floating charge amounts to a legal transplant from England[22] and is therefore a familiar concept to anyone with knowledge of English personal property security law. Of course floating charges also extend to land held by the granter. As in England, only a limited category of persons can grant floating charges, the principal ones being companies and limited liability partnerships. While the floating charge has been welcomed by the banks,[23] given the state of the Scots common law of security referred to at the start of this chapter, it has proved controversial. Floating charges are creatures of equity. As we have already noted,[24] Scots law does not recognise equity in the sense that it is recognised in England. Making the floating charge fit against a civilian background has been problematic. For example, as we have seen, true rights in security in Scots law are real rights, but a floating charge only becomes real on crystallisation.[25] At one point efforts to make the floating charge fit shook the very foundations of Scottish property law.[26]

[18] For a recent appraisal, see HL MacQueen, 'Two Toms and an Ideology for Scots Law: TB Smith and Lord Cooper of Culross' in E Reid and DL Carey Miller (eds), *A Mixed Legal System in Transition: TB Smith and the Progress of Scots Law* (Edinburgh, Edinburgh University Press, 2005) 44–72.

[19] *Carse v Coppen* 1951 SC 233, 239.

[20] Companies (Floating Charges) (Scotland) Act 1961 and the Companies (Floating Charges and Receivers) (Scotland) Act 1972. The current legislation is the Companies Act 1985 ss 462–466 and the Insolvency Act 1986 ss 50–71.

[21] Eighth Report of the Law Reform Committee for Scotland (Cmnd 1017, 1960) para 2.

[22] Notwithstanding Lord Cooper's comments, one similar security was already recognised in Scotland, namely the agricultural charge. It was introduced by the Agricultural Credits (Scotland) Act 1929, following equivalent legislation in England and Wales in the previous year, the Agricultural Credits Act 1928. An agricultural charge can be granted by agricultural cooperatives over 'stocks of merchandise', but we understand that in practice it is not used. Instead, agricultural cooperatives grant floating charges.

[23] See, eg, RB Jack, 'The Coming of the Floating Charge to Scotland: An Account and an Assessment' in DJ Cusine (ed), *A Scots Conveyancing Miscellany: Essays in Honour of Professor JM Halliday* (Edinburgh, W Green, 1987).

[24] See Section B(i).

[25] *National Commercial Bank of Scotland Ltd v Liquidators of Telford Grier Mackay & Co Ltd* 1969 SC 181.

[26] See the House of Lords case of *Sharp v Thomson* 1997 SC (HL) 66, where the fundamental principle that ownership of land only transfers on registration of the conveyance was undermined. But a later House of Lords rowed back in *Burnett's Trustee v Grainger* 2004 SC (HL) 19. In the meantime the matter had been referred to the Scottish Law Commission. See Scottish Law Commission, *Report on* Sharp v Thomson (Scot Law Com No 298, 2007).

Academic commentators have called for the floating charge to be abolished and replaced,[27] but attempts at reform have so far not succeeded.[28]

(d) Aircraft Mortgages and Ship Mortgages

Scotland has more or less the same statutory regime for aircraft mortgages and ship mortgages as the rest of the United Kingdom.[29] These securities are non-possessory but require registration in order to have third-party effect.

(iii) Functional Securities

(a) Introduction

The limited menu of true securities has led to widespread use of functional securities. Here ownership[30] of the asset will be used for security purposes. Typically the creditor will hold the property, but, in the case of the trust, ownership is vested in the debtor and the creditor is a beneficiary under the trust.

(b) Transfer

True security (apart from the uncomfortable case of the floating charge) does not seem possible in relation to incorporeal moveable property such as claims,[31] company shares and intellectual property rights. Thus security is achieved in relation to such property by transferring it to the creditor, either by means of an assignation[32] in security, or by complying with the transfer rules which are applicable in specific cases.[33] The practical difficulties resulting from this are discussed below.[34] An assignation in security can either state expressly that the purpose of the transfer is security or it can purport to be an absolute assignation but be qualified by a separate agreement between the parties.[35] Where the asset that is being transferred is a claim, in other words the right to the performance of an obligation

[27] See GL Gretton, 'Should Floating Charges and Receivership Be Abolished?' 1986 *SLT (News)* 325 and D Cabrelli, 'The Case Against the Floating Charge in Scotland' (2005) 9 *Edinburgh Law Review* 407.

[28] See Section D(ii).

[29] Merchant Shipping Act 1995 s 16 and sch 1; Civil Aviation Act 1982 s 86; the Mortgaging of Aircraft Order 1972 (SI 1972/1268) and The International Interests in Aircraft Equipment (Cape Town Convention) Regulations 2015 (SI 2015/912).

[30] Note, however, some scholars take the view that only corporeal property is capable of ownership, whereas incorporeal property, being a right (or rights), is 'held'. See GL Gretton, 'Ownership and its Objects' (2007) 71 *Rabels Zeitschrift* 802.

[31] Claims are broadly equivalent to choses in action. They are rights to the performance of an obligation, normally to pay money.

[32] Assignation is the Scottish equivalent of what is known as 'assignment' in common law jurisdictions.

[33] Such as a transfer of shares in a company, which has to be registered in its register of members, or in the CREST register for dematerialised shares.

[34] See Section C.

[35] Gloag and Irvine (n 1) 490–94.

(typically payment of a debt), an assignation is only completed by notifying the obligant (the account debtor).[36] There is no equivalent in Scotland to equitable assignment in English law.

As regards corporeal moveables entering into a sale and leaseback arrangement makes the delivery required in pledge unnecessary to 'secure' the purchaser/lessor. But this runs the risk of being struck down by the Sale of Goods Act 1979 section 62(4) as a sham sale.[37]

(c) Retention

As in other parts of the United Kingdom, it is typical for the seller of goods in a commercial sales contract to have a clause retaining ownership until the price is paid. It is also common to retain title until all sums due to the seller are paid, thus giving the seller a high level of protection in the event of the buyer's insolvency.[38] While valid in themselves, such clauses are vulnerable to sub-sales to third parties in good faith[39] and can also be defeated by forms of original acquisition such as accession (eg bricks being used to build a house accede and become owned by the landowner).[40] Other examples of ownership retention (common also in consumer transactions) are hire purchase, under which ownership of vehicles or other goods is kept until the final instalment is paid by the hiree/purchaser, or leasing, when ownership never passes to the lessee.

(d) Trusts

While, as mentioned, Scots law does not admit equity, it has a long history of accepting the trust.[41] The accepted conceptual basis for this is now the 'dual patrimony' theory. Ownership of trust property is held by trustees as a 'special patrimony' and thus separately from their private assets, which are in their 'ordinary patrimony'.[42] This means that if a trustee becomes personally insolvent the trust assets cannot be touched by the trustee's personal creditors because they are ring-fenced in the special patrimony. While the use of trusts for security purposes

[36] See, eg, RG Anderson, *Assignation* (Edinburgh, Education Legal Education Trust, 2008) ch 6.

[37] For discussion, see Scottish Law Commission, *Discussion Paper on Moveable Transactions* (Scot Law Com DP No 151, 2011) paras 6.37–6.44 and the references given therein.

[38] *Armour v Thyssen Edelstahlwerke AG* 1990 SLT 891.

[39] The leading provision is the Sale of Goods Act 1979 s 25 but the Hire Purchase Act 1964 s 27 has particular rules on motor vehicles.

[40] See DL Carey Miller with D Irvine, *Corporeal Moveables in Scots Law*, 2nd edn (Edinburgh, W Green, 2005) para 12.14.

[41] See G Gretton, 'Trusts' in Zimmermann and Reid (eds) (n 15) 480–517.

[42] See G Gretton, 'Trusts without Equity' (2000) 49 *International & Comparative Law Quarterly* 599; KGC Reid, 'Patrimony Not Equity: The Trust in Scotland' (2000) 8 *European Review of Private Law* 427; KGC Reid, 'Smoothing the Rugged Parts of the Passage: Scots Law and its Edinburgh Chair' (2014) 18 *Edinburgh Law Review* 315, 335–38; and Scottish Law Commission, *Report on Trust Law* (Scot Law Com No 239, 2014) para 3.4. See also *Ted Jacob Engineering Group Inc v Johnston-Marshall and Partners* [2014] CSIH 18 [90] per Lord Drummond Young and *Glasgow City Council v The Board of Managers of Springboig St John's School* [2014] CSOH 76 [16] and [17] per Lord Malcolm.

was condemned by the Inner House of the Court of Session in one case over 30 years ago,[43] it seems unlikely that a similar approach would be taken today given the vast number of commercial transactions that are based on trust structures.[44]

(iv) True versus Functional Securities

As will be seen in other chapters in this volume, many systems take an entirely functional approach to the creation of security rights over moveable property. These include the Uniform Commercial Code Article 9 in the United States and the Personal Property Security Acts (PPSAs) in Canada, Australia and New Zealand.[45] Registration is generally required for third-party effect, in order to publicise the security. Scotland, like its southern neighbour, continues to take a binary approach, recognising both true and functional securities. What is intriguing about this is the comparison between the very restrictive approach to true securities and the very generous approach to functional securities. Thus while it is generally essential that pledged property is in the possession of the pledgee[46] so as to publicise the pledge to third parties there is apparently no such worry as to publicity in the case of an all-sums retention of title clause (or hire purchase or a trust). Other legal systems take a stricter approach as to what can be secured in retention of title.[47] Some commentators have questioned how rational current Scots law is.[48]

C. Difficulties in Practice

In this section we consider the practical difficulties in the current law, beginning with securities over corporeal moveables. As is well known, the true security of pledge is not generally convenient for either debtors or creditors.[49] The former will

[43] *Clark Taylor & Co Ltd v Quality Site Development (Edinburgh) Ltd* 1981 SC 111.

[44] Scottish Law Commission (n 42) para 3.16. See also *Tay Valley Joinery Ltd v CF Financial Services Ltd* 1987 SLT 207.

[45] For a valuable recent monograph considering the functional approach taken in the US against the non-functional approach in the Netherlands, see DJY Hamwijk, *Publicity in Secured Transactions Law: Towards a European Public Notice Filing System for Non-possessory Security Rights in Movable Assets?* (Rotterdam, published privately, 2014).

[46] An exception is *North-Western Bank Ltd v Poynter, Son and Macdonalds* (1894) 22 R (HL) 1 but for criticism of that decision, see AF Rodger, 'Pledge of Bills of Lading in Scots Law' 1971 *Juridical Review* 193 and GL Gretton, 'Pledge, Bills of Lading, Trusts and Property Law' 1990 *Juridical Review* 23.

[47] eg Germany. See M-R McGuire, 'National Report on the Transfer of Movables in Germany' in W Faber and B Lurger (eds), *National Reports on the Transfer of Movables in Europe Volume 3: Germany, Greece, Lithuania, Hungary* (Munich, Sellier, 2011) 164.

[48] See WM Gordon, 'Roman Influence on the Scots Law of Real Security' in R Evans-Jones (ed), *The Civil Law Tradition in Scotland* (Edinburgh, Stair Society, 1995) 167–75.

[49] See, eg, A Morell and F Helsen, 'The Interpretation of Transparency and Availability of Collateral: German and Belgian Laws of Non-possessory Security Interests' (2014) 22 *European Review of Private Law* 393, 398.

normally struggle to run their businesses if they have to surrender key assets such as equipment or vehicles as a necessary requirement of obtaining secured finance. The latter will not want to have to store large quantities of assets. Pledge in practice is generally only a viable option for goods already stored on third-party premises such as whisky in warehouses;[50] for property in transit, for example goods being shipped where the bill of lading can be pledged;[51] and for pawnbrokers.[52]

As noted already,[53] however, security by retention of ownership of corporeal moveables is widely used in Scotland, whether by retention of title by suppliers of goods on sale, or by finance leasing of vehicles or equipment purchased direct by lessors from manufacturers and leased to end-users who cannot or do not wish to purchase the vehicles or equipment direct.[54] While most funders and commercial third parties will assume that vehicles, equipment and stock used by a business may not be owned by that business and many third parties will be protected as good faith purchasers,[55] verifying the contrary position can be time consuming and unreliable.

It can also be time consuming to verify the existence of transfers for security purposes[56] of incorporeal moveable property. Nevertheless, checking the register of members of a company for a security transfer of shares or that an account debtor has received notice intimating an assignation of a claim are reasonably reliable. The actual practicalities of making such registrations and intimations is in practice of more concern, particularly when bulk completion of security is required over large volumes of shares or claims, or there is concern about the reaction of a share issuer or account debtor to registration or intimation. Doubts regarding the effectiveness of transfers of future claims create further problems for financing companies, such as debt factors or invoice discounters, wishing to take such transfers and those wishing access to revolving working capital funding backed by revolving trade debts owed.

In addition, transfer for security purposes can create consequential problems for transferors and transferees. While a transfer of shares for security purposes will not normally turn the transferee into a holding company of the share issuer,[57] mechanisms require to be put in place to ensure that, prior to default, voting rights

[50] *Inglis v Robertson & Baxter* (1898) 25 R (HL) 70.

[51] But whether a bill of lading can be pledged under Scots law is not certain because of *Hamilton v Western Bank* (1856) 19 R 152. The Scottish Law Commission (n 37) paras 15.3–15.6 recommends that the law is clarified to ensure that such a pledge is valid.

[52] As in England and Wales, pawnbroking is mainly regulated by the Consumer Credit Act 1974 ss 114–122. See also www.thenpa.com/.

[53] See Section B(iii)(c).

[54] Retention of title and leasing of course are also common in England, where the equitable fixed charge is available as a true security. Aircraft are frequently leased in the United Kingdom, although a registered mortgage is available (see Section B(ii)(d)). Sale and leaseback is also used in Scotland, but less commonly because of the risks indicated at Section B(iii)(b).

[55] See Section B(iii)(c).

[56] Bearing in mind that true securities over incorporeal moveables (other than floating charges) are not normally possible in Scots law (see Section B(iii)(b)).

[57] Companies Act 2006 sch 7, para 8.

can be exercised by and dividends paid to the transferor and communications from the issuing company are passed on. Similarly, when intellectual property is transferred in security it will normally be necessary for licences to be granted back to the transferor.

When security is constituted by transfer, multiple parallel security interests over the same assets are not possible and a further security interest can only be created by transferring the right to have the secured assets retransferred (sometimes known as the 'reversionary right'). This makes complex security priority arrangements problematic. This issue also arises to some extent regarding corporeal moveables as it is not clear whether possession by or for several pledgees is competent.

While floating charges do not fit comfortably into Scots law,[58] they do not suffer from the issues described already in this section. It is accordingly possible for several floating charges with complex priorities to be granted over existing and/or future corporeal and/or incorporeal moveables without any need for possession or intimation or for registration in a register relating to shares or other assets charged.[59] Floating charges are often taken in parallel with other security arrangements, partly to address the shortcomings of those arrangements or to facilitate realisation following default. The relatively uniform operation of floating charges throughout the United Kingdom also makes them attractive from the practical perspective. However, there are also ways in which a floating charge is less attractive to creditors than a pledge or security transfer. First, the grantor is able (prior to the crystallisation of the charge) to dispose of charged assets free from the charge. Secondly, the charge is subject to diligence executed by the chargor's creditors prior to crystallisation, to the expenses of an administrator and to certain preferred but unsecured creditors.[60]

D. Reform

(i) Introduction

The main subject of this section is the current moveable transactions law reform project of the Scottish Law Commission. Before discussing that something will be said of the various previous unsuccessful reform attempts which have been made since the introduction of the floating charge in 1961.

[58] See Section B(ii)(c).

[59] Though floating charges granted by companies registered under the Companies Acts and UK limited liability partnerships will require to be registered at Companies House under Part 25 of the Companies Act 2006. Assignations and other transfers in security by such entities also require to be so registered but pledges do not.

[60] Companies Act 1985 s 463 and Insolvency Act 1986 ss 55, 59, 175 and 176A and sch B1, para 116.

(ii) Previous Law Reform Attempts

The last half century has seen a veritable procession of non-implemented reports on reform of security over moveables, some made on a United Kingdom basis and others Scotland-only.[61] The first was the Crowther Report of 1971,[62] some of which was implemented by the Consumer Credit Act 1974. It proposed a functional approach based on the notice filing system under the Uniform Commercial Code Article 9. It recommended that this should be introduced in both England and Wales, and Scotland, but that the differences between the legal systems would make it desirable to have separate legislation.[63] The then government's response to this was lukewarm.[64] A working party was subsequently set up under the auspices of the Scottish Law Commission to examine how a notice-filing scheme might work in Scotland. Its chair was Professor John (Jack) Halliday, a former Scottish Law Commissioner, and its report was published in 1986,[65] but its recommendations were never taken forward. A similar fate befell the Diamond Report of 1989,[66] which proposed notice filing for both England and Wales, and Scotland.

In 1994 the Murray Report was published.[67] It was confined to Scotland only and, in contrast to the earlier reports, had a draft Bill. It rejected notice filing for several reasons, including the fact that it 'involved a radical departure from the current law, and [was] very complex'.[68] Instead it recommended a new fixed security over both corporeal and incorporeal moveable property which would be created by registration in a new 'Register of Security Interests' to be kept by the Registrar of Companies. In addition, the floating charge was to be rolled out to non-company debtors but only for moveable property and not consumer goods. But like all its predecessors there was no implementation.

The final story of non-implementation is perhaps the most remarkable one. We have noted earlier the awkward fit between floating charges and Scots law. The Scottish Law Commission was asked to look at the subject to see what could be done to improve the law. In 2004 the Commission produced its *Report on Registration of Rights in Security by Companies*.[69] This proposed a new legislative

[61] This section owes much to the Scottish Law Commission, Discussion Paper on Moveable Transactions ch 10. On unimplemented reports in England and Wales, see J de Lacy, 'The Evolution and Regulation of Security Interests over Personal Property in English Law' in De Lacy (ed) (n 7) 3.

[62] Report of the Committee on Consumer Credit (Cmnd 4596, 1971).

[63] Crowther Report para 5.2.21.

[64] White Paper on Reform of the Law on Consumer Credit (Cmnd 5427, 1973).

[65] The report is available at www.scotlawcom.gov.uk/publications/consultation-papers-and-other-documents/1965-2000/.

[66] AL Diamond, *A Review of Security Interests in Property* (Department of Trade and Industry, 1989).

[67] *Security over Moveable Property in Scotland: A Consultation Paper* (Department of Trade and Industry, 1994). Both of the present chapter's authors felt moved to comment on it. See H Patrick, 'Reform of Security over Moveable Property: Some General Comments' 1995 *SLT (News)* 42 and AJM Steven, 'Reform of Security over Moveable Property: Some Further Thoughts' 1995 *SLT (News)* 120.

[68] *Security over Moveable Property in Scotland: A Consultation Paper* para 2.5.

[69] Scot Law Com No 197, 2004.

scheme. Central to this was the establishment of a new Scottish Register of Floating Charges to be run by Registers of Scotland.[70] Floating charges affecting assets in Scotland would require to be registered there and not at Companies House.

The scheme was implemented by the Bankruptcy and Diligence etc (Scotland) Act 2007 Part 2. But after the 2007 Act was passed by the Scottish Parliament, the Committee of Scottish Clearing Bankers wrote to the Cabinet Secretary for Justice objecting to the legislation being brought into force on the basis that it would result in increased cost to business.[71] The principal argument was that whereas a UK company with assets in Scotland and England only has to register once at Companies House under the current law, under the 2007 Act Part 2 two registrations would be required. This view was supported strongly by the City of London Law Society and the Financial Markets Law Committee among others.

The Scottish Government established a technical working group under the auspices of Registers of Scotland to consider the matter.[72] Its report proposed three options: (1) implement Part 2 without amendment; (2) implement with amendments; and (3) do not implement. The Scottish government carried out a consultation on the report in 2012 and has said nothing since. It appears highly unlikely that the 2007 Act Part 2 will ever be brought into force.

(iii) Scottish Law Commission Project on Moveable Transactions

The Scottish Law Commission was established by the Law Commissions Act 1965 with the task of promoting the reform of the law of Scotland.[73] The Commission primarily carries out its work under ongoing programmes of law reform, which are agreed with the Scottish Government. The present practice is for a new programme to be agreed every few years, following wide-ranging consultation by the Commission as to the areas that it should examine, using the criteria of importance, suitability and resources.[74]

When the Commission published its Seventh Programme of Law Reform in 2005 it announced its intention 'to review the law of assignation of, and security over, incorporeal moveables'.[75] It noted that this project had originally been suggested by the Law Society of Scotland and had the support of a number of other legal bodies.[76] It then set out the justifications for the project, in particular the

[70] The department responsible in Scotland for various registers, including the Land Register.

[71] See *Register of Floating Charges Technical Working Group: Report to Scottish Government* (2011) Appendix 3, available at www.scotland.gov.uk/resource/doc/254430/0121799.pdf.

[72] See ibid. Dr Patrick was a member of this technical working group.

[73] Law Commissions Act 1965 s 2. The 1965 Act also set up the Law Commission for England and Wales.

[74] See www.scotlawcom.gov.uk/law-reform-projects/ninth-programme-of-law-reform/.

[75] Scottish Law Commission, *Seventh Programme of Law Reform* (Scot Law Com No 198, 2005) para 2.31.

[76] ibid para 2.32.

importance of incorporeal moveables as a source of wealth and potential source of security for credit, and the fact that the current Scottish rules generally date back to before the Industrial Revolution and are not fit for modern commerce.[77] It highlighted the fact that the requirement of intimation (notification) to the account debtor for there to be an assignation was cumbersome and that since there was no equivalent to the English fixed charge, the only way to use incorporeal moveable property for security purposes was to assign it.[78]

While the Seventh Programme ran from 2005 to 2009 little progress was made by the Commission in relation to the project due to the need to concentrate on its work on land registration.[79] When the Commission came to publish its Eighth Programme of Law Reform in 2010 it set out its decision to widen the project to include security over corporeal moveable property on the basis that that area of law was also 'outmoded'.[80] This had the support of a number of key respondents to the Eighth Programme. Lord Hamilton, who at the time was Lord President of the Court of Session, Scotland's most senior judge, stated that the topic 'appears to be in urgent need of consideration'.[81] The Society of Writers to Her Majesty's Signet[82] argued that this should be the first priority for the Commission in its Eighth Programme as there is 'no workable fixed security in Scots law'.[83] Thus the moveable transactions project was commenced in earnest, comprising of three strands:

(a) assignation (transfer) of incorporeal moveable property;
(b) security over incorporeal moveable property; and
(c) security over corporeal moveable property.

It can immediately be seen that there is a lack of symmetry in the project because transfer of corporeal moveable property is excluded. The reason for this is that most cases of transfer of this type of property are governed by the Sale of Goods Act 1979. This is a UK-wide statute and it would not make sense to proceed here on a Scotland-only basis.

The Commission published a substantial Discussion Paper in relation to the project in May 2011.[84] The paper's principal author was Professor George Gretton,

[77] ibid paras 2.33–2.34.

[78] ibid paras 2.31–2.38.

[79] This project led to Scottish Law Commission, *Report on Land Registration* (Scot Law Com No 222, 2010), which was implemented by the Land Registration etc (Scotland) Act 2012. The same small team at the Commission is responsible for all property law-related projects, consisting of a Commissioner, a project manager (who is a lawyer on secondment from the Scottish Government Legal Directorate) and a legal assistant (who is a recent law graduate on a fixed one-year contract).

[80] Scottish Law Commission, *Eighth Programme of Law Reform* (Scot Law Com No 220, 2010) para 2.5.

[81] Submission of Lord Hamilton on *Eighth Programme of Law Reform* (on file at Scottish Law Commission).

[82] See www.thewssociety.co.uk/.

[83] Submission of WS Society on *Eighth Programme of Law Reform* (on file at Scottish Law Commission).

[84] Scottish Law Commission, *Discussion Paper on Moveable Transactions* (Scot Law Com No 151, 2011).

who had just completed his five-year term as a Commissioner.[85] He was succeeded as lead Commissioner by the first-named author of the current chapter. There followed the usual consultation period of three months following publication. A seminar was held to discuss the security aspects of the project in October 2011.[86] At the time of writing work is well underway on a final report and a draft Bill.[87] The Commission team is being assisted by an advisory group of legal practitioners and academics who have expertise in the area. In due course, the draft Bill could, if the Scottish Government chose to implement the report, then form the basis of a Bill to be considered by the Scottish Parliament, as rights in security is an area of devolved law.[88]

As the final report has yet to be approved by Commissioners what can be said at the present time is limited. But it is likely that the Commission will recommend a scheme broadly based on that proposed in the 2011 Discussion Paper, because this commanded widespread support from consultees. Under this scheme there would be a new register, to be known as the Register of Moveable Transactions (RMT) and administered by Registers of Scotland. The RMT would be an electronic register. A new security over both corporeal and incorporeal moveable property would be introduced, which would be created by registration in the RMT. In respect of corporeal moveables there would be no requirement for the creditor to have possession. In respect of incorporeal moveables, because the new security would be a true security, the property would not be transferred to the creditor. It would therefore be possible for more than one new security to be granted over the same property. Broadly speaking the new security would be the equivalent of the English fixed charge, but it could be granted by any person and not just companies and certain other bodies. However, there would be special protections for consumer granters. Floating charges would remain competent.

The RMT would also have a second role. It would be possible to register assignations of claims (including assignations in security) in this register as an alternative to intimation to the account debtor. This would make bulk assignations of claims under Scots law far more commercially practical as there would only need to be the one simple registration rather than numerous individual intimations.

It might be observed that the scheme is not particularly radical or ambitious. In particular the plan is not to introduce the functional approach to security exemplified by the Uniform Commercial Code Article 9 in the United States and the PPSAs in Canada, Australia and New Zealand. Why? First, the Commission is very conscious of the number of previous attempts to reform moveable security law in

[85] His 'Of Law Commissioning' (2013) 17 *Edinburgh Law Review* 119 is a valuable insight into the Commission.

[86] The papers are published at (2012) 16 *Edinburgh Law Review* 261–82. The speakers were Professor Gretton, Dr Patrick, Dr Ross Anderson and Professor Hugh Beale.

[87] For the project webpage, see www.scotlawcom.gov.uk/law-reform-projects/security-over-corporeal-and-incorporeal-moveable-property/.

[88] But some aspects of the scheme, eg any provisions relating specifically to companies, may require legislation by Westminster as the law of business associations is currently a reserved matter.

Scotland which have been unsuccessful, several of these being along functionalist lines.[89] Secondly, it is also acutely aware of the English experience and the desire for commercial law in Scotland and in England and Wales to be broadly similar.[90] The Law Commission for England and Wales, in papers published in 2002[91] and 2004,[92] proposed a radical reform of personal property security law based on a functionalist notice-filing approach. In a subsequent report of 2005,[93] after significant opposition from stakeholders, it changed tack and recommended a more limited set of proposals. But even these were largely not implemented.[94] While that Commission's work was on securities granted by companies, whereas the moveable transactions project is not so limited, it remains highly relevant to Scotland. The reality is that it would be unacceptable to banks, other financial institutions and other stakeholders for there to be a functionalist approach in Scotland requiring retention of title clauses, hire purchase, trusts and the like to be registered when there was no such requirement in the rest of the United Kingdom. If there were any doubt on that matter, the experience of the Bankruptcy and Diligence etc (Scotland) Act 2007 Part 2 removes it.[95]

The challenge for the Commission in its Report on Moveable Transactions is to recommend a scheme which is acceptable in UK commercial law terms but also works effectively within Scottish property law where there is an absence of equity. It also has to take account of the fact that there is growing dissatisfaction with the current state of English personal property security law evidenced by the establishment of the Secured Transactions Law Reform Project[96] and ongoing work by the City of London Law Society.[97]

E. Conclusion

This chapter has attempted to set out the shortcomings of the current Scottish law on security over moveable property. In many ways the law is not fit for current practice, most notably in the absence of a true non-possessory security over

[89] See Section D(ii).

[90] Several areas of law which are relevant to the moveable transactions project, including consumer credit law, corporate insolvency law and intellectual property law operate currently on a UK-wide basis and are reserved to the Westminster Parliament.

[91] Law Commission, *Registration of Security Interests: Company Charges and Property other than Land* (Law Com CP No 164, 2002).

[92] Law Commission, *Company Security Interests: A Consultative Report* (Law Com CP No 176, 2004).

[93] Law Commission, *Company Security Interests* (Law Com No 296, 2005).

[94] See H Beale, 'The Exportability of North American Chattel Security Regimes: The Fate of the English Law Commission's Proposals' (2006) 43 *Canadian Business Law Journal* 177.

[95] See Section D(ii).

[96] See Ch 1.

[97] On which, from a Scottish perspective, see AJM Steven, 'Secured Transactions Reform' (2013) 17 *Edinburgh Law Review* 251.

corporeal moveables and the requirement for notification to account debtors in relation to assignation (including assignation in security). The last decade or so has seen the overhaul and modernisation of Scottish land law resulting from the work of the Scottish Law Commission.[98] It is to be hoped that the Commission's recommendations on moveable transactions, when published, will provide the basis upon which Scottish moveable security law can also be brought into the twenty-first century.[99] The complaint made by Gloag and Irvine at the end of the nineteenth century and quoted at the start of this chapter can then finally be addressed.

[98] Most recently, the Land Registration etc (Scotland) Act 2012, which came fully into force on 8 December 2014. See generally AJM Steven, 'A Golden Era? The Contribution of the Scottish Law Commission to Property Law' in W Barr (ed), *Modern Studies in Property Law: Volume 8* (Oxford, Hart Publishing, 2015) 13.

[99] Further, once the Commission completes the moveable transactions project it will then review the law of heritable securities (mortgages of land). See Scottish Law Commission, *Ninth Programme of Law Reform* (Scot Law Com No 242, 2015).

Part II

The Current State of Affairs: the English Law of Secured Transactions

12

The English Law of Personal Property Security: Under-reformed?

LOUISE GULLIFER AND MAGDA RACZYNSKA

A. Introduction

The use of proprietary interests as a means of securing performance of obligations is a critical part of financial transactions and of the economy. Evidence suggests that provision of security for credit promotes macroeconomic growth by facilitating access to finance and plays an important role in the risk-management and risk-mitigation practices[1] of financial institutions.[2] The English law of personal property has developed a range of techniques that are used to protect against credit risk, some of which arose solely to secure credit (traditional security interests: charge, mortgage, pledge, lien) while others developed originally in contexts other than security but are used as such (for example, retention of title agreements in contracts of sale, hire purchase or leases). This law is to a large extent found in cases although to some extent it is based on statute. Of particular importance are the Companies Act 2006, Part 25, which governs the law on registration of charges created by companies and limited liability partnerships (LLPs) across the United Kingdom[3] and the Bills of Sale Acts 1878–1891[4] governing security granted in writing by individuals, including groups of individuals such as unincorporated associations.

[1] Institute of International Finance, *Principles of Liquidity Risk Management* (March 2007) 9. See also *Asset Encumbrance, Financial Reform and the Demand for Collateral Assets* (Report submitted by a Working Group established by the Committee on the Global Financial System, Paper No 49, May 2013) available at www.bis.org/publ/cgfs49.pdf (last accessed April 2016).

[2] R Levine, 'Finance and Growth: Theory and Evidence' in P Aghion and S Durlauf (eds), *Handbook of Economic Growth*, 1st edn (Amsterdam, Elsevier, 2005) vol 1, ch 12, 865.

[3] The law on rights in security in Scotland is a devolved matter but the law on registration of charges created by companies is reserved to the UK Parliament as a matter concerning regulation of companies under the Scotland Act 1998. For discussion of reform in Scotland see Ch 11.

[4] Bills of Sale Act 1878, Bills of Sale 1878 (Amendment) Act 1882, Bills of Sale Act 1890 and Bills of Sale Act 1891.

Given the importance of security in achieving economic growth, it is particularly important to have a modern law governing the use of proprietary interests as protection against credit risk. This law should be responsive to, and insofar as possible predictive of, the practical and economic needs of market participants. The commercial and financial community is entitled to expect the modern law to enable them to create and enforce security as efficiently (simply and cheaply) as possible, with minimum formality and maximum flexibility while balancing the interests of those affected by the transactions. The debate on how the law in this area can be improved has a long history. No fewer than three reports going back over a period of over 40 years[5] have recommended that English law should be reformed in a fundamental way. The first was the Crowther Report in 1971,[6] which criticised the law as incoherent and inefficient and recommended the adoption of a scheme essentially based on Article 9 of the US Uniform Commercial Code. These recommendations were supported by the Cork Report in 1982[7] and amplified by the Diamond Report in 1989.[8] Some proposals of the latter were included in the Companies Act 1989 but the relevant part of this Act was never brought into force because of technical difficulties, particularly in relation to the land registration system. More recently, at the suggestion of the Company Law Review Steering Group,[9] the issue of fundamental reform was referred to the Law Commission, which proposed a draft scheme based on the revised Article 9/PPSA model in its consultative report in 2004.[10] Due to time constraints its final recommendations were more limited,[11] and were not enacted in the Companies Act 2006. The 2006 Act included a power to make amendments to Part 25, which covered the registration of company charges.[12]

Following a period of consultation by the Department for Business, Innovation and Skills ('BIS'), reforms were brought in pursuant to that power.

5 For a historical development of the statutory framework of the law of security interests in personal property in England see J de Lacy, 'The Evolution and Regulation of Security Interests over Personal Property in English Law' in J de Lacy (ed), *Personal Property Security Law Reform in the UK: Comparative Perspectives* (London, Routledge-Cavendish, 2012) 3–82; P Graham, 'Registration of Company Charges' [2014] *Journal of Business Law* 175, 179–82.

6 Report of the Committee on Consumer Credit (Cmnd 4596, 1971).

7 *Insolvency Law and Practice: Report of the Review Committee* (1982, Cmnd 8558). Although it was concerned primarily with insolvency, the report made some proposals for far-reaching changes to security, including expressing broad support for the scheme proposed by the Crowther Committee.

8 A Review of Security Interests in Property (1989).

9 Company Law Review (CLR) (1998–2001) launched with the DTI consultation document, *Modern Company Law for a Competitive Economy* (London, DTI, 1998); see also the CLR consultation document, *Modern Company Law: Registration of Company Charges* (London, DTI, 2000); the CLR Steering Group Document No 7 (URN 00/1213); and the CLR Steering Group, *The Final Report* (London, DTI, URN 01/942, 2001), 2 vols, ch 12 (focused on charges).

10 Company Security Interests: A Consultative Report (Law Com Consultation Paper No 176, TSO, 2004). See also Registration of Security Interests: Company Charges and Property other than Land (Law Com Consultation Paper No 164, TSO, 2002).

11 Company Security Interests: Final Report (Law Com No 296, TSO, 2005).

12 Companies Act 2006 s 894.

The Companies Act 2006 (Amendment of Part 25) Regulations 2013 introduced sections 859A–859Q to replace sections 860–892 of the Companies Act 2006. The new sections apply to charges created on or after 6 April 2013, the date on which the Regulations came into force. The 2013 Regulations constitute the most substantive change in the registration of charges granted by companies since 1900. In that sense it is right to refer to them as 'a milestone … in the history of UK company law'.[13]

The reform, while generally welcome, was, however, limited. Some opportunities to clarify the law were missed and some wider issues were not considered at all. One reason for this was the restrictive interpretation of the scope of the amendment power mentioned earlier. While it would be undeserved to criticise a reform for not achieving what it never set out to achieve, it is justified to continue to seriously consider the need for a wider reform. This is the task currently undertaken by the Secured Transaction Law Reform Project,[14] as well as by a working party set up by the City of London Law Society chaired by Richard Calnan. The purpose of this chapter is twofold. First, it sets out to identify and evaluate the extent of the changes made under the 2013 reforms. Our second aim is to explain where further work is needed.

B. The 2013 Reforms

Motivated by a desire to remove obstacles to companies' access to finance, the 2013 reforms set out to reduce uncertainty as to what charges are registrable and to improve procedures by reducing the cost for those filing for registration.[15] One of the main purposes of the reform was to update the system to take full advantage of advances in technology, so that fully electronic registration and searching would be possible. Another purpose was to establish one regime which would apply to registration of charges throughout the United Kingdom: previously Scotland had had a separate system from England, Wales and Northern Ireland. It will be seen that while there have been some changes in the requirements, the basic scheme, based on the principles governing registration of security granted by companies in the Companies Act 1900, remains.

(i) What Charges and Other Matters are Registrable?

Under the new section 859A, all charges and mortgages created by companies are registrable unless specifically exempt. Previously, there was a closed list of

[13] Graham (n 5).
[14] See Ch 1.
[15] BIS, Registration of Charges. Impact Assessment (BIS, IA No BIS0136, 2012).

registrable charges, which was a product of successive additions[16] to the original set of four types of registrable security instituted by the Companies Act 1900.[17] The list was unsuited to modern needs of finance. It contained some outdated definitions; for example, registration of 'a charge created or evidenced by an instrument which, if executed by an individual, would require registration as a bill of sale' was required.[18] Although in many circumstances this amounted to a fixed charge over goods of which the debtor was the owner at the time of creating the charge, uncertainty existed in relation to some assets as to whether they fell within the notion of 'personal chattels' under the Bills of Sale Acts.[19] The registrable charges included all floating charges but only some fixed charges. Although the distinction between the two still exists in the context of insolvency, it is welcome that the line no longer needs to be drawn for the purposes of registration, the rationale for which in modern times was never entirely clear.[20]

The exemptions from registration specifically mentioned in section 859A include rent security deposits,[21] charges securing underwriting obligations of corporate members of Lloyds and charges exempted under other legislation. The most significant exemption in that category involves security financial collateral arrangements which fall within the Financial Collateral Arrangements (No 2) Regulations 2003 (FCARs).[22]

Earlier drafts of the 2013 Regulations also exempted pledges from registration (for the avoidance of doubt) while providing that pledges created by pledgors who remained in possession but attorned to the pledgee would be registrable.[23] Pledges were omitted from the final draft: this was because the registration requirements applied to charges and it was not thought that pledges were charges. However, uncertainty remains in relation to registrability of pledges and liens where a debtor in actual possession attorns in writing to the pledgee because they may be characterised as a charge.[24]

[16] Companies Act 1907 s 10 (adding security in land and book debts); Companies Act 1928 s 43 (adding security in calls made but not paid; ships; goodwill; some intellectual property); Mortgaging of Aircraft Order 1972 (adding security over an aircraft); Copyright, Designs and Patents Act 1988 (extending the intellectual property in which security can be taken). See further de Lacy (n 5) 27–37.

[17] Companies Act 1900 s 14 (registration was required of charges on unpaid or uncalled share capital, floating charges, charges on a series of debentures and charges that would have required registration under the Bills of Sale Acts had they been created by an individual).

[18] Companies Act 2006 s 860(7)(b) (repealed).

[19] See Section D(i).

[20] R Calnan, 'Floating Charges: A Proposal for Reform' [2004] *Journal of International Banking and Financial Law* 341.

[21] It was thought that landlords taking or holding cash to secure tenants' liabilities under a lease would not be familiar with, or anticipate, the requirement to register (BIS Impact Assessment, (n 15) para 62).

[22] As amended by the Financial Markets and Insolvency (Settlement Finality and Financial Collateral Arrangements) (Amendment) Regulations 2010.

[23] BIS, Revised Scheme for Registration of Charges Created by Companies and Limited Liability Partnerships: Proposed Revision on Part 25, Companies Act 2006 (BIS, August 2011, URN 11/1108) ('BIS 2011 paper') section 860B.

[24] See *Re Welsh Irish Ferries Ltd* [1986] Ch 471 (a shipowner's lien over sums payable to a charterer as sub-freights was a registrable charge); applied in *Western Bulk Shipowning III A/S v Carbofer Maritime Trading ApS (The Western Moscow)* [2012] EWHC 1224 (Comm). Also noted in Graham (n 5) 185.

What is not entirely clear under the 2013 Regulations is whether any of the exempted security interests can be registered even though they need not be registered. Section 859A(2) provides that the registrar must register a charge when the relevant documents are presented, but section 859A does not apply to exempted charges, and there is no power in the 2013 Regulations nor the Registrar's Rules enabling the registrar to register any other charges. On the other hand, the law now makes more specific provisions for registration of statements that are voluntarily delivered.[25] Exempted charges are not one of them. This could suggest that exemption of charges imposes a ban on their registration so they cannot be registered if voluntarily filed. Although there is no express statement that the statutory list of voluntarily delivered statements is exhaustive, there is also no express power for the registrar to register any matters other than those listed. Whatever the outcome of this academic argument, anecdotal evidence[26] suggests that the practice of Companies House is to refuse such registration when it decides that the charge falls within an exemption although it is not clear how far the nature of the transaction is investigated before it is decided that it is exempted. Such decisions are sometimes hard to make. For example, whether a charge falls within the FCARs or not can be a matter of great uncertainty,[27] and it would be very unfortunate if the registrar had to make this very difficult decision in order to decide whether the charge could be registered.[28] Under the previous law many security financial collateral arrangements were prophylactically registered. This change in the approach creates a risk to the lenders that their security will not be valid against creditors and insolvency officers should the court not agree with Companies House's characterisation of the transaction.[29]

There is another potential problem. If a lender is not sure whether an arrangement falls within the FCARs, it may seek to register as a precaution. If the registrar allows the registration on the basis that the transaction is outside the FCARs, a question arises whether this provides grounds for estopping the lender from relying on the transaction as being within the FCARs or even characterises the transaction as outside the FCARs for all purposes. It would be very unfortunate if this were the case. At the very least, it could prevent the lender from arguing later

[25] Companies Act 2006 s 859C (charges to which acquired property is subject: the section, is, however, limited to charges which would have been registrable under s 859A), s 859J (statement that chargor is a trustee), s 859L (entries of satisfaction and release), s 859O (notification of addition to or amendments of a charge).

[26] A telephone conversation in January 2015 with a helpline adviser at Companies House discussing their practice but see G Yeowart and R Parsons, *Yeowart and Parsons on the Law of Financial Collateral* (Cheltenham, Edward Elgar, 2016) para 4.21.

[27] See generally H Beale, M Bridge, L Gullifer and E Lomnicka, *The Law of Security and Title-based Financing*, 2nd edn (Oxford, Oxford University Press, 2012) ch 3; L Gullifer, 'What Should We Do about Financial Collateral?' (2012) 65 *Current Legal Problems* 377.

[28] The fear of such unfortunate practice has been expressed by one of us before, L Gullifer, 'Personal Property Security Law: Where Next? Part 1' (2012) 8 *Journal of International Banking and Financial Law* 465.

[29] In some situations, permitting prophylactic registration can also serve as a way for technical difficulties in the law to be ironed out by 'stealth', see Canada Ch 4 D(iii)(b).

that the arrangement did fall within the FCARs in order, for example, to rely on a clause providing for appropriation of collateral.[30] This prevention could be on the basis that the lender was estopped from making such an argument on the grounds that registration was not possible unless a security arrangement did not fall within the FCARs.[31]

A range of statements can now voluntarily be delivered to the registrar. This includes particulars of a charge subject to which property has been acquired.[32] Previously, it was mandatory to register such a charge.[33] Compulsory registration was seen as unnecessary given the small number of cases where it applies. In most cases when property subject to a charge is transferred, the chargee demands a new charge to be granted, which requires new registration anyway.[34] Further, the chargor may now file voluntarily a statement that it is acting as trustee of property or undertaking subject to charge,[35] which is simply a codification of existing practice to avoid misleading records.[36]

(ii) The Process of Registration

(a) Electronic Filing

The most important step taken towards modernisation in the 2013 reforms is the introduction of electronic registration. Although it was previously possible to conduct searches online via WebCHeck and CompaniesHouseDirect, documents needed to be delivered in paper format. It is still possible to do this, but it is also possible to deliver the necessary documents online, thus saving time and the costs associated with paper documentation. Electronic registration of charges takes place via the Companies House WebFiling, which is a system also used for filing other information such as a company's annual accounts, annual return and changes in a company's directors or secretary. To file a charge electronically it is necessary to apply for an authentication code.[37] The person making the filing pays a registration fee to the registrar (currently £10 for electronic by contrast to £13 for paper registrations).[38] The law no longer provides for a right to recover the

[30] Such a clause would be valid under reg 17 of the FCARs.

[31] This point arose in a discussion with Oxford BCL students, in particular, Jialong Ying.

[32] Companies Act 2006 s 859C.

[33] ibid s 862; as to the effect of non-registration generally, see also below.

[34] BIS consultation paper, Registration of Charges Created by Companies and Limited Liability Partnerships: Proposals to Amend the Current Scheme and Relation to Specialist Register (BIS, March 2010) ('BIS 2010 paper') para 29, referring to Law Commission Report (n 11) paras 3.62–3.63. Compare, however, the position in the US and Canada, discussed in Ch 4 C(iii)(c).

[35] Companies Act 2006 s 859J.

[36] BIS 2010 paper (n 34) para 29 (indicating that it was the registrar's practice anyway) and BIS 2011 paper (n 23) 14.

[37] The process is quite complex, and many law firms are, at present, continuing to register using paper documentation.

[38] www.gov.uk/government/organisations/companies-house/about/about-our-services#wf-forms.

amount of fees from the company if a person other than the company delivered the documents to the registrar.[39] This change is consistent with the idea that it is no longer the company's duty to register a charge.

(b) Documents To Be Delivered

Under the new regime, the person registering the charge must deliver a statement of particulars and a certified copy of the charge instrument (if the charge has been created or evidenced by one) to the registrar within 21 days of the creation of the charge.[40] The registrar includes in the register all the documents filed which are required to be filed.[41] The registrar gives the charge a unique identification code, which enables the particulars, the instrument and any other documents filed to be 'tied' together on the register. The registrar no longer checks the charge documents delivered against the prescribed particulars,[42] thus saving costs and also eliminating the risk of the registrar being liable for negligence.[43] The requirement that a company should keep a separate register of charges has now been abolished although companies are required to keep copies of the full instrument available for inspection.[44]

The registration of the entire charge instrument, where there is one, was intended as a means to increase transparency.[45] It is questionable, however, to what extent this purpose is achieved. First, after the charge instrument is registered, parties may decide to amend it. There is no requirement to register any additions or amendments. While it is possible to deliver to the registrar a notification that terms of the charge have been changed or new ones added, the registrar is not compelled to register them and in any case this facility is limited to certain types of term.[46] This creates a risk that the charge instrument registered is not reflective of the terms governing the parties' relationship at the time the register is searched, which makes it necessary to conduct further due diligence.

Secondly, placing the entire charge instrument on the register raises an issue about the confidentiality of the terms of the charge and information included in it. This risk has been addressed by a provision for redaction of some personal information such as an individual's name, residential address, email address and telephone number, bank account identifier or signature.[47] This does not,

39 Under Companies Act 2006 s 860(2), (3) (repealed).

40 The date of creation is now statutorily defined, see Section B(ii)(c).

41 Companies Act 2006 s 859I.

42 The 'prescribed particulars' differed slightly from the particulars that needed to be entered on the register previously under ibid s 869(4). For discussion, see Section B(ii)(d).

43 The risk was small given the possible difficulty with establishing the existence of duty of care on the part of the registrar in the light of *Yuen Kun Yeu v A-G of Hong Kong* [1988] AC 175 (PC) (a body supervising a deposit-taking business owed no duty of care to the depositors). For discussion of where the risk of mistakes now lies, see Section B(ii)(f).

44 Companies Act 2006 ss 859P and 859Q.

45 BIS 2010 paper (n 34).

46 See Section B(iv).

47 Companies Act 2006 s 859G.

though, deal with the wider problem of commercial confidentiality[48] and there is a strong incentive now for the charge instrument to be as short as possible, with most details of the transaction documented elsewhere. It is not clear whether documents referred to in the charge document are required to be registered, but they may contain relevant information. For example, a negative pledge is often included in the loan agreement rather than the charge instrument.[49] This uncertainty undermines the transparency objective of the register.

In addition, the inability to redact commercially sensitive information on the Companies House register is at odds with the existing legislation governing registration of security interests in specialist registers. When registering security in a patent, registered trade mark or a registered design in a specialist register,[50] it is possible for the secured party to apply to have the security agreement designated confidential,[51] an option which is not open when registering in the Companies House register. At the same time, a secured party cannot merely register the security in the specialist register if the grantor is a company or an LLP. Registration in the specialist register only protects priority of the security; in order to ensure the security is not void against liquidator, administrator or other creditors it is necessary to register at Companies House. The need to register twice alone is unsatisfactory (and a matter for a separate debate) but that commercially sensitive information can be protected on one register but not the other seems entirely unjustifiable and prejudicial to the commercial interests of the parties involved.

Security in intellectual property aside, the availability of the entire charge agreement on public record with Companies House may of course be a matter of convenience in some cases but any such advantage should be weighed against all the risks it imports. Apart from the problems described above, there is also the issue of constructive notice of the charge instrument, which merits separate discussion below.[52]

Although it is debatable to what extent placing the charge instrument on the register is beneficial, it is certainly an improvement on the previous law that the original charge document no longer needs to be filed. This saves the time and cost

[48] The earlier drafts of the 2013 Regulations included the possibility to redact a limited amount of commercially sensitive information. It was not possible to redact information required as part of the prescribed particulars, for example the description of the property or undertaking charged necessary to identify the charged assets. Redaction of such information was to result in the invalidity of the charge (2011 BIS paper (n 23) 12, draft s 860A(3)). This was not included in the final draft for fear that the provision would, first, introduce an uncertainty whether a charge is valid or not and secondly, that it would lead to costly negotiations between the contracting parties over which information should be redacted: BIS, Impact Assessment (n 15) paras 173–74.

[49] See L Gullifer, 'Piecemeal Reform: Is It the Answer?' in F Dahan (ed), *Research Handbook on Secured Lending in Commercial Transactions* (Cheltenham, Edward Elgar, 2015). We are indebted to Marisa Chan of Clifford Chance for this point.

[50] Patents Act 1977 s 32; Trade Marks Act 1994 s 25; Registered Designs Act 1949 s 19.

[51] Patents Rules 2007 (SI 2007/3291) reg 53; Trade Marks Rules 2008 (SI 2008/1797) reg 59; Registered Designs Rules 2006 (SI 2006/1975) reg 30.

[52] See Sections C(ii) and D(iii).

associated with delivering the charge document to the registrar and returning it. It also facilitates registration in title registers, which require the original document to be filed within a particular period in order to preserve priority.

(c) Period for Delivery

There has been no change in the permitted period for delivery of documents[53] except that charges created outside the UK no longer benefit from an extended period.[54] The 21-day period begins with the day after the date of creation of the charge. Unlike under previous law, what constitutes the date of creation is now comprehensively defined.[55] This brings English and Scottish laws in line for the purposes of UK-wide registration and deals with some previously existing uncertainties, for example those surrounding the date of creation when the charge was created by deed delivered into escrow.[56] The definition does not clarify, however, what the date of creation is if a charge agreement is conditional despite inclusion in earlier drafts.[57] It is a shame that this has been omitted, resulting in some uncertainty in the law.[58] The period for delivery may be extended by the court[59] on the same grounds as before,[60] namely where the failure to deliver was accidental or is not of a nature to prejudice creditors or shareholders or a relief is just and equitable.

(d) Prescribed Particulars

The format in which particulars are filed has now been streamlined.[61] The delivered statement of particulars must identify the chargor, the chargee and the date of creation of the charge. Where the charge is created or evidenced by an instrument, most particulars are now entered in a prescribed 'tickbox' format, limiting opportunity to provide 'free text', which simplifies the filing process and makes searching easier, especially for those who do bulk downloads and broad-brush analyses.[62] The 'yes-no' tickboxes are provided to indicate:

- whether the charge instrument creates a fixed charge over any other property;
- whether the charge instrument creates a floating charge and, if so, whether it is over all the property and undertaking of the company;

[53] See Section D(iii).
[54] This used to be 21 days beginning with the day after the date of receipt of the charge instrument in the UK.
[55] Companies Act 2006 s 859E.
[56] See Beale et al (n 27) para 10.14.
[57] BIS 2011 paper (n 23) 17.
[58] Contrast *Re Jackson v Bassford Ltd* [1906] 2 Ch 467, 476–77 (Buckley J) and *Smith (Administrator of Cosslett (Contractors) Ltd) v Bridgend CBC* [2001] UKHL 58 [61] and [63] (Lord Scott).
[59] Companies Act 2006 s 859F.
[60] ibid s 873 (repealed), where the late delivery procedure was referred to as 'rectification'.
[61] ibid s 859D.
[62] BIS 2011 paper (n 23) 10–11.

- whether the terms of the charge include a negative pledge clause, that is, a clause prohibiting or restricting the chargor from creating security which ranks equally with or ahead of the charge;
- whether the company is acting as trustee in relation to the charged property (it is optional to include this information).

There is also a box to provide a short description of any land, ships, aircraft or intellectual property which are subject to a fixed charge in the charge instrument.

In the less common cases where the charge is not created or evidenced by an instrument, it is necessary to describe the nature of the charge, the property charged and the obligations secured by the charge. There is an optional tickbox to indicate whether the company is acting as trustee in relation to the charged property. Further details must be included if the charge is in a series of debentures.[63]

In terms of content, under the previous law the prescribed particulars were, in some ways, more extensive as they included the amount secured by the charge.[64] This information is no longer required, even in relation to charges without an instrument.[65] Although the amount secured is potentially useful information, it does, of course, change frequently so that any searcher would have to check with the charge anyway for up-to-date information. Similarly, the old law required a description of the property charged, which was useful but at the same time gave rise to difficulties of abbreviating complex and lengthy descriptions of property. The particulars need now only include a short description of charged property in certain cases.[66] Charges over such property can (and in some cases must) be registered in another UK register, so searchers can consult a specialist register if they wish. There is scope for further modernisation in this area by interconnecting the registers, and this is discussed below.[67]

(e) Negative Pledge

Another improvement is the new facility to indicate the existence of a negative pledge in the particulars. This change should, however, be approached with cautious enthusiasm. Not all forms of negative pledge are registrable; only those where the terms of the charge prohibit or restrict the company from creating security that would rank equally or in priority to the charge are registrable. Such clauses are typically found in the standard form of floating charge, where their main purpose is to preserve the priority of the chargee. Other forms of negative pledge clauses, which are not formulated as prohibiting or restricting the debtor from creating higher-ranking or rateable security, are not registrable as part of the particulars.

[63] Companies Act 2006 s 859B.

[64] ibid 869(4), now repealed.

[65] An indication of the obligation secured is required, but this need not, presumably, include the amount secured.

[66] ibid s 859D(2)(d).

[67] See Section D(v).

These include a clause in a fixed charge agreement to prevent the chargor from granting a subordinated security without the lender's prior consent[68] or the so-called affirmative negative pledge, ie a clause whereby the borrower agrees to create equal or rateable security in the asset if and when security is created in favour of another party. This means that the person searching the register should not assume that all negative pledge clauses are revealed in the particulars.

As mentioned earlier, it is very likely that there will be other documents relating to the financing transaction of which the charge is part. One is the loan agreement, which is likely to be on Loan Market Association or other standard terms. It is common practice to include a negative pledge in such a document and therefore it may not be included in the charge document. It is unclear whether such a negative pledge is registrable or not. Either way there could be confusion: if it is registered but not included in the charge document, a searcher may draw the conclusion that the 'yes' box is wrongly ticked, while if it is not registered, the searcher has no notice of it.[69]

An issue has arisen in practice as to whether it is possible to register a negative pledge clause taken by an unsecured lender. It is suggested that it is not. This is because section 859D refers to the negative pledge clause being expressed *in the terms of the charge*, not any other agreement between the borrower and the lender. For a negative pledge to be registrable, the lender must take a charge over an asset, even if it is of small value, and include the negative pledge clause in the terms of the charge. It similarly is not possible to register an agreement to create a charge at some point in the future with a negative pledge clause. Such an agreement does not seem to create a charge.[70] Consequently, the negative pledge clause would not be expressed in the terms of the charge but merely an agreement to create a charge.

(f) Conclusive Certificate

Under the old regime, having checked the particulars against the charge document, the registrar issued a conclusive certificate, which was 'conclusive evidence that the requirements of [Part 25 of the Companies Act] as to registration have been satisfied'.[71] This provision was interpreted to mean that the charge was valid against creditors, liquidator and administrator even if the particulars delivered were inaccurate, for example as to the property charged[72] or the date of creation so that the charge was not actually delivered within the 21-day period.[73] The risk of

[68] Their purpose is to trigger a range of rights and remedies upon breach rather than to secure priority, especially given that a fixed charge already has priority over subsequent interests except that of a bona fide purchaser of legal interest, L Gullifer (ed), *Goode on Legal Problems of Credit and Security*, 5th edn (London, Sweet & Maxwell, 2013) para 1–77.

[69] See Gullifer (n 49).

[70] *cf* G Hill, 'Negative Pledge with Provision for "Automatic Security" on Breach: A Form of Floating Charge?' (2008) 10 *Journal of International Banking and Financial Law* 528; *cf* the cases cited in n 58.

[71] Companies Act 2006 s 869(6)(b) (repealed).

[72] *National Provincial and Union Bank of England v Charnley* [1924] 1 KB 431.

[73] *Re Eric Holmes (Property) Ltd* [1965] 1 Ch 1052; *Re CL Nye Ltd* [1971] Ch 442 (CA).

inaccuracy was, therefore, on the searcher rather than on the chargee, and redress against the registrar was very unlikely.[74]

Under the new regime, it will be recalled that the law no longer provides for the registrar to check the particulars against the charge document, although this does still seem to occur, in that submission of the registration documents can be either accepted or rejected by Companies House.[75] Once the prescribed particulars and document have been delivered, the registrar must issue a certificate to the person who made the delivery, identifying the company who granted the charge and the unique reference code allocated to the charge.[76] The certificate is conclusive evidence only as to the fact that the charge is not invalid as a result of late delivery (or, in the case where leave for late delivery has been granted by the court, that any timing condition provided by the court has been satisfied). The certificate is not conclusive evidence that any of the particulars registered are correct.[77] It would seem that the risk of inaccurate particulars still falls on the searcher, but, of course, the inaccuracy could normally be discovered by a careful reading of the registered charge document. The current system, therefore, assumes that any searcher likely to be adversely affected by any matter covered by the particulars will read the entire charge document. Despite what was said earlier about the incentive to register short charge documents, some, at least, will be lengthy and complex. It might be thought that it would be better for the risk of inaccuracy to be placed on the person registering, as it is, for example, under a notice-filing regime.[78]

(iii) Consequences of Failure to Register

The sanction for failure to deliver the particulars and any charge instrument within the prescribed period is invalidity against creditors, liquidator or administrator.[79] The formulation of this civil sanction has not changed. Therefore, as under the old regime,[80] 'creditors' means secured creditors and execution creditors. An unregistered charge is valid against unsecured creditors until they acquire a right or interest in the charged property, that is until execution, appointment of a liquidator or before the company goes into administration.[81] Also, as before, when a charge becomes invalid for failure to deliver, the sums secured by it are immediately payable.[82]

[74] See n 43.

[75] See the demonstration video at http://resources.companieshouse.gov.uk/webfiling/demoVideos/chargeDocuments.shtml, and the anecdotal evidence mentioned in Section B(i) above.

[76] Companies Act 2006 s 859I(3) and (4).

[77] BIS 2011 paper (n 23) 19.

[78] See Ch 2 D(iii).

[79] Companies Act 2006 s 859H.

[80] ibid s 874 (repealed).

[81] Beale et al (n 27) para 10.34.

[82] Companies Act 2006 s 859H(4).

Previously, failure to register attracted an additional—criminal—sanction. It amounted to an offence committed by a company and every officer of it who was in default as well as attracting a sanction of invalidity against specified persons.[83] The criminal sanction was the original sanction when registration was first introduced in the Companies Act 1862 and until 1900 it was the sole sanction for lack of registration.[84] It was consistent with the register's role as a means to prevent fraud on those seeking to deal with the company. While the abolition of the old-fashioned criminal sanction is very welcome, it may have introduced an uncertainty in the context of constructive notice discussed below.

(iv) Amendment, Enforcement and Release of Security[85]

It is important that the register reflects accurate information as to the status of the charge in relation to the borrower's assets, and so it is important to enable parties to record relevant changes to the terms of the charge agreement. It is possible to register an amendment to the charge after its creation or the addition of certain types of terms, namely a negative pledge clause and a variation of priorities agreement.[86]

Where security is enforced by the appointment of a receiver and manager, the registrar must be given notice together with details of the charge within a prescribed period.[87] This largely mirrors the previous law, including the preservation of a criminal sanction for non-delivery of such notice to the registrar.

When the debt is paid or property otherwise released from the charge it is critical to the borrower that the records reflect this. On the other hand, there is a risk of fraudulent filing by the borrower. The current law does not deal with this any differently to the previous law: the registrar includes in the register a statement of satisfaction or release when filed.[88] However, the law now requires particulars of the person delivering the statement. This would give searchers notice of a possible moral hazard if that person were the chargor but these particulars are not placed on the register. A suggestion was made during consultation that supporting evidence such as the deed of discharge should be required to be filed with a statement of satisfaction or release as a safeguard against fraudulent filing and that the absence of the evidence would be publicly recorded. However, this was not followed.[89] Therefore, as under the old regime, the only safeguard against fraudulent filing is the offence under section 1112 of the Companies Act, which prescribes sanctions for false statements made to the registrar.

83 ibid 860(4) and (5) (repealed).
84 *Wright v Horton* (1887) 12 App Cas 371 (HL) esp 376–77 (Lord Halsbury LC).
85 For discussion of the comparable issues in the US and Canada, see Ch 4 C(iii)(a).
86 Companies Act 2006 s 859O.
87 ibid s 859K.
88 ibid s 859L.
89 BIS 2011 paper (n 23) 21.

C. Missed Opportunities—Greater Uncertainties

There are some issues which were omitted in the final regulations even though they were considered in previous drafts. This was probably because of a restrictive interpretation of the power to amend Part 25 of the Companies Act 2006,[90] so as to exclude any issues concerning priorities.

(i) Whether an Unregistered Charge Binds Purchasers

An unregistered charge is not invalid for all purposes. Section 859H, like its predecessor, lists those against whom an unregistered charge is invalid but is silent as to purchasers of property. This is an omission, which was rectified in the Companies Act 1989,[91] the relevant part of which was never brought into force. In the 2010 proposals BIS suggested making an unregistered charge void against a buyer, except in certain specified cases of property subject to specialist registers,[92] but the provision was unfortunately not included in the final draft. Since there has been no change, it is likely that the previous prevailing view will be adopted, which is that an unregistered charge is not void against a purchaser.[93]

(ii) Constructive Notice

Another opportunity, regrettably missed, is a clarification of the extent to which registration is constructive notice. At drafting stages various provisions clarifying this were suggested[94] but in the end none were included. This omission leaves the existing law in a state of even greater uncertainty than previously existed.[95]

Prior to the 2013 Regulations there were also no statutory provisions regarding notice but it was reasonably well established that the registration of a charge was notice of the existence of the charge. Third parties reasonably expected to search the register had constructive notice of all particulars that were required to be filed

[90] See Section A.

[91] Companies Act 1989, s 399.

[92] BIS, *Government Response—Consultation on Registration of Charges created by Companies and Limited Liability Partnerships* (BIS, December 2010) (referred to as BIS 2010 response) proposal F and see the scheme proposed in BIS 2011 paper (n 23) para 37 (stating that the proposal was rejected following discussion with the stakeholders).

[93] *Stroud Architectural Services Ltd v John Laing Construction Ltd* [1994] 2 BCLC 276 145 (Sir John Newey QC); see also Beale et al (n 27) para 13.26; E McKendrick (ed), *Goode on Commercial Law*, 4th edn (London, Penguin Books, 2010) 710.

[94] See BIS 2010 response (n 92) proposal F ('any person taking a charge over the company's property is deemed to have notice of any previously registered charge') and see BIS 2011 paper (n 23) para 37 (stating that the proposal was rejected following discussion with the stakeholders).

[95] See generally Gullifer (ed) (n 68) paras 2.25–2.31.

under the Companies Act 2006. On the other hand, there was notice of particulars which were voluntarily filed (such as negative pledge clauses accompanying floating charges) only to those parties who actually searched the register[96] although arguments were made that they should constitute notice more widely.[97] Registration was not notice of contents of the charge instrument,[98] which in any case was not accessible from the register although a party searching the register had a right to inspect a copy of the charge instrument at the company's registered office.[99]

(a) Of What is Registration Notice?

Under the current law, a person *actually* searching the register probably has notice of both the particulars and the charge instrument, although the position where the particulars are inaccurate is unclear.[100] It is much harder to establish who has constructive notice and of what. Using the pre-2013 logic that constructive notice applied to the information that was required to be registered, it is at least arguable that under the current law the register does not constitute constructive notice of anything since no information is 'required' to be registered in the sense of there being a legal duty to register.[101] This would be very unsatisfactory, and this argument is not likely to succeed, though its existence creates uncertainty.

It is also possible to make an argument that while the registration is not compulsory, once a commercial decision to register is made, the law provides which documents need to be delivered to the registrar and when, so that they are 'required to be registered'.[102] If this is true, there is constructive notice of information contained in both the statement of particulars and the charge instrument (if any). Some argue that this might take the doctrine of constructive notice too far.[103] Yet, an argument that constructive notice applies only to the particulars, or only to the instrument, is difficult to justify if the basis for application of the doctrine is the duty to deliver certain documents, which covers both the particulars and the instrument (if there is one).

As mentioned above, there is a lack of clarity as to the position where the charge instrument is inconsistent with the registered particulars, for example where the

[96] *English & Scottish Mercantile Investment Co v Brunton* [1892] 2 QB 700; *Wilson v Kelland* [1910] 2 Ch 306; *Siebe Gorman & Co Ltd v Barclays Bank* [1979] 2 Lloyds Rep 142, 160; *Welch v Bowmaker, Re Salthill Properties Ltd* (2004) IEHC 145.

[97] JH Farrar, 'Floating Charges and Priorities' (1974) 38 *The Conveyancer* 315, 319; see, however, Beale (et al) (n 27) paras 12.16–12.17 (suggesting that the doctrine of inferred knowledge finds no support in cases and would be undesirable).

[98] *English & Scottish Mercantile Investment* [1892] 2 QB 700; *Standard Rotary Machine Co Ltd* (1906) 95 LT 829; *Wilson v Kelland* [1910] 2 Ch 306; *Siebe Gorman & Co Ltd v Barclays Bank* [1979] 2 Lloyds Rep 142.

[99] Companies Act 2006 s 877 (repealed).

[100] See Section B(ii)(f).

[101] Gullifer (ed) (n 68) para 2.29.

[102] If they are not, the charge is unregistered and the civil sanctions apply.

[103] Graham (n 5) 192.

particulars indicate there is no fixed charge but the terms of the instrument create one.[104] First, if the particulars are inaccurate, do they constitute a 'statement of particulars' at all for the purposes of the Companies Act 2006? If the answer is negative, the entire charge would be invalid, which would seem disproportionately harsh a consequence. Second, does the person searching have notice of the inaccurate particulars or the accurate instrument? If she were taken to have notice of the charge instrument, the regime would encourage (or even require) detailed diligence, which would increase cost and effort on the part of the searching party and render the registered particulars (almost) for guidance only. Not only could this become a disincentive to accurate completion of the registered particulars, but there would be a risk of incentivising portrayal of particulars shedding a better, if untrue, light on the company.

This raises the question of the role of the particulars. It appears that BIS regarded them as particularly useful for bulk downloaders and credit rating agencies, especially as they are searchable, which the charge instrument is not.[105] This suggests a lesser role of particulars in giving notice to potential secured creditors compared to the charge instrument, and maybe that if the charge instrument were inconsistent with the particulars the former would prevail. If this is correct, the position under current law is that constructive notice applies to the entire charge instrument, which raises the question of the cost-effectiveness of the system.[106]

(b) To Whom is Registration Notice?

Assuming that only a person who is reasonably expected to search the register would have constructive notice,[107] further lack of clarity surrounds the question of who counts as such a person. Under the old regime, a buyer of goods subject to the charge in the ordinary course of chargee's business is probably not reasonably expected to search: the position now seems unchanged.[108] Although it seems that lenders seeking to take registrable security are reasonably expected to search, it is unclear whether this extends to those taking non-registrable security such as pledgees (who probably should reasonably be expected to search)[109] or those

104 Gullifer (ed) (n 68) para 2.30.

105 BIS 2011 paper (n 23) 5, 11.

106 See further Section D(iii).

107 Such seemed to be the position under previous law, see G McCormack, *Secured Credit under English and American Law* (Cambridge, Cambridge University Press, 2004) 106–07; *contra* W Gough, *Company Charges*, 2nd edn (London, Lexis Nexis Butterworths, 1996) ch 32 (arguing that registration is constructive notice to the entire world); for rebuttal see Beale et al (n 27) paras 12.05–12.14.

108 See also Graham (n 5) 191; under previous law see, for example, Beale et al (n 7) para 12.05; G McCormack, 'The Nature of Security over Receivables' (2002) 23 *Company Lawyer* 64, 86; see also *Feuer Leather Corp v Frank Johnstone & Sons* [1981] Comm LR 251.

109 Beale et al (n 27) para 14.06, suggesting that there has been a shift from the previous view that it would not be reasonable to expect a pledgee, who is not himself registering, to check the register (citing Lord Hacking in the House of Lords debate on the 1989 Companies Act (HL Deb 6 April 1989, vol 505, col 1217) and *Joseph v Lyons* (1884) 15 QBD 280, 286 (Cotton LJ)).

taking security financial collateral arrangements under the FCAR (who probably should not be so expected). This has also been problematic pre-2013, so it is a shame that an opportunity to clarify this has been missed.[110]

It is probably fair to observe that the doctrine of constructive notice has proved to be ill-suited to the secured transactions law in England given the extent and persistence of uncertainty affecting this area. A much wider reform is needed, abolishing the doctrine of constructive notice in this area and replacing it with an alternative set of rules determining priority between various third parties. Although the opportunity to conduct such a reform was not open to BIS given the limited scope of the power within which it was operating, nevertheless such a reform is needed.[111]

D. The Persisting Need to Consider a Wider Reform

The 2013 reform did not tackle some important issues, as a result of which a range of pressing problems and inefficiencies continue to persist. We address the key areas in turn.

(i) Security Granted by Non-corporate Debtors

Security interests over tangible movable assets (goods) granted in writing by individuals or groups of individuals (consumers, sole traders and partnerships) must comply with the Bills of Sale Acts 1878–1891.[112] The Acts have been criticised for over a century for the technical pitfalls they have created, attracting the first negative judicial commentary just a few years after the introduction of the 1882 Act,[113] and were recommended for repeal by the Crowther Committee in 1971[114] and BIS in 2009.[115] The Law Commission also called for a serious consideration of reform in this area.[116] Although the Bills of Sale Acts continue unscathed,[117] the discussion is far from finished.[118] Having launched its two-year review of the Acts in

[110] Draft proposals were made prior to 2013 Regulations to deal with this issue (BIS 2010 response (n 92) proposal F). See also Gullifer (ed) (n 68) para 2-31.

[111] See further Section D(iv).

[112] This applies also to general assignments of book debts (see n 128 below).

[113] *Thomas v Kelly and Barker* (1888) LR 13 App Cas 506 (HL) 517 (Lord Macnaghten).

[114] See n 6.

[115] BIS 2009 Consultation Paper, *A Better Deal for Consumers* (BIS, December 2009, URN 09/1595).

[116] Law Commission Consultation Paper 2002 (n 10).

[117] Following the 2009 BIS consultation focused on consumer lending, a voluntary code of practice was adopted under the auspices of the Consumer Credit Trade Association.

[118] General support for reform was noted by the Law Commission Report (n 11) para 1.48. For academic calls for reform, see L Gullifer and S Hurst, 'Bills of Sale Acts: Ripe for Reform?' (2013) *Journal of International Banking and Financial Law* 685; G McBain, 'Repealing the Bills of Sale Acts'

September 2014, the Law Commission published a consultation paper in 2015.[119] A recommendation was made to repeal the Acts and to replace them with new legislation regulating non-possessory security granted by individuals over goods they already own. The security would take the form of a "goods mortgage", registrable in a broadly similar way to the current registration of bills of sale, and a "vehicle mortgage", registrable at a designated asset finance registry.[120] An electronic registration of security granted by individuals was not recommended for fear of the reform taking longer than desirable to deal with some urgent problems. The final report is due to be published later in 2016.

In our view it is unfortunate that Bills of Sale Acts continue to apply to security granted by individuals, especially those running a business: sole traders and partnerships. The scale of the problem is staggering and probably underrated. Of an estimated 5.4 million private sector businesses, the latest available figures from the start of 2015 show that 62 per cent of them are sole proprietorships (3.3 million) and 8 per cent self-employed partnerships.[121] These statistics suggest that 70 per cent of businesses are not subject to the Companies Act regime and may be subject to the Bills of Sale regime when seeking to grant security over goods to obtain credit.

Security in the form of a bill of sale is far less flexible and more onerous than security granted by companies. There are strict and complex formalities for a security bill,[122] creating a trap even for solicitors.[123] The slightest slip in complying with the formalities can result in the invalidity of the security or even of the personal covenants contained in the bill of sale.[124] By contrast, there are no formalities for creation of security by companies, only requirements to make security valid against creditors, liquidators and administrators. In comparison to companies, those lending to unincorporated businesses run a greater and unnecessary risk that the security is not created, which might influence their decision whether or not to lend against a bill of sale.

The Acts prohibit granting security in future assets (except growing crops) as security is void against everyone except the grantor unless goods covered in the

(2011) 5 *Journal of Business Law* 475; D Sheehan, 'The Bills of Sale and Company Charges Consultations: An Opportunity Missed?' (2011) 26 *Journal of International Banking and Financial Law* 347; D Sheehan, 'The Abolition of Bills of Sale in Consumer Lending' (2010) 126 *Law Quarterly Review* 356.

[119] Law Commission, *Bills of Sale Call For Evidence* (October 2014), available at www.lawcom.gov.uk; Law Commission, *Bills of Sale* (Law Com, Consultation Paper No 225, London, TSO, 2015), available at www.lawcom.gov.uk.

[120] The private registries already doing such registration (HPI, Experian and CDL) would be invited to apply to be designated, see Law Commission Consultation Paper (n 119) paras 10.43–10.61.

[121] *Business Population Estimates for the UK and Regions 2015* (BIS, October 2015, URN15/92) available at www.gov.uk.

[122] Prescribed in sch 1 to the Bills of Sale Act 1882.

[123] *Chapman v Wilson* [2010] EWHC 1746 (Ch) (where a document drafted by a solicitor was held invalid for lack of formality).

[124] Bills of Sale Act 1882, 1878 (Amendment) s 9.

bill are specifically listed in the schedule.[125] If future goods are not sufficiently described in the prescribed form, the bill of sale is void against the debtor too. This is also usually seen as precluding unincorporated businesses from granting a floating charge,[126] which is available in relation to companies. Moreover, by contrast to companies, unincorporated businesses are subject to uncertainty and limitations when creating security over certain assets. The Acts apply to 'personal chattels'[127] and general assignment of book debts.[128] It is unclear, for example, whether the Acts apply to a charge over a houseboat (given that transfers and assignments of ships and vessels are excluded)[129] or aircraft (which could not have been contemplated by the drafters of the Acts). There is also no possibility to register security in a range of intangible assets, eg single book debts, insurance contracts or intellectual property, although, of course, security over these assets can be created by non-corporate debtors. Those lending against such assets are, therefore, less well protected than when lending to companies.

The registration process is cumbersome, involving witness attestation and paper filing.[130] The register of bills of sale, maintained by the Royal Courts of Justice, is manual, difficult to search and lacks transparency.[131] Repayment of the debt does not extinguish the bill automatically as a satisfaction certificate must be issued. Anecdotal evidence suggests that it is almost impossible to match bills with the certificates due to physical cataloguing and recording problems. This stands in stark contrast to the electronic register for companies.

For these reasons, it is very likely that the ability to borrow by unincorporated entities is limited and that borrowing is more costly than secured borrowing by companies. There seems to be no good reason to continue to differentiate between lending to corporate and incorporate business.[132] A restricted ability to borrow may also create an unnecessary pressure to incorporate. In our view, the Bills of Sale Acts should be repealed and replaced with an alternative system of registration of security along the lines suggested by the Law Commission in 2004,[133] at least in relation to sole traders and partnerships.[134] We fear that the 2015 Law Commission recommendations for a more modest reform[135] do not go far enough to deal with the problems effectively. It would be regrettable if the drive for short-term solutions were to hamstring the prospect of a wider modernisation in this area. The practical issues of a deeper reform are being considered by the Secured

[125] ibid ss 4, 5.

[126] See P Giddins, 'Floating Charges by Individuals: Are They Conceptually Possible?' [2011] *Journal of International Banking and Financial Law* 125.

[127] Bills of Sale Act 1878 s 4.

[128] Insolvency Act 1986 s 344.

[129] Bills of Sale Act 1878 s 4.

[130] ibid s 10.

[131] See Gullifer and Hurst (n 118); McBain (n 118) 506, esp fn 250.

[132] Also noted in the Diamond Report (n 8) para 16.15.

[133] Law Commission Consultative Report (n 10).

[134] Consumer lending may raise different issues, which are not considered here.

[135] Law Commission Consultation Paper (n 119).

Transactions Law Reform Project. The most significant issues specific to this group of debtors are (1) how to identify the grantor of the security and (2) how to accommodate a floating charge-type security in bankruptcy of a sole trader or partners.

In relation to the first issue, one way would be to use existing identifiers such as the debtor's name (as ascertained in documentation, which would have to be prescribed and hierarchised), a VAT number (although not every business would have one) or a national insurance number, or a combination of at least two of these.[136] Another would be a separate registration number for the purposes of registration of a security. Limited partnerships, for example, already register at Companies House even though they remain unincorporated.[137] The second main issue is closely related to the wider issue of who should pay the price of insolvency.

(ii) The Need to Increase Transparency of Registrable Interests

English law lacks transparency in two aspects: there are too many different interests used as security and too few proprietary interests that are registrable. The multiplicity of interests, each governed by different rules accumulated over the centuries, has made the law more complicated than it needs to be and difficult to navigate, especially for non-English lawyers. One of the most problematic areas is the distinction between fixed and floating charges, which is tricky to apply in practice and of critical importance in insolvency.[138] One solution would be to streamline the rules that apply to the so-called traditional forms of security, which would remove the need to draw lines between fixed and floating security or legal and equitable security. But such an approach would miss the opportunity to achieve an even greater transparency. In our view, a scheme governing the traditional form of security interests should also extend to other proprietary interests used as protection against credit risk, the most important of which are retention and transfer of title in asset finance, as is the case under Article 9/PPSA schemes, although not necessarily by adopting the regulatory framework found in those schemes.

At present, financiers may hold various interests in assets to give them proprietary protection against default, but only charges and mortgages are registrable. As a result, financiers looking to an asset for security have no cheap and easy way of knowing whether an unregistered interest such as a retention of title under conditional sale or hire purchase has been created ahead of them. This may lead to the financiers unexpectedly finding their interest subject to another interest. In some cases they can rely on searches with certain non-statutory bodies such

136 For discussion of how this problem was addressed in Australia, see Ch 7 E(iii).

137 See Limited Partnerships Act 1907, ss 8 and 8A. This does not make them legal entities, see *Re Barnard* [1932] 1 Ch 269; 272 (Farwell J).

138 See Calnan (n 20) (arguing that the problems would be diminished if fixed and floating charges were not treated differently on insolvency).

as HPI or Experian. However, their records are confined to motor vehicles with failure to register having no legal sanction and registration having an uncertain effect. Financiers can, of course, carry out extensive due diligence, but the costs of this are heavy compared with the cost of searching a register.

It is unconvincing that retention of title in asset-based finance ought to be treated differently to a charge solely on the ground that it constitutes no more than a contractual stipulation as to when the title to goods is to pass whereas a charge is a grant of an interest. The law was criticised for regulating transactions according to their form and not their substance as early as the Crowther Report in 1971. Registration of retention of title was recommended by the Cork Report and the Law Commission, although the latter thought it should be part of a wider registration scheme available not only to interests functionally equivalent to security, but also a range of other interests (such as sales of receivables and commercial consignments). Extending registration to proprietary interests that function as security and certain other interests used in financing transactions (such as sales of receivables), coupled with a rule that priority is determined by the date of registration, could improve the transparency and reduce the costs of due diligence.

(iii) The Registration Process: Not as Cheap and Modern as It Could Be

The purpose of the registration system instituted originally by the Companies Act 1900 was to ensure that companies could not conceal from creditors, suppliers and customers the extent to which their assets were charged to others.[139] Historically, the register was treated as a means to provide public notice in order to prevent fraud, which otherwise was thought likely to occur purely because the debtor remained in possession.[140] Modern systems of secured transactions move towards the idea that the purpose of registration is to enhance certainty and transparency.[141] A slight shift towards such thinking was visible in BIS prior to the enactment of the 2013 Regulations. It noted that as well as preventing fraud, registration is meant to support transparency by facilitating access to information about changes through a public record to anyone who might benefit from it, hence the concern about providing searchable particulars for bulk downloaders and credit rating agencies.[142]

[139] See Gullifer (n 49).

[140] Before the Bill of Sale Act 1854, which was the first to introduce registration (it was for non-corporate debtors), the non-possessory chattel mortgage was typically taken as conclusive evidence of the intent to defraud creditors within the Fraudulent Conveyance Act 1571.

[141] *cf* the objectives of a modern secured transactions law set out in the UNCITRAL Legislative Guide on Secured Transactions 2007, available at www.uncitral.org, paras 46–59.

[142] BIS Impact Assessment (n 15) paras 3 and 15.

In the context of registration, 'certainty and transparency' means timely availability of relevant information on which one can rely. In a financial transaction, the most important piece of information that a prospective creditor wants to know is whether the borrower's assets are subject to interests which would bind the prospective lender. Under the current system, lenders cannot obtain this information with certainty due to the risk that a charge ranking ahead was created within the last 21 days. Although the risk of invisibility of a charge has not been reported to cause problems in practice,[143] it would be naïve to infer that it will never do so in the future. Moreover, expectations change with the development of technology. In a system where it is possible to record information almost instantaneously, it is not difficult to imagine that there will soon be an expectation that the record should instantaneously be transparent and where it is not, one ought to be able to rely on the record accordingly if one is to rely on it at all. A system which fails to catch up with the technological advances and the ensuing expectations will soon look outdated.

Certainty and transparency of transactions would be enhanced if the register served as means of determining priority. Making registration a priority point would also obviate the need to require registration within a stated period, to provide for a late registration procedure and to issue a conclusive certificate. This would reduce the cost of the registration process further as the court and registrar would not need to be involved.

Making registration a priority point goes in tandem with a notice-filing system.[144] Under both notice filing and transaction filing it is possible to secure priority in advance of a security agreement but it is cheaper to do so under notice filing; in a transaction-filing system an advance filing must be followed up with a separate filing of a charge document.[145] On the negative side, the charge instrument is not available on the register in a notice-filing system, so the question becomes to what extent provision of the charge instrument on the register adds value to the registration process. Indeed, it is this point that is the bone of contention between the proponents and critics of a notice-filing system.[146]

It is undoubtedly true that filing a charge instrument provides more information. Yet, quantity is not necessarily better than quality. The questions we should really be asking are (1) why place the information on the register (presumably,

[143] Lenders tend to protect themselves by withholding advances for 21 days; this can be problematic for borrowers and lenders frequently advance earlier, taking (and, no doubt, pricing in) the risk of competing interests.

[144] See Ch 2.

[145] This two-stage registration has been introduced in Ireland, see Ch 10.

[146] For arguments against notice filing see R Calnan, 'The Reform of the Law of Security' (2004) 3 *Journal of International Banking and Financial Law* 88; G McCormack, 'The Law Commission Consultative Report on Company Security Interests: An Irreverent Riposte' (2005) 68 *Modern Law Review* 286, 298–300; G McCormack, 'American Private Law Writ Large? The UNCITRAL Secured Transactions Guide' (2011) 60 *International and Comparative Law Quarterly* 597, 615.

treating the registrar merely as a repository of data which does not give notice would be a waste of resources) and (2) assuming the purpose of registration is to give notice, what sort of information should give notice. We saw earlier that in the United Kingdom at the moment there are difficulties in relation to notice.[147] Any advantage of filing a copy of the charge document should be weighed against the increased transaction costs associated with redacting personal information (more billable hours spent on a transaction by legal advisors who need to delete sensitive data before the instrument is filed). There is also the concern that the redaction rules will not permit sufficient removal of information to retain confidentiality: no redaction system can ever be perfect, and parties will develop methods of working around the issue, such as including all commercially sensitive material in other documents.

A notice-filing model is proving increasingly more popular across the world, having been adopted in the United States, Canada, New Zealand and more recently Australia, Jersey, Malawi and many other jurisdictions.[148] It is also preferred as a model at international level.[149] In England, it has been recommended by the Crowther Report 1971, Diamond Report in 1989, the Company Law Review Steering Group's final report in 2001 and by the Law Commission. During the latest reforms the notice-filing model was not considered but this was to due to the fact that the mandate to change the law was very narrow.[150] There are compelling economic reasons to consider its introduction in the United Kingdom.

(iv) Unnecessarily Complex Priority Rules

In English law, priority as between competing secured creditors and other financiers is determined under the general law, not the statute. The basic rule is that whoever created an interest first wins but there are numerous exceptions. Rules of priority are more complex than they need to be, partly because of the many different forms of security each of which has its own set of priority rules. A number of rules are unclear and unsatisfactory such as the rules of priority as between the holder of a fixed charge and an innocent buyer or lessee of the charged property, the rules on tacking of future advances or the rules on priority of security in intellectual property.[151] Other rules may be clearer but are unworkable

[147] See Section C(ii).

[148] See Chs 2, 4, 6, 7, 8, 9 and http://securedtransactionslawreformproject.org/reform-in-other-jurisdictions/.

[149] eg Book IX of the Draft Common Frame of Reference; EBRD Model Law on Secured Transactions (1994) (see Ch 22), UNCITRAL Legislative Guide on Secured Transactions (2007) and UNCITRAL Draft Model Law on Secured Transactions (see Ch 24).

[150] BIS Impact Assessment (n 15) paras 20–21.

[151] A Tosato, 'Security Interests over Intellectual Property' (2011) 6 *Journal of Intellectual Property Law & Practice* 93.

in practice without incurring substantial expense. This is so in respect of trade receivables, where priority is determined on the basis of the date of giving notice to the debtor.[152] As a result, the practical outcome is frequently uncertain. This often makes it necessary for the parties to enter into a priority agreement, which increases the transaction costs and which would not be needed under a clearer system of priorities.

A rule whereby priority is determined by the date of perfection rather than creation, is a simpler and clearer solution.[153] Where interests are registered, priority is simply determined by the date of registration. Critics have argued that to the extent that such a rule would amount to an abolition of the distinction between legal and equitable interests for the purposes of priority, the distinction should also be abolished in relation to outright transactions.[154] But this is only a question of different starting point.[155] A well-devised system would need to provide rules to resolve priority disputes in the context of outright transfers where they are relevant.

(v) Absence of Connection Between Registers

Separate registries exist in the United Kingdom in relation to certain types of asset, the most important of which relate to land,[156] ships,[157] aircraft[158] and certain intellectual property rights (patents,[159] trademarks[160] and registered designs).[161] The registries record dispositions with respect to each asset, including transfers of title and creation of encumbrances including security. It is not compulsory to register security over these types of asset at a specialist registry but doing so has some important effects on priority. At the moment, if a debtor is a company or LLP, it is necessary to record the security twice: in a specialist register and at Companies House. The advent of electronic registration and the fast-developing technology opens the door to introducing information-sharing arrangements between the registers, the effect of which would be to facilitate making one registration that

[152] *Dearle v Hall* (1828) 3 Russ 1, 38 ER 475.

[153] See Ch 2 F.

[154] Calnan (n 146); *Discussion Paper: Secured Transactions Reform* (City of London Law Society, 2012) Part 5.

[155] H Beale, 'Reform of the Law of Security—Another View' (2004) 4 *Journal of International Banking and Financial Law* 117.

[156] Land Registration Act 2002 s 27.

[157] Under the Merchant Shipping Act 1995 sch 1 and Merchant Shipping (Registration of Ships) Regulations 1993 (SI 1993/3138).

[158] UK Register of Aircraft Mortgages under the Mortgaging of Aircraft Order 1972 (SI 1972/1268).

[159] Patents Act 1977 s 33.

[160] Trade Marks Act 1994 s 25.

[161] Registered Designs Act 1949 s 19.

would appear on both registers. It would further save cost not only to those who file, but also to those who search.

E. Conclusion

There are different approaches to evaluating a reform. One is to consider whether it achieved the purposes it was meant to fulfil. The 2013 reform to a large extent fulfilled the objectives it set out to achieve: it clarified a list of registrable charges and streamlined the process of registration, notably by introducing the long-overdue electronic filing. Although in realising these objectives some opportunities were missed and new uncertainties have been introduced, on balance it would be difficult to condemn the 2013 reform as a failure.

Another approach is to look more broadly at the purposes which an area of law should fulfil and measure the extent to which the reformed law achieves them. The broad objectives of the secured transactions law have been set on a number of occasions by various bodies engaged in the debate on reform across the world, at national and international level. Many are uncontroversial. It would be hard to disagree that the modern secured transactions law should (1) be as simple as possible but not simpler; (2) be as transparent and certain as possible; (3) promote contractual freedom and flexibility of transactions; (4) promote efficiency of transactions and their enforcement; (5) balance the interests of those affected by the transactions; (6) not unduly discriminate between market participants; and (7) make full use of technology as far as possible.[162]

Measured against those broad objectives, the 2013 reform left much scope for improvement: the wider law relating to the range of registrable interests, priority, non-corporate grantors of security and the process of registration, as this chapter has shown. It would be naïve to think that waiting for the 2013 reform to settle would somehow make us better prepared to debate the need and shape for further changes given how narrow the scope of the 2013 reform was.

Not reforming the law further would seem a very risky and rather short-sighted option. Given that London is one of the world's leading financial centres and English law is one of the world's leading systems of both transactional law and the enforcement of contractual rights through the English courts, it is particularly important to consider the reasons for and shape of a more radical reform while keeping in mind the developments in Europe and worldwide. The number of jurisdictions significantly modernising their laws is growing across the world.

[162] *cf* the objectives of a modern secured transactions law set out in the UNCITRAL Legislative Guide on Secured Transactions 2007, available at www.uncitral.org, paras 46–59; objectives set out by R Calnan, 'What Makes a Good Law of Security?' in F Dahan (ed), *Research Handbook on Secured Lending in Commercial Transactions* (Cheltenham, Edward Elgar, 2015).

The process of modernisation of secured transactions laws worldwide is likely to continue to develop given the current work of UNCITRAL on the Draft Model Law on Secured Transactions.[163] These international developments set certain standards of expectations of the commercial and financial community of today and if they are not given due consideration the United Kingdom might be left behind. It is therefore time to be more ambitious in the aspirations. If the public is to derive much benefit from the substantial amounts of public money spent on law reform it is necessary to reform our approach to reform.[164] Comparative law work in this area has probably never been more important than now.

[163] M Raczynska, 'A New Model Law of Secured Transactions: Worldwide Modernisation in the Making?' [2014] *Journal of International Banking and Financial Law* 697.

[164] Paraphrasing JN Lyon, 'Law Reform Needs Reform'(1974) 12 *Osgoode Hall Law Journal* 421.

13

An Uneasy Case of Multiple Tracing Claims in English Law

MAGDA RACZYNSKA*

A. Introduction

The English law of security and title-based finance is complex and uncertain in a number of areas.[1] One such area involves the rules governing claims to traceable proceeds arising from dispositions of assets subject to security. The law of tracing in England is not codified but has been developed over the centuries by the courts. Jurisdictions that adopted Personal Property Security Acts (PPSAs) sought to deal with this area expressly in the statutes.[2] However, even under these Acts various problems exist in relation to claims to traceable proceeds, as shown elsewhere in this volume.[3] The purpose of this chapter is to discuss some of the uncertainties arising under English law. A recurring theme in the following account is that it is sometimes necessary to consider altering the interpretation of precedents to take into account the fact that the organisational concepts in law change as the legal system develops. This is particularly true in English law in which many concepts developed as part of a remedial system founded on forms of action but those concepts may not necessarily be suited to a system concerned with substantive rights. This chapter argues that the law governing cumulation of proprietary claims to traceable proceeds and original asset in the context of secured transactions is in a state of confusion, unnecessarily perpetuated in a relatively recent case[4] and stemming from the use of old organisational concepts without due consideration of alternative ones.

* I would like to express my gratitude to Professor Louise Gullifer and Professor Duncan Sheehan for comments on earlier drafts of this chapter. All errors remain my sole responsibility.

[1] See also Ch 12 C, D.

[2] For example, Saskatchewan PPSA 1993 s 28; New Zealand PPSA 1999 ss 45–47; Australian PPSA 2009 ss 31–34; Security Interests (Jersey) Law 2012, ss 24–26.

[3] Ch 5; Ch 6; Ch 8 E.

[4] *Buhr v Barclays Bank plc* [2001] EWCA Civ 1223.

Let us consider the following scenario. A debtor company borrows £5,000 from a lender, who takes a charge over the debtor company's van as security for the loan. The company is based in England and the charge is registered in Companies House. The debtor company sells the van to a third party without the secured creditor's consent. The market value of the van at the time of sale is £2,700 but the agreed price is £1,000. The price is deposited in an account in which there are no other funds, so the price is identifiable as traceable proceeds of the van.[5] Can the secured creditor assert security in both the original asset and the traceable proceeds of misappropriated collateral? No statute in English law provides an answer to this question while the judicial guidance is sparse. An existing view seems to be that the secured creditor cannot claim both the traceable proceeds and the original asset because the remedies are inconsistent. The secured creditor is thought to adopt the unauthorised sale when he claims traceable proceeds and to reject the sale when he claims the original asset. Some judicial support for this reasoning can be gathered from the decision in *Buhr v Barclays Bank plc*.[6] However, this point was considered only obiter. In the literature, while there are views that claims to traceable proceeds are inconsistent with parallel claims to the original asset, the basis for the inconsistency has not been explored. This is unfortunate because it results in an uncertainty of when a proprietary remedy is available. This chapter aims to fill this gap by identifying the relevant distinctions with a view to enhancing the rigour of theoretical analysis and certainty of practical application in this difficult area. In so doing, it makes a contribution to the law of tracing as might apply to secured transactions but it does not simplify it. The persisting complexity may well be seen as unwarranted in a modern system of secured transactions law.

One reason for the current complexity and uncertainty of the law governing proprietary claims contingent on tracing in English law is that a number of basic issues remain controversial while bearing on more detailed questions in this area. It is, therefore, useful to begin with an outline of the controversy surrounding the existing explanations of claims to traceable proceeds in English law in order to see if any analysis sheds light on whether claims to traceable proceeds and to the original asset can coexist or whether they are inconsistent. As we shall see, none of the explanations is determinative, which prompts an investigation into analogies that can be drawn with other areas where multiple claims are available. It is shown that the idea of the grantor of security becoming an agent of the creditor retrospectively, akin to the ratification of an unauthorised act by an agent, is an unsatisfactory explanation of claims to traceable proceeds in the context of security and that such an analogy should be taken cautiously. Consequently, this chapter shows first, that *Buhr* should not be treated as good authority for the basis of claims to traceable assets and secondly, following on from this, that it is at least open to debate

[5] See also the tracing scenarios set out in the examples used in Ch 5 D, which this chapter purposefully draws parallels with.

[6] *Buhr* (n 4).

that the secured creditor in English law may be able to assert cumulative claims to both proceeds and the original collateral so long as he does not recover excessively.

This chapter deals only with proprietary claims to traceable proceeds, excluding any personal claims. Also outside the scope of this chapter is the much-discussed basis of proprietary claims contingent on tracing, with the debate split primarily between the proponents of the unjust enrichment view[7] and the vindication of property view.[8] Consequently, discussion on the possible defences of third parties is also omitted.

B. Explanations of Claims to Traceable Proceeds

Claims contingent on tracing have attracted considerable attention, both judicial and academic, in the context of claims by owners with legal title and claims by trust beneficiaries claiming traceable proceeds of unauthorised dispositions by the trustee.[9] To some extent, the principles and debates that developed in those contexts

[7] P Birks, *Unjust Enrichment*, 2nd edn (Oxford, Oxford University Press, 2005) 35; P Birks, 'Receipt' in P Birks and A Pretto (eds), *Breach of Trust* (Oxford, Hart Publishing, 2002) 216–22; P Birks, 'On Taking Seriously the Difference between Tracing and Claiming' (1997) 11 *Trusts Law International* 2, 7–8; P Birks, 'On Establishing a Proprietary Base' (1995) 3 *Restitution Law Review* 83, 91–92; P Birks, 'Property, Unjust Enrichment and Tracing' (2001) 54 *Current Legal Problems* 231; A Burrows, 'Proprietary Restitution: Unmasking Unjust Enrichment' (2001) 117 *Law Quarterly Review* 412; A Burrows, *The Law of Restitution*, 3rd edn (Oxford, Oxford University Press, 2011) 185–89; R Chambers, 'Tracing and Unjust Enrichment' in J Neyers, M McInnes and S Pitel (eds), *Understanding Unjust Enrichment* (Oxford, Hart Publishing, 2004); L Smith, *The Law of Tracing* (Oxford, Oxford University Press, 1997) 300; but see L Smith, 'Restitution: The Heart of Corrective Justice' (2001) 79 *Texas Law Review* 2115, which represents a more nuanced approach leaning towards the vindication view; L Smith, 'Unravelling Proprietary Restitution' (2004) 40 *Canadian Business Law Journal* 317, 327–28.

[8] G Virgo, *The Principles of the Law of Restitution*, 2nd edn (Oxford, Oxford University Press, 2006) 11–17; G Virgo, 'Vindicating Vindication: *Foskett v McKeown* Reviewed' in A Hudson (ed), *New Perspectives on Property Law, Obligations and Restitution* (London, Routledge-Cavendish, 2004); G Virgo, 'Restitution through the Looking Glass' in J Getzler (ed), *Rationalizing Property, Equity and Trusts* (London, Butterworths, 2003) 82; J Penner, 'Value, Property and Unjust Enrichment: Trusts of Traceable Proceeds' in R Chambers, C Mitchell and J Penner (eds), *Philosophical Foundations of the Law of Unjust Enrichment* (Oxford, Oxford University Press, 2009) 313–14; R Grantham and C Rickett, 'Property and Unjust Enrichment: Categorical Truths or Unnecessary Complexity' (1997) 2 *New Zealand Law Review* 623; R Grantham and C Rickett, 'Property and Unjust Enrichment' (1997) *New Zealand Law Review* 668, 675–84; P Millett, 'Proprietary Restitution' in S Degeling and J Edelman (eds), *Equity in Commercial Law* (Sydney, Lawbook Co, 2005) 314; P Millett, 'Property or Unjust Enrichment' in A Burrows and L Rodger (eds), *Mapping the Law: Essays in Memory of Peter Birks* (Oxford, Oxford University Press, 2006) 265, 273 (arguing that the law of tracing is itself part of the law of property); L Ho, Book Review of 'Mapping the Law: Essays in Memory of Peter Birks' (2007) *Trusts Law International* 110; W Swadling, 'Property and Unjust Enrichment' in J Harris (ed), *Property Problems from Genes to Pension Funds* (London, Kluwer, 1997) 130; W Swadling, 'A Claim in Restitution?' (1996) 1 *Lloyd's Maritime and Commercial Law Quarterly* 63. See also L Smith, 'Unjust Enrichment, Property and the Structure of Trusts' (2000) 116 *Law Quarterly Review* 412, 413; L Smith, 'Transfers' in P Birks and A Pretto (eds), *Breach of Trust* (Oxford, Hart Publishing, 2002) 121, fn 42.

[9] The key work in this area is L Smith, *The Law of Tracing* (n 7).

apply to security interests. One such area concerns methods of asserting interests in traceable proceeds, which we consider in turn to see whether any light is shed on the inconsistency of claims to traceable proceeds and to the original asset. The following account also serves to illustrate the complexity of this area of law. Since there is no authority in English law determining which analysis best explains the mechanism of asserting proprietary claims to traceable proceeds in the context of security interests, any of these explanations could theoretically apply. However, if an analogy between security interests and trusts in the context of tracing holds, the explanation consistent with vindication would likely be preferred.[10]

(i) The Immediate Interest Explanation

The immediate interest explanation is the earliest way of analysing claims to traceable proceeds. The claimant is seen as having an immediate proprietary interest in traceable proceeds from the moment of substitution.[11] The reasoning behind this approach is that the substitute follows the nature of the original asset, so when the original asset is subject to a particular proprietary interest, no change of the state or form of the asset can divest it from that interest.[12] On this approach, the claimant may end up with an automatic proprietary interest in both traceable proceeds and the original asset followed in the hands of the third party so long as the third party has no defence to the chargee's claim. In the example considered at the start of this chapter, the secured creditor would be able to claim a lien in both the van in the hands of the buyer and the £1,000 deposited in the debtor's account.

This approach is no longer considered as a robust explanation of tracing claims because of the problems it gives rise to in the context of ownership claims:[13] with each substitution the claimant comes to own a new asset. Conceptually, on this view, multiple claims are not inconsistent with one another given that the claimant merely claims what he already has a right to. However, with multiple substitutions the claims are geometrically multiplied. For example, a stolen car can be sold to a buyer, who knows about the theft while the thief buys a Rolex watch with the sale proceeds from a seller, who also knows about the theft. It may be that the claimant can claim the car, the Rolex and the sale proceeds. Recovering all of them simultaneously would likely exceed the value of the car originally misappropriated, which could be seen as a problem of excessive recovery.[14] Another

[10] *Foskett v McKeown* [2001] 1 AC 102 (HL) 127 (Lord Millett).

[11] *Cave v Cave* (1880) 15 Ch D 639. This model is also known as the exchange product theory.

[12] See *Taylor v Plumer* (1815) 3 M&S 562, 574 (Lord Ellenborough C); *Scott v Surman* (1743) Willes 400, 404, 125 ER 1235, 1239 (Willes LJ), cited more recently in *Triffit Nurseries (a Firm) v Salads Etcetera Ltd (in administrative receivership)* [2001] BCC 457, 461 (Robert Walker LJ).

[13] For objections to the exchange theory see S Worthington, 'Justifying Claims to Secondary Profits' in EJH Schrage (ed), *Unjust Enrichment and the Law of Contract* (The Hague, Kluwer Law International, 2001) 451, 462.

[14] A similar problem of excessive recovery is raised later in relation to security interests, see Section E.

(more serious) objection to the immediate interest approach is that the claimant might become an owner of an asset without knowing about it or wanting it. Such ownership might attract liabilities to the owner, giving rise to the so-called 'involuntary ownership' problem.[15] For example, a van stolen from the owner could be substituted for a lion or some illegal substances. The owner of the stolen car might not want to own a dangerous animal or drugs. This objection is not of primary concern in the context of security interests to the extent that a secured creditor does not normally bear the liabilities in relation to the asset. However, the weakness of this explanation in the context of ownership might undermine its use in the context of security interests in English law at present.[16]

(ii) The Explanation Based on Power *In Rem*

The problems raised by the immediate interest approach can be resolved in two ways.[17] One is to say that there is no interest in traceable proceeds until the claimant makes an informed decision to assert the interest. This would be done by way of exercising the power *in rem*[18] to vest the interest. This power is similar to the power to revest title under a voidable contract.[19] Another is to say that the claimant has an immediate interest subject to a power to release title (election), discussed in (iii) below. On the 'power to revest' view, the claimant would not acquire an interest in the traceable proceeds until the power was exercised. It is not clear when the exercise of power would occur: when the court adjudicates,[20] when the defendant is informed of the duty towards the claimant[21] or some other time. Whenever the power is exercised, it would not of itself be inconsistent with a parallel claim to the original asset, whether the original asset were claimed using the same (power *in rem*) approach or was based on an immediate interest explanation.

[15] See *Dexter Motors Ltd v Mitcalfe* [1938] NZLR 804 (CA).

[16] It does not necessarily mean that English law would be precluded from adopting the immediate interest explanation in the context of security interests in the future. It seems that such an approach underlies PPSAs (n 2) which provide that security interests automatically extend to proceeds. See, for example, Ch 5 D.

[17] See Smith, *The Law of Tracing* (n 7) 323–26.

[18] P Birks, *An Introduction to the Law of Unjust Enrichment*, revised edn (Oxford, Clarendon Press, 1989) 393–94; P Birks, 'Mixing and Tracing' (1992) 45 *Current Legal Problems* 69; P Birks, 'Overview: Tracing, Claiming and Defences' in P Birks (ed), *Laundering and Tracing* (Oxford, Clarendon Press, 1995) 307–11; P Birks, 'Property and Unjust Enrichment: Categorical Truths' (1997) *New Zealand Law Review* 623, 629, 662–63.

[19] D Fox, 'Overreaching' in Birks and Pretto (eds) (n 7) 102; D Sheehan, *The Principles of Personal Property Law* (Oxford, Hart Publishing, 2011) 252. See also B Häcker, 'Proprietary Restitution after Impaired Consent Transfers: A Generalised Power Model' (2009) 68 *Cambridge Law Journal* 324 (arguing that proprietary restitution after impaired consent transfers should always take the form of a power to vest and not an immediate interest).

[20] Smith, *The Law of Tracing* (n 7) 323.

[21] B McFarlane, *The Structure of Property Law* (Oxford, Hart Publishing, 2008) 325. This would make the power a purely factual power.

One problem with this approach is the weak protection it bestows upon the claimant prior to the exercise of the power. If a third party were to acquire an interest in the traceable proceeds prior to the exercise of the power, the claimant's interest would be defeated by the time the power was exercised.[22] In addition, in the context of security interests, it is not clear how the interest based on a power *in rem* arises. The interest, which is based on a unilateral act of the creditor, would clearly not arise consensually. Since it may arise even against the will of the owner of the assets, it cannot be argued, for instance, that the exercise of the power to vest an interest gives rise to a presumption that a charge is created by the chargor.[23] In any case it would be very unlikely that a fresh registration in Companies House would be necessary to preserve the effectiveness of the security if the grantor were a company. The current wording of the Companies Act 2006 indicates that a charge is registrable where it is created by a company[24] and the word 'create' does not ordinarily include a situation where a company is liable to have its assets encumbered with a charge because the creditor exercised a power to create such an interest.[25] Given that the new interest arises upon the exercise of a power by the creditor, it is difficult to see that it would arise by operation of law, at least not in a remedial sense.[26] It could be described as arising by operation of law in a sense analogous to the constructive trust in English law (ie a non-remedial constructive trust).

(iii) The Explanation Based on Election

Election is in some ways a halfway house between the immediate interest explanation and the power *in rem* explanation. The claimant is seen as having an immediate and vested property right in traceable proceeds of the original property subject to the requirement of election.[27] Objections to this model, voiced by a proponent of the power *in rem* explanation, Professor Peter Birks, included an observation[28]

[22] *Re French's Estate* (1887) 21 LR Ir 83 (mere equity). The power would have a proprietary effect if it could be exercised by vesting the title in the proceeds retrospectively, as suggested by Bogert, GG Bogert and GT Bogert, *The Law of Trusts and Trustees*, 2nd revised edn (West Publishing Co, 1978) §472, cited in Smith, *The Law of Tracing* (n 7) 324–25 fn 128.

[23] See *Re Wallis & Simmonds (Builders) Ltd* [1974] 1 All ER 561, 574 (Templeman J).

[24] Companies Act 2006, s 859H.

[25] The terms 'power' and 'liability' are used in the Hohfeldian sense as jural correlatives. See WN Hohfeld, 'Some Fundamental Legal Conceptions as Applied in Legal Reasoning' (1913) 23 *Yale Law Journal* 16, 44–54.

[26] In any case remedial proprietary interests are not currently recognised in English law and given the opposition to them, they are not likely to be recognised in the future, see H Beale, M Bridge, L Gullifer and E Lomnicka, *The Law of Security and Title-based Financing*, 2nd edn (Oxford, Oxford University Press 2012) para 6.163 citing R Goode, 'Ownership and Obligation in Commercial Transactions' (1987) 103 *Law Quarterly Review* 433; G McCormack, 'The Remedial Constructive Trusts and Commercial Transactions' (1996) 17 *Company Lawyer* 3; P Birks, 'The End of the Remedial Constructive Trust' (1998) 12 *Trust Law International* 202.

[27] Smith, *The Law of Tracing* (n 7) 322–24, 358–61.

[28] Birks, 'Overview' (n 18) 309–10.

that the vested interest model, albeit subject to election, is inconsistent with the choice that the claimant owner typically has between an equitable ownership or a lien when asserting an interest in traceable proceeds.[29] One response to this is that the claimant from the moment of substitution has multiple vested interests in proceeds: equitable ownership and a lien and by exercising the power releases one of them. Alternatively, the choice between ownership and a lien could be seen as a new (secondary) election that arises after the claimant exercised the power to release the title to other assets. However, this reasoning makes this secondary election look like a choice between remedies, which would be problematic because equitable ownership cannot be asserted as a remedy in English law.[30] Thus, the former is preferable. All vested interests are subject to election.

Conceptually, election works like a power to release title (retroactively, from the moment of the unauthorised disposition)[31] but with simultaneous acquisition of full rights and liabilities at the point of election in relation to the asset, which is not released. This avoids the problem of involuntary ownership, so that, for example, if land constitutes traceable proceeds, the claimant does not need to pay stamp duty until, and if, he elects ownership.[32]

On the election model, the claimant chooses between claiming traceable proceeds or the original asset. What is not clear is whether the claimant exercising the power *can* release or *must* release her interest in the original asset in order to acquire the full interest in traceable proceeds. Smith seems cautiously to suggest that he must so release.[33] The authorities for the claimant's right to elect are inconclusive on this point,[34] so it should be treated as open to question.

[29] As to availability of the choice (also referred to as election) see *In re Hallett's Estate* (1880) 13 Ch D 696 (CA) 709 (Sir George Jessel MR): 'the beneficial owner has a right to elect either to take the property purchased, or to hold it as a security for the amount of the trust money laid out in the purchase'; *Foskett* (n 10) 130–31 (Lord Millet).

[30] See, eg, *Williams v National Bank of Nigeria* [2014] UKSC 10 [9] (Lord Sumption JSC); A Burrows, *The Law of Restitution*, 3rd edn (Oxford, Oxford University Press, 2011) 193–94; but *cf* W Swadling, 'The Fiction of Constructive Trust' (2011) 64 *Current Legal Problems* 399 (arguing that constructive trusts should be treated as informal express trusts). The traditional English rejection of remedial constructive trust is often contrasted with other jurisdictions which recognise remedial constructive trusts, eg in the US: *Restatement of Restitution: Quasi Contracts and Constructive Trusts* (1937) para 160 and *Restatement (Third) of Restitution and Unjust Enrichment* (2011) para 55 comment b, and Canada (*Rawluk v Rawluk* [1990] 1 SCR 70).

[31] It is a power in the Hohfeldian sense, as noted by Smith, *The Law of Tracing* (n 7) 324 fn 124.

[32] The claimant may of course prefer to elect for a lien, precisely for this reason, as seen in *Fern Advisers Ltd v Burford* [2014] EWHC 762 (QB) at [19] (Mackie J).

[33] Smith, *The Law of Tracing* (n 7) 324.

[34] *Foskett* (n 10) 127 (Lord Millett): 'Where one asset is exchanged for another, a claimant can elect whether to follow the original asset into the hands of the new owner or to trace its value into the new asset in the hands of the same owner. In practice his choice is often dictated by the circumstances'. Smith, *The Law of Tracing* (n 7) 324 also cites *Marsh v Keating* 131 ER 1094 (HL), (1834) 1 Bing NC 198, which seems to be authority for the point that a claim can be made to traceable proceeds even if the original asset was not lost and that the interest in the proceeds exists from the moment of substitution. It does not seem to be an authority for the point that once proceeds are claimed, the original asset cannot be.

Even if the claimant must release the interest in the original asset and even if this is due to an inconsistency between claims to the original asset and the proceeds, it is far from clear what the rationale for such a proposition would be.

C. How to Determine Whether Claims to an Asset and its Traceable Proceeds are Inconsistent

We saw above that none of the explanations of proprietary claims to traceable proceeds are determinative of whether claims to the misappropriated asset and to traceable proceeds of the misappropriation are consistent.

(i) The Judicial and Academic Views on Inconsistency of Claims in the Law of Security Interests

There is some judicial and academic support for the argument that the secured creditor cannot successfully claim both the proceeds and the original asset following an unauthorised disposition. A statement to that effect was made by Professor Sir Roy Goode in *Legal Problems of Credit and Security*.[35] This was founded on a view that claims to traceable proceeds of an unauthorised disposition are based on an implied adoption of the wrongful act and one cannot simultaneously adopt a wrongful act and make a claim based on the wrongful adoption.[36] While the latest edition generally embraced Professor Goode's formulation, the reference to adoption of a wrongful sale was removed.[37]

Professor Goode's views expressed in the first edition of *Legal Problems of Credit and Security* and in the 1995 edition of *Commercial Law*[38] were considered in the case of *Buhr v Barclays Bank*.[39] Although it concerned charges over unregistered land, the principles enunciated in this case are of wider application.[40] The case was factually straightforward. Mr and Mrs Buhr executed a charge by way of legal

[35] R Goode, *Legal Problems of Credit and Security*, 1st edn (London, Sweet & Maxwell, 1988) 16.

[36] *cf* the use of the language of adoption in the parallel context of trusts, *Ultraframe (UK) Ltd v Fielding* [2005] EWHC 1638 (Ch), [2006] FSR 17 at [1514]–[1515], [1518] (Lewison J); see also J Penner, 'Duty and Liability in Respect of Funds' in J Lowry and L Mistelis (eds), *Commercial Law: Perspectives and Practice* (London, Lexis Nexis Butterworths, 2006) 207, 217 paras 12.26–12.27.

[37] L Gullifer (ed), *Goode on Legal Problems of Credit and Security*, 5th edn (London, Sweet & Maxwell, 2013) para 1-66.

[38] R Goode, *Commercial Law*, 2nd edn (London, Butterworths, 1995) 667–88.

[39] *Buhr* (n 4).

[40] ibid at [37] (noting a parallel between the consequences of non-registration of land charges over unregistered land and charges granted over any asset by a company that are registrable in Companies House).

mortgage in favour of Barclays Bank over their farm, which was unregistered land.[41] This was a second charge, which Barclays sought to protect as a puisne mortgage by entry of a Class C1 land charge under the Land Charges Act 1972, but the entry was in the wrong name, which meant the land charge was not registered and was void against a purchaser.[42] The Buhrs later sold the farm to a third party, who discharged the first mortgagee, leaving a balance of £27,500 in the solicitors' account.[43] Mr Buhr subsequently went bankrupt. Barclays Bank sought to affirm that it had a proprietary interest, enforceable against the purchaser, in the traceable proceeds of sale and succeeded at the High Court and later at the Court of Appeal.

In relation to asserting claims to both proceeds and the original collateral, it is reasonably clear that Judge Weeks QC in the first instance agreed with Professor Sir Roy Goode that the secured creditor cannot have both.[44] Lady Arden in the Court of Appeal was less unequivocal, saying only that it was not true to say that the secured creditor had a right to elect between proceeds and the original asset in every case, giving an example of authorised dispositions in which the secured creditor has no right to claim proceeds.[45] Importantly, Her Ladyship did not say that, where the sale was unauthorised, the secured creditor had to elect and release title to the asset it did not choose. In any case, any such comment by Lady Arden would have been (and in the case of Judge Weeks QC was) obiter. Barclays Bank's claim to traceable proceeds was the only available claim on the facts in the absence of a duly registered land charge and the purchaser taking free of it.

This does not fully resolve the issue of inconsistency of claims to traceable proceeds and the original asset because it is not clear why adoption should be the basis for claims to traceable proceeds. However, this points us to a method which could be used to determine the issue. We need to look for analogies with scenarios where multiple claims to different assets are made. There is a strong sense that in *Buhr* the analogy drawn was with that of a principal adopting an unauthorised act of an agent. But other analogies could work too. Smith, for example, suggested an analogy with the way in which proprietary rights are protected by personal rights.[46] If we explore the possible analogies in more detail, we shall be able to shed some light on the inconsistency of claims to the asset and its proceeds.

[41] It was decided before the Land Registration Act 2002 introduced compulsory registration of land upon disposition. If analogous facts came before the court today, the grant of a legal charge would trigger the requirement to register.

[42] Land Charges Act 1972 s 4(5).

[43] One curious aspect of this case is that factually it appears unclear whether Barclays consented to the sale although it is clear that the courts found the sale unauthorised. See *Buhr* (n 4) at [45] and [49] (Arden LJ). But *cf* L McMurtry, 'The Extent of Security: Sale, Substitutions and Subsequent Mortgages' [2002] *Conveyancer and Property Lawyer* 407, 411.

[44] *Buhr* (n 4) at [11] and [13].

[45] ibid at [45]–[46].

[46] Smith, *The Law of Tracing* (n 7) 324.

(ii) Where to Search: the Alternative and Cumulative Remedies Elsewhere in Law

Drawing analogies can be problematic because there may be scenarios that more closely resemble one with which a parallel is to be drawn. One way to address this risk is to contrast a range of similar scenarios. So, on the one hand, we have a secured creditor seeking to claim an asset that was wrongfully sold to a third party and traceable proceeds of this unauthorised disposition (in the hands of the wrongdoer or, perhaps, passed to a third party). On the other, we have three possible scenarios with which to draw an analogy:

(1) A contractual party seeks to avoid a contract voidable for fraud or to affirm it, or a principal seeks to ratify an unauthorised act done on his behalf or to disaffirm it and treat the person who acted as accountable.
(2) An owner, whose stolen goods were sold on by the thief to a third party, seeks to recover from the thief sale proceeds as gain-based damages (in the common law form of money had and received or equity's form of account of profits) and compensatory damages for the tort of conversion[47] to compensate the loss suffered, measured with reference to the value of the misappropriated goods at the time of conversion.[48]
(3) As in (2) but the owner seeks to sue not only the thief, but also the buyer for damages for conversion.

Much of the law applying to the availability and recoverability of remedies that underlies these scenarios was clarified in the House of Lords' decision in *United Australia Ltd v Barclays Bank*.[49] Prior to this decision all three scenarios would have been viewed as examples of substantially inconsistent remedies. The inconsistency is clear in the first scenario. In relation to a contract voidable for fraud, the claimant cannot simultaneously elect to bring the parties' respective obligations to an end and to leave the contract effective.[50] Similarly, where a contract is concluded by an agent without any authority from the principal, the principal cannot choose to continue not to be bound by the contract and at the same time to ratify it and become bound. The inconsistency is less obvious in (2) and (3). Early cases employed the doctrine of waiver of tort to demonstrate the

[47] English law does not know a common law action of vindication of misappropriated assets as Civilian jurisdictions do. An owner is left with conversion, ie a claim that the defendant interfered with the claimant's right to immediate possession of the asset, the typical remedy being damages, Torts (Interference with Goods) Act 1977 s 3.
[48] *BBMM Finance (Hong Kong) v Eda Holdings* [1990] 1 WLR 409 (PC).
[49] *United Australia Ltd v Barclays Bank* [1941] AC 1 (HL).
[50] *Car and Universal Finance Co Ltd v Caldwell* [1965] 1 QB 525, 550 (Sellers LJ): 'The disaffirmation or election to avoid a contract changes the relationship of the parties and brings their respective obligations to an end, whereas an affirmation leaves the contract effective though subject to a claim for damages for its breach'.

substantial inconsistency.[51] According to the doctrine, when the claimant sued for sale proceeds he was seen to have adopted the wrongdoer's acts as those of an agent and could not sue for damages for conversion. The decision in *United Australia* made it clear that the owner may pursue claims for both compensatory damages and gain-based damages together as alternative remedies and need not elect until the judgment is made (which corresponds to scenario (2)).[52] The House of Lords rejected the doctrine of waiver because it imported a fiction that the claimant adopts an act of a wrongdoer where in fact he is not adopting but protesting;[53] in fact, the action for money had and received 'lies only because the acquisition of the defendant is wrongful and there is thus an obligation to make restitution'.[54] By recovering sale proceeds from the thief, the claimant has merely waived the right to recover another remedy—damages—from the thief.[55] At the very least *United Australia* makes the explanation of adoption of a wrongful act 'a redundant embellishment'[56] to the explanation of recoverability of alternative remedies.

Another issue clarified in *United Australia* is that by recovering sale proceeds from the wrongdoer *in full* the claimant elects not to recover compensatory damages for conversion of the same goods from the same wrongdoer. One question, which was not answered in *United Australia* and which merits consideration before we proceed to the next part of the chapter, is on what basis the claimant can obtain judgment for only one remedy if more claims can be pursued against one wrongdoer. In the Privy Council decision *Tang Man Sit v Capacious Investments Ltd*, Lord Nicholls suggested that judgments for money had and received (gain-based damages) and compensatory damages were 'alternative and inconsistent remedies'[57] but did not explain what he meant by 'inconsistent'. Although the authorities do not offer extensive explanations of inconsistency there is some useful analysis in the literature.[58]

One approach is that the remedies are inconsistent because they have different aims (one to compensate the claimant for losses, the other to deprive the

[51] See *Smith v Baker* (1873) LR 8 CP 350, 355 (Bovill CJ), followed by Lord Smith in *Rice v Reed* [1900] 1 QB 54 (CA).

[52] *United Australia* (n 49) 21 (Viscount Simon LC) and 30 (Lord Atkin), approving the dicta of Lord Russell CJ and Vaughan Williams LJ in *Rice v Reed* [1900] 1 QB 54 (CA) 63 (Lord Russell CJ) and 67 (Vaughan Williams LJ) and disapproving the dictum of Smith LJ in that case at 65–66 that to bring an action for money had and received waives the tort. See also *Halifax Building Society v Thomas* [1996] Ch 217.

[53] *United Australia* (n 49) 29 (Lord Atkin), 34 (Lord Romer).

[54] ibid 18 (Viscount Simon LC).

[55] See *Hunter v Prinsep* (1808) 10 East 378, 391, 103 ER 818, 824 (Lord Ellenborough CJ) cited with approval in *United Australia* (n 49) 32 (Lord Atkin) and 34 (Lord Romer).

[56] S Watterson, 'An Account of Profits or Damages? The History of Orthodoxy' (2004) 24 *Oxford Journal of Legal Studies* 471, 472.

[57] *Personal Representatives of Tang Man Sit v Capacious Investments Ltd* [1996] AC 514 (PC) 521, 522, 525 (Lord Nicholls).

[58] S Watterson, 'Alternative and Cumulative Remedies: What is the Difference?' (2003) 11 *Restitution Law Review* 7. The account in this section draws on this work.

defendant of the benefit), which the law should not pursue simultaneously.[59] This approach has rightly been criticised in the literature;[60] the mere fact that the aims are different does not mean, without more, that the aims are mutually exclusive. Another and preferable view is that the term 'inconsistent' does not add anything to the remedies being alternative and the reason they are alternative is to ensure the claimant does not make a double recovery,[61] ie both '*full* damages and *complete* restitution'.[62] For that reason the claimant has to elect when the judgment is entered. The question that arises is whether the claimant is debarred from recovering *some* compensatory damages if he recovered *some* restitution. The authorities are clear that the claimant is not precluded from suing third parties, for example third- and fourth-party buyers from the thief.[63] There are suggestions in *United Australia* that the claimant may sue third parties (in tort or for money had and received) and recover from them even when the claimant already recovered in full from the original wrongdoer.[64] As against one defendant, there are some arguments in favour of not precluding the claimant from recovering partially under both remedies from the same defendant. For one thing, the ability to recover under both remedies partially is not necessarily inconsistent with the principle of prevention of double recovery. Further, there are some authorities that at least admit the possibility of this rule. It is hinted in *Lythgoe v Vernon*[65] that the claimant need not be prevented from recovering under both remedies against the same wrongdoer. In that case the owner, whose hops were wrongfully sold, recovered part of the proceeds of sale. He subsequently sought to sue the wrongdoer in tort for damages for the rest. Although the claimant was precluded from suing in tort, this was on the basis that he accepted part of the proceeds in *full* satisfaction of the recovery of proceeds of sale.[66] Counsel for the defendant admitted that if the

[59] *Redrow Homes Ltd v Betts Bros Plc* [1997] FSR 828 (CtSn, IH) 831 (Lord Clyde) (suggesting that damages and an account of profits are inherently inconsistent remedies for copyright infringement because they are different); *Devenish Nutrition v Sanofi-Aventis* [2007] EWHC 2394 at [110]–[111] (Lewison J) upheld by CA [2008] EWCA Civ 1086 at [103] (Arden LJ).

[60] Watterson (n 58) 15; D Sheehan, 'Competition Law Meets Restitution for Wrongs. Case Comment' (2009) 125 *Law Quarterly Review* 222, 224–25 (critique of *Devenish* (n 59)).

[61] *Watson Laidlaw & Co Ltd v Potts, Cassells & Williamson* (1914) 31 RPC 104 (HL) 119–20 (Lord Shaw); *Mahesan v Malaysia Government Officers' Co-operative Housing Society* [1979] AC 1 (HL) 28 (Lord Diplock). See also P Birks, 'Inconsistency between Compensation and Restitution' (1996) 112 *Law Quarterly Review* 375, 378. This explanation is seen as insufficient, see Watterson (n 58) 17.

[62] See G Treitel, *Remedies for Breach of Contract* (Oxford, Oxford University Press, 1988) 98–100, cited in P Birks, 'Inconsistency between Compensation and Restitution' (1996) 112 *Law Quarterly Review* 375, 378.

[63] *Burn v Morris* (1834) 2 Cr & M 579, 149 ER 891 (A lost a £20 banknote, which B found and took to C to change. Subsequently, B gave A £7. A sought to recover damages in tort (trover) from C and succeeded); *Davies v Petrie* [1906] 2 KB 786 (CA) (claims by the trustee in bankruptcy against third parties for debts are not altered even if the assignee received part payment and accounted for it to the trustee in bankruptcy).

[64] *United Australia* (n 49) 31 (Lord Atkin) and 50–51, 54 (Lord Porter) (indicating that the problem was posed but not solved by Lord Haldane in *John v Dodwell* [1918] AC 563 (PC) 570).

[65] *Lythgoe v Vernon* (1860) 5 H & N 180, 157 ER 1148.

[66] See also *Brewer v Sparrow* (1827) 7 B & C 310, 313, 108 ER 739, 740 (Holroyd J); *United Australia* (n 49) 43 (Lord Porter).

proceeds had not been taken in full satisfaction of the obligation to pay the entire sum, the claimant would have been able to sue the same wrongdoer in tort.[67] Stronger support can be found in *United Australia*, where Lord Porter held:

> [Some cases including *Lythgoe v Vernon*] are instances of a plaintiff electing to receive something in satisfaction of his claim, and thereby precluding himself from denying that he has obtained his chosen remedy. On the other hand, where the proceeds are received by the plaintiff but not accepted in full discharge, he may still sue for the original wrong.[68]

While Lord Porter goes on to illustrate the principle with authorities that involved cumulation of restitution against the wrongdoer and damages against third parties,[69] which strengthens further the support for cumulation of remedies against multiple defendants, it might cast a shadow on the strength of authority of these obiter dicta regarding recoverability against the same wrongdoer. However, it seems clear that Lord Porter had in mind recovery of damages against the same wrongdoer as he refers to 'the original wrong', not that of a third party, and talks earlier in the same paragraph about recovering against the same wrongdoer.[70] While cases are not decisive, there is at the very least a suggestion that the claimant who recovered under one remedy in partial satisfaction is not precluded from recovering under the other remedy for the balance.

In addition, there are arguments in the literature that the doctrine of election should not be seen as logically inevitable where remedies are alternative. Watterson argues that the true mischief of cumulations of compensatory and gain-based damages is to prevent excessive recovery for the same wrongful conduct by achieving the minimum necessary to fulfil the aims of each remedy, so that a recovery of gain-based damages would reduce the claimant's losses and, conversely, a recovery of compensatory damages would reduce the wrongdoer's wrongful enrichment.[71] On that view, election is not a logical necessity[72] but one of the techniques of avoiding excessive remedial cumulations, the other being a judgment for both remedies with a non-discretionary[73] judicial adjustment to the amount of the award, which could be based, for example, on a rule that the award of a sum equal to the higher of the full compensatory damages or the full gain-based damages for the same wrongful conduct.

The argument that the mischief of the rule against cumulation of alternative remedies is to prevent excessive recovery is a welcome refinement of the established view that the rule's rationale is to prevent double recovery; while excessive recovery includes double recovery, it allows for inclusion of more nuanced

[67] *Lythgoe* (n 65) 181–82.
[68] *United Australia* (n 49) 43 (Lord Porter), see also further 48 and 49 (Lord Porter).
[69] *Burn v Morris* (n 63); *Davies v Petrie* (n 63).
[70] See further *United Australia* (n 49) 49 (Lord Porter).
[71] Watterson (n 58) 17–19.
[72] ibid 21–23.
[73] Reliance on judicial discretion in awarding remedies would have been open to objection, see P Birks, 'Three Kinds of Objection to Discretionary Remedialism' (2000) 29 *University of Western Australia Law Review* 1, noted by Watterson (n 58) 24.

scenarios. As to the techniques of preventing excessive cumulations, there seems no practical advantage to choosing judicial adjustment over a claimant's election[74] and there would probably have to be a compelling reason for abandoning the doctrine of election as a deep-rooted technique of preventing double (or excessive) recovery without a good reason. The difficulty that arises is to determine in which circumstances cumulation of remedies would be excessive.[75]

Returning to the three groups of scenarios outlined above, the election by a contractual party seeking to avoid a contract or by a principal seeking to ratify an agent's unauthorised act (scenario (1)) stands in a stark contrast with the election in scenarios (2) and (3). The causes of action in scenario (1) are mutually exclusive and so the rights and remedies are inherently inconsistent,[76] and thus when the claimant is entitled to one of two inconsistent rights and with full knowledge does an act unequivocally showing which he has chosen, he cannot afterwards pursue the other.[77] By contrast, in scenarios (2) and (3) the remedies are based on different causes of action that can be concurrent, so claims for alternative remedies can be pursued together and no question of election arises until either claim has been brought to judgment and, we can add based on the discussion above, unless the recovery would be excessive.[78] In what follows we examine the possible analogies between the scenarios of recovering under one or more available remedies discussed in this section and claims to traceable proceeds of unauthorised dispositions of collateral.

D. An Analogy to Adoption of Unauthorised Act of an Agent by a Principal

While there is some support for the analogy between an agent and a grantor of security in *Buhr*, there are also important objections to maintaining that parallel.

(i) Support in Authority for the Analogy

In *Buhr v Barclays Bank* Lady Arden, with whom Lord Woolf CJ and Lord Tuckey concurred, held:

> The Buhrs' disposition was unauthorised. They purported to sell with full title guarantee and thus free from Barclay's charge. Barclays (if indeed it has already done so by

74 See Watterson (n 58) 23.
75 This is discussed in Section E in the context of security.
76 See *United Australia* (n 49) 4 (as argued by the counsel—Denning KC, as he then was).
77 See ibid 30 (Lord Atkin).
78 See ibid.

commencing these proceedings) could adopt this transaction and thus retrospectively make the Buhrs its agent.[79]

Lady Arden did not explain why the secured creditor had a power to adopt the unauthorised transaction. The reference to retrospective agency suggests that the idea of adoption was used as a parallel with the doctrine of ratification of an act performed without authority by an agent (A) in the name of the principal (P).[80] If the parallel between the chargor and the agent holds, the position of the chargor claiming traceable proceeds would be similar to a position of the principal ratifying an unauthorised disposition: the secured creditor could either ratify and claim proceeds or do nothing and treat the transaction as unauthorised, in which case he would continue to have rights in the original asset. Suing simultaneously for remedies in the original asset and in its proceeds would be inconsistent.

(ii) Critique of the Analogy

(a) Objections of a General Nature

The use of ratification to explain proprietary claims to traceable proceeds in general law is not new. There are some early authorities, in which the right to recover proceeds was based on the rule that a wrongdoer, like an agent, had to account for money had and received when he sold property on his principal's behalf.[81] The claimant could, however, waive or ratify the wrongful disposal and, in so doing, claim the original asset from the wrongdoer and, where possible, the third party. This line of reasoning was based on the doctrine of waiver of tort, which we saw was rejected in *United Australia Ltd*. An action to recover proceeds of an unauthorised act is a method of obtaining a remedy, not an expression of a mental state of forgiveness of an unauthorised act.[82] In other words, there is *no intention* on the part of the claimant to *adopt* the unauthorised transaction, whether expressly or impliedly. Yet, it is important to explore in more detail whether an analogy can nevertheless be drawn between the agent and the chargor.

(b) Specific Objections to the Analogy

A parallel between an agent and the chargor works to a certain extent: both the agent and the chargor can act with or without authority given by the other contractual party. For example, just as an agent can contract on behalf of the creditor,

[79] *Buhr* (n 4) at [49].

[80] R Munday, *Agency. Law and Principles* (Oxford, Oxford University Press, 2010) para 6.01.

[81] *Lamine v Dorrell* (1705) 2 Ld Raym 1216, 1217, 92 ER 303, 303–04 (Holt CJ).

[82] See also D Fox, 'Common Law Claims to Substituted Assets' (1999) 7 *Restitution Law Review* 55, 56 (referring to the right to proceeds as originating in 'a fictitious extension of the doctrine of rectification and in the general rule that an agent had to account for the money he received when he sold property on his principal's behalf').

the chargor has the power to sell the asset subject to security in a way that may affect the legal position of the chargee. But the parallel does not go very far. First, ratification is only available where the agent acted on behalf of the principal, which is considered from the perspective of the third party with whom the purported agent deals, not from the perspective of the agent or the principal.[83] When the chargor sells the asset subject to a charge in an unauthorised way, his action is anything but on behalf of the chargee. Secondly, when the principal chooses not to ratify, he is not bound by the agent's act. When the secured creditor 'elects' not to 'ratify', he is still bound by the consequences of the chargor's act: the third party acquired the asset subject to the charge and may or may not have a defence of a bona fide purchaser for value without notice, which is a matter of an exception to the *nemo dat* principle. The chargor's disposition of the asset subject to security will, at the very least, amount to the change of the person of the chargor, but it may, in some cases, lead to the destruction of the charge over the asset where the third party buyer will be able to raise an exception to the *nemo dat* rule effectively. Thirdly, it is arguable that even if the above objections to ratification can be overcome, the explanation of claims to proceeds based on ratification is inconsistent with the existing rules governing dispositions under fixed and floating charges in English law. This requires explanation.

A fixed charge requires the chargor to be restricted in dealing with the collateral free of security without the chargee's consent.[84] Consequently, the holder of a fixed charge acquires an interest in the proceeds of authorised dispositions where he consented to the specific disposition on the basis that he would acquire an interest in the proceeds. A blanket consent to disposal of charged assets given in advance is unlikely to be consistent with a fixed charge because such consent may be interpreted as giving the chargor a right to dispose.[85] By the same token, if an agreement provided that a consent were to be given *after* dispositions of charged assets, the charge created would unlikely be fixed. Conversely, where the chargor disposes of the asset without the chargee's prior consent, there is no reason why the chargee should not be able to provide a retrospective consent. However, it is far from clear that such retrospective consent would (or even could) operate as ratification. The situation is straightforward if the chargor did not acquire any proceeds in the unauthorised disposition. By providing retrospective consent, the chargee adopts the withdrawal of the asset from security, making it authorised *ab initio*, just as adoption of an unauthorised act by the principal makes it authorised *ab initio*.[86]

[83] *Keighley Maxstead & Co v Durant* [1901] AC 240 (HL). Note that the issue of ratification of an act by an undisclosed principal stimulates some academic interest.

[84] See *Re Spectrum Plus Ltd (in liquidation)* [2005] UKHL 41, [2005] 2 AC 680. See also the discussion in Beale et al (n 26) paras 6.106–6.112; S Worthington and I Mitchkovska, 'Floating Charges: The Current State of Play' (2008) 9 *Journal of International Banking and Financial Law* 467.

[85] Beale et al (n 26) para 6.111.

[86] *Koenigsblatt v Sweet* [1923] 2 Ch 314, 325 (Lord Sterndale MR); *Wilson v Tumman and Fretson* 134 ER 879, (1843) 6 M&G 236, 242 (Tindal CJ); *Bird v Brown* (1850) 4 Exch 786, 154 ER 1433.

It is more difficult to see how ratification would work if the unauthorised disposition by the chargor yielded proceeds in the hands of the chargor. When providing retrospective consent, the chargee is free to choose whether to consent to the withdrawal of the asset with or without acquiring a right to proceeds. This follows from the fact that, depending on the terms of the agreement authorising the disposition, a fixed chargee is free to consent to a disposition of a charged asset on the basis that he has a security interest in the proceeds or, albeit unusually, on the basis that he does not. An obstacle to viewing retrospective consent as ratification is that it is not certain on what terms the chargee would have consented to the authorised disposition. Although it could be argued that the terms of the retrospective consent would run backwards to the terms of the authorised disposition (ie the terms on which the chargee retrospectively consented would be deemed the same as the terms on which he would have consented prior to the disposition), such reasoning would not be easily reconcilable with the rule in agency law that ratification is made on the terms corresponding to what would have been an authorised disposition.[87] In other words, ratification must carry the terms of the authorised disposition, not the other way round. If the terms on which the chargee would have consented to an authorised disposition are not known, it is impossible to tell what ratification in full would have looked like.

Another difficulty with using ratification is the possible inconsistency with the rules on characterisation of fixed and floating charges. While characterisation of a charge as fixed or floating is typically a matter of interpretation of the charge agreement and any contemporaneous agreements,[88] post-contractual agreement or conduct may be relevant to the characterisation of the charge in some circumstances.[89] A one-off retrospective consent to an unauthorised disposition is not likely to cast a shadow of doubt on whether the charge is fixed but repeated unauthorised disposals and subsequent retrospective consents might. They are likely to indicate that the parties varied their agreement to one where the chargor has freedom to use the charged assets. To show variation it would be necessary to demonstrate an offer, acceptance and certainty of terms.[90] If each retrospective consent operated as ratification, each disposition would be considered as having been authorised *ab initio*. This would preclude or at least weaken any argument that parties varied an agreement because the chargor would not be seen as

[87] This follows from the rule that when the principal chooses to ratify an unauthorised transaction he must do so in full and cannot choose to ratify only the parts which are favourable to him: see *Smith v Hodson* (1791) 4 Term Rep 211, 100 ER 979; *Peru v Peruvian Guano Co* (1887) 36 Ch D 489, 499 (Chitty J); *Re Mawcon* [1969] 1 WLR 78, 83 (Pennycuick J).

[88] *Spectrum* (n 84) at [158] (Lord Walker).

[89] See S Atherton and R Mokal, 'Charges over Chattels: Issues in the Fixed/floating Jurisprudence' (2005) 26 *Company Lawyer* 10; A Berg, 'The Cuckoo in the Nest of Corporate Insolvency: Some Aspects of the Spectrum Case' [2006] *Journal of Business Law* 22, 33–44; L Gullifer and J Payne, 'The Characterization of Fixed and Floating Charges' in J Getzler and J Payne (eds), *Company Charges: Spectrum and Beyond* (Oxford, Oxford University Press, 2006) 69–73; Beale et al (n 26) paras 6.115–6.119.

[90] See *Glencore Grain Ltd v Flacker Shipping Ltd (The 'Happy Day')* [2002] EWCA Civ 1068 at [61] (Potter LJ).

having had freedom to use charged assets beyond the most recent unauthorised disposition. So, each unauthorised disposition would look as if it were one-off, not one in a series. If this is correct, using ratification as an explanation of retrospective consent undermines the rules on characterisation of fixed and floating charges and could, arguably, be used to circumvent the existing rules on the interpretation of parties' agreement as creating a floating charge.

If the role of ratification in explaining claims to proceeds is doubtful in the context of the fixed charge, it is even more so in the context of a floating charge. Under an uncrystallised floating charge the chargor has a power to dispose of assets free from security to the extent permitted in the charge agreement, usually in the ordinary course of business, so the dispositions of assets subject to a floating charge are likely to be for the account of the debtor.[91] Whether the floating charge extends to the proceeds of such authorised dispositions depends on the terms of the agreement, usually where proceeds of authorised dispositions are within the description of the subject matter of the floating charge. Where the charge agreement is silent about proceeds, the floating chargee is not automatically entitled to proceeds purely because they are proceeds of authorised dispositions[92] although this view is far from settled or uncontroversial.[93] Where the disposition of assets subject to a floating charge is unauthorised, there is authority to suggest that the disposition is for the account of the disponee from the chargor, not the chargee. In *Hubbuck v Helms*[94] assets subject to a floating charge were sold outside the ordinary course of business. Unusually, the unauthorised sale did not crystallise the charge. It was held that the chargee could obtain an order for the appointment of a receiver restraining the purchaser from selling assets outside the ordinary course of business of the chargor company. It follows that the purchaser was free to deal with the assets in the ordinary course of business. There was certainly no question of retrospective consent to unauthorised dispositions or ratification. Given that dispositions of assets subject to a floating charge are almost always for the account of the chargor, there seems to be no scope for an argument that the floating chargee could be in a position to adopt an unauthorised transaction as authorised. Even if we assume, for the sake of argument, that the floating chargee could do so, ratification of an unauthorised disposition as authorised would yield proceeds for the account of the chargor, not the chargee, which means that ratification would have no role to play in explaining a floating chargee's rights to proceeds of unauthorised dispositions where the charge is floating (if such rights can be asserted at all).

[91] Gullifer (ed) (n 37) para 1-68.

[92] Beale et al (n 26) para 15.05; see also Gullifer (ed) (n 37) para 1-68.

[93] For a contrary view see R Nolan, 'Property in a Fund' (2004) 120 *Law Quarterly Review* 108 (arguing that substitutes of authorised dispositions automatically fall within an uncrystallised floating charge and that this is an implied, though silent, default rule, which emerged through the use of precedents).

[94] *Hubbuck v Helms* (1887) 56 LJ Ch 536.

The weight of arguments suggests that the explanation of an interest in traceable proceeds based on adoption of an unauthorised disposition is unsatisfactory. It remains unclear to what extent, if at all parallels can be drawn between secured transaction and agency. An examination of such parallels is beyond the scope of this chapter. However, if the objections to ratification undermine any analogy between an agent and the charged, then it is also unsatisfactory to say that the chargee's claims to proceeds and to the original asset are inconsistent (as they are in scenario (1) in Section C(ii) above). The obiter dictum in *Buhr* in this respect must be doubted.

E. Cumulative Claims to Traceable Proceeds and the Original Asset

(i) Drawing the Correct Analogy: is the Chargor More Like a Thief than an Agent?

Given the difficulties with making the chargor retrospectively an agent for the creditor, it may be more appropriate to compare the position of the secured creditor to a claimant suing a thief for money had and received and a third party for damages in conversion of the original asset. If true this means that in English law the secured creditor may not be precluded from making claims to assert an interest in the original asset and in the traceable proceeds. The remedies sought by the secured creditor are alternative but the claims may not be inconsistent. A full recovery under one would prevent the secured creditor from recovering under the other. We saw above that the mischief of the rule against cumulation of alternative remedies is prevention of double or excessive recovery.[95] Where the claimant recovers under one remedy in part, there is nothing to stop them from recovering under the other for the balance. Although there were some doubts in relation to recovering under alternative remedies against one wrongdoer, the rule seems reasonably well established and uncontroversial where the claimant sues different defendants (for example, the thief and a buyer of stolen goods or, in the secured transactions scenario, typically the grantor of security who holds traceable proceeds and the third party buyer).[96] If the argument advanced here is correct, the analysis of recovery in relation to the key types of approaches to claims to traceable proceeds discussed in section B is as follows. If claims are based on a power *in rem* the claimant is not prevented (subject to any defences) from exercising a power in relation to the original asset or in relation to the proceeds or in

[95] See Section C(ii).
[96] See ibid.

relation to both unless the claimant would recover excessively. If claims are based on election, the claimant can, *but need not*, elect to release his interest in relation to the original asset while preserving his interest fully in traceable proceeds.[97]

(ii) The Problem of Determining Excessive Recovery

The difficulty in the context of secured transactions is establishing what constitutes an excessive recovery. An associated consideration is whether the assessment of what amounts to excessive recovery should vary depending on the context. In American literature, for example, it was pointed out that cumulation of claims in original collateral in the hands of a third party and its proceeds does not give rise to a problem of a 'windfall' or 'double recovery' because the creditor cannot recover beyond the amount of the secured debt.[98]

However, the ability to resort to multiple assets may be seen as a windfall where the value of the assets which the secured creditor is able to claim exceeds the value of the original collateral prior to disposition. This 'oversecuritisation' might create an economically inefficient result. The argument about economic inefficiency could go something like this: the greater value of the collateral does not necessarily translate to a benefit to the secured creditor because he can only resort to the assets up to the amount of the secured debt. Probability of repayment does not increase infinitely with the increasing number of assets. There comes a point where any added extra asset that inflates the value of the collateral will not increase the probability of repayment.[99] The benefit to the secured creditor is marginal at most. At the same time the debtor (and, indeed, a third party against whom the creditor claims interest in the original asset or traceable proceeds) ceases to be able to offer these assets as first-ranking security for new loans, which—the argument could go—may mean he will be unable to raise finance or to raise it as cheaply as would otherwise be possible. The debtor (or a third party), therefore, bears an opportunity cost and is worse off. This situation is economically inefficient (more specifically, Pareto inefficient) because the debtor (or a third party) can be made better off by freeing up some of the assets from the security without making the secured creditor worse off. The issue just described has been identified as a problem and addressed in Canada by a provision that the amount secured by the security interest in the disposed-of original collateral and the proceeds is limited to the market value of the collateral at the date of the dealing.[100]

[97] See Section B(iii).

[98] S Harris and CW Mooney, Jr, *Security Interests in Personal Property. Cases, Problems and Materials*, 5th edn (New York, Foundation Press, 2011) 286. See also Ch 5 D(iii).

[99] For example, if Andy lends £5 to Jenny, who gives security over her watch worth £100, the likelihood of repayment will not increase substantially (if at all) just because Jenny adds security over her computer worth £500.

[100] See, for example, the Saskatchewan Personal Property Security Act 1993 s 28(1) and the Ontario case *Bank of Nova Scotia v IPS Invoice Payment System Corporations* (2010) 318 DLR (4th) 751 (Ontario

There is an important caveat to the economic efficiency argument described above: it assumes that the amount of the secured debt does not change or, if anything, diminishes as the debtor repays the debt. However, many secured transactions are more complex in practice than that. For example, parties may have agreed that the secured creditor could make further advances, enlarging the amount of the debt secured against the assets. This alters the economic efficiency argument because the ability to resort to the original collateral and to proceeds would provide the secured creditor with a benefit.[101] The benefit may be so considerable that the ability to resort to the original asset and to the proceeds would be more economically efficient than if the creditor were limited in some way. This illustrates the importance of understanding commercial reality underlying any economic efficiency analysis whenever one considers what the legal rules should be. Some commentators also note that the additional protection of (or the 'windfall' to) the secured party is justified because when the debtor sells without authorisation, the original collateral as well as the proceeds are likely to be in jeopardy.[102] These arguments strengthen Professor Duggan's criticism of a statutory limitation on the secured party's cumulative enforcement rights except where the secured party takes enforcement action to recover proceeds.[103]

In the context of enforcement actions of proprietary claims to traceable assets in English law discussed in this chapter, it has been argued that the claimant ought not to be able to recover excessively if resorting to both proceeds and original asset. The authorities have tended to use the reference to 'prevention of double recovery' or 'achievement of full satisfaction' as a way of determining how much, and what, should be recovered. While their instructive value is modest, they seem to focus on recovery from the perspective of the claimant. If this were to apply in the context of secured transactions, full recovery short of excessive recovery would mean recovery of an interest in assets (original, traceable proceeds of both) up to the amount of the outstanding secured debt.

F. Conclusion

To say that the English law of tracing is complex is far from an overstatement. A number of issues remain controversial or uncertain while others are unearthed only through the detailed questioning of the existing orthodoxies and assumptions. This chapter falls into this last-mentioned category. It questioned

Superior Court of Justice) (in which the limitation was held to be implied in the absence of codification of the rule akin to the Saskatchewan PPSA) discussed in Ch 5 D.

[101] See further Ch 5 D(ii).

[102] L LoPucki and W Warren, *Secured Credit. A Systems Approach*, 7th edn (New York, Wolters Kluwer, 2012) 170.

[103] Ch 5 D(ii).

the judicial and academic view that the secured creditor's interest in traceable proceeds of an unauthorised disposition is based on adoption. This was accomplished by looking at how the organisational concepts in law have changed and by considering the possible new distinctions and analogies. In relation to security, the analogy with ratification of an unauthorised transaction in agency law has been questioned based on the current understanding of fixed and floating charges. The feasibility of drawing analogies between secured creditor and a person claiming against a thief was considered. If true, it would seem possible to hold cumulative remedies. The transition from the fiction of waiver of tort to the consideration of recovery based on prevention of excessive recovery signifies a transition from a legal system governed by forms of action to a system in which courts are able, but are not free in their discretion, to take into account the aims and bases of the substantive rights. If the same applied in relation to security interests, the rules under English law would have effect that is much closer to that of the rules found in the PPSAs than previously thought. However, any enthusiasm should be weighed against at least two factors. One is the significant number of problems that persist in the law of tracing, the issue of the correct basis being only one example. Another is the possible conceptualisation of secured transactions as giving rise to issues analogous to those arising in agency law, different to the analysis based on retrospective agency considered in *Buhr* but detailed debate of those issues must wait for another day.

The question which ought to be asked, and which has not been considered in this chapter, is whether the rules governing claims contingent on tracing in the context of secured transactions ought to be codified, as took place under the PPSAs. This requires careful consideration. The discussions in this chapter, focused on the existing uncertainties in the law of tracing shows that the law is much more complex than previously thought and the analysis presented here may help provide a direction for the future discussion of reform in the area. Opponents of codification of tracing rules in the context of the law of security and title-based finance sometimes argue that if any such codification were to take place, it should cover the entirety of the law of tracing and not be limited to secured transactions. One theme that began to emerge in this chapter was that the policy considerations relevant to claims contingent on tracing in the context of security are often different from those which would apply to ownership. If this is so, an argument against codification of tracing rules based on the extent of that codification falls away.

14

Should Clauses Prohibiting Assignment be Overridden by Statute?

LOUISE GULLIFER*

A. Introduction

Many contracts for the supply of goods or services include a clause prohibiting assignment by the supplier of its rights under the contract. The existence of such clauses, both in particular contracts and more generally, can have a chilling effect on the use of receivables as collateral to obtain financing. Thus, in many jurisdictions, there is a legislative override for such clauses, so that they are not enforceable against third parties. There is an ongoing debate as to whether English law should follow suit and, if so, what form the override should take, which has now led to a power to make reforms being included in sections 1 and 2 of the Small Business, Enterprise and Employment Act 2015.[1] This chapter examines the arguments for and against an override in English law, informed by two small-scale surveys undertaken by the author and others over the last four years.[2]

* An earlier version of this chapter has appeared in the *Penn State Journal of Law and International Affairs*, vol 4.

[1] Draft Regulations have now been published (n 4). However, the need for statutory reform is not universally accepted. The Financial Law Committee of the City of London Law Society argue that any practical problems in financing transactions relating to anti-assignment clauses can be dealt with by consensual means, see R Calnan, 'Ban the Ban: Prohibiting Restrictions on the Assignment of Receivables' [2015] *Journal of International Banking and Financial Law* 136.

[2] One was carried out by Hugh Beale and Louise Gullifer in 2011 ('the 2011 study'), with the assistance of Anna Kloeden. It was funded by the Asset Based Finance Association (ABFA), who stressed from the outset that it wanted a completely independent view to be taken. The second was carried out in 2014 as part of the work of the Secured Transactions Law Reform Project ('the 2014 study') by Sarah Paterson. I am grateful to both Hugh Beale and Sarah Paterson for permitting me to use this material in this chapter, and for many useful discussions. For further discussion of the results of the surveys, see H Beale, L Gullifer and S Paterson, 'Ban on Assignment Clauses: Views from the Coalface' (2015) 30 *Butterworths Journal of International Banking and Financial Law* 463; H Beale, L Gullifer and S Paterson, 'A Case for Interfering with Freedom of Contract? An Empirically Informed Study of Bans on Assignment' [2016] *Journal of Business Law* 203.

The form of an override is not discussed in detail, for reasons of space. One model is that found in Personal Property Securities Acts (PPSAs) such as the Saskatchewan Personal Property Securities Act,[3] which provides that an anti-assignment clause is binding on the assignor, but only to the extent of making it liable for damages for breach of contract, and is unenforceable against third parties. Another model is that found in the Uniform Commercial Code (UCC) Article 9, which provides that an anti-assignment clause is ineffective to the extent that it prohibits or restricts assignment, or the creation of a security interest, and also to the extent that it provides that an assignment is a breach of contract. The recent draft Regulations circulated by the UK Department for Business, Innovation and Skills[4] follow the UCC model.

In this chapter, the arguments for and against an override are examined in section B. Sections C to F discuss the reasons why an override has not been a policy imperative in England and Wales until recently. Section G considers whether there should be a statutory override and section H concludes that, on balance, such an override would be beneficial.

B. The Arguments

If the availability of finance and credit in the economy is to be maximised, it is important that as many sources of wealth as possible can be used as collateral. To do this, the source of wealth (the asset) must be able to be alienated to the secured creditor. In the past, the obvious assets which could be alienated were tangible assets: goods and land. However, sources of wealth also included intangible assets, most importantly, rights to be paid by another. Thus, many centuries ago, it became possible to use obligations owed to a borrower as collateral for a loan, first by pledging a document which represented that obligation (a documentary intangible) and then by enabling the benefit of obligations to be assigned, either absolutely or by way of security. A major difference between the use of tangible property (goods and land) as collateral and the use of such obligations, known in English law as choses or things in action,[5] is that in the latter case there is another person to consider, namely the obligor. There is no real problem when the obligor undertakes an obligation which is designed to be transferred, for example a negotiable instrument. But where the obligation can be transferred without the agreement, or even the knowledge, of the obligor, a policy imperative arises in

[3] Section 41.

[4] Available at www.gov.uk/government/uploads/system/uploads/attachment_data/file/383538/draft-statutory-instrument-business-contract-terms-restrictions-on-assignment-of-receivables-regulations-2015.pdf.

[5] Also known as intangibles, but the category of intangibles is potentially wider than just choses in action, including, for example, intellectual property, carbon trading units etc.

competition to that of maximising available collateral by permitting alienability: that of protection, where necessary, of the obligor. This latter policy is demonstrated in English law, for example, by the rule that only an assignee who has taken a statutory assignment can sue the debtor[6] (if an equitable assignment is taken, the assignor must be joined in any action). The main criteria for a statutory assignment, namely that the assignment is in writing, that it does not relate to part of a debt or a future debt and that notice of the assignment has been given to the debtor, all serve some function in protecting the debtor. The policy is also shown by the rule that the benefit of a contract for personal services cannot be assigned,[7] and, more widely, by permitting the obligor to protect himself by restricting the ability of the obligee to assign the benefit of the obligation to another. This permission is also justified by another, even wider policy: that of freedom of contract.

Thus, whether there should be a statutory override of anti-assignment clauses can be seen as a matter of balancing competing policy imperatives: alienability of assets, which maximises available collateral, and freedom of contract, which allows obligors to protect themselves against adverse effects of assignment of the right to which their obligation correlates. In assessing that balance, many jurisdictions and transnational instruments have come down in favour of alienability.[8] Gilmore described the view in favour of the unrestricted and unrestrictable alienability of contract rights as 'so fundamental an order [that] belief is instinctive and irrational, not logical and reasoned'.[9] This argument has been used to justify a statutory provision making an anti-assignment clause unenforceable against third parties.

It is suggested here that the policy position is not so simple. At least from the English law perspective, there is a view that the policy imperatives can be satisfied without any statutory interference.[10] It is also thought that legislative change has to be justified by economic arguments based on the effects of uncertainty of outcome and on evidence that the availability and the cost of borrowing is actually affected by the existence, or potential existence, of anti-assignment clauses in contracts giving rise to receivables. These views are held for various interconnected reasons:[11] first, that the current law, to a large extent, accommodates the

[6] Law of Property Act 1925 s 136.

[7] *Tolhurst v Associated Portland Cement Manufacturers* (1900) Ltd [1903] AC 414.

[8] See, in relation to the Australian Personal Property Securities Act 2009, A Duggan and D Brown, *Australian Personal Property Securities Law*, 2nd edn (Sydney, LexisNexis, 2016) 42; UNCITRAL Legislative Guide on Secured Transactions, II.107; See also, in relation to the UNCITRAL Convention on Assignment of Receivables in International Trade, UNCITRAL A/CN.9/397 (report of Secretary-General) para 23, A/CN.9/489 (analytical commentary on the draft Convention) para 100).

[9] G Gilmore, *Security Interests in Personal Property* (Boston, Little, Brown & Co, 1965) 7.6 p 212.

[10] See Calnan (n 1) 136. See, however M Bridge, 'The nature of assignment and non-assignment clauses' (2016) 132 Law Quarterly Review 47, who argues that the current law is uncertain and accepts that a statutory override will restore marketability.

[11] Another reason, which is not examined here in detail, is a fundamental belief in freedom of contract. The question whether such freedom should be statutorily interfered with is examined throughout this chapter.

protection of the obligor and the validity of a proprietary interest of the assignee; second, that receivables financiers in England and Wales have managed reasonably well up to now by adopting 'workarounds' enabling them to function within the current system; third, that the main concern about anti-assignment clauses relates to borrowers who are small businesses, and is part of a wider problem of inequality of bargaining power; and fourth, that anti-assignment clauses play an important and justifiable role in loan agreements, in derivative contracts and in other financial transactions, and there is real concern over defining the scope of statutory controls so that these benefits are not lost.

Each of these reasons will now be considered.

C. The Accommodation of the Current Law

In discussing the law in this area, terminology can be confusing. In this analysis, terms are adopted which relate to receivables arising from supply contracts, since this is the context in which anti-assignment clauses are said to cause most problems.[12] The parties to the contract giving rise to the receivable are called the 'supplier' (the obligee) and the 'customer' (the obligor). The supplier is the client of the 'financier' to whom it assigns, or attempts to assign, the receivable.

A financier is concerned about three things in relation to the receivables it takes as collateral. The first is that it has a proprietary interest in the receivables and their proceeds which will survive the insolvency of the supplier. The second is that it has priority over any subsequent assignee, or other person claiming an interest in the receivables. The third is that, if the customer does not pay, the financier can ensure that the debt is enforced, and that it has a proprietary claim to the proceeds of that enforcement. The following paragraphs examine the extent to which these are achievable under English law.

(i) Statutory Assignment

Under English law there are two types of assignments. A statutory assignment under section 136 of the Law of Property Act 1925 takes place when certain conditions are satisfied.[13] The most important, for current purposes, is that there must be notification to the obligor (the customer). Once this has occurred, the customer will, and indeed must, pay the financier rather than the supplier.[14] If the customer fails to pay, the financier is able to sue the customer direct. In effect, the supplier

[12] Another context, that of receivables under loan agreements, is considered in Section F.

[13] See Section B.

[14] If the customer pays the supplier, it will have to pay the financier as well and try to recover the payment made to the supplier.

drops out of the picture. A statutory assignment will also give the financier a proprietary interest in the receivable in the event of the insolvency of the supplier, or of a competing interest.[15] There is clear authority that a receivable which contains an anti-assignment clause cannot be the subject of a statutory assignment,[16] so that the customer can continue to pay the supplier, and cannot be sued (at law) by the financier.

(ii) Equitable Assignment: No Anti-assignment Clause

The other type of assignment is an equitable assignment. An assignment will be equitable when one of the conditions for a statutory assignment is not fulfilled; for example, a valid equitable assignment can take place without notification of the customer. A financier who takes an equitable assignment has a proprietary interest in the receivable which survives the insolvency of the supplier, and will also have priority over a competing interest, subject to the rules on priority. Until the customer is notified, if it pays it will, of course, pay the supplier, and will obtain a good discharge by so doing. The supplier, though, will hold those proceeds on trust for the financier.[17] Moreover, valid set-offs can continue to arise between the supplier and the customer until the customer receives notification of the assignment;[18] after this, only set-offs arising from the contract itself or closely connected claims can arise.[19] If the customer does not pay, the financier cannot (at least in theory) sue the customer for non-payment without joining the supplier to the action, although this rule is less restrictive than it sounds. It is easy to join a party to an action (no consent is needed if they are joined as a defendant) and the court will not require joinder if there is no good reason.[20] Also, if the financier wishes to enforce, it will give notice of the assignment to the customer, which will not only require the customer to pay it rather than the supplier,[21] but will also, in

[15] The priority rules, which depend on those set out in the nineteenth-century case of *Dearle v Hall* (1828) 38 ER 475, are somewhat complex.

[16] *Linden Gardens Trust Ltd v Lenesta Sludge Disposals Ltd* [1994] 1 AC 85, 106–09. Of course, the true effect of a clause will always depend on its exact wording, and the case of *Linden Gardens*, though laying down certain principles, was considering a particular form of words.

[17] This trust is often expressly declared, but would arise in any event: *GE Crane Sales Pty Ltd v Commissioner of Taxation* (1971) 126 CLR 177, 213–14; *Barclays Bank Ltd v Willowbrock International Ltd* [1987] 1 FTLR 386.

[18] *Roxburghe v Cox* (1881) 17 Ch D 520.

[19] *Government of Newfoundland v Newfoundland Rly Co* (1888) LR 13 App Cas 199; *Business Computers Ltd v Anglo-African Leasing Ltd* [1977] 1 WLR 578, 585.

[20] *William Brandt's Sons & Co v Dunlop Rubber Co Ltd* [1905] 2 AC 454; *Sim Swee Joo Shipping Sdn Bhd v Shirlstar Container Transport Ltd* (unreported) 17 February 1994; *Raiffeisen Zentralbank Österreich AG v Five Star General Trading LLC* [2001] EWCA Civ 68 at [60]. Good reasons would include the possibility that the supplier might contest the assignment, or that the assignment is only of part of the debt, so that, unless the supplier is before the court, the customer might face more than one action.

[21] *Jones v Farrell* (1857) 1 De G & J 208; *Brice v Bannister* (1878) 3 QBD 569; *William Brandt's Sons & Co v Dunlop Rubber Co Ltd* [1905] 2 AC 454.

most cases, convert the equitable assignment into a statutory assignment,[22] thus enabling the financier to sue the customer direct. Of course, where the financing is on a non-notification basis, such as invoice discounting,[23] the financier will normally expect the supplier to enforce against the non-paying customer, and, if the financing is with recourse, will have contractual rights against the supplier so that the risk of non-payment is on the supplier.[24] It is only where the supplier either refuses to sue or is insolvent that the financier will be concerned to have the right to sue the customer itself. Even then, the financier might not need to enforce directly, if there is an efficient means of enforcing against the customer through the insolvency process of the supplier.[25]

(iii) Purported Equitable Assignment: Anti-assignment Clause Present

If the receivable contains an anti-assignment clause, some, but not all, of the above analysis changes. The customer, who is discharged by paying the supplier before notification of the assignment, is also similarly discharged by paying the supplier after notification: it is entitled to ignore the notification. Once the debt is paid, though, the supplier will hold the proceeds on trust for the financier despite the anti-assignment clause: there is little *direct* authority on this point in English law, but there are a number of dicta supporting this view,[26] and much academic support.[27] In fact, it is extremely common for invoice discounting agreements to include an express provision that the proceeds are held on trust for the financier, and an anti-assignment clause will not prevent this being effective.[28] It is thought

[22] This would not be the case if the conditions for a statutory assignment were not fulfilled, for example if the assignment was for part of a debt.

[23] See Section D(i).

[24] See H Beale, M Bridge, L Gullifer and E Lomnicka, *The Law of Security and Title-Based Financing*, 2nd edn (Oxford, Oxford University Press, 2012) para 7.127.

[25] See Section D.

[26] *Re Turcan* (1888) 40 Ch D 5, 10–11, supported by Lord Browne-Wilkinson in *Linden Gardens Trust Ltd v Lenesta Sludge Disposal Ltd* [1994] 1 AC 85, 106 and Waller LJ and Rix LJ in *Barbados Trust Co Ltd v Bank of Zambia* [2007] EWCA Civ 148 at [28], [77]. See also *Devefi Pty Ltd V Mateffy Perl Nagy Pty Ltd* (1993) 113 ALR 225, 236 and *Don King Productions Inc v Warren* [2000] Ch 291, 312, 321–22, 332.

[27] B Allcock, 'Restrictions on the Assignment of Contractual Rights' [1983] *Cambridge Law Journal* 328, 335–36; G Tolhurst, 'Prohibitions on Assignment and Declaration of Trust' [2007] *Lloyd's Maritime and Commercial Law Quarterly* 278; G McMeel, 'The Modern Law of Assignment: Public Policy and Contractual Restrictions on Transferability' [2004] *Lloyd's Maritime and Commercial Law Quarterly* 483, 507–08; M Smith, *The Law of Assignment* (Oxford, Oxford University Press, 2007) 347. P Zonneveld, 'The Effectiveness of Contractual Restrictions on the Assignment of Contractual Debts' (2007) 22 Journal of International *Business and Financial Law* 313; C Tham, 'Notice of Assignment and Discharge by Performance' [2010] *Lloyd's Maritime and Commercial Law Quarterly* 38, 77; L Gullifer (ed), *Goode on Legal Problems of Credit and Security*, 5th edn (London, Sweet & Maxwell, 2013) para 3-39.

[28] *Don King Productions Inc v Warren* [2000] Ch 291, 321; M Smith and N Leslie, *The Law of Assignment* (Oxford, Oxford University Press, 2013) paras 25.33–25.36.

that even if the clause purported to prohibit such a declaration, this would be ineffective to prevent such a trust arising, since the customer has no interest in preventing the alienation of the proceeds and such a clause would be against public policy.[29] However, this point has never been litigated, so the position is not entirely clear.

If the customer does not pay, it is clear that the financier cannot sue it directly, as there can be no statutory assignment. Provided, however, that the agreement between the supplier and the financier can be said to give rise to a trust of the unpaid receivable (either expressly or impliedly),[30] it is likely that the financier can sue the customer, joining the supplier as defendant to the action, under a procedure known as the *Vandepitte* procedure. A beneficiary under a trust of a right can bring an action to force the trustee to bring an action to enforce that right for its benefit; the *Vandepitte* procedure merely short-circuits this process by enabling the beneficiary to instigate an action which brings all parties before the court.[31] In a case dealing with the purported assignment of a syndicated loan containing a restriction on assignment, a majority of the Court of Appeal decided that the *Vandepitte* procedure was available to the 'assignee',[32] but doubt as to its appropriateness in this context has been expressed by other judges.[33]

Further, if there is an effective trust of the receivable, the financier will have a proprietary interest which survives the supplier's insolvency, and against competing interests in the receivable. What is not entirely clear, however, is whether it is possible for a carefully drafted anti-assignment clause to prevent a trust of the receivable from arising. The judges in the *Barbados Trust* case were divided on this issue,[34] and although a strong case can be made for an analysis whereby the trust is invalid to the extent that it affects the customer, but arises validly between the financier and the supplier,[35] there is still considerable uncertainty.[36]

[29] R Goode, 'Inalienable Rights?' (1979) 42 *Modern Law Review* 553; *Linden Gardens Trust Ltd v Lenesta Sludge Disposals Ltd* [1994] 1 AC 85, per Lord Browne-Wilkinson at 108. The supplier would be in breach of contract by declaring the trust, but it is hard to see what the damages would be.

[30] Whether this is the case depends on the interpretation both of the anti-assignment clause and the purported assignment. Two recent cases show that this is fact specific, and therefore subject to considerable uncertainty: *Co-operative Group Limited v Birse Developments Limited* [2014] EWHC 530 (TCC); *Stopjoin Projects Ltd v Balfour Beatty Engineering Services (HY) Ltd* [2014] EWHC 589 (TCC).

[31] It is named after the case of *Vandepitte v Preferred Accident Insurance Corp of New York* [1933] AC 70 in which it was first used.

[32] *Barbados Trust Co Ltd v Bank of Zambia* [2007] EWCA Civ 148.

[33] *Don King Productions Inc v Warren* [2000] Ch 291, 321 per Lightman J and *Barbados Trust Co Ltd v Bank of Zambia* [2007] EWCA Civ 148 at [139] per Hooper LJ.

[34] *Barbados Trust Co Ltd v Bank of Zambia* [2007] EWCA Civ 148 at [44]–[47], [88], [129]–[139].

[35] Gullifer (ed) (n 27) para 3-42. See also Bridge (n 10).

[36] A contrary view, namely that the clause renders the receivable inalienable, so that a valid trust cannot be declared of it, is expressed in A McKnight, 'Contractual Restrictions on a Creditor's Right to Alienate Debts' [2003] *Journal of International Banking Law and Regulation* 43; G McMeel, 'The Modern Law of Assignment: Public Policy and Contractual Restrictions on Transferability' [2004] *Lloyd's Maritime and Commercial Law Quarterly* 483; P Turner, 'Charges of Unassignable Rights' (2004) 20 *Journal of Contract Law* 97; GJ Tolhurst and JW Carter, 'Prohibitions on Assignment: A Choice to be Made' (2014) 73 *Cambridge Law Journal* 405.

From the point of view of the customer, the anti-assignment clause protects its position by enabling it at all times to get a good discharge by paying the supplier: it will never be required to pay anyone else. Even if it is sued by the financier under the *Vandepitte* procedure,[37] the order will be that the customer must pay the supplier (the trustee), who will then hold the proceeds on trust for the financier. Further, a notice of assignment received by the customer is probably ineffective to prevent set-offs arising between the supplier and the customer.[38]

(iv) The Current Level of Protection for Financier and Customer Under Current English Law

The legal position, therefore, is that, on the whole, the interests of the financier and the customer can both have a certain degree of protection if an anti-assignment clause is used. This is subject to several caveats. First, the law is complex, and, in some areas, quite uncertain. There are few cases precisely on the relevant points, and even those that there are have not arisen in the context of receivables financing.[39] Second, the legal position will depend on the precise wording of the anti-assignment clause, and of the purported assignment or declaration of trust.[40] Third, even if in theory a financier is protected by the rule that the proceeds are held on trust, this will not help if the supplier has not kept the proceeds in an identifiable state so that they can be traced on its insolvency. A financier might be better off with a proprietary right to a debt owed by a solvent customer, than to proceeds which may or may not be held by an insolvent supplier.

It should be pointed out that the fact that there is a reasonable degree of protection in the current law does not necessarily rule out statutory intervention. For example, UCC former Article 9-318(4) (which contained an override of anti-assignment clauses)[41] was included in the original UCC to reflect the existing US law rather than to change it.[42] This was, however, in the context of a

[37] This would only occur if, despite the clause, a valid trust of the receivable existed.

[38] If, despite the clause, there is a valid declaration of trust, this will break the mutuality required for set-off. If the clause renders a trust invalid to the extent that it affects the customer, then the notification of the trust could be said to be ineffective for all purposes, including preventing set-offs, see J Marshall, 'Declaring a Trust over Rights to an "Unassignable" Contract' (1999) 12 *Insolvency Intelligence* 1; A Tomson and A Rose, 'No Assignment Clauses and Bank Insolvency' [2014] *Corporate Rescue and Insolvency* 228. The position is not, however, completely certain.

[39] The one exception is *Stopjoin Projects Ltd v Balfour Beatty Engineering Services (HY) Ltd* [2014] EWHC (TCC) 589, which did concern receivables financing.

[40] *Linden Gardens Trust Ltd v Lenesta Sludge Disposals Ltd* [1994] 1 AC 85; *Don King Productions Inc v Warren* [2000] Ch 291; *Barbados Trust Co Ltd v Bank of Zambia* [2007] EWCA Civ 148; *Co-operative Group Limited v Birse Developments Limited* [2014] EWHC 530 (TCC); *Stopjoin Projects Ltd v Balfour Beatty Engineering Services* (HY) Ltd [2014] EWHC 589 (TCC).

[41] This provision is the forerunner of revised Art 9-406(d), which is currently in force.

[42] This is made clear by the official comment to the old Article 9, which says: 'It can be regarded as a revolutionary departure only by those who still cherish the hope that we may yet return to the view entertained some two hundred years ago by the Court of the King's Bench'. Even this, however, is an

codification of commercial law, and the introduction of a whole new system for secured financing. To make a case for free-standing legislation there has to be a policy imperative.

D. Industry Workarounds

(i) Financing Structures

Until recently, there were two types of receivables financing: factoring, which is on a notification basis, and invoice discounting, which is non-notification.[43] Factoring tends to be used for smaller suppliers, where a financier has concerns about the ability of the supplier to run its ledger properly and to operate a trust account, and also where the financier has concerns about the supplier's financial position.[44] Since it involves a statutory assignment, factoring gives the financier much more control over the collection of the debts. Factoring is more expensive for the supplier than invoice discounting, and a supplier can pay even more for extra services, such as the taking on by the financier of the credit risk of the customer.[45] In invoice discounting, the collection of the receivables is carried out by the supplier, who holds the proceeds in a trust account for the financier.

Recently, two variations on these structures have become more popular, although the details vary in each case. One is discounting of individual invoices over an online platform: this takes place on a non-notification basis, with the platform merely acting as an intermediary. Another is supply chain financing, whereby a customer arranges with a financier that the latter purchase receivables owed by the customer to its suppliers at the point when the receivables arise, once the invoice has been confirmed by the customer. This has the advantage that there are less likely to be disputes about the invoice, and also that the financing can be based on the credit rating of the customer rather than the (smaller) supplier.[46] Having said that, this kind of financing is usually only offered to established suppliers whose invoices reach a certain, reasonably high, level and is also only offered by large

overstatement. There were contrary cases which were overruled by the legislation, such as *Alhusen v Caristo Construction Corp* 303 NY 446, 103 NE 2d 831 (1952).

[43] Much of the information in this section comes from the 2011 study, updated to take into account recent developments.

[44] Sometimes a financier will shift a client from an invoice-discounting basis to a factoring basis if the client gets into financial difficulties.

[45] Most receivables financing is on a recourse basis, whereby the supplier either guarantees payment of the receivables or agrees to repurchase unpaid receivables.

[46] The UK government launched a scheme in 2012 to encourage businesses and government agencies to offer supply chain financing, see www.gov.uk/government/news/prime-minister-announces-supply-chain-finance-scheme.

customers.[47] There is also a concern that supply chain financing encourages large customers to extend the credit period they require, forcing small businesses to pay for a longer period of financing, albeit at a lower rate.[48]

(ii) Checking for Anti-assignment Clauses

Although some of the workarounds discussed below are adopted regardless of whether particular receivables arise from contracts containing an anti-assignment clause, English financiers very frequently check for the presence of anti-assignment clauses (and for other problematic clauses) in the invoices they finance.[49] Thus, one of the major arguments for a statutory override made in other jurisdictions (that it is not feasible for a receivables financier to discover about anti-assignment clauses,[50] so the whole cost of financing rises as a result) is not really made out in England and Wales. However, checking contracts is burdensome and takes time, particularly if it is necessary to consult lawyers about the effect of a particular clause.[51] The need to do so clearly increases costs, although it is probably the case that some checking would still take place even if there were to be a statutory override of anti-assignment clauses. It is also the case that most supply contracts are on a customer's standard terms, and financiers get to know the terms of large customers and whether they contain an anti-assignment clause, so checking involves merely looking at who the customers are rather than reading individual contracts.

(iii) Workarounds Used by Financiers: Non-notification Financing

If the financing is on a non-notification basis, the presence of an anti-assignment clause does not create problems for the financier on a day-to-day basis, since the customer does not know of the assignment, and continues to pay the supplier.[52] Of course, the supplier would be in breach of contract: this could be of concern, for example, if it enabled the customer to terminate the supply agreement.[53] The

[47] 2011 study.

[48] See www.telegraph.co.uk/finance/yourbusiness/9634184/Payment-concerns-over-supply-chain-finance-move.html; http://realbusiness.co.uk/article/15791-the-supply-chain-finance-scheme-hit-or-miss; www.selectfactoring.co.uk/supply-chain-finance-scheme.

[49] Those interviewed for the 2011 study all said that they checked, while the picture was more mixed in relation to the 2014 study, although most said that they checked, at least in many cases.

[50] Australian Personal Property Securities Act 2009; Duggan and Brown (n 8) 42.

[51] 2011 study.

[52] In the 2011 study we were told that anti-assignment clauses created great problems for online auctions. However, the 2014 study revealed that since then this part of the industry has developed workarounds similar to those in regular invoice discounting, and so what is said in relation to that applies also to online auctions.

[53] Although such a breach is unlikely to be repudiatory, it could fall within a clause entitling the customer to terminate for 'any material breach' (which is quite common) or could trigger a cross-default

financier might worry about two situations: if the supplier becomes insolvent, and if the customer does not pay and the supplier refuses to enforce.[54]

In relation to the first situation, financiers almost universally protect themselves by taking a security interest over all the assets of the supplier.[55] This has the effect, under English law, of enabling the financier to appoint an administrator of the supplier were it to become insolvent.[56] The financier is then in a good position to direct the administrator to collect in the receivables, and to pass the proceeds to it. There seems to be little concern among financiers about the collecting in of debts if an administrator is appointed (even if he is not appointed by that particular financier), although the costs are sometimes a problem if the supplier is a very small business.[57] Financiers also see an 'all-assets' security interest as having an additional benefit, namely that it will cover receivables which are not assigned to the financier because of an anti-assignment clause: sometimes they will specify that such 'non-vesting debts' fall within a fixed charge, while much of the all-assets security interest will be a floating charge. This ignores the fact that, depending on the wording of the clause, an anti-assignment clause may prevent the creation of a valid security interest to the same extent that it prevents a valid assignment.[58]

Another mode of protection often coupled with the all-assets security interest is for financiers to take a personal guarantee from the directors of the supplier company.[59] To be effective this of course depends on the creditworthiness of the directors, and also might entail costs in enforcing the claims under the guarantees, to which there could be arguable defences.

Yet another possibility is for the financier to take a power of attorney enabling it to sue the customer in the name of the supplier.[60] This protection tends to be more useful in the second situation: when the supplier is solvent but refuses to

clause. The absence of a general duty of good faith in English law could mean that a customer could rely on such a termination clause even if its real motivation for termination was something entirely different. In theory, a breach could entitle a customer to obtain an injunction to prevent further breaches (although this is unlikely) or to sue for damages. However, it is hard, usually, to see what loss is suffered by the customer.

[54] The 2014 study indicated that the latter concern is at least as important, and, for invoice discounters, more important than the former, although the sample for this particular question was small.

[55] 2011 study and 2014 study.

[56] Paragraph 14 of sch B1 to the Insolvency Act 1986 provides that a qualifying floating charge holder can appoint an administrator out of court.

[57] Discussion at seminar for receivables financiers hosted by the Secured Transactions Law Reform Project on 8 May 2014, and 2014 study.

[58] Although a charge is not, in theory, an assignment, many charges are drafted as equitable mortgages, which are. A fixed charge has been treated as an assignment in a number of cases, *Biggerstaff v Rowatt's Wharf Ltd* [1896] 2 Ch 93; *NW Robbie & Co v Witney Warehouse Co* [1963] 1 WLR 1324, CA; *Foamcrete (UK) Ltd v Thrust Engineering Ltd* [2000] EWCA Civ 351, [2002] BCC 221. See also *Re Turner Corporation Ltd (In Liq)* (1995) 17 ACSR 761 where the Federal Court of Australia took the view that a clause prohibiting assignment also prohibited a charge.

[59] 2011 study and 2014 study.

[60] 2014 study.

sue. For the power of attorney to be irrevocable on the insolvency of the supplier, the financier would need to have some sort of proprietary right in the receivables or would need to be owed the receivables directly.[61] Where there is an anti-assignment clause, the latter is clearly not the case, and it is unclear whether a right under a trust is a sufficient proprietary interest to render the power irrevocable. The legal position is uncertain and untested.[62]

(iv) Workarounds Used by Financiers: Notification Financing

An anti-assignment clause causes much greater problems for financiers who operate on a notification basis. Here, there is a likelihood that the customer will refuse to pay the financier when notified, and will, instead, pay the supplier. The financier is then at risk of the proceeds being dissipated by the supplier, leaving the financier at the credit risk of the supplier. As a result, such financiers often refuse to finance receivables arising from contracts containing such clauses, or demand that the customer agrees to a waiver.[63] The evidence from the 2014 study is that financiers only sometimes pursue a waiver. There was considerable agreement[64] that the time and effort involved in obtaining a waiver was substantial or significant, and that by no means all customers were willing to agree to a waiver. Some customers would only agree to a waiver on terms which were disadvantageous to the supplier: this depended on the bargaining power between them and also on whether the financing was being sought at the beginning of the supplier/customer relationship.

(v) Supply Chain Financing

In one sense, the increasing availability of supply chain financing is a workaround. It is customer driven: the customer waives the anti-assignment clause to enable supply chain financing with its nominated financier, but relies on it to prevent the supplier obtaining financing elsewhere. This means that the supplier is locked into the supply chain financing deal, which could be seen as anti-competitive. The discount rate for such financing is usually reasonably low, since it is based on the credit rating of the (large) customer, but the period for which financing is required may be increased.[65] However, supply chain financing does achieve protection for

[61] Powers of Attorney Act 1971 s 4.

[62] See discussion in M Bridge, L Gullifer, G McMeel and S Worthington, *The Law of Personal Property* (London, Sweet & Maxwell, 2013) para 29-043.

[63] 2011 study. It should be pointed out that invoice discounters also sometimes refuse to finance receivables if they contain an anti-assignment clause, or will only finance them on a factoring basis, or demand a waiver. This is particularly true if, for some reason, a security interest over the supplier's assets is not taken.

[64] 12 out of the 18 respondents.

[65] See Section D(i).

the customer; only invoices approved by the customer are financed, which reduces disputes, and the customer does not have to deal with a financier with whom it has no relationship.

(vi) Effect of Workarounds

It can be seen that the industry has developed a number of workarounds which mean that, with the exception of factoring where the financier cannot or does not try to obtain a waiver, receivables containing anti-assignment clauses are usually financed. However, the workarounds are costly in terms of time and effort, and also create more uncertainty, which can lead to costly disputes. In fact, one concern of the industry is that the existence of an enforceable anti-assignment clause may give a customer traction in disputes which it would not otherwise have, or will enable the customer to negotiate benefits for itself which would otherwise not exist. Although it is hard to prove, it seems likely that the existence of enforceable anti-assignment clauses increases the cost of financing.[66]

E. Inequality of Bargaining Power

(i) Reasons for the Inclusion of Anti-assignment Clauses

At this point it is necessary to consider the reasons why a customer might want to include an anti-assignment clause in a supply contract. The reasons usually given in the literature are that the customer wishes to avoid paying the wrong party, that it wishes to make sure that set-offs can continue to arise between it and the supplier, and that it wishes to continue to deal with the supplier rather than the financier, who is an unknown quantity.[67] The information gathered from the two surveys (which came from all three constituencies: customers, suppliers and financiers) shows that the motivations are more mixed. There appeared to be little

[66] In the 2014 study, 11 out of 18 answered 'always' or 'sometimes' to the question: Do you consider that (a) receivables are purchased at a greater discount to face value, or (b) the advance rate applied to the purchase of receivables will be reduced, as a result of the possibility that the contract governing the receivable may contain a valid prohibition on assignment, than would apply if such prohibitions on assignment were not binding as against an assignee? However, only a small minority answered 'yes' to the question: Do you consider that the cost of finance is increased as a result of the inclusion of a prohibition on assignment within funded ledgers? This discrepancy may be explained by the latter question being interpreted as relating only to where receivables with anti-assignment clauses were actually included in the funded ledger, which is seldom the case in factoring arrangements.

[67] See eg O Akseli, 'Contractual Prohibitions on Assignment of Receivables: An English and UN Perspective' [2009] *Journal of Business Law* 650, 656; L Gullifer and J Payne, *Corporate Finance Law: Principles and Policy* (Oxford: Hart Publishing, 2011) 378–79; R Goode, 'Contractual Prohibitions against Assignment' [2009] *Lloyd's Maritime and Commercial Law Quarterly* 300, 302.

concern about paying the wrong party per se,[68] but there did appear to be genuine concern about incorrect invoicing and the sorting out of disputes.[69] It was thought that financiers would be more concerned that the invoice was paid, and would wish disputes to be sorted out afterwards between the customer and the supplier. The problem of incorrect invoicing was being tackled both by self-invoicing and by electronic invoice platforms.[70] However, the desire to retain the relationship with the supplier in order to sort out disputes is ongoing.[71] Opinions, not surprisingly, varied as to how helpful the financiers were in sorting out disputes and how aggressively they sought payment.

Perhaps also surprisingly, the issue of set-off did not seem to be of great importance.[72] This may reflect the fact that transaction set-off, that is, set-off of cross-claims arising out of the same contract or closely related to the claim, is not affected by assignment of the receivable. The desire to lock the supplier into a supply chain finance agreement was mentioned by one respondent to the 2014 study, and one respondent to the 2011 study mentioned one customer who wanted total confidentiality, so did not want its identity revealed to a financier. However, there seemed to be considerable consensus that in many cases customers did not really include anti-assignment clauses to prevent receivables financing at all, but to prevent 'assignment' (or subcontracting) of suppliers' obligations under the contract. Of course, under English law an obligation cannot be assigned, and so such a clause would be unnecessary, but it might be included out of ignorance or in order to make the subcontracting of obligations a repudiatory breach which would entitle the customer to terminate the relationship. In any event, many financiers felt that the clauses, in the form where they precluded receivables financing, were included without a great deal of thought: out of 'habit' or 'fear of the unknown', or out of an over-abundance of caution by lawyers who drafted the boilerplate contract.[73]

(ii) Balance of Bargaining Power

It is certainly the case that anti-assignment clauses are generally found in standard-form contracts used by large companies for their small and medium-sized suppliers.[74] The suppliers cannot negotiate the terms of the contracts and, as previously discussed, may find it difficult to obtain a waiver. Where the balance

[68] This was mentioned by the financiers in the 2011 study but by no one else.

[69] 2011 study, especially evidence from customers.

[70] Such as www.tungsten-network.com/uk/en/expertise/e-invoicing/.

[71] It was mentioned by a number of respondents to the 2014 study.

[72] This was the view of the customers in the 2011 study, though one supplier thought that it was critical.

[73] 2014 study.

[74] All the respondents to the 2014 study selected either large companies or government agencies (or both) as likely to include anti-assignment clauses in their contracts, although four also selected 'small companies'.

of bargaining power is reversed, so that the supplier is a large company and the customer is a small company or a consumer, the latter are not able to bargain for the protection of an anti-assignment clause. Control of anti-assignment clauses therefore raises a wider question of protection of small businesses against potentially unfair terms. Under English law, unreasonable exclusion and limitation clauses included in standard-form contracts are unenforceable against businesses (of all sizes),[75] and penalty clauses are, in some circumstances, unenforceable,[76] but otherwise any control of unfair terms relates to consumer contracts. The Law Commission suggested in 2005[77] that some control should be extended to contracts with micro businesses,[78] but this suggestion has not been implemented. Some of the suppliers who responded to the 2011 study suggested that there was a problem with unfair terms in supply contracts[79] which was wider than just with anti-assignment clauses, and that either legislation, or maybe wider codes of practice,[80] were needed.

If it is right that inequality of bargaining power enables large customers to impose potentially unfair terms on small suppliers, then statutory control of anti-assignment clauses could have the effect that, deprived of this protection, the customers just imposed more swingeing terms in other areas.[81] This is a reason for reform to be approached with care, but not a clinching reason against statutory reform.

F. The Role of Anti-assignment Clauses in Financial Transactions

In many financial transactions, there are specific reasons for the inclusion of anti-assignment clauses which are important for the proper functioning of the market. In some cases, the clause does not ban assignment, but permits it to certain entities and requires consent for assignment to others. Thus, for example, in syndicated loan agreements, it is very common for a clause to permit assignment to certain financial institutions, but to require consent for assignment to others. This stems from a concern that were the loan to be assigned to, for example, a hedge fund

[75] Under ss 3, 6(3) and 7(3) of the Unfair Contract Terms Act 1977.

[76] E Peel (ed), *Treitel on The Law of Contract* 14th edn (London, Sweet & Maxwell, 2015) paras 20-129–20-145.

[77] Law Commission Report 292, *Unfair Terms in Contracts* (2005).

[78] Businesses with nine or fewer employees.

[79] One example is a term making large sums payable on termination of the contract by the supplier.

[80] For example, the Groceries Supply Code of Practice, see www.gov.uk/government/publications/groceries-supply-code-of-practice.

[81] Such as a term that an invoice for goods or services is not payable until the invoice has been approved by the customer. This possibility was discussed with the respondents to the 2011 study, but is, of course, speculation: there can be no hard evidence.

specialising in distressed debt, it would be enforced in a much more aggressive way than it would be by a bank,[82] and also from a concern that a loan might be sold to one of the competitors of the borrower.[83] In derivatives contracts, which depend on close-out netting to protect against credit risk and for enforcement, it is critical that mutuality of parties is maintained, and so restrictions on assignment are very important.

The existence of these good reasons for anti-assignment (or restrictions on assignment) clauses to be enforceable means that any statutory override of anti-assignment clauses should be limited in scope to the context in which such clauses cause most problems, namely receivables financing. This, of course, raises definitional issues: for example, how do you exclude contracts for financial products without also excluding contracts for the provision of services relating to finance (such as computing services and financial advice)? The difficulties that such definitional issues pose, and the concern about the effects on the financial industry for getting the limitation of scope wrong, have led to considerable opposition to the statutory control of anti-assignment clauses from City lawyers and bankers.

G. Should there be a Statutory Override?

As indicated, the debate in England and Wales has largely moved from a clash of policies to a discussion based on pragmatism and cost-benefit analysis. In most situations, the presence of anti-assignment clauses does not prevent suppliers financing their receivables. This is because the law has developed in such a way that generally a financier will have an equitable interest in, at least, the proceeds of the receivables and probably in the receivables themselves. Further, the industry has developed a number of workarounds, which means that the receivables will be collected for the ultimate benefit of the financier both where the customer does not pay and when the supplier is insolvent. None of this is surprising. In the absence of any statutory control of anti-assignment clauses it is to be expected that both the law and the industry will accommodate the interests of all parties, to the extent that they can.

This, however, is not the end of the story. If the current position imposes costs on the industry, and thus on financing, which are not outweighed by the benefit of such clauses to the customers, then this would be a good reason for legislation. A further reason could be if certain suppliers were unable to obtain financing. Moreover, if it were felt that legislation could do no or little harm, but would have the beneficial effect of clarifying the existing law and making the balance of

[82] The market has therefore developed ways of transferring the risk and benefit of the loan without actually assigning it, such as loan participation and, more commonly now, credit default swaps.

[83] Law Commission, *Company Security Interests*, Law Com No 296 (2005) 5.33.

protection between all parties clear, this could also justify legislative change. All three of these arguments pertain in England and Wales today.

It is reasonably clear from both surveys[84] that some small suppliers, whom financiers will not finance on the basis of invoice discounting because of concerns about their ability to collect in the receivables and hold them on trust for the financier, are unable to have certain invoices financed because they contain anti-assignment clauses. The only way round this problem is for the customer to waive the clause, and this is not possible on some occasions, either because the costs of doing so outweigh the benefits to both the supplier and the financier, or because the supplier has so little bargaining power compared with the customer. The UK government is very concerned about the funding of small businesses at the moment: they are seen critical to economic recovery.[85] This, then, is a good reason for a statutory override of anti-assignment clauses.

It is also clear that the presence of such clauses leads to costs for the financing industry. There is the cost of discovering such clauses, although it should not be overemphasised.[86] Waivers can be costly, as is the development and execution of the workarounds discussed above. Moreover, the existence of the workarounds themselves increases *ex ante* uncertainty, both in terms of the law[87] and also in that it increases the possibility of disputes. Finally, the law itself is complex and uncertain. A financier cannot be sure that it has a valid interest in a receivable containing an anti-assignment clause. It is clearer that it has an equitable interest in the proceeds, but this is not any good if the proceeds are not traceable.

Are these costs outweighed by the benefits of the clauses? It is clear that such clauses are of value in the context of financial contracts. However, some of the reasons why customers seem to include them in their contracts are of little merit[88] and the results from the (small-scale) surveys suggest that some do not seem of concern in the real world.[89] The concern about preserving a relationship with the supplier in the event of dispute or incorrect invoices is a real one, but the latter point can be overcome with modern invoicing techniques, and the former argument is undermined by the fact that customers are prepared to permit assignment to a financier of their choice under a supply chain finance scheme. The argument that a financier might be more aggressive in enforcing invoices than a supplier is also flawed, since the risk of a third party influencing enforcement is an ever present one: the supplier could be taken over by a more aggressive management.

[84] The 2011 study and the 2014 study. It should be borne in mind that both surveys were fairly small scale.

[85] www.gov.uk/government/news/small-business-big-support-confirmed-by-prime-minister.

[86] This is because the financiers are familiar with the standard terms of the big customers, and also because they would read the contracts anyway for other adverse clauses.

[87] For example, whether a power of attorney will be enforceable on insolvency of the supplier, or whether an anti-assignment clause renders a charge void.

[88] The prevention of subcontracting does not require an anti-assignment clause, and the 'habit' or 'fear of the unknown' reasons seem unmeritorious.

[89] There seems to be little concern about set-off, or about the danger of paying the wrong party.

The customer's concern to remain in a relationship with the supplier may have more to do with the fact that the supplier is a small business compared with it, the customer, and therefore the customer is likely to have more of an upper hand in negotiations than it would have with a financier. The use of an anti-assignment clause to lock a supplier into supply chain financing also seems unmeritorious. If the supply chain financing was sufficiently attractive to the supplier, it would choose it anyway in preference to other sources of financing.

This brings us to the argument that a statutory override would do little harm, and could do some good in clarifying the law. One possibility of harm is that the override is not sufficiently limited, and causes problems in the financial markets. This is a serious risk, but could be overcome by careful drafting, even if this were at the expense of not including some borderline cases within the override.[90] Another possibility is that an override leads to harsher terms being imposed by large customers on small suppliers in other areas. This again would be serious, but could be controlled by a code of practice.[91] It therefore seems that the benefit in clarifying the law would outweigh any possible detriment.

H. Conclusion

This chapter has sought to elucidate the arguments both for and against a statutory override of anti-assignment clauses in English law. It is suggested that the arguments are not ones of principle, or even policy, but are more pragmatic. Since such clauses have not ever been the subject of statutory intervention, the common law has developed in such a way as to give all parties limited protection, and the industry has worked around the law to enable receivables financing to take place. However, on the basis of two recent surveys, the pragmatic arguments are assessed, and, on balance, it appears that a statutory override would be beneficial.

[90] The power included in the Small Business, Enterprise and Employment Act 2015 s 1 excludes financial services contracts, as do the draft Regulations (n 4).

[91] See, for example, the UK Groceries Supply Code of Practice (4 August 2009) available at www.gov.uk/government/publications/groceries-supply-code-of-practice/groceries-supply-code-of-practice.

Part III

Modernisation of the Law of Secured Transactions in Selected European Civil Law Jurisdictions

15

The Peculiar Approach of German Law in the Field of Secured Transactions and Why it has Worked (So Far)

MORITZ BRINKMANN*

A. Introduction

To include a chapter on German law in this book, which is devoted to the modernisation of the law of secured transactions in European jurisdictions, may be perceived as superfluous, as there is currently no reform debate in Germany. Lenders and borrowers are by and large satisfied with the system as it is. For two reasons, however, a brief discussion of the situation in Germany might nevertheless be appropriate here. First, the peculiar approach of German law, namely the complete lack of publicity, provides some interesting insights into the function of publicity requirements with respect to security rights. Secondly, it is possible, if not likely, that the discussion about law reform in the field of secured transactions will before long gain momentum in Germany as well: some of the factors that are crucial to the functionality of the German regime may lose traction as business practices are changing. Furthermore, the integration of (financial) markets will eventually put pressure on Germany to bring its law into line with international standards.

I shall begin with a brief overview of the German secured transactions law and in particular its lack of publicity. I shall then attempt to explain the mechanisms the courts have developed to address the repercussions of secret security rights, as well as the specific conditions of the German economy without which the 'secret pledge' approach would not have functioned. Lastly, I shall identify the factors which may support future law reform.

* Professor of Civil Law, German and European Civil Procedure and Insolvency Law, University of Bonn and the representative of Germany at the UNCITRAL Working Group VI (Security Interests).

B. Brief Overview of the German Law of Secured Transactions

Louise Gullifer described the English law of secured transactions in an interview in the following terms: 'It is complex, difficult to understand—even for English trained lawyers—and pretty impenetrable for lawyers from other jurisdictions'.[1] This sentence is—*mutatis mutandis*—also true of the German law on security over movable property. The rules in this field are special in two ways. Deviating from the general approach in German private law, the rules applicable to securities over movables are to a great extent not codified, but judge made. One could go as far as saying that with respect to secured transactions—as far as movables are concerned—Germany is a common law jurisdiction.

The other particularity is the fact that Germany is one of the very few jurisdictions that do not require publicity with respect to security rights over movables. It is puzzling, especially for lawyers trained in jurisdictions that maintain a registry of security rights, that the German law nevertheless functions well (by and large) and that there is no evidence of the costs of credit in Germany being higher than in other jurisdictions.

Notwithstanding Uniform Commercial Code (UCC) Article 9-type systems, German law does not follow a functional approach, in the sense that all transactions which aim at securing an obligation are characterised as a security right. Instead, German law provides for a number of different types of right that may be used in order to secure payment of an obligation. In practice, however, some of these types of right only play a marginal role, or are used only with respect to certain classes of assets. Hence, the following rough overview is not structured along the different types of right, but along the different types of collateral, as this approach gives a more realistic and complete picture of German law in the field of secured transactions.

(i) Tangibles as Collateral

The uninitiated reader of the BGB (*Bürgerliches Gesetzbuch*—German Civil Code)[2] might be misled into believing that under German law the possessory pledge is the only, or at least the most important, type of security right over tangibles. Sections 1204–1259 BGB deal indeed in great detail with all questions relating to a pledge, and the Code is silent regarding any other type of security over movables. In practice, however, these provisions are largely irrelevant, as the pledge is—outside

[1] Available at www.vimeo.com/101077553.

[2] An English translation of the provisions of the BGB may be found at www.gesetze-im-internet.de/englisch_bgb/german_civil_code.pdf.

of pawnshops—rarely used to create a security right over movables. Due to the transfer-of-possession requirement enshrined in section 1205 BGB, the pledge is unsuitable for most types of transaction.

Grantors and secured creditors can avoid the transfer-of-possession requirement by resorting to a fiduciary transfer of ownership (*Sicherungsübereignung*). Such a transfer of title for the purpose of securing an obligation has been held to be permissible by German courts, even prior to the adoption of the BGB in 1896.[3] The courts not only maintained their liberal attitude after 1900—the year the BGB came into force—but went further, accepting a fiduciary transfer of ownership with respect to future goods and inventory.[4]

Under a *Sicherungsübereignung* the grantor transfers his title in the collateral to the secured creditor. For such a transfer, sections 929–930 BGB require an agreement between the parties that title shall pass to the secured creditor. In addition, a supplementary agreement whereby the grantor possesses the collateral on behalf of the secured creditor is also required. This secondary agreement is known as a *Sicherungsabrede*. Through the *Sicherungsabrede* the creditor acquires indirect possession of the collateral; the grantor, however, retains actual possession. The secured creditor is obliged to transfer title to the collateral back to the grantor, after the secured claim is extinguished.

It is important to further underline that there is no registration requirement or any other form of publicity with respect to a *Sicherungsübereignung*. Under sections 929–930 BGB, the agreement to transfer title, together with the acquisition of constructive possession of the collateral, suffice to render the secured creditor the new owner as long as the transferor is the owner. Only a good-faith acquisition of title would require actual possession by the transferee (section 933 BGB). In insolvency, however, the position of the secured creditor is characterised on the basis of a functional approach: a person who owns property for security purposes does not in insolvency enjoy the rights of a full owner, but only the rights of a secured creditor.[5] The position of a secured creditor is weaker than the position of a full owner in the sense that he cannot demand transfer of possession with respect to the collateral. Instead, the trustee may use or even sell the collateral.[6] The trustee may also retain a certain share of the proceeds, to the benefit of the estate for the purpose of covering enforcement and administrative expenses.[7]

[3] Reichsgericht, 9.10.1880, RGZ 2, 168 ff; Reichsgericht 10.1.1885, RGZ 13, 200 ff; Reichsgericht 2.6.1890, RGZ 26, 180 ff.

[4] Reichsgericht, 15.5.1911, *Juristische Wochenschrift* 1911, 762; Reichsgericht 14.11.1911, *Juristische Wochenschrift* 1912, 144 ff. For a more comprehensive analysis of the case law's development see M Brinkmann, *Kreditsicherheiten an beweglichen Sachen und Forderungen* (Tübingen, Mohr Siebeck, 2011) 93 ff.

[5] German Insolvency Code s 51 No 1. An English translation of the provisions of the German Insolvency Code may found at www.gesetze-im-internet.de/englisch_inso/.

[6] German Insolvency Code s 166 para 1.

[7] ibid ss 170–171.

(ii) Receivables as Collateral

With respect to receivables the situation is very similar. Again, the BGB contains extensive provisions on the pledge over receivables (sections 1279–1290 BGB). In practice, however, the pledge is rarely used. Security over intangibles other than receivables, ie shares, intellectual property rights, negotiable instruments and certificated securities, is the only field in which the BGB pledge plays a significant role. With respect to receivables legal practice largely avoids the pledge, as its creation requires notification of the debtor of the receivable (section 1280 BGB). There are few things that German borrowers dread more than disclosing their financing methods to their business partners. Hence, lenders and borrowers resort to the fiduciary assignment in order to create a security right over a receivable. The assignment is particularly attractive as it requires (under German law) neither registration nor the notification of the debtor. The mere agreement between the transferor and the transferee suffices to assign the receivable. Such an agreement may also cover a bulk of receivables, as well as future receivables.

As long as the debtor meets his obligations arising from the credit agreement, the grantor is allowed to collect the receivable in his own name without having to disclose the assignment. Only if the debtor defaults will the secured creditor revoke the grantor's collection right and collect the receivable himself. In insolvency, however, the creditor to whom a receivable was assigned for security purposes is treated as a secured creditor.[8] As a result, the right to collect the receivable is vested in the trustee,[9] and the estate receives a 9 per cent share of the proceeds as compensation for its expenses.[10]

(iii) Retention of Title

Nearly all contracts for sale under German law contain a clause to the effect that title to the sold item does not pass before the buyer has paid the purchase price. There are no formalities which must be observed concerning such retention of title (ROT) clauses. In particular, the contract does not need to be in writing, let alone carry a certified date.

At least with respect to credit sales, eg instalment sales or other situations in which payment is not immediately due, these clauses function as a security right: if the buyer ultimately fails to pay the purchase price, the seller will enforce his rights in the sold item by reclaiming it on the basis that he still is the owner.

It may be helpful to explain the legal structure of ROT clauses in more detail. Under German law the sales contract must be distinguished from the question of who is the owner of the sold item: the sales contract as such merely creates an

[8] ibid s 51 No 1.
[9] ibid s 166 para 2.
[10] ibid ss 170–171.

obligation on the part of the seller to transfer ownership to the buyer. For this transfer, ie for the performance of the seller, a second agreement is required. In a title retention situation, the parties will conclude this second agreement together with the sales contract. The effectiveness of this secondary agreement, however, is reliant on a condition to the effect that title only passes if the buyer pays the purchase price in full.

Regarding equipment, the practical importance of ROT devices is fairly limited, as today's equipment is usually leased rather than bought. With respect to inventory, however, the situation is very different. Inventory is often purchased by way of a credit sale. In many instances, the supplier will even allow the buyer to sell on the inventory before he has paid the purchase price. The receivable thereby generated is assigned in advance to the supplier.[11] These devices are designed to give the seller a security right in the proceeds of the inventory.

There is also a second type of extended ROT, clause which is relevant concerning inventory in the form of raw material. Here, the supplier permits the buyer to process the raw materials even before he has paid the purchase price. In return, the sales contract contains a clause whereby the supplier acquires automatic ownership of the goods that are manufactured from the materials delivered. Again, the clause is aimed at giving the supplier a security right in the proceeds of the goods sold and delivered by him.

C. The Most Striking Feature: The Complete Lack of Publicity

The very rough description of the German law of secured transactions given above shows that German law completely disregards any publicity requirement with respect to security rights over movables. The transfer-of-possession requirement that is associated with the pledge is, to all intents and purposes, irrelevant as borrowers and lenders in practice rely exclusively on the (secret) fiduciary transfer of title. Not only did the judiciary give its blessing to these devices, they were also (implicitly) accepted by the legislator in the nineteenth century. When the BGB was drafted, the legislator was aware of the practice of using the fiduciary transfer of ownership to create a security right. It nevertheless did not adopt a provision along the lines of Article 717 of the Swiss Civil Code, explicitly prohibiting such practices. Hence, the courts felt (legitimately) invited by the legislator to continue permitting the *Sicherungsübereignung* (fiduciary transfer of ownership for security purposes) under the new law. Therefore, the transfer-of-possession requirement provided for in section 1205 BGB did not prevent the practice of creating non-possessory security rights over movables.

[11] Such an extended ROT clause featured prominently in English law in *Aluminium Industrie Vaassen BV v Romalpa Aluminium* [1976] 1 WLR 676 per Roskill LJ.

The approach of the BGB's legislator seems, at first glance, half-baked, or even contradictory. It appears nonsensical to require transfer of possession with respect to the creation of a pledge, while simultaneously (implicitly) allowing the creation of a non-possessory pledge through a fiduciary transfer of ownership. It has been said that this puzzling approach is comparable to the behaviour of a man who diligently locks the door to his garden, but at the same time leaves the fence wide open.[12] In hindsight, however, the solution adopted by the legislator was in all likelihood a very pragmatic and sensible approach, although it could be criticised it for its lack of dogmatic rigour.[13] It was clear that a possessory pledge would be useless in practice, as it does not meet the needs of borrowers and lenders. On the other hand, the legislator was aware that a registry for security rights over movables would have been extremely expensive and cumbersome to work with, at least judging by the land registry, which was the only example of a registry at the time.

The door was deliberately left open by the legislature so that courts and legal practice would be able to develop a non-possessory security right based on the fiduciary transfer of ownership. The legislator of the BGB entrusted the courts with the task of resolving any problems such a non-possessory security right might create.

The result of this approach was that borrowers and lenders had a security device at their disposal that did not require any formalities, and proved to be extremely flexible. The downside, however, was a certain degree of uncertainty, in a legal as well as in a factual sense. The lack of publicity creates a factual uncertainty in that a borrower may have difficulties assessing whether a given piece of property is already encumbered. The legal uncertainty stemmed from the fact that—at least in the first few years after the adoption of the BGB—there was neither codified law nor any case law on which the parties could rely. This uncertainty was of course reduced over time as the case law developed. However, a degree of uncertainty remains, as the Bundesgerichtshof (BGH—German Federal Court of Justice) has once more fairly recently had to decide on quite fundamental questions in the field of security over movables. As late as 2007, for example, the BGH had to determine the circumstances under which a global assignment for security purposes may be set aside in insolvency by the trustee. The BGH 'saved' the global assignment and ruled that it is, by and large, insolvency proof.[14]

D. Why the German Approach has Worked (So Far)

There are essentially two reasons why the uncertainty described above has—as far as we know—not significantly hampered lending activities or raised the costs

[12] See G Frotz, Gutachten zum 4. Österreichischen Juristentag 1970, part 3, vol 1, 110.

[13] H Koziol, 'Glanz und Elend der deutschen Zivilrechtsdogmatik' (2012) 212 *Archiv für die civilistische Praxis* 1, 27 ff.

[14] BGH, 29.11.2007, BGHZ 174, 297 ff.

of credit in Germany. One has been the German courts' proficiency at developing doctrines which have helped to overcome some of the potential hurdles secret security rights based on the fiduciary transfer of title might create (Subsection (i) below). The other is the so-called *Hausbankprinzip*, which has shaped German financing practices (Subsection (ii) below) in such a way that the lack of publicity of German security rights does not create severe problems.

(i) Judge-made Workarounds

For two reasons it might be interesting to highlight some of the most important decisions that have shaped the German law of secured transactions as it stands today. First, the law is still largely uncodified, so it is difficult—not only for non-German trained lawyers—to access and understand. Secondly, an overview of the most important decisions might point out some of the policy choices a legislator has to make when drafting a secured transactions law.

(a) Rules on the Enforcement of a Security Right

One of the first questions that had to be decided by the courts was the issue of whether the provisions on the enforcement of the pledge were to be applied by way of analogy to the fiduciary transfer of ownership for security purposes (*Sicherungsübereignung*). These provisions disallow the *lex commissoria* and provide only for sale by public auction. The Reichsgericht—the highest German court at the time—decided in 1913 that an agreement between a grantor and a secured creditor whereby the secured creditor becomes the full owner of the collateral should the debtor default, is permissible in the context of a *Sicherungsübereignung*.[15] This decision paved the way for parties to provide for various out-of-court enforcement mechanisms in their security agreements, in particular for a private sale.

(b) After-acquired Property

Another important step was to permit security rights that automatically attach to future collateral, such as inventory subsequently acquired by the grantor or receivables subsequently created by the grantor against his customers. The Reichsgericht accepted such transactions provided that the parties clearly specified the assets to which the security right ought to attach.[16] Parties may meet this requirement by either simply encumbering all assets (present and future), or by providing for the encumbrance of certain assets. For example, all inventory stored in certain rooms or of all claims (existing and future) against debtors whose names begin with certain letters.

[15] Reichsgericht, 11.10.1913, *Juristische Wochenschrift* 1914, 76.

[16] Reichsgericht, 23.12.1902, RGZ 53, 218; Reichsgericht, 14.11.1911, *Juristische Wochenschrift* 1912, 144.

(c) Competing Security Rights

A third fundamental issue was, and to some extent still is, the resolution of conflicts over competing security rights. Here, one of the main shortcomings of a title-based security rights regime becomes apparent: as the grantor can transfer his title to an asset to one creditor only it is impossible—or at least very difficult—to create junior security rights. Hence, a conflict between two competing security rights can only produce an all-or-nothing result: either the creditor acquires title to the collateral or he is completely unsecured. In other words, the option of having a junior security right does not exist in a title-based system. To amend this, German courts developed a sophisticated and complicated device, called the *Anwartschaftsrecht*. This term is a somewhat mysterious legal concept not to be found in the BGB. It describes the position a buyer has in goods he has acquired under ROT before he has paid the purchase price in full. As the condition for the acquisition of ownership is not met, the seller remains the owner. The buyer, however, has a contingent entitlement to the goods in the sense that title automatically passes to him once the purchase price is paid. This contingent entitlement gains value with every instalment paid. The buyer can use this *Anwartschaftsrecht* as collateral by transferring it to, eg, a bank to secure another loan.

(d) The Problem of Over-security

The 'invention' of the *Anwartschaftsrecht* could, however, resolve only one of many repercussions the title-based approach carries with it. The fact that multiple security rights in the same asset are not feasible under German law creates a lock-in effect for the grantor/debtor. Imagine a debtor who has used his only piece of equipment, which is very valuable, to secure a loan. If the value of the collateral exceeds the amount of the loan, and if the grantor subsequently needs more credit, he has no option other than to ask the secured creditor for a larger loan. Nobody else would lend him money as he cannot offer even a junior security right to other parties. This lock-in effect might have adverse effects on the availability and costs of credit.

To address this problem the judiciary has developed intricate rules on 'over-security' (*Übersicherung*). According to these rules a security right in tangibles is void if the value of the collateral 'grossly' exceeds the amount of the loan at the time the security right was granted.[17] The courts have refrained from providing a specific ratio, and as there is only very limited case law on this question,[18] the limits of this doctrine are a subject of debate in the literature.[19]

In the years prior to 1997 there was great uncertainty as to what effects a subsequent disparity between the amount of the loan and the value of the collateral

[17] BGH, 12.3.1998, *Neue Juristische Wochenschrift* 1998, 2074.

[18] Besides the decision of the BGH from 12.3.1998, see OLG Hamm, 9.10.2001 *Neue Juristische Online Zeitschrift* 2002, 1398; OLG Köln, 27.1.2009—3 U 84/08, OLGR Köln 2009, 571.

[19] P Bülow, *Recht der Kreditsicherheiten*, 8th edn (Heidelberg, CF Müller, 2012) para 1112.

might have. Such a subsequent 'over-security' may arise where the loan has been reduced by instalments paid by the debtor, or where the collateral has gained value because the debtor stores more inventory than at the time the security was granted. In 1997 the BGH decided that in such instances the security right is not void. The grantor merely has a personal right against the creditor to release a part of the collateral.[20] If the grantor exercises this right he can use the released collateral to seek financing from a different creditor. Thus, the lock-in effect of title-based security rights can be overcome in part.

(e) Superpriority for Acquisition Financing with Respect to Proceeds

For reasons I will deal with in Subsection (d) the typical conflict between secured creditors in German practice is not between two competing banks, but between a bank and a supplier. Where an asset is delivered to the debtor by the supplier, the supplier will usually win the priority conflict as he still is the owner of the asset by virtue of an ROT clause. As long as the seller retains ownership, the bank cannot acquire rights in the asset.

With respect to proceeds, however, the situation is less straightforward: if the buyer/debtor sells the collateral in the ordinary course of business to one of his customers he creates a receivable against a third party debtor. This receivable may be the subject of two competing assignments for security purposes: one assignment is in favour of a bank to which the debtor has assigned all his present and future claims against his customers, the other assignment is an extended ROT clause in favour of the supplier, which I have described in Section B(iii).

The question to be determined is whether the bank or the supplier should have a security right in the receivable. If one tries to apply a first-in-time rule, one could ask which of the two competing assignments was first. In many instances the assignment in favour of the bank will pre-date the sales contract that contained the extended ROT clause with the assignment in favour of the supplier. Hence, under a first-in-time rule, the bank would usually win the priority contest with respect to proceeds.

In 1950 the German law professor Werner Flume published a paper on this question.[21] He concluded that the assignment in favour of the bank is void where the bank knew or ought to have known that the debtor has to acquire inventory from his suppliers under extended ROT clauses, as this is the dominant practice in the industry in question. Flume argued that in such situations the bank induces its debtor to breach his contract with the supplier, as the bank asks for an assignment also with respect to those receivables which stem from the sale of inventory delivered to the debtor under an extended ROT clause. In other words, Flume argued for a solution that would give suppliers a superpriority extending to the

[20] BGH 27.11.1997, BGHZ 137, 212 ff.

[21] W Flume, 'Der verlängerte und erweiterte Eigentumsvorbehalt' (1950) *Neue Juristische Wochenschrift* 841 ff.

proceeds of the inventory they had delivered to the debtor. In 1959 the BGH adopted this approach.[22] Since then, this doctrine (in German: *Vertragsbruchtheorie*) has become part of the German case law in the field of secured transactions. Hence, under German law the supplier (as the prototype acquisition financier of inventory) has a superpriority not only in the supplied goods, but also in any proceeds where the parties have included an extended ROT clause in their contract.

It might be interesting to compare the German approach to the solution adopted by the UNCITRAL Model Law. The UNCITRAL Draft Model Law addresses the particular question in Article 39.[23] The Model Law suggests two alternatives. Under Alternative B the priority of an acquisition security right in a tangible asset that is effective against third parties does not extend to its proceeds. Alternative A distinguishes (similar to Article 9-324 UCC) between acquisition security rights in inventory and in goods other than inventory:

1. In the case of an acquisition security right in assets other than inventory, consumer goods and intellectual property or rights of a licensee under a licence of intellectual property that is held by the grantor for sale or licence in the ordinary course of the grantor's business or that that is used or intended to be used by the grantor primarily for personal, family or household purposes, a security right in proceeds has the same priority as the acquisition security right.
2. In the case of an acquisition security right in inventory and intellectual property or rights of a licensee under a licence of intellectual property that is held by the grantor for sale or licence in the ordinary course of the grantor's business, a security right in proceeds has the same priority as the acquisition security right, except where the proceeds take the form of receivables, negotiable instruments, or rights to payment of funds credited to a bank account.
3. The priority of a security right in proceeds referred to in para 2 is conditional on the acquisition secured creditor notifying non-acquisition secured creditors that have registered a notice in the Registry with respect to a security right created by the grantor in an asset of the same kind as the proceeds that, before the proceeds arose, the acquisition secured creditor registered a notice with respect to assets of the same kind as the proceeds in the Registry.

The German law provides for an 'Option C' and goes beyond both alternatives provided for by the Model Law in the sense that the supplier automatically enjoys priority, also with respect to receivables as proceeds.

The reasons why German courts in the 1950s adopted Flume's idea and bestowed an automatic superpriority upon suppliers cannot be fully understood without taking the German financial market in the years after the introduction of the Deutsche Mark in 1948 into consideration. During those years the German economy was booming, growing faster than the banks, which could not satisfy the hunger for credit of German businesses. Hence, suppliers had to function as

[22] BGH, 30.4.1959, BGHZ 30, 149 ff.
[23] A/CN.9/884/Add.2.

financiers of their customers.[24] For this arrangement to function, it was essential that the suppliers had a security right not only in the inventory they delivered, but also in whatever proceeds those assets generated. This economic situation changed of course, as the German banking sector developed. The doctrine of induced breach of contract, however, survived these changes and is still applied today.[25]

(ii) Financing as a One-Stop Shop: The *Hausbankprinzip*

A key factor underpinning the functionality of the German approach, ie the lack of publicity, is the so-called *Hausbankprinzip*.[26] The term *Hausbankprinzip* describes the fact that traditionally many German small and medium-sized enterprises have a strong and long-term commitment with one particular bank (relationship banking). The *Hausbank* will usually be the exclusive supplier of all financial services. In addition to lending and corporate financing the *Hausbank* supports the day-to-day business activities of the company through electronic and international banking services, receivable management and treasury activities. Additional services may include rating, and support with applications for public funding.

Even though the importance of the *Hausbank* concept is slowly declining—not least because of the Basel Accords—it still is a dominant factor, in particular with respect to small and medium-sized enterprises. In many situations a business will rely exclusively on its *Hausbank*, usually a savings bank (*Sparkasse)* or a cooperative bank, as a source of credit. Hence, inventory financing, receivables financing, financing of the acquisition of real property or other investments will often be done with the same creditor.

This tradition of extreme relationship banking significantly reduces the need for publicity. Due to the long-term nature of the relationship between the *Hausbank* and its customer, it is a relationship characterised by a substantial degree of mutual trust. This trust is based on the fact that the bank has access to all information regarding the financial situation of the borrower. Consequently, the bank will usually become aware of any attempts by the borrower to obtain credit from another party and to create security rights in assets that are already pledged to the *Hausbank*.

Moreover, not only would it be difficult for the borrower to deceive its bank by using the same collateral twice, it would also be a very risky gamble as in doing so the borrower's relationship with the *Hausbank* would be jeopardised, and with it the very financial foundation on which the business is based. Thirdly, a prospective borrower will have great difficulty obtaining credit from a bank or another source that is not its *Hausbank*. A bank other than the *Hausbank* will be very cautious about giving credit to a business with which it has no pre-existing relationship.

[24] K Melsheimer, *Sicherungsübereignung oder Registerpfandrecht* (Cologne, Springer Fachmedien, 1967) 122.

[25] See eg BGH, 8.12.1998, *Neue Juristische Wochenschrift*, 1999, 940 ff.

[26] On the role of the *Hausbank* in the context of the German financial market see R Elsas, *Die Bedeutung der Hausbank* (Wiesbaden, Deutscher Universitäts Verlag, 2001).

In particular, it will ask for confirmation by the business's *Hausbank* that an asset offered by the business as collateral is not already pledged to the *Hausbank*. In this sense, the *Hausbank* concept fulfils by and large the functions of a notice-filing system: a prospective lender only needs to be aware of the borrower's *Hausbank* in order to know where to turn to for information on the existence of a security right in a given asset. It would make for an interesting research project to explore the role played by the German system of secret security rights in the development of the *Hausbank* concept.

It is obvious, however, that the *Hausbank* concept has ramifications for credit market competition. While it might reduce transaction costs, it potentially hampers the costs of credit as it creates lock-in effects. As we have seen, it is very difficult for a borrower to obtain credit from a source other than its *Hausbank*. In this sense the *Hausbank* has a monopoly over the supply of credit as well as other financial services to the business. This could have the effect that credit costs are higher due to the financial system being based on a strong version of relationship lending. These costs, however, might be offset by gains (from the perspective of the business) through lower financing costs at the beginning of the financial relationship. In this sense, relationship lending may even increase credit availability for emerging or distressed businesses, as a monopolistic creditor envisages that it will be able to share in the future surplus generated by the firm.[27]

This is not an appropriate forum to further examine the efficiency of relationship lending or the German *Hausbank* concept. For the purposes of this chapter, it suffices to draw attention to the fact that the lack of publicity in German secured transactions law is partly compensated for by the strong relationship between a business and its *Hausbank*, which is typical of the German financial market, at least with respect to SMEs. In this sense, secret security rights and relationship lending go hand in hand.

E. New Challenges in a Changing Environment

All in all, the peculiar approach of German law in the field of secured transactions has worked quite well during the last 120 years. There is no evidence that the costs of credit are higher in Germany than in other jurisdictions due to the uncertainty resulting from the non-existence of a registry, or from the fact that the law in this field is not codified but judge made.

For two reasons, however, it is nevertheless not advisable to advocate German law in this field as a role model for law reform in other countries. The first reason is that the German law of secured transactions functions well because it is

[27] M Petersen and R Rajan, 'The Effect of Credit Market Competition on Lending Relationships' (1995) *Quarterly Journal of Economics* 407, 408.

tailor made to fit the very specific conditions of the German financial market and German financing practices. (The sentence is probably also true in reverse, in the sense that the law shaped the financing practices.) In countries with other practices, and in particular in countries where relationship lending plays a less dominant role than in Germany, a registry is probably an indispensable tool to reduce uncertainty.

The other reason is that it is doubtful to what extent the German approach is fit to meet current and future developments. In the following Subsections (i) and (ii) I shall point out two of these trends, which might eventually create pressure on Germany to reform its law in order to bring it into line with the modern approaches to the law of secured transactions.

(i) Growing Importance of Cross-border Transactions

The most obvious disadvantage of German law is the fact that security rights that have been created under German law are largely useless in situations where there is a chance that the collateral will eventually leave German territory.

As virtually all jurisdictions use the *lex rei sitae* to determine the law applicable with respect to property rights in tangibles,[28] the transfer of an asset from one country to another leads to a change in the applicable law. This change often has fatal consequences for German security rights: when an asset that was located in Germany and which is the subject of a (secret) transfer of ownership for security purposes is relocated to another country, the law of the place where the asset is situated will govern the question concerning which security rights exist in the asset. In many instances the new *lex rei sitae* will not recognise the German transfer of ownership for security purposes for its lack of publicity. Hence, the secured creditor loses its security right as a consequence of the relocation of an asset.[29]

Some laws,[30] however, provide for a grace period during which the security right has to be made effective according to the new *lex situs*. If the requirements of the new applicable law to make the security right effective against third parties are satisfied prior to the end of that period, the security right continues to be effective against third parties thereafter under the law of the state where the asset is now located. If, however, the grace period lapses, the creditor will lose his security right.

A similar fate awaits German sellers who have sold goods to a buyer in another jurisdiction. While a simple ROT clause will within the EU often be recognised by

[28] H-P Mansel, Staudinger BGB—EGBGB/IPR Einführungsgesetz zum Bürgerlichen Gesetzbuche/IPR Artikel 43-46 EGBGB (Internationales Sachenrecht) (Berlin, Sellier-de Gryuter, 2015), Art. 43 paras 90 ff.

[29] ibid para 1306.

[30] eg UNCITRAL Legislative Guide on Secured Transactions, Recommendation 45.

the jurisdiction in which the buyer resides,[31] sellers cannot rely on extended ROT clauses in international transactions as other jurisdictions usually do not accept these clauses, at least so far as the security right in the proceeds is concerned.[32] With respect to English law, the *Romalpa* decision,[33] which upheld such a clause, has been 'distinguished out of existence'[34] by subsequent cases.[35] Today, extended ROT clauses are only effective under English law to the extent that they can be characterised as a charge[36] and meet the conditions for third-party effectiveness of a charge, ie registration.[37]

The upshot of this situation is that German exporters cannot use the security rights provided for by German law, as these rights will not be recognised (with the exception of simple ROT clauses) in the jurisdiction of the buyer where the assets will eventually be situated. As a consequence, parties to international sales contracts have to have recourse to letters of credit or other substitutes. Functionally, letters of credit of course go beyond security rights in the sense that they also eliminate the risk of the seller needing to enforce his rights in the buyer's jurisdiction. This function of letters of credit is crucial, particularly if enforcement of a security right may be time consuming and expensive. In such situations, the additional costs of a letter of credit are justified. In other situations, however, it might be more efficient for the parties not to turn to a bank for a letter of credit, but rather to create a security right in the asset. To use a security right, however, is only a viable option if this right will be recognised wherever the asset is subsequently located. Hence, a security right that is recognised worldwide could greatly reduce transaction costs of international sales contracts as it makes letters of credit superfluous, at least in some situations.

This effect gains importance with the ongoing integration of markets worldwide and the growing competition in international trade. In the future, German exporters might perceive it as a structural disadvantage compared to their international competitors that German law cannot offer them security rights (other than ROT clauses) that are recognised internationally. In this sense the internationalisation

[31] In Switzerland according to Art 102 Abs 2, 3 Bundesgesetz über das Internationale Privatrecht [IPRG—Federal Code on Private International Law] only if the ROT clause is registered within three months after the asset has been brought to Switzerland. If that period lapses before registration is effected, the seller loses his rights in the collateral.

[32] Brinkmann (n 4) 334 ff.

[33] *Aluminium Industrie Vaassen BV v Romalpa Aluminium* [1976] 1 WLR 676 per Roskill LJ.

[34] M Bridge, 'Case 5: Motor Cars Supplied and Resold (I), England' in E-M Kieninger (ed), *Security Rights in Movable Property* (Cambridge, Cambridge University Press, 2009), 329.

[35] *Hendy Lennox (Industrial Engines) Ltd v Grahame Puttick Ltd* [1984] 1 WLR 485; Re Andrabell Ltd [1984] 3 All ER 407. See also G McCormack, Secured Credit under English and American Law (Cambridge, Cambridge University Press, 2004) 183.

[36] U Drobnig, 'Recognition and Adaptation of Foreign Security Rights' in U Drobnig, H Snijders and E-J Zippro (eds), *Divergences of Property Law* (Munich, Sellier, 2006) 105, 111.

[37] *Pfeiffer Weinkellerei-Weineinkauf GmbH & Co v Arbuthnot Factors Ltd* [1988] 1 WLR 150; *Compaq Computer Ltd v Abercorn Group Ltd* [1991] BCC 484; Bridge (n 34) 327.

and integration of economic relations will eventually trigger a trend towards the harmonisation or even unification of security rights regimes. German exporters in particular may have much to gain from such a reform.

(ii) New Players on the German Credit Market

German lenders, ie German banks, are by and large satisfied with the status of secured transaction law. They certainly do not push for reform along the lines of the UNCITRAL Model Law or Art 9 UCC.[38] The current system provides not only for very flexible, cost-efficient and at the same time reliable security rights, it also protects—to some extent and probably inadvertently—the market share of German banks as it creates a kind of closed shop on the German credit market. The system as it is makes it very difficult for foreign banks to get a foothold on the German market as it favours—for the reasons described above—lenders that are in the position of a *Hausbank*. For banks that do not yet have an established position on the German market it is very difficult to become the *Hausbank* for a given business as businesses will prefer a bank that is experienced over a newcomer on the market when it comes to selecting a future *Hausbank*. For this reason the German law of secured transactions raises the barriers to entry on the German credit market. For German banks this is advantageous as it is an impediment to prospective competitors.

There are, however, a few symptoms of the demise of the *Hausbank* concept. One is that under the Basel III Accord it might be difficult, or at least unattractive, for a bank to hold all of the risks associated with one borrower in its books. As Basel III promotes the diversification of risks on the part of banks, we might see a trend away from the *Hausbankprinzip* in Germany over the coming years.

Another symptom of the diminishing importance of the *Hausbank* is that over the last few years not only large, but also medium-sized enterprises are beginning to turn to the capital markets for the acquisition of new capital. Hence, the importance of bank credit, and with it the described effect, is—albeit very slowly—declining. A third trend is that some German enterprises such as Siemens or the machinery manufacturer Trumpf have over recent years begun to establish their own banks, particularly since they were dissatisfied with the assistance regarding export financing offered by traditional banks.[39] In order to meet certain regulatory conditions, Siemens, Trumpf, and others established banks that have the purpose of providing finance to their international customers. The success of this new

[38] H-J Lwowski, 'Quiet Creation of Security Interests or Filing' in H Eidenmüller and E-M Kieninger (eds), *The Future of Secured Credit in Europe* (Berlin, De Gruyter, 2008) 174, 178.

[39] *Die Welt*, article dated 4 April 2014, www.welt.de/wirtschaft/article126762093/Warum-Mittelstaendler-jetzt-eigene-Banken-gruenden.

type of bank could prove to be crucial to the future of secured transactions law in Germany. These banks may have a strong interest in the availability of a security right that is recognised not only within Germany, but also in the countries where their business partners are based.

F. Summary

The German law of secured transactions is peculiar, particularly for the fact that under German law secret security rights are permissible. While the pledge provided for in the BGB requires transfer of possession of collateral, parties in practice use the fiduciary transfer of ownership to create security rights. Such a transfer requires neither transfer of (actual) possession nor registration. There is, however, no evidence that the uncertainty which secret security rights might generate has hampered the availability of credit in Germany. This is most probably due to the traditionally strong role relationship lending plays in Germany, particularly with respect to SMEs.

The importance of the *Hausbank*, however, might decline over the following years as financial markets become increasingly integrated. If the described trends gain momentum the tide might eventually shift and the call for a reform of the law of secured transactions will also be heard in Germany.

16

Italian Secured Transactions Law: the Need for Reform

ANNA VENEZIANO

A. Introduction

In recent years, a significant number of national legislators in various parts of the world have undertaken wide-ranging structural reforms in the field of secured transactions. The resulting legal regimes are still quite divergent, especially when European legal systems are compared with each other[1] and with common law jurisdictions that followed the model of Uniform Commercial Code Article 9, as modernised by the Canadian Personal Property Security Acts.[2] All of them, however, shared the assumption that a reform of the outdated, often complex and incoherent pre-existing rules was necessary and would benefit the economy by facilitating access to credit. Secured transactions have also recently been the focus of international harmonisation initiatives, which, while differing in nature (from hard law[3] to various degrees of soft law[4]),

[1] For a comparative overview see U Drobnig, 'Security Rights in Movables' in AS Hartkamp, MW Hesselink, E Hondius, C Mak and E Du Perron (eds), *Towards a European Civil Code*, 4th edn (Alphen aan den Rijn, Wolters Kluwer, 2010) ch 43, 1025; E-M Kieninger (ed), *Security Rights in Movable Property in European Private Law* (Cambridge, Cambridge University Press, 2009). The more recent French and Belgian reforms are discussed in Chs 18 and 19 respectively.

[2] See the contributions in Part I of this volume.

[3] The most successful hard law instrument being, so far, the 2001 Cape Town Convention on International Interests on Mobile Equipment and its Protocol on Matters Specific to Aircraft Equipment (adopted jointly by the Institute for the Unification of Private Law (UNIDROIT) and the International Civil Aviation Organization (ICAO)), with, respectively, 71 and 64 contracting states and the approval of the European Union as Regional Economic Integration Organisation, and more than 700,000 filings in the dedicated electronic international registry operated by Aviareto (a joint venture between the private company SITA SC and the Irish government). On the Cape Town Convention see R Goode, *Convention on International Interests in Mobile Equipment and Protocol Thereto on Matters Specific to Aircraft Equipment, Official Commentary*, 3rd edn (Rome, UNIDROIT, 2013). The texts of the Cape Town Convention and its Protocols and their updated status are available at the UNIDROIT website (www.unidroit.org).

[4] In particular, at a global level, the 2010 Legislative Guide on Secured Transactions and its 2012 Supplement on Electronic Registries by the UN Commission on International Trade Law UNCITRAL (a soft-law product with the aim of paving the way to domestic law reforms) available at www.uncitral.org/pdf/english/texts/security-lg/e/09-82670_Ebook-Guide_09-04-10English.pdf.

scope[5] and geographical sphere of application (both global *and* regional),[6] all recognise the economic relevance of implementing a sound and efficient secured transactions regime (and, if dealing with cross-border transactions, the need to ensure recognition and enforcement of creditors' rights at an international level).[7]

In this context, the Italian legislator has been notably absent. Until recently, it has shown little interest in reconsidering what is, as will be seen in more details below, an admittedly obsolete regime, and limited itself to ad hoc interventions that have not always fulfilled original expectations. Things changed at the end of 2014, when a proposal to entrust the government with the task of drafting an organic reform following a number of predetermined general directions was included in a legislative package mainly devoted to simplifying, modernising and introducing more efficiency in certain aspects of procedural and enforcement law.[8] This action, undertaken directly by the Ministry of Justice, came in the wake of a wider reflection on the inefficiencies of current Italian procedural and substantive creditor protection and their detrimental effect on (foreign) investments.[9] It explicitly mentioned the aim of facilitating access to credit on more favourable conditions, especially for small to medium-sized enterprises. A further element considered in the proposal was the recent reforms undertaken

[5] They range from addressing specific collateral and markets (ie the Cape Town Convention and its Protocols dealing with specific high-value mobile equipment such as aircraft, railway rolling stock and space assets, as well as the instruments in the field of financial markets such as the 2006 Hague Convention on the Law Applicable to Certain Rights in Respect of Securities Held with an Intermediary and the 2009 UNIDROIT (Geneva) Convention on Substantive Rules for Intermediated Securities), to encompassing general secured transactions law (as is the case for the UNCITRAL *Legislative Guide*).

[6] Interestingly, secured transactions have been the object of harmonisation efforts at regional level in various parts of the world, particularly through the technique of the Model Law. As examples see the 2002 Organization of American States (OAS) Model Inter-American Law on Secured Transactions, as well as the 1994 European Bank for Reconstruction and Development (EBRD) Model Law on Secured Transactions aimed at facilitating the transition to capital market economies and the introduction of efficient systems of security rights over movables in Central and Eastern European countries. Additionally, an entire book of the Draft Common Frame of Reference for a European Private Law project (a soft-law academic endeavour) was dedicated to 'Proprietary security in movable assets' (Book IX, in Ch von Bar and E Clive (eds), *Principles, Definitions and Model Rules of European Private Law, Draft Common Frame of Reference (DCFR)*, vol 6 (Munich, Sellier, 2009) 5389 ff; and most recently U Drobnig and O Böger (eds), *Proprietary Security in Movable Assets* (Munich, Sellier, 2015).

[7] This was the primary purpose of the Cape Town Convention and its Protocols. See RCC Cuming, 'International Regulation of Aspects of Security Interests in Mobile Equipment' [1991] *Uniform Law Review* 75; R Goode, 'Transcending the Boundaries of Earth and Space: the Preliminary Draft UNIDROIT Convention on International Interests in Mobile Equipment' [1998] *Uniform Law Review* 52.

[8] Schema di disegno di legge di delega al governo recante disposizioni per l'efficienza del processo civile, la riduzione dell'arretrato, il riordino delle garanzie mobiliari, nonché altre disposizioni per la semplificazione e l'accelerazione del processo di esecuzione forzata (approved on 17.12.2013 and presented to the Parliament on 12.02.2014).

[9] This reflection was shared by the Bank of Italy and the Italian Banking Association (ABI). See also the Document on structural reforms to facilitate economic growth released by the Council of Ministries on 8 April 2014 (Documento di Economia e Finanza 2014–riforme strutturali per favorire la crescita).

(or at the time still pending) in other European countries, in particular France and Belgium, whose secured transactions regime before the reform showed some similarities with Italian law.

In this chapter, I will first give a brief overview of current Italian secured transactions law, with no pretence of completeness, but in order to underline the urgent need for reform; secondly, I will, again briefly, discuss some of the suggestions contained in the most recent legislative proposals. The original draft presented in 2014 was finally not approved as it stood. Despite this, and the fact that the suggested changes were, in some respects, less incisive than they could have been, the proposal is certainly interesting from a comparative perspective and should be considered a reasonable starting point for any future endeavours towards structural improvement of the Italian legal framework on secured transactions.[10]

B. Brief Overview of Current Italian Secured Transactions Law

Italian secured transactions law is characterised by two aspects, which are, at least apparently, in contradiction. On the one hand, the legal devices at the disposal of an enterprise wishing to raise financing using the value of its assets (be they equipment, inventory or receivables) are limited and inefficient. On the other hand, the rules are complex and confused, since a number of exceptions to the equal treatment of creditors (*pari passu* rule) have been incrementally introduced in specialised sectors with no general rethinking of the whole system.[11]

[10] And indeed, two independent legislative initiatives were launched when this volume was in the final stages of editing. The idea of a structural reorganisation in this field resurfaced in a legislative proposal of 12 February 2016 dealing with insolvency law. The proposal contained a provision entitled 'non-possessory security rights' (garanzie non possessorie) which reproduced, but in a shortened and more cautious form, the main directions contained in the 2014 text. Most recently, a new registered non-possessory pledge for enterprises was introduced by Art 1 of governmental Decree 3 May 2016 No 59. The Decree follows at least some of the directions of the previous proposals, especially regarding flexibility of the collateral, publicity and enforcement. It is however still awaiting parliamentary confirmation and some amendments are expected. Both for this reason and the fact that it was approved when this volume had already been typeset, it will not be specifically addressed here.

[11] For an appraisal of current Italian secured transactions law see (in English and French): M Bussani, 'Le présent et l'avenir des sûretés réelles' in *Rapports nationaux italien/Italian National Reports, XVI International Congress of Comparative Law, Brisbane 2002* (Milan, Giuffrè, 2002) 245; G Ferrarini, 'Changes to Personal Property Security in Italy: A Comparative and Functional Approach' in R Cranston, (ed), *Making Commercial Law. Essays in Honour of RM Goode* (Oxford, Oxford University Press, 1997) 477; G Tucci, 'Towards a Transnational Commercial Law for Secured Transactions: the Preliminary Draft UNIDROIT Convention and Italian Law' [1999] *Uniform Law Review*, 371; A Veneziano, 'Italy' in HC Sigman, and E-M Kieninger, *Cross-Border Security over Tangibles* (Munich, Sellier, 2007) 159; M Graziadei and A Candian, 'Italian Report' in Kieninger (ed) (n 1).

(i) Traditional Security Rights over Movables

The 1942 Italian Civil Code in principle only allows for possessory pledges as far as tangible assets are concerned (*pegno con spossessamento*).[12] There is no general consensual non-possessory security right on assets either held for use or to be resold. An exception was, and still is, represented—as is the case in other civil law jurisdictions—by chattel mortgages on easily identifiable goods of relatively high unit value and for which a title registry is set up: ships, aircrafts and motor-vehicles.[13] Such mortgages are, however, subject to cumbersome rules as to their creation, effectiveness and enforcement, which substantially deprive them of commercial attractiveness.

The 'Italian way' of developing new devices in order to satisfy the growing needs of the modern economy was, as has rightly been pointed out, haphazard.[14] As far as tangible goods are concerned, the legislator did not introduce new non-possessory pledges (with limited, more recent exceptions regarding certain specific products of the food industry).[15] Nor did judges (and scholars) recognise parties' freedom in constituting new forms of security over tangibles playing on the relationship between contract and property law. Transfer of property by way of security was indeed struck down by courts as contrary to general principles, among which the well-known prohibition of *pactum commissorium* contained in the Civil Code.[16] Under the impulse of interested economic lobbies or for reasons of national interest, a plethora of so-called 'consensual liens' (*privilegi consensuali*) were incrementally added by special legislation, mostly dealing with enterprise crises and restructuring. Such liens differed markedly as to their scope (but were always limited to specific industry sectors) and were subject to different formal and publicity requirements (invariably cumbersome) as well as to different rules on their priority vis-à-vis competing interests.

Assignment of debt, to which the prohibition of *pactum commissorium* was not deemed to apply, received a less restrictive treatment. The traditional assignment rules in the Civil Code were, however—and still are—incompatible with modern receivable financing techniques, given that formal notice to the account debtor (or the acceptance of the latter in a document containing a certified date) is a strict requirement for effectiveness towards competing third parties and in insolvency.[17] Nor was the problem solved by the legislative introduction of

[12] Italian Civil Code Art 2740(1).

[13] See Italian Maritime Code Art 565 (mortgage over ships) and Art 1027 (mortgage over aircraft); Royal Decree 15.3.1927, No 436, implemented by Law 19.2.1928, No 510; and Italian Civil Code Art 2810 (consensual lien—ie, a mortgage—over motor vehicles).

[14] Tucci (n 11) 378.

[15] See the statutory non-possessory pledges on PDO products kept in warehouses for long periods and subject to transformation, such as cured ham or cheese. More details in Veneziano (n 11) 166.

[16] Italian Civil Code Art 2744.

[17] ibid Art 1265.

simpler rules applicable to commercial receivables, which were in practice only applied to factoring contracts.[18]

(ii) Recent Developments and their Limitations

More recently, the need to adapt the obsolete Italian legal framework to the growing needs of economic operators, and financial institutions especially, has led to some interesting developments. I will focus here on two of them: the introduction of a special 'Bank Charge' on enterprise assets, and the recognition of revolving pledges and transfer of property (also) by way of security for financial collateral. They certainly represent important steps towards a modernisation of a clearly outdated regime. They are, however, confined to specialised and restricted sectors; the first of them, moreover, failed to achieve its practical purpose.

A reform of the Banking Law in 1993 introduced a special 'non-possessory lien' in favour of banks only, regulated in its Article 46 (*privilegio ex Art 46*, hereinafter 'Article 46 Bank Charge') to secure medium- to long-term financing to enterprises. The Article 46 Bank Charge replaced a veritable maze of different pre-existing consensual liens and is indeed more accurately described as a 'charge', being the result of an agreement between the parties, connected to a loan, and requiring publicity (though registration) in order to be opposable to third parties. Whilst, in theory, Article 46 could have been the basis for the creation of a veritable enterprise floating security, the uncertainties regarding the revolving effect as pertains to future inventory,[19] its priority against other security rights,[20] and the limited effectiveness of its enforcing procedures[21] have rendered its use unattractive in practice.

A second important step forward was the judicial and scholarly recognition (at least to some extent and with some interpretative uncertainties) of the revolving pledge on intangibles (in particular, financial collateral). This development was subsequently backed by the legislator and finally sanctioned by the implementation of the EU Directive on Financial Collateral Arrangements ('Collateral Directive').[22]

[18] Law of 21.02.1991, No 52. See Ferrarini (n 11) 477.

[19] A literal reading of the legislative provision, backed by the Bank of Italy, denies the revolving character of the security as to inventory, see critically Tucci (n 11).

[20] As between Art 46 creditors, a simple first-to-file rule would be applied. All other competing limited rights on the assets prevail over the Bank Charge if created with an 'ascertained date' (*data certa*) that antedates registration of the charge. In practice, it would be difficult for a lender to determine whether a prior-in-time interest prevails over its security since the ascertainment of the date is not done through a public filing but through notarisation or authentication by a public official, and is mainly a way to prevent fraud. In insolvency, moreover, the creditor is postponed to a number of preferred claims that enjoy higher priority. For more details see Veneziano (n 11).

[21] The Banking Law did not in fact modify the ordinary rules of enforcement (Civil Procedural Code Arts 502 ff), which require a judicial decision and formal (and lengthy) enforcement proceedings, aiming at liquidation. On enforcement see in particular Tucci (n 11) 378.

[22] Directive 47/2002/CE [2002] OJ L168/43 was implemented in Italy by Legislative Decree 21.05.2004, No 170. Its subsequent amendment through Directive 2009/44/EC [2009] OJ L146/37 was implemented by Legislative Decree 24.03.2011, No 48.

In the context of this contribution regarding general secured transaction laws, two elements relating to the specialised field of financial collateral are particularly worth mentioning.

The first one is that the implementation of the Collateral Directive introduced a number of relevant derogations from the general rules applicable to secured transactions in Italy. Among other things, it sanctioned the admissibility and enforceability of both pledges and transfers of title or assignments of debt, also by way of security; it dramatically reduced the formalities for constituting and enforcing the security; it confirmed the right to use the encumbered financial collateral without requiring further action to ensure the validity or effectiveness of the pledge; it dramatically reinforced creditors' rights in insolvency; finally, it allowed self-help enforcement provisions, including appropriation if parties so agree and provided an objective evaluation mechanism. This in turn forced the legislator to formally repeal the traditional prohibition of *pactum commissorium* as regards financial collateral. It is especially the latter aspect concerning enforcement measures that, in my opinion, may be of particular interest in the perspective of an organic reform of secured transactions law, as will be seen below.

The second element concerns the scope of application of the Collateral Directive. Originally, the Directive only applied to financial collateral defined as 'financial instruments' and 'cash', where at least one of the parties was a public authority, central bank or financial institution (and the secured party had possession or 'control' over the collateral).[23] In 2009 the European legislator amended the Directive, inter alia expanding the notion of financial collateral to encompass not only financial instruments and cash, but also 'credit claims', ie loans granted by banks to firms.[24] In relation to this latter type of financial collateral, however, not all the provisions of the Directive apply: this is notably the case for right of use of financial collateral under security financial collateral arrangements.[25] In addition, Member States were given the option to introduce further exceptions to the general regime and to continue requiring formal acts for the effectiveness of collateral arrangements concerning credit claims in relation to (the debtor and) third parties. It is worth noting that the Italian legislator took advantage of the latter option and retained the publicity requirements of the Civil Code on third-party enforceability of assignments of credit claims.[26] I believe that this choice, while

[23] See H Beale, M Bridge, L Gullifer and E Lomnicka, *The Law of Security and Title-Based Financing*, 2nd edn (Oxford, Oxford University Press, 2012) 34.

[24] According to Art 2(1)(o) of the Directive, 'credit claims' are 'pecuniary claims arising out of an agreement whereby a credit institution, as defined in Art 4(1) of Banking Consolidation Directive 2006/48/EC of 14 June 2006 relating to the taking up and pursuit of the business of credit institutions [2006] OJ L 177, including the institutions listed in Art 2 of that Directive, grants credit in the form of a loan'.

[25] Article 5 of the Directive.

[26] See the new paragraph in Art 3 of Legislative Decree 21.05.2004, No 170, introduced by Legislative Decree 24.03.2011, according to which enforceability as against third parties for collateral arrangements on credit claims is still subject to the publicity requirements of the Italian Civil Code (notification to or acceptance by the account debtor).

effectively retaining an antiquated rule regarding enforceability of assignments of debts against third parties, may be seen, in perspective, as a blessing in disguise. It would enable a future legislator undertaking an organic reform to consider in that wider context which publicity and priority rules may be more suitable for general secured transactions law as opposed to a specialised sector such as that of financial markets.

(iii) Asset-based Acquisition Finance Devices

Italian law does recognise some title-based devices in the context of acquisition finance, in particular retention of title and financial lease. They are usually not classified as security rights but as ownership vested in the vendor/lessor. Thus, the requirements for admissibility and effectiveness are completely different from those applicable to traditional security devices.[27]

The 1942 Italian Civil Code, adopting a rather modern approach for the time, already provided specific rules on instalment sales and the effects of retention of title clauses in a sales contract.[28] Unlike in most other (especially European) jurisdictions, retention of title in certain items, ie 'machinery'[29] whose value exceeds what has now become a negligible sum[30] is also subject to registration, in the registry kept at the Tribunale (first instance court) of the place where the asset is located at the time of the stipulation. It is important to note, however, that the seller's rights are protected only as against *sub-buyers* (superseding the general bona fide acquisition provision in Article 1153 of the Civil Code), only in relation to the specific asset that was sold, and only if that asset remains within the jurisdiction of the same Tribunale.[31] In relation to competing creditors (in particular execution or judgment creditors) and also as against an insolvency administrator, the retention of title does not have to be filed, though it must be previously agreed upon in writing between the parties, confirmed in the sale invoices, with ascertained date prior to the date of attachment and duly registered in the buyer's accounts.[32] Moreover, only simple retentions of title not extending to proceeds or products of the original assets are allowed.

[27] Graziadei and Candian (n 11).

[28] Italian Civil Code Arts 1523–1526.

[29] With the exception of assets that are registered in public registries.

[30] Italian Civil Code Art 1524(2): € 15.49—the amount has never been adjusted to the decrease in value of the nominal sum in Italian old *lire*.

[31] In the case of equipment exceeding the value of €258.23 an additional requirement of a marking—a plate containing the seller's name and its property right in the machine as well as particulars concerning the machine—is provided for by special legislation, but again only to protect the title-retaining seller from sub-buyers.

[32] This is the resulting regulation after the implementation of the 35/2000/EC Late Payment Directive (Legislative Decree No 231/2002, Art 11(3)) and the decision of the European Court of Justice of 26.10.2006, *Commission v Italy*, C-302/05, according to which Italy did not fail to implement the Directive by providing for additional acts on the part of the seller in order for the title retention to be opposable to the buyer's creditors.

It is interesting to note that the registry for the retention of title is the same one that should be used also for an Article 46 Bank Charge. This did not result, however, in any coordination of the priority rules, even as between the two registrable interests, and was apparently done solely to avoid the setting up of another registry.[33] The question is considered to be of little practical importance due to the scant attention that the Article 46 Bank Charge has received until now in financing practice.

In sum, as far as retention of title under a sales contract is concerned, its statutory rules make it impractical to use on a large scale in commercial transactions.

Leasing, on the other hand, is widely used for equipment assets. The main reasons for its success, besides the fiscal ones, are the relatively rapid conclusion of the contract, the lack of formalities (as opposed to the granting of a traditional security right but also of a retention of title), the simple enforcement procedures and its high priority in insolvency, the lessor being deemed the 'true owner' of the goods.

C. Some Thoughts on Recent Plans for Legislative Reform

As already noted, the legislative proposal presented in February 2014 had the—limited—purpose of empowering the government to embark on an organic reform of secured transactions law, following a number of fundamental principles and directions on which any subsequent legislative act should have been based. It represented, therefore, a 'kick-off' of sorts for further governmental action. It is my belief that the vast majority of goals it wished to achieve are still worth considering within the framework of the wider comparative reflection provided in this volume and, despite some shortcomings and limitations, should at least provide a useful starting point for any future reform project in Italy.[34]

(i) The Reform Strategy: Generalisation of a Non-possessory Security Right, Publicity, Flexibility and Easier Enforcement

The explanatory report to the legislative proposal highlighted the reasons for a reform in the area of security rights over movables referring both to the fragmentary nature of current law and to its inability to meet the needs of modern

[33] For this comment and a review of what could be the abstractly possible solutions as to the relative priorities see Veneziano (n 11) 173.

[34] As witnessed by the legislative proposal approved by the Council of Ministries on 12 February 2016 (n 10) which basically followed, though with a less detailed and more cautious approach, the main directions contained in the older text. For the most recent Decree on a 'non-possessory pledge' see above (n 10).

economy. The overall goals of the reform endeavour should therefore be a simplification and rationalisation of the applicable rules, to enhance their predictability and accessibility, as well as the introduction of a regime that would be more flexible and efficient, thereby aligning Italian law with the most recent developments at European and international level.

In order to reach these goals, Article 4 of the proposal listed several criteria that would serve as a general guidance for future governmental legislative activity. First and foremost, it envisaged a generalisation of a non-possessory security right over movables,[35] which is currently only admissible on specific collateral (and with different rules depending on the collateral). Thus, from being considered an exception to the general rule that the debtor should be dispossessed, the non-possessory pledge would became the norm, independently of the type of asset on which it were created.

More precisely, the opposability of the security right against third parties would not depend on dispossession anymore, but the latter would be replaced by a new publicity mechanism based on a unified, debtor-based, publicly accessible and entirely electronic registry, devoted only to security rights over movables and enabling electronic consultation and filing (including modifications, renewals and termination). Such a registry would determine the opposability and priority rank of the security right vis-à-vis third parties.[36]

Furthermore, it would be possible to constitute a valid and enforceable security not only on precisely identified assets, but also on collateral determined by reference to a general category or type (such as stock, inventory etc) and to an overall value, provided that mechanisms for the subsequent identification of future assets were included.[37]

Unless otherwise agreed by the parties, the security provider would have the right to use the collateral (in keeping with its intended use) as well as to dispose of the collateral. The creditor's priority would be transferred on to the proceeds or products. The same kind of flexibility would be admitted in relation to the secured credit or credits (be they present or future and even resulting from a not-yet-existing relationship), provided that a maximum amount of indebtedness were established.

[35] Interestingly, the proposal does not use the expression *pegno non possessorio* (non-possessory pledge) but the more neutral term *garanzia mobiliare* (security right over movables). A similar terminology is used in the new legislative proposal of 12 February 2016 (*garanzia mobilare senza spossessamento*). See also Section ii.

[36] The new proposal of 12 February 2016, unlike the previous one, seems to indicate that registration may be required also for the creation of the security right and not only for its opposability to third parties. Whether such a requirement would end up being too burdensome for the parties will depend on additional factors including the type of documents or information that should be registered, the accessibility of the registry and the measures introduced to preserve the confidentiality of the information.

[37] The reference to a general category or type and to an overall value is not reproduced in the new proposal of 12 February 2016.

A further point connected to the flexibility of the secured credit concerned the introduction of a so-called 'rechargeable hypothec on movables', a special type of security based on the example of the French reform of 2006[38] (but recently repealed and then reinstated with a more limited scope by the French legislator)[39] that would extend to different or additional credits with no need to determine them in advance.[40]

As regards enforcement of the security right, the proposal abolished the prohibition of the *pactum commissorium* contained in the Italian Civil Code and advocated that the efficiency of enforcement measures be strengthened, with due consideration for the protection of the debtor's interests. More generally, a substantial part of the proposal was devoted to the simplification and acceleration of credit enforcement procedures (regardless of the existence of a proprietary security right).

In conclusion, Article 4 strongly enhanced party autonomy. As a balance, it introduced both a publicity system that would guarantee transparency and predictability, and rules protecting the debtor's interest, by limiting the extent of its liabilities and both debtor and third parties by monitoring creditors' actions in enforcement proceedings. A final point in Article 4, moreover, entrusted the government with the general task of including further limitations of parties' autonomy in consumer credit contracts.

(ii) An Appraisal of the Reform Strategy: A Step in the Right Direction with Some Caveats

Before considering the merits—and shortcomings—of the legislative proposal, it should be noted once again that it did not contain a fully-fledged statutory reform, but delegated the power to draft a legislative decree following specified policy goals to the government. Should such guidance ever be implemented, it would be necessary to address a number of additional issues, some of them requiring further policy decisions that were not directly envisaged. Thus, while many of the criteria that were listed may represent desirable outcomes, their general nature makes it difficult to understand how exactly they would be translated into detailed legislative action.[41]

[38] The French *hypothèque rechargeable* was introduced by Ordonnance 23.6.2006 No 346, portant réforme des sûretés (Art 2422 Code civil and Arts L313-14, L313-14-1, L313-14-2 Code de la consommation). Its aim was to allow that a plurality of credits be secured by a single deed, with the possibility to add new credits or substitute old ones at any time during the duration of the security. See L Aynés and P Crocq, 'Les suretés—la publicité foncière' in P Malaurie and L Aynés (eds), *Droit civil*, 9th edn (Paris, Defrénois, 2015) 353.

[39] Article 46 of Law 17 March 2014 (JO 18 mars 2014), loi relative la consommation. The Parliament decided to repeal it essentially because it was feared that it could easily lead to over-indebtedness of the consumer. In practice, however, this device was rarely used. The legislator decided to reintroduce it with Article 48 of Law 20 December 2014 limiting it to professional credits only. Aynes and Crocq (n 38) 356.

[40] This device was wisely dropped in the new reform proposal of 12 February 2016.

[41] The same caveat applies in regard to the new proposal of 12 February 2016.

Having said this, an appraisal of whether the proposal was a step in the right direction is certainly possible. To this end, I will focus on two points in particular that I see as veritable cornerstones for any future reform: the setting-up of a public electronic registry on the one hand, and the enhancement of parties' autonomy in the enforcement of the security right on the other. I will also, however, attend to what were, in my opinion, the most relevant drawbacks of the proposal, namely the failure to expressly address the issue of the opposability of creditors' rights in insolvency proceedings (including any conflicts with non-consensual liens), and the failure to clearly define what was meant by 'security right' and to expressly adopt a 'functional' approach as regards the scope of the intended reform. It should be underlined that such limitations were by no means unintentional: in particular, the proposal was purposely silent on insolvency law, since additional legislative changes had just been introduced and a wider organic reform in this field was in the pipeline.[42]

The proposal, as was seen above, expressly directed the government to tie the third-party effects of a security right with a public registration system and to set up a dedicated registry for this purpose. Public registration of a security right is indeed a time-honoured solution to the problem of admitting non-possessory security rights in Italian law, and not only for uniquely identifiable, high-value mobile collateral such as aircraft or ships, for which a title registry exists. Consensual 'liens' or charges provided by special legislation were and are characterised by registration, and even sales with retention of title are supposed to be registered (though only for the purpose of superseding the good-faith acquisition rule). The main differences with the more modern approach envisaged in the reform proposal lie in several interconnected factors: the introduction of a unified registry for the general non-possessory security right, which would displace the fragmented and inefficient current regimes; the development of sophisticated software for electronic filing, which would provide a more efficient and cost-effective solution; the exclusive purpose of the registry (ie solving the priority conflicts between the secured creditor and third parties, and not addressing other aspects such as the validity of the security right as such or title issues);[43] and finally, the acceptance of a clear-cut first-to-file priority rule.[44]

Admittedly, a number of key aspects of the future publicity regime were not clarified. In particular, while the proposal admitted the creation of a floating lien on inventory (and probably also book debts), there was no mention of whether

[42] The proposal of 12 February 2016 does address, in a separate provision, the issue of the simplification of the existing non-possessory liens in insolvency. The Government is entrusted with the task of reducing their number, taking into account that some of them may be obsolete, and of rearranging the priority rules. Nothing is expressly stated, however, on the opposability of the new security right in insolvency, except that the relationship between enforcement procedures and insolvency proceedings should be regulated.

[43] As already noted (n 36) this issue is not as clear in the new proposal of 12 February 2016.

[44] On this point the new proposal of 12 February 2016 appears to take a step back and only directs the Government to 'regulate the priority conflict arising from multiple filings'.

the priority rules should be differentiated according to whether the third parties were creditors with security rights on the same asset, lien or judgment creditors, or subsequent buyers in the ordinary course of business. Moreover, a correct functioning of the priority rules as envisaged would, in my view, require the adoption of a 'notice-filing' in lieu of the more traditional 'transactional-filing' approach, but nothing was specified on this point either. All these aspects should be kept in mind when proceeding with an organic reform. Furthermore, the accompanying explanatory report to the proposal aptly envisaged that the registry fee be diversified depending on the operation (a lower fee would be levied for mere consultation) but should not in any case be excessive. This is again an element that should be considered in future legislation.

Overall, however, the new publicity system would be perfectly compatible with existing Italian law and would provide a more efficient solution to priority issues than the current haphazard and diversified regimes.

Turning to the issue of enforcement of secured creditors' rights upon debtors' default, the need to improve and modernise Italian law in this area is undeniable. The current regime is excessively cumbersome when the suppler provisions of the possessory pledge are not applicable, and relies on outdated techniques to protect the debtor and third parties, namely imposing formal judicial proceedings and public enforcement measures as well as sanctioning the invalidity of certain parties' agreements. The clear statement in the proposal that the general prohibition of *pactum commissorium* should be abandoned is to be welcomed, also in light of the fact that even the most traditionally oriented national laws in this respect show a clear tendency to move away from a strict interpretation of the requirement, not only in very specialised areas, such as financial collateral, but in general.[45]

The proposal is admittedly rather vague on the issue of how to achieve more simplicity and efficiency in enforcement and on what would be the measures to protect the debtor (and, I would add, third parties),[46] though it does emphasise the need to introduce stricter limitations on party autonomy when the debtor is a consumer. I would submit that using *ex post* evaluation of the exercise of enforcement rights through the application of a standard of 'commercial reasonableness' in business-to-business transactions would be perfectly acceptable in Italian law.

As already mentioned, there is one aspect of secured transactions law on which the proposal was silent, ie the opposability of the security right in insolvency proceedings. It almost goes without saying that any structural reform in this area should expressly determine the extent to which a security right survives insolvency and address the interaction with insolvency legislation. Furthermore, additional thought should be given to reorganising the current opaque and extremely

[45] See for example Art 2348 of the French code civil, as modified by the 2006 French secured transactions law reform, which considers such agreements valid.

[46] The need to introduce measures to protect 'third parties who contracted with the debtor when it was in possession of the collateral' is expressly mentioned in the new proposal of 12 February 2016, though nothing more specific is provided at this stage.

complex regime of non-consensual liens, especially in insolvency. The recent creation of an ad hoc Commission to study the feasibility of an organic reform of insolvency law, including a possible simplification of the rules applying to non-consensual liens, is a welcome step in this direction. It would be important that this work be properly coordinated with any substantive law reform efforts in this area.[47]

Finally, a word about the definition of what is meant by 'security right over movables' and the scope of application of the proposed reform. Article 4 purposely avoided the use of technical terminology to refer to the type of agreement that should be covered by the new regime. It did not use any of the traditional terms (*pegno* ('pledge'), *ipoteca mobiliare* (hypothec over movables), *privilegio consensuale* (consensual lien)) but preferred to adopt the more neutral expression *garanzia mobiliare* (security right over movables), an innovation as far as Italian legislative and judicial language is concerned. Effectively, any issue regarding a more precise definition of the scope was shifted to the future drafters.[48]

In principle, this left open the opportunity of embracing (or at least discussing the feasibility of) a more functional approach to secured transactions. Retention of title devices, especially in sales contracts, leap to mind in this regard. On the one hand, existing international instruments have clearly opted for an inclusive approach concerning retention of title devices.[49] On the other hand, this issue in relation to national law is far from uncontroversial, especially as regards European jurisdictions,[50] and it represents a difficult point on which one should tread carefully. In any case, however, it is my firm belief that a legislator considering an organic reform of secured transactions should—at the very least—openly acknowledge that there are other contractual devices that, in practice, despite a different formal allocation of title on the assets as between the two parties, fulfil the function of securing a creditor's claim with an *in rem* right that is opposable to third parties. There may be good reasons to treat retention of title differently from more traditional security rights, and indeed uniform law instruments in this

[47] This remains true also under the proposal of 12 February 2016, which does not regulate the issue either.

[48] The new proposal of 12 February 2016 follows a similar approach, referring to 'non-possessory security rights' (*garanzie non possessorie*).

[49] See the Cape Town Convention on International Interests in Mobile Equipment (n 3) covering not only traditional (limited) rights *in rem* (an agreement granting—or transferring—a property right to secure a loan), but also finance devices based on retention of title, such as a conditional sale and a lease (Conv Art 2(2)). Likewise the UNCITRAL Legislative Guide on Secured Transactions (n 4) shows a marked preference for including retention of title devices in the overall secured transactions regime (see in particular paras 101–112 and Recommendation 8). A similar approach is followed by regional instruments. Particularly interesting, in this respect, is Book IX of the Draft Common Frame of Reference (n 6), which covers both contractual 'security rights' and 'ownership retained under retention of ownership devices': DCFR, Art IX 101.

[50] A discussion of this issue in respect to European jurisdictions can be found in E-M Kieninger, 'Evaluation: A Common Core? Convergences, Subsisting Differences and Possible Ways for Harmonisation' in Kieninger (n 1) 647.

field have all recognised some degree of flexibility in this respect.[51] Such a choice, however, should be embraced in a transparent way, taking into account the economic purpose of the device rather than, exclusively, its formal legal structure. The seller's claims should be openly weighed against the interests of other competitors over the value of the assets, and, possibly, all devices fulfilling an analogous economic purpose should be subject to the same treatment, at least regarding priority rules, again notwithstanding their formal legal structure.

D. Concluding Remarks

In this contribution, the need for an organic reform of Italian secured transactions law was highlighted and the key points of a recent attempt to put this subject on the legislative agenda were critically discussed. Notwithstanding the limitations that were flagged in the preceding paragraphs, I believe that the general criteria contained in the recent legislative proposals are still of value and could indeed be seen as a sound basis on which to build more comprehensive reform.

[51] For the Cape Town Convention see M Deschamps, 'The Perfection and Priority Rules of the Cape Town Convention and the Aircraft Protocol—A Comparative Law Analysis' (2013) *Cape Town Convention Journal* 51, 53, available at www.ingentaconnect.com/content/hart/ctcj/2013/00002013/00000001/art00004. For the UNCITRAL Legislative Guide see S Bazinas, 'The UNCITRAL Draft Legislative Guide on Secured Transactions' [2005] *Uniform Law Review* 141.

17

The Still Uncompleted Evolution of the French Law on Secured Transactions Towards Modernity

JEAN-FRANCOIS RIFFARD*

A. Introduction

Did the French law of secured transactions miss the turn of modernity? Such a question must still be asked after the reform that occurred on 23 March 2006 with the adoption of a governmental ordinance relating to security rights in general. For almost two centuries the French law presented only few differences from the secured transactions laws of other countries, all of these laws based on the single figure of the possessory pledge. But the situation changed radically in the late twentieth century, when the legislatures of most Western countries forced them to adapt their secured transactions laws to the new requirements of commercial practice, within a context of increasing globalisation. Some chose to ignore the past and built a brand new and original law. Others preferred to adapt their existing laws. The French Parliament chose a middle way based on its history and traditional concepts of personal property security law, but modified in such a manner as to fit the requirements of commercial practice. Many commentators feared, however, that these legislative efforts were insufficient for a competitive French law.

The adaptation of the law on secured transactions to the evolution of the French, and even international, economic and commercial environments has always been problematic. The evolution of the law has long been hindered by the absolute requirement of the dispossession of the grantor. As a first step towards a necessary modernisation, the French legislator chose to circumvent the rule in an indirect and fragmentary manner through limited statutory exceptions. It was not until 2006 that the legislature finally agreed to abandon the rule of dispossession by establishing a non-possessory pledge.

* Professor of Law, University of Auvergne, School of Law.

Should we conclude that the reform was not a success, or worse, a complete failure? Such an overly pessimistic conclusion should be moderated. Even though there were mistakes and regrettable shortcomings that have somewhat weakened its scope, the reform is based on solid and modern fundamental principles in line with the key fundamental principles of most of the reforms implemented in foreign countries, and recommended by international bodies such as the United Nations Commission on International Trade Law (UNCITRAL).

B. The Origins: The Era of Dispossession

(i) The Reign of the Dispossession Rule

Until the nineteenth century, the French secured transactions law was governed by the fundamental rule of dispossession of the grantor. Article 2076 of the Civil Code of 1804 stated that 'the pledge remains efficient as long as this pledge has been and still remains in the possession of the creditor or a third party agreed upon by the parties'. Until 2006 the French Cour de cassation deduced/assumed from this text that the dispossession of the grantor was a condition for the validity of the pledge.

This establishment of the rule of dispossession was, however, the result of a long struggle for influence between proponents of Germanic customs, which only recognised the possessory pledge, and supporters of the chattel mortgage. A brief reminder of this evolution will allow a better understanding of the relationships between French law and non-possessory security rights.

From an historical point of view, there was no fundamental reason for not recognising a chattel mortgage in French law. The Romans, indeed, knew such a mortgage, designed as an improvement on the pledge (pignus). Its regime was very flexible and efficient as it gave full protection to the creditor despite its occult nature.

With the collapse of the Roman Empire in the fifth century, the chattel mortgage disappeared from French law under the influence of the barbaric custom '*meuble n'ont pas de suite par hypothèque*'. After the official drafting of the custom, the possessory pledge became the unique security right recognised by French law. The desire to protect both third parties and the secured creditor motivated this consecration. The security of commercial transactions was a guarantee that third parties could trust in the ostensible ownership of the possessor of a tangible asset. In addition, it was not conceivable to organise an effective system of publicity of non-possessory rights in movables, because the encumbered assets were generally of little value and easily saleable. Lastly, the requirement of dispossession was reinforced by the consecration of the rule that in matters of movables, possession is equivalent to title.[1]

[1] Code civil (C civ) Art 2276.

The pledge has nonetheless for a long time held a central place in the French law, as it was adapted to the needs of an agricultural society. However, the regime of the pledge was extremely rigorous, particularly with regard to the form. The secured creditor could not enforce his pledge against third parties unless it was established by deed or under private deed, duly registered, containing the statement of the amount of the secured claim, as well as the species and nature of the encumbered assets.

Reflecting the ancestral distrust of the creditor, drafters of the Civil Code had strictly regulated the enforcement of the pledge. According to former Article 2078, the creditor could not freely dispose of a pledge after default of the debtor. He could either have a court request that the encumbered asset remain in payment and up to the amount of the debt, according to an estimate by experts, or he could be authorised to sell the assets by auction. Any clause allowing the creditor to appropriate the pledge *pacte commissoire* or dispose of it without the formalities of the auction *clause de voie parée* was null and void, unless it was agreed after the conclusion of the security agreement.

At the beginning of the nineteenth century, dispossession appeared as a necessity; however, the traditional form of pledge would soon reach its limits, particularly due to the emergence of new types of personal property of high value, especially in the commercial field. The formal requirements slowed the conclusion of commercial transactions and the requirement of dispossession was incompatible with the need for the merchant to continue to dispose of the encumbered assets. Industrial development and the development of credit that followed led to a crucial need for non-possessory security devices. Under pressure from traders and bankers, the French legislator was made to adapt the old pledge to this new environment.

(ii) First Attempts to Adapt the Pledge to Business Practices

As a first step, the French legislator chose to relax the regime of the pledge without abandoning the requirement of dispossession. In the face of such a lack of ambition, merchants tried by themselves to adapt the requirement of dispossession through conventional agreements.

(a) Creation of a Commercial Pledge

The commercial pledge[2] was established by the law of 23 May 1863. Contrary to what the business community had hoped, this law did not establish a comprehensive and homogeneous regime, but had on a few points relaxed the regime of the pledge when it secured a commercial claim, regardless of the nature of the encumbered asset and the quality of the parties. These special provisions, which

[2] J Hamel, 'Le gage commercial, Etudes de droit commercial' (Dalloz, 1953).

survived the reform of 2006, focus on two points.[3] First, the commercial pledge may be proved by any means when the grantor and the creditor are traders. Second, enforcement of the pledge has been made easier. Upon the default of the debtor, the creditor must simply notify to the grantor his intention to sell the collateral by auction and wait for a period of eight days. An auction is not necessary if the collateral can be traded on a stock exchange. Except for these provisions, the commercial pledge remains subject to the rules of the Civil Code.

(b) *Softening of the Rule of Dispossession*

One of the most important consequences of the Industrial Revolution was the development of inventory. It was important that manufacturers could enhance their inventory, providing them with the guarantee of credit necessary for the development of their businesses. However, they were quickly confronted by the limits of the possessory pledge. It was obviously not an option for the grantor to transfer the possession of his stocks to the creditor, as they were essential to his activity. Similarly, the creditor had neither the will nor the material capacity to store the encumbered goods.

Using the notion of symbolic dispossession, French traders developed the technique of the pledge with no shifting of inventory.[4] A creditor usually leased a grantor's room or part of a grantor's room in which the inventory was stored. To inform third parties about its rights, the secured creditor could post a notice on the wall or organise a permanent guard.

This technique was improved in 1848 with the field warehousing system, *warrant des magasins généraux*, which still exists. The grantor can store his goods in a warehouse, approved and controlled by the State, in exchange for a receipt that he must deliver to his creditor. With this receipt, the creditor can, in case of default, take possession of the goods and sell them. In 1863,[5] the pledge of Bill of Lading, which is another good example of pledge on symbolic instrument, was established in the same way.

(iii) Limited Statutory Exceptions to the Requirement of Dispossession

All these different mechanisms were only an expedient, not challenging the rule of dispossession. Nevertheless, the dogmatic position of the legislator became more and more untenable with the Industrial Revolution. There was a strong demand from traders and merchants for the recognition of a new non-possessory security

[3] Commercial code (C com) Arts L521-1 and L521-3.

[4] R Roblot, Les sûretés mobilières sans déplacement', in Liber Amicorum G. Ripert "Le droit privé français au milieu du XXe siècle", t. 2, (Paris, 1950) 362

[5] Statute of 23 May 1863.

right, and, at the beginning of the nineteenth century, the legislator had no choice but to accept the passing of statutes that enabled lenders to acquire certain non-possessory interests in their debtors' property. However, he refused to abandon the general rule of dispossession and he only created, on a case-by-case basis, special non-possessory security devices. Unfortunately, this was done in a disordered way. As a result, it led to a very disparate set of security rights, as shown by the terminological vagueness. Some of these new security devices have been named *gage sans dépossession* (non-possessory pledge) or *hypothèque mobilière* (chattel mortgage), and others *nantissement* or even *warrant.*

The common point of all these new devices lies in the creation of a system of registries organised on a real basis. This has been made possible because the assets subject to these non-possessory rights are easy enough to identify and dissociate. Unfortunately, the legislator created for each of these securities a special registry managed by different agencies.

It may be useful, therefore, to have a quick overview of these special non-possessory security devices, as they all survived the 2006 reform.

(a) Security Rights on Agricultural Equipment

It was in the agriculture sector that Parliament created the first non-possessory security right in 1898 in the form of the *warrant agricole*, now ruled by Article L. 342-1 of the Rural Code.[6] At that time, it was a necessity to enable farmers to encumber their crops and harvests in order to access credit. This non-possessory pledge allowed the grantor to engage both his inventory and professional assets and gave to the secured creditor a fictitious right of retention over the assets. The *warrant agricole* is made effective against third parties by a registration on a special register, held by the clerk's office of the local county court (Tribunal d'Instance). Even though this form of pledge has some advantages, it has not been a success in practice.

A simplified variant of the *warrant agricole* appeared in 1935[7] in the winery sector. Called *engagement de garantie du stock de vin* by the law and 'warrant vinicole' in business practice,[8] this device is strictly reserved to producers of wines, excluding traders. The encumbered assets can only be a stock of wine in a cellar and not a growing crop. The *warrant vinicole* must be registered in a special registry held by the *Administration des contributions indirectes* but, curiously, it is still a secret security right as this registry is not accessible to the public. Nevertheless, the 'warrant vinicole' is opposable *erga omnes.*

[6] A Dupuis-Fiore, 'Le warrant agricole, une sûreté à redécouvrir' in *Clés pour le siècle* (Dalloz, 2000) 789 ff; I Couturier, v° 'Warrant Agricole' in *Répertoire de droit civil (Dalloz, 2009).*

[7] Decree-Law of October 23, 1935 repealed by Decree 2003-851 of 1 September 2003, now Art. 661 and 662 Code Rural Ancien

[8] A De Brosses, 'Les garanties réelles vinicoles' (1998) 58 *Banque et Droit* 9 ff; A Jauffret, 'Les sûretés réelles sur les vins' in *Liber Amicorum VOIRIN (LGDJ, 1967)* 423.

(b) Non-possessory Security Rights on Transportation Vehicles

Transportation vehicles such as motor cars, shipping and aircraft are easily identifiable movables and with significant value. Therefore, they fit perfectly all the requirements for setting up a registration system based on a real criterion similar to the real estate recording system that already existed. The legislator created a chattel mortgage on boats in 1874, on ships in 1917 and finally on aircraft in 1926.[9] These different chattel mortgages are all subject to a similar regime. They must be evidenced in writing and registered in specialised asset-based registers held in the local commercial court or in the ministry in charge of civil aviation for the chattel mortgage on aircraft.

To support the automotive industry sector, Parliament also established in 1934 a new non-possessory pledge in favour of sellers of motor vehicles. Any sale of a motor vehicle should, on pain of nullity, automatically and legally establish a non-possessory pledge in favour of the seller/creditor. Notwithstanding the undeniable benefits to the creditor, the *gage automobile* fell into disuse, and this is the reason why its regime was improved by the reform of 23 March 2006.[10]

(c) Non-possessory Security Rights on Professional Equipment

All the assets of a business, both intangible and tangible, have to be maximised in order to secure all the credit necessary to its proper functioning, however it is also impossible for a business to transfer, as a security purpose, the possession of certain of its assets. In consequence, the legislature created a new *nantissement du matériel et de l'outillage*[11] by statute of 18 January 1951.[12] The regime of this new non-possessory pledge was not attractive enough to make it a success. The *nantissement* can be granted only to the seller of professional equipment, and must be registered in a special register held by the clerk's office of the local commercial court. This registration is a condition of validity of the security rights and not only a question of third-party effectiveness. Contrary to what he had decided for other special non-possessory rights, the legislator did not recognise a fictitious right of retention, which weakens the position of the secured creditor. Finally and most importantly, the *nantissement* is today supplanted by the use of leasing or the retention of title clause.

(d) Non-possessory Security Right on Business

Another important example of special non-possessory devices created by the French legislator is the pledge on business, *nantissement du fonds de commerce*.[13]

[9] P Lamoureux, La garantie offerte par l'hypothèque sur les navires, bateaux et aéronefs, (1953) in Le gage commercial: Études (ss. dir.) de J. Hamel (Dalloz, 1953) 262

[10] E Le Corre-Broly,' Le gage sur véhicule automobile source d'interrogations' (2014), *Recueil Dalloz* 440.

[11] G Cornu, 'La loi du 18 janvier 1951 relative au nantissement de l'outillage et du matériel d'équipement' in Le gage commercial: Études (ss. dir.) de J Hamel (Dalloz, 1953) 442

[12] Now C Com Art L 525-1 ff.

[13] C com Art L 142-1.; P de Couliboeuf, Le nantissement de fonds de commerce (1995), *Droit et Patrimoine*, sept 1995, 35

This non-possessory pledge encumbers all the elements of a business, for example the brand, commercial name, customer and goodwill. The parties may agree to extend the scope of the *nantissement* to furniture, equipment, tools and industrial property rights, but in no case to inventory. The pledge is created by a written agreement and must be registered at the clerk's office of the local commercial court. Registration is not only a question of third-party effectiveness, but also a condition of validity of the security right. After default, the secured creditor may enforce his security rights through a public sale of the business. There is no possibility for him to acquire the business in satisfaction of the secured obligation.

(e) Non-possessory Security Rights in Intellectual Property

With the development of intellectual property, the legislator could not remain inactive, and considered some new non-possessory devices on this kind of property. However, the existence of the moral rights of the author makes such creation more difficult. Two types of pledge on intellectual property have been established with some success in practice. The first is the pledge on films, *nantissement des films cinématographiques*. A debtor can encumber the future rights of exploitation of his film in order to finance its production. The *nantissement* is registered in a special register and gives to the creditor a direct claim on the future income generated by the film. The second is the pledge of software. Once again, it is the future exploitation rights that can be pledged. This pledge is created by a written agreement and registered to the *Institut National de la Propriété Intellectuelle* for a renewable period of five years.

C. The Present: The 23 March 2006 Reform

The French law of secured transactions, which was governed by rules mostly dating from the Napoleonic Code (1804), badly needed to be modernised. It was essential to confer on it a new attractiveness and make it more competitive in the context of strong international competition. This reform occurred on 23 March 2006 with the adoption of a governmental ordinance relating to security rights in general.[14]

(i) The Genesis of the Reform

The reform of March 2006 is the logical result of the work done by the Grimaldi Committee, which had been asked in 2003 to suggest certain modifications to the

[14] Grimaldi's Commitee Official Report, Pour une réforme globale du droit de sûretés, (2005) *Droit et Patrimoine*, n° 140, adde Commentaries to the 2006 march 23 ordinance relating to security rights, (2006) JCP ed. G, supplément au n°20 17 mai 2006.

Civil Code to make the secured transactions law more coherent and more efficient. The committee report, issued on 31 March 2005, suggested a general rewriting of the regime of the main security devices (eg guarantees, pledge, mortgage and retention of title). The proposed reform would not have constituted a revolution in the French law. The main goal of the committee was to propose, in the light of professional practice, the modernisation of rules that had become obsolete and to innovate only when necessary.

The report was unfortunately not completely followed through. For reasons based on the urgency of the reform, the government chose to legislate by ordinance. Jealously safeguarding its privileges, Parliament, by the law of 26 July 2005, authorised the government to reform but excluded from the scope of the reform guarantees, fiduciary transfer for purposes of security, and the pledge of financial instruments. Parliament also authorised only a *codification à droit constant* of retention of title, thereby excluding any substantial modification of that regime.[15] Be that as it may, this reform brought significant modifications and improvements to the law related to security rights over movables.

(ii) The Security Rights Over Movables in the Ordinance of 23 March 2006

The main goal of the legislator was to give a new coherence to the secured transactions regime. It commenced with a clarification of the terminology used in the Civil Code. Now the term *gage* (pledge) refers exclusively to a security over tangible movables, while *nantissement* refers to a security over intangibles. This terminological clarification, however, did not lead to a substantial unification. The legislator did not wish to unify the various security rights over movables and adopt a unitary approach as done in the United States with Uniform Commerical Code Article 9 or as suggested by the UNCITRAL Model Law on secured transactions. On the contrary, he chose to rebuild the new law in the Civil Code around four fundamental devices: liens, retention of title and, primarily, the new pledge (Subsection (a) below) and the *nantissement* (Subsection (b) below).

(a) A Major Innovation: The Non-possessory Pledge

The new regime of the pledge *gage* can be found in the new Articles 2333–2350 of the Civil Code. Its key objective was to confer two features regarded as essential to any modern security regime: flexibility (see (1) below) and efficiency (see (2) below).

[15] D Legeais, 'La réforme du droit des garanties ou l'art de mal légiférer' *Liber Amicorum Ph. Simler*, (Litec Dalloz, 2006), 367; L Aynès, 'Le gage des meubles corporels', (2005) *Droit et Patrimoine* 61.

1. A Flexible Regime

Dispossession of the grantor is no longer a condition of validity of the *gage*. This major change has two important consequences. The dispossession of the grantor is now a simple method for achieving third-party effectiveness, in the same way as registration, and it is now possible to grant a pledge on future goods or several pledges on the same collateral. This new pledge may encumber any type of tangible assets, including present or future, individualised or fungible assets, provided that they are in trade. The grantor must have the ability to dispose of the encumbered asset. Actual ownership of the grantor is only required for the pledge of present goods. When the pledge is created on future assets, the collateral will be encumbered automatically and without further formality, as soon as the grantor becomes owner of the collateral. According to Article 2335 of the Civil Code, the pledge of a thing belonging to another is void. It may give rise to damages where the creditor did not know that the collateral belonged to another.

The pledge can secure any type of obligations, whether present or future, determined or determinable, conditional or unconditional. With regard to formal requirements, the pledge is created, on pain of nullity, by a written agreement which contains the description of the debt secured, the quantity of the encumbered assets, as well as a description of their species or nature.[16]

In application of the specificity principle, the security agreement must include the designation of both the collateral, whether present or future, and the secured obligation. This requirement prohibits the 'omnibus' pledge, ie a pledge that encumbers all the grantor's movable assets, present and future, in order to secure all types of obligation, present and future, owed to the secured creditor.

The pledge may now be made effective against third parties through two methods, the choice being left to the parties. First, in tangible assets, the pledge may be made effective by the secured creditor's or agreed third party's possession of the encumbered assets.

The second and main method for achieving third-party effectiveness is registration. Article 2238 of the Civil Code provides that the pledge can be offered to public notice through registration in a special registry whose details shall be regulated by a decree in the Conseil d'Etat.

A decree dating from December 2006 established the new system of registries.[17] This new regulation appointed the clerk's offices of the local commercial courts as registrar. The court's registries are centralised at a national level in order to make available online to the public all information relating to security rights in movable assets.

Registration confers an efficient protection against other competing claimants. Where a pledge has been duly registered, the particular successors of the grantor

[16] C civ Art 2336.

[17] R Boffa, L'opposabilité du nouveau gage sans dépossession, (2007) *Recueil Dalloz, Chron.* 1161.

may not avail themselves of Article 2276, which states that in matters of movables, possession is equivalent to a title. In other words, a pledge made effective against third parties by registration always has priority over any other claimant such as a buyer, transferee, lessee or donee of the encumbered assets, even in good faith.

The purpose of the registry is not only to receive, store and make information relating to pledges available to the public. It assists in providing rules for determining the priority of a pledge with regard to/over competing pledges granted by the same grantor in the same encumbered asset. Where the same asset has been the subject matter of several non-possessory pledges, the rank of the secured creditors is determined by the order of their registration.

Article 2340 of the Civil Code deals with the conflict between a pledge made effective by registration and a pledge made effective by dispossession of the grantor. It states that where an asset first encumbered by a registered non-possessory pledge is subsequently the subject matter of a possessory pledge, the right of preference of the first secured creditor is enforceable against the subsequent creditor in possession notwithstanding the right of retention of the latter.

With regard to rights and obligations of the parties to a security agreement, the Code provides several mandatory rules, dependent upon whether the pledge is with or without dispossession. Where the secured creditor is in possession of the tangible assets, he shall be legally considered as a depositary. As a consequence, he has the obligation to ensure the conservation of the collateral and take all reasonable steps to preserve the assets and their value, on condition that he recovers useful and necessary expenses incurred for the preservation of the pledge. He must maintain these assets separated from goods of the same nature which belong to him, or the grantor would be entitled to claim the return of the encumbered assets, without prejudice of damages. Unless otherwise agreed, the secured creditor collects the natural or civil fruits or revenues of the encumbered asset and he must charge them to the interests or, in their absence, to the capital of the secured debt.[18]

When the grantor remains in possession, he cannot dispose of the encumbered assets, unless the secured creditor authorises him to do so, or the encumbered assets are fungible goods. In this case, the grantor may dispose of them, if the security agreement so provides, on condition of replacing them with the same quantity of equivalent goods. The grantor must also ensure the preservation of the encumbered assets. In the event of breach of this obligation, the secured creditor may avail himself of the forfeiture of the term of the secured debt and make it immediately payable or request an additional pledge.

2. The Efficiency of the New Pledge

Traditionally, the indivisibility of the pledge confers an effective protection to the secured creditor. Indeed, a pledge is indivisible notwithstanding the divisibility of the debt between the heirs of the debtor or those of the secured creditor.

[18] C civ Art. 2345.

With the reform, the secured creditor now has two new interesting prerogatives. Firstly, he legally has a right of retention on the collateral. It is logical that the creditor in possession, either directly or through an agreed third party, has such a right. It is more surprising that the 4 August 2008 Act gave a fictitious right of retention to the creditor not in possession. This Act was justified by the necessity to improve the attractiveness and the efficiency of the non-possessory pledge especially in a case in an insolvency proceeding. Nevertheless this advantage is today illusory since this right of retention was declared ineffective three months later by an ordinance of 18 December 2008[19] in the event of bankruptcy of the debtor.

The main improvement brought by the reform is the new set of provisions on enforcement of the pledge after default. In principle, the creditor may enforce his pledge through a judicial disposition of the encumbered asset. The secured creditor must first obtain an order of the court before organising the sale of the collateral at a public auction.[20] This sale shall take place following the rules on enforcement proceedings from which the security agreement may not derogate. This disposition is intended to avoid the risk of the secured creditor selling off the encumbered assets. It seems that the grantor can, after the conclusion of the security agreement, waive this protection and expressly authorise the secured creditor to sell or otherwise dispose of the encumbered asset without applying to a court. Before the reform, the Cour de cassation enforced such clauses (*clause de voie parée*) when they were concluded subsequent to the pledge contract. The reform seems to have maintained this solution. A public auction is not necessary if the price of the collateral can be determined by reference to an official quotation.

In the case of a non-possessory pledge, the grantor in possession has a duty to transfer the possession of the collateral after default in order to allow him to dispose of the asset. If he does not, the secured creditor cannot obtain possession of the collateral without applying to a court. There is no self-help repossession in French law, but the creditor may alternatively apply for a court order ruling that the property of the encumbered asset will be vested in him in total or partial satisfaction of the secured obligation, up to a maximum of the due debt. This judicial acquisition of the encumbered assets is very popular in practice, not only because it allows the risks and costs inherent in public sales to be avoided, but mainly because it excludes any competition with other competing claimants. If the value of the encumbered asset, determined officially by an expert, is greater than the amount of the secured claim, the secured creditor must pay a cash balance to the grantor or deposit the surplus if there are other secured creditors.

Another major contribution of the 23 March 2006 ordinance is undoubtedly the validation of the *pacte commissoire*, ie an extrajudicial acquisition of an encumbered asset in satisfaction of the secured obligation. According to Article 2348 of

[19] C com Arts L 622–7 I.

[20] C civ Art 2346.

the Civil Code, it may be agreed in the security agreement or afterwards that in case of default, the secured creditor will become owner of the encumbered assets in total or partial satisfaction of the secured debt.

The value of the encumbered assets has to be determined on the day of the transfer by an expert designated by amicable agreement or judicially, in the absence of an official quotation of the property on a regulated market. Where that value exceeds the amount of the secured debt, the sum which equals the difference shall be paid to the debtor or, if there are other secured creditors, shall be deposited.

A *pacte commissoire* cannot be concluded for a pledge securing a consumer credit. It also becomes ineffective as soon as the insolvency proceedings commence. With this late limitation, the *pacte commissoire* has undoubtedly lost much of its interest, at least in commercial matters.

(b) A Modernised Regime: The Pledge on Receivables

According to Article 2329 of the Civil Code, a pledge on intangibles is called a *nantissement*.[21] It is important to note that, according to Article 2355, a conventional pledge which attaches to intangible movables other than receivables is, unless proved otherwise, regulated by the rules governing the pledge on tangibles. Such a provision is quite confusing, for the regime of the pledge will be applied to most of the security rights on intangibles, even though they will be called *nantissements*. A unique terminology would probably have been more appropriate.

It is all the more confusing that the only *nantissement* considered by the Civil Code is the pledge on receivables.[22] Until the reform of 2006, security rights on receivables had been particularly neglected by the Civil Code. Except for a single special provision, the regime was exactly the same as that of the pledge of tangible assets, which was obviously inappropriate. To remedy this situation, the legislator passed the Dailly Act in 1981, which established a special regime of pledge but limited to professional receivables. The 23 March 2006 reform went further with an original and reliable regime of pledge on non-professional receivables, called a *nantissement de créances*. This new security right must be seen as a complement, not an alternative, to the Dailly Act. In other words, a creditor taking security over professional receivables can choose whether to use the new *nantissement* or the Dailly Act

This *nantissement* may encumber any type of receivable, whether civil or commercial, contractual or non-contractual, present or future. The grantor may choose to encumber a single or a number of receivables, provided that each of them should be sufficiently identified. The *nantissement* extends to all accessories of the debt unless otherwise agreed.[23]

[21] J Stoufflet, Le nantissement de biens incorporels (2006), JCP E. n°20-21, étude n°5, 19.
[22] P Crocq, Le nantissement de créance (2006) Revue Lamy de Droit civil, n°29, 13.
[23] C civ Art 2359.

Similar to the pledge on tangible assets, the *nantissement* shall on pain of nullity be concluded in writing. The security agreement must contain details of the debts secured or, in case of future debts, must allow their individualisation or contain elements that allow it, such as the indication of the debtor, the place of payment, the amount of the debts or an estimate thereof and, if appropriate, their due date.[24]

The most important feature of this *nantissement* and its originality is probably the methods for achieving its third-party effectiveness. The *nantissement* is effective *erga omnes*. Article 2361 states that it takes effect between the parties and is enforceable against third parties from the date of the conclusion of the security agreement. In order to be enforceable against the debtor of the encumbered debt, the pledge must be notified to him or he must intervene in the security agreement, failing which the grantor alone duly receives payment of the debt. This choice is questionable. However, in order to simplify this notification of the debtor of the secured debt, the reform of 2006 substituted a simple notification by letter for notification by a bailiff.

If the pledged receivable comes to maturity before the secured claim, the legislature establishes the principle that the secured creditor should collect this amount as receivable, for him to retain the collected sums on an account with an institution authorised to receive. If the obligation secured is thereafter executed by the debtor, the secured creditor will then have the obligation to return the funds to the grantor.

If the pledged receivable will come to maturity after the secured claim, and if there is a default, the secured creditor may first wait until the pledged receivable becomes due and thereafter collect the sums. He may also have the pledged debt assigned to him, by the judge or by a *pacte commissoire*, as well as all the rights which attach to it, in satisfaction of the secured obligation.[25] The collected sums are deducted from the secured debt when due. If the secured creditor who enforces his pledge collects a sum higher than the secured debt, he must return the surplus to the grantor.

It should be noted that the secured creditor benefits from an original right of retention over the encumbered receivable. Conceptually speaking, it may be strange to assert the existence of a right of retention on a receivable which is an intangible movable. It would have been more appropriate to refer here to the notion of 'control'.

(iii) The Weaknesses of the 2006 Reform

Notwithstanding some welcome innovations, the reform contains some underdeveloped changes. A certain hesitancy on the part of the legislator, and even

[24] C civ Art 2356 al 2.

[25] S Hébert, Le pacte commissoire après l'ordonnance du 23 mars 2006, (2007), *Recueil Dalloz, Chron.* 2052.

some mistakes, resulted in many factors undermining the basis of what should have been a major change in the French law on secured transactions. This weakening of the reform found some of its causes within the new law on secured transactions itself (Subsection (a) below) but also outside (Subsection (b) below).

(a) Endogenous Factors: Heterogeneity and Competition

Two internal factors can explain the mixed success of the reform. First, the legislator did not go far enough in his attempt at rationalisation within the Civil Code. While Parliament had the opportunity to unify all the forms of security over movables by grouping them together under the exclusive regime of the *gage* and *nantissement* of the Civil Code, the legislator chose instead not to abrogate all the pre-existing special non-possessory security rights. This preservation is doubtless a source of confusion and conflict. In addition, the legislator decided to add further confusion by creating some new special non-possessory pledges. As a result, heterogeneity is still a landmark of the French secured transaction law (see (1) below).

Second, while the legislator intended to strengthen the attractiveness of the new pledge, it has at the same time strengthened and extended the scope of a rival system based on the use of property rights such as retention or transfer of title. This new regime now creates unfair competition between the security rights, aggravating the disenchantment of those in business with the pledge (see (2) below).

1. The Unnecessary Creation of a Special Pledge on Inventory

In order to remedy the lack of non-possessory rights over inventory, the legislator established in the Commercial Code a new special pledge: *le gage des stocks*. The creation of this special pledge is, at the very least, surprising. Indeed, it is obviously duplicative of the new pledge of the Civil Code,[26] which can perfectly encumber inventory. This redundancy would be acceptable if the special pledge of the Commercial Code was more adapted and more flexible than the pledge of common law. On the contrary, the special regime[27] was, in its first version, more rigorous and less efficient than the regime of the civil pledge. For example, the pledge of stocks was subject to a very rigorous formalism. The security agreement must include, as a condition of validity of the contract, certain information[28] such as the exact name, 'Act of Pledge of Inventory', and the name of the insurance company that insures the inventory against fire and destruction.

The secured creditor had to register his pledge of inventory on a specialised registry kept at the office of the clerk of the commercial court of the seat or residence of the debtor, within 15 days of the conclusion of the contract. The failure to advertise within the time limit was not sanctioned by the simple

[26] *cf* Section C (ii) a.
[27] C com L 527-1.
[28] C com L 527-5 para 2.

non-enforceability of security vis-à-vis third parties, but by its nullity. At last, and very curiously, Parliament had prohibited the *pacte commissoire* so that the parties were unable to agree in the security agreement that the secured creditor will acquire the encumbered assets in total or partial satisfaction of the obligation.

The question then arises as to whether the parties can through an express clause decide to submit their pledge on inventory to those provisions of the Civil Code. As the provisions of the Commercial Code are not mandatory, nothing seems to prevent such a choice. However, the Plenary Assembly of the Cour de cassation held recently[29] that a creditor who wants to take a warranty on stocks of goods of the debtor may only submit its security to the special regime of the pledge on stocks.

Fully aware of the difficulty, the French legislator reformed the regime of the 'Gage des stocks' by the 29 January 2016 ordinance.[30] The objective of this reform was to bring the regime of the pledge of inventory into line with the regime of the Civil Code pledge. If this legislative intervention which corrects a legal anomaly must be approved, the method chosen by the Legislator is questionable. Why maintain a special security regime which is redundant with the Code civil pledge of common law? Indeed, the inventory-specific rules, that could justify such a special regime are very few and limited to the 'Spraying Clauses'. According, Article L527-6 of the Commercial Code, when the stocklist reflects a decrease of at least 10% of their value as outlined in the security agreement, the creditor may require the debtor, after formal notice, to either to restore the inventory or to reimburse of a portion of the loan in proportion of the observed decrease. When the stocklist reflects a decrease of at least 20 per cent of their value, the creditor can require, after formal notice of the debtor, the total reimbursement of the debt considered as due. However, the security agreement may provide rates higher than those fixed by the law. As the pledge of stocks should not paralyse the activity of the grantor, the legislature expressly provided for the possibility for him to freely dispose of encumbered elements, on the condition that they be restored to the inventory.

After default, the secured creditor may now enforce his security rights following the Civil Code rules. The creditor may thus apply to a court to either sell the inventory by auction or be authorised to acquire the inventory in full satisfaction of the secured obligation. The parties can now include a '*Pacte commissoire*' in their security agreement.

2. The Unwelcome Integration of the *Gage Automobile* in the Civil Code

In order to modernise the old pledge on motor vehicles, the legislature has taken advantage of the 2006 reform to add to the Civil Code several provisions especially

[29] Cass. ass. plén., 7 déc. 2015, n° 14-18.435

[30] A Reygrobellet, Les nouveaux habits du gage de stocks, (2006) JCP éd Notariale et Immobilière, act. 261

dedicated to a new form of *gage automobile*[31] as a replacement for the old one. Once again, this is regrettable given that the common law pledge was perfectly adapted for motor vehicles, without the need for special provisions. Moreover, the effects of this special regime are minimal. The only difference is as regards the method of achievement of third-party effectiveness. The pledge is effective against third parties by a declaration made by the secured creditor to the administrative authority. The secured creditor in possession of the receipt of the declaration is entitled to a fictitious right of retention.

3. The Creation of Special Security in the Financial Sector

It was crucial, in a context of competition between financial markets, to offer to the participants in the financial and banking field some effective and modern security rights on bank accounts and financial instruments.

The pledge on bank accounts has been considered by the legislator as a special form of the *nantissement de créances*. According to Article 2360, where the asset subject to a *nantissement* is a bank account, the encumbered debt must be understood as being the credit balance, provisional or final, on the day of the enforcement of the security with the reservation of the regularisation of the current transactions. With the same reservation, in the event of insolvency proceedings being commenced against the pledgor, the rights of the secured creditor attach to the balance of the account on the date of the opening judgment.

The legislator created a pledge on an account of securities by an ordinance of 8 January 2009. This pledge is quite original, insofar as it encumbers not the securities in the account but the account itself. In that sense, it looks like a floating security interest. The *nantissement* is established both between the parties with respect to the issuing corporation and third parties, by a statement[32] signed by the holder of the encumbered account (ie the grantor). This statement contains certain information, on pain of nullity, such as identification of the pledged account, the secured obligation, and the nature and number of securities in the account at the date of the agreement.

As soon as the receipt of the declaration by the bank is issued, the *nantissement* becomes fully effective against third parties. The grantor is then deprived of the free disposal of the assets. However, it is possible for him to continue to operate on condition that the parties have agreed upon the conditions on which the grantor may dispose of securities contained in the encumbered account.

In case of default, the secured creditor will enforce his security rights following the two modes of common law. However, if the securities are listed on an official stock exchange, they may be transferred directly by the secured creditor, without any judicial proceeding.

[31] C civ Arts 2351–2353.

[32] L 211-20 of the Monetary and Financial Code.

4. Competition of Security Rights Based on Property Rights (*Propriété-Sûretés*)

Even though the retention of title has long been used by sellers and enforced by judges, it was only in the 2006 reform that a *clause de réserve de propriété* was expressly recognised, in the Civil Code, as a security.[33] Four articles now dictate its regime. However, there is here almost no innovation since the legislator confirmed the pre-existing case law solutions according to the law of July 2005. On this point the reform is more symbolic than substantive.

According to Article 2367 of the Civil Code, ownership of property may be retained as security through a clause of retention of title, which defers the transferring effect of a contract until payment in full of the secured obligation.

The formal requirements are negligible. A retention of title shall simply be agreed upon in writing. The clause is opposable *erga omnes*, as it is effective against third parties as soon as it is established in writing. Nevertheless, the legislature has organised a system of optional registration, whose only interest is to ease the repossession of the encumbered asset. If the clause is registered, the secured creditor may require the return of the goods sold without applying to a court.

In case of default, the secured creditor is entitled to claim the restoration of the property and take possession of the encumbered assets. But the goods must still exist in nature in the debtor's estate. The attachment of the encumbered asset to another asset is not a bar to the rights of the creditor where those assets may be separated without suffering damage. If the retention of title is on fungible goods, the secured creditor can claim the return of property of the same nature, up to the amount of the debt remaining due.

The secured creditor may also claim the equivalent of the value of the original encumbered asset in two circumstances. First, it may claim the price still in the hands of the sub-purchaser. The secured creditor may then claim any indemnity under an insurance policy which is subrogated to the encumbered asset.

The security right being, by essence, indivisible, the secured creditor is entitled, in the event of default, to claim the repossession of all the assets, regardless of the amount of debt still due. As a security right cannot be a source of enrichment, Article 2371 states that where the value of the asset taken back exceeds the amount of the secured debt still due, the creditor owes to the debtor a sum equal to the difference.

Retention of title is not the only security device based on the use of a property right. In 2009 the French legislator established for the first time in French law a new form of transfer of title as a purpose of security. The *fiducie sûreté,*[34] inspired by the common law trust, is a transfer of title of the encumbered asset by the grantor to a *fiduciaire* (trustee) for the benefit of the secured creditor. The trustee can

[33] P Crocq, La réserve de propriété, (2006), *JCP n° spécial* 18 mai 2006, n°6.

[34] F Barrière, La Fiducie-sûreté, (2009), *JCP éd. E*, 1808; S de Silgy, La fiducie, une réussite? (2013) *Revue Lamy de Droit civil*, 59.

be the secured creditor himself. The *fiducie sûreté* may be with or without dispossession. In this last case, the grantor and the trustee will conclude an agreement whereby the trustee, as the legal owner of the collateral, will transfer upon conditions the possession of the goods to the grantor. The 30 January 2009 ordinance created a 'refillable' *fiducie-sureté*, which is used to secure obligations others than those mentioned in the initial security agreement.

In the event of a default of the debtor, and unless otherwise provided in the agreement, the trustee, when he is the creditor, acquires the full property of the assets transferred as security. Where the trustee is not the creditor, the latter may require that the property be returned to him, or if so provided by the trust agreement, the sale of the encumbered assets. The value of the assets transferred as a purpose of security has to be determined by an expert designated by agreement or judicially, unless the collateral is a sum of money. In all cases, if the value of the acquired or transferred asset exceeds the amount of the secured debt still due, the secured creditor owes to the debtor a sum equal to the difference.

Even if it seems very effective, the *fiducie sûreté* does not seem to have been as successful as expected, especially because of its costs and questions about the nature of the rights of the trustee over the encumbered assets transferred as security.

5. Competition from Statutory Liens

Security rights are today weakened by the proliferation of statutory liens on movables: *privilèges mobiliers*. These liens are divided into two categories. The first includes the *privilèges généraux* that encumber all movables, tangible or intangible, of the debtor. Some of them are based on considerations of humanity, like the old *privilège des frais de dernière maladie*, which secures costs incurred for the cure of a terminal illness.[35] But most of them are based on fiscal and social considerations such as public treasury or social security liens.[36] These liens are harmful to other creditors because they have a superpriority and are usually secret except for the social security lien, which must be registered when the secured obligation is above a sum fixed by the law.

The second category includes special liens—*privilèges spéciaux*—granted on specified types of debtors' movables. Some of these liens are based on the concept of pledge, such as that granted to a landlord as security for the payment of rent, that granted to a hotel proprietor over all a traveller's luggage, or finally the lien granted to a carrier over goods transported. Others are based on the addition or the preservation of an asset in the debtor's estate, such as the lien granted to the seller of movables, which participates in the growth of the estate of the purchaser, for the benefit of all creditors.

[35] C civ Art 2331-3.
[36] Articles L 243-4 and L.243-5 of the Social Security Code.

(b) Exogenous Factors: The Impact of Bankruptcy Laws

Finally, at a more general level, it is regrettable that the legislator chose to reform the law on secured transactions and the insolvency law separately, even though both reforms were simultaneous. This absence of general reflection on the balance between these intimately related fields of law is very harmful. It is particularly delicate, from the legislative point of view, to reconcile insolvency laws and secured transactions laws, as these two branches have contradictory goals. Protecting insolvency assets against the actions of creditors, whether secured or unsecured, appears as an imperative to ensure at most the debtor's reorganisation, and at least an equitable and collective treatment of all similarly situated creditors. This objective leads inevitably to the sacrifice of secured creditors, especially those who have security rights over debtors' collateral.

The decision to commence insolvency proceedings may challenge the existence of conventional security rights. Pledges and others security rights will fall within the avoidance provisions of the suspect period[37] applying to any security interests that were perfected within the time period between the date of cessation of payments and the decision to commence the insolvency proceeding. Even A security right granted before the date of cessation of payments can be declared void by a judge if it is found to be out of proportion to the secured claim, and if the liability of the secured creditor is recognised.[38]

In addition, the secured creditor must satisfy a duty of declaration. Like any creditor, he has to submit his secured claim for admission to the insolvency representative within the period of two months from the commencement decision. If he does not do so, the claim and the attached security rights are not effective against the insolvency representative.

The secured creditor, like all other creditors, is subject to an automatic and mandatory stay or suspension of actions and proceedings against the assets of the debtor for a limited period of time. Therefore he cannot enforce his security rights in any way (sale or acquisition in satisfaction of the secured obligation). It is only after a decision on liquidation that he will regain the right to seek a court order ruling that the property of the encumbered asset will be vested in him in satisfaction of the secured obligation.[39] It should be recalled that the commencement of insolvency proceedings makes voidable any *pacte commissoire* agreed by the parties.

A secured creditor will also be in competition with new legal creditors with superpriority. As a matter of fact, a new creditor who consents to a post-commencement credit to the insolvent debtor will have a statutory lien (*privilège de conciliation* or 'new money') with a superpriority. The only way for a secured

[37] C com Art L 632-1.
[38] C com Art L.650-1.
[39] C com Art L 642-20.

creditor to avoid the consequence of insolvency proceeding is therefore to take a security right over an asset which is not or not yet in the insolvency estate. This simple fact explains the success of the security property rights such as retention of title or transfer of title for a security purpose, which then appears as the only effective way for creditors to protect themselves against the risks inherent in bankruptcy.

Indeed, the position of the secured creditor with retention of title, in the event of a bankruptcy of the buyer, is particularly advantageous. On the condition that the goods can still actually be found in the estate of the debtor, the creditor may immediately demand the return of his property if he has registered his security right.[40]

With regard to the *fiducie sûreté*, the 18 December 2008 order tempered the benefits by operating a distinction between possessory transfers of title and transfers of title with the debtor remaining in possession of the collateral. Regarding the *fiducie sûreté* with dispossession, the creditor's right of retention gives him a very advantageous position. The non-possessory *fiducie sûreté* is on the other hand subject to the rule of continuation of contracts. Therefore the insolvency representative can suspend the effect of the *fiducie sûreté* by performing the financial obligations so that the creditor may not recover the encumbered asset.

In case of liquidation, the trustee must however transfer the property to the secured creditor, without restriction, whether the *fiducie sûreté* is with or without dispossession.

Since the pledges and traditional security rights remain sacrificed in case of insolvency proceedings, and the retention or transfer of title for a security purpose are the only effective devices for financing the acquisition of goods in case of bankruptcy of the debtor, it is doubtful that creditors will make extensive use of the new *gage* or *nantissement* provided by the reform.

D. The Future: Just One More Go! A Reform to be Continued

The study of the French secured transactions law leaves a feeling of incompleteness. While it contained some remarkable and modern provisions, the reform was marred by a series of errors and oversights that have weakened its impact. We should, however, remain optimistic. The correction of these technical errors, today well identified and condemned, could easily be done through a future and short reform. The main objective of this complementary reform should be to abrogate all special security interests created before 2006 that overlap with the new pledge of the Civil Code. Only the question of the fate of the system of security rights

[40] C com Art L 624-10.

based on property could be more problematic. But the non-unitary approach as advocated by the UNCITRAL Legislative Guide on security operations could be an interesting source of inspiration. Moreover, the French legislator would be well advised to consider some reforms that have recently occurred in other civil law countries. These reforms are indeed based on the best of the French model, but they were able to draw many lessons from the French experience and correct defects. The Uniform Act of OHADA (Organization for the Harmonization of Business Law in Africa) and the recent reform of the Belgian secured transactions law by the Act of 11 July 2013 are very good examples.

May the legislator have the desire and the courage to go one step further. But, as Rudyard Kipling would say, this is another story!

18

The Belgian Reform on Security Interests in Movable Property

ERIC DIRIX

A. Introduction

Belgian law on secured transactions was fundamentally changed in 2013. It is fair to say that this reform came as somewhat of a surprise. Legal writers had argued over the years for a modernisation of the law, and models such as Article 9 of the Uniform Commercial Code (UCC), with its functional and integrated approach, were very attractive in academic circles. Belgian law before the reform was indeed very complex and fragmented. Some aspects such as its enforcement proceedings were even completely obsolete. However, a reform of this part of the law was not of the highest importance for the business community. The requirement of possession for the creation of a security right on movables posed difficulties, but in practice these could be circumvented by using devices such as negotiable documents representing the goods or by using special purpose vehicles.[1] Furthermore, banks were perfectly happy with the current situation since they were the only group of creditors who could be granted a non-possessory pledge on the enterprise. In case of bankruptcy of their clients, the banks very often made *pari passu* agreements to avoid conflicts about ranking and the like.

The complexity of the system and the outdated legislative framework did not mean that the system did not work. Banks, enterprises and practitioners were accustomed to it and case law has dealt with most of the questions that were left unanswered by the legislator. As is often the case, legal rules live on regardless of whether they are efficient or in the best interest of the community. As Professor Watson has poignantly told us, obsolete laws 'are kept in existence by factors such absence of effective machinery for radical change, by indifference, by juristic fascination with technicalities, and by lawyers' self-interest'.[2] Legal change very often

[1] E Dirix, 'Belgian Report' in E-M Kieninger and H Sigman (eds), *Cross-Border Security over Tangibles*, (Munich, Sellier, 2007) 221–41.

[2] A Watson, *Society and Legal Change* (Edinburgh, Scottish Academic Press, 1977) 8.

only comes about as a result of external events. In Belgium the reform of the law of secured transactions was triggered by the financial crisis and the credit crunch that resulted from it.

B. Current Situation

Before this reform, Belgian law on security interests was that of a typical civil law jurisdiction and very similar to French law before its 2006 reform. The fundamental device used to grant a security interest over a movable asset is the possessory pledge (Article 2073 Civil Code). In the system of the *Code Napoléon* the existence of a pledge without taking control of the collateral is inconceivable (*pas de gage sans dépossession*). Accordingly, it was not possible under Belgian law to create a non-possessory pledge of a movable asset or a group of movable assets. The only non-possessory pledge under Belgian law is the pledge over a business (*pand handelszaak/gage sur fonds de commerce*), which covers all movable assets of the enterprise except for 50 per cent of the inventory (Act of 25 October 1919).[3] This pledge can only be granted to banks and financial institutions and it is effective against third parties through registration. This form of publicity is not a 'filing' system and is rather outdated. The publicity is not organised on a national scale but on the level of the 'arrondissement'. A similar security right exists for agricultural enterprises (Act of 15 April 1884).[4]

The basic principles of the Belgian law on security rights—both before and after the reform—are: publicity, accessority and specificity.

Traditionally, *publicity* is considered to be a fundamental aspect of the Belgian system of security interests. Belgian law has always been opposed to undisclosed security interests. The purpose of publicity is to dispel the false impression of wealth and to inform the other creditors about the extent of their right of recourse. This approach explains the traditional hostility towards fiduciary transfers.[5] It was also the reason why Belgium was one of the last countries in Europe to recognise retention of title clauses, which was only achieved as a result of the insolvency reform of 1997.[6] Recent legislation reveals that Belgian law has shifted away from this traditional position. The 1994 Act on assignment of claims[7]

[3] Official Gazette, 21 November 1919.

[4] Official Gazette, 11 May 1884.

[5] According to Cass 17 October 1996, *Pas* 1996 I 992 a security assignment is only valid inter partes and has no legal effect in relation to third parties. In a recent case the court repeated the principles formulated in the 1996 decision, but it recharacterised the security transfer as a pledge. A security assignment is valid, but in regard to competing creditors it can never procure more to the assignee than the entitlements of a pledgee (Cass 3 December 2010, www.juridat.be). It is interesting to note that the French Cour de cassation came to the same result (Cass Fr 19 December 2006, *D* 2007 344, *RTDCiv* 2007 160: 'en dehors des cas prévus par la loi, l'acte par lequel un débiteur cède et transporte à son créancier, à titre de garantie, tous ses droits sur des créances, constitue un nantissement de créance').

[6] Act of 8 August 1997, Official Gazette, 28 October 1997.

[7] Act of 6 July 1994, Official Gazette, 15 July 1994.

abolished the formal requirements of the old Article 1690 Civil Code. According to the new Article 1690 Civil Code an assignment is valid and in principle effective against third parties as from the agreement of assignment. Accordingly, the same Act also changed the rules concerning the pledging of claims. The new Article 2075 Civil Code states that the pledgee takes 'possession' of the claim as from the conclusion of the pledge agreement. Retention of title clauses were recognised by the Bankruptcy Act of 1997.[8] According to Article 101 of this Act retention of title clauses are valid and binding on other creditors in bankruptcy proceedings without any publicity requirements. The same Act disposed also of the publicity requirement for the statutory preference of the unpaid seller of movables. Finally, the Act of 15 December 2004[9] implementing the Directive on Financial Collateral Arrangements (2002/47/EC) is another step in the same direction. The pledge and the security transfer of financial assets are valid and binding upon third parties without any publicity. Furthermore, the Belgian legislator did not use the right to restrict the scope of the Directive to financial institutions. The new rules on the pledging of financial collateral apply in principle to all legal and natural persons. As a result of all these developments Belgian law lacks coherence.

Security rights are also considered to be *accessory* rights. The underlying obligation should not necessarily exist at the moment of the creation of the security right. It is sufficient that it exists when the creditor enforces the security right. The creation of security rights to guarantee future or conditional debts poses no problems. As a consequence of the accessority principle the annulment of the underlying obligation leads to the termination of the security right. According to the law of obligations the transfer of the claim also entails the accessories of the claim such as the security rights (eg legal preference, pledge, mortgage, retention of title). The means of judicial enforcement of the claim are also considered to be accessory rights, which are transferred to the transferee.

Another principle is that of *specificity*. The recognition of a security right requires that the object is specified or can be specified. This condition is applied in a strict manner regarding immovable property and corporeal property in general. Regarding incorporeal movables the principle of specificity is applied less strictly. A pledge agreement can cover both present and future claims. It is sufficient that the agreement provides the necessary elements to determine the claims. General descriptions are valid as long as they describe the claims in such a manner that they can be identified without further discussion between the parties.

A less attractive feature of Belgian law is the complex system of *statutory preferences*. As in France, but in contrast to Germany or the Netherlands, statute law creates numerous classes of creditors that are protected by a specific or a general statutory preference on the debtor's assets (or part of them). Claims such as the unpaid balance of a purchase price, unpaid rent, claims of subcontractors, claims of carriers, costs incurred for the conservation of specific assets and

[8] Official Gazette, 28 October 1997.

[9] Official Gazette, 1 February 2005 (2nd edn).

unpaid insurance premiums, among many other types of claim, are secured by a statutory preference. General preferences covering the totality of the (movable) estate of the debtor are granted to the tax authorities, employees and social security agencies. The number of these exceptions on the *pari passu* principle is still increasing. Even in 2014 a legal preference was introduced to protect compensation claims of victims of crimes causing physical or mental damage (new Article 27, 5*bis* Mortgage Act). There are also other statutory mechanisms that result in the preferential treatment of certain categories of creditors such as 'direct actions' (*actions directes*). An important example can be found in Article 1798 Civil Code, which allows an unpaid subcontractor to claim moneys owed to him by the main contractor directly from the employer although there is no contractual connection between the subcontractor and the employer. If the main contractor goes bankrupt, the subcontractor is entitled to the proceeds of the claim of the main contractor against the employer prior to all other creditors of the main contractor.

To have a more complete picture of the rights of security holders one must also keep in mind that Belgian insolvency law is rather debtor friendly. Recent developments of Belgian insolvency law have resulted in limiting the rights of enforcement of the holders of security rights. Traditionally, pledgees and mortgagees were considered to be so-called 'separatists', which meant that they were simply not concerned by the insolvency proceedings of their debtor. They could enforce their security rights as if there were no collective proceedings. The new Bankruptcy Act (1997) provides for a stay of the right of enforcement of those creditors (Articles 26 and 100 Bankruptcy Act). This does not affect the right of the secured creditors to be paid by priority of the proceeds. The administrator must hand over those proceeds minus the costs that were incurred by him in the course of realisation. In case of reorganisation proceedings, all creditors, including secured creditors, are submitted to a moratorium during the so-called 'observation period' of up to 12 months (Article 38 §1 Continuity of Enterprises Act 2009). When a reorganisation plan is adopted, the rights of enforcement of secured creditors, creditors with a specific legal privilege and the title retention of the unpaid seller remain further suspended during a period of 24 months on the condition that the plan provides in the payment of the current interests (Article 50 Continuity of Enterprises Act 2009). Similar restrictions on the rights of secured creditors exist in consumer insolvency proceedings (see Article 1675/7, §2 Judicial Code).

C. The New Pledge Act

The new Belgian Pledge Act of 11 July 2013 ('the Act') changes the Belgian Civil Code as to security rights over movables in a fundamental way.[10] The Act will

[10] Official Gazette, 2 August 2013 (2nd edn) www.juridat.be. For the official German translation: Official Gazette, 14 August 2014 (2nd edn).

replace the old provisions regarding pledge in the Civil Code (Articles 2071–2091) but with a new numeration. The Act will enter into force by Royal Decree. It contains a complete modernisation of the legal framework regarding security rights over movables including the retention of title and the legal lien. The most important innovation is that Belgian law now recognises the pledge over movable goods without dispossession of the pledgor. In order to affect the rights of third parties, the pledge needs to be registered in a fully electronic national pledge register, which will be put in place by the Ministry of Finance. It was, at the time of the adoption of the Act, expected that the new register would be operational towards the end of 2014, but this timing has been readjusted by the legislator postponing the ultimate date until towards the end of 2016.[11] The entry into force of the entire Act is suspended until that point.

D. The French 2006 Reform

For Belgium the recent French reform of the provisions of the Civil Code regarding security rights was of great importance. In France the bicentenary of the *Code civil* in 2004 was used as an opportunity to modernise the Code. In the event, priority was given to the modernisation of the provisions on personal and real security rights. Those provisions had remained more or less unaltered since 1804. A committee of experts chaired by Professor Grimaldi drafted a proposal that was swiftly introduced by way of ordinance—and without parliamentary debate—as the new Book IV 'Des sûretés' in the Civil Code (Articles 2223–2488-5).[12] Its main innovation is the introduction of a non-possessory security right that acquires binding effect on third parties through registration (Article 2338 Civil Code). However, French law still remains complex as a non-possessory security right on inventory (*gage des stocks*) was introduced into the Commercial Code (Article L 527-1-11), the existing non-possessory pledges were not abolished and the trust-like *fiducie*, which was introduced in 2007, can also be used for security purposes.[13]

E. Reasons for Reform

The arguments for the reform in France also apply to Belgium. As in France prior to the 2006 reform, there is no general non-possessory pledge. Before the reform

[11] Article 2 Act 26 November 2014, Official Gazette, 1 December 2014.

[12] Ordonnance no 2006-346 du 23 mars 2006 relative aux sûretés, *JO* no 71, 24 March 2006.

[13] See P Ancel, 'La réforme du droit des sûretés en France' in *La réforme du droit privé en France* (Brussels, Larcier, 2009) 29–47; J Leavy, 'France' in HC Sigman and E-M Kieninger (eds), *Cross-Border Security over Tangibles* (Munich, Sellier, 2007) 101–23; Ph Simler, 'La réforme du droit des sûretés' *Jurisclasseur périodique*, edn E, 2006, 662–66.

of 2013 the law concerning security rights on movables was also very complex due to the distinction between civil law and commercial law, regulatory fragmentation, the proliferation of legal preferences, the difficulty of accommodating security mechanisms based on property within the system and the outdated rules of enforcement. Furthermore, the present system is not very efficient (eg existing publicity systems are not organised on a national scale) and sometimes it is even archaic (eg rules of enforcement). As has been said before, the reform was triggered by the financial crisis and the ensuing credit crunch. The Belgian government was convinced that an efficient system of security rights could serve as an important tool to facilitate the extension of credit to businesses and families and would have a beneficial effect on economic growth and employment. This also explains the fact that the reform was achieved in a relatively short time.

In accordance with the UNCITRAL Legislative Guide on Secured Transactions the purpose of the Act is to create a system that enables the parties to create security interests in a simple and efficient manner, allows the utilisation of a broad range of assets for security purposes, makes it possible to secure all types of obligation, abolishes the requirement of withdrawing the possession of the security provider, creates an integrated and consistent system and provides for efficient enforcement rules with as little court intervention as possible. Of course all this has to be achieved by striking the right balance between debtor and creditor, while paying attention to the legitimate interests of affected third parties. In regard to certain issues the new Act provides for protective rules for consumers (eg formation and proof of contract, over-collateralisation, enforcement).

The group of experts behind the reform also recommended a complete revision of the numerous statutory preferences. In the end the government did not follow this recommendation.

F. Main Features of the Act

The Act extensively reforms the law relating to security rights on movables. In contrast to the Draft Common Frame of Reference (DCFR) and Article 9 UCC, the Act does not introduce a general notion of 'security interest' but still maintains the traditional terms and concepts of pledge (*droit de gage/pandrecht*), retention of title (*réserve de propriété/eigendomsvoorbehoud*) and legal lien (*droit de rétention/retentierecht*).

The new rules apply to all types of movable property (eg specific assets, a business, future claims, intellectual property rights). Security interests on ships and financial assets (see 2004 Act on financial security transactions and Financial Collateral Directive) are not affected by the Act.

The fundamental distinction is that between the *validity* of the pledge (between the parties) on the one hand and its *effectiveness against third parties* (filing, possession or control) on the other hand. The parties may create a valid pledge simply by an agreement (Article 2). If one of the parties is a consumer, the agreement must be in documentary form signed by both parties (Article 4). In order to affect third party rights the pledge agreement needs to be registered. To facilitate this a new pledge register (Article 26) will be set up by the Belgian Finance Ministry. As from the moment of registration the pledge will affect third party rights. The pledge will normally take priority over the rights of third parties as from the date of registration (but with some exceptions, eg purchase money security).

Registration of the pledge will be the most straightforward and usual way to obtain priority over third parties. The debtor remains in possession of the collateral and has, in principle, the right to dispose of it 'in the ordinary course of business' (Article 21). A transferee takes the collateral free of the security right if the transfer took place in the ordinary course of business or he acquired it in good faith (Article 2279 Civil Code). Only banks and professionals (business persons and enterprises) have an obligation to check the register in order to satisfy the good faith requirement (Article 25).

However, it is still possible for a security right to bind third parties without registration and in other ways, by virtue of:

— corporeal property: the taking of possession of the movable property by the creditor (Article 39);
— receivables: the taking of 'control' by the creditor (Article 60); the security holder is in 'control' when he is entitled to notify the debtor of the encumbered claim;
— retention of title by the unpaid seller over movable property (Article 69): the only requirement is a document prior to the delivery of the goods stating that the seller retains possession.

A pledge is an accessory right and can secure all types of obligation. A pledge can guarantee both existing and future debts (so-called 'pledge of all sums') provided that they can be determined at the moment of the enforcement of the pledge. The agreement needs to mention the maximum amount of the secured claims (Article 10). If the secured claim is transferred to a third party, the security right also passes to the transferee.

The new Act also strengthens the economic stability of the security interest: the interest will continue to exist notwithstanding the transformation of the encumbered assets. If the transformation was not authorised by the pledgee, the rules of *specificatio* will be applied in order to assess whether the security interest can continue over the result of the transformation (Article 18). The same goes for commingling of the assets: the commingling does not affect the security interest. If there are several security interests with the same priority ranking that are affected by the commingling, they will be entitled *pro rata proportionis* (Article 20). With these rules, the legislator has to the largest possible extent aimed to connect economic certainty to legal certainty.

The Act also determines the rights and obligations of parties. The pledgor has the duty to take care of the pledged assets in his possession and the pledgee is entitled to inspect these assets at any time (Article 16). If the pledgor seriously fails to fulfil his obligations, the judge may at the request of the pledgee order that the encumbered goods are handed over to him (Article 22). In regard to the possessory pledge, the pledgee must keep the pledged assets segregated from his own assets in order to guarantee that the pledgor can exercise his rights of ownership in the event that the pledgee has become insolvent. If the goods have been commingled, the pledgee has to return the same quantity of similar goods to the pledgor at the end of the contract (article 44). In the event of bankruptcy or attachment by other creditors, the pledgor may exercise his rights on the separated goods. If the goods have been commingled, the goods that are available at that time are considered to be the pledged assets in the amount of the pledged quantity. If there are several pledgors, they will assert their claims to the commingled assets in proportion to their rights (Article 44). Under the new Act the pledgee is not entitled to use the encumbered assets (Article 42).

Other innovations of the new Act are:

- the adoption of the 'functional approach' to security interests;[14]
- the prohibition of enrichment of the creditor as a general principle of security rights regardless of their nature (eg retention of title: Article 72): the surplus is to be handed over to the debtor or is subject to the right of recourse of the other creditors;
- the introduction of swift rules of enforcement (except in regard to security interest agreements where one party is a consumer): enforcement will, in principle, take place without court intervention, but access to the court remains possible when such is needed—the fundamental requirement is that enforcement takes place in a commercially reasonable manner (Article 47);
- the introduction of the possibility that security interests may be held for third parties (known as a security trust);[15]
- the right of retention (legal lien) is qualified as a security interest (Article 76);
- the recharacterisation of a security transfer as a pledge (Article 62); and
- the treatment of non-assignment clauses as ineffective in regard to third parties (Article 64).

G. Registration

The new pledge register is broadly speaking in accordance with the principles of the DCFR: available and searchable online, and registration, renewal and

[14] Good examples are the prohibition of enrichment of the secured creditor as a general principle, the recharacterisation of a security transfer as a pledge (Art 62) and Art 70, which applies different rules on the pledge (eg real subrogation, commingling, transformation of the goods) on retention of title.

[15] See A Thiele, *Collective Security Arrangements—A Comparative Study of Dutch, English and German Law* (Deventer, Kluwer, 2003).

deletion may all be done online.[16] Entries in the register can be made directly by the secured creditor who has to notify the debtor (Article 29). The register can be described as an intermediate step between 'transactional filing' and 'notice filing'. The Act enumerates the relevant data which need to be reported in the register. Registration requires the existence of the pledge agreement. All the basic elements of the pledge agreement need to be registered. As a consequence, advance filing is not possible.

Access, fees and so on are to be determined by Royal Decree (after consultation with the Commission on Privacy) (Article 34). Access to the registry to submit registrations or to make searches can take place without the assistance of the registry staff. The role of the registrar is strictly passive; only the formal requirements of the filing are examined.

The creditor is liable for any incorrect entry (Article 31) and the debtor can ask the creditor to remove any incorrect information (Article 33).

The registration expires after 10 years, unless renewal (for a further period of 10 years) takes place during the first period (Article 35). Once the entry expires it no longer appears on the register. Registration is in the name of the debtor.

The pledgee may at any time delete the entry. He is obliged to do so if the secured debt is paid. In the event of a dispute between the parties only the court can order the deletion of the registration.

With regard to the consultation of the register, the Act remains rather vague and much is left to Royal Decree. The expert committee argued for a public register that would be accessible to all and at low cost in line with modern standards.[17] In the end the legislator opted for a more restrictive approach due to privacy arguments. Foreign examples show us that registries that are easily accessible and at low cost ultimately lead to more transactions, which is positive for economic activity and also generates higher revenues.

H. Priority Conflicts

Security rights are real rights and accordingly the priority rule of property law applies (*prior tempore*—'first in time'—rule). According to the 'first in time' rule an older security right beats a newer one (Article 57). The ranking of the subsequent pledgees is determined by reference to the moment they fulfilled the requirement for enforceability vis-à-vis third parties (through registration, possession or control).

[16] For a comparison of notice filing under Art 9 UCC and European developments, see D Hamwijk, *Publicity in Secured Transactions. Towards a European Public Notice Filing System for Non-possessory Security Rights in Movable Assets* (Amsterdam, University of Amsterdam, 2014).

[17] Recommendations 4–10 *UNICITRAL Guide on Implementation of a Security Rights Registry* (Vienna, UN, 2014) 35–43.

The 'first in time rule' is, however subject, to a number of exceptions. A special status is conferred on the unpaid seller (Article 58). The so-called 'purchase money priority' applies both to the seller with a statutory privilege (Article 20, 5° Mortgage Act) and to the seller under retention of title. It concerns a conflict between two financing methods of a different nature: the seller under title retention provides credit on the basis of 'asset-based financing', which means that the object of the security right is also the object of the financing. In contrast, the pledgee has provided credit ascertained by a security right over assets which are not 'objectively' related to the credit itself. The legislator adhered to a legal-economic argument in support of the unpaid seller: financial institutions are generally better equipped than professional sellers to investigate the proprietary status of assets belonging to their debtor. The economic loss due to the bank's investigation is therefore smaller than the economic loss due to an investigation effected by a seller. Moreover, the claim of the seller is more closely connected to the encumbered asset than the claim of the bank.

Another special position is conferred to the statutory priority right of the subcontractor over the claims of the main contractor against the principal (Article 20, 12° Mortgage Act). In a conflict between the subcontractor and the pledgee of these claims, the subcontractor will have priority (Article 58). Finally, a 'superpriority' is granted to creditors who have possession of assets which they have repaired (Article 58).

I. Receivables as Collateral

With regard to receivables, both registration and possession are means to achieve third party effects. According to Article 60 the pledgee takes possession ('control') by entering into the pledge agreement provided that he is entitled to notification of the pledge to the debtor of the pledged asset. As we have seen above, Belgian law introduced in 1994 the 'silent' pledge on receivables. Prior to that reform the pledge agreement needed to be notified by a bailiff to the debtor of the pledged claim or accepted by him. Under the new provision the notion of 'control' is strengthened: the pledgee must be entitled to notify the debtor of the claim.

Other notable provisions are that a security assignment is reclassified as a pledge (Article 62)[18] and that a clause not to assign or pledge a claim has no external force (Article 64). Clauses restricting or prohibiting assignment or pledge are not effective towards third parties, except if the latter knew or should have known about these clauses. In other words: such clauses have, according to the new Act, no proprietary effect, but are solely governed by the law of obligations. A third party who knowingly violated the clause could be held liable in tort for unlawful

[18] This outcome was already accepted by case law, see n 5.

interference with a contract. This provision aims to enhance legal certainty in favour of financial institutions and other vehicles for transactions of assignment or pledge of receivables.

J. Retention of Title

An important innovation is that retention of title is now fully recognised and was given its legal basis in the Civil Code. Under current Belgian law, there is no general concept of title retention. The retention of title was only recognised in Belgium in 1997 by Article 101 of the Bankruptcy Act. This has resulted in case law of the Belgian Cour de cassation rejecting the third party effects of title retention in insolvency proceedings other than bankruptcy.[19] The reasoning of the Supreme Court was that, since retention of title only figures in the Bankruptcy Act, it cannot be recognised outside bankruptcy (eg other insolvency proceedings).

Retention of title will, under the new Act, be generalised (and not only in the event of bankruptcy, but in all insolvency proceedings, attachments etc). Furthermore, the effects of such clauses are dealt with under a functional approach in which retention of title is considered as a security right. Numerous rules governing the pledge are also applicable to retention of title. An example is the prohibition of unjust enrichment of the seller. The seller is under the obligation to refund the surplus value (Article 72).

Although the law integrates retention of title into the Civil Code and defines it as a security interest, it is not necessary to submit it to the registry. The only formal requirement which has to be fulfilled is that an agreement on the suspension of the property transfer must be agreed upon at the latest at the moment of delivery of the goods. Only in regard to consumers does the legislator require a document signed by the buyer (Article 69).

This exception to the publicity requirement was made for practical reasons. Both in Belgium and in the legal systems of its neighbours, the seller's retention of title is effective against third parties without any publicity requirement. Given its interconnected economy it was argued that it would be difficult for Belgium unilaterally to introduce such a system. Imposing registration for the perfection of title retention would have burdened the competitive position of Belgian sellers if, unlike their foreign trade partners, they were only entitled to a title retention after registration. Moreover, such a publicity requirement would hinder rapid commercial business transactions and be a burden for small businesses.

These arguments are not totally convincing. It would be preferable for retention of title to be included in the registry in the future. This would make the registry far

[19] Cass 7 May 2010, *Arr Cass* 2010, no 321, *Rechtskundig Weekblad* 2011–12, 271, note ME Storme (www.juridat.be).

more useful and make the law more realistic and functional. This result would also be more consistent with the traditional Belgian antipathy towards undisclosed security rights.

K. Legal Lien

The legal lien (*droit de rétention/retentierecht*) has up to now not been regulated by the Belgian Civil Code and its effects have remained uncertain. The right of retention is an application of the *exceptio non adimpleti contratus*, which allows a contracting party to suspend the performance of its obligations as long as the other party has not performed its obligations. The Civil Code only provided for specific applications of this right of retention. However, case law and legal scholarship have acknowledged for many decades the possibility for a creditor in possession of movable assets to withhold the assets until the moment that all obligations connected to these assets have been met by the debtor. As a result, the *exceptio* and the 'right of retention' are considered as 'general principles of law'. However, the right of retention stands or falls with the possession of the goods and does not create a legal preference on its proceeds. It is for good reason that the right of retention has often been described as an 'uncompleted' security right. According to case law, the right of retention can also be made effective in relation to third parties (eg other creditors, owner, seller). The new Act codifies this case law and give the right of retention a legal basis in the Civil Code. The main innovation is that following the example of the Dutch Civil Code, the legal lien is treated as a 'preferential right' similar to the pledge (Article 76).

L. Remedies and Enforcement

The new rules of enforcement are in line with modern standards.[20] According to the new Act the secured creditor is entitled to carry out extrajudicial enforcement unless otherwise agreed. Court intervention is no longer necessary except in the case of consumers (Article 46). The pledgee is entitled through the pledge agreement to exercise his right of recourse without the need of an enforceable instrument or judicial authorisation. Access to the court remains possible, but

[20] See for a comparative overview, E Dirix, 'Remedies of Secured Creditors outside Insolvency' in H Eidenmüller and E-M Kieninger (eds), *The Future of Secured Credit in Europe* (Berlin, De Gruyter, 2008), 223–41.

only if one of the parties asks for it. Another innovation is that more space is given to freedom of contract.

The pledgee is free to choose the method of realisation (sale, rent). He can opt for a public or private sale. The main principle is that the foreclosure must take place in an economically sound manner (Article 47). Efficient remedies whereby as little economic value as possible is lost serve the interests of both parties and those of other creditors. This does not mean that the courts have no further role to play. The principle is that access to the court remains possible when it is needed. Each party has the right at any stage of the enforcement to seek court intervention (Article 54). After the termination of the proceedings *a posteriori* control by the court remains possible for up to one year.

M. Importance of Comparative Law

The new Act is, as has already been said, to a large extent inspired by foreign examples and international models. This is a clear example of how private law in Europe is moving away from national sources towards new common ground and taking into account a great variety of information (eg model laws, soft law, comparative research).[21] The importance of the French reform has already been pointed out. Other models were the UNCITRAL Legislative Guide on Secured Transactions, Article 9 of the UCC, the Model Law on Secured Transactions of the European Bank for Reconstruction and Development and the UNIDROIT Convention on International Interests in Mobile Equipment.[22] An important source of inspiration was also the DCFR. Book IX of the DCFR is also based on a functional approach.[23] The rules apply in principle to any security right in movable property and any security mechanism, whatever the name or legal basis (security right, ownership retained or transferred) (Book IX, Article 1:101-102). A striking difference with the Belgian Act is that under the DCFR the retention of title is also subject to the registration requirement.

Because the new Belgian Act is largely based on foreign examples and international models it can undoubtedly contribute to a harmonisation of the law on security rights over movable property. The Belgian legislator has indeed expressed this ambition.[24]

[21] See J Milo, J Lokin and JM Smits, 'Introduction' in J Milo, J Lokin and JM Smits (eds), *Tradition, Codification and Unification* (Cambridge, Intersentia, 2014) 1.

[22] *Parl Doc*, Chamber of representatives, 2012–13, 53-2463/001, 11 (www.fed-parl.be).

[23] See A Veneziano, 'Security Rights in Movables in the DCFR' in V Sagaert, ME Storme and E Terryn (eds), *The DCFR: National and Comparative Perspectives* (Cambridge, Intersentia, 2012) 305–312.

[24] *Parl Doc*, Chamber of representatives, 2012–13, 53-2463/001, 11.

N. Conclusions

With the new Act Belgium will be equipped with a modern system of movable collateral that meets contemporary international standards. It is regrettable that the complex system of privileges remains unaltered. Here the work is not finished and Belgium is lagging behind its neighbouring countries.

Furthermore, one can express the hope that for the future the unitarian and functional approach is further developed and that also retention of title and financial leasing will be submitted to the registry.

Finally, it remains uncertain whether the new Act will attain fully the economic objectives of the reform. The answer to that question also depends on the manner in which the pledge registry is organised and the costs of establishing security rights and access to the registry.

19

Secured Transactions Law Reform in Lithuania

ANDRIUS SMALIUKAS

A. Introduction

Lithuania has recently made considerable efforts to reform its secured transactions law, covering security over both movable and immovable property. The reform started in the late 1990s and was finalised in 2012. Three distinct legislative stages of the reform took place during these years, each bringing new features in development and modernisation of secured transactions law. The end result of the reform can neatly be described in the words of Professor Roy Goode as the 'confluence of legal concepts and philosophies' of a modern security law.[1]

The purpose of this chapter is to discuss the main conceptual features of secured transactions law reform in Lithuania, starting with a brief description of developments in Lithuanian secured transactions law prior to 2012 and, most importantly, focusing on the challenges and achievements of the last stage of reform in 2012.[2]

B. The Beginnings of Modern Secured Transactions Law in Lithuania

The first phase, which culminated in the enactment of the Law on charge of movable property (*Kilnojamojo turto įkeitimo įstatymas*)[3] and creation of the

[1] R Goode, 'The Unidroit Draft Mobile Equipment Convention: Confluence of Legal Concepts and Philosophies' in Société de législation comparée (ed), *Mélanges en l'honneur de Denis Tallon. D'ici, d'ailleurs: harmonisation et dynamique du droit* 69, 72–74 (Paris, Société de législation comparée, 1999).

[2] For more detailed analysis of the first two stages of the Lithuanian reform, see A Smaliukas, 'Reform of Security over Movable Property in Lithuania: Evaluation de lege lata and Proposals de lege ferenda' (2004) 15 *European Business Law Review* 879; A Smaliukas, 'Reform of Laws on Security Interests in Lithuania: Convergence of Legal Concepts' in Iwan Davies (ed), *Issues in International Commercial Law* (Aldershot, Ashgate, 2005) 31.

[3] The title of this Act is sometimes translated into English using the umbrella term 'pledge' instead of 'charge'.

modern Hypothecary Register (*Hipotekos registras*), which started functioning from 1 April 1998, was inspired by two major sources, namely the European Bank for Reconstruction and Development's (EBRD) Model Law on Secured Transactions[4] and the Norwegian system of registration of security rights.[5] However, the EBRD's Model Law was not transplanted mechanically—rather, it served (together with the EBRD's Core Principles for a Secured Transactions Law) as an inspiration for the drafters of the rather simplified Lithuanian version of security law.

The aim of the first stage was to provide for a general framework of secured transactions law and, most importantly, to create a modern registry system for publication of security over movable property. This goal was partially achieved.

In the EBRD's Regional Survey of Secured Transactions Laws this stage of Lithuanian reform was positively evaluated and Lithuania was included in a small group of 'advanced reform' countries, ie those that had undertaken a sound reform of their respective legislation, followed by coherent practical implementation of recent legal enactments.[6]

Conceptually, however, the new system lacked coherence, as it was a mix between Uniform Commercial Code (UCC) Article-9 inspired functionalism of security rights (the charge over movable property was defined from the functionalistic perspective)[7] and very formal registration process where in practice only formal non-possessory pledges were created and perfected. Moreover, the new law was not much longer and detailed than the EBRD's Core principles for a Secured Transactions Law, so many important aspects of modern secured transactions law were not sufficiently regulated (if regulated at all) and were thus not applicable in practice. Also the new law functioned in parallel with the old Lithuanian Civil Code of 1964, still based on the Soviet model of security rights, which allowed non-possessory pledges to be created and perfected *erga omnes* without the need

[4] On the EBRD Model Law and its impact on security law reform in the region see, eg, J Simpson and J Menze, 'Ten Years of Secured Transactions Law Reform' (2000) (Autumn) *Law in Transition* 20; LA Mistelis, 'The EBRD Model Law on Secured Transactions and its Impact on Collateral Law Reform in Central and Eastern Europe and the Former Soviet Union' (1998) 5 *Journal of East European Law* 455, 460; C Dageförde, 'Das besitzlose Mobiliarpfandrecht nach dem Modellgesetz für Sicherungsgeschäfte der Europäishen Bank für Wiederaufbau und Entwicklung' [1998] *Zeitschrift des Europäischen Privatrechts* 686; F Dahan and G McCormack, 'International Influences and the Polish Law on Secured Transactions: Harmonization, Unification or What?' [2002–03] *Uniform Law Review* 713, 718–22. Lithuanian law on charges over movable property was discussed in G Bartkus and D Petrauskaite, 'Lithuania's Law on Pledge over Movable Property' (2000) (Autumn) *Law in Transition* 50; D Petrauskaitė, 'Secured Transactions in Lithuania' in U Drobnig, M Roth and A Trunk (eds), *Mobiliarsicherheiten in Osteuropa* 87, 87–90 (Berlin, Arno Spitz, 2002).

[5] See M Exner, 'Norvegische Pfandrechte als Alternative zum deutschen Eigentumsvorbehalt?' [1992] *Recht der internationalen Wirstchaft* 811–14. For information on the Norwegian registration of security system see www.brreg.no/english.

[6] See generally MG Bridge, RA Macdonald, RL Simmonds and C Walsh, 'Formalism, Functionalism, and Understanding the Law of Secured Transactions' (1999) 44 *McGill Law Journal* 567–664. Another major reason for the second stage of reform to be commenced was the need to amend a number of particular inadequacies of the novel legislation on security interests.

[7] Pursuant to Art 19 of this law, the uniform concept of a registered charge embraced retention of title devices and leases for security purposes.

to register them in a public registry.[8] This obviously created huge uncertainty for creditors since 'silent' non-disclosed non-possessory pledges could technically be created under the old rules of the 1964 Civil Code.[9] In practice this 'false wealth' risk rarely materialised (because the business community started to use the 1998 Law and to register all the non-possessory charges at the Hypothecary Register), yet it was evident that further reform was needed.

However, the Soviet model was an ideal starting point for the comprehensive security law reform. First, it was not hostile towards the non-possessory security interests. The Civil Code allowed the creation of a non-possessory security without the imposition of any specific limitations on the scope of collateral and it was not required to record this form of security right in a public registry. Secondly, prior to the reform Lithuania had not had a working system of real security, hence there were no parties, who could influence the law-making process, interested in keeping the status quo. Consequently, the process of reform was impeded neither by the desire of practitioners to save the system, which, though not ideal, still often functioned well enough, nor the negative influence of many traditional legal concepts: the factors that undermined security law reform in numerous economically advanced jurisdictions.[10]

C. The Second Stage of Reform in 2003—Secured Transactions Regulated by the New Civil Code

In 2003 the Law on charge of movable property was codified into the new Lithuanian Civil Code and the Code of Civil Procedure.[11] The codification was the

[8] This was not only different from the absolute majority of the civil law jurisdictions, but also from other former socialist states of Central and Eastern Europe, which were not part of the USSR. Soviet civil law ignored the problem of the 'false wealth' that is deemed to be created by the undisclosed non-possessory security rights. See PR Wood, 'Comparative Financial Law: A Classification of the Worlds' Jurisdictions' in R Cranston (ed), *Making Commercial Law. Essays in Honour of Roy Goode* (Oxford, Clarendon Press, 1997) 38–41; S Kaufhold, *Internationales und europäisches Mobiliarsicherungsrecht. Eine Analyse des gegenwärtigen Rechtszustands und der Möglichkeiten internationaler Koordinierung* (Würzburg, Würzburger rechtswissenschaftliche Schriften, 1999) 34. The main reason for such a fundamental difference in the treatment of security interests in socialist law is that the drafters of the socialist legislation on secured transactions did not intend it to be widely used in practice. *Cf* H Oda, *Law and Practice of Real Security Rights in Russia* (2001) 42 *Jurisprudentie Onderneming & Recht* 305; U Drobnig, 'Mobiliarsicherheiten in Osteuropa—Materielles Recht' in Drobnig, Roth and Trunk (eds) (n 4) 1–4.

[9] *cf* H Oda, *Russian Commercial Law* (The Hague, Martinus Nijhof, 2002) 174; A Dovgert, 'Das ukrainische Recht der Mobiliarsicherheiten' in Drobnig, Roth and Trunk (eds) (n 4) 229–230; N Csizmazia, 'Reform of the Hungarian Law of Security Rights in Movable Property (2008) I *Juridica* 181–98.

[10] See F Dahan, 'Secured Transactions Law in Western Advanced Economies: Exposing Myths' (2001) 16 *Butterworths Journal of International Banking and Financial Law* 60.

[11] On the reform of Lithuanian private law in general see V Mikelėnas, 'Unification and Harmonization of Law at the Turn of the Millennium: the Lithuanian Experience' [2000–02] *Uniform Law Review* 243–61; V Mizaras and V Nekrošius, 'Das neue Zivil-und Zivilprozessrecht in Litauen' [2002] *Zeitschrift des Europäischen Privatrechts* 466–88.

pinnacle of the general reform of Lithuanian private law and all the codified legal provisions, inter alia the secured transactions rules, were fine-tuned considerably and redrafted.

This second stage of reform finally crystallised the concept of Lithuanian secured transactions law: Lithuania did not opt for the functionalistic approach of UCC Article 9, yet it pursued wholesale formalistic reform, now also reflecting the experience of the civil law revision in Quebec.[12] Consequently, the Lithuanian Civil Code covered not only the charges *stricto sensu*, but also their functional equivalents—the so-called quasi security interests, which, apart from generally being registered in a single register, might have some characteristics of a charge.

A charge is defined as a uniform concept: a possessory or non-possessory real right that secures the performance of an obligation by vesting in the creditor priority to satisfy his claim out of the value of the collateral. All non-possessory charges must be registered in the Hypothecary Register. Major functional equivalents to a charge, such as retention of title devices, financial leasing and arrangements that transfer ownership for security purposes, despite having retained their traditional legal identity, should, with a few exceptions, also registered.

Charges were regulated by Book 4 of the new Civil Code, which is devoted to the rights *in rem*.[13] It stems from the legal definition of a charge,[14] extended by the jurisprudence of the Lithuanian Supreme Court:[15] a charge is a real right belonging to the creditor and encumbering the ownership of the security provider, be it a debtor or a third party, created to secure the performance of an obligation. Thus, the charge is an absolute right that can be enforced against everyone, entitling its holder to rights of pursuit and preference. Moreover, the fact that the charge is held to be a real but not a personal right determines its enforceability in the debtor's insolvency. Nevertheless, the Civil Code upholds the accessory nature of the charge, expressly stating that the charge extinguishes when the secured obligation ceases to exist.[16] Apart from consensual charges the Code also covers charges imposed by law. It is noteworthy that a charge over movable property was legally distinguished from a non-possessory security over immovables, which was called a hypothec[17] and regulated in a separate section of Book 4 of the Civil Code.[18]

[12] See generally Bridge et al (n 6); M Boodman and R Macdonald, 'How Far is Article 9 of the Uniform Commercial Code Exportable? A Return to Sources?' (1996) 27 *Canadian Business Law Journal* 250–77; P Ciotola, 'La Réforme des sûretés sous la Code civil du Québec' in *La Réforme du Code Civil*, vol III (Sainte-Foy, Presses de l'Université Laval, 1993) 303–443.

[13] Articles 4.198-4.228 of the Civil Code (in force until 1 July 2012).

[14] Article 4.198 of the Civil Code (in force until 1 July 2012).

[15] See dictum of the decision of the Lithuanian Supreme Court delivered on 15 May 2000 in *AB Lietuvos žemės ūkio bankas v AB Šėtos sūrinė* (case no 3K-3-545/2000).

[16] Article 4.200 of the Civil Code (in force until 1 July 2012).

[17] In many of the official translations from Lithuanian into English 'hypothec' is translated as 'mortgage', this, however, being incorrect. Under hypothec, unlike the mortgage, there is no conveyance of title, since the creditor de jure only receives limited proprietary rights and the ownership of collateral is vested in the debtor.

[18] Articles 4.170–4.197 of the Civil Code (in force until 1 July 2012).

In principle, the new secured transactions law functioned well: security could be created over almost any movable assets, both tangible and intangible; the principle of specificity of collateral had its limits allowing (although with some notable restrictions) the floating charge over universality of assets;[19] the creation inter partes and perfection *erga omnes* of security rights was relatively fast (up to five days) and cheap (depending on the value of the property, maximum notary duty and registration fee combined could not exceed the statutory cap of approximately 200 EUR); both possessory and non-possessory charges were legally recognised; all non-possessory charges were registered in the single public registry; and all perfected charges (ie the charges with an *erga omnes* effect) had absolute priority over all other creditors of the debtor (inter alia such preferential creditors as employees, tort victims and state tax authority) and this priority was retained even in case of the insolvency of both corporate and individual debtor. The enforcement of a duly registered security interest was also relatively fast and cheap—a special hypothecary judge supervised the enforcement procedure, which per se was a special type of non-contentious proceedings where the debtor could only make limited objections to enforcement (ie the debtor could not challenge the validity of the security right but could only claim that the secured obligation was not yet due or that the debtor had already duly settled the secured debt).

The new security law created at the second stage of reform was considerably more modern and sophisticated than the 1998 legislation, but its practical application (as monitored by both the government and academia) still revealed considerable room for improvement.[20]

One of the major issues was the cumbersome two-tier procedure of perfection of security rights, where all instruments creating non-possessory charges (called charge deeds and per se heavily and impractically formalised as the form and even paper colour(!) of the deed was approved by the Minister of Justice) had first to be approved by the notary public and then presented to a hypothecary judge for scrutiny before their registration at the Hypothecary Register. Although this awkward-sounding procedure in practice did not take that long (as mentioned, up to five days), it was still extremely inefficient as both the notary public and the hypothecary judge performed essentially the same function—legal scrutiny of the charge deed. It also meant that it was not feasible to create and perfect a non-possessory charge the same day. In order to make the system more efficient for both parties to a secured transaction and the government, one of the two institutions involved had to go—the perfection of security interests should either become the exclusive

[19] In the words of Professor Wood, it was the embryo of the concept of a 'universal charge'. See PR Wood, *Comparative Law of Security and Guarantees* (London, Sweet & Maxwell, 1995) 10–11; However, only goods and raw materials owned by an enterprise could be charged pursuant to the rules on charge over stock in trade. Such a limited form of universal charge was somewhat similar to the French *nantissement du fonds de commerce* and the Russian *залог товаров в обороте*. See P Malaurie and L Aynès, *Les sûretés. La publicité foncière*, 10th edn (Paris, Cujas, 2000) 210–34; A Zevrev, 'Security Issues under Russian Law' in JJ Norton and M Andenas (eds), *Emerging Financial Markets and Secured Transactions* (The Hague, Kluwer Law International, 1998) 298–99.

[20] See Smaliukas (n 2) 879.

responsibility of notaries public, or alternatively security instruments could be presented for scrutiny directly to a hypothecary judge, without the need for prior notarisation.

The formalisation of the charge deed itself was only explained by the fact that the Hypothecary Register can only efficiently register a formalised document. Thus, the registration system was designed as the title registration system based on a document registration. Registration both created and perfected the security right and the deed itself had to be registered at the Hypothecary Register. This could not be done online—the deed, first approved by the notary public, then upheld by the hypothecary judge, had to be physically presented to one of the divisions of the Hypothecary Register for public registration. Only access to the register data could be obtained easily online by any interested person (for a small fee). Obviously, the technical advances in the IT industry allowed the e-registration of any data online, thus the document registration system could be efficiently altered into a modern notice registration system.

Also, although the universal security interest was recognised, it was extremely rudimentary and undeveloped. For example, neither immovable property nor trade receivables could be part of the charged pool of assets. This was not compatible with principles of modern security law.[21]

Another shortcoming was that the enforcement procedure lacked the necessary flexibility. Private sale and foreclosure of collateral were not allowed and the only method of enforcement (although generally fast and rather efficient) was a sale of collateral by public auction, conducted by the bailiff. It was especially troublesome in cases where intangible property (such as dematerialised shares, receivables or intellectual property (IP) rights) served as collateral.

All of these issues led to the third stage of security law reform, which came into force in July 2012.

D. The Reform of 2012: An Advanced Secured Transactions Law

The reform of 2012 was a coherent and comprehensive effort to reform and harmonise security over both movable and immovable property. The drafters of new Lithuanian secured transaction laws inter alia relied on the UNCITRAL Legislative Guide on Secured Transactions.[22]

[21] R Goode, 'The Protection of Interests in Movables in Transnational Commercial Law' (1998) 2/3 *Uniform Law Review* 458–59. For the position to the contrary see JH Dalhuisen, 'The Conditional Sale is Alive and Well!' in Norton and Andenas (eds) (n 19) 86–87; U Drobnig, 'A Comparative Introduction to Security over Movables and Intangibles' in Norton and Andenas (eds) (n 19) 11–12.

[22] The author of this chapter was one of the drafters of the 2012 legislation. For the UNCITRAL Legislative Guide on Secured Transactions, which was adopted by consensus on 14 December 2007, see www.uncitral.org/pdf/english/texts/security-lg/e/09-82670_Ebook-Guide_09-04-10English.pdf.

Prior to 2012, the Lithuanian Civil Code had two completely separate security rights: a hypothec (*hipoteka*) and a charge (*įkeitimas*). A hypothec was a non-possessory security over immovable property only. A charge, as discussed earlier, allowed the creation of possessory or non-possessory security rights over movable property. Rules on hypothecs had all the problems described above plus a number of issues of their own.

After the reform, a hypothec is now an umbrella security right that allows the creation of security over both movable and immovable property.[23] This mechanism is similar to the one provided in the Civil Code of Quebec. However, differently from Quebec, a separate security right—a charge over movable property (also reformed along the same lines)—does remain. Therefore, the parties can choose whether to charge movable collateral under the rules of hypothec, or to create a charge. In practice, when movable property is charged together with immovable, parties often create a single security in the form of a hypothec. Also a hypothec must be chosen where a security is created over an enterprise—ie a pool of various assets changing in the ordinary course of business—if immovable property is part of the collateral. This type of security is called an enterprise hypothec. Charge of movable property is now mainly used as a possessory security. However, since the rules on charge are more flexible (especially as regards enforcement), the parties still have an interest in continuing to create non-possessory charges in their own right.

Reform was not functionalistic—it further expanded the modern formalistic approach taken by the drafters of the Civil Code in the early 2000s. The quasi security interests such as retention of title, transfer of title as security, and financial leasing arrangements continue to be regulated separately from hypothecs and charges. However, they are perfected by registration in the public registry (called the Contracts Register), which is integrated with the Hypothecary Register. The main feature and achievement of the reform—the system of creation, perfection and enforcement of security—was simplified and became more efficient.

Hypothecs and non-possessory charges over movable property are created by a notarised security agreement.[24] A formalised charge deed is no longer required. Parties may now exercise a broad freedom of contract, which inter alia means that a security agreement need not even be a separate contract—it may be part of a loan, sale and purchase or any other financial arrangement. The law only requires express agreement on certain perfection-related clauses, such as the legal type of security (eg if an enterprise hypothec or an enterprise charge is created, it must be expressly stated so in the agreement), fixed or maximum amount of secured obligation, or description (which must not always be specific) of collateral.

[23] The main legislative provisions of the new reform are Articles 4.170–4.197 of the Civil Code (on hypothecs); Articles 4.198–4.228 of the Civil Code (on charges over movables); Articles 745–748 of the Code of Civil Procedure (on enforcement with the assistance of the bailiff); Articles 26, 43 and 46 of the Law on Notaries (on the functions of the notary public related to creation, perfection and enforcement of a security right). The texts of the laws can be accessed online at www3.lrs.lt/dokpaieska/forma_l.htm.

[24] Articles 4.185–4.188 and 4.29–4.210 of the Civil Code.

The law provides no special requirements for the legal standing of the parties to the secured transaction. Any natural or legal person (corporate or non-corporate) may receive or provide a security. A third party may provide its property as collateral to secure the debtor's obligation.

Security agents are now allowed, thus in the case of secured syndicated loans or secured bonds a security agent may create and perfect a security interest (both in the form of a hypothec and a charge) without the need to identify the secured creditors.

Any monetary obligation (present and future) can be secured. Future property may serve as collateral (either property that does not yet physically exist or property that is not yet owned by the debtor). Such a security is perfected (ie has an *erga omnes* effect) once the fact that a debtor owns the collateral is notified to the Hypothecary Register. Shares, other securities and financial instruments, receivables, IP rights and other intangible property may serve as collateral without any restrictions.[25]

The principle of specificity is reduced to the requirement that collateral may be sufficiently identifiable. Thus, a description of a class of assets is usually sufficient—for example, 'all receivables from this group of contracts', 'all IP rights of the debtor'. Also a single security agreement can create security over multiple objects as collateral (or a pool of assets in the case of an enterprise hypothec or an enterprise charge) in order to secure the performance of one or multiple obligations. The new rules on the enterprise hypothec were drafted under the model of Quebec, also learning from the experience of the English floating charge. When the pool of assets consists only of current and future movables, an enterprise charge (and not an enterprise hypothec) shall be created, yet the difference here is minimal as the rules of enterprise hypothec are applied mutatis mutandis.[26]

The law allows agreement on a fixed or maximum secured amount. Most commonly the maximum hypothec or a maximum charge are created, since this type of security secures the principal obligation plus interest, default interest and related contractual damages. An unlimited extension of security right to cover default interest and contractual damages may prejudice the legitimate interests of other creditors (especially unsecured ones) of the debtor. Therefore, the requirement to indicate the maximum secured amount serves as a balancing act—on the one hand, a secured creditor has an extended priority in the event of the debtor's default, extending the security to more than just the principal obligation plus contractual interest; on the other hand, other creditors of the debtor may see from the Hypothecary Register what is the maximum secured amount and thus take a more rational and measured decision as to whether (and on what conditions) to extend credit to the debtor. The exact amount of the maximum security is only established at enforcement (subject to its maximum ceilings).

[25] Articles 4.171 and 4.201–4.202 of the Civil Code.
[26] See Articles 4.177 and 4.202 of the Civil Code.

A hypothec and a non-possessory charge are perfected by registration, whereas a possessory charge is perfected by a creditor taking possession of collateral (actual or symbolic, such as in case of charges of intangible securities or money in a bank account). Only perfected security rights may be invoked against third parties (ie used *erga omnes*).

Registration in the Hypothecary Register now functions as a notice registration system. It is an online registration done by the notary public on the same day (actually, immediately after) the notary approves the security agreement in question. The position and function of a hypothecary judge were discontinued and the notary is now solely responsible for orderly creation, perfection (with the technical support of the hypothecary registry) and enforcement of non-possessory security.

Thus, the creation and perfection of non-possessory security rights is now much faster and even less expensive than before July 2012. It also has much broader scope as regards the property that may be used as collateral and more flexibility in general. The enforcement procedure has also been substantially improved.[27]

Unlike the most common theoretical model of a notice registration system, which shall merely perfect a security interest and put the searcher 'on notice' that the secured party might claim a security interest in the collateral,[28] a current Lithuanian model maintains the presumption that all the data at the hypothecary registry is materially correct.[29] This is achieved because the parties may only do the notice filing via the notary public, who first approves the security agreement (after satisfying herself as to its legality). Therefore, such variation of a notice filing system allows to justify the out-of-court enforcement of security rights—since the notary checks the factual and legal accuracy of the registered data, in the event of default a secured creditor may rely on these data without the need to prove their accuracy and may apply for out-of-court enforcement on the basis of the data from the Hypothecary Register.[30]

[27] See Articles 4.192, 4.192(1) and 4.21–4.222 of the Civil Code.

[28] *cf* ET Wohlers, 'The Registry: Essential Element in Secured Lending' (2001) 18 *Arizona Journal of International & Comparative Law* 711–19; Ronald CC Cuming, 'Considerations in the Design of an International Registry for Interests in Mobile Equipment' [1999–92] *Uniform Law Review* 275, 281; Charles W Mooney Jr, 'Relationship between the Prospective UNIDROIT International Registry, Revised Uniform Commercial Code Article 9 and National Civil Aviation Registries' (1999–92) *Uniform Law Review* 335, 337–39.

[29] See V Nekrošius, 'Vorschriften über die Verpfändung von Mobilien sowie über das Prinzip der Prozeßkonzentration' in Drobnig, Roth and Trunk (eds) (n 4) 99.

[30] Justification of the out-of-court enforcement of security rights historically used to be one of the central security law issues in the civil law jurisdictions. On the one hand, it would be desirable to ensure the speedy and very cheap registration of security interests, which, as the practice of the US, Canadian common law jurisdictions and, more recently, New Zealand indicates, can be achieved with electronically conducted notice registration, which serves merely as a warning to the interested parties, enabling them to make further enquiries. On the other hand, such notice registration-based system could be deemed incompatible with the need for fast and efficient enforcement of the security right, because the civil procedure laws would require that a creditor prove his case—registration like this only presumes the debt and, hence, a security might still exist. See J Ziegel, 'The New Provincial Chattel Security Law Regimes' (1991) 70 *Canadian Bar Review* 683; G McCormack, 'Personal Property Security Law Reform in England and Canada' [2002] *Journal of Business Law* 113, 122–23;

The enforcement procedure for hypothecs and non-possessory charges is more efficient and diverse than it used to be prior to the reform. It has become a fast and cheap out-of-court procedure supervised by the notary public. In order to start the enforcement of the security, a secured creditor applies to the notary to issue an enforcement notice. The notary conducts a limited legal due diligence (only checking the information disclosed at the Hypothecary Register and other public registers) in order to establish whether the security is still valid, is duly perfected and what its conditions are. However, a notary does not verify whether a debtor is in default—the creditor is solely responsible for starting the enforcement only when contractual and statutory grounds are present. Thus, the said due diligence is a fast process, conducted in one day or even in a matter of hours. After the notary is satisfied with the due diligence outcome, she informs the debtor in writing, giving the debtor a grace period of 20 days to voluntarily settle the secured obligation. If it is not settled during the grace period, the notary issues the enforcement notice. It is a special document which is per se enforceable. Importantly, the only valid objection the debtor may have to stop the enforcement is that the secured obligation is discharged. No other objections are relevant for the notary, even if the debtor goes to court to challenge the enforcement. Only interim measures (an injunction to stop the enforcement) issued by the court may stop the out-of-court enforcement procedure. However, it rarely happens in practice since the court needs solid grounds for such an injunction.

After the enforcement notice is issued, foreclosure of collateral is legally permissible. The parties may ask the notary to approve the foreclosure agreement, which the notary does approve provided the value of the collateral is not manifestly disproportionate to the secured amount.

Alternatively, an enforcement notice may be presented to the bailiff, who, in the case of a hypothec, sells the collateral by public auction. In the case of a non-possessory charge, however, an enforcement notice allows the creditor more flexibility and options: the creditor may exercise the foreclosure without the need for the debtor's agreement; or the creditor may conduct a private sale of collateral; finally, public sale with the help of the bailiff is also available.

Enforcement of an enterprise hypothec has some specific features: here an enforcement notice contains the appointed receiver, who is recommended by the creditor (actually, the creditor or its representative may be appointed as receivers). A receiver has to establish the most efficient way to satisfy the secured claim—preferably, from the administration of the proceeds that are generated by the enterprise (where it is feasible for the enterprise to remain a going concern). If this option is not viable, the receiver shall consider selling the collateral as a whole (ie selling the entire pool of assets if that helps to maximise value) or, as a last resort, selling the assets piecemeal.

E-M Kieninger, 'Evaluation: a Common Core? Convergences, Subsisting Differences and Possible Ways for Harmonization' in E-M Kieninger (ed), *Security Rights in Movable Property in European Private Law* (Cambridge, Cambridge University Press, 2004) 647.

Possessory charges may now be enforced as agreed by the parties in the security agreement (or an ad hoc agreement reached once the debtor is in default). The law has no special mandatory provisions, except the general rules aimed to protect the debtor from the creditor's unjust enrichment.

Finally, the reform integrated the Law on financial collateral arrangements into the general security law system.[31] It remains a separate law, to which the Civil Code now expressly gives a status of *lex specialis*.

Among the rules that were not changed during the reform is the rule of an absolute priority of a secured creditor. Creditors secured by both a hypothec and a charge continue to enjoy absolute priority against all other creditors of the debtor even in the bankruptcy proceedings. An enterprise hypothec has the same priority. Although the absolute priority rule has been extensively criticised for unjustifiably overprotecting the interests of secured creditors at the expense of all others, in particular non-adjusting creditors of a debtor,[32] the decision of the Lithuanian Parliament to opt for the principle of absolute priority should be considered the right one at the right time. There are two major reasons to support this submission. First, this rule increased the practical application of charges over movable property and thus promoted the development of the Lithuanian economy.[33] Value of the movable property used as collateral has already increased exponentially following the first two stages of the reform and, as of July 2012, secures a considerably larger amount of debts than hypothecs over immovables.[34] Secondly, prior to the reform of security law, the Lithuanian legal system was obviously too heavily debtor oriented. Security interests, though rarely used, were subordinated to a number of preferential claims, including taxes and customs duties. Creditors lacked reliable official information on the legal status of debtors and their property. The bad-faith debtor could unjustly undermine the legitimate interests of his creditors. The atmosphere of legal uncertainty made the country's credit market less attractive for lenders, particularly foreign ones. Absolute priority of security, coupled with the broad definition of collateral and effective enforcement, continue to contribute to Lithuanian economic growth.[35]

[31] This law transplanted into Lithuanian national law by EU Directive 2002/47/EC on financial collateral arrangements (as amended by EU directive 2009/44/EC).

[32] See inter alia LA Bebchuk and JM Fried, 'The Uneasy Case for the Priority of Secured Claims in Bankruptcy: Further Thoughts and a Reply to Critics' (1997) 82 *Cornell Law Review* 1281–349; J Drukarczyk, 'Secured Debt, Bankruptcy, and the Creditors' Bargain Model' (1991) 14 *International Review of Law and Economics* 204–05; H Kanda and S Levmore, 'Explaining Creditor Priorities' (1994) 80 *Virginia Law Review* 2103–54; LM LoPucki, 'The Unsecured Creditor's Bargain' (1994) 80 *Virginia Law Review* 1892–915.

[33] For a theoretical discussion on whether security is really efficient and contributes to the country's economic growth, see P Ali, *The Law of Secured Finance. An International Survey of Security Interests over Personal Property* (Oxford, Oxford University Press, 2002) 33–46; HW Fleisig, 'Economic Functions of Security in a Market Economy' in Norton and Andenas (eds) (n 19) 15–36.

[34] This is evidenced by the annual data published by the hypothecary registry—see www.hipotekosistaiga.lt/index.php?3069019307.

[35] See the data from Lithuanian Bank at www.lb.lt/latest_lithuanian_macroeconomic_indicators.

E. Conclusion

The path that Lithuania took in its attempt to modernise secured transactions law can best be summarised in Lord Denning's quotation from *Packer v Packer*:

> What is the argument of the other side? Only this, that no case has been found in which it has been done before … [but] [i]f we never do anything which has not been done before, we shall never get anywhere. The law will stand still whilst the rest of the world goes on: and that will be bad for both.[36]

Despite many theoretical and practical 'mysteries, myths and monstrosities'[37] of security law that are still so common in a large number of the jurisdictions in the world (including economically developed states), Lithuania has managed to absorb the good international practice, to learn from its own mistakes (as well as some mistakes of its neighbours) and to create a modern and uniform secured transactions law, covering security over both movable and immovable property. No negative legal or economic effects of the reform have been reported—quite the contrary: the reform has led to much wider availability of cheap credit for businesses and households. One could conclude that at present Lithuanian security law reform is a success that could serve as an inspiration (if not a roadmap) for those unreformed jurisdictions that are contemplating and debating the security law reform effort but just somehow still cannot commence the process.

[36] Lord Denning in *Packer v Packer* [1953] 2 All ER [127], [129] (CA).

[37] See DE Allan, 'Security: Some Mysteries, Myths and Monstrosities' [1989] *Monash University Law Review* 915, 337–360.

20

Modernisation of the Law of Secured Transactions in Spain

TERESA RODRÍGUEZ DE LAS HERAS BALLELL AND JORGE FELIU REY*

A. Law of Secured Transactions in Context

Modern economies are critically dependent on the existence and the proper functioning of the credit market. Credit availability and access to finance in reasonable conditions heavily rely on a sound, reliable and efficient secured transactions legal system. Secured credit strengthens creditors' position, minimises risks involved in financing transactions and fosters the credit offer in efficient conditions. On the contrary, a poor, inefficient or outdated system governing secured transactions would very likely distort the funding market, reduce credit availability and worsen finance conditions. Therefore, in recent decades, close attention has been paid to modernising existing laws and to unifying rules governing secured transactions in order to facilitate access to credit and to attenuate divergences among legal traditions, and important efforts have been made and are still in progress, both at the domestic and supranational levels, in this regard. Supranational efforts from the end of the 1960s have led to the adoption of an important variety of international/regional instruments on security interests (Conventions, Model Laws, Principles, Legislative Guides).[1] At the same time, mainly encouraged by the international harmonising process, several domestic jurisdictions have embarked on projects to modernise their rules on secured transactions.

Spain has not remained oblivious to such an international context. As in its neighbours, new legislation has been adopted and existing rules have been amended to modernise the law of secured transactions, particularly during the last 70 years. The main reforms have been driven by one of the following three motives:

* This chapter has been elaborated within the framework of the Research Project DER2013-46070-P Modernisation of Spanish Law of Secured Transactions to Facilitate Access to Credit in an International Context.

[1] NO Akseli, International Secured Transactions Law. Facilitation of Credit and International Conventions and Instruments (London, Routledge, 2011).

the need to meet new financing needs and repair market failures, to counteract economic situations entailing financing constraints and to enable local businesses access to international financial markets by ratifying international instruments and implementing uniform solutions in domestic legislation.

Like other continental civil law jurisdictions and honouring Roman law tradition,[2] historical security interests rules, embodied in the codes and some ancillary regulations, governed only possessory pledges (in movable property) and mortgages (in immovable property).[3] The need to facilitate access to credit without dispossessing the debtor of the most valuable assets of his/her business activity led to the adoption of rules on non-possessory pledge and movable mortgage (mortgage in movable property) in 1954 (Non-Possessory Pledge Act, NPPA).[4] Consequently, a registry system for movable property had to be established to replace the role of possession with registration. The registry system has evolved significantly towards the current Registry of Personal Property (*Registro de Bienes Muebles*, RPP)[5] and widened its scope. In the absence of codified rules dealing with receivables and other intangible personal property, gaps have been filled by scholars, case law and legislative reforms. Likewise, the expansive use in commercial practice of title-based devices has entailed the adoption of a few rules on title reservation and financial leases,[6] albeit they are insufficient and unsystematic. More recently, and among others, Royal Decree Law 5/2005 of 11 March[7] (RDL2005), which implements in Spain Directive 2002/47/EC of the European Parliament and of the Council of 6 June 2002 on financial collateral arrangements, has been adopted. In parallel, insolvency laws have experienced a succession of amendments in response to unfavourable economic circumstances, market needs and modern principles of business reorganisation. Interestingly, the enforcement system has also evolved to make realisation of security interests more flexible and enable the efficient assessment of reasonable value for assets. Thus, along with public auction, realisation agreements and sale by specialised entity,[8] the Spanish legal system is also familiar with extrajudicial enforcement

[2] AM Garro, 'Security Interests in Personal Property in Latin America: A Comparison with Article 9 and a Model for a Reform' (1986–1987) 9 *Houston Journal of International Law* 157.

[3] Technically, code provisions do not regulate pledge and mortgage as security interests but those security agreements by which the grantor grants or agrees to grant to a chargee either a pledge or a mortgage. Á Carrasco Perera, E Cordero Lobato, MJ Martin López, *Tratado de los Derechos de Garantía, Tomo I*, 3rd edn (Cizur Menor, Thomson Reuters Aranzadi, 2015) 643.

[4] *Ley sobre Hipoteca Mobiliaria y prenda sin desplazamiento de posesión* of 16 December 1954, published in Official Bulletin (BOE) 18 December 1954.

[5] Additional Provision of the Royal Decree 1828/1999, December 3, por el que se aprueba el Reglamento del Registro de Condiciones Generales de la Contratación, BOE 23 December 1999.

[6] Currently, leasing agreements lack comprehensive substantive regulation. They are, however, contracts legally nominated in an Additional Provision of the legislation on bank supervision *Ley* 26/1988, July 29, *de Disciplina e Intervención de las Entidades de Crédito*, BOE 30 July 1988.

[7] BOE 14 March 2005.

[8] Civil Procedural Act (Law 1/2000, *de Enjuiciamiento Civil*), BOE 8 January 2000, Arts 640–675.

procedures. Notary-supervised proceedings are extensively acknowledged by statutes in both security devices and title-based ones.[9] In addition, realisation of collateral by netting and by appropriation (mainly, under RDL2005) will also be discussed below.

Notwithstanding the number and relevance of reforms undertaken to date, a comprehensive modernising project of Spanish law of secured transactions is pending and highly desirable. The accession of Spain to the Cape Town Convention (CTC or 'Convention')[10] on 28 June 2013, on the terms and under the conditions that will be further explained, and subsequently the accession to its Aircraft Protocol in on 27 November 2015, have been a salutary impetus to reopen the domestic debate about the need to modernise the Spanish legal system on secured transactions and entailed the adoption of some implementation actions aimed to apply that international instrument (CTC as regards to aircraft equipment) that has finally entered into force for Spain on 1 March 2016. Very recently, an unofficial draft of a general law on secured transactions, which was essentially based on the concept of a multifunctional registered pledge, has circulated among scholars, registrars and other professionals; but, at the time of completing this chapter, there is no official initiative to produce a new legal text on the matter.

Thus, the current Spanish law of secured transactions still portrays an unsatisfactory image. The system is fragmented with rules scattered in a palette of laws and regulations governing (both possessory and non-possessory) security interests, hire purchase agreements[11] (Law 28/1998, HPAA), title-based devices (in particular, title reservation and financial leases), insolvency issues, registration and formalities for creation, validity and perfection. As parts of the system have evolved at different paces, a reasonable level of consistency is lacking. So, modern rules in certain areas are contrasted with antiquated solutions and obsolete processes in others. As a consequence, the system is complex to apply and construct but, at the same time, poor in scope.

The evolution of the Spanish law of secured transactions will be traced below through the highlighting and explanation of the most relevant milestones in the modernising process up to the present day. Reforms, as further discussed, are focused on substantive rules as well as registration and insolvency-related ones.

[9] Illustratively, Art 1872 Civil Code (Cc), Arts 86–88 and 95–96 NPPA, Art 16 Law on Hire-Purchase Agreements (HPAA) (see n 11).

[10] The Convention on International Interests in Mobile Equipment was adopted at a diplomatic conference held in Cape Town, South Africa, on 16 November 2001 under the auspices of UNIDROIT (International Institute for the Unification of Private Law/*Institut International pour l'Unification du Droit Privé*) and ICAO (International Civil Aviation Organization). Pursuant to Art 49(1) CTC, the Convention entered into force on 1 March 2006 together with the Protocol thereto on matters specific to aircraft equipment (hereinafter, Aircraft Protocol).

[11] Law 28/1998, July 13, on Hire-Purchase Agrements (*Ley de Venta a Plazos de Bienes Muebles*), BOE 14 July 1998.

B. A Portrait of the Spanish Law of Secured Transactions

The current Spanish law of secured transactions seems to be based more on formal criteria than on functional ones.[12] Therefore, at first sight, the Spanish legal system as regards secured transactions could quite reasonably be characterised as a formalist model. Notwithstanding this, it might well be worth noting that substance-over-form solutions,[13] providing for the same rules for transactions pursuing equivalent economic aims, exist in Spanish legislation.[14] Hence, a functional approach is familiar and is indeed adopted in certain issues. As a consequence, even if differences between 'what is owned' and 'what is owed'[15] are not definitively ignored, the distinction between traditionally pure security interests and title-based devices is not totally undisputed. Surprisingly, although both leasing agreements and conditional sales would traditionally be deemed title-based devices, today the legal nature of title reservation[16] or of the title held by the lessor in a leasing agreement[17] is disputed among scholars (and in case law), discussing whether the lessor and the conditional seller should be treated as a pure owner[18] or as a mere creditor holding a security interest over the asset instead.

Likewise, an express reference to 'functional equivalence' can even be found in Spanish legal rules for the purposes of registration. Thus, it is laid down (Article 4(a)

[12] For a more thorough study of the concept of international interest and the circular model adopted by the Convention to incorporate national categorisation, see T Rodríguez de las Heras Ballell, 'El concepto funcional de garantía en el Convenio de Ciudad del Cabo relativo a garantías internacionales sobre elementos de equipo móvil' [2012] *Anuario de Derecho Civil* 1605.

[13] R Goode, *Legal Problems of Credit and Security* (Louise Gullifer ed), 4th edn (London, Thomson Sweet & Maxwell, 2008, reprinted 2011) 3.

[14] As an example, Article 3 of Act 28/1998 of 13 July on instalments sales (*Ley de Venta a Plazos de Bienes Muebles*) when stating, after the definition of 'instalments sales' for the purposes of the law, that any agreement or act, regardless of the legal form or the denomination given by parties, will fall within the scope of the law provided that economic goals pursued by parties are the same as an instalment sale.

[15] MG Bridge, RA Macdonald, RL Simmonds, C Walsh, 'Formalism, Functionalism, and Understanding the Law of Secured Transactions' (1998–99) 44 *McGill Law Journal* 567.

[16] R Bercovitz, La cláusula de reserva de dominio. Estudio sobre su naturaleza jurídica en la compraventa a plazos de bienes muebles (Madrid, Editorial Moneda y Crédito, 1971); Á Carrasco Perera, E Cordero Lobato, MJ Martin López, Tratado de los Derechos de Garantía, Tomo II: Garantías Mobiliarias, 2nd edn (Cizur Menor, Aranzadi, 2008) 416–17.

[17] R Bercovitz, 'El pacto de reserva de dominio y la función de garantía del *leasing* financiero' in U Nieto Carol, JI Bonet Sánchez, *Tratado de Garantías en la Contratación Mercantil*, Tomo II, vol 1 (Madrid, Civitas, 1996) 377–416; A Cabanillas Sánchez, 'La configuración del arrendamiento financiero (leasing) por la Ley de 29 de julio de 1988, en la jurisprudencia y en el Convenio sobre Leasing Internacional' (1991) *III Anuario de Derecho Civil* 961; F González Castilla, *Leasing financiero mobiliario. Contenido del contrato y atribución del riesgo en la práctica contractual y la jurisprudencia* (Madrid, Civitas, 2002) 156–78; MJ Morillas Jarillo, 'Algunos aspectos del leasing de aeronaves en España' (1993) 208 *Revista de Derecho Mercantil* 471; R Illescas Ortiz, 'El *leasing:* aproximación a los problemas planteados por un nuevo contrato' (1971) 119 *Revista de Derecho Mercantil* 74; R Jiménez de Parga, MT de Gispert Pastor, 'La operación de *leasing* "es una operación de crédito?"' (1988) 31 *Revista de Derecho Bancario y Bursátil* 487.

[18] JM Miquel González, 'La reserva de dominio' in Esteve Bosch (ed), *Nuevas Perspectivas de Derecho Contractual* (Barcelona, Bosch, 2012) 139.

Ordinance of 19 July 1999)[19] that, along with pure hire purchase agreements on identifiable assets, any other agreement by virtue of which parties pursue the same economic goals as those of a hire purchase agreement will be registered in the RPP. These examples reveal that even if the Spanish model cannot properly be described as a functionalist one on secured transactions, it can be asserted that a functional approach is not totally unknown and that the equivalence of economic effects in legal transactions is certainly not disregarded in the Spanish jurisdiction.

Such uncertainty as to the nature of the different security interests, especially those created by title-based devices, is particularly relevant for the purposes of the application of the Cape Town system. According to Article 2, the applicable law shall determine whether an international interest will be deemed granted by the chargor under a security agreement; vested in a person who is the conditional seller under a title reservation agreement; or vested in a person who is the lessor under a leasing agreement. Consequences will result from that categorisation, insofar as, for instance, default remedies provided for by the Convention will be different depending on the type of agreement. Therefore, an open domestic debate about the nature of those interests (as security interests or pure ownership) would be relevant for the application of Cape Town provisions upon its proper entering into force for Spain.

C. The Modernisation of the Spanish Law of Secured Transactions: Milestones

Traditional security devices were divided in two categories depending on the nature of the collateral: on the one hand, the pledge (*prenda*) for movable property and, on the other hand, the mortgage (*hipoteca*) and the antichresis (*anticresis*)[20] for real property.

The pledge, as regulated in Articles 1857 to 1873 of the Civil Code[21] (Cc), typified a consensual asset-based security device under two main characterising features: it is a security interest in movable property and it requires dispossession of the debtor. Then, the pledge in Spanish law was traditionally devised as a possessory pledge in tangible personal property. In practice, its use as a security device was constrained by its possessory operation. In fact, as the perfection of the pledge entailed the displacing of the possession of the collateral to the creditor or a third party designated by the parties, pledged assets had necessarily to be

[19] Ordinance of 19 July 1999 on the Registry of Hire-Purchase Agreements in Movables, BOE 20 July 1999.

[20] The antichresis is not deemed a security interest however. A Carrasco Perera, E Cordero Lobato, MJ Martin López, *Tratado de los Derechos de Garantía, Tomo I*, 3rd edn (Cizur Menor, Thomson Reuters Aranzadi, 2015) 643.

[21] Royal Decree 24 July 1889, BOE 25 July 1889.

tangible ones, that is, susceptible of being possessed. Interestingly, if possession of the asset is not passed to the creditor or the designated third party, the pledge is not perfected. Without possession, neither inter partes effects nor effects against third parties arise. Then, without possession, no in rem right (security interest) has been created;[22] parties have only personal obligations and can exercise personal actions accordingly.

Soon, nevertheless, the traditional concept of pledge had to evolve to meet new financing needs and embrace emerging market practices. To that end, first, alongside the possessory pledge, non-possessory security devices were introduced. Secondly, intangibles assets had to be admitted as collateral as well.

(i) The Transition from Possessory Devices to Non-possessory Ones

Under the classical form of pledge (possessory pledge), the displacement of possession played a relevant two-fold role. As the debtor lost possession of the asset, any unauthorised transaction in relation to the asset was prevented. Simultaneously, the dispossession of the debtor gave notice and warned his/her creditors that the debtor's patrimonial capacity was limited. In addition, the possessory pledge made enforcement in case of default easier and more efficient.

Particularly in the second half of the twentieth century, the Spanish legal system joined the modernisation trend which had driven the Code-based jurisdictions towards a new conceptualisation of traditional security interests. Two main driving forces guided the transition from possessory devices to non-possessory ones. First, the possessory pledge was revealed as being an uneconomic institution,[23] designed for a market of small credit but unsuitable for post-industrial economies. Secondly, movable property superseded the monopolistic position of real property in the economy and proved that the old maxima *res mobilis res vilis* was overcome.

Under the NPPA, two non-possessory security devices were created: the chattel mortgage and the non-possessory pledge. The chattel mortgage is simply a mortgage-like non-possessory security device that can be granted over uniquely identifiable assets as listed in the NPPA (Article 12). The non-possessory pledge is a pledge-like security interest that can be granted over movables whose identification is weaker and expressly included in the NPPA without dispossessing the debtor. In sum, uniquely identifiable assets could be mortgaged, whereas over

[22] Spanish Supreme Court judgment of 21 July 2006 (RJ 2006, 5139).

[23] Nonetheless, it is critically noted that dispossession does not always entail the unproductivity of the collateral, for an ordinary exploitation is a natural expression of the duty to diligently conserve the pledged asset. Besides, it should be recalled that some rules governing possessory pledge are still applicable by default to all asset-based security devices to the extent that they have not been absorbed by special legislation. Á Carrasco Perera, E Cordero Lobato, MJ Martín López, *Tratado de los Derecho de Garantía, Tomo II*, 3rd edn (Cizur Menor, Thomson Reuters Aranzadi, 2015) 156.

those assets whose identification is weaker a non-possessory pledge should be granted. These two non-possessory devices are mutually exclusive, insofar as the law specifies which movables can be given as collateral under a chattel mortgage and which ones under a non-possessory pledge. The different nature of goods leads as well to different rules on creation and perfection. Thus, in a chattel mortgage, the movable can be uniquely identified and registered in the RPP. Nonetheless, in the case of a non-possessory pledge, the movable cannot be individualised on a specific basis and therefore publicity provided by registration is weaker. Hence, registration is supplemented by the determination of the *status loci*. That is, the debtor keeps possession over the movable as a depositary and the pledged asset cannot be moved to a place other than the *status loci* as fixed in the security agreement.

According to the aforementioned identification criteria, a chattel mortgage can be granted only over the following assets (Article 12 NPPA): business premises, automobile and motor vehicles, trams, train cars (provided that they are owned by private entities), aircraft, industrial equipment and intellectual property rights. Non-possessory pledges, on the other hand, can be granted (Articles 52–54 NPPA) by the owner of farms and livestock installations over expected crops and fruits, animals and offspring, equipment and tools; by any business over equipment identifiable by unique characteristics (model, trademark, number), other than equipment that can be mortgaged, and stored merchandise; and finally, over collections of artistic or historical value, receivables and future credit rights.

The desired clarity in the legal delimiting of the scope of both non-possessory security devices is however obscured by further amendments and by commercial practice. The original scope of application was expanded by the reform undertaken by Law 41/2007 of 7 December (Third Final Provision). Accordingly, the amended Article 2 NPPA declares unenforceable any contractual provision banning the grant of subsequent pledges or mortgages over goods that were already pledged or mortgaged. Hence, pledged or mortgaged goods have since then been included within the material scope of the law. Likewise, upon the reform, the law permits the granting of pledges and mortgages over those goods whose price is still due (not totally paid). By lifting that traditional limit, two different regimes are in force. On the one hand, as per the NPPA, any covenant forbidding subsequent pledge or mortgage of those goods that are already encumbered is unenforceable. On the other hand, however, according to the HPAA (Law 28/1998, 13 July), any hire purchase agreement shall necessarily include a prohibition on transferring or in any way disposing of (creating a security interest) the movable whose price is not totally paid yet without the prior written consent of the seller or, if applicable, the financer (Article 7 HPAA).

Commercial practice reveals that, despite the legal compartmentalisation of security devices by types of goods, several security interests can be created over the same asset with differing legal effects. Conflicts of rules arise in those situations where movable and immovable mortgages and non-possessory pledges may concur over the same asset. The following example can better illustrate those conflicting situations.[24] Over industrial equipment, several security interests can be created. First, unless agreed otherwise, a chattel mortgage over commercial premises covers equipment, tools and machines (Article 21)—as well as trademarks, commercial names and other intellectual property rights—provided that some conditions are met. Secondly, equipment and machines can be covered, if agreed, by the chattel mortgage over commercial premises as merchandise devoted to the running of the business activity (Article 22). Thirdly, equipment can be encumbered by a specific chattel mortgage of industrial equipment (Article 42). Fourthly, to the extent that equipment is not devoted to an industrial activity, a non-possessory pledge could also be created over it (Article 53) when the conditions laid down by Article 42 are not satisfied. Finally, a real mortgage could be extended by agreement to cover equipment (Article 111.1. Mortgage Act).[25]

Likewise, the process of building a legal regime for non-possessory security interests required from its outset the establishment of a registry system aimed at filling the gap left by the absence of dispossession. Hence, the evolution and use in practice of such non-possessory security devices passed in parallel to the shaping and implementation of the RPP.[26] Currently, the RPP comprises six sections whose scope and nature appreciably differ: ships and aircraft; automobile and other motor vehicles; industrial machinery, commercial premises and equipment; other security interests; other registrable movable property; standard contract terms.[27] From its inception, the RPP does not properly operate as a 'title registry', insofar as the prior registration of ownership of the object as a condition to register further interests on it is not compulsory (save for ships and aircraft) but merely facultative.[28]

(ii) Types of Collateral: From Tangibles to Receivables

The requirement of possession not only played the role of controlling perfection but also indirectly demarcated the material scope of eligible collateral. Unavoidably, as the collateral had to be delivered to and possessed by either the creditor or

[24] As brilliantly further explained by Encarna Cordero Lobato, 'Prenda sin desplazamiento e hipoteca mobiliaria' in ME Lauroba and J Marsal (eds), *Garantías reales mobiliarias en Europa* (Madrid, Marcial Pons, 2006) 80–89.

[25] Decree of 8 February 1946 approving Mortgage Act (*Ley Hipotecaria*), BOE 27 February 1946.

[26] Excellent analysis of the registry system for personal property can be found in L Fernández del Pozo, *El registro de bienes muebles. Los bienes muebles y la preferencia registral de los derechos inscritos* (Madrid, Marcial Pons, 2004).

[27] Thus, currently, the scope of the RPP is the registering of the following: agreements relating to personal property, such as sales, with or without deferred payment, ordinary leasing agreements and special leasing agreements (financial leasing, renting, lease-back), movable mortgages and non-possessory pledges, naval mortgages, notices of seizure and notices of lawsuits and any other security interest, encumbrance or limitation on such assets with effects against third parties. Likewise, standard contract terms and judgments about them are registrable as well.

[28] E Vázquez de Castro, *La publicidad registral en el tráfico de bienes muebles* (Madrid, Thomson Reuters Civitas, 2012) 87.

the designated third party, only tangible goods could be possessed and therefore used as collateral. The same rationale would exclude the pledge of future goods, albeit tangible ones, insofar as the pledge would not arise until the delivery of the good. Likewise, generic goods cannot be pledged due to fact that the object is undetermined. The pledge is not perfected until the debtor specifies the collateral and delivers it to the creditor or designated third party. Nevertheless, a universality (or group) of goods (eg a collection of paintings) can be pledged as a whole. In those cases, the specification of each item is not needed. Simply, the universality (the collection of goods) securing the obligation can be delimited by volumetric parameters, value or number (eg all Picasso paintings at the museum, the engine pool owned by an airline, stock of goods up to a certain value, the volume of a container). Then, items can be separated and replaced within the agreed limits without entailing either the termination of the security interest or the modification of the relationship. Finally, purely operative reasons explain why those goods that are previously used as collateral in a non-possessory pledge cannot be pledged subsequently, for the debtor possesses the good and is supposed to need it for the running of the economic activity.

Conceptually, the classical model of pledge was not designed for intangible or fungible goods. Business and professional debtors' patrimony, however, includes valuable intangible assets that might remain unproductive under the traditional possessory security devices. The use of money/money claims and receivables as collateral under the traditional possessory pledge represented a conceptual challenge.

First, unlike the 'regular pledge', a traditional possessory pledge where pecuniary collateral is individualised (a set of identified coins), the delivery of money or other fungible goods as collateral under an 'irregular pledge' implies that the secured creditor becomes the owner but not only the possessor. The 'irregular pledge' is not expressly regulated but parties can validly agree on it in exercise of their contractual autonomy. Whether this security device is really a pledge is questionable. Considering that the creditor becomes the owner of the collateral, important consequences arise. On the one hand, the creditor takes on any risks on the asset if the asset (the money) is lost or perishes anyhow (*res perit domino*). On the other hand, in case of default, the (pledged) money will pay off the debt. In banking practice, it is common that the bank, as a secured creditor, pledges the fixed-term deposit of its client, who is the debtor. Despite the divergence of scholars' opinions, in those cases, the 'irregular pledge' seems to become in practice a 'pledge of credits'.[29]

Secondly, the admission of the use of receivables as collateral was conceptually complex as possession over them is not possible. Besides, although some provisions refer laterally to the pledge of receivables (Articles 1868 and 1872 Cc), the Code is reluctant to admit such a possibility. The legislative refusal was indeed

[29] A Carrasco et al (n 23) 225. Likewise, Spanish Supreme Court judgment 19 April 1997 (RJ 1997, 2054).

initially reaffirmed by the Supreme Court (judgment of 27 December 1985 RJ 1983, 6654). But a decade later the Supreme Court did finally recognise the admissibility of pledge of receivables (judgment of 19 April 1997 (1997, 3429). Today, the pledge of receivables is expressly mentioned in the Insolvency Act (Article 90.1.6º), in RDL2005, on financial collateral arrangements (Article 8.1), and in the NPPA (Article 54).[30] Although a comprehensive set of rules is not provided for by legislation currently in force, the aforementioned provisions outline with thick lines the legal regime of the pledge of receivables.

As further discussed below, such provisions, insofar as they do in any way allude to the pledge of receivables, succeed in closing, in some cases, preceding debates among scholars and jurisprudence. But, in other cases, they incorporate in the legal system new elements for discussion. The most relevant issues will be elaborated on below.

The nature of the pledge of receivables is still up for debate. In the absence of a legal regime, the use of receivables as collateral is non-typified.[31] Consequently, scholars usually treat as synonymous pledge of receivables and assignment of receivables for security purposes. It is contended, additionally, that the assignment is the consensual mechanism to pledge receivables. So, pledge of receivables and assignment would be functionally interconnected. Even more, it is contended that 'assignment' is indeed a common effect for two different consensual devices. Nevertheless, such terminological confusion and their functional connection are not innocuous. Legal effects differ depending on legal nature. Hence, whereas in the case of pledge of receivables a real security interest is granted to the creditor (the chargee), under an assignment agreement, the creditor only holds a personal right (not an in rem right).

Likewise, the overlapping of legal regimes (pledge and assignment) makes required formalities uncertain. As a starting point, it is well worth noting that a possessory pledge can be validly granted under a private document or even orally, since no special formality is required. However, no effects against third parties arise until the date of the security agreement is stated in a public document.[32] With such a rule, secret or sham agreements against creditors' interests would be prevented. Therefore, scholars discuss whether *erga omnes* effects (against third parties) of the pledge of receivables require a certain date in a public deed as the pledge legal regime provides for (Article 1865 Cc) or a simple private document reliably fixing a date[33] (Article 1526 Cc) as provisions governing assignment

[30] Likewise, it is expressly regulated in the Catalonian Civil Code (Arts 569-12, 569-13.3 y 569-18).

[31] R Aranda. Rodríguez, *La prenda de créditos* (Madrid, Marcial Pons, 1996) 21–61.

[32] Some pledges, according to their particular legislation, do not need a public document: pledges by way of endorsement for security purposes of nominative shares, of bills of exchange and of life insurance policies and financial collateral arrangements under RDL2005.

[33] *Ex* Articles 1218 and 1227 Civil Code, a date is deemed certain in the following cases. A public document proves, even against third parties, the date when it was signed. The date of a private document will not be certain against third parties until any of the following events occurs: it is registered in a public registry; the death of any of the contracting parties; it is delivered to a public servant due to his/her position.

permit. Commercial practice is particularly prudent and, *ad cautelam*, both the public document and notification to the debtor are usually considered. Nonetheless, the current Insolvency Act, in Article 90.1.6º, seems to have opted for the latter option when recognising as privileged credits those secured by pledge of receivables as agreed in a private document. Along the same lines, RDL2005 (Article 8.1) stipulates that financial collateral arrangements have to be provided in writing, but no further formality can be required for the creation, validity, perfection, enforceability or admissibility in evidence of a financial collateral arrangement or the provision of financial collateral under a financial collateral arrangement.

Under the possessory pledge, the requirement of the dispossession of the debtor in a pledge of receivables has to be replaced by a functionally equivalent mechanism. Classical doctrine[34] maintained that the notification of the assignment to the debtor whose credit had been assigned for security purposes replaces the role of possession. The notice would prevent the debtor upon being informed from paying his/her original creditor (the debtor granting the pledge) and ensure that the credit was not disposable. Modern scholarly opinions,[35] nevertheless, describe the notification as an obligation of the debtor/assignor; hence, it is not an essential element for the valid creation of the pledge.

In 2007, Article 54 NPPA was amended by Law 41/2007 of 7 December to expressly admit non-possessory pledges of receivables, even over future credit rights (excluding negotiable instruments and financial instruments under RDL2005). Additionally, it was stated that, for a valid perfection, non-possessory pledges had to be registered in the RPP. The reform triggered a lively debate about the real impact of the amended provision in the legal regime for pledges of receivables. On the one hand, it was discussed whether the new legal recognition entailed that only non-possessory pledges can be granted over credit rights or if parties are entitled to freely decide to grant either a possessory pledge or a non-possessory one over receivables. On the other hand, it was debated if the reform had intended to establish a compulsory registration system for pledges of receivables, since validity and perfection are subject to registration. The opinion defended by scholars[36] and followed, for instance, by the General Directorate of Registries and Public Notaries[37] is that both possessory pledges

[34] M Albadalejo, *Derecho Civil. Derecho de Bienes* (Madrid, Edisofer, 2012) 725.

[35] N Moralejo Imbermón, 'Los contratos constitutivos de derechos reales de garantía', in *Tratado de Contratos* (Valencia, Tirant lo Blanch, 2009) 4260; Á Carrasco et al (n 23), 875; V Guilarte, 'Comentario a los artículos 1857 a 1886 CC' in *Comentarios al Código Civil y Compilaciones Forales* (Madrid, Edersa, 1979) 415.

[36] A Carrasco et al (n 23) 239.

[37] *Resolución de la Dirección General de Registros y del Notariado* of 18 March 2008, por la que se responden las consultas presentadas por la Asociación Española de Banca y por la Confederación Española de Cajas de Ahorro relativas al párrafo tercero del artículo 54 de la Ley de 16 de diciembre de 1954, de hipoteca mobiliaria y prenda sin desplazamiento según la redacción dada por la Ley 41/2007, de 7 de diciembre (BOE 29 March 2008).

and non-possessory pledges can be granted over credit rights according to their specific legislation. Thus, only non-possessory pledges will have to be registered for validity purposes. Nonetheless, in order to avoid uncertainties, it is common practice to combine both legal regimes (possessory pledge and non-possessory pledge) and proceed to register as well, with the resulting increase of costs though.

Interestingly, after the initial reticence regarding the validity of security interests over credit rights, in recent years, not only have legal obstacles been removed to affirm their admissibility, but three alternative legal regimes have even been provided for by current Spanish legislation: possessory pledge, non-possessory pledge and financial collateral arrangements.

(iii) Financial Collateral Arrangements: A Revolution of Principles

In Spain the regulation of financial collateral arrangements and the bilateral close-out netting has been framed within several packages of productivity-stimulus measures and reform programmes for financial markets.

The precedent for the current legal regime can be found indeed in Law 37/1998 of 16 November, modifying the Securities Act of 1998, as amended by Law 44/2002 of 22 November (Reform of Financial Markets Act). Upon the reform of 2002, Law 37/1998 in Additional provision 10 ('Flexibilisation of security interests legal regime') did succinctly regulate financial collateral arrangements, bilateral close-out netting provisions and insolvency effects. RDL2005, which aims to belatedly incorporate, among others, Directive 2002/47, derogates from previous provisions and intends to provide a systematic legal framework for financial collateral arrangements and bilateral close-out netting in Title I, Chapter II, Articles 2–17.[38]

RDL2005 represents one of the most profound reforms in the Spanish legal system for secured transactions. Not surprisingly, its hasty adoption, an inaccurate translation of the Spanish version of the Directive and the use of highly specialised financial terms drew strong criticism[39] from the outset. Additionally, an imprecise definition of financial collateral arrangements and a generous scope of application initially gave rise to some uncertainties. Certainly, the Spanish legislator opted for

[38] The legal regime for financial collateral arrangements and close-out netting provisions was included, relatively intact, within the Proposal for a Commercial Code presented in 2013. However, it was finally excluded from the scope of the envisaged Commercial Code in the last version of 30 May 2014 (Draft Bill of Commercial Code), whose enactment is still pending.

[39] F Redondo Trigo, 'El pacto marciano, el pacto ex intervallo y la fiducia cum creditore en las garantías financieras del Real Decreto-ley 5/2005' (2007) 699 *Revista Crítica de Derecho Inmobiliario* 357; A Sánchez Andrés, 'Algunos aspectos de la directiva sobre garantías financieras en relación con el derecho español de los mercados de valores' in *Estudios jurídicos sobre el mercado de valores* (Madrid, Civitas, 2008) 1258; BA González Navarro, 'Reintegración concursal y normas especiales: el Real Decreto-Ley 5/2005, de 11 de marzo' in *La reintegración en el concurso de acreedores* (Cizur Menor, Aranzadi, 2009) 434; A Veiga Copo, 'Hacia la globalidad de las garantías reales. De las garantías omnibus, globales y futuras a las garantías financieras' in *Créditos, garantías y concurso* (Madrid, Civitas, 2010) 87.

delimitating the legal scope to the maximum without resort to any of the limits at the disposal of Member States under Directive 2002/47. The decision of the Spanish legislator on that issue, far from being anecdotal, gauges the extent and the level of impact of the new regime in the traditional principles and rules governing secured transactions at the domestic level. In fact, those financial collateral arrangements falling within the scope of RDL2005 will benefit from a relaxation of formalities for creation, efficiencies in enforcement and a particularly benevolent treatment in insolvency. Interestingly, from the time of its adoption, some reforms have been undertaken regarding issues pertaining to the material scope of the legal regime.

The RDL2005 regime is applicable to financial collateral arrangements, close-out netting provisions and financial collaterals which satisfy a set of objective and subjective conditions. In this regard, two recent judgments of the Spanish Supreme Court[40] of 20 and 26 June 2012 respectively provide that RDL2005 conditions are met; the legal regime for financial collateral arrangements applies regardless of how it has been qualified or named by the parties.

For the purposes of RDL2005, like the Directive, financial collateral arrangements can be security financial collateral arrangements and title transfer financial collateral agreements. Under the former (Article 6.3), a collateral provider provides financial collateral by way of security in favour of, or to, a collateral taker, and where the full ownership of the financial collateral (object or credit right) remains with the collateral provider when the security right is established. Accordingly, RDL2005 provides for a pledge of financial collateral as an alternative to the ordinary pledge as regulated in the Civil Code and more likely to the non-possessory pledge as well. Under the latter, a collateral provider transfers full ownership of financial collateral to a collateral taker for the purpose of securing or otherwise covering the performance of relevant financial obligations. The recognition of such a title transfer formula for security purposes, anticipated by Law 40/2002, gave rise to controversy initially insofar as it conflicted with the traditional treatment of *fiducia cum creditore* by scholars and courts as a 'sham transaction'. Interestingly, the Spanish Supreme Court in its judgment of 24 June 2010 (RJ 2010, 5410) held that its express recognition for financial collateral arrangements has ousted the traditional rule prohibiting the secured creditor from appropriating or disposing of the collateral (Article 1859 Cc) as a classical public order rule. Therefore, it is arguably upheld that the Supreme Court judgment might enable the extension of the title transfer device to collateral other than financial collateral. Hence, it would also entail the admission of the validity of *pactum commissorium*. It would mean an important revolution of principles underpinning the domestic secured transactions system.

[40] J Hormaechea Alonso, 'Ejecución de garantías financieras y compensación en el concurso. Comentario a las sentencias de la Sala de lo Civil del Tribunal Supremo de 20 de junio de 2012 y de 26 de junio de 2012' (2013) 18 *Revista de Derecho Concursal y Paraconcursal* 272.

Notwithstanding the foregone assertion and without disregarding the revolutionary essence of RDL2005 in some issues for the Spanish system, it has to be recalled that the realisation of collateral by netting and by appropriation had been admitted since the last century by scholars and case law provided that collateral is cash or publicly listed companies' shares. That is, the prohibition of *pactum commissorium* had been heavily relaxed under the Spanish legal system in the above-mentioned transactions even before the implementation of the special regime for financial collateral arrangements. Nevertheless, the open question is whether non-listed companies' shares are included within RDL2005 and whether they might benefit from realisation mechanisms as well. The most likely answer seems to be negative insofar as rights of the collateral provider cannot be properly protected in the absence of an official (or unofficial) market where objective criteria enable valuation of the collateral for the purposes of enforcement or the exercise of the right of use. Nevertheless, scholars' opinions and case law are divergent.[41]

Regarding the personal scope, RDL2005 has been significantly generous not only in opting for the broader option offered by the Directive, but even going further, including in some cases individuals as well, excluded, however, by the Directive. Thus, RDL2005 applies to financial collateral arrangements and close-out netting provisions between parties listed in Article 4.1 (in line with Article 1.2.(a) to (d) Directive); and between any legal entity and one of those entities listed in Article 4.1; to close-out netting provisions between any parties even if one of the parties is an individual; and to financial collateral arrangements between an individual and one of the entities listed under letter (d) of Article 4.1 (authorities managing exchange markets, registry entities, a central counterparty, settlement agent or clearing house, including similar institutions acting in the futures, options and derivatives markets).

In 2013[42] a new entity was added to the list covered by RDL2005: the Banking Restructuring Assets Management Society (SAREB). The SAREB is a private entity[43] whose mission was to assist in the recovery of the Spanish financial sector. To that end, for the purposes of recovery, financial collateral arrangements, originally provided in favour of financial entities duly falling within the personal scope of RDL2005, might be transferred to SAREB. As a consequence, upon the transfer, the financial collateral arrangements would not be covered anymore by RDL2005 and would accordingly lose its special protection, as SAREB was not an

[41] In favour of the admissibility, A Veiga Copo, *Tratado de la prenda* (Cizur Menor, Thomson Reuters Civitas, 2011) 280 and José Manuel Cuenca Miranda, 'Los valores no cotizados en el Real—Decreto Ley 5/2005 y el principio de interpretación conforme' (2014) 1 *La Ley Mercantil* 172. Against, Carrasco et al (n 23), 608; K Lyczkowska, *Garantía financieras. Análisis del Capítulo II del Título I del Real Decreto-Ley 5/2005, de 11 de marzo* (Cizur Menor, Thomson Reuters Civitas, 2013) 91–94.

[42] Royal Decree Law 6/2013 of 22 March, modifies Law 9/2012 of 14 November (Restructuring and Resolution for Financial Institutions Act) to apply the RDL2005 regime to the Banking Restructuring Assets Management Society (SAREB) as well.

[43] According to most recent data available at www.sareb.es, 55 per cent of SAREB equity capital is contributed by private entities and the remaining 45 per cent is held by FROB (Bank Restructuration Fund).

included entity. Therefore, in order to make the restructuring and recovery measures package effective, SAREB was expressly added to the list of entities covered by RDL2005.

As regards eligible types of financial collateral, at the time of the enactment, RDL2005 laid down, like the Directive, that a financial collateral could exclusively consist of cash or financial instruments (Article 7). More recently, in 2011, the incorporation in Spain of Directive 2009/44/EC of 6 May by Law 7/2011[44] made changes in the aforementioned legal provision to increase the pool of available collateral by adding credit claims. Thus, financial collateral can consist of credit rights/claims as well, provided that certain conditions are satisfied. In particular, credit claims mean 'pecuniary claims arising out of an agreement whereby a credit institution grants credit in the form of a loan'. In this case, Spain has resorted to the limiting option provided by the Directive to exclude from the scope credit claims where the debtor is a consumer or a micro- or small enterprise, unless the collateral taker or the collateral provider is any of the entities listed under Article 4.1(b).[45]

In order to achieve the main goals of the Directive and to enhance the position of creditors, provisions dealing with enforceability, insolvency issues and rights arising from financial collateral arrangements have to be adopted. In particular, the incorporation into the domestic system of some of these provisions deserves closer attention, as it entails a departure from domestic rules and traditional principles.

First, the right of use of the financial collateral under the financial collateral arrangement, if provided by the terms of the arrangement, used to be unfamiliar for the classical security model.

Second, the realisation of financial collateral by appropriation appeared to conflict with the prohibition of the *pactum commissorium*. Currently, under Article 11 RDL2005, appropriation is possible only if agreed by the parties in the security financial collateral arrangement; and the parties have agreed in the security financial collateral arrangement on the valuation of financial instruments and credit claims. Meaningfully, RDL2005 acknowledges the validity of *pacto marciano* and *pacto ex intervallo*, which were already variations of *pactum commissorium* admitted in Spain's legal tradition.[46]

Thirdly, the fact that RDL2005 encapsulates a special insolvency regime, parallel to general insolvency rules, drew strong criticism at the beginning. Privileges conferred on financial collateral creditors, even higher than those of the privileged 'ordinary' creditors, were deemed exorbitant (against the *par conditio creditorum*

[44] BOE 12 April 2011.

[45] Article 4.1(b) RDL2005: 'The European Central Bank, the Bank of Spain, a central bank, the Bank for International Settlements, a multilateral development bank, the International Monetary Fund and the European Investment Bank'.

[46] F Redondo Trigo, 'El pacto marciano, el pacto ex intervallo y la fiducia cum creditore en las garantías financieras del Real Decreto-ley 5/2005'.

principle). As expected, nonetheless, following the European mandate, RDL2005 set up a special insolvency regime for financial collateral based on three main pillars. First, financial collateral agreements (or the provision of the financial collateral under such agreement) will not be declared null and void or be reversed on the sole basis of an insolvency proceeding (winding-up proceeding or restructuring measures) under the conditions laid down. Second, financial collateral arrangements shall not be limited, restricted or in any way affected by the commencement of an insolvency proceeding and they will be separately enforced, outside of the insolvency proceeding, in conformity with the terms of the arrangements and the rules provided for by RDL2005. Third, financial collateral arrangements and the provision of financial collateral, concluded or provided prior to the commencement of the insolvency proceeding, can be rescinded or contested under Article 71 of the Insolvency Act only by the 'insolvency receivers' (*administración concursal*) and on the sole grounds of fraud of creditors. The stricter criterion of 'fraud of creditors' was introduced by Law 7/2011 of 11 April to replace the previous lower threshold of 'detrimental to creditors'. Upon the amendment, arrangements are less exposed to rescission actions.

D. Insolvency

Insolvency situations represent the most conclusive testing ground to assess the soundness and the effectiveness of secured transactions. The treatment of secured transactions within the insolvency framework is not only a helpful tool to gauge the actual level of protection[47] for creditors' interests,[48] but also a criterion that indirectly helps to categorise any secured transaction as a pure security interest or a title-based device, in those legal system acknowledging such a distinction. Thus, illustratively, the analysis of the provisions currently in force[49] related to the enforcement of a title reservation clause in an insolvency proceeding projects a blurred image. It arguably seems that, albeit disputed among scholars, the conditional seller, as a title reservation holder, is treated as other in rem secured creditors holding security interests over personal property instead of being deemed a real owner. In sum, the conditional seller would be entitled to a *separation ex iure*

[47] One of the most compelling reasons indeed for taking security, in particular, H Beale, M Bridge, L Gullifer and E Lomnicka, *The Law of Security and Title-Based Financing*, 2nd edn (Oxford, Oxford University Press, 2012) 7.

[48] It might well be worth noting that creditors holding interests over ships and aircraft will be entitled to enforce their privileges, in conformity with special legislation, on a separate basis. Upon the separate enforcement, the remainder will be reintegrated to the debtor's estate for the purposes of the insolvency proceedings (Art 76 IA).

[49] The precedent regime prior to the enactment of the current legislation (Insolvency Act of 2003) seemed, however, to contemplate the opposite solution by providing the conditional seller and the financier with a right of *separatio ex iure dominii*.

crediti but not to a *separation ex iure domini*. Similar reasoning would lead to the categorisation of the position held by the lessor in insolvency proceeding in the same terms and with equivalent consequences.

The Spanish legal framework for insolvency was profoundly reformed in 2003 by the enactment of the Insolvency Act (hereinafter, IA).[50] It signified a landmark legislative achievement that responded to a long-awaited aspiration to modernise archaic, dispersed and complex precedent rules governing a diversity of institutions with a new systematic, unified and flexible system. Since the entering into force on 1 September 2004, nonetheless a number of further amendments have been undertaken to better meet market needs, to counteract effects of economic crisis or to enable refinancing arrangements and debt restructuring. Some of them do directly affect secured transactions.

Significantly, the pre-insolvency stage was widely ignored in the original version of 2003. Therefore, 2009, 2011 and 2013 reforms aimed to change that model. In order to foster preservative solutions, pre-insolvency arrangements were enabled and an actual pre-insolvency system has been designed. Several modalities of pre-insolvency solutions are available: individual refinancing arrangement (Article 71.*bis* 2 IA); plural refinancing arrangement (Article 71.*bis* 1 IA); collective refinancing arrangement (Additional Provision 4 IA); and Extrajudicial Arrangement proceeding (Articles 231 IA ff). The collective arrangement is the only one that could affect secured creditors with or without their consent. Apart from that, it can be argued that overall secured creditors' interests were protected and immune from the arrangement to the extent of the secured obligation. Nevertheless, 2014 and 2015[51] reforms have had a notable impact on the position of (asset-based) secured creditors.

First, Law 17/2014 of 30 September,[52] aimed to enable financial 'deleverage' in conjunction with due protection of creditors' reasonable expectations. To that end, certain improvements had to be made to rules governing the pre-insolvency stage and refinancing arrangements. Thus, enforcement might be stayed at the commencement of negotiations leading to the reaching of an agreement with creditors. Nonetheless, the enforcement of secured transactions will not be stayed,

[50] Law 22/2003 of 9 July on Insolvency, BOE 10 July 2003. Needless to say, European Union legislation on bankruptcy (Council Regulation (EC) No 1346/2000 of 29 May 2000 on insolvency) also applies in Spain.

[51] Royal Decree Law 1/2015 of 27 February, BOE 28 February 2015, introducing a 'fresh start' solution in insolvency laws and Law 9/2015 of 25 May, BOE 26 May 2015. 'Fresh start' solutions had previously been introduced, for certain debtors and under specific conditions, by Law 14/2013 providing support to entrepreneurs and promoting internationalisation. The extent of the 'fresh start' is nonetheless limited. The debtor was required, among other requirements, to entirely pay off secured creditors (mortgage and pledges). Under the RDL 1/2015, the 'fresh start' model has been substantially amended. Interestingly, the total payment to privileged creditors is not always required for the cancellation of debts. Other formulas are laid down to allow the debtor to be eligible for 'fresh start' benefits.

[52] BOE 1 October 2014. The enactment of Law 17/2014 derives from the legislative processing as an ordinary law of the Royal Decree Law 4/2014 of 7 March, adopting urgent measures in refinancing arrangements and debt restructuring.

as a general rule, unless they were related to assets needed for the continuity of the business or professional activity. This protection rule had been previously enhanced by replacing the old criterion of 'assets attached to the business or professional activity' by the new threshold of 'assets necessary for the continuation of the business of professional activity'. Interestingly, the scope of relevant assets will be further reduced.[53]

Secondly,[54] Royal Decree Law 11/2014 of 5 September,[55] expanded the relaxing measures provided for by Royal Decree Law of March 2014 to the insolvency arrangement as well.[56] In this regard, in the case of an asset-based security interest, the special privilege of the secured credit will not exceed the value of the collateral (ie if there is a secured credit of 50 over an asset valued up to 30, the remaining 20 will not be deemed privileged). The remaining part of the credit will be treated according to its nature (Article 90.3 IA). To that end, some valuation rules are laid down to assess the reasonable value of assets (Article 94.5 IA). The most visible result of this reform is that privileged creditors, who used to be indifferent to the adopting of the arrangement, should be more active in the process to the extent of the part of their credits transpiring to be ordinary or non-privileged.

E. The Modernisation of the Spanish Legal System in the International Context: Current Situation and Perspectives

From a supranational approach, the course of the Spanish legal system's evolution is certainly determined by the European Union rules, Spain having been a Member State since 1986, and by international initiatives. On the one hand, relatively late incorporation of Directive 2002/47 on financial collateral arrangements by RDL2005 is, for instance, an illustrative sign of profound reform of traditional principles and domestic rules on secured transactions. On the other hand, beyond the implementation of European legislation, the compact and multifaceted movement of international harmonisation of rules governing secured transactions is triggering an open debate about the existing model and impelling efforts towards the modernisation of the domestic legal system. Although no specific legislative

[53] R Cabanas Trejo, 'La garantía real en el preconcurso de acreedores' (2014) *Diario La Ley*, No 8317, 23 May 2014.

[54] R Cabanas Trejo, 'Una nueva reforma de la legislación concursal (RDL 11/2014, de 5 de septiembre, de medidas urgentes en materia concursal) (2014) *Diario La Ley*, No 8406, 24 October 2014.

[55] Likewise, Royal Decree Law 11/2014 was subsequently processed as an ordinary law (*Proyecto de Ley de medidas urgentes en materia concursal* 1121/000117): Law 9/2015 of 25 May, BOE 26 May 2015.

[56] J Pulgar Ezquerra, 'Ley 17/2014 de medidas urgentes en materia de refinanciación y reestructuración de deuda empresarial y Real Decreto-Ley 11/2014 de reformas urgentes en materia concursal: nuevos paradigmas' (2014) *Diario La Ley*, No 8391, 3 October 2014.

initiative is ongoing, several circumstances reveal that attention has been focused on diagnosing the domestic system and attentively observing international instruments with the aim of guiding an envisaged modernisation.

Along with the participation of Spain in international forums and the ratification of other Conventions, the accession to the Cape Town Convention in 2013 and to its Aircraft Protocol in 2015 (effective since 1 March 2016) is an especially meaningful landmark in the process of modernisation with reference to international coordinates. The peculiar conditions under which the accession has been carried out require further analysis.

(i) The *Staggered* Accession to the Cape Town System

On 28 June 2013, together with several declarations, Spain deposited the instrument of accession to the Convention with UNIDROIT. The instrument of accession was published in the Official Bulletin dated 4 October 2013, along with the entire text of the Convention, the list of Contracting States and all declarations made to date.[57] Nevertheless, no Protocol was ratified, either simultaneously or as a immediate continuation of the accession, until the deposit of the instrument of accession with UNIDROIT on 27 November 2015. Consequently, Spain is a Contracting State of the Convention since October 2013 but no instrument of ratification, approval, acceptance or accession to any of the Protocols was deposited in two years. Upon the accession to the Aircraft Protocol, the Convention in relation to aircraft object is, since 1 March 2016, finally part of Spanish legal system and its provisions are effective and fully operational—previously, Convention's provisions could not be applied on an isolated basis without a Protocol.

Due to the original and pragmatic multidivisional[58] structure under which the Cape Town system works, the staggered ratifying process followed by Spain resulted in an anomalous situation to the extent that the expected ratification of any of the Protocols was deferred. Today, the transitional situation is totally concluded and the CTC is effective in Spain, but it might well be worth analysing the effects that derived from the staggered and prolonged process of ratification.

Along the transitional period, the Spanish position in relation to the CTC was displaying dysfunctional effects.[59] The Convention was considered to enter in force for Spain from 1 October 2013 and Spain was treated as a Contracting State for the purposes of the Convention; but in practical terms, the CTC could not be applied to any category of mobile equipment within its sphere of application and its provisions remained inactive as from the time of the entry into force

[57] BOE 4 October 2013 (www.boe.es).

[58] Following my description of the system in T Rodríguez de las Heras Ballell, Las garantías mobiliarias sobre equipo aeronáutico en el comercio internacional. El Convenio de Ciudad del Cabo y su Protocolo (Madrid, Marcial Pons, 2012) chapter I.F, 42.

[59] Further analysed in T Rodríguez de las Heras Ballell, 'The Accession by Spain to the Cape Town Convention: A First Assessment' [2014] *Uniform Law Review* 1–23.

of a Protocol for Spain (1 March 2016) and then as regards the corresponding category of equipment (aircraft object), as the Convention provisions cannot have any effect unless linked to a specific category of equipment as covered by a Protocol.

The accession to the CTC was a critical decision for Spanish strategic economic sectors, which has to be applauded. Upon the deposit of the instrument of accession, Spain confirmed its firm support for the Cape Town system as a stimulus of strategic industries and an enabler of a modernisation process in domestic legislation. The deferred ratification of any of the Protocols was arguably justified by the need to carry out a prior reform of domestic legislation (both in material rules and in a registry system) dealing with issues involved in and related to secured transactions over mobile equipment in order to be prepared for adopting the Protocols subsequently.

Certainly, the proposal for a modernisation of the existing system on secured transactions is timely and very convenient, but it has proved to require a longer time and entail a complex process. Notwithstanding this, from the outset an early adoption of the Protocols was highly desirable without making it dependent on the success of a all-embracing reform. Even more importantly, the CTC and the Protocol can reasonably work in Spain with a limited number of amendments to domestic rules. As a matter of fact, the CTC is already in force considering that the actions adopted so far aimed to implement the uniform system have been essentially focused on and led to enable the functioning of the designated national entry point. Although a profound and comprehensive reform of the secured transactions domestic framework has to be encouraged and is still an urgent undertaking that the Spanish legislator should not avoid, it proved not to be a *conditio sine qua non* for the Convention to take effect. Even if it is our understanding that a truly effective implementation of the Convention does still require further reform regarding certain issues. In particular, to align insolvency provisions with Alternative A of Article XI of the Protocol aiming to produce an equivalent result, to review domestic rules in the light or Article X, to ensure that procedural rules are suitable for the exercise of all remedies provided for by the Convention and the Protocol, and to amend the inadequate rules applicable to the national entry point.

(ii) The Implementation of the Cape Town System in Spain: Selected Topics

A total exploitation of economic benefits and strategic advantages required completing the international commitment with the prompt ratification of any of the Protocols. Insofar as the reason for postponing the ratification of the Protocol seemed to be the need for a prior reform in the domestic legal framework and the registry system, seminars, workshops and professional meetings have been organised to discuss critical issues, contrast opinions and disclose concurring interests.

On the occasion of those meetings, the importance of paying careful attention to implementation has been emphasised repeatedly. If the Convention provisions are not properly implemented or the existing domestic rules or practices hamper the functioning of the International Registry, the expected benefits of the Convention and its Protocols may greatly diminish.

Particular concerns have been raised in relation to the registry system and registration rules. Although Spain can count on a sound, modern, efficient and highly computerised registry system and some existing registry regulations are already in the process of reform[60] to contemplate the operation of the International Registry, registry models and philosophies are visibly divergent, albeit not irreconcilable. Put simply, where the systems diverge, the Spanish registration model is overall based on a document-filing registry (with some nuances) conducted by active registrars who substantially review the registration. As Spain has decided to designate a national entry point (*Registro de Bienes Muebles*) and principles governing national registry systems which may differ from the registry model designed by the CTC, the proper operation of the national entry in critical in order to anticipate and minimise contradictions (including areas such as eventual fees, required documentation and registrar review).

In relation to this matter, for a proper implementation it was crucial to conduct discussion in professional and institutional forums. A proper implementation relies on two dimensions: on the one hand, a carefully pondered list of declarations and an adequate wording of them; on the other hand, a reform of the national system as to those aspects likely, if not duly amended, to hamper the full exploitation of the uniform instrument's expected efficiencies.

(a) *Scope of Application: Categories of Objects and Types of Security Agreement*

As far as the material scope is concerned, all objects covered by the Cape Town system in the three Protocols—aircraft equipment, railway rolling stock and space assets (Article 2 CTC)—adopted so far can be used as collateral in the different security devices provided for by the Spanish legal system on secured transactions. Some of them are expressly mentioned in specific legislation (such as aircraft or train carriages) but most of them fall easily into the general category of movable or personal property susceptible of being pledged or subjected to other forms of security interest under the domestic law even before Spain became a Contracting State. Therefore, mobile equipment as described by the CTC is subject to the same asset-based secured transactions rules as personal property in general.

Notwithstanding this, it might well be worth pointing out some considerations. First, in certain cases, when assets are expressly mentioned in special legislation,

[60] The old Decree 419/1969, of 13 March 1969, regulating the Registry of Aircraft is in the process of reform. The new text would include express provisions regulating interconnection between the Registry of Aircraft and the RPP aimed at enabling the application of the CTC.

parties are not free to choose the most appropriate security agreement. For instance, according to legislation regulating non-possessory pledges and mortgages on chattels (movable mortgage), train carriages and aircraft can only be mortgaged (using movable mortgage) but not pledged under the same law (non-possessory pledge).

Secondly, according to the scope of application of the Aircraft Protocol, an aircraft in its entirety is not treated as an object in conformity with the Protocol. Aircraft equipment comprises airframe, helicopter, and engines. On the contrary, aircraft are expressly contemplated in Spanish legislation on non-possessory pledges and chattel mortgages. Aircraft equipment could alternatively be subject to different security forms other than movable mortgage (leasing, conditional sale with title reservation, non-possessory pledge). However, since aircraft are described as a compound asset, the principle of accession by incorporation entails that the interest is presumed to extend over all component parts. As a consequence, once the engine is installed, it would become part of the aircraft and lose autonomy. Despite that traditional principle, there is not an insurmountable obstacle to adopt CTC classification. Additionally, the separate registration of engines and even of component parts has been admitted,[61] provided that they meet identifiable criteria sufficiently to access the RPP.[62] As a matter of fact, contracting parties who decide to depart from legal provision and agree on a different extension of the interest frequently include in their security agreements provisions limiting the legal extension of a mortgage and separating engines, due to its high value and in accordance with industry practices.[63] By all means, once the CTC and the Aircraft Protocol are in force in Spain, their provisions are part of the Spanish legal system replacing, and hierarchically prevailing, over domestic rules contradicting them.

Thirdly, with regard to space assets, even if no specific references to this category of objects are found in existing secured transactions rules' there is no reason to question that these assets may be pledged or subjected to other forms of security agreements with the full extent of effects (lease agreements, title reservation sales, non-possessory pledge, depending on the nature of each specific asset). Likewise, mining, agricultural and construction equipment likely to fall within the scope of the envisaged Protocol on matters specific to mining, agricultural and construction equipment (MAC Protocol), in case of adoption, would easily be subject to all forms of security agreements as described above.

In relation to the asset-based financing schemes, in secured transactions relating to aircraft equipment, an overall preference for leasing contracts and title reservation agreements can be asserted, whereas the use of security agreements, in particular mortgage agreements, over aircraft equipment is definitively more limited. In the aviation market, the usual security packages present in

[61] Resolution of 29 January 2001, Dirección General de Registros y del Notariado.

[62] Article 6 Ordinance of 19 July 1999 regulating the Registry of Hire Purchase of Movables. *Ordenanza para el Registro de Venta a Plazos de Bienes Muebles.*

[63] Rodríguez de las Heras (n 58) 51–57.

internationally developed aircraft finance structures are applied (SOL—Spanish Operating Lease,[64] as an alternative to the traditional Japanese Operating Leases and German Leverage Leases).

(b) *Analysis of the Declarations Made by Spain on the Occasion of the Accession*

Spain's instrument of accession to the Convention was deposited with UNIDROIT together with declarations under Articles 52 and 54(2) of the Convention. Other than the classical declaration regarding Gibraltar's status under Article 52, the declaration made under Article 54(2) is particularly pertinent for enforcement purposes.

Framing the declaration under Article 54(2) within the Spanish legal context may give rise to some unexpected results. Should the scope of the declaration literally mean that only purely judicial remedies can be applied in the enforcement of security interests, an undesirable consequence might result. Out-of-court enforcement, as enshrined by domestic legislation, would be deactivated in the international context. It makes no sense, and it is very unlikely to inspire Spain's instrument of accession, an intentional decision to grant worse treatment to international security interests than that provided for by domestic rules. Considering that notary-supervised proceedings are purportedly preferable in terms of speed and efficiency, it might be contented instead that, either under Article 13, as additional remedies permitted by the applicable law, or under Article 14, creditors would benefit from exercising any remedy provided by the Convention, subject to Article 54(2), in conformity with the procedure prescribed by the law of the place where the remedy is to be exercised, and, consequently, following the procedural requirements of those enforcement procedures to be conducted before a notary public when applicable. It is the author's contention that the latter interpretation should take priority.[65]

The instrument of ratification of the Protocol has represented the opportunity to clarify the scope of the declaration. On the occasion of depositing an

[64] J López Quiroga and A Cabellos Ballenilla, 'Spanish Aviation Finance Market' (2006) *Air Finance Journal*, 27 October, explain the functioning of the SOL: 'under the SOL structure, on its delivery date, a leasing company acquires the aircraft ordered by the airline under normal commercial terms pursuant to a sale and purchase contract entered into with the manufacturer (Airbus, in the case of Iberia). The leasing company will in turn lease it, under a financial leasing agreement, to a third party (financial lessee), which will then enter into an operating lease agreement (which may or may not have a purchase option) with the airline. The use of a finance lease agreement allows the financial lessee to benefit from an accelerated tax depreciation of the leased asset and to benefit from the financial effect of a deferral of the Spanish income tax (set at 35%, although it is to be reduced progressively to 30% in the coming years). In this case, the financial lessee may transfer some of the financial advantage to the airline as lower rental payments under the operating lease or as a reduced exercise price of the purchase option held by the airline, for example'.

[65] In contrast, however, Encarna Cordero considers that the wording of the declaration entails that CTC remedies could not be enforced before a notary: Cordero, 'Garantías internacionales sobre elementos de equipo móvil' (2013) 8189 *Diario La Ley*.

instrument of ratification, further declarations to the Convention can be made. Specifically, according to Article 53 a Contracting State may, at the time of ratification, acceptance, approval of, or accession to the Protocol, declare the relevant 'court' or 'courts' for the purposes of Article 1 and Chapter XII of the Convention. Hence, in the instrument of ratification Spain has rightly declare that *all of the competent courts of the Kingdom of Spain, as determined in accordance with the Spanish laws and regulations*, are the relevant courts for the purposes of Article 1 and Chapter XII of the Convention. The circular expression 'all the competent courts' is not particularly transparent but at least provides a helpful interpretative instrument to avoid the exclusion of notary-supervised proceedings by the declaration under Article 54(2) insofar as any organ, tribunal or authority empowered to enforce security interests in accordance with Spanish laws and regulations will be covered by the 'leave of the court' requirement. The aim of the declaration under Article 53 seems to be to defuse the undesirable rigidity of the previous declaration under Article 54(2); nevertheless, it is doubtful whether it is enough to satisfy Article X of the Protocol with a substantially similar domestic solution. It has to be pointed out here that, as a subsequent declaration, the declaration under Article 53 does not become effective until 1 June 2016. Since any subsequent declaration can be made at any time after the entering into force of the Convention, any further declaration will take effect under the conditions laid down by Article 57.

On the occasion of the accession to the Convention, Spain made no declarations under Articles 39 and 40. Nevertheless, declarations under such Articles were expected in further instruments of ratification of any of the Protocols. It was reasonable to expect that Spain would take the opportunity of the ratification of the Aircraft Protocol (most likely the first one) to make some declarations to the Convention. In particular, declarations under Articles 39(1)(a), 39(1)(b) and 40 were highly probable. In fact, the actual accession to the Aircraft Protocol has confirmed such expectations and Spain has made subsequent declarations under Articles 39(1)(a) and (b) and 40.

On the one hand, with regard to the Aircraft Protocol, Spain has made declarations under Article XIX(1) designating a national entry point (*Registry of Movables—Registro de Bienes Muebles*); Article XXIX regarding the status of Gibraltar; and Article XXX(1) on the irrevocable de-registration and export request authorization (IDERA). The initial implementation of the national entry point was, however, certainly incorrect and dysfunctional.[66] Subsequent actions

[66] As critically noted and discussed in other publications: T Rodríguez de las Heras Ballell, 'El nuevo Reglamento de matriculación de aeronaves civiles, y el Convenio de Ciudad del Cabo y su Protocolo sobre garantías internacionales en elementos de equipo aeronáutico' [2015] 15 *Revista de Derecho de Transporte: Terrestre, Marítimo, Aéreo y Multimodal* 235; and T Rodríguez de las Heras Ballell,

have tried to amend the effects of such wrong provisions and ensure today a normal functioning of the national entry point on a regular basis.

F. Conclusions

The Spanish law of secured transactions has evolved in recent decades and experienced several reforms mainly aimed at better meeting new financing needs and facilitating access to credit, at counteracting economic situations entailing financing constraints and at allowing local businesses access to international financial markets in competitive conditions. With such goals, substantial amendments in domestic legislation and accession to international instruments have taken place in recent years. As a whole, the current Spanish legal system covers possessory and non-possessory (including title-based) security devices over tangibles and intangible assets (receivables).

Likewise, the registry system has carried out a significant modernising process resulting in modern, professional and highly computerised registries. In particular, the establishment of the PPR has appreciably facilitated the evolution of the secured transactions system towards non-possessory security devices. Nonetheless, a comprehensive reform aimed at modernising, unifying and providing consistency in the legal framework governing secured transactions is long awaited and still pending.

Despite the latest reforms, Spanish rules governing secured transactions are scattered, fragmentary and, in some cases, even antiquated. The modernising impetus has not affected all areas of secured transactions laws uniformly. Whereas reforms in insolvency laws have been numerous and substantial, the legal regime of traditional security interests has remained largely intact, except for the modern rules on financial collateral arrangements.

In 2005 the incorporation into Spanish jurisdiction of European rules on financial collateral arrangements entailed a profound reform in the secured transactions system. Although the scope of that reform is limited, some basic principles underpinning the whole legal conception of secured transactions have been challenged and put under consideration. Particularly, the realisation of collateral by netting and by appropriation gave rise to some initial concerns in relation to the traditional prohibition of *pactum commissorium*. Nonetheless the contrast is only

'La adhesión de España al Protocolo Aeronáutico del Convenio de Ciudad del Cabo y su implementación: una primera valoración del nuevo Reglamento de Matriculación de Aeronaves' [2015] 2 *Bitácora Millenium DIPr* 88—Part I http://www.millenniumdipr.com/ba-29-la-adhesion-de-espana-al-protocolo-aeronautico-del-convenio-de-ciudad-del-cabo-parte-i, Part II: www.millenniumdipr.com/ba-30-la-adhesion-de-espana-al-protocolo-aeronautico-del-convenio-de-ciudad-del-cabo-parte-ii-.

apparent, for Spanish laws are familiar with extrajudicial enforcement procedures, and the realisation of collateral by netting and by appropriation had been admitted since the last century by scholars and case law when collateral is cash or publicly listed companies' shares. In sum, the prohibition of *pactum commissorium* had been largely relaxed in such transactions under the Spanish legal system even before the implementation of the special regime for financial collateral arrangements. Consequently, a debate is open about the need to undertake a deep and all-embracing reform of the existing legal system.

The accession by Spain to the CTC in 2013 and the subsequent and long-awaited accession of the Aircraft Protocol in 2015 have also significantly contributed to triggering discussion and fostering proposals for reform among practitioners, scholars and market players beyond the simple adoption of the minimum modifications required for an effective implementation of the CTC. Today, it can be affirmed that the need for a comprehensive reform is more visibly and widely felt.

Part IV

The Potential Influence of International Legislative Texts on Law Reform

21

The EBRD's Experience in Secured Transactions Reform: How Can Outsiders Help?

FREDERIQUE DAHAN

A. Introduction

In 2000 John Simpson and Joachim Menze, then working at the European Bank for Reconstruction and Development (EBRD), published an article, 'Ten Years of Secured Transactions Reform',[1] which described the EBRD approach to secured transactions legal reform projects and some of the results of its work. It recalled how, at the first annual meeting of the EBRD held in Budapest in April 1992, the Office of the General Counsel of the EBRD led a round-table discussion on economic law reform which had, as its particular topic, 'Creditors' Rights and Secured Transactions in Central and Eastern Europe'.[2] The choice of that topic indicated that the potential role of security in easing the chronic shortage of credit in the former communist countries had already been recognised. A legal system that enabled recovery from assets of the borrower could provide a solution which would not only increase the availability of credit, but also improve the terms attached to it, notably the duration and the cost. One of the outcomes of the round-table discussion was a request that the EBRD propose a basis for uniform or similar regulation of secured transactions across the region. As a direct result, the EBRD embarked on the preparation of a Model Law on Secured Transactions ('Model' or 'Model Law') which was published in April 1994.[3]

It was stressed from the outset that the Model was *not* intended as detailed legislation for direct incorporation into local legal systems. It was intended to form a

[1] John Simpson and Joachim Menze, 'Ten Years of Secured Transactions Reform' (2000) Autumn, *Law in Transition*, EBRD, 20–27.

[2] The EBRD is a financial institution which invests in the region and by doing this fosters transition towards market economy—for more information about the EBRD, see www.ebrd.com.

[3] The Model Law for Secured Transactions, EBRD, 1994.

basis from which national legislation for transition countries could be developed: in other words, a starting point which would indicate through a detailed legal text how the principal components of a secured transactions law could be drafted but which would allow for a high degree of flexibility to enable adaptation to local circumstances; and a reference point which could be turned to for guidance and illustration. The drafting of the Model was not seen as an isolated exercise, but as the first step in the Bank's effort to foster legal transition in the field of secured credit.

The EBRD's objective was clear: it consisted of improving the legal framework for secured transactions in all the countries in which the EBRD operates in order to facilitate the availability of credit. The ways of achieving that objective had to be tailored to take advantage of the role of the EBRD within the region, making optimum use of the limited resources available and acting as a catalyst for reform. The emphasis had thus been on developing tools for reform that can be used in different countries and on giving support and assistance in specific cases. This has not been limited to secured transactions only: progressively, the Office of the General Counsel of the EBRD has developed a continuing programme, the 'Legal Transition Programme', which includes other areas where reform is essential to the investment climate in the countries where it invests.[4]

It is apposite in 2016—25 years after the inception of these efforts—to take stock of what has been achieved but also, perhaps most importantly, to reflect on the role of an organisation like the EBRD—which, after all, is an outsider to jurisdictions which ultimately decide and shape their own legal framework. This chapter will argue the nature of such a role. First, it will start by explaining why countries do not need models any longer but instead can still benefit from exposure to a wealth of legal texts, data and other comparative materials. Then it will go on to show that standard setting is still needed to ensure that the system put in place is coherent given the different facets of secured transactions—something which may require the perspective and overview that organisations like the EBRD may be well placed to have. Thirdly and finally, it will explain that third-party assessment (which can be carried out by the EBRD or others) can be very helpful for countries which may need technical guidance as to what aspect of their system may need fine-tuning or significant reform and where the largest economic benefits may lie.

B. Why Models may be Outdated but Comparative Experience Sharing Remains Very Useful

(i) Development of the EBRD Model Law

When the EBRD Model Law was developed, the need for a model which could be used as an example was perhaps greater for secured transactions than for other

[4] See www.ebrd.com/law.

areas of law. Apart from the US and some countries which had followed the US example, there were few countries in the world which had a coherent, comprehensive and effective legal framework for non-possessory security over movable assets. In the rest of the world this area had been filled by an array of laws and practices built up over decades, even centuries, often providing different rules for different kinds of assets, sometimes satisfactory, sometimes not. These may have enabled the taking of security but often at the cost of a substantial economic inefficiency and these systems certainly did not provide a suitable template for transition countries to draw on. This is where the Model was at its most useful.

One principle which guided the drafting of the Model was to produce a text which was compatible with civil law concepts and, at the same time, to draw on common law systems which have developed many useful solutions to accommodate modern financing techniques. It was by deliberate design that the Model was prepared by a civil lawyer and a common lawyer—John Simpson and Jan-Hendrik Röver—under the guidance of an international Advisory Board comprising 20 eminent lawyers from 15 different jurisdictions, which enabled the work to draw on the experience of many countries with widely varying laws and traditions.[5]

Another guiding principle was that the Model had to be simple in order to be of practical use for economies in transition where the needs of legislative reform dwarf the available resources. It sought to illustrate a basic system on which more sophisticated rules could be developed. Therefore, it was clearly stated that the Model could not be used in a 'cut and paste' exercise but would entail significant development and tailoring for the needs of the jurisdiction in which it was going to be used.

Was the Model used? And which countries adopted it? This is a question that is often raised. It is beyond doubt that the Model has served as a basis for reform in several reform initiatives across Central and South East Europe,[6] and even beyond, but it is more interesting to dwell on other, more defining facts.

(ii) The World has not Stood Still

As reforms started to happen across the region, reference materials started to become available which could more readily serve as a source of inspiration for other transition economies. In other words, rather than using the Model, which was precisely just a model, not a 'living' Act, policymakers and their advisers undertaking reforms found it as useful, if not more so, to read and study laws newly adopted in neighbouring countries. For instance, when reform took place in the early 2000s in the Slovak Republic, the country naturally turned towards

[5] See www.ebrd.com/cs/Satellite?c=Content&cid=1395238855784&d=&pagename=EBRD%2FContent%2FDownloadDocument, viii.

[6] For example, Georgia, Hungary, Kyrgyz Republic, Moldova, Russian Federation, Serbia and Slovak Republic.

Hungary, Poland and Latvia as potential source of transplants for their own new provisions. Not only had these laws been drafted in a legal system that was very close to their own, but they could also benefit from the implementation experience in these exporting countries—something that the Model obviously could never have delivered.

Further, the world has evolved significantly since 1994 in this area, and not just in transition economies. As this very volume testifies, a number of jurisdictions in Western Europe and also beyond have successfully completed secured transactions reform to modernise their existing systems. New Zealand and Australia are two examples.[7] The OHADA Uniform Act for Secured Transactions, which was reformed in 2010, is another, very potent model since the Uniform Act applies directly in 17 countries in Africa, primarily of French law tradition.[8] France (2006)[9] and Belgium (2013)[10] are important markers which provide a source of inspiration that did not exist 20 years ago. For Morocco, which is in the process of reforming its secured transactions framework, it is natural to turn towards the French reform for guidance but also to be able to learn from the experience that has been amassed since the adoption of the new law and avoid the pitfalls and issues that have arisen.[11]

These examples show that the appeal of a model law, however well drafted and influential it may be, has significantly diminished since the mid-1990s because countries which are embarking on reform now have access to newly adopted, modern and living systems from which lessons and inspiration can be derived.

(iii) Models are No Substitute for Policy Choices and Robust Implementation

To many people the term 'legal reform' implies only the process of drafting legal provisions, and yet in practice this is often one of the easiest stages. It is not that the drafting of legislation is in any way easy but it is a technical process where the needs and the results are largely capable of definition and assessment. But before drafting of legislation can usefully begin, there has to be a broad consensus among all concerned on *what* the law is to achieve and *how* it is to achieve it. That involves a learning process. Typically those from the country whose law is to be changed have to learn about the issues that have to be addressed if a secured

[7] See Chs 6 and 7.

[8] Uniform Act of 15 December 2010 on secured transactions, which replaced the 1997 Uniform Act on the same subject. See www.ohada.org/.

[9] See Ch 17.

[10] See Ch 18.

[11] See P Stoffel-Munk, 'Premier bilan de la réforme des sûretés en droit francais' (2012) 231 *Droit et Patrimoine* 56. See also M Mourahib and O Lemseffer, 'Reforming an established secured transactions legal system: Why and how Morocco is approaching the challenge' in F Dahan (ed), *Research Handbook on Secured Financing in Commercial Transactions* (Cheltenham, Edward Elgar, 2015).

transactions law is to be compatible with the needs of modern secured financing. This is typically what a model does not deliver: the learning is unlikely to be derived from the reading of a series of legal provisions. Policymakers are unlikely to have either the time or the inclination to do so. Besides the Model, the EBRD has developed a set of 'Core Principles' and 'Guidelines', which can be drawn upon during the reform process.[12] It became evident that whereas the Model was an important and helpful instrument for local reformers, *a more general formulation* of the goals and principles of successful reform was needed to help foster economic development. There is no substitute for the long and painstaking process of legal reform, which implies designing a law that really suits the local circumstances and interfaces efficiently with existing laws and meets the objectives of the policymakers.[13] The Core Principles are based on the assumption that the role of a secured transactions law is to encourage and facilitate access to credit, but they do not seek to impose any particular solution on a country and only to indicate the result that should be achieved.

Further, implementation of a new law is just as important as the passing of the law itself. This covers everything that needs to be done to enable a newly adopted law to operate effectively—and in the domain of collateral, that means to offer maximum economic benefit to borrowers and lenders, and more indirectly to the economy as a whole. The biggest issue is usually the setting up of a system for collateral registration, but every aspect of carrying out secured credit transactions under the new law has to be examined, from the administrative requirements of creation, to the steps that can be taken to enforce, from the manner of giving requisite notices, to the method for determining priority between competing claims in the charged assets. A new collateral law brings with it changes in the practice of granting credit and the impact the law has on potential users at the moment it becomes effective is critical to its success. If the perception is not favourable at this stage it is likely that the new law will not be fully utilised. Finally, every legal system is dependent on application and enforcement of the law by the courts. A law will not lead to the results for which it has been designed if judges fail to interpret it in the way that is intended or if the court procedures prevent it from operating effectively—in the context of secured transactions the courts have in addition a specific and fundamental role when it comes to enforcement. Procedures for enforcement without court involvement may reduce that role but it remains essential that the courts can support and, when necessary, take control of the enforcement procedure.

All this points towards a much deeper understanding and absorption of secured transactions systems from the reforming country than a model can ever provide. In fact, a model law may give the erroneous idea that reform consists of nothing

[12] See www.ebrd.com/what-we-do/legal-reform/access-to-finance/transactions.html.

[13] See Frederique Dahan, 'A Single Framework Governing Secured Transactions? Comparative Reflections' in Dahan (ed) (n 11).

other than adopting a law—in fact, in this area, like any other, reforming requires knowledge transfer—and this is complex and often lengthy.

(iv) Guidance and Illustration is Better than Copying and Pasting

If 'outsiders' are included into the reform process, they also have to learn about the context in which the law is to operate: existing laws, institutions and practice and the underlying culture. Moreover, outside advisers can give assistance, support and encouragement but they cannot assume primary responsibility for the introduction of a new law. Many good projects have foundered because of the absence of a local champion within the country who is committed to achieving the reform and who can act as a driving force to pursue the project to a successful conclusion. When the commitment is present, it is fundamentally important to divide responsibilities between the different contributors to the reform process clearly and for each to understand what is expected of them. Outside advisers should only feed in with their knowledge and experience, and they should not be a substitute for policymakers. Similarly, the law has to fit the country and reflect the local traditions and culture, and that is only likely to happen if the drafters belong to that country. This does not mean, however, that external sources and advice may not add much value. Outsiders with expertise in secured transactions law and experience in reform can help the jurisdiction to define the results it wants to achieve, ensuring that these results are never lost sight of, and provide multiple examples of ways to achieve the results.

This is where outside organisations such as the EBRD can be most useful: it benefits from a considerable amount of materials which it can share as and when required. For example, when discussing the reform of a register where security rights over collateral would be recorded, and the fees that may be appropriate to charge, it can be very useful indeed for the country in question to benefit from the experience of a number of other jurisdictions. It becomes quite clear that the trend across the world is moving away from fees that are calculated as a percentage of the secured debt or the value of the secured assets towards fixed fees, often nominal, which tariff is established to only cover the costs of registration. This information is often difficult to obtain as it requires conducting research in a number of jurisdictions in order to establish what tariffs apply. Organisations like the EBRD or the International Finance Corporation (IFC) often conduct surveys and special studies which provide a wealth of data on many specific aspects of reform (see below). Naturally, only in-depth expertise allows for the provision of comparative advice that is balanced and to the point. Comparative exercises can be very lengthy, expensive and ultimately pointless unless they are carefully targeted and the materials gathered are meaningful in the context of the jurisdiction which intends to use them.

These remarks point to the very limits of a model law. In the EBRD experience, the importance and usefulness of the Model has diminished over the years as the reform process has expanded in the region and the EBRD itself, together with others, has built a deep understanding of the role they could play in the reform.

C. The Missing Links: Coherence of the Framework which Spans Over Different Instruments

Another, perhaps less obvious, role for outsiders advising on secured transactions reform lies with the need to be able to advise on the coherence of the legal framework that is being put in place, often in a disjointed fashion, by the country in question. What makes the EBRD approach to secured transactions perhaps unique is the fact that the EBRD has recognised and emphasised the role of collateral in a number of different transactional contexts. As an international financial institution which lends primarily to the private sector, the Bank has promoted the use of a variety of investment products (or has supported local financial institutions, which in turn use these products), which very often rely on collateral. This has been fed into the advisory arm of the EBRD, in particular the Legal Transition Programme, and has thus positively affected the way secured transactions law reform has been shaped.

Indeed, secured transactions reform cannot limit itself to the mere taking of security over movable property in generic terms. This would first ignore the fact that the taking of security over real estate (immovable property) when available is the backbone of any security package. Secondly, it must be understood that secured transactions will apply beyond corporate finance, but that the same techniques will also be relevant in structured finance or capital markets instruments. Thirdly, some types of collateral, or the context in which they are used (for example, agriculture financing), can present their own set of challenges, which must be taken into account when reforming. Specific rules will need to be put in place, while the overall system must be kept consistent and coherent. This can be a challenge if different government authorities and advisers have worked on the separate respective pieces of legislation. Finally, the area of secured transactions has also been captured at an international/regional level, which ought to be taken into account too: the local law thus must, if the country aims to be integrated regionally or internationally, access, ratify or at least adopt the key principles of the international treaty, directive or other instrument. We will examine each proposition in turn.

(i) Mortgage is a Security Interest

At the start of the transition process, most of the countries of Central and Eastern Europe provided for the possibility of taking security over immovable property, usually on the basis of laws which had their origins in the pre-communist era.

The reform priority at that time was to enable movable property to be used as collateral. Not only was there an absence of rules governing security over movables, but also many borrowers did not have suitable real estate to offer as security. But the EBRD approach has always been to treat mortgages as an integral part of secured transactions and to apply the same legal principles to this form of security. The context for pledge law reform has been different, yet, economically speaking, pledge and mortgage fulfil the same purpose and it is illogical that the reform of the legal framework for each should be conducted in isolation.

Mortgage financing has always been a favourite form of financing for banks. The primary credit risk is supported by solid security which does not move and which normally maintains its value. The incentive to avoid default is high, especially for residential property because a borrower will make every effort to avoid losing their home. Mortgage law reform is not necessarily high on the agenda of many countries, because giving security by mortgage is not a new concept. Yet the rules for mortgage have not always developed in the most rational and legally efficient way, and this may be particularly visible in developed economies with a variety of different systems, mostly shaped in a different era, which have been more or less adapted over the years to accommodate market changes. One of the opportunities that transition countries have is precisely the ability to avoid the kind of obsolete provisions or concepts that often hinder development in advanced economies.

This holistic approach as to the scope of secured transactions is in contrast with other reference materials, such as the UNCITRAL Legislative Guide on Secured Transactions, or indeed the IFC Toolkit on Secured Transactions and Collateral Registries, published in 2010,[14] both of which specifically exclude security of immovable property from their scope. The danger of such an approach is that it does not encourage convergence of legal provisions governing the two types of security, thus often leading to different stances on matters where logically there should be no inherent difference. For example, if it is possible to describe the secured debt generally and for the secured debt to be fluctuating during the duration of the obligation, it should not matter at all whether the assets given as collateral are movable or immovable. The sharing of security rights among creditors, including via the administration of the security by a syndicate (often referred to as a security trustee) should be possible for the entire security package. Similarly, if the law has allowed enforcement of the pledge over movable property to take place out of court, enforcement of the mortgage over immovable property out of court should also be contemplated. The principal aim of enforcement is to realise the mortgaged property promptly at market value. The mortgagor and the mortgage creditor should share a similar interest that the mortgaged property be realised at the best price.

All too often, one finds differences between regimes applicable to mortgages and pledges which are simply born out of legal conservatism rather than

[14] www1.ifc.org/wps/wcm/connect/industry_ext_content/ifc_external_corporate_site/industries/financial+markets/publications/toolkits/secured+transactions+systems+_+collateral+registries+tool kit. See also Ch 23.

economic rationale. When outsiders' support for the reform is called in, there is an opportunity to discuss with the authorities the desirability of seeking harmony between the two regimes (except naturally over the aspects where specific rules are necessary—such as registration of the security right).

(ii) Security Rights in Securities

The relevance of secured transactions law and its versatility is particularly striking as far as securities are concerned, in particular those that are secured by assets (asset-backed securities), be they mortgage loans, auto-loans, or credit cards. Covered bonds operate on the same, simple basis that assets strengthen the likelihood of the bondholder's claim being honoured as per the terms of the bond. It is often overlooked that secured transactions law will play an important role in the feasibility of both covered bonds and asset-backed securities. In covered bond transactions, the rights of bondholders to the assets loans in the cover pool will often be given by way of pledge. In an asset-backed securities structure, the special purpose vehicle will typically give a pledge over the assets in favour of the noteholders. A good secured transactions law should avoid pitfalls which, in some jurisdictions, have made these transactions unnecessarily complex or costly. For example, it should not be necessary to obtain consent from the obligors (eg the mortgage borrower or credit card holder) for the validity of the pledge, nor should notice to the obligor be required by law. Because the cover pool for covered bonds may well be dynamic and fluctuating, it may be necessary in the pledge to describe the collateral generally, including future loans, so as to avoid any formality whenever the cover pool is amended. Generally, the ability to easily and effectively give security by way of pledge can greatly facilitate the risk-mitigating arrangements in asset-backed securities transactions, which rest on contractual arrangements over the cash flows. Pledges over cash, bank accounts and accounts receivable are all necessary building blocks of asset-backed securities.

Countries that have a modern framework for secured transactions, enabling the giving of an enforceable, first-ranking pledge right that remains effective on the insolvency of the pledgor (be it the issuer or the originator), will have a great advantage. This is where working with an international financial institution with a broad exposure to a diversity of financing techniques could be a distinct advantage to draw the attention of the policymakers and technical experts involved in the reform to the far-reaching consequences of their work.

(iii) The Special Case of Warehouse Receipts

Food security and warehouse receipts systems are key objectives for the EBRD, especially as the region in which the EBRD operates has such considerable potential in primary agriculture.[15] In the late nineteenth and early twentieth centuries, warehouse receipt finance played a major role in enabling the development of US agriculture. Warehouse receipts (WHR) systems constitute an alternative solution for commodity producers, processors and traders to access short-term financing, take advantage of price fluctuations, and secure the storage of their produce. Broadly speaking, the system is based on storage of commodities in a warehouse where the warehouse operator issues a receipt upon delivery of the commodity. The receipt can then be used as collateral—typically, the receipt would be issued in two parts, one part evidencing the commodity ownership, the other part, the right of pledge created against the commodity for the benefit of the holder of that part. There are different approaches in the development of legislative frameworks. In some cases, legislators build upon existing laws but usually the effort begins with new legislation. Lenders are more likely to feel comfortable when there is strong legislation in place protecting the rights and interests of depositors in public warehouses; a legal basis for the recognition, perfection and enforcement of the collateral; the negotiability of the receipts; strong safeguards over the integrity of the system; and clear procedures in case of default and ultimately bankruptcy of the warehouse.[16]

Warehouse receipts themes are reminiscent of secured transactions, in particular enforcement over the commodities. The attractiveness of the WHR system depends to a very large extent on the enforcement system. Since the financier has extended credit comforted by the availability of grain stored in a regulated warehouse, it is essential that, should the borrower/debtor default on the credit, the creditor is able to sell such grain to repay the debt. Enforcement mechanisms should be quick, reliable, simple and adapted to the local context—with its specific risks and perception of risks. This is very important as commodities are easily moved and highly liquid. In legal terms, the means of enforcement will depend on the legal instrument that the creditor holds in the receipt—and thus the legal right such instrument gives him on the grain. In some markets, the receipt will be double and in practice, the lender is granted with a pledge over the grain; in other markets, lenders are handed the simple warehouse receipts, thereby receiving ownership of the grain (such transfers should not have tax or accounting implications).

These reform discussions would be greatly facilitated by a modern legal basis for secured transactions where the means of enforcement have been made effective and are creditor driven. In particular, enforcement should be allowed to start when the creditor decides. There should not be a statutory, compulsory grace period, or a subjective assessment by the court, for instance of the seriousness of the default. Once the creditor has given notice to the warehouse on the commencement of enforcement, the effect of this notice should be to freeze the grain in the warehouse and to prevent the sale, transfer, pledge or any other actions over the grain by the

[15] www.ebrd.com/pages/sector/agribusiness.shtml.

[16] For more detail, see EBRD-FAO, *The use of warehouse receipt finance in agriculture in transition countries*, 2009, www.eastagri.org/publications/detail.asp?id=33.

debtor and the warehouse. Ideally, the sale of grain could be done directly (private sale) or by auction organised by the creditor, as long as the grain is sold at or close to market price. The creditor should be entitled to transfer ownership of the grain to the purchaser (whether because the law made him the owner of the grain or on the behalf of the borrower). And finally, there should be a clear ranking order for allocation of the sale proceeds, which should preferably be (1) any unpaid costs to the warehouse and storage fees that may be due; (2) payment to the creditor of outstanding secured debt, plus interest, penalties and enforcement expenses; (3) any surplus paid to the debtor.

However, WHR reform presents specificities, which call for a differentiated approach whilst ensuring coherence. First, the system must focus on structural components, which include licensing and inspection of public warehouses and insurance and indemnity funds. Ideally, one would want to see a strong system of licensed and supervised public warehouses. In the absence of such a system, the financial institution is exposed to the risks related to the warehouse operation, such as improper handling, damage or loss of the collateral, or fraud. These operating risks could be mitigated through a highly selective choice of warehouses and close monitoring by specialist collateral managers (where a third party is liable for the continued presence of the commodities in the warehouse). This means that, in practice, a good deal of effort on this reform will be spent on building a robust and credible licensing and supervising system, which of course is totally absent from a 'classic' secured transactions reform.

Secondly, it is questionable whether it would be apposite to include the registration of the right of pledge over the grain (via the second part of the warehouse receipt used as collateral) into a pledge register. There is no question that the management of WHR finance is much improved if an electronic warehouse receipt system is adopted. However, the system is not geared primarily to the pledging aspects of the system. It is also to be used for receipt issuance—bringing a significant level of protection against fraud by preventing the double use of WHR to obtain finance from two different banks, the transfer of previously pledged receipts, or attempts to take delivery with a fake receipt when the real receipt has already been sold or pledged. Banks would only be prepared to accept it as security because the issuance of a receipt establishes with certainty the existence of the commodity as described in the receipt. This is in sharp contrast to the notice-filing approach of a pledge register, where title of the assets offered as collateral is not evidenced by the registration/filing of the security right. Finally, the electronic system could be used for the trading functionalities of the receipts (legally qualified as securities), offering users possibilities to invest and trade in existing commodities through a safe and easily acceptable electronic system.[17] Because of these

[17] 'They may be a good first step (pending integration into a full-fledged regional exchange network) for countries that are too small for a comprehensive commodity exchange, or where local investors are unable to pay the costs of such a system', EBRD-FAO, *The use of warehouse receipt finance in agriculture in transition countries*, 2009, www.eastagri.org/publications/detail.asp?id=33.

similarities and differences, secured transactions law and WHR law need to be closely coordinated for the overall system to be coherent, but they also need to be clearly differentiated on aspects where it is appropriate.

(iv) Financial Collateral and the EU Directive on Financial Collateral Arrangements

Another area where coordination and coherence are required concerns financial collateral. Financial collateral is an increasingly important tool by which financial assets are provided by a borrower (the collateral provider) to a lender (the collateral taker) to minimise the risk of financial loss to the lender in the event of the borrower defaulting on its financial obligations to such lender. Financial collateral is increasingly used in all types of transaction, including capital markets, bank treasury and funding, payment and clearing systems and general interbank lending. The concept of financial collateral has not necessarily come high on the agenda of secured transactions law reformers because in many jurisdictions (such as the UK), the transactions are structured as title finance. *Title transfers* (including repurchase agreements—'repos') occur where ownership of the collateral passes to the collateral taker, on terms that it or equivalent assets will be transferred back when the obligations are discharged. *Security arrangements* occur where the collateral taker obtains a security interest in the collateral, coupled with physical possession or control, but does not become the owner. One of the reasons for using title finance as opposed to security rights was to allow the buyer to have the right to use the securities transferred to it.

However, the development of the EU Financial Collateral Directive in 2002 (amended in 2009)[18] has made the distinction irrelevant when it applies. The assets covered by the Directive are: cash, financial instruments (eg shares, bonds, securities) and credit claims.[19] The Directive applies to the collateral taker and the collateral provider provided that both are either a public authority, public sector body, a central bank, a financial institution subject to prudential supervision, or a legal entity (not a physical person). The Directive has created a set of substantive rules which will apply to all EU Member States, but these rules are mostly permissive rules and they leave undisturbed the core mechanisms as to creation/attachment, priority and enforcement principles which exist in each jurisdiction. Precisely, the Directive's objective has been to recognise the arrangements entered into by the parties, regardless of whether these arrangements are made in the form of a title transfer of or a pledge over the collateral. There is some effect on perfection to the extent that formalities are eliminated (ie no registration of the

[18] Directive 2009/44/EC of the European Parliament and of the Council of 6 May amending Directive 98/26/EC on settlement finality in payments and securities settlement systems and Directive 2002/47/EC on financial collateral arrangements as regards linked systems and credit claims, OJ L146/37.

[19] The credit claims concept was introduced by Directive 2009/44/EC.

pledge should be required, 'possession' or 'control' is sufficient). The Directive also prescribes that the right for the collateral taker to use or appropriate the financial collateral has to be given effect. The aim of the Directive is also to provide for rapid and non-formalistic enforcement procedures designed to limit contagion effects in the event of default by one of the parties to the arrangement. Thus, Member States are required by the Directive to ensure that the collateral taker is able to realise financial collateral in one of the following ways:

— for financial instruments, by sale or appropriation and by setting off their value against, or applying their value in discharge of, the relevant financial obligations;
— for cash, by setting off the amount against or applying it in discharge of the relevant financial obligations;
— for a credit claim, by sale or appropriation (if so agreed between the parties) or by setting off their value against or applying their value in discharge of, the relevant financial obligations.

Moreover, Member States must recognise the applicable close-out netting provisions, even if the collateral taker or provider is already subject to insolvency proceedings, and specifically disapply insolvency law provisions which would impede the realisation of such collateral, eg any moratorium on enforcement.

The benefits that the Directive has brought to the use of financial collateral are undisputable. However, the intersection with, or indeed the full application of, secured transactions law will be unavoidable and thus must be managed. In the US, for instance, security over financial collateral falls within the scheme created by Article 9 of the Uniform Commercial Code, along with many other types of collateral, although special rules will apply. This is because Article 9 has adopted the so-called functional approach to secured transactions, which subjects to the same regime all transactions which have as their function to provide security, regardless of the form (security right or transfer of title, etc) used by the parties' agreement.[20] However, the majority of financial collateral arrangements in the European market are done on the basis of title transfers.

One problem which has arisen in England concerns the impact of the Directive (and its implementing provisions contained in the Financial Collateral Arrangements (No 2) Regulations 2003) over floating charges. Indeed, since the Directive prevents Member States from requiring the performance of a formal act for perfection of a financial collateral arrangement (ie registration), the Regulations have thus disapplied section 860 of the 2006 Companies Act (which requires floating charges to be registered at Companies House) as long as they fulfil the other requirements of the Directive of 'possession or control' over the financial collateral. This is quite tricky because the distinction between fixed and floating charges, under English law, although subject to much uncertainty, rests to a large extent on the control that the chargeholder may or may not have over the

[20] See Ch 2.

property.[21] Since it is indeed possible to take a floating charge over investment property that will permit the chargeholder to deal with the property, there is a need to determine whether or not such a floating charge falls under the jurisdiction of the Financial Collateral Arrangements (No 2) Regulations (in which case, no registration at Companies House will be necessary) or not (in which case, if the floating charge was not registered as prescribed, it would be void against the liquidator and other creditors). A good deal of literature has been written on the difficulty, and indeed at times undue complexity, of these questions.[22]

But such complexity is not simply the result of the English floating charge. All countries which have adopted the Directive will have to ensure that there is full clarity on the boundaries between the financial collateral regime derived from the Directive, and the regime which will be drawn from the secured transactions regime and may also apply to financial instruments (such as in the case where a bank takes security over credit claims held by a corporate). Furthermore, for a country like Morocco, which does not aspire to become an EU Member but seeks nevertheless to adopt a financial collateral regime that would mirror the one in place in the European Union so as to remain an attractive investment destination for European investors, the dilemma is whether the legal framework should impose the title transfer as the sole structure possible between financial market participants; whether financial arrangements should be defined, as is the case in the EU Directive, based on the type of collateral and the nature of the parties; or whether it would be preferable to attempt a definition of the financial collateral arrangements instead—which would be a challenging task but which would have the distinct advantage of drawing clearer boundaries between secured transactions and other transfer titles arrangements.[23]

Here again, it is believed that outside organisations like the EBRD can play a positive role in advising the jurisdiction on the specific challenges of sophisticated security instruments and the need to ensure a comprehensive yet coherent regime where investors and other market players have complete clarity on the rules that apply, and certainty as to the validity of their arrangements.

In conclusion, the more sophisticated a jurisdiction's financial sector becomes, especially when integrated into a regional and international economic space, the more complex its legal framework and the greater the risk of incoherence and inconsistency. An external organisation may be well placed to assist in ensuring coherence and harmony, especially if this organisation operates in many sectors and thus has first-hand understanding of the challenges. The small and painstaking amendments and review of legal acts may not sound as impressive as the building of systems from scratch but it is essential for a sound investment climate.

[21] Hugh Beale, Michael Bridge, Louise Gullifer and Eva Lomnicka, *The Law of Security and Title-Based Financing*, 2nd edn (Oxford, Oxford University Press, 2012) 35, 58.

[22] See L Gullifer, 'What Should We Do About Financial Collateral?' (2012) 65(1) *Current Legal Problems* 377–410.

[23] See Edward Murray, 'Financial Collateral Arrangements and the Financial Markets' in Dahan (ed) (n 11).

D. Monitoring, Evaluating and Fine-tuning

Perhaps the greatest myth of all in legal reform is that a new law once passed and implemented will achieve everything that is expected of it. There is no country where new laws can be guaranteed to operate perfectly from day one. In transition countries where the pace of change is rapid, the experience needed to absorb new laws and regulations is still developing and the maturity of new institutions is often lacking, the monitoring of a newly implemented law is an essential part of the reform process. Monitoring can enable defects and deficiencies to be identified and remedied. It implies not only following the mechanical operation of the law, but more broadly assessing the effectiveness of the law in achieving its purpose.

A monitoring programme will be most effective if it is closely linked to the work that has gone into the preparation of the law and if it involves a wide range of people. It should include an assessment of the performance of the law against the objectives that it was originally designed to achieve at the consensus-building stage; a systematic review of the practical operation of the law and the perception of its intended users and those involved with its implementation; and a study based on hard evidence of the use that is made of collateral under the law; the improvement in processes such as registration or enforcement that the reform has achieved; the new financial products that have been created based on new provisions; or the change in credit risk assessment and other risk management tools that the reform has permitted.

Input will ideally be sought from lenders, borrowers and their advisers, from lawyers and the administrators of the collateral registry, from judges and court officers, from government departments and the central bank, from economists and outside observers. This is likely to require some not insignificant resources, both monetary and time-wise, and the support of an external organisation which can mobilise such resources and organise the work can be critical. For example, when the EBRD provided assistance to the Office of the Prime Minister in the Slovak Republic in early 2000, such assistance included a programme of interventions post adoption of the reform. The programme included:

- the production of FAQs on the registry website to guide and advise users, especially at the outset of the registry's operations;
- the publication of a legal commentary on the new Civil Code provisions aimed at guiding their legal and judicial interpretation;
- a judicial training programme (administered by the United States Agency for International Development (USAID)) to inform the judiciary of the new legal provisions and how they were to contribute to dispute resolution, especially in the case of out-of-court enforcement;
- the publication of a Practical Guide on Taking Security in the Slovak Republic, which provided suggestions on how the new law could be used in practice to reap the maximum economic benefits from the new possibilities it offered;

- a detailed review of the functioning of the register and recommendations as to the measures necessary to iron out teething problems—including processes, software, IT systems, etc—for the benefit of the Chamber of Notaries who operates the register as well as that of the Ministry of Justice, which was in charge of the project;
- collection of feedback from users as to their perception of the new system—especially banks;
- an attempt to collect the Central Bank's data on the reported collateral usage by banks in their lending before and after the reform, in an attempt to be able to assess the impact of the reform on lending, whilst disentangling the externalities of such usage. It turned out that this attempt was not successful because of the way the Central Bank was collecting information on collateral so we had to wait a decade to have some insight on this key question (see below).

Even if such a programme cannot always be put in place, comparative studies represent very important, and perhaps overlooked, tools to provide policymakers with objective, dispassionate assessment of the systems in place, and ultimately promote reform. The most well-known source of such assessment is the *Doing Business Reports* produced by the World Bank Group. Chapter Six on 'Getting Credit' may have many inherent flaws and limitations, but has had formidable influence over all countries in the world which, as a direct or indirect result of such assessment, have amended their laws on collateral (and credit bureaus). In 2013–14, for instance, nine economies had improved access to credit by strengthening the legal rights of borrowers and lenders—either by reforming secured transactions legislation or by enhancing secured creditors' rights in bankruptcy proceedings.[24] More granular studies can also be extremely helpful to policymaking: for example, the World Bank Group published a study on collateral registries in 35 jurisdictions, which analyses in detail how these registries have been set up and are functioning against defined best practices.[25]

The EBRD has also undertaken a number of surveys and reports with the intention of drawing the attention of policymakers to the strengths and weaknesses of their secured transactions systems.[26] In 2005 the Polish Central Bank asked the EBRD and the World Bank to prepare studies looking at the Legal Framework for Credit Market and the Judiciary in Poland and to make a number of recommendations anchored on best international practices.[27]

24 See www.doingbusiness.org/data/exploretopics/getting-credit.

25 Alejandro Alvarez de la Campa, Santiago Croci Downes and Bettina Tirelli Hennig, *Making Security Interests Public: Registration Mechanisms in 35 Jurisdictions*, The World Bank/IFC, 2012, www.doingbusiness.org/~/media/GIAWB/Doing%20Business/Documents/Special-Reports/Making-Security-Interests-Public.pdf.

26 See www.ebrd.com/what-we-do/legal-reform/access-to-finance/transactions.html.

27 See www.ebrd.com/legal-reform/where-we-work/poland.html#anchor1; Frederique Dahan and John Simpson, 'The Impact of the Legal Framework on the Secured Credit Market in Poland' (2006) April, *Butterworths Journal of International Banking and Financial Law* 174–81.

More generally, the EBRD regularly produces surveys of the laws and practices underpinning secured transactions. These surveys focus on the legal efficiency of the system in place, that is to say, the extent to which a law and the way it is used provides the benefits that it was intended to achieve. Since the prime purpose of a secured transactions law is economic and essentially facilitative, the basic legal framework should be *conducive* to a flexible market for secured credit. A relatively simple indicator of the success of a secured transactions law reform (or primary motive for undertaking the secured transactions law reform) would be the subsequent increase in the *volume* of secured lending. This is a crude and narrow indicator, inadequate by itself. The intended function of the secured credit market may be more than just to boost the amount of credit granted against security. It may also include, for example, opening up credit to new sectors of society, increasing efficiency and productivity, or allowing privately funded infrastructure projects. The intended function of a law has thus to be looked at in the context within which it is to operate, that is to say the degree to which the legal framework enables secured transactions: first, to achieve their basic legal function, and secondly, to operate in a way which maximises economic benefit—see such a study focusing on mortgage markets.[28]

Finally, economic studies on the impact of reform are still too often neglected, despite the importance of the subject—although this is slowly changing. In particular, in the last 10 years, financial literature has included several studies which, in different contexts, attempt to explore the correlation and even causality between secured transactions law reform and access to credit. Such examples include the following:

— Research, which was carried out in a broader context, to investigate the effect of legal change on the lending behaviour of banks in 12 transition economies. The authors found that banks increase the supply of credit subsequent to legal change and that changes in collateral law matter more for increases in bank lending than changes in bankruptcy law (although one of the authors found in a separate study that very strong creditors' rights could have a negative impact on lending).[29]

— A World Bank paper which, using firm-level surveys for up to 73 countries—some of which had introduced collateral registries for movable assets and some which had not—explored the impact of introducing collateral registries for movable assets on firms' access to bank finance.[30]

[28] Frederique Dahan and John Simpson, 'Legal Efficiency of Secured Transactions Reform: Bridging the Gap between Economic Analysis and Legal Reasoning' in Frederique Dahan and John Simpson (eds), *Secured Transactions Reform and Access to Credit* (Cheltenham, Edward Elgar, 2008) 122–138.

[29] Rainer Haselmann, Katharina Pistor and Vikrant Vig, 'How Law Affects Lending' (2010) 23(2) *Review of Financial Studies* 549–80; Vikrant Vig, 'Access to Collateral and Corporate Debt Structure: Evidence from a Natural Experiment' (2013) 68(3) *Journal of Finance* 881–928.

[30] Inessa Love, María Soledad Martínez Pería and Sandeep Singh, 'Collateral Registries for Movable Assets: Does Their Introduction Spur Firms' Access to Bank Finance?', Policy Research Working Paper

— An academic paper, which was able to exploit the loan database from a large international bank operating in 60+ countries in the world to test the effect of cross-country differences in collateral laws regarding movable assets on lending and sectorial allocation of resources. The authors found that loan-to-value (LTV) of loans collateralised with movable assets are on average 21 percentage points higher in countries with weak collateral laws relative to immovable assets. Further, stronger collateral laws tilt collateral composition away from immovable to movable assets.[31]

Although such studies have their limitations and one should exercise caution in drawing too rigid lessons for future reform endeavours, they remain extremely valuable to feed into the global pool of knowledge around the world.

E. Conclusion

Secured transactions reform is an expert subject which continues to raise considerable interest, both in term of content and of process. A number of international organisations have entered the arena and made their own specific contribution. In parallel, a number of key jurisdictions have also embarked on or completed reform of their legal framework. More than ever, cross-fertilisation opportunities arise and, as this chapter has shown, outside organisations such as the EBRD have a role to play, even if this role may not be that of standard setter as it was in the early years of transition when the Model Law was published.

Instead, the EBRD can play a distinct and crucial role by undertaking focused assessment of existing legal systems, including their coherence, which can thus

No 6477, The World Bank Development Research Group, Finance and Private Sector Development Team, June 2013. Public.

[31] Charles W Calomiris, Mauricio Larrain, José Liberti and Jason Sturgess, 'How Collateral Laws Shape Lending and Sectoral Activity', Working Paper, Draft, 2014. The study examines in detail the loans that a bank had made in a number of countries, including the Slovak Republic, with full details on the collateral that was taken at the time of the origination, including the value of the assets being pledged as collateral. The data thus allow comparison of the LTV ratio applied by the bank on collateral made of immovable property (buildings and land) against the LTV ratio applied when the collateral included movable property only (such as machinery, inventory, accounts receivable, bank accounts). By carefully comparing the data before and after the 2003 secured transactions reform which took place in the Slovak Republic, and by controlling for all other factors that could have affected these results, the researchers found that prior to the reforms, the value of movable collateral that firms needed to offer to get a loan of a certain size was fully 20 percentage points higher than the value of immovable collateral. After the reforms, this difference was almost entirely eradicated. There was also a small increase in the volume of lending against movable assets post reform but this was not so significant—which may have been due to the fact that such increase takes more time to materialise. The broader study, covering 12 countries across the world, identified similar impacts from good collateral laws elsewhere.

lead to fine-tuning and adjustments. This requires accepting that reform is not a linear process but a continuous effort to fit the legal provisions with the local circumstances, which are continuously evolving under internal and external pressures. Furthermore, organisations must also accept that they need to evolve too: their knowledge of secured transactions and reform beliefs must be attuned to the changes that occur across the world. They must be prepared to recognise that practices and structures now require a different approach from that which was promoted 10 or 20 years ago.

Whether in London, Washington DC, Paris, Cairo or Moscow, who said the last word on secured transactions has been heard …?

22

The United Nations Convention on the Assignment of Receivables in International Trade and Small Businesses

N ORKUN AKSELI*

A. Introduction

Receivables are important assets for small and medium-sized businesses. Their utilisation as collateral for credit has grown since the 1980s. Raising finance through assignment of receivables is a vital financing technique for small businesses and routinely used by companies in financing their businesses.[1] It has been pointed out that raising finance through assignment of receivables 'is simply bigger business than the financing of mobile goods'.[2] Receivables financing has seen considerable growth as 'receivables are self-liquidating and … [a] short-term source of cash'.[3] Studies conducted by the World Bank, however, have revealed that the use of receivables or intangibles as collateral has not reached its full potential, as banks in developing economies do not widely recognise receivables as acceptable collateral.[4] Divergence in the regulation of the law of assignment in national

* Some of the arguments in this chapter are partly based on N.O. Akseli "*The Utility and Efficacy of the UN Convention on the Assignment of Receivables and the Facilitation of Credit*" in Availability of Credit and Secured Transactions in a Time of Crisis (N.O. Akseli ed.) (CUP, 2013).

[1] Law Commission Report on Company Security Interests No 296 (2005), para 4.1 ('Law Commission Report').

[2] NB Cohen, 'Harmonizing the Law Governing Secured Credit: The Next Frontier' (1998) 33 *Texas International Law Journal* 173, 185.

[3] S Schwarcz, 'Towards a Centralized Perfection System for Cross-Border Receivables Financing' (1999) 20 *University of Pennsylvania Journal of International Economic Law* 455, 456. For the significance of receivables financing, see also F Oditah, *Legal Aspects of Receivables Financing* (London, Sweet and Maxwell, 1991) 2.

[4] See, eg, M Safavian, 'Firm-level Evidence on Collateral and Access to Finance' in F Dahan and J Simpson (eds), *Secured Transactions Reform and Access to Credit* (Cheltenham, Edward Elgar, 2008) 110, 113 ff. M Safavian, H Fleisig and J Steinbuks, 'Unlocking the Dead Capital' (2006) March, *View*

systems causes uncertainty and increases the cost of credit in cross-border assignment of receivables contracts. Hence the need to have an international instrument that promotes cross-border flow of goods and services by facilitating access to credit as well as acting as an example for domestic law reform activities.

The majority of world trade relies on credit supplied by banks and other financial institutions to SMEs, which comprise 90 per cent of businesses and 50 per cent of employment globally.[5] It can be argued that the use of movable and intangible assets as collateral may have a positive impact on production and growth.[6] With the continuous effects of the credit crisis, the access to credit for businesses has become a significant problem in both developed and developing economies.[7]

While the United Nations Convention on the Assignment of Receivables in International Trade ('the Receivables Convention') has been signed by three countries and ratified by one,[8] feasibility studies as to the possibility of adoption of the Receivables Convention have been underway in North American jurisdictions.[9] On 10 February 2016, the President of the United States Barack Obama sent the Convention to the US Senate for ratification.[10] It is believed that other countries will follow suit soon.[11] Recently, support for the Receivables Convention has also gained momentum with endorsements[12] from influential business and

Point Note Number 307); S Simavi, 'Making Finance Work for Africa: The Collateral Debate', *World Bank PDP Forum* (2007); 'Vietnam Increasing Access to Credit through Collateral (Secured Transactions) Reform' (IFC/MPDF, 2007); 'Reforming Collateral Laws and Registries: International Best Practices and the Case of China' (FIAS/IFC PEP China, March 2007).

5 www.ifc.org/wps/wcm/connect/a16f4f004f36e8539c3cde032730e94e/SM2015_IFCIssueBrief_SMEs.pdf?MOD=AJPERES and www.ifc.org/wps/wcm/connect/967d26804b7eee0986a5c6bbd5788 91b/IFC-SME-Factsheet2012.pdf?MOD=AJPERES.

6 H Fleisig, 'The Economics of Collateral and of Collateral Reform' in Dahan and Simpson (eds) (n 4) 81, 89 ff.

7 According to the Federation of Small and Medium Sized Businesses statistics, small businesses in the UK have serious problems in gaining access to credit. www.fsb.org.uk/ Report on *Number Crunching the Credit Crunch.*

8 www.uncitral.org/uncitral/uncitral_texts/security/2001Convention_receivables_status.html. Five actions (ratification, accession, approval, acceptance, succession) are necessary for entry into force. So far the Convention has received one ratification (Liberia) and three signatures (US, Luxembourg and Madagascar).

9 For calls urging the US to adopt the Receivables Convention see, eg, RM Kohn, *Convention to Bolster Exports and Jobs. UN Pact Would Increase Business Loans Based on Receivables, The Washington Times*, 6 March 2012. See, eg, Uniform Law Conference of Canada www.ulcc.ca/en/us/Assignment_Receivables_International_Trade_En.pdf. Particularly in the US the self-execution method of implementation may be chosen. See www.uncitral.org/pdf/english/colloquia/3rdSecTrans/Ed_Smith_Implementation.pdf.

10 https://www.whitehouse.gov/the-press-office/2016/02/10/message-senate-un-convention-assignment-receivables-international-trade

11 See generally S Bazinas, RM Kohn, LF del Duca, 'Facilitating a Cost-Free Path to Economic Recovery—Implementing a Global Uniform International Receivables Financing Law' (2012) 44 *Uniform Commercial Code Law Journal* 277. www.ulcc.ca/en/uniform-acts-new-order/current-uniform-acts/639-uncitral-assignment-of-receivables-international.

12 The Convention has received endorsements from legal bodies as well such as the American Bar Association (www.americanbar.org/content/dam/aba/migrated/intlaw/policy/investment/receivablesconvention113C.authcheckdam.pdf).

professional bodies including the International Factors Group[13] and the International Chamber of Commerce (ICC).[14] It is argued that the general principles of the Receivables Convention have been widely accepted in national laws.[15] Thus, it is fair to say that these general principles have become international customary law.

The central argument in this chapter will focus on three significant general principles of the Receivables Convention that may assist small businesses' access to finance. These are: Article 8, which recognises the validity of bulk assignments of receivables and assignment of future receivables; Article 9, which aims to override anti-assignment clauses; and the registration of security interests over receivables (Annex of the Receivables Convention). The chapter will first present the background of the Receivables Convention and its general principles. This will be followed by an evaluation of the provisions that aim to override anti-assignment clauses and those that enable the registration of security interests over receivables. Conclusions will summarise the arguments.

B. Background and General Principles of the Receivables Convention

The United Nations Commission on International Trade Law (UNCITRAL) drafted the Receivables Convention after almost a decade of careful work.[16] It was adopted in 2001.[17] The Receivables Convention has a dual purpose. First, the explicit purpose of the Receivables Convention is to harmonise the law of

[13] www.ifgroup.com/wp-content/uploads/2014/12/IFG-endorsement-for-the-UN-Convention-on-the-Assignment-of-Receivables-in-International-Trade.pdf.

[14] www.iccwbo.org/News/Articles/2014/ICC-endorses-UNCITRAL-Convention-on-the-Assignment-of-Receivables-in-International-Trade/.

[15] The general principles of the Receivables Convention, in addition to being settled in most civil and common law jurisdictions, have also been followed in the modernisation of secured transactions law in China, Colombia, Malawi, Mexico, Ghana, India, Japan and South Korea. For example, in Latin free assignability is called *Pactum de non cedendo*. Free assignability is generally recognised by some of the Roman law-influenced civil law systems, for instance the Swiss Code of Obligations (Art 164) and the Turkish Code of Obligations (Art 162(1)) and the PPSA and the UCC Article 9 regimes: see, eg, UCC §9-406(d) and UCC §9-408(a). In the UK, under the Small Business, Enterprise and Employment Act 2015 s 1, bans on assignment are nullified. For a comparative work on the assignment of receivables see also H Sigman and E-M Kieninger, *Cross Border Security over Receivables* (Munich, Sellier, 2009). See also Chs 15, 16 and 18 on Germany, Italy and Belgium respectively.

[16] For the background of the project and its inception point, see Report of the Secretary General: Study on Security Interests (A/CN.9/131 and Annex). Previous attempts were a uniform conditional sales Act enacted by Norway, Sweden and Denmark between 1915 and 1917; Unidroit Draft provisions of 1939 and 1951 concerning the impact of reservation of title in the sale of certain goods; provisions regarding the effect of bankruptcy of reservation of title in the sale of goods in the draft EEC Bankruptcy Convention of 1970; and model reservation of title clauses contained in several General Conditions elaborated by the UN Economic Commission for Europe. HS Burman, 'The Commercial Challenge in Modernizing Secured Transactions Law' [2003] *Uniform Law Review* 347, 348–49.

[17] A/RES/56/81.

assignment of receivables in international trade. Secondly, its implicit purpose is to provide a model for the modernisation of domestic assignment laws. This is achieved by its general principles and key provisions, which may be taken as an example in domestic modernisation or reform activities. Therefore, with these two purposes, the Receivables Convention aims to facilitate increased access to low-cost credit by reducing legal obstacles. Reduction of legal obstacles provides greater certainty to lending transactions.

UNCITRAL observed that:

> [T]he diversity of national laws and the lack of standard transnational rules creates significant additional expenditure, delays and uncertainty [in] many international business transactions … [and] parties may be dissuaded from using receivables financing at all and are then forced to rely on … more expensive arrangements, such as overdraft facilities, letters of credit or export guarantees.[18]

There is divergence in the way national legal systems regulate taking security over, or sale of, receivables. These divergences are deeply rooted in the cultural, legal and historical traditions of nations. They have the tendency to increase the cost of credit in the global markets and affect the competitiveness of businesses. These divergences are felt in the creation, third-party effectiveness, priority and enforcement of a security right.[19] These differences relate to the proprietary effects of security.[20] Particularly, the role of possession in some civil law jurisdictions as the significant element in proprietary rights[21] is considered to be an obstacle to the development of receivables financing and its harmonisation. This aspect of the law is regarded as one of the reasons for the lack of recognition of the Receivables Convention. The reluctance of a country to adopt the Receivables Convention may be linked to the following two broad observations: adopting a different set of principles than the ones that have been well established, and the familiarity of the legal and financial community with this new set of principles.[22] However, the Receivables Convention provides a number of solutions that enable countries to modernise their laws in order to respond to the needs of small businesses. These include, particularly, promoting secured financing of receivables financing,

[18] 'UN Investigates Receivables Financing', *International Trade Finance*, 3 June 1994; 213 ABI/INFORM Global, 4 ff.

[19] Report of the Secretary General: Study on Security Interests (A/CN.9/131 and Annex), reprinted in (1977) 8 *Yearbook of the United Nations Commission on International Trade Law*, 180 ff. For a similar view see also generally HL Buxbaum, 'Unification of the Law Governing Secured Transactions: Progress and Prospects for Reform' [2003] *Uniform Law Review* 322.

[20] For a comparative analysis of cross-border receivables financing, see, eg, Sigman and Kieninger (n 14).

[21] See generally R Goode, 'Reflections on the Harmonization of Commercial Law' in R Cranston and R Goode (eds), *Commercial and Consumer Law: National and International Dimensions* (Oxford, Clarendon Press, 1993) 3, 12. For example, receivables are intangible assets which cannot be transferred using traditional methods of transfer or security.

[22] HD Gabriel, 'Commentary on the Availability of Credit and the Utility and Efficacy of UNCITRAL's Legislative Efforts in Secured Transactions' in O Akseli (ed), *Availability of Credit and Secured Transactions in a Time of Crisis* (Cambridge, Cambridge University Press, 2013) 217, 222–23.

overriding anti-assignment clauses and enabling the use of future receivables in assignment and the bulk assignment of receivables.

There is a link between the borrower's financial strength and the attraction to secured credit. It has been pointed out that 'borrowers exhibit an increasing tendency toward unsecured debt as their financial strength increases'.[23] Public companies usually borrow on an unsecured basis. The reasons for this are that they have sufficient credit strength and can spread their sources of finance. Large companies rather prefer to use negative pledge clauses in their contracts.[24] The Law Commission observed this tendency by reporting that 'well-established public companies are able to borrow readily on an unsecured basis, but for many smaller enterprises credit can be obtained on significantly better terms … if the borrower is able to offer security to the lender'.[25] This observation is supported by empirical studies which suggest that security is mainly used by small businesses that pose default risk.[26] Small businesses are mainly able to offer receivables owed to them as their only meaningful collateral. Thus, there is a policy reason to modernise secure credit laws to promote the availability of capital and make credit at affordable rates.[27] Professor Gabriel succinctly notes on this point as follows:

> [T]he [Receivables] Convention, by providing for a source of secured credit should favor smaller borrowers in less developed economies. Most importantly, by opening up new potential markets for capital, and thereby creating a wider number of potential borrowers in a greater number of jurisdictions, the Convention should serve the larger goal of providing a vehicle for capital to move toward its most efficient use by finding borrowers who can best use the resources.[28]

The general principles of the Convention aim to create simplicity in the law of assignment of receivables. By simplifying the rules on the assignment of receivables, the Convention, prevents complexity and achieves certainty and accessibility.[29]

[23] RJ Mann, 'Explaining the Pattern of Secured Credit' (1997) 110 *Harvard Law Review* 625, 674 where Mann concludes that secured credit '[enhances] the borrower's ability to give a credible commitment to refrain from excessive future borrowing and by limiting the borrower's ability to engage in conduct that lessens the likelihood of payment'.

[24] P Wood, *Law and Practice of International Finance* (London, Sweet and Maxwell, 2008) 253. Fleisig empirically provides that in the US one-third of credit is unsecured and about two-thirds is secured. HW Fleisig, 'The Economics of Collateral and of Collateral Reform' in Dahan and Simpson (eds) (n 4) 81, 88.

[25] Law Commission Report No 296 (2005) para 1.2.

[26] J Armour, 'The Law and Economics Debate About Secured Lending: Lessons For European Law-making?' in H Eidenmüller and E-M Kieninger (eds), *The Future of Secured Credit in Europe* (Munich, De Gruyter Recht, 2008) 3, 9; MA Lasfer 'Debt Structure, Agency Costs and Firm's Size: An Empirical Investigation', Working Paper, Cass Business School (2000) 18. Lasfer concludes that small firms hold more secured and less unsecured debt than larger companies.

[27] See, eg, the Preamble of the Receivables Convention '*Being of the opinion* that the adoption of uniform rules governing the assignment of receivables would promote the availability of capital and credit at more affordable rates …'.

[28] Gabriel (n 21) 222.

[29] For a similar argument in terms of an ideal law of security, see R Calnan, 'What Makes a Good Law of Security?' in F Dahan (ed), *Research Handbook on Secured Financing in Commercial Transactions* (Cheltenham, Edward Elgar, 2015) 451, 453 ff.

It recognises the validity of assignments of future receivables and bulk assignment of receivables.[30] The Convention also partially nullified contractual limitations to the assignment of receivables. Certainty is achieved with respect to the rights of the assignor and assignee, as well as with respect to the effectiveness of the assignment as against the debtor. The Receivables Convention establishes a conflict-of-laws provision on priority of competing claims. It also provides a substantive law regime as an optional annex governing priority between competing claims and offers a model for the registration of security interests for the purposes of obtaining priority,[31] as well as covering outright and security transfers of receivables.[32]

C. Assignment of Future Receivables and Bulk Assignment of Receivables

Eliminating restrictions on the use of receivables as collateral to obtain finance is important for small businesses. In this context, the Receivables Convention recognises the validity of bulk assignments of receivables and present assignments of future receivables as well as assignments of partial or undivided interests in receivables. These restrictions are generally known as *statutory limitations* as they are found in legislation dealing with assignment of receivables.

The Receivables Convention Article 8 aims to facilitate the flow of credit by eliminating statutory limitations in national laws. In this context, the Convention focuses on financing practices such as securitisation, project financing, factoring and asset-based financing by recognising the validity of the assignment of future receivables and bulk assignment of receivables. Certain legal systems restrict the assignment of future receivables and receivables assigned in bulk in order to protect the assignor from over-charging its assets.[33]

[30] Article 8.

[31] Article 42(4).

[32] On these issues see, eg, S Bazinas, 'Key Policy Issues of the United Nations Convention on the Assignment of Receivables in International Trade' (2003) 11 *Tulane Journal of International & Comparative Law* 275; S Bazinas, 'UNCITRAL's Work in the Field of Secured Transactions' (2004) 36 *Uniform Commercial Code Law Journal* 67; S Bazinas, 'An International Legal Regime For Receivables Financing: UNCITRAL's Contribution' (1998) 8 *Duke Journal of Comparative & International Law* 315; S Bazinas, 'Lowering the Cost of Credit: the Promise in the Future UNCITRAL Convention on Assignment of Receivables in International Trade' (2001) 9 *Tulane Journal of International & Comparative Law* 259; S Bazinas, 'UNCITRAL's Contribution to the Unification of Receivables Financing Law: The United Nations Convention on the Assignment of Receivables in International Trade' [2002] *Uniform Law Review* 49; F Ferrari, 'The UNCITRAL Draft Convention on Assignment in Receivables Financing: Applicability, General Provisions and the Conflict of Conventions' (2001) 1 *Melbourne Journal of International Law* 1; F Ferrari, 'The UNCITRAL Draft Convention on Assignment in Receivables Financing: Critical Remarks on Some Specific Issues' in J Basedow, I Meier, AK Schnyder, T Einhorn and D Girsberger (eds), *Private Law in the International Arena—Liber Amicorum Kurt Siehr* (The Hague, TMC Asser Press, 2000) 179; M Deschamps, 'The Priority Rules of the United Nations Receivables Convention' (2002) 12 *Duke Journal of Comparative & International Law* 389.

[33] For a similar assertion see Bazinas, 'Lowering the Cost of Credit' (n 32) 265.

These restrictions tend to increase the cost of credit as every single receivable upon its creation has to be described and the debtor for every receivable needs to be notified. This activity requires administrative work to ensure an effective transfer. Costs associated with administering this process arise when the assignor and the assignee create new agreements each time a receivable comes into existence. Thus the Receivables Convention does not require each receivable to be described in the contract of assignment and does not require a new contract of assignment to be concluded when a future receivable is created.

Legal systems provide certain reasons for restricting these types of assignment. First, restriction protects 'the assignor from excessive limitations on its economic activity, addressed by requirements for a specific description of the assigned receivable'.[34] Second, concerns over bulk assignments and assignments of future receivables gather around the fact that these types of financing practice may have an impact 'on the economic freedom of the assignor or related specificity concerns'.[35] The restriction of security over future receivables arises out of 'the desire to restrict security and … the desire to prevent future property being caught up as a security for pre-existing debt'.[36] Third, statutory prohibitions on bulk assignments have been justified with the 'concerns about the advantage gained by [large] financing institutions, obtaining a bulk assignment … and future receivables from their borrowers, over small suppliers, who are often protected by retention of title arrangements'.[37]

Specificity and publicity requirements limit the use of future receivables as collateral in traditional Napoleonic legal systems.[38] Otherwise, most legal systems recognise the assignability of future receivables. It can be argued that specificity and publicity doctrines may not be compatible with the requirements of modern finance. The specificity doctrine[39] requires the identification, specification and separation of the asset from the transferor's assets in order for the assignment to be valid.[40] Specification of the debtor and the information on the receivable are

[34] ibid 265.

[35] S Bazinas, 'Multi-Jurisdictional Receivables Financing: UNCITRAL's Impact on Securitization and Cross-Border Perfection' (2002) 12 *Duke Journal of Comparative & International Law* 365, 371.

[36] P Wood, *Comparative Law of Security and Guarantees* (London, Sweet & Maxwell, 1995) 41.

[37] Bazinas (n 35) 372.

[38] K Zweigert and H Kötz, *An Introduction to Comparative Law*, 3rd edn (Oxford, Clarendon Press, 1998) 445 ff; see also P Wood, 'World-Wide Security—Classification of Legal Jurisdictions' in J Norton and M Andenas (eds), *Emerging Financial Markets and Secured Transactions* (London, Kluwer, 1998) 39, 40 ff.

[39] This doctrine was abolished in England by *Tailby v Official Receiver* (1888) LR 13 App Cas 523 and *Holroyd v Marshall* (1861) 10 HLC 191, All ER Rep 414 [1861]–[1873]. The doctrine has three basics. First, one cannot transfer an asset unless the asset is identified. Secondly, if a security is created over a future asset at the present time to cover an existing debt, then this actually is a creation of security for pre-existing debt when the asset comes into existence and is treated as a potentially voidable preference. Thirdly, there may be a prejudice against debtors granting security over all of their future receivables and thereby either destroying their means of income or weakening the cushion available to unsecured creditors, see Wood (n 35) 40 ff.

[40] P Wood, *Maps of World Financial Law* (London, Allen & Overy LLP, 2005) 83.

elements of separation. The specification requirement is based on the idea that the owner of assets needs to be known in order for a valid transfer. Publicity depends on specificity. This is because publicity may require some form of creditor's control or possession over the assets. In order to achieve creditor's control assets need to be specifically identified otherwise the transfer cannot be publicised.[41] Under the publicity requirement, if an assignment requires notification of the debtor, whose identity may not be known at the time of the contract of assignment, that may be considered as an obstacle to the assignment of future receivables. The critical problem with notification to underlying obligors is that it provides no means of constituting a present pledge of the future accounts of a business since there is no debtor to notify until the right to payment arises.[42]

The Receivables Convention Article 8(1) recognises the validity of assignment of future receivables and bulk assignment of receivables (receivables that are not identified individually). An assignment cannot be deemed as ineffective against the assignor, the assignee, and the debtor or a third party just because it is an assignment of future receivables or a receivable that is not individually identified at the time of the assignment. The Receivables Convention sets a condition in Article 8(1)(a) and (b) that these receivables should be identified as receivables to which the assignment relates. The Convention does not require specific description of the receivables. The description can be general so long as the receivables may be identified to the contract of assignment. If the parties provide general descriptions in an assignment, this will be effective as long as receivables are described in such a manner that they can be identified as receivables to which the assignment relates, which means that the debtor and the amount owed should be identifiable in order for the assignments made in bulk to be valid.

Article 8(1)(b) provides that assignments of future receivables are to be recognised provided that the receivables can, at the time of the conclusion of the original contract, be identified as receivables to which the assignment relates. In relation to bulk assignments, receivables should be identifiable at the time of the assignment, if they cannot be identified individually by virtue of Article 8(1)(a). Identification of the exact moment at which the transfer becomes effective would clarify doubts in those legal systems where bulk assignments and assignments of future receivables are not recognised. Recognising the assignment of future receivables as of the time of the conclusion of the original contract does not compromise the rights of the assignee. This is because 'in practice credit was extended at the time when an

[41] Wood (n 23) 258.

[42] See R Serick, *Securities in Movables in German Law: An Outline* (Deventer, Kluwer, 1990) 81–82 (where he argues that this sort of limitation as to future accounts rather than a desire to maintain secrecy is the main reason why pledges of intangibles are not generally used in German financing practice); see also J Rakob, 'Germany' in Sigman and Kieninger (eds) (n 14) 63 (noting that 'the creation of a pledge over receivables requires that notice of the pledge be sent to the third party debtor. This … made pledges unpopular—loss of possession deprives the pledgor of the chance to work with the collateral, notice to third party debtors of receivables may damage the reputation and credit of the pledgor or may confuse the debtor about who to pay to'. See Ch 15.

actual transaction from which receivables might flow was concluded'.[43] This also makes sense as the assignor might assign the same receivable to another person; therefore the Convention protects the interests of the assignee.[44]

Article 8(2) dispenses with the need for a new contract of assignment to be executed when there is an assignment of future receivables. The future receivable must arise or be created after and be identified to the contract of assignment. The rationale is that future receivables arise after the contract of assignment therefore there is no need to have a new assignment document covering that receivable. Article 10(1) supplements the position and provides that a personal or property right securing payment of the assigned receivable is transferred to the assignee without a new act of transfer.

D. Anti-assignment Clauses

One of the general principles of the Receivables Convention, under the Effects of Assignment chapter, is its recognition of an assignment made notwithstanding an anti-assignment clause. The Receivables Convention under Article 9(1) provides that an anti-assignment clause in a contract dealing with certain types of trade receivable is not enforceable against the assignee. However, the rights of the debtor against the assignor are not affected.[45] Trade receivables mentioned in this provision are trade receivables other than those arising from financial services, construction or real estate; receivables arising from intellectual property transactions; credit card receivables; and receivables arising from multi-party netting agreements. The Convention's treatment of anti-assignment clauses also means that small businesses may be able to further utilise financing techniques such as factoring and securitisation in order to access finance.

Under the Convention's treatment, an assignment made notwithstanding an anti-assignment clause will be effective as against the debtor and third parties such as the creditors of the assignor and his trustee in bankruptcy. Recognising

[43] See A/CN.9/434, para 118.

[44] See generally B Markell, 'UNCITRAL's Receivables Convention: The First Step, But not the Last' (2002) 12 *Duke Journal of Comparative & International Law* 401. See also A/CN.9/445, para 224 (where it was noted that 'There was general support for the principle that a future receivable should be deemed as having been transferred at the time of the contract of assignment. It was observed that, in view of the risk that, after the conclusion of the contract of assignment, the assignor might assign the same receivables to another assignee or become insolvent, it was essential to set the time of the transfer of the assigned receivables at the time of the conclusion of the contract of assignment … in practice, the assignee would acquire rights in future receivables only when they arose, but in legal terms the time of transfer would be deemed to be the time of the contract of assignment'.

[45] For a more detailed treatment of anti-assignment clauses under the Receivables Convention see, eg, O Akseli, 'Contractual Prohibitions on Assignment of Receivables: An English and UN Perspective' (2009) 7 *Journal of Business Law* 650. In the US under the UCC Art 9 regime UCC §9-406(d) provides free alienability of rights to payment and that any agreement between an account debtor (*debtor*) and an assignor is ineffective.

the effectiveness of an assignment made notwithstanding an anti-assignment clause poses a question at the juncture of freedom of contract and the ability to create security. The Receivables Convention, the UNCITRAL Legislative Guide on Secured Transactions, and common and civil law systems have recognised the effectiveness of an assignment made in violation of an anti-assignment clause.[46] Under English law an assignment made in violation of an anti-assignment clause is ineffective.[47] However, recently section 1 of the Small Business, Enterprise and Employment Act 2015 has nullified bans on invoice assignment clauses in order to facilitate small businesses' access to finance.[48] It is argued that in the refinement of the implementation of this provision, the Receivables Convention's approach could be helpful.

Recognising the effectiveness of an assignment made in violation of an anti-assignment clause would not adversely affect small debtors, as 'they do not have the bargaining power to insert anti-assignment clauses in their contracts and … would continue paying the same bank account or post office box'.[49] This approach would not affect large debtors as they have sufficient bargaining power.[50] The Receivables Convention protects the assignee, under Article 9(2), by providing that the breach of an anti-assignment clause by the assignor is not in itself a sufficient reason for the avoidance of the original contract by the debtor. The liability of the assignor for breach of the anti-assignment clause is preserved under the Receivables Convention. However, the debtor may not terminate the agreement on the grounds of breach of an anti-assignment clause (Articles 9(2) and 10(3)). This prevents the debtor avoiding the contract and strengthening his bargaining power.[51] This approach also provides certainty to the assignee in relation to the outcome of the transaction. The assignor may be held liable for breach of contract of anti-assignment. However, the right to compensatory damages that the debtor may have under the applicable law has been left outside the Receivables Convention.[52] Article 9(2) aims to protect a person who is not party to an agreement between the assignor and the debtor on the sole ground that he had

[46] UCC Article 9 §9-406(d); Australian Personal Property Securities Act 2009 s 81; Swiss Code of Obligations Art 164; Turkish Code of Obligations Art 162(1); UNCITRAL Legislative Guide on Secured Transactions Recommendation 24.

[47] *Linden Gardens Trust v Lenesta Sludge Disposals* [1994] 1 AC 85.

[48] www.gov.uk/government/uploads/system/uploads/attachment_data/file/408130/bis-15-165-nullification-of-ban-on-invoice-assignment-clauses-summary-of-responses.pdf; www.gov.uk/government/uploads/system/uploads/attachment_data/file/392477/bis-14-1232-nullification-of-ban-on-invoice-assignment-clauses-consultation.pdf; for evidence supporting the nullification of bans on anti-assignment clauses www.publications.parliament.uk/pa/cm201415/cmpublic/smallbusiness/memo/sb76.htm; www.publications.parliament.uk/pa/cm201415/cmpublic/smallbusiness/memo/sb13.htm; see also Chs 2 and 14.

[49] A/CN.9/WG.II/WP.105, para 83; see also A/CN.9/489, para 103.

[50] A/CN.9/WG.II/WP.105, para 83. The Addendum to the Draft Legislative Guide on Secured Transactions para 230 clearly indicates that a debtor such as a consumer may protect itself through statutory prohibitions. A/CN.9/631/Add.1.

[51] Bazinas, 'Key Policy Issues' (n 32) 287.

[52] A/CN.9/489, para 99.

knowledge of the agreement. The knowledge by the assignee of the existence of the anti-assignment clause is irrelevant. The assignee cannot be held liable on the sole ground of knowledge of the anti-assignment clause. There must be additional grounds of knowledge in order for the assignee to be held liable as the third party. However, knowledge may be relevant in the case of tortious liability of the assignee such as for malicious interference with advantageous relations.[53] Article 18(3) does not allow the debtor to make a claim for breach of an anti-assignment clause against the assignee by way of set-off so as to defeat the assignee's demand for payment.

The Contracting States are not permitted to make a declaration to override the effectiveness of the provision of free assignability. A Contracting State is permitted to make a declaration as to whether an assignment of a receivable owed by a governmental debtor in that state will be excluded from the Convention's anti-assignment rules (Article 40). Article 9 will not be effective vis-à-vis a sovereign debtor who is located in a Contracting State if that state makes a declaration under Article 40. Article 9 does not apply to restrictions arising by statute or other rule of law.

E. Registration

The Convention also offers a model for the registration of security interests for the purposes of obtaining priority.[54] The Convention's optional annex contains substantive law priority rules, which the Contracting States may opt into if they 'wish to modernize or to adjust their laws to accommodate assignments under the Convention'.[55] The rules are based on Uniform Commercial Code Article 9 (*first registration in time*), English law (*Dearle v Hall*) and the civil law system (*first assignment in time*). The registration system proposed by the Convention under Article 42(4) is intended to modernise national laws. States may apply their own priority rules and they can still utilise the registration system. The rationale for preparing an optional annex is that some states may have no priority rules, or the existing rules may be outdated or not fully adequate in addressing modern financing techniques.[56] A general registry of security interests system that provides notice to potential financiers may present clear advantages to small businesses. Small businesses do not radiate information about their credit unlike large firms who release information through their access to stock market, financial statements, ratings conducted by the rating agencies or registration of earlier security interests by previous creditors.[57]

[53] A/CN.9/470, para 102; see also A/CN.9/WG.II/WP.105, para 85.

[54] Article 42(4).

[55] Bazinas (n 35) 380 ff.

[56] A/CN.9/489/Add 1, para 72.

[57] B Carruthers and L Ariovich, *Money and Credit: A Sociological Approach* (Cambridge, Polity, 2010) 85, 149 ff.

Financiers or investors do not have credit data information.[58] Asymmetric information is a critical matter in small businesses' access to finance. It is also one of the reasons why small businesses are refused finance.[59] Investors incur transaction costs in due diligence, which leads to reduction in funding causing an 'equity gap'.[60] Clear information about the financial strength and the status of small business could encourage lending and reduce the financial vulnerability of lenders.[61] Financiers lend to small businesses provided there is clear information about their previous transactions with lenders. Although banks have their own reliable information systems (credit card information, exclusive and informal relationships with small businesses etc), it is important to reduce the effectiveness of information asymmetry as a ground for refusing finance to small businesses. One way to obtain clear and reliable information about incorporated and unincorporated businesses is to register security interests created by these businesses.

(i) Priority Rules Based on Registration

Optional Annex sections 1 and 2 provide priority rules based on registration. The rules detailed in these sections aim to provide notice to potential financiers that certain receivables may have been assigned. The rule on priority among several assignees (Section I, Article 1) is that the assignee who registers the information about the assignment first gains priority. If no such information is registered, priority will be determined by the order of conclusion of the respective contracts of assignment. The rationale underlying such registration is 'not to create or constitute evidence of property rights, but to protect third parties by putting them on notice about assignments made and to provide a basis for settling conflicts of priority between competing claims'.[62] The rationale for the priority between the assignee and the insolvency administrator or creditors of the assignor (Section I, Article 2) is that if registration takes place and the receivable is assigned before the commencement of insolvency proceedings in relation to the assets and affairs of the assignor, the assignee will have priority. Section II Article 3 details how a registration system should be established. This is an especially important guide for Contracting States that do not have a general registration system. The registry is open to any person for search of the records according to identification of the assignor and a search in writing can be obtained. The written search result issued

[58] For reform discussion in sharing credit data with alternative financiers, see, eg, www.gov.uk/government/consultations/competition-in-banking-improving-access-to-sme-credit-data; www.gov.uk/government/consultations/competition-in-banking-improving-access-to-sme-credit-data.

[59] *The SME Financing Gap Theory and Evidence*, v 1 (OECD Publishing, 2006) 19.

[60] JE Stiglitz, 'The Contributions of the Economics of Information to Twentieth-Century Economics' (2000) 115(4) *Quarterly Journal of Economics* 1441; JE Stiglitz and A Weiss, 'Credit Rationing in Markets with Imperfect Information' (1981) 71 *American Economic Review* 393.

[61] Carruthers and Ariovich (n 56) 155.

[62] A/CN.9/489/Add 1, para 74.

by the registry is admissible as evidence and is proof of the registration of the data to which the search relates. The registration is proposed to be simple and inexpensive and requires a limited amount of data by virtue of Article 4, which establishes the basic characteristics for an efficient system and therefore an assignee and an assignor would not be required to register information that is too detailed. These basic characteristics are 'the public character of the registry, the type of data that need to be registered, the ways in which the registration-related needs of modern financing practices may be accommodated and the time of effectiveness of registration'.[63]

(ii) Priority Rules Based on the Time of the Contract of Assignment

Articles 6 to 8 of the Optional Annex regulate priority rules based on the time of the contract of assignment. Article 6 deals with priority among several assignees based on the order of the conclusion of the respective contracts of assignment. Article 7 regulates priority between the assignee and the insolvency administrator or creditors of the assignor. The right of the assignee has priority over the right of an insolvency administrator and creditors, provided that the receivable is assigned before the commencement of insolvency proceedings. The time of the assignment may be established by any method of proof under Article 8.

The time of the assignment determines priority. Although under the *nemo dat* rule, after the first assignment the assignor cannot assign the same receivable to another assignee as he has no right to assign, there is a disadvantage to this approach. Third-party creditors may not be able to determine whether certain receivables have been assigned. This is because there is no registration system that they can check with. This may have a negative impact on the availability and the cost of credit. Third-party creditors would need to protect themselves against the risk of a previous assignment having taken place. On the other hand 'in a closed market, banks can still rely on borrowers' representations and gain knowledge about their clients' financial transactions [and] and the penalty for double financing of receivables in these markets outweighs the potential benefits'.[64]

(iii) Priority Rules Based on the Time of Notification of Assignment

In this approach, priority is determined by the order in which the debtor receives notifications of the respective assignments. However, the knowledge of a prior assignment by an assignee makes it impossible for that assignee to obtain priority

[63] A/CN.9/489/Add 1, para 78.
[64] Bazinas, 'Lowering the Cost of Credit' (n 32) 284.

over that prior assignment even if the subsequent assignee notified the debtor first. The priority between the assignee and the insolvency administrator or creditors of the assignor is governed by Article 10. According to Article 10, the assignee will have priority over the right of an insolvency administrator if the receivable was assigned and notification was received by the debtor before the commencement of such insolvency proceeding. It is possible that potential assignees may inquire from the debtor as to whether receivables have been assigned previously. In terms of bulk assignments and assignment of future receivables the system may not be ideal for assignees. This is because the identity of the debtor will be unknown or there will simply be multiple debtors. Thus it can be argued that this system may not be cost-effective for assignees.[65]

Under English law,[66] an assignment made by a company will only be registrable if it is an assignment by way of security (charge) over book debts of the company.[67] If it is an assignment by way of sale it is not registrable. On the other hand, all types of assignments (outright or for security purposes) by an individual are registrable.[68] The Law Commission in its Report recommended that sales of receivables by companies should also be registered.[69] Functionally, sale of receivables is similar to charge over receivables; it seems perfectly reasonable to make the sale of receivables registrable. Registration can, at least, be on a voluntary basis. Lack of registration causes certain problems such as subsequent creditors or assignees having to rely on the representations of the assignor and possibly not being informed of the existence of a functional equivalent of charge over receivables.[70] The rule in *Dearle v Hall*,[71] which regulates priority over receivables, is not suitable for modern financing techniques.[72] Failure to notify debtors will result in the loss of priority status in subsequent assignments under *Dearle v Hall* and in civil law jurisdictions the assignment could become void in the insolvency of the assignor.[73] According to Professor Oditah: 'bulk assignees of receivables, especially lenders as opposed to invoice discounters generally do not give notice of their bulk assignments until the assignor defaults and it is necessary for the assignee to collect the assigned receivables itself'.[74] In the assignment of future

[65] For criticism of the rule in *Dearle v Hall* see, eg, J de Lacy, 'The Priority Rule of Dearle v Hall Restated' (1999) 63 *The Conveyancer* 311.

[66] For more information see Ch 2.

[67] Companies Act 2006 s 860(7)(f).

[68] Insolvency Act 1986 s 344.

[69] Law Commission Report No 296, paras 4.7 ff.

[70] ibid.

[71] *Dearle v Hall* (1828) 3 Russ I.

[72] Nevertheless, the rule also applies to assignment of bulk receivables *Compaq Computer Ltd v Abercorn Group Ltd* [1993] BCLC 602.

[73] For a similar assertion see F Oditah, 'Recurrent Issues in Receivables Financing' in J Armour and J Payne (eds), *Rationality in Company Law: Essays in Honour of DD Prentice* (Oxford, Hart Publishing, 2009) 321, 351. This is because formal validity and publicity requirements are considered as condition of priority and they have not been met.

[74] ibid.

receivables this rule is not ideal either. It is not possible to notify debtors who are unknown at the time of conclusion of the contract of assignment. Even when the identities of future debtors are known and notice is given prior to the receivables coming into existence, this may not be sufficient to secure its priority. It is because a notice given to the debtor after the receivables have come into existence will have priority.[75]

F. Conclusions

The Receivables Convention is a sophisticated piece of legislative work which has not yet received the praise it deserves. While it has not yet received sufficient ratifications and entered into force, its general principles, some of which have been further discussed in this chapter, have been incorporated in developed legal systems that support the facilitation of credit. The principles have also been incorporated into the UNCITRAL Legislative Guide on Secured Transactions and the UNCITRAL draft Model Law on Secured Transactions. Thus, it can be argued that it has perhaps achieved its mission.

[75] *Re Dallas* [1904] 2 Ch 385.

23

The UNCITRAL Legislative Guide on Secured Transactions and the Draft UNCITRAL Model Law on Secured Transactions compared

SPYRIDON V BAZINAS*

A. Introduction

At its October 2015 and February 2016 sessions,[1] Working Group VI (Security Interests) of the United Nations Commission on International Trade Law (UNCITRAL or the 'Commission')[2] adopted and submitted to the Commission for final consideration and adoption a draft model law on secured transactions (the 'DML').[3] The DML is based on the recommendations of the UNCITRAL Legislative Guide on Secured Transactions (the 'ST Guide'), including the Supplement on Security Rights in Intellectual Property (the 'IP Supplement'), the UNCITRAL Guide on the Implementation of a Security Rights Registry (the 'Registry Guide'), and the provisions of the United Nations Convention on the Assignment of Receivables in International Trade (the 'CARIT').[4] The purpose of this chapter

* Spyridon (Spiros) V Bazinas is Senior Legal Officer at the International Trade Law Division of the Office of Legal Affairs of the United Nations, which functions as the Secretariat of the United Nations Commission on International Trade Law (UNCITRAL). The views expressed in this article are the personal views of the author and do not necessarily reflect the views of the United Nations or UNCITRAL. This chapter is based on S Bazinas, 'The draft UNCITRAL Model Law on Secured Transactions', in *The Draft UNCITRAL Model Law on Secured Transactions—Why and how?* B Foëx (ed), (Geneva, Schulthess) 2016, 19–44.

[1] The reports of the Working Group on its work at those sessions are contained in documents A/CN.9/865 and A/CN.9/871 (see http://www.uncitral.org/uncitral/commission/sessions/49th.html).

[2] For the origin, mandate, composition and methods of work of UNCITRAL, see www.uncitral.org/uncitral/en/about_us.html.

[3] This chapter refers to the DML contained in documents A/CN.9/884 and Addenda 1-4 (see www.uncitral.org/uncitral/commission/sessions/49th.html).

[4] See www.uncitral.org/uncitral/uncitral_texts/security.html.

is to briefly discuss the DML and compare its provisions with the key recommendations of the ST Guide.

B. The ST Guide and the Need for a Model Law

UNCITRAL prepares various types of uniform law texts, such as Conventions, model laws and guides (legislative and contractual).[5] Those texts differ in a number of respects, including as regards the certainty and flexibility they provide. A Convention provides the highest degree of uniformity and the lowest degree of flexibility, as it has to be implemented as is, except to the extent it allows declarations with respect to one or the other of its provisions.[6] To the contrary, a legislative guide provides the lowest degree of uniformity but the highest degree of flexibility in the sense that it contains an analysis of issues to be addressed in legislation and mere recommendations to the legislator.[7] In the scales of uniformity and flexibility, a model law is between a Convention and a legislative guide. While it contains legislative provisions, it is sufficient if the thrust, the philosophy of the model law is reflected in a national enactment. A model law does not need to be implemented verbatim, in one and the same law, or in a way that would not fit the legislative technique and method of each state. And with respect to certain issues, a model law may also include alternatives for the enacting state to choose from. All this is certainly the case with respect to the DML.

The question arises as to why the DML is necessary now that we have the ST Guide, a text that has rightly been described as a remarkable achievement[8] and is already having a significant impact on the development of national laws.[9] The answer is that, with its 248 recommendations and almost 500 pages of commentary (with the IP Supplement), the ST Guide may not be easy for states to implement. In addition, the ST Guide addresses all issues with respect to security interests in all types of movable asset with very few exceptions (e.g., receivables arising under financial contracts and securities).[10] Moreover, the ST Guide offers alternatives with respect to important issues, such as those relating to acquisition security interests.[11] The DML is much shorter, has a broader scope and contains less

[5] See www.uncitral.org/uncitral/en/uncitral_texts.html.

[6] For example, CARIT allows States to declare that they will not be bound by the conflict-of-laws chapter (Art 39) or article 9 dealing with the contractual limitations on assignments (Art 40, only if the debtor of the receivable is a Government or a public entity located in the state making the declaration).

[7] Other than the guides mentioned in this article, the UNCITRAL Legislative Guide on Insolvency Law is a good example (www.uncitral.org/uncitral/en/uncitral_texts/insolvency/2004Guide.html).

[8] N Cohen, 'Should UNCITRAL Prepare a Model Law on Secured Transactions?' [2010] *Uniform Law Review* 326.

[9] SV Bazinas, 'The Influence of the UNCITRAL Legislative Guide on Secured Transactions' in F Dahan (ed), *Research Handbook on Secured Financing in Commercial Transactions* (Cheltenham, Edward Elgar, 2015) 26.

[10] ST Guide rec 4, subpara (c).

[11] ST Guide recs 178–202.

exceptions. Thus, the DML is easier to implement and will usefully complement the ST Guide in providing more focused and specific guidance to states. The DML will also provide states with another authoritative text prepared by an international legislative body like UNCITRAL and adopted by consensus.[12]

Yet, a number of concerns or objections have been expressed with respect to a model law on secured transactions as compared to the ST Guide. For example, it has been argued that the DML might not add enough value to the ST Guide to justify the additional efforts, be eventually inconsistent with the ST Guide, create a disincentive for states to implement the recommendations of the ST Guide, be impossible to prepare, or reduce the flexibility of states in preparing a law that would meet their needs and thus not be as widely implemented as the ST Guide already is.[13] It has also been argued that a model law might not be desirable as there cannot be a 'one size fits all' law on secured transactions,[14] or feasible as it would not create an international normative regime (like the Convention on International Interests in Mobile Equipment) or a regime with a narrowly defined area of law (such as letter of credit financing), and could create a difficult dilemma for states as regards revisiting issues already addressed in the ST Guide and refusing to address valid concerns.[15] Finally, it has been argued that the time is not right to prepare a model law as there is an oversupply and an under-demand for model laws.[16]

The work of Working Group VI so far has proven that all these otherwise reasonable concerns have not created insurmountable difficulties. There can certainly not be a 'one size fits all' secured transactions law. But, as an UNCITRAL Model Law, the DML leaves states sufficient flexibility and is not a 'one size fits all' law. States may implement it in various ways as long as they implement the key concepts of the DML (including the comprehensive scope, the simple creation of security interests, notice registration for third-party effectiveness, a complete set of priority rules, an efficient enforcement regime, and the main conflict-of-laws rules). As already mentioned, at its October 2015 and February 2016 sessions, the Working Group adopted and submitted the DML to the Commission for final consideration and adoption.[17]

[12] The long-standing practice in the Commission is to reach decisions by consensus (see A/65/17—Report of the United Nations Commission on International Trade Law, Forty-third session (A/65/17, Annex III, para 2) www.uncitral.org/uncitral/en/about/methods_documents.html. Consensus in the practice of the Commission does not mean that any state can veto a decision, but rather that, while starting from the majority view, the Chairman makes an effort to address all concerns so that all states can accept or at least be able to live with the decision.

[13] For a discussion of the considerations in favour of and against a model law, see Cohen (n 8) 329–35.

[14] RA Macdonald, 'A Model Law on Secured Transactions' [2010] *Uniform Law Review* 421. In fact, Macdonald accepts the idea of 'many model laws' and raises the question whether UNCITRAL should prepare them or simply provide technical assistance to states implementing the recommendations of the ST Guide.

[15] ibid 422–23.

[16] ibid 423–24.

[17] For the relevant reports of the Working Group, see (n 1) The Commission is expected to consider and adopt the DML at its forty-ninth session, in 2016 (New York, 27 June–15 July 2016).

The DML simply reflects the policy of those recommendations of the ST Guide that have a normative character and thus belong in a model law. Other recommendations that are mere admonitions to the legislator have been left out or are discussed in the Guide to Enactment of the DML.[18] In addition, several recommendations have been revised for their policy to be reflected in legislative language. Moreover the DML addresses issues not addressed in the ST Guide (e.g., security interests in non-intermediated securities).

As to the timing of the work by the Working Group or the lack of a sufficient demand for a model law, the fact that so many states are currently reviewing their secured transactions law seems to suggest that the timing is perfect and the demand rather high. For these reasons, at its forty-eighth session, in 2015, the Commission approved the substance of the registry-related provisions of the DML and asked the Working Group to expedite its work so as to submit the DML to the Commission for final consideration and adoption at its forty-ninth session in 2016.[19] As to the alleged oversupply of model laws, because of the existence of regional secured transactions laws (such as the model laws prepared by the European Bank for Reconstruction and Development (EBRD), the (Organization of American States (OAS) or the Organization for the Harmonization in Africa of Business Law (OHADA)), this does not seem to be an obstacle. Regional texts meet regional needs. An international text by UNCITRAL will meet international needs. This is particularly true if the regional texts were prepared many years ago (as is the case with the model laws prepared by the EBRD the OAS or OHADA) as states are looking for up-to-date guidance, which they can find in the ST Guide and the DML.[20]

C. The Scope of the DML

(i) The Unitary, Functional and Comprehensive Approach

In line with the ST Guide, the DML follows a modern approach to secured transactions that can be described as a unitary, functional and comprehensive

[18] Contained in documents A/CN.9/885 and Addenda 1–4 (see www.uncitral.org/uncitral/commission/sessions/49th.html).

[19] Report of the Commission at its forty-eighth session, in 2015, A/70/17, para 216.

[20] 'Acknowledging the importance of modern secured transactions law for the availability and cost of credit and the need for urgent guidance to states, in particular those with developing economies and economies in transition, the Commission expressed its satisfaction for the considerable progress achieved by the Working Group in its work. The Commission thus requested the Working Group to expedite its work so as to complete the draft model law, including the definitions and provisions on non-intermediated securities, and to submit it to the Commission for adoption together with a guide to enactment as soon as possible.' (see Report of UNCITRAL on the work of its forty-seventh session, in 2014, Official Records of the General Assembly, Sixty-ninth Session, Supplement No. 17 (A/69/17), para 163 www.uncitral.org/uncitral/en/commission/sessions/47th.html).

approach. The unitary approach means that the DML uses a single, unitary concept of 'security right' rather than several terms (e.g., pledge, hypothec, etc). The functional approach means that the DML applies to all types of right in movable property created by agreement to secure payment or other performance of an obligation. In other words, the form of the transaction or the terminology used by the parties (e.g., transfer of title for security purposes, retention-of-title sale or financial lease) is not decisive. Moreover, the DML follows a comprehensive approach in the sense that security interests may: (a) secure all types of obligation, present or future, determined or determinable, including fluctuating obligations and obligations described in a generic way; (b) encumber assets described specifically or generally, or even all of the assets of a grantor, present and future, including a changing pool of assets; and (c) be created or acquired by any legal or natural person, including a consumer.[21]

This unitary, functional and comprehensive approach to secured transactions is not dictated by ideological considerations or preferences for one or the other national legal system. It is a practical response to the main problem of secured transactions laws around the world, that is, the fragmentation of secured transactions law into multiple laws dealing differently with transactions that fulfil security functions. The result of this fragmentation is the creation of gaps and inconsistencies, which cannot but have a negative impact on the availability and the cost of credit (even if judges, practitioners and business people do their best to minimise the negative impact). In addition, the unitary, functional and comprehensive approach is the approach typically followed in modern secured transactions legislation.[22] Moreover, it is the approach that facilitates harmonisation of the laws of various states as it deals in a comprehensive and similar way with all types of security interest.

However, the unitary, functional and comprehensive approach does not mean that borrowers, such as consumers, that deserve special protection are not protected. In line with the ST Guide, the DML provides that nothing in the DML affects the rights and obligations of the grantor and the debtor of the receivable under other laws governing the protection of parties to transactions made for personal, family or household purposes.[23] In addition, the unitary, functional and comprehensive approach does not mean that unsecured creditors are not protected. In line with the ST Guide, with the exception of limitations based solely on the ground that an asset is a future asset, the DML preserves statutory limitations to the creation or enforceability of a security interest in certain types of asset (e.g., household items or employment and retirement benefits, at least up to a certain amount).[24] Unsecured creditors may also be protected by way of statutory privileges (preferential claims) and, in line with the ST Guide, the

[21] ST Guide rec 2 and DML Art 1.

[22] See, for example, the new PPSA of Australia www.comlaw.gov.au/Details/C2012C00151.

[23] ST Guide rec 2, subpara (b), and DML Art 1, para 5.

[24] ST Guide rec 18 and DML Art 1, para 6.

DML only recommends that such privileges should be limited and set out in the law in a transparent way for parties to be able to take them into account when deciding whether to enter into a transaction and on what terms.[25] Finally, the comprehensive, unitary and functional approach does not mean that retention-of-title sales and financial leases need to be recharacterised as secured transactions for all purposes (ie, tax, accounting, etc.). It is sufficient to subject them to secured transactions law for its limited purposes (ie, creation, third-party effectiveness, priority and enforcement). Nor does coverage of these devices in the ST Guide or the DML mean that suppliers of goods on credit cannot be protected. In fact, in line with the ST Guide, the DML generally provides that, once they register, within a short period of time after delivery of the goods, suppliers of goods on credit have priority over other secured creditors even though they registered a notice before the suppliers of goods on credit but within that time period.[26]

(ii) The Scope of the DML and the Scope of the ST Guide Compared

Generally, the scope of the DML is the same as the scope of the ST Guide. However, there are certain exceptions. First, unlike the ST Guide, the DML deals with security interests in non-intermediated securities, such as shares and bonds other than those credited in a securities account.[27] The reasons are that: (a) such securities are regularly used in commercial finance transactions;[28] (b) there are wide divergences among the various national regimes in that regard;[29] and (c) neither the ST Guide nor other texts prepared by other organisations deal with non-intermediated securities.[30]

Second, unlike the ST Guide, the DML does not deal with security interests in letters of credit. The reason is that letter of credit financing is a very specialised and narrow area that is subject to specialised regulation and does not need to be addressed in the DML. States interested in letter of credit financing can still find some guidance in the ST Guide.

Third, unlike the ST Guide, the DML does not deal with security interests in attachments to movable or immovable property. The reason is that, while

[25] ST Guide recs 83 and 239 and DML Arts 33 and 34.

[26] ST Guide recs 180 and 182 and DML Arts 47 and 48.

[27] DML Art 2(v).

[28] R Kohn, 'The Case for Including Directly Held Securities within the Scope of the UNCITRAL Legislative Guide on Secured Transactions' (2010) XV(2) *Uniform Law Review* 413–18, at 417

[29] ibid.

[30] See Report of Working Group VI on the work of its twenty-fifth session (A/CN.9/802), paras 72 and 73 (www.uncitral.org/uncitral/en/commission/working_groups/6Security_Interests.html). The Unidroit Convention on Substantive Rules for Intermediated Securities (2013) and the Convention on the Law Applicable to Certain Rights in Respect of Securities held with an Intermediary (206) do not deal with non-intermediated securities.

attachments are important, the recommendations of the ST Guide provide sufficient guidance for the benefit of states that would like to deal with attachments in their law and there is a need to keep the DML as short and simple as possible.

D. Creation of a Security Interest

(i) General Rules

One of the key objectives of an effective secured transactions law is 'to enable parties to obtain security rights in a simple and efficient manner'.[31] So, in line with the ST Guide, the DML provides that a security agreement is sufficient for the creation of a security interest, although in the case of assets in which the grantor acquires rights or the power to encumber after the time of the conclusion of the security agreement ('future assets'), the security interest is created at that later time.[32] The DML also provides that the security agreement must identify the parties, and describe the secured obligation and the encumbered assets.

In view of the importance of the required description of the encumbered assets, the DML deals with it in a separate provision that implements the policy of the ST Guide.[33] The assets must be described 'in a manner that reasonably allows their identification'. What is a reasonable identification of the assets may differ according to the circumstances and the type of asset involved. For example, in the case of inventory, a generic description, such as 'all my present and future inventory' or 'all my present and future inventory of personal computers' or 'all my present and future inventory of personal computers in warehouse X', may be enough. However, in the case of intellectual property, a specific description, such as 'my patent X', may be necessary (the same rule applies to the description of the encumbered assets in the notice to be submitted to the registry).

Similarly flexible is the DML with respect to the form of a security agreement. A security agreement need be in writing only if it is not accompanied by delivery of the encumbered assets to the secured creditor.[34] This approach combines flexibility (no need for written agreement) with the protection of the legitimate interests of the secured creditor (written agreement only if the secured creditor is not in possession of the assets). The flexibility goes even further. First, it is enough if the agreement is concluded or, at least, evidenced in writing. Second, the writing need only indicate the grantor's intent to create a security interest, that is, the secured creditor's signature is not required. Third, the writing may lead to that

[31] ST Guide rec 1, subpara (c).
[32] ST Guide recs 13 and 14 and DML Art 6.
[33] ST Guide rec 14, subpara (d), and DML Art 9.
[34] ST Guide rec 15 and DML Art 6, para 3 and 4.

result by itself or in conjunction with the course of conduct of the parties, that is, an order, shipment, delivery and acceptance of the goods may be enough. And fourth, writing includes an electronic communication and signature includes an electronic signature.

To facilitate financing practices, such as revolving credit arrangements, the DML provides that it should be possible for a security interest to secure any type of obligation, including future, conditional or fluctuating obligations.[35] Also, to reduce risks and ensure better credit terms for borrowers, the DML provides that it should be possible to create a security interest in future assets, that is, assets created or acquired by the grantor after the creation of a security interest.[36] In order to facilitate consideration of the matter by the national legislator, the commentary of the ST Guide discusses the various approaches taken in different legal systems in this regard to ensure that grantors are not over-committed.[37]

In order to simplify the creation of security interests in all assets of an enterprise the DML provides that a security interest may be created in all assets of a grantor. There are two characteristic elements of such transactions: (a) a security interest may be created in all assets of a grantor with a single agreement; and (b) a grantor may still dispose of certain of its assets (e.g., inventory) in the ordinary course of its business.[38] The ST Guide discusses over-collateralisation, suggesting ways in which it could be addressed, but makes no recommendation as the appropriate response may vary widely from state to state.[39]

In any case, recognising the need to protect certain parties or exclude certain types of asset from the scope of secured transactions law, as already mentioned, the DML defers to consumer protection legislation and to legislation according to which certain types of asset (e.g., employment benefits or household goods) may not be transferred or encumbered.

To protect the secured creditor from unauthorised transfers by the grantor (in which a security interest follows the asset but the asset may be removed from the secured creditor's reach) or transfers in the ordinary course of business or in good faith (in which the transferee takes the asset free of the security interest), the DML provides that, unless otherwise agreed by the parties of the security agreement, the security interest automatically extends to any identifiable proceeds of the encumbered assets.[40] Even in cases in which the security interest follows the assets in the hands of the transferee, it makes sense for the security interest to extend to the proceeds where, for example, the proceeds may be of higher value than used assets. This approach ensures that the secured creditor is sufficiently secured and

[35] ST Guide rec 16 and DML Art 7.

[36] ST Guide rec 17 and DML Art 8.

[37] ST Guide, Ch II, paras 51–55.

[38] ST Guide, Ch II, para 63, and Art 8, subpara (d).

[39] ST Guide, Ch II, para 69.

[40] ST Guide rec 19 and DML Art 10. The term 'proceeds' is defined to mean 'whatever is received in respect of encumbered assets' and includes proceeds of proceeds (see DML Art 2, subpara (bb)).

thus is more likely to offer better credit terms to the borrower. However, this does not mean that the secured creditor will ever obtain more than what it is owed.[41]

(ii) Asset-specific Rules

The DML contains a series of asset-specific provisions dealing with creation issues. First, in line with the ST Guide,[42] an agreement limiting the creation of a security interest in a receivable does not invalidate a security interest created despite that contractual limitation.[43] This essentially means that the agreement between the creditor and the debtor of the receivable does not affect third parties and thus the creditor of the receivable continues to bear the risk of insolvency of its contractual partner, the debtor of the receivable. It does not mean, however, that, for example, the debtor of the receivable is deprived of any claim for damages against the creditor of the receivable for breach of contract. A similar rule applies to security interests in rights regarding the payment of funds credited to a bank account.[44]

Second, also in line with the ST Guide, the DML provides that a security interest in a negotiable document extends to the goods covered by the document.[45] And third, also in line with the ST Guide, the DML provides that a security interest in assets containing an intellectual property asset (e.g., inventory of personal computers containing copyrighted software) does not automatically extend to the intellectual property asset and vice versa. This means that, in the absence of agreement, if the grantor defaults, the secured creditor can repossess and sell the inventory as is, but not use the copyrighted software in other personal computers.[46]

(iii) The Treatment of Creation Issues in the ST Guide and the DML Compared

There is no policy change in the treatment of creation issues in the DML as compared with their treatment in the ST Guide. However, there are several changes of a drafting nature. For example, because of its importance, the issue of the description of the encumbered assets in a security agreement is addressed in a separate provision.[47]

There is also a potential change to the treatment of independent personal or property rights securing or supporting the payment of the secured obligation (e.g., an independent guarantee or stand-by letter of credit). Unlike the ST Guide which

[41] ST Guide, Ch II, paras 72–89.
[42] ST Guide rec 24.
[43] DML Art 13(1).
[44] DML 15.
[45] ST Guide rec 28 and DML Art 16.
[46] IP Supplement rec 243 and DML Art 17.
[47] DML Art 9.

provides that the security interest automatically extends to such an independent personal or property right, under the DML (which in this respect follows CARIT) the grantor is obliged to transfer the benefit of that right to the secured creditor.[48]

E. Third-party Effectiveness of a Security Interest

(i) General Rules

Following the approach of the ST Guide, the DML distinguishes between effectiveness of a security interest as between the grantor and the secured creditor, on the one hand, and its effectiveness as against third parties (such as other secured creditors, buyers of the encumbered assets, judgment creditors and the mass of creditors or the insolvency administrator in the grantor's insolvency), on the other.

In addition, this approach makes it possible for the DML to apply to all devices serving security purposes, including form-free types of transaction, such as retention-of-title sales and financial leases. In this way, the DML establishes a comprehensive and rational regime that addresses the problems of uncertainty and inconsistency created by multiple regimes or a piecemeal approach to secured transactions. This approach does not harm the rights of parties to these title devices. Once a retention-of-title seller registers a notice, within a short period of time after delivery of the goods to the buyer, its priority goes back to the time of delivery of the goods. Such a notice may cover a multiple transactions between the same parties for a long period of time. In a cross-border situation, it ensures that the retention-of-title seller will not lose its rights or its priority. Whether the remedies of the seller or the secured creditor are more efficient depends on the specific situation (e.g., whether the residual value of the used goods is higher than the part of the purchase price paid by the buyer minus the value of the use of the goods).

In legal systems in which a security interest has by its nature as a property right effects *erga omnes*, the DML may be implemented in the following way: upon its creation, a security interest may be effective against all of the grantor's creditors as long as the priority of competing rights is determined on the basis of the time when registration or another third-party effectiveness step occurred.[49]

The general method for achieving the third-party effectiveness of a security interest is the registration of a notice of the security interest in a publicly accessible registry. However, to avoid undermining well-functioning practices, the DML recognises that the third-party effectiveness of a security interest may also be achieved: (a) in a tangible asset by a transfer of the possession of the asset to

[48] ST Guide rec 25(b), CARIT Art 10(2) and DML Art 14.
[49] ST Guide, Ch II, para 4 and Ch III, para 8.

the secured creditor;[50] and (b) another method (see below under E(ii)); and (c) automatically upon the creation of the security interest In certain types of asset, such as cash proceeds,[51] and consumer goods.[52]

(ii) Asset-specific Rules

While the general rules apply to all types of asset, the DML also includes a set of asset-specific third-party effectiveness rules that are intended to accommodate specific financing practices. Thus, the third-party effectiveness of a security interest may also be achieved: (a) in a right to payment of funds credited to a bank account by the transfer of the bank account to the secured creditor, the creation of a security interest in favour of the depositary institution or the conclusion of a control agreement;[53] (b) in a negotiable instrument or a negotiable document by transfer of possession of the instrument or the document to the secured creditor;[54] and (c) in a non-intermediated security by registration in the books of the issuer or conclusion of a control agreement.[55]

(iii) The Treatment of Third-party Effectiveness Issues in the ST Guide and the DML Compared

Generally, the DML follows the policy of the ST Guide with respect to third-party effectiveness. Most of the differences are of a drafting nature and cannot be avoided as the DML is a legislative text, and not a recommendation to the legislator. The main difference between the DML and the ST Guide relates to the provision dealing with the third-party effectiveness of a security interest in non-intermediated securities. The general methods of third-party effectiveness (notice registration and transfer of possession) apply also to non-intermediated securities. Two asset-specific methods are added with respect to non-intermediated securities, registration in the books of the issuer and a control agreement (among the issuer, the secured creditor and the grantor according to which the issuer agrees to follow instructions from the secured creditor without further consent from the grantor).[56] The DML also includes a new provision according to which acquisition security interests in consumer goods are effectively automatic upon its creation.[57] This rule is intended to exempt from registration consumer transactions (possibly below a certain value).

[50] ST Guide rec 37 and DML Art 16, subpara (b). No reference is made to specialized registration though ST Guide rec 38 and DML Art 16, subpara (a).
[51] ST Guide rec 39 and DML Art 19, para 1.
[52] DML Art 23.
[53] ST Guide rec 49 and DML Art 24.
[54] ST Guide recs 37 and 51–53 and DML Arts 16, subpara (b), and 25.
[55] DML Art 26.
[56] DML Art 2, subpara (g)(i) and Art 26.
[57] DML Art 23.

F. The Registry System

(i) The DML and the Registry Act

The DML provides for the establishment of a publicly accessible security interests registry (the 'Registry').[58] The details of the registry system are set out in a set of rules entitled 'Draft Model Registry-related Provisions'. These rules are based on the recommendations of the ST Guide and the Registry Guide. They are included in a distinct part of chapter IV of the DML as they may be implemented in the secured transactions law, another statute or another type of legal instrument such as a decree or regulation, or partly in the former and partly in the latter.

In line with the ST Guide, the DML avoids imposing unnecessary formalities on the creation of a security interest. Thus, registration is not necessary for the creation of a security interest.[59] And, as the legal consequence of registration is to make a security interest effective against third parties (provided that there is a valid security agreement), there is no need to register the security agreement but only a notice thereof. As the commentary to the ST Guide points out, 'registries based on a notice-registration concept exist in an increasing number of States and have also attracted considerable international support'.[60] It is worth noting that notice-based registration has been so successful that it has been adopted even in the context of specialised (including asset-based) registration systems, such as the registration systems for the types of high-value mobile equipment covered by the Cape Town Convention on International Interests in Mobile Equipment and its Protocols,[61] and patent and trademark registries.[62] For the same reason, notice registration is even advocated for immovable property registries.[63]

In such a notice-based registration system, quick and easy registration is ensured by requiring registration of a notice that contains a limited yet sufficient amount of data, that is, the identifier and address of the grantor and the secured creditor or its representative, a description of the encumbered assets and, if permitted by the law, a selection of the period of effectiveness of the registration and, if a state chooses the option offered, the maximum amount for which the security interest

[58] DML Art 27.

[59] ST Guide rec 34 and DML Art 16.

[60] ST Guide, Ch IV, para 14.

[61] These registries are asset-based rather than debtor-based registries. Briefly, asset-based registration has the disadvantage that it is necessary to have a unique identification and cannot accommodate a generic description or after-acquired property. But it has the advantage that it shows all registrable interests, not merely those created by the debtor. See Art 31 of the Convention and s 5 of the Aircraft Registry Regulations and Official Commentary (Revised Edition) by R Goode, Unidroit, Rome, 2008, p 122. The Aircraft Registry is a particularly successful example of such a registry (see www.internationalregistry.aero/irWeb/Controller.jpf).

[62] IP Supplement, paras 132–34.

[63] J Simpson and F Dahan, Mortgages in Transition Economies, Secured Transactions Reform and Access to Credit (EBRD, 2008) 195.

may be enforced.[64] First, the information in a notice is sufficient for a potential third-party financier to determine whether some assets of the grantor may be encumbered by a security interest in the sense that it provides a warning. Second, notice registration does more than that, and allows a potential third-party financier to request more information from the grantor and, with the grantor's consent, from secured creditors on the registry record. Third and most importantly, notice registration provides an objective method for determining priority. Fourth, notice registration preserves the confidentiality of the details of the relevant transaction.

Document registration is also discussed in the commentary on the ST Guide, but is not recommended. The reason is that a notice registration system is inherently more efficient. It simplifies the registration and searching process, minimises the administrative burden, delays and costs, reduces the risk of error and liability is sufficient in view of the legal consequences of registration, that is, third Party effectiveness and preserves the confidentiality of the relevant transaction.[65]

With regard to the amount of information required in a notice, the DML balances the rights and interests of searchers and secured creditors.[66] In an effort to ensure the confidentiality of the transaction and avoid use of the registry by lenders to obtain information about the clients of competitors, the DML provides that a search be made possible only by the identifier (e.g., name or any identification number) of the grantor, and not by the identifier of the secured creditor.[67] In a further effort to ensure confidentiality, the DML provides that the secured creditor may choose not to identify itself on the notice but give the identifier and address of a representative.[68] The possibility to identify a representative also facilitates secured transactions that involve multiple lenders that appoint one of them to be their representative for the purpose of registration and possibly other purposes.

Same as in a security agreement,[69] encumbered assets must be described in a manner that reasonably allows their identification.[70] Whether the notice should describe the encumbered assets by stating their serial numbers, if any, is left to each enacting state. For example, description of the encumbered assets by serial number should be possible in the case of high-value mobile equipment, such as ships or aircraft, or intellectual property rights, such as patents or trademarks,

[64] ST Guide rec 57 and Registry Act Art 7.

[65] ST Guide, Ch IV, paras 10–14.

[66] For a comparison of the registry systems under UCC §9, the Canadian PPSAs, the OAS Model Law on Secured Transactions and the OAS Registry Regulations, on the one hand, and the ST Guide, on the other, see M Dubovec, 'UCC Article 9 Registration System for Latin America' (2011) 28(1) *Arizona Journal of International & Comparative Law* 117.

[67] ST Guide rec 54, subpara (h) and recs 58–60 and Registry Act Art 21. The ST Guide explains that this approach is intended to prevent lenders from using the registry in order to identify the clients of their competitors. The ST Guide also explains that this approach does not prevent a state from designing a registry so as to permit search by secured creditor identifier for internal purposes of the registry, such as, for example, for making a global amendment of notices at the request of the secured creditor to whom the notices relate (*see* ST Guide, Ch IV, paras 29 and 30).

[68] ST Guide rec 57, subpara (a), and Registry Act Art 7, subpara (b).

[69] DML Art 9.

[70] ST Guide rec 63 and Draft Model Registry-related Provisions Art 11, para 1.

but not in the case of inventory. With respect to indexing and searching, the DML provides that reference should be made mainly to the grantor identifier (or the registration number assigned to an initial notice and associated with any related notice).[71] The reason is that grantor indexing and searching greatly simplifies the registration process to the extent that a single registration can cover a changing pool of assets and future assets.

(ii) The Treatment of Registration Issues in the ST Guide and the Registry Act Compared

Generally, the Draft Model Registry-related Provisions follow the policy of the ST Guide and the Registry Guide. Most of the differences are of a drafting nature. However, there are some new rules.

First, the Draft Model Registry-related Provisions address the impact of a transfer of an encumbered asset on the effectiveness of a registration, that is, whether in the case of a transfer of an encumbered asset a registration of a new notice is necessary for the security interest to continue being effective against third parties.[72] This issue had been discussed in the commentary but not addressed in the recommendations of the ST Guide.[73] Three options are offered: one requiring registration of a new notice; another requiring registration of a new notice within a certain period after the secured creditor acquires knowledge of the transfer; and a third one that does not require registration of a new notice (which is the approach followed where the encumbered asset transferred is intellectual property).[74]

Second, the Draft Model Registry-related Provisions address the question whether the secured creditor's authorisation is required for the registration of an amendment or cancellation notice.[75] This question had been discussed in the commentary of the Registry Guide but not addressed in a recommendation as it is a question for the law (not the Registry regulations).[76] Four different options are offered for discussion, requiring the secured creditor's authorisation or not with different conditions.

Third, the Draft Model Registry-related Provisions address two more related issues—correction of errors and limitation of liability of the Registry. Those issues too had been discussed in the Registry Guide but not addressed in a recommendation.[77] With respect to correction of errors, options are offered, dealing with the following questions: (a) whether the Registry should be able to correct an error itself or inform the registrant to enable the registrant to correct the error; and (b) the time of effectiveness of a notice correcting an error.[78] Also with respect to

[71] Draft Model Registry-related Provisions Art 22. The ST Guide discusses in the commentary but does not recommend indexing and searching by serial number (see Ch IV, paras 31–36).

[72] Draft Model Registry-related Provisions Art 26.

[73] ST Guide, Ch IV, paras 78–80. Recommendation 62 simply states that the matter should be addressed!

[74] IP Supplement, rec 244.

[75] Draft Model Registry-related Provisions Art 21.

[76] Registry Guide, paras 249–259.

[77] Registry Guide, paras 135–144.

[78] Draft Model Registry-related Provisions Art 31.

the limitation of liability of the Registry, options are offered ranging from limitation of the basis or the amount of the liability to excluding liability altogether.[79]

Finally, while there is no policy change with regard to the registry fees, the Draft Model Registry-related Provisions emphasises the two options foreseen in the ST Guide and the Registry Guide.[80] The first option foresees fees at a cost-recovery level, to be specified by the enacting state. It is based on the assumption that one of the key objectives of a modern secured transactions regime, that is, transparency with respect to secured transactions, cannot be achieved if the Registry is used as an opportunity to generate revenue. The second option foresee no fees and is based on the assumption that the Registry is a key component of a modern secured transactions regime, which would enhance the availability of credit at a lower cost, and thus should be treated as a public service and not a benefit to the parties to secured transactions.[81]

G. Priority of a Security Interest

(i) General Rules

The DML includes a comprehensive set of rules dealing with priority conflicts between a secured creditor and every possible competing claimant. In a conflict between two security interests in the same asset, the one that was made effective against third parties (by registration or otherwise) earlier has priority.[82]

A transferee of an encumbered asset takes the asset subject to the security interest, with the exception of situations that have to do with the good faith acquisition of an encumbered asset or its acquisition in the transferor's normal course of business.[83] Subject to insolvency rules, in principle a security interest preserves its third-party effectiveness and priority.[84]

In line with the approach taken in the ST Guide,[85] the DML takes no position as to whether there should be any statutory preferential claims. It simply includes an article for enacting states to list their preferential claims.[86] The right of an unsecured creditor that has obtained a judgment and taken the steps necessary to have it enforced before a security interest became effective against third parties has priority over that security interest.[87]

[79] Draft Model Registry-related Provisions Art 32.
[80] ST Guide rec 54, subpara (i), and Ch IV, para 37; Registry Guide rec 36 and paras 274–280.
[81] Draft Model Registry-related Provisions Art 33.
[82] DML Art 28.
[83] DML Art 32.
[84] DML Art 33.
[85] ST Guide, Ch V, paras 90–93.
[86] DML Art 34.
[87] DML Art 35.

Generally, an acquisition security interest with respect to which a notice had been registered within a short period of time after delivery of the goods has priority as of the time of delivery of the goods, not the time of registration.[88] Priority among competing acquisition security interests is determined on the basis of the general rules, with the exception that an acquisition security interest of a seller or lessor has priority over a competing acquisition security interest of a person other than a seller or lessor.[89] Alternatives are provided with respect to whether the priority of an acquisition security interest (in goods or intellectual property) extends to its proceeds.[90]

(ii) Asset-specific Rules

The DML includes detailed priority rules with respect to security interests in certain types of asset. First, to avoid interfering with the negotiability of negotiable instruments, the DML provides that a security interest in a negotiable instrument made effective against third parties by possession of the instrument has priority over a security interest in the same instrument made effective against third parties by registration.[91]

Second, with respect to rights to payment of funds credited to a bank account, the DML sets out the priority of a security interest depending on the method by which it was made effective against third parties. The order is as follows: the transferee of the account, the depositary institution, a secured creditor with a control agreement, in the case of several control agreements, the secured creditor with the earlier control agreement, and the secured creditor that registered a notice.[92]

Third, again to avoid undermining the negotiability of negotiable documents, a security interest in tangible assets covered by a negotiable document made effective against third parties by possession of the document has priority over a competing security interest made effective against third parties by registration or possession of the assets covered by the document.[93]

(iii) The Treatment of Priority Issues in the ST Guide and the DML Compared

Other than changes of a drafting nature, a few new provisions have been included in the DML. The first is a proposed rule dealing with priority conflicts between security interests granted by different persons (i.e. the initial grantor and a transferee of an encumbered asset). In the case of such a priority conflict, priority is

[88] DML Art 36.
[89] DML Art 37.
[90] DML Art 39.
[91] DML Art 44, para 1.
[92] DML Art 45.
[93] DML Art 47.

determined according to the time when third-party effectiveness was achieved, provided that the initial secured creditor registers an amendment notice adding the name of the transferee within a short period of time after the transfer or after the secured creditor acquires knowledge of the transfer.[94]

The second is a rule dealing with priority conflicts between security interests in non-intermediated securities. According to that rule, a security interest in certificated securities made effective against third parties by possession of the certificate has priority over a security interest made effective against third parties by registration of a notice in the security interests registry. With respect to uncertificated securities, there is a cascade of rules according to which a security interest made effective against third parties by registration in the books of the issuer has priority over a security interest made effective against third parties any other method and a security interest made effective against third parties by a control agreement has priority over a security interest made effective against third parties by any other method except registration in the books of the issuer. The rule also provides that it does not affect the rights of holders of non-intermediated securities under the relevant securities law to be specified by each enacting state.[95]

The priority rule with respect to security interests in rights to payment of funds credited to a bank account is not new. However, it is interesting to briefly discuss it to provide some comparison with the priority rule with respect to security interests in non-intermediated securities and to explain its usefulness for transactions such as non-notification factoring and undisclosed invoice discounting. This provision also contains a cascade of rules, according to which the priority order from high to low is as follows: a security interest made effective against third parties by the secured creditor becoming the account holder, a security interest of the depositary institution, a security interest made effective against third parties by the conclusion of a control agreement, a security interest made effective against third parties by the registration of a notice in the security interest registry. The depositary institution's rights of set-off have priority over any security interest, except one made effective against third parties by the secured creditor becoming the account holder. Finally, in the case of a transfer of funds from an encumbered bank that is initiated or authorised by the grantor, the transferee acquires its right free of the security interest, unless it had knowledge that the transfer violates the rights of the secured creditor under the security agreement.[96]

Under this rule, in the case of non-notification factoring or undisclosed invoice discounting, the factor or invoice discounter need not register a notice in the security interests registry. To have priority over all competing claimants, the factor will need to become the holder of its client's account to which the relevant receivables are being paid. To have priority against all except the depositary institution and a secured creditor that has become the account holder, the factor will need to take a control agreement. To have priority over the depositary institution (including for

[94] DML Art 28, para 2 and Draft Model Registry-related Provisions Art 26, para 1, options A and B.

[95] DML Art 49.

[96] DML Art 45.

its set-off rights), the factor will need to obtain a subordination agreement.[97] Of course, all these rules are sufficient to protect a factor only if the receivables are paid into a bank account. If a third-party creditor interferes and obtains payment of a receivable, priority of the security interest of that creditor and the factor will have to be determined on the basis of the general priority rules governing receivables (that is, according to the order of registration).

H. Enforcement of a Security Interest

(i) General Rules

Following the ST Guide, the DML recognises that an enforcement regime that results in delays or excessive costs is likely to affect the availability and the cost of credit.[98] At the same time, the DML recognises that the judicial enforcement regime does not lend itself to harmonisation at the international level. Thus, the DML leaves enforcement before a court or other authority (eg a chamber of commerce) largely to other law to be specified by each enacting State, making one recommendation, that is, that the judicial enforcement regime should also foresee expedited enforcement proceedings. The DML also allows enforcement out of court or another authority (e.g. by way of self-help remedies), while at the same time it introduces safeguards for the grantor and other parties with interests in encumbered assets.

The first such safeguard is that the enforcing secured creditor must act in good faith and in a commercially reasonable manner (eg, avoid selling the encumbered assets outside the relevant market with the result that a price below their actual market price is obstained).[99] To protect the grantor from undue pressure on the part of the secured creditor, the DML provides that the grantor may not waive the general standard of conduct.[100] Other rights existing under the enforcement provisions of the DML may be waived, but only after default, not at the time of the negotiation of the security agreement, to avoid putting the grantor in the position of having to give up its rights to obtain a concession from the secured creditor.[101]

The second safeguard is that the enforcing secured creditor cannot obtain possession of the encumbered assets out of court, unless: (a) the grantor has consented in the security agreement to the secured creditor obtaining possession of the encumbered assets out of court; (b) the secured creditor has given the grantor

97 DML Art 41.
98 ST Guide, Ch VIII, para 6.
99 DML Art 4.
100 DML Art 3.
101 DML Art 70, para. 3.

and any person in possession of the encumbered assets notice of default and extra-judicial repossession; and (c) at the time of repossession, the grantor and any person in possession of the encumbered asset does not object.[102]

The third safeguard is an elaborate notice system according to which notice of the secured creditor's intention to dispose of the encumbered assets out of court must be given well in advance to the grantor, the debtor (if it is a person other than the grantor), a secured creditor on the registry record, a creditor that notifies the enforcing secured creditor and any other secured creditor in possession of the encumbered assets.[103] Any of those persons may pay the secured obligation in full and obtain a release of the encumbered assets.[104] And a secured creditor with a security interest that has priority over the interest of the enforcing creditor may take over enforcement and decide to continue the same method of enforcement or initiate a new method of enforcement.[105] Similar safeguards for the grantor and other parties with interests in the encumbered assets are foreseen in the case of a proposal by the secured creditor to acquire the encumbered assets in satisfaction of the secured obligation.[106]

The fourth set of safeguards relates to the distribution of proceeds from the disposition of encumbered assets out of court. The DML provides that the enforcing secured creditor must apply the net proceeds (after deducting the reasonable costs of enforcement) to the secured obligation; if there is a shortfall, the grantor remains liable, but the secured creditor then has the position of an unsecured creditor; and any surplus remaining must be turned over to the grantor or to other creditors announced during the enforcement proceedings, or, in case of doubt, be deposited with a competent judicial or other authority.[107]

To ensure finality of the rights acquired pursuant to an out-of-court disposition, the DML recommends that the transferee acquire the encumbered assets free of any security interests that are subordinate to the security interest of the enforcing secured creditor, but subject to any security interests with priority over the security interest of the enforcing secured creditor.[108]

(ii) Asset-specific Rules

The DML contains only one asset-specific rule, which deals with the right of the secured creditor to collect payment under a receivable, negotiable instrument, right to payment of funds credited to a bank account or non-intermediated security.[109]

102 DML Art. 75, para. 3.
103 DML Art. 76, para. 4.
104 DML Art 73.
105 DML Art. 74.
106 DML Art. 78.
107 DML Art. 77.
108 DML Art. 79, para. 3.
109 DML Art. 80.

(iii) The Treatment of Enforcement Issues in the ST Guide and the DML Compared

The addition of collection of payment under a non-intermediated security constitutes the main difference between the ST Guide and the DML enforcement provisions. Collection may take place not only after default, but also before default provided that the grantor has consented. In addition, collection of funds from a bank account may take place out of court only if the security interest has been made effective against third parties by the secured creditor becoming the account holder or by a control agreement, that is, with the consent of the depositary bank.

I. Law Applicable to a Security Interest in Movable Property

(i) General Rules

The draft Model Law contains a complete set of conflict-of-laws rules, which are intended to enhance certainty as to the law applicable to security interests in movable property and facilitate the movement and the financing of movable property across national borders with a regime that would allow the cross-border recognition of national security interests.

The law applicable to the creation, third-party effectiveness and priority of a security interest in a tangible asset is the law of the state in which the asset is located (except if the asset is covered by a negotiable document, where the applicable law is the law of the location of the document). There are a few exceptions to the *lex situs*. The law applicable to a security interest in mobile goods that typically cross national borders is the law of the state in which the grantor is located. The law applicable to goods, rights in which are subject to registration in a title registry (such as ships or aircraft), is the law of the state under whose authority the registry is maintained. Finally, the law applicable to a security interest in goods in transit or export goods is the law of the state of destination, provided that the goods reach their destination within a short period of time.[110] Following generally applicable rules, enforcement of a security interest in a tangible asset is referred to the law of the state in which enforcement takes place.[111]

With the exception of security interests in receivables related to immovable property, bank accounts, assets subject to registration, intellectual property and non-intermediated securities that are subject to special rules, the law applicable

[110] DML Art 79. The conflict-of-laws provisions of the DML are contained in document A/CN.9/853 (see www.uncitral.org/uncitral/en/commission/sessions/48th.html).

[111] DML Art 82.

to security interests in intangible assets is the law of the grantor's location.[112] Location of the grantor is defined by reference to its place of business and, in the case of places of business in more than one state, by reference to the place where the grantor has its central administration.[113] The rationale of this rule is that it is the rule that: (a) is most likely to lead to the application of the law of one state; (b) can reasonably be determined in most cases; and (c) is the law of the state in which the main insolvency proceeding with respect to the grantor will most likely be commenced. The relevant time for determining location of the asset or the grantor is, with respect to creation issues, the location at the time of the putative creation of a security interest, and, with respect to third-party effectiveness and priority issues, the location at the time the issue arises.

(ii) Asset-specific Rules

Following the approach of the ST Guide, the DML contains a number of asset-specific conflict-of-laws rules (including rules dealing with the law applicable to security interests in bank accounts and intellectual property).[114]

(iii) The Treatment of Conflict-of-laws Issues in the ST Guide and the DML Compared

The main difference with the ST Guide is the new rule on the law applicable to security interests in non-intermediated securities. This rule offers three options for discussion. Under the first option, the law applicable to security interests in certificated securities is the law of the state in which the certificate is located; and the law applicable to security interests in uncertificated securities is the law of the state under which the issuer is constituted (to which also matters relating to the effectiveness of a security interest as against the issuer are referred, both with respect to certificated and uncertificated securities). Under the second option, the law applicable to all issues with respect to all types of non-intermediated securities is the law of the issuer's location. Under the third option, the law applicable to all issues with respect to equity securities (ie shares) is the law of the issuer's location and the law applicable to all issues with respect to debt securities (ie bonds) is the law governing the securities.

Each option has advantages and disadvantages. The first option appropriately distinguishes between certificated and uncertificated securities, but the law of the issuer's location may not be appropriate for debt securities. The second option

[112] DML Art 80.
[113] DML Art 84.
[114] DML Arts 90 and 92.

refers all issues to the law of the issuer's location, but again that law may not be appropriate for debt securities. The third option distinguishes between debt and equity securities, but the distinction may not always be clear (as in the case of convertible securities) and, in any case, while it focuses on the contractual nature of debt securities that are analogues to receivables in a generic sense, it provides for the application of a law other than the law applicable to security interests in receivables.

J. Conclusions

The ST Guide, including the IP Supplement, and the Registry Guide, have become the main reference tools for the modernisation and harmonisation of secured transactions law.[115] However, the Guide is a long and complex text and thus not always easy to implement. The DML is intended to assist states in this regard. This chapter briefly introduced the DML and its main differences from the ST Guide, the IP Supplement and the Registry Guide. These differences may be summarised as follows: (a) several recommendations have been revised to be reflected in legislative language; (b) a number of recommendations that do not belong in a legislative text have been left out or referred to the Guide to Enactment of the DML; (c) no provisions were included in the DML on security interests in stand-by letters of credit and attachments to movable and movable property; (d) a number of provisions have been added to the DML to address security interests in non-intermediated securities; and (d) the recommendations of the ST Guide and the Registry Guide have been reflected in a separate set of model registry rules, which may be implemented in the secured transactions law, a separate act, or partly in the former and partly in the latter.

[115] Bazinas (n 9).

Part V

Conclusions and Recommendations

24

Conclusions and Recommendations

LOUISE GULLIFER

An ideal secured transactions law is one that is clear, certain and easily accessible. A creditor should be able to obtain a security interest over any asset, including future assets, as cheaply as possible. There should be transparency, to enable others to know about the existence of a security interest, and the publicity process should also enable a creditor to know with certainty that his interest, once perfected, will take priority over any interest he does not know about. It should also be possible to enforce a security interest effectively whether or not the borrower is insolvent. Lastly, although it should be possible for creditors to contract out of most default rules in relation to priority and enforcement, that default position should be the one most likely to be required in general, so as to minimise transaction costs.

To obtain and maintain such an ideal law, the existing law needs to be constantly under review, and the possibility of change for the better should be ever present.[1] The jurisdictions considered in this volume have been engaged in this process, and many have introduced reforms to bring their law more in line with this ideal. The purpose of this chapter is to draw out the implications from the foregoing chapters for reform of secured transaction law generally, and for reform of English law in particular. Discussion of reform initiatives breaks down into three questions: why was reform needed? how was reform effected? and what was the substance of the reform? This chapter will consider each of these in turn.

A. The Drivers for Reform

The drivers for reform are more varied than might be imagined. This section seeks to disentangle the common reasons which appear from the discussion in this volume. Obviously, in any particular jurisdiction, there will be a combination of these reasons, and there may also be other, more localised, imperatives for reform.

[1] The discussion in chapter 3 (United States) demonstrates how UCC Article 9 is kept under constant review, as does Ch 4 B and Ch 5, in relation to Canada. A statutory review was built into the Australian reforms, see Australia (Ch 7 B).

(i) The State of the Unreformed Law

Many reasons for reform, of course, relate to the state of the unreformed law. Particular problems with the law tend to lead to piecemeal reform (however unsatisfactory); the imperatives that lead to wholesale reform are usually more generic. They arise either from the structural state of the law, which is, usually, complex, fragmented and inaccessible, and/or from the fact that the law does not function well in modern markets.

(a) *Complexity and Fragmentation*

Secured transactions law tends to be very path dependent; it is also, however, often the focus of lobbying by interest groups, and the close connection between the ability to take security and economic growth[2] means that if a change in the law is required to enable a particular industry to thrive, that change is often made, without too much consideration of whether it fits with the rest of the law. Thus unreformed secured transactions law tends to be very fragmented, with different types of interest (each with their own set of rules) available for different assets and different transactions,[3] and sometimes even different parties.[4] It is common for there to be different security interests for land and for personal property,[5] and for tangibles and intangibles,[6] while local differences have led to much more limited interests, such as those over specific types of foodstuff important in particular jurisdictions.[7] Another demarcation line is often between possessory and non-possessory interests,[8] while another is between those involving a transfer of ownership and those merely involving a lesser proprietary interest.[9] A further common distinction is different treatment for security interests created by companies and those created by non- corporate debtors (which can be further divided

[2] See Ch 1.

[3] See, for example, the description of the plethora of security interests that existed in the pre-Article 9 US law (Ch 3 A).

[4] See, for example, the position in Italy, where there is a charge which can only be granted to a bank (Ch 16 B(ii)): a similar charge existed in Belgium before the 2013 reforms, see Belgium (Ch 18 B).

[5] This distinction remains in all the jurisdictions considered, although in many of the reformed systems it is possible to have a single security interest over land and personal property (see, for example, New Zealand (Ch 6 E(ii)), Lithuania (Ch 19 C)).

[6] In relation to security interests, see, for example, Germany (Ch 15 B(i) and B(ii)), Italy (Ch 16 B(i)) and in relation to functional equivalents see, for example, Scotland (Ch 11 B(iii)).

[7] Italy (Ch 16 B(i) n 15), France (Ch 17 B (iii)(a)).

[8] Most, if not all, systems which do not have a unitary concept of security make this distinction. For example, English law has the pledge and lien, which are possessory, and the mortgage and charge, which are non-possessory; Ireland has a similar structure (see Ch 10 A). Scotland also has this distinction, see Ch 11 B(ii), as do the unreformed European jurisdictions (see Spain (Ch 20 C), Italy (Ch 16 B(i)), Germany (Ch 15 B(i)).

[9] This distinction exists in English and Irish law, where the mortgage involves a transfer of ownership and a charge does not, and also existed in the US, Canada, Australia and New Zealand before the law was reformed. Security transfers also exist, for example, Scotland (Ch 11 B(iii)(b)), France, (Ch 17 C(iii)(a)(4)), Germany (Ch 16 B(ii)).

into businesses and consumers).[10] Still further, a federal jurisdiction may have different secured transactions laws in each province or state.[11]

Fragmentation leads to complexity, which in its turn means that the law is hard to understand and access, especially for those who cannot afford extensive legal advice, and also for business partners from other jurisdictions. Moreover, if there are a number of different security interests, each with their own characteristics, demarcation lines have to be drawn and have to be interpreted by courts and parties. As parties attempt to extend or manipulate these lines, courts can either respond by recharacterising interests which do not fully correspond to the labels put on them, or the courts can permit a wide freedom of contract leading to further complexity and uncertainty. All of these factors can increase the cost and availability of credit.

Fragmentation and complexity have clearly been drivers for reform in many of the jurisdictions discussed in this volume,[12] and are a cause for concern and call for reform in others.[13] The obvious response is to move to a system where there is just one single security interest to which the same rules apply, as in the Article 9/PPSA type systems.[14] However, this has been a step too far for some jurisdictions, such as Belgium and Lithuania: each have kept two types of 'true' security interest,[15] as well as delineating retention of title devices.[16] The options available for a reforming jurisdiction are further discussed below.[17]

(b) Lack of Functionality

In some jurisdictions, there are, or have been, deep-seated problems with the substance of the law, which have acted as barriers to finance. In civil law jurisdictions, the lack of an effective non-possessory security interest has been, and in some cases still is, a source of considerable difficulties,[18] and has led to a variety of

[10] This type of distinction is particularly evident in common law jurisdictions: it was the case before reform in the US, Canada, Australia and New Zealand, and is still the case in English, Irish and Scottish law (see English law (Ch 12 D(i)), Ireland (Ch 10 A), Scotland (Ch 11 D): the reform proposals are for a fixed charge which can be granted by any person, legal or natural).

[11] This factor was a major driver in the Australian reforms, see Ch 7 A. It was also a driver behind the US and Canadian reforms (see US Ch 3 A, Canada Ch 4 B (iii)): secured transactions law is still governed by state or provincial law in those jurisdictions, but there is much more commonality than there was before the law was reformed. (See Ch 3 generally. For discussion of the issues raised by harmonisation and unification, see Ch 4 B (iv) and (v)).

[12] See, for example, US (Ch 3 A and B), Canada (Ch 4 B (i)), New Zealand (Ch 6 A), Australia (Ch 7 A), Belgium (Ch 18 A).

[13] See, for example, English law (Ch 12), France (Ch 17 B (iii)(a)), Spain (Ch 20 A), Italy (Ch 16 B).

[14] For a recent example, see the Jersey law (Ch 9 B(ii)), and see also the approach of the UNCITRAL Legislative Guide and Model Law (Ch 23 C(i)). For discussion of the history of the single security interest concept, see US Ch 3 B (iv) and Canada Ch 4 A).

[15] In Belgium, the pledge (*droit de gage*) and the legal lien (*droit de rétention*) (Ch 18 F) and in Lithuania the hypothec (*hipoteka*) and the charge (*ikeitimas*) (Ch 19 D)

[16] ibid.

[17] Section C(i)(a).

[18] Scotland (Ch 11 C), France (Ch 17 B(i)), Belgium (Ch 18 B), Spain (Ch 20 A), Italy (Ch 16 B (i)).

workarounds, which lead to complexity.[19] Another feature of civil law which has caused difficulties is the requirement that the subject matter of a security interest be identified specifically, which made taking security over future property either difficult or impossible.[20]

Once a jurisdiction permits non-possessory security to be taken, there is a need for registration to provide publicity, and the lack of an effective registration system is another major problem which has led to wholesale reform (or to calls for reform). In some jurisdictions there is no register at all,[21] and the reforms have involved creating a registry from scratch.[22] In others, the registration system was fragmented or incomplete: the effect of reform has been streamlining and modernisation of the system.[23]

Unless enforcement of security interests is reliable and effective, lenders will not be willing to reduce the cost of credit just because the loan is secured. In particular, the lack of ability to enforce without court proceedings, which can be lengthy, uncertain and expensive, has been a driver towards reform.[24] Effective enforcement, however, is dependent on insolvency law, and the interrelation between a reformed law and the national insolvency system is critical.[25]

(ii) International Concerns

As well as shortcomings in a jurisdiction's own law, another driver for reform is the move towards greater internationalisation. There are at least two aspects to this: the effect of an increase in cross-border transactions and the pressure imposed by reform in other jurisdictions and at a transnational level.

(a) Cross-border Transactions

One obvious problem arising from cross-border transactions is if a security interest which is valid under the domestic law of a jurisdiction is not recognised

19 France (Ch 17 B(iii)), Spain (Ch 20 C(i)), Italy (Ch 16 B(i)).

20 See, for example, the position in Spain under the 1954 Act, where the goods under a non-possessory pledge including future property have to be stored and kept in a particular identified place (Ch 20 C(i)).

21 For example, Germany: see Ch 15 D(ii) for discussion of why this is the case and Ch 15 E for discussion of why calls for reform may soon occur in Germany.

22 See, for example, Jersey (Ch 9, Part 1 K), Malawi (Ch 8 B(iii) and C).

23 Particular examples are Belgium (Ch 18 E and L) and Lithuania (Ch 19 D). See also Australia (Ch 7 A).

24 See, for example, Jersey (Ch 9, Part 1 N) and Lithuania (Ch 19 D). The civil law prohibition on the *pacte commissoire* (extrajudicial acquisition) is a particular example of the difficulties of enforcement mentioned in the text: this prohibition has been abolished in France (Ch 18 C(ii)(a)(2)) (and, recently, even in relation to the special pledge on inventory (Ch 18 C(iii)(a)(1)). See also the 2014 Italian reform proposal discussed in Ch 16 C(ii)). The approach of the UNCITRAL Model Law recognises the potential problems with judicial enforcement, and provides for out of court enforcement, while including safeguards for the grantor and others with an interest in the encumbered assets, see Ch 23 H).

25 See Sections B(vi) and C(vi) below.

by the law of another jurisdiction to which the asset which is the subject of the security interest may be moved. This was a major driver in relation to the Cape Town Convention on International Interests in Mobile Equipment, which itself has been a factor in calls for reform in various jurisdictions.[26] A similar argument can be made about the EU Financial Collateral Directive,[27] and other EU harmonisation initiatives.[28] It is also one reason why there are likely to be calls for reform of the German law of secured transactions in the near future.[29]

Cross-border transactions work best if the law in each jurisdiction is similar, and there is therefore often a desire for at least some harmonisation between the law of neighbouring states. Reform in a neighbouring jurisdiction can be a driver to reform, as can be seen in Australia and Belgium.[30]

(b) International and Transnational Moves to Reform

While, in the end, reform must be driven by local champions,[31] international efforts can both promote reform and influence its content. The fact that jurisdictions around the world are reforming and modernising their law is an incentive to states to do the same, especially as much available finance is now global and lenders will lend where they feel most certain that they will have good credit protection. Despite many flaws, the Doing Business rankings produced by the World Bank are influential, and one of the chief components of the ranking of 'Getting Credit' is the legal strength of an economy's secured transactions regime.[32] There is increasing international agreement as to, at least, the minimum requirements of a modern secured transactions law, based in large part on the principles refined by UNCITRAL in its Legislative Guide.[33]

International harmonisation efforts are also influential as to the method and content of reform. For many jurisdictions, the actual process of drawing up a reformed law, educating the relevant participants, including the judiciary, the lawyers and the business community, and setting up structures such as a registry, is seen as too expensive and difficult. Thus, reform is not attempted

[26] Spain, for example, has acceded to the Cape Town Convention and has ratified the Aircraft Protocol, and this has reopened the domestic debate on secured transaction law reform, see Ch 20 A and E.

[27] See, for example, Spain (Ch 20 C(iii)), Italy (Ch 16 B(ii)).

[28] See, for example, the EU Initiative on Insolvency, 2nd March 2016 (public consultation launched on 24th March 2016 and impact assessment (2nd March 2016) available at http://ec.europa.eu/smart-regulation/roadmaps/docs/2016_just_025_insolvency_en.pdf.

[29] See Germany Ch 15 E(i).

[30] The New Zealand reforms were an important driver towards reform in Australia, see Ch 7 B, and the French reforms were an encouragement to Belgium to reform its law, see Ch 18 D. The argument can work both ways. Lack of reform of English law has been a reason for the shape of the proposed Scottish reforms, which are relatively modest, see Ch 11 D(iii).

[31] This point is made in relation to the EBRD reform project (see Ch 21 B(iv)). For an example of a local champion, see the work of David Allen in Australia, mentioned in Ch 7 B.

[32] See www.doingbusiness.org/methodology/getting-credit. The methodology is particularly favourable to a PPSA-type system, as it gives high marks for a unitary, functional regime with a notice-based register, as well as for effective coverage and enforcement. See Ch 21 D.

[33] See discussion in Ch 23 C(i).

despite the benefits it would bring. The work of transnational organisations such as the EBRD,[34] the World Bank[35] and UNCITRAL[36] in overcoming these negative factors is therefore actually a major driver towards reform.[37] The influence of the Cape Town Convention has already been mentioned.

(iii) General Reasons

In this section more general reasons for reform, which have affected many areas of law, are discussed.

(a) Advances in Information Technology

Much secured transaction reform relates to setting up or improving a registration system, and the ever-increasing advances in information technology both make possible highly sophisticated systems and enable effective systems to be set up cheaply and easily. Modernisation of a registration system, for example, to enable electronic filing and sophisticated searching, is therefore an imperative leading to secured transaction law reform. A reformed system can include registration and searching based on both debtor and, in appropriate cases, asset,[38] and, in some cases, registers can be made to communicate with each other. It is perfectly possible to have a system which runs on virtually no human input provided that the particulars registered are not checked by anyone, and any risk of mistake falls on the person registering.[39] These features make the system cheap and simple to set up and run: this reduction in costs is an added factor leading towards reform.

(b) The Desire for Economic Growth

Economic growth is an imperative for all countries, but for some it is very clear that reforming the legal framework will have a direct effect on its financial position. For example, the Malawian reforms were driven by its low ranking in the Doing Business surveys and the consequent recommendations of the World Bank to help it improve economic growth.[40] Further, where the current system is little used, the transitional costs and disruption are less worrying.[41]

For other, more developed, economies, the immediate link between reform and economic growth is perhaps less obvious, and the costs and disruption of reform

[34] See Ch 21.

[35] See Ch 21 D.

[36] See Ch 23.

[37] See M Raczynska, 'A New Model Law of Secured Transactions: Worldwide Modernisation in the Making?' [2014] *Butterworths Journal of International Banking and Financial Law* 697.

[38] See, for example, the registration against serial-numbered property in Australia (Ch 7 E(iii)) and Malawi (Ch 10 B (iii)). See also the position in Canada (Ch 4 D(i)).

[39] See, for example, the systems in New Zealand (Ch 6 F(ii)).

[40] See Ch 8 A.

[41] See the Malawian experience in Ch 8 and also that of Lithuania (Ch 19 A).

are perceived to be much greater. For example, it is pointed out in the chapter on the Belgian reforms that an outdated law can be worked around by those involved in the credit markets until some kind of external catalyst triggers a move towards reform.[42] In Belgium, this was the financial crisis, and the perception of the Belgian government that an efficient system of security rights would aid economic growth.[43] It is, however, unfortunate if a major external catalyst is required for reform, as this often leads to rushed or skewed reform, which arises as a reaction to a particular set of circumstances and which may not be best in the long run.

(iv) Lessons for English Law

To what extent do the drivers mentioned above apply to the law of England and Wales? Some of the reasons why attempts at wholesale secured transactions law reform have not succeeded so far are that the current law works reasonably well in most respects, that particular problems can be dealt with by piecemeal reform[44] and that the process of wholesale reform is perceived as potentially disruptive and expensive, outweighing the economic benefits. None of the drivers discussed in this section apply to such an extent that, on their own, they compel reform. The case for reform in England and Wales depends on an accumulation of long-term advantages over the present system, which outweigh the short-term costs.

English law certainly suffers from complexity and fragmentation, as discussed in Section A(i)(a), as it is heavily path dependent. Skilled lawyers are trained to overcome this, and even to exploit it, as the corollary is that the different concepts can be manipulated to achieve whatever outcome is required. Only occasionally do the courts step in and recharacterise transactions.[45] The priority rules, which are particularly complex, are often contracted around. However, this not only increases costs, but is only possible if the rules are known in the first place.[46] It is very unfortunate that the law is impenetrable and incomprehensible to business people and to those from other jurisdictions. Simplification and clarification would be great benefits, and a codification of the law could be combined with substantive reform to take account of some of the other drivers which are present in this jurisdiction.

It cannot be said that English law suffers severely from the examples of lack of functionality outlined in Section A(i)(b). It is possible to take a non-possessory interest over all kinds of asset, including future ones, and to take a security interest over all the assets of a company. There is a functioning register in relation to company security interests, although there is no doubt that it could be improved by

[42] Chapter 18 A.

[43] Chapter 18 E.

[44] For example, the 2013 reforms to the registration system (Ch 12) and the proposed statutory override of anti-assignment clauses (Ch 14).

[45] An example of this is the recharacterisation of fixed charges as floating, see *Re Spectrum Plus* [2005] 2 AC 680.

[46] See Ch 12 D(iv).

the use of more innovative technology, as well as by a widening in scope.[47] Security interests can be enforced without judicial input, and insolvency law is creditor friendly. However, as mentioned in Chapter 12,[48] there are sufficient problems with the current law to warrant further reform.

In terms of international developments, English law is rather out on a limb. The current law is not particularly compatible either with that of its European neighbours,[49] or with other common law jurisdictions which have reformed along PPSA lines. More wholesale reform is possible in Europe, driven by the current national trends and also the move towards a capital markets union:[50] English law is not in a position at the moment to act as any sort of model for a harmonised law, or even to exert much influence over the form of such law.

The availability of information technology to improve the registration system, and other national and international models to assist with the content of reform, mean that the costs of reform of English law could be reduced, and thus could be outweighed by the undoubted economic benefits of simplification and clarity. It is, however, imperative that any reform of English law takes account of the lessons learnt from other jurisdictions both in method and in content. This volume is a contribution towards this learning process.

B. The Method of Reform

Secured transaction reform is, in one sense, like any private law reform and needs to be undertaken by whatever system a jurisdiction has in place for such reform. It cannot be effected by the courts, but must involve legislation. This is because registration will be at the heart of the regime, and, to be properly effective, a central register must have rules which bind everyone, not just the users who are parties to the system.[51] It will also, probably, involve public funding. Further, since one of the main imperatives for reform is usually the fragmentation and complexity of the previous law, the enactment of a comprehensive code will usually be required.[52] Choices then have to be made as to what falls within the code, as discussed below.[53]

47 See Ch 12 D(iii).

48 Chapter 12 C.

49 Or even its Scottish neighbour.

50 See the EU Green Paper 'Building a Capital Markets Union' COM (2015) 63 final, http://eur-lex.europa.eu/legal-content/EN/TXT/?uri=CELEX:52015DC0063.

51 This is the one of the weaknesses of the HPI private registration system of interests in motor vehicles which operates in England and Wales: it needs the support of legislation, in this case, the Hire Purchase Act 1964, but would be much more effective were it a national state-regulated system. The register set up in Dublin in relation to international interests in mobile equipment under the Cape Town Convention is run by a private company, but is governed by the Cape Town Convention and the Aircraft Protocol, which has become part of Irish national law.

52 The system in Italy, for example, is largely established by legislation, but it is rightly criticised for being fragmented and unclear, see Ch 16 B.

53 Section C.

It is very clear from the discussion of reform in the chapters in this volume that there are a number of pitfalls to avoid when carrying out secured transactions reform, and these, together with the correlative good practice, will now be discussed.

(i) Law Reform Takes Time

This point is made forcefully by Roy Goode in his chapter on the reforms in Jersey,[54] but appears from a number of the accounts of reform in this volume.[55] This is hardly surprising. Secured transaction law is complex, and its efficacy depends on it being as certain and predictable as possible, so it is not advisable to legislate in haste and to allow mistakes to rise to the surface (although a degree of this is inevitable). The French experience is, perhaps, an example of this latter approach.[56] The process of interaction between government officials, academic and private lawyers and business and other stakeholders is, and should be, lengthy to allow for relevant issues to be discussed and the necessary compromises reached. The process could, perhaps, be shortened by the models now available to aid the drafting process,[57] although note must be taken of the dangers of using a model without the lengthy process of knowledge transfer that is also necessary.[58]

The major reforms discussed in this volume have been wholesale reforms, which have resulted in an entirely new system of secured transactions law, including rules on registration, priorities and enforcement. Of course, reform can also take place in a more piecemeal fashion,[59] and this has taken place in some of the jurisdictions

[54] Chapter 9 A.

[55] Australia (Ch 7 B) (reform mooted since the 1970s and finally took effect in 2012), Lithuania (Ch 19 A) (reform started in the late 1990s and was finalised in 2012), Scotland (the first report on wholesale reform was in 1971, and the latest report on the proposed reforms is yet to be released). The reforms in Malawi (where there was a very significant economic imperative towards reform) have been quicker: the work on legal reform started in 2008 (although more general economic work had preceded this) and the reforms became operational in late 2015 (see Ch 8 A). The French reforms were also quicker (work started in 2003 and the reforms were enacted in 2006) but it is clear that this is just the first stage, and the chapter on France argues that another round of reform is necessary (see Ch 17 D, although note that the latest reform in January 2016 has not reduced the problematic complexity of the law, see Ch 17 C(iii)(a)1). The Belgian reforms, which are expected to come into force in 2016, were also relatively quick: work started as a result of the financial crisis in 2008.

[56] See the analysis in Ch 17.

[57] This includes both models of actual laws, such as the New Zealand legislation which has been used as a model in, for example, Jersey (Ch 9 A) and Malawi (Ch 8 A), and transnational initiatives such as the UNCITRAL Legislative Guide and draft Model Law (see Ch 23), used particularly in Malawi (Ch 8 A) and Belgium (Ch 18 M) and the Cape Town Convention. The Belgian legislator has expressed the view that the Belgian reforms, which themselves used these transnational models, can contribute to harmonisation (see Ch 18 M), which they undoubtedly will do, especially in relation to reform in European and other civil law jurisdictions.

[58] This point is made clearly in Ch 21 B(iii) on the experience of the EBRD in secured transaction law reform.

[59] For the drawbacks of piecemeal reform, see L Gullifer, 'Piecemeal Reform: Is It the Answer?' in F Dahan (ed), *Secured Lending in Commercial Transactions* (Cheltenham, Edward Elgar, 2015).

discussed in which wholesale reform has not yet taken place.[60] Piecemeal reforms might be seen as a staging post on the way to wholesale reform, but they may also hold back the process, for two reasons. One is that piecemeal reform may fix an immediate problem, and thus take away the imperative for wholesale reform, in a situation where this comes from an accumulation of drivers rather than from one major catalyst. The second is that piecemeal reform usually adds to the complexity of the law. While this may be, in one way, a driver for reform, when a law is very complex, the transitional costs of reform can be great and this can be a disincentive to reform.

(ii) Consultation with Business People and their Legal Advisers

It is clear from the recently reformed jurisdictions that one key to the success of a new system is to involve the business community in discussions and design from the start.[61] One example of this being done successfully is Jersey, where practitioners were involved in designing the law and the register and in drawing up a market standard security agreement.[62] The importance of consulting with local experts is also noted in the chapter on the work of the EBRD, both initially and after implementation as part of an ongoing monitoring process.[63] It is clear from the experience in the US and Canada that even a reformed system requires constant monitoring, both to discover problems and to make sure that the system caters for current business practices.[64]

(iii) Education and Training Before and After Implementation

The critical importance of educating those who are to use a reformed system is stressed in a number of the chapters.[65] This may seem obvious, but it may not be so obvious that the level of education goes beyond teaching the legal rules and running tutorials on how to use the register. Most wholesale reforms will require the application of a new legal mindset to familiar situations, even if the end result is not very different from that under the previous regime.[66] Not only do users of

[60] Examples of this are English law (Ch 12), Ireland (Ch 10), Spain (Ch 20) and Italy (Ch 16).

[61] The inclusion of the business and practising community in the drafting of UCC Article 9 is discussed in US (Ch 3 B(iii)).

[62] See Ch 9, Part 2 A.

[63] See Ch 21 B(iv) and D. Note, as well, the involvement of the practising and business community in the statutory three year review of the Australian law reforms, see Australia Ch 7 B.

[64] See US (Ch 3) and Canada (Ch 4 B), and the specific example described in Ch 5 A of the work of the Ontario Bar Association PPSL Committee.

[65] See, particularly, the chapters on Australia (Ch 7 C(ii)), Malawi (Ch 8 F) and the work of the EBRD (Ch 21 B and D).

[66] One example is the treatment of what was formally the floating charge under the PPSA systems: the result is very similar, but the conceptual structure is very different, see New Zealand (Ch 6 C(ii)).

the system need to be educated, the judiciary need to internalise the new system.[67] Education also needs to continue after implementation: for example, the statutory review of the Australian reforms has recommended a fresh and ongoing education campaign.[68]

(iv) Level of Complexity of Drafting

Since one of the reasons for reform is simplification and clarity, one might have thought that a reforming statute that is too complex would be counterproductive. As Roy Goode points out, there is a choice between complex and lengthy legislation that attempts to 'provide solutions to every conceivable problem' and 'a simpler set of provisions which would be rough round the edges and leave more leeway for the court'.[69] Jersey chose the latter course, and the legislation (of course, dealing only for the moment with security interests over intangible property) is relatively simple and short. Examples of the former are UCC Article 9, which has been amended and revised over the years to take account of problems that have arisen,[70] and the Australian PPSA. The latter has been criticised as being too long and complex:[71] this seems to have been a result of a laudable attempt to cover every eventuality, but it has resulted in confusion. The statutory review has therefore recommended a series of measures to reduce the complexity of the legislation and the registration process.[72] The choice, however, is not a straightforward one. Simpler legislation does lead to gaps, as illustrated by the discussion in Chapter 5 on Canada,[73] which highlights a number of unresolved issues in the Ontario legislation, many of which have been expressly covered in other legislation, such as the Saskatchewan PPSA and Article 9.

(v) Interrelationship with Other Areas of Law

It is critical that any reformed system of secured transactions interacts properly with the rest of the national law, and many reforming jurisdictions have had to execute reforms in corporate law, in the law relating to dispute resolution and, probably most importantly, in insolvency law.[74] The effect of failure to amend

[67] The benefits of this are stressed in the New Zealand chapter (Ch 6 H). The discussion also gives some examples of where judges have failed to take account of the conceptual changes. One of the tasks of the EBRD in reforming jurisdictions has been to work with the judiciary, both before and after reform (see Ch 21 B(iii) and D).

[68] B Whittaker, Review of the [Australian] PPSA 2009 Final Report (2015) recommendation 392.

[69] Chapter 9, Part 1 A.

[70] Chapter 3 C and D.

[71] See Ch 7 C(ii).

[72] Chapter 7 J.

[73] Chapter 5.

[74] See Australia (Ch 7 H), Malawi (Ch 8 E).

insolvency law depends on how well that law functions before reform: there was little reform in New Zealand but this does not seem to have caused any problems.[75] On the other hand, it is thought that the failure to amend the system of statutory preferences in insolvency may hamper the operation of reforms in France and Belgium.[76] In Australia, considerable efforts were made to harmonise terminology and substantive law between the secured transaction regime and the insolvency regime. Considerable difficulty has been caused by the definitions and terminology chosen to replace the 'floating charge' trigger for the preferential status of certain creditors: it was sought to retain the same policy but merely to change the wording. The resulting complexity has been criticised,[77] and has been the subject of recommendations in the statutory review.[78]

In English law, the distinction between fixed and floating charges has been a source of great uncertainty, yet because this distinction usually determines who pays for the expenses of the insolvency process, any change in the law (whether as part of a wholesale reform or not) would require a review of the policy behind the funding of insolvencies. The difficulty of doing this is likely to be a disincentive to reform in this area, and is a good example of the close interrelation between secured transaction law (which is more easily harmonised) and insolvency law (which is difficult to harmonise substantively).

(vi) Lessons for English Law

There is no doubt that reform of the English law of secured transactions is taking time.[79] The first impetus for reform came in 1971, with the Crowther report,[80] and the first report recommending a PPSA scheme was in 1989.[81] Since then, the Law Commission has examined the issue and made recommendations,[82] yet actual reform has been limited.[83] In many ways, the issues discussed in this section explain why that has been the case. There have been (sometimes abortive) attempts at piecemeal reform.[84] Despite considerable efforts, especially on the part of the Law Commission, to consult with business people and to explain the consequences of reform, there is still a resistance to change. There is concern over

[75] See New Zealand (Ch 6) and the comparison made in the Australia chapter (Ch 7 H).

[76] France (Ch 17 B(iii)(b)) and Belgium (Ch 18 B and E). See also the comment on the Italian proposals in Ch 16 C(ii).

[77] See Australia (Ch 7 H(ii)).

[78] Whittaker (n 68) recommendation 356.

[79] See Section B(i).

[80] Report of the Committee on Consumer Credit (1971) Cmnd 4596. Although primarily concerned with consumer credit, this report also considered reform of personal property law more generally.

[81] AL Diamond, A Review of Security Interests in Property (HMSO, 1989).

[82] Law Commission, Company Security Interests (Law Com No 296, 2005).

[83] See Ch 12.

[84] Companies Act 1989 part IV; the Financial Collateral Arrangements Regulations 2003 (and the later amending legislation); the 2013 reforms discussed in Ch 13.

the resulting complexity of drafting, and the consequences for other areas of law, particularly insolvency law.[85] These points must be taken on board in any proposed reform. However, the costs of a reformed system are ever decreasing, thanks to technological advances, and the benefits are increasing, as outlined in the first section of this chapter. It is worth, therefore, taking the time required to consult widely with business people and financiers, to engage in education and explanation, and to make sure that the scheme proposed and drafted is the most suitable for England and Wales both now and for the rest of the twenty-first century. The Secured Transaction Law Reform Project is now engaged in this process.

C. The Substance of Reform

Much of the discussion in this volume is about the substance of reform, or likely reform, and it is impossible to discuss it all in this concluding chapter. Instead, issues will be highlighted that any potential reforming jurisdiction has to address, but the discussion will concentrate on some issues which are of particular significance to English law.[86] On at least some of these issues, a different view can be taken as a result of policy choice, legal culture and local business conditions.

(i) The Scope of the Regime

(a) Single Security Interest

One of the first decisions that must be made is whether there will continue to be a number of different types of security interest, each with their own rules, or a single security interest governed by one set of rules. There are three approaches that have been followed by the reforming jurisdictions: first, retaining the different types of security and quasi-security interests, albeit with some rationalisation;[87] second, creating a single type of security interest, but leaving quasi-security interests (usually retention of title devices) separately delineated;[88] third, a functional approach treating all interests which have the purpose of security in the same way.[89]

[85] The Law Commission's terms of reference did not include revision of insolvency law, and this limited the changes that could be recommended in relation to fixed and floating charges.

[86] Thus, for example, there is no discussion of whether it should be possible to take security over future assets or circulating assets, since this is already permitted under English law.

[87] For example, Lithuania (Ch 19); Ireland (Ch 10) and England and Wales (Ch 12), although in both systems all non-possessory true security interests are treated the same for registration purposes); Scotland (Ch 11).

[88] See, for example, Belgium (Ch 18) (retention of title devices are treated separately and are not registrable, but are subject to many similar rules to 'true' security interests).

[89] This is the approach of the PPSA jurisdictions, and the US, as well as the UNCITRAL Model Law (Ch 23), though the UNCITRAL Legislative Guide included a non-unitary approach (Option B), which treated retention of title devices separately.

The advantage of a single security interest is the reduction of complexity.[90] The rules are the same whatever interest is created. This, of course, is not entirely true since possessory interests are perfected in a different way from non-possessory interests, and there is often an option, or a requirement, to perfect an interest in intangible property by control. Further, certain interests attract the purchase money security interest priority rules, which are an exception to the general rules. However, these differences are based on easily recognised functional distinctions, rather than concept-based legal distinctions, which are often subject to fine, path-dependent, distinctions.[91]

(b) What Interests Are Registrable?

A separate issue, which is not logically related to whether there is a single security interest, is what interests are included in the registration system. The PPSA systems include all security interests (defined according to the functional approach) but also include other interests, partly because they are thought to give rise to publicity concerns and partly because the line is difficult to draw between them and functional security interests. The width of scope has grown as the PPSA concept has developed, so that, for example, UCC Article 9 does not include leases over one year, which are 'deemed security interests' under the Canadian system.[92] The scope of what else could fall within 'deemed security interests' is very wide: most jurisdictions include outright assignment of receivables[93] and commercial consignments, for example, but Australia went further and included a 90-day lease of serial-numbered goods: this was the subject of much lobbying from the plant hire industry and has now been removed from the scope.[94] How wide a registration regime should be is a matter of balance between what is useful to be recorded on the register, and the cost and uncertainty engendered by requiring registration of interests which previously had not been subject to this requirement.

One of the main difficulties in introducing a wide-ranging registration requirement is that those taking such interests are concerned that they may be very adversely affected on the insolvency of the counterparty if they have failed to register. This concern is ameliorated if the sanction for non-registration is not unenforceability on insolvency but is merely a loss of priority: registration then becomes a genuine choice.[95] This is the position in New Zealand, and it is pointed

90 The importance of this as a driver for reform has already been noted (Section A(i)(a)).

91 This point is made elegantly in Grant Gilmore, "The Secured Transactions Article of the Commercial Code" (1951) 16 Law & Contemp. Probs. 27, at 27 (the quotation is set out in Ch 4 A). As discussed below at Section C (i)(c), deemed security interests can be included within a registration regime without being recharacterised for all purposes.

92 See Ch 4 D(v). The same is true for the other PPSA systems, see New Zealand (Ch 6 E(i)), Australia (Ch 7 C(vi)) and Malawi (Ch 8 B(i)).

93 The scope of such inclusion can, however, vary, see Canada Ch 4 D(iv).

94 Australia (Ch 7 C(vi)).

95 The sanction for non-registration more generally is a matter for decision for a reforming jurisdiction. To some extent this will depend on whether the perceived purpose of registration is to make information available to creditors in general (in which case the sanction for non-registration

out that this has meant that there was less hostility from the leasing industry to the introduction of registration than might otherwise have been the case.[96] The Australian PPSA has followed suit in relation to some deemed security interests,[97] and the review has suggested that this be extended to all leases which are in this category.[98]

Of course, another technique that can be used in a codified system is for interests to be brought into the general scheme, providing for priority and enforcement, without them being subject to a registration requirement. The PPSA schemes permit perfection by possession and by control, and some interests are brought within the scheme but are said to be 'automatically perfected'.[99]

Decisions have also to be made about the exclusion of interests which might otherwise be thought to fall within the code: these exclusions can be principled but can also be pragmatic.[100]

(c) Treatment of Title-based Interests

There are, therefore, a number of choices which have to be made in relation to title-based interests. The first is whether any title-based interests are to be included in the code. If they are, then it is necessary to decide whether any are to be registrable, and, if so, which ones. A line can be drawn between those interests which have the purpose of securing an obligation ('quasi-security interests') and those which do not, but, when stated like this, the line is difficult to draw. Another possibility is to consider whether or not all or substantially all the usual risks and rewards of an owner are transferred to the debtor: this test has been used in accounting practice to distinguish between finance leases and operating leases.[101] As we have seen, many systems include the former category (finance leases etc.) within the registration scheme,[102] and the PPSA systems include other title-based interests. Once an interest is within the registration scheme, the priority rules of the scheme would normally also apply to it, so that an unregistered interest loses priority to

would normally be that the security interest will be ineffective in the debtor's insolvency), or merely to protect subsequent secured creditors and other purchasers (in which case registration might be only a priority point).

[96] Chapter 6 F(i).

[97] APPSA s 268, see Ch 7 C(v).

[98] Whittaker (n 68) recommendation 330.

[99] For example, under the Jersey law there is automatic perfection of an interest in favour of a securities intermediary if it is to finance the purchase of investment securities for a customer before the customer has paid for them, see Ch 9, Part 1 J(ii).

[100] Malawi, for example, excluded fixtures on strategic grounds, see Ch 8 B(i). For discussion of the treatment of fixtures under Article 9, see US Ch 3 C(iii).

[101] See UK GAAP SSAP21. Note that the International Accounting Standards Board has decided to propose a new accounting standard with a single model of a lease, so that operating leases over one year would appear on the balance sheet.

[102] As well as the PPSA systems, see the Lithuanian scheme (Ch 19 D). There is optional registration of retention of title devices in France, see Ch 17 C(iii)(a)(4). See also the discussion of the Italian proposals in Ch 16 C(ii).

a registered one, and, subject to the purchase money security interest rules,[103] the first to register will have priority.

The next decision, however, is whether any title-based interests are treated like security interests in other respects. Two important issues are the location of title and whether, on enforcing its interest, the creditor can keep any surplus value over and above the unpaid payment obligation. The PPSA systems 'recharacterise' quasi-security interests, so that the debtor has title and the interest of the secured party is by way of grant.[104] The most visible sign of this is the obligation to account for surplus value on enforcement, as well as the imposition of duties on enforcement, such as to obtain the best price reasonably obtainable.[105] A system can, however, impose such duties on a creditor relying on a quasi-security title-based interest without changing the location of title, or, for that matter, requiring registration of such an interest.[106] It should be remembered that it is not necessarily just to the debtor that a secured creditor must account for a surplus: it could be to a junior secured creditor. As pointed out in the chapter on German law, one of the drawbacks of a title-based system is that any surplus value cannot be used to secure other loans: in Germany, where title-based devices are very prevalent, a workaround has been developed so that this surplus value can be used to a limited extent.[107]

A system can also make quasi-security interests registrable without recharacterising them, that is, without changing the location of title or obliging the 'creditor' to account for surplus value.[108] The advantage (from the point of view of the 'creditor') is ease of enforcement, since there is no duty to sell or to obtain a reasonable price, and the 'creditor' has an entitlement to the surplus.[109] On the insolvency of the debtor, this is a detriment to its other creditors. The competing policies, therefore, are between protection for title-based financiers and making assets available to other creditors.[110]

From a formal point of view, it should not be difficult to include quasi-security interests within a registration scheme without recharacterising them. This technique is already used in the PPSA schemes in relation to title-based interests which

[103] For an explanation of these, see Ch 2 F(ii).

[104] This is not spelt out in some legislation but has been held by the courts to be implicit, see New Zealand (Ch 6 E(i)), especially at n 40.

[105] Australia (Ch 7 G). See also Malawi (Ch 8 B(v)).

[106] Examples of such a system are France (Ch 17 C(iii)(a)(4): Civil Code Art 2371); Belgium (Ch 18 J).

[107] See Germany (Ch 15 D(i)(c)). Under English law, of course, a security interest can be granted in the lessee's or hirer's rights under the lease or hire-purchase agreement.

[108] This is the position under Option B of the UNCITRAL Legislative Guide, for example. Note that Option B is not included in the Draft Model Law.

[109] While this can look like a windfall, it may be valuable to a financier who finances a number of assets for the debtor. While some assets may produce a surplus, others may produce a deficiency, so the financier can 'cross-collateralise'. In fact, where this is not the case, even straight retention of title devices often contractually oblige the financier to return any overall surplus to the debtor.

[110] See paras 211–213 UNCITRAL Legislative Guide, where the effect on reorganisation of an insolvent debtor is also examined.

are not for the purpose of security, such as leases over one year: it is expressly provided that the provisions on enforcement do not apply to them.[111]

(ii) The Structure of the Registration System

(a) Advance Filing?

There are a number of choices which have to be made about the structure of the registration system, even if it is assumed that a reformed system will make full use of information technology to achieve its aims. The question of what interests should be registrable has already been considered. One major issue is whether registration should be permitted in advance of the creation of a security interest. This is, of course, a major component of a notice filing scheme.[112] It has the advantage that a creditor can protect itself while negotiating an interest, and will not be vulnerable during any period between creation of its interest and its own registration. It also avoids the 'invisibility' period that exists under current English law.[113] An additional advantage is that there can be one registration for a whole series of transactions with the same debtor.[114] This is particularly important if retention of title devices are included in the scheme. For advance filing to be effective, registration must be a priority point.

There are two other approaches to this issue as well as notice filing. One is for the interest to be created by registration.[115] Coupled with registration being a priority point (which it would be as it coincides with creation), the creditor is protected provided that it checks the register immediately before registration. Another is to permit advance filing in relation to a specific transaction, so that once the transaction is entered into, the priority point is the advance date rather than the date of creation of the interest.[116] Other reformed jurisdictions do not seem concerned about creditors being unprotected between creation and registration. They differentiate between creation and perfection (validity against third parties), and provide that registration is the priority point.[117] Given the ease and speed of electronic registration, the risk posed by the delay between creation and registration may now not seem to be significant, provided that the creditor acts swiftly.

A considerable disadvantage of a notice filing scheme is that a search may reveal a registration which does not relate to an actual security interest (a false

[111] Note, as well, the similar position adopted under Option B of the UNCITRAL Legislative Guide, and under the Cape Town Convention, depending on the treatment of leases by the applicable law, see Spain (Ch 20 B).

[112] See Ch 2 D(i).

[113] Chapter 12 D(iii).

[114] See Ch 2 D(i).

[115] Scotland (Ch 11 D(iii)).

[116] Ireland (Ch 10 B(ii)). This technique is also used in the Cape Town Convention registry.

[117] France (Ch 17 C(ii)(a)(1)); Belgium (Ch 18 F).

positive) or may not reveal a registration relating to an actual security interest (a false negative).

The dangers of false positives arise from advance filing itself, but also from the nature of the notice filing process, since where advance filing relates to a specific transaction, it will usually lapse unless the transaction is in some way confirmed. In a notice filing system, it is possible for interests that are never actually created to remain on the register, and for a notice to be registered against a party maliciously or carelessly even if there is not a secured transaction pending. There are various methods of dealing with these problems adopted by the PPSA jurisdictions.[118]

The dangers of false negatives are not specific to a notice filing system but apply to any type of registration system. For example, a paper registration system includes the inherent danger that a registration may not be correctly entered on the register or that entry may be delayed: this is obviated by the use of a fully electronic system.[119] Further, the 'invisibility' period under current English law clearly raises the possibility of false negatives. Moreover, in any debtor based system, where a debtor has changed its name or the secured asset has been transferred to a third party subject to the security interest, a search may not reveal the security interest. The extent to which this problem is addressed by requirements to amend the register depends on how much a jurisdiction is concerned that the register gives accurate public notice.[120]

(b) *What Information Should be Provided?*

Another choice to be made is how much and what information is to be provided on the register. The choice, from a functional point of view, is reasonably free since information technology allows as little or as much information to be registered very easily. The advantage of a great deal of information, as under the English system where the charge document is registered,[121] is that a searcher can find out most (though not all) of what he wants to know without making further enquiries. If advance registration is permitted, the information will necessarily have to be less detailed.[122] With a notice filing system, where very little information is registered, the searcher will have to make enquiries from the debtor or the registered secured creditor.[123] All reformed systems, even the English system, have moved away from

[118] For example, the debtor may be required to give consent to registration, or may have the right to insist that an interest is taken off the register (see Ch 2 D(iv) and Canada Ch 4 C(ii)), which discusses the differences between Article 9 and the Canadian PPSAs in this regard) or it may be wrongful to register if there is no intention to create an interest (see Australia (Ch 7 E(iv))).

[119] See Canada Ch 4 C(iii)(b).

[120] For discussion of the methods used to deal with this problem under Article 9 and in Canada see Ch 4 C(iii)(b). See also Ch 23 F(ii) on the alternatives suggested under the UNCITRAL Draft Model Law. Registration by asset, where available, also overcomes this problem.

[121] Chapter 12 B(ii)(b).

[122] Note that in Ireland, where there is an optional two stage advance registration process, relatively little information is required to be registered, see Ireland (Ch 10 B(ii)). More information could, however, be required at the second stage.

[123] Chapter 2 D(iii).

a procedure where the registrar has to check the accuracy of the information, and in most electronic systems the role of the registrar is entirely administrative.[124]

(c) Registration by Asset

Although debtor-based registration is necessary in any scheme which permits security interests over future property, and over all the assets of the debtor, where an asset can be individually identified, it is useful for a scheme to permit registration against that asset.[125] While such registration can only be optional (as a creditor with a security interest over future property could not register against the asset, and its interest should not be void in the debtor's insolvency), there is a strong incentive on those who can register in this way to do so, if it preserves their priority over those who do not register.[126] With modern technology, it should be possible for asset registers to be linked with debtor-based registers, to enable 'one-stop' searches.[127]

(iii) Other Methods of Perfection

Most reformed systems allow perfection by possession[128] and many allow some form of control in relation to certain intangible property.[129] What amounts to control, and what kind of security interests can be perfected by it, vary from system to system. Canada, for example, does not make provision for perfection by control of a security interest over a bank account,[130] while other PPSA systems do.[131] While most systems permit registration as an alternative to control, the US does not in relation to a security interest over a bank account.[132]

(iv) The Priority Rules

Simplifying the priority rules is a major driver for many reform initiatives.Once an efficient and comprehensive registration system is in place, the best basic priority

[124] See, eg, Malawi (Ch 8 B(iii)), Canada Ch 4 C(iii)(b).

[125] For discussion of some of the benefits of this, see Ch 2 H(ii).

[126] See, for example, Australia (Ch 7 E(iii)). Registration by serial number, however, is prone to human error when inputting the number, which can result in exact match searches not being complete, see ibid.

[127] See Ch 12 D(v).

[128] This is either by a direct provision in legislation, as under the PPSA systems, or by permitting a possessory security interest, such as the English or civil law pledge.

[129] In EU countries, the Financial Collateral Directive requires 'possession or control' as, effectively, an alternative mode of protection. See, for example, Spain (Ch 20 C(iii)), Italy (Ch 16 B(ii)).

[130] Chapter 5 C.

[131] Ch 4 E(iii). Australia (Ch 8 E(i)), Malawi (Ch 9 D(i)), Jersey (Ch 10, Part 1 J(iii)). New Zealand, by contrast, has no concept of control.

[132] Chapter 4 E(iii), Ch 5 C. The position in this regard under English law is unclear, see Ch 12 B(i).

rule is clearly one based on the order of registration,[133] and for unified systems the rule is not just 'first to register', but 'first to register or perfect by another means'.[134] Systems also all have some sort of purchase money security interest rule, either overtly in the legislation[135] or because the location of title in title-based devices is not changed, and so, because the debtor never owns the asset, it cannot grant a security interest over it as future property.[136] Most systems also provide that dispositions of assets which are subject to a security interest can be made free of that interest in the ordinary course of business, thus replicating the operation of a floating charge.[137] Whether the recipient has notice of the security interest is irrelevant: most reformed jurisdictions eschew reliance on notice as part of the priority rules, and rely instead on the integrity of the register,[138] although there are some cases where notice can be reintroduced as determining priority. For example, a buyer taking with notice that the disposition is in breach of the security agreement takes subject to the security interest.[139] Further, the corollary of an advance filing system is that a secured creditor can 'tack' any further advances onto its original priority.[140] Ireland has attempted to prevent this by introducing priority rules related to future advances based on notice, which seems to jeopardise the certainty of the whole system of priorities.[141]

There are, however, additional rules which vary among jurisdictions and in relation to which a reforming jurisdiction would have to make choices. For example, in some PPSA jurisdictions, security interests perfected by control have priority over those perfected by registration.[142] There are also variations in the detailed rules regarding the treatment of the proceeds of the collateral.[143]

133 Not only is this the rule in the PPSA jurisdictions, but also in Ireland (Ch 10 B(v), though note that, as enacted, the position is still not entirely clear), Scotland (Ch 11) although in that jurisdiction creation and registration are at the same moment, so the priority rule could also be described as first in time), France (Ch 17 C(i)(a)(1)), although this only applies to registrable non-possessory pledges, Belgium (Ch 18 H). Cf the current English law rules (Ch 12 D(iv)).

134 For the PPSA systems, see Ch 2 F(i); see also Belgium (Ch 19 H).

135 As in the PPSA systems (see Ch 2 F(ii)) and in Belgium (see Ch 18 H). There are, however, variations as to what must be done to obtain PMSI status, see, for example, New Zealand (Ch 6 D).

136 This reasoning still applies in Belgium in relation to retention of title devices (see Ch 18 H) and applies in unreformed jurisdictions, such as under English law and Italian law (see Ch 16 B(iii)).

137 Chapter 2 H(i). See also Belgium (Ch 18 F).

138 Note that there are differences as to the relevance to buyers of notice of unperfected security interests: in Australia and New Zealand a buyer defeats an unperfected security interest regardless of the buyer's knowledge, while in Canada a buyer with knowledge takes subject to the interest. See Ch 6 D n 32.

139 See Ch 2 H, Australia (Ch 7 F(v)), Jersey (Ch 9, Part 1 L(v)), Malawi (Ch 8 B(iv)). Such rules can become very complex, see Whittaker (n 68) 7.6.2 who sets out a table of different situations in which knowledge is relevant under the Australian PPSA and recommends some simplification (see recommendation 188).

140 See Ch 2 F(i)).

141 See Ch 10 B(v).

142 US (in relation to bank accounts), see Ch 5 C, US and Canada (in relation to securities) see Ch 4 E(ii), Australia (Ch 7 F(i)), UCC §9-328, Jersey (Ch 9, Part 1 L(ii)), UNCITRAL Draft Model Law (see Ch 23 G(ii). Cf New Zealand (which does not have a concept of control) and Malawi.

143 See Canada Ch 5 D, Jersey Ch 9, Part 2 D, English law Ch 13.

(v) Anti-assignment Clauses

Overriding clauses prohibiting assignment has been part of nearly all the PPSA systems,[144] although this is not strictly or logically necessary as part of a secured transaction law codification. For example, the Lithuanian reforms do not include such a provision,[145] and nor does the Malawian PPSA. In contrast, such a provision is likely to become part of English law in the near future, without there being any other wholesale reform of secured transactions law, for the reasons explored in Chapter 14.

(vi) Enforcement Mechanisms

For many jurisdictions, reforming the law in relation to enforcement and remedies was a very important driver towards reform. These are jurisdictions where, previously, self-help, out-of-court remedies were non-existent or limited and/or where the available remedies were complex and fragmented.[146] The main differences on enforcement in reformed jurisdictions arise from the intersection with insolvency law.[147] If there are too many statutory priorities or other carve-outs, this not only reduces creditors' ability to recover (this is a matter of policy for a particular state),[148] but it also adds to the complexity and uncertainty of the whole system.[149]

(vii) Lessons for English Law

This section has not sought to identify all the choices which have to be made when reforming a secured transactions law, but to highlight some of the main areas in which different jurisdictions have made different choices, and some areas which are common to all, which must therefore be considered as fundamental to any modern reform.

Many of the changes made in other reformed jurisdictions are not necessary under English law, in that the functionality already exists. For example, it is possible to take security over future property and to enforce security without court involvement. However, for a reform to achieve the aims of clarity and lack of fragmentation, it is likely to be necessary for the form of English law to change even

[144] See, for example, Jersey (Ch 9, Part 2 M(i)), UNCITRAL draft Model Law, Ch 23.

[145] Although note that the Belgian reforms do, see Ch 18 F.

[146] See particularly Belgium (Ch 18 E and L), Lithuania (Ch 19 D) and Malawi (Ch 8 B(v)).

[147] See Section B(vi).

[148] For discussion of the policy debate in the US in relation to Article 9 see Ch 3 D(ii)(b).

[149] See Belgium (Ch 18 B and E); France (Ch 17 C(iii)(b)). Note also the points made about Australian and English law in Section B(vi).

in these areas in which there is already functionality. A good example of this is the treatment of floating charges by the PPSA jurisdictions.[150]

By identifying the substantive choices that can be made when reforming secured transactions law, it is possible to address the arguments in relation to such choices more clearly. As mentioned earlier, there are benefits in using models rather than trying to reinvent the wheel, but it cannot be assumed that everything that works in another jurisdiction will work in English law. Analysis of the choices made by other jurisdictions, and the reasons for those choices, will enable the suitability of each part of a model to be properly assessed and assimilated.

D. Conclusion

For a proposed reform of English law to be robust it is important to learn the lessons from other jurisdictions, both as to the need for reform, the process of reform and the substance of reform. The collected wisdom from around the world in this volume will be able to inform not only the work of the Secured Transaction Law Reform Project, but the deliberations of anyone interested in law reform in England and Wales, and around the world. The jurisdictions included are merely samples of a much bigger process of law reform which is being undertaken around the globe. It would be unfortunate if English law were to be left behind: advantage should be taken of the opportunity to profit from the experiences of others.

[150] See Ch 2 I and Ch 6 C.

INDEX

www.ingramcontent.com/pod-product-compliance
Lightning Source LLC
LaVergne TN
LVHW052209200926
848481LV00001B/61
9781509927517